Shakespeare's Books

STUDENT SHAKESPEARE LIBRARY

Series Editor
Sandra Clark (Birkbeck College, University of London)

Shakespeare's Legal Language	B. J. & Mary Sokol
Shakespeare's Military Language	Charles Edelman
Shakespeare's Theatre	Hugh Richmond
Shakespeare's Books	Stuart Gillespie

Shakespeare's Books

A Dictionary of Shakespeare Sources

STUART GILLESPIE

continuum
LONDON • NEW YORK

Continuum
The Tower Building   15 East 26th Street
11 York Road   Suite 1703
London SE1 7NX   New York 10010

First published in 2001 by
THE ATHLONE PRESS

This edition 2004

British Library Cataloguing in Publication Data
*A catalogue record for this book is available
from the British Library*

ISBN 0 8264 7775 5

Library of Congress Cataloging-in-Publication Data
*A catalog record for this book is available
from the Library of Congress*

Distributed in The United States, Canada and South America by
Transaction Publishers
390 Campus Drive
Somerset, New Jersey 08873

Previously published in hardback in the
Athlone Shakespeare Dictionary series

Typeset by RefineCatch Limited, Bungay, Suffolk
Printed and bound in Great Britain by
Antony Rowe Ltd, Chippenham, Wiltshire

Contents

Illustrations

Series Editor's Preface

The Athlone Shakespeare Dictionaries aim to provide the student of Shakespeare with a series of authoritative guides to the principal subject-areas covered by the plays and poems. They are produced by scholars who are experts both on Shakespeare and on the topic of the individual dictionary, based on the most recent scholarship, succinctly written and accessibly presented. They offer readers a self-contained body of information on the topic under discussion, its occurrence and significance in Shakespeare's works, and its contemporary meanings.

The topics are all vital ones for understanding the plays and poems; they have been selected for their importance in illuminating aspects of Shakespeare's writings where an informed understanding of the range of Shakespeare's usage, and of the contemporary literary, historical and cultural issues involved, will add to the reader's appreciation of his work. Because of the diversity of the topics covered in the series, individual dictionaries may vary in emphasis and approach, but the aim and basic format of the entries remain the same from volume to volume.

Sandra Clark
Birkbeck College
University of London

Acknowledgements

Brian Southam and Gordon Williams invited me to write this volume and helped lay the foundations for my work. Advice and practical assistance, including the loan of books and other material, has come, sometimes even before I thought to ask, from John Durkan, John Gardner, Ernst Honigmann, David Hopkins, Willy Maley, Rob Maslen, David Pascoe and Peter Walsh. Others have been patient enough to read and comment closely on a range of draft entries, in some cases kindly allowing me to make use of ideas and suggestions without specific acknowledgement: Alastair Fowler, Peter France, John Jowett, Donald Mackenzie and David Newell. Elisabeth Leedham-Green scrutinized a penultimate draft of the complete book. My greatest debt is to Bob Cummings, whose other kindnesses great and small have been surpassed by his reading and discussion of the whole volume as it has taken shape, resulting in many important suggestions, corrections and redirections. I am of course solely responsible for remaining shortcomings. My thanks to all of these, and to my family, which has been growing alongside this book, for a full range of diversions.

Acknowledgement is also made to the Librarian, Glasgow University Library, for permission to reproduce the illustrations (actual size except where stated), all of which are drawn from the Glasgow University collections.

SFG
University of Glasgow
March 2000

Abbreviations

Periodicals

ANQ	*American Notes and Queries*
CahiersE	*Cahiers Elisabéthains*
CompD	*Comparative Drama*
CompLit	*Comparative Literature*
EinC	*Essays in Criticism*
ELH	*ELH: A Journal of English Literary History*
ELN	*English Language Notes*
ELR	*English Literary Renaissance*
ES	*English Studies*
HLQ	*Huntingdon Library Quarterly*
JEGP	*Journal of English and Germanic Philology*
JMRS	*Journal of Medieval and Renaissance Studies*
MLN	*Modern Language Notes*
MLQ	*Modern Language Quarterly*
MLR	*Modern Language Review*
MP	*Modern Philology*
N&Q	*Notes and Queries*
PMLA	*Publications of the Modern Languages Association of America*
PQ	*Philological Quarterly*
RenD	*Renaissance Drama*
RenQ	*Renaissance Quarterly*
RES	*Review of English Studies*
SEL	*Studies in English Literature, 1500–1900*
ShJ	*Shakespeare Jahrbuch* (previously *Jahrbuch der Deutsche Shakespeare-Gesellschaft* and *-Gesellschaft West*)
ShQ	*Shakespeare Quarterly*
ShSt	*Shakespeare Studies*
ShSu	*Shakespeare Survey*
SP	*Studies in Philology*
TSLL	*Texas Studies in Language and Literature*
YES	*Yearbook of English Studies*

Frequently Cited Works

Baldwin (1944)	T. W. Baldwin, *William Shakspere's Small Latine and Lesse Greeke*, 2 vols. Urbana, IL.
Baldwin (1950)	T. W. Baldwin, *On the Literary Genetics of Shakspere's Poems and Sonnets*. Urbana, IL.
Bullough	Geoffrey Bullough, *Narrative and Dramatic Sources of Shakespeare*, 8 vols. London, 1957–75.
Jones (1977)	Emrys Jones, *The Origins of Shakespeare*. Oxford.
Martindale (1990)	Charles and Michelle Martindale, *Shakespeare and the Uses of Antiquity: An Introductory Essay*. London.
Muir (1977)	Kenneth Muir, *The Sources of Shakespeare's Plays*. London.
Satin (1966)	Joseph Satin, ed., *Shakespeare and his Sources*. Boston.
Tillyard (1944)	E. M. W. Tillyard, *Shakespeare's History Plays*. London.

Introduction

A number of excellent books on this topic already exist: why compile another? All students of Shakespeare must be eternally grateful for, in particular, T. W. Baldwin's *Shakspere's Small Latine and Lesse Greeke* (1944) and Geoffrey Bullough's *Narrative and Dramatic Sources of Shakespeare* (1957–75), but they and their companions on the library shelf (such as Kenneth Muir's *The Sources of Shakespeare's Plays*, 1957–77, and Emrys Jones' *The Origins of Shakespeare*, 1977) do not meet all needs. The scholarly work these volumes reflect appeared a generation or more ago, and there has been no shortage of new contributions in recent decades; moreover, all are selective in some way or ways. Baldwin's monumental study is confined to the influence of the classics, and Jones specializes in the early plays. Muir's attention is more evenly spread, though more glancing, but still he offers no more than thirty pages on all the Late Plays and none on the poems. Bullough's eight-volume set, because it is essentially a collection of documents, deals with certain kinds of sources and analogues only, and often, as it happens, those with limited intrinsic interest – nothing by so important a figure for Shakespeare as **Virgil**, for example, is included.[1] Finally, these existing works simply do not allow easy reference to information on many of the writers who affected Shakespeare and how they did so, because they arrange their information not by source-author but by individual Shakespeare text; a plethora of index entries must be consulted before an overview can be formed. However unfashionable the notion of the author may be today, **Chaucer** or **Seneca** or **Marlowe** were as Shakespeare conceived them real individuals responsible for a range of different works, and it follows that one way of understanding the nature of his conceptions is to consider each of these ranges of textual entities as a group, instead of pondering Shakespeare's use of them one instance at a time.

This book is not intended to replace, or rehash, the invaluable volumes of Bullough or Baldwin or Jones, then, but supplies something different. In 1964 Kenneth Muir wrote a short article 'The Future of Shakespeare Source-Hunting' for the *Shakespeare Newsletter*. He suggested

1

that once Bullough's eight volumes were complete, little would remain to be discovered about Shakespeare's plot sources, but that scholars ought methodically to investigate the area of Shakespeare's reading, about which knowledge is only fragmentary. Both areas are, in fact, fruitful for scholarship. Since Muir's essay, large numbers of studies have appeared on new aspects of previously recognized Shakespearean sources, and, partly because understanding of the nature of a source has been changing to embrace intertextuality more loosely conceived, fresh texts have been brought into conjunction with Shakespeare's. The present compilation, through attending to both acknowledged plot sources and other kinds of material he was acquainted with, aims to be a digest of information on Shakespeare's literary knowledge in general. This knowledge will usually, but not always, have been acquired through reading (he saw plays on stage, for example). Hence this is a guide not only to what we customarily think of as Shakespeare's immediate 'sources'; many writers (such as **Cicero**, **Daniel** or **Marlowe**) who have or seem to have more diffuse effects on Shakespeare's work than what this term usually tends to suggest (such as Arthur **Brooke**, **Cinthio** or **Lodge**) can nevertheless be of great interest and importance in understanding that work.

Or we may think of 'creative and imaginative' sources as opposed to 'narrative and dramatic ones', as Hal Jensen has recently distinguished them:

> Look into any volume of Geoffrey Bullough's invaluable *Narrative and Dramatic Sources of Shakespeare* and you will find few works that have an eminent place of their own on the literature shelves. These plays, poems and histories interest us largely to the extent to which they fail to be Shakespeare . . . It is different for those which belong in that as yet unwritten compendium, Shakespeare's Creative and Imaginative Sources, which would present those works – by Marlowe, say, and Ovid – to which Shakespeare owed a profound artistic debt.[2]

But the two categories do not have to be separated thus (indeed they cannot be, and Bullough does in fact include several texts from Ovid). Scholarly ideas of how one work may leave its mark on another, of the range of possible things a 'source' may be, are changing. What Robert S. Miola calls 'our recently expanded understanding of sources' involves the assumption, generally made now, that a text may derive from a source quite obliquely, when it is part of a 'tradition' or 'context' for a work; and the understanding, now common enough, that evidence about a source can be derived from 'scenic form, thematic figuration, rhetorical strategy, structural parallelism, ideational or imagistic concatenation' as well as more straightforward kinds of 'verbal iteration'.[3] These changes in our presuppositions do not invalidate earlier work, but they do lead – have already led – to a different range of possible effects on Shakespeare being identified in acknowledged sources, and to new sources being proposed. This compendium takes account of such developments – necessarily so, since its basis throughout is the recent findings of other scholars. In other words, it is based on a broader sense of how literary texts can relate to one another than is reflected in the standard earlier studies.

While it seems that commentators will always overplay their hands, and more works will always be claimed as Shakespearean sources than will be widely credited, it is the case that the present generation of scholars has tended to accept a greater number of these claims than has ever been acknowledged before. But there are still limits on what can usefully be included in this volume, which is not conceived as a general guide to what the English read in the second half of the sixteenth century, and is in fact not intended to stray very far from what the Elizabethans would have thought of as literary, 'letters', a category which includes, in particular, history, but tends not to extend to, for example, most popular songs, chapbooks, pamphlets and tracts. It deals primarily with works of this kind that we know or can on current evidence suppose Shakespeare read in whole or in part, and which affected his own writing in some way. 'Negative' influences, when a work is read and reacted *against*, are sometimes said to be intrinsically less susceptible to investigation than 'positive' ones, but strongish reactions at least are often traceable, and are discussed under a number of headings here. Analogues, on the other hand, however interesting in their own right, are not covered.

Discrimination between hard-to-distinguish phenomena, such as 'affinity' and 'echo', is of course crucial in determining, so far as it can be done, whether we should believe a given work affected Shakespeare. Discrimination between other phenomena, such as 'allusion' and 'imitation', is crucial in determining, so far as it can be done, what kind of effect it was. In both cases, informed interpretation depends greatly on appropriate historical contextualization. At the simplest level, the likelihood of Shakespeare's having knowledge of a work available only in a Polish-language edition is more remote than in the case of a French-language one. One section of each main entry in this dictionary is devoted to the availability, presentation, reputation and use of each writer or text in Shakespeare's time.

Like Geoffrey Bullough's compendium, this book aims in the main 'not to discover new sources but to make those already known accessible' – or rather, to make information about them, including samples of them, accessible. Quantities of fresh discoveries are not to be expected in a compilation of this kind, though some ideas are aired. Needless to say, though, no book of this kind can be neutral or impersonal: the compiler's own judgement about what to include in each entry is engaged at every step. Constructing entries regularly involves assembling the available information in new ways, or sometimes supplying new pieces of information; and in selecting and prioritizing material, this volume deliberately differs from most bibliographies.

Scope and Arrangement of Entries

Some difficult choices have presented themselves where it seemed that two or more alternative entries could be constructed. A full entry on **The Bible** seems obviously preferable to a series of entries on Tyndale, Coverdale, and so on, whereas separate entries on **Livy**, **Pliny** and **Camden** are needed rather than one on Philemon Holland, the translator of all three. The choice is less straightforward where a single translator and a single work are concerned. Should there be an entry for Thomas North, or for Plutarch? At the risk of neglecting the translator, the entry is usually on the source: an entry on **Plutarch** is supplied, but not one on North. There are several justifications. In many cases (not as it happens including this one) there is uncertainty about which translation Shakespeare used; Shakespeare will in probably most cases have known more about the source-author than the translator; the reader is more likely to look up the source first. In all cases cross-references are supplied, and in many cases a specimen of the translator's work is quoted in the entry under the source-author.

For similar reasons, sections of one writer's work later incorporated into another's (for example in the chroniclers' constant recycling of material) are generally treated under the original writer where there is a likelihood Shakespeare knew he was reading him, even if he would have done so as part of a later compilation. Hence **More** has an entry on account of his *History of King Richard III*, as well as there being a separate entry for **Hall**, through whose Chronicle Shakespeare must have known More's work. Adapters and imitators whose work had largely broken free of connections with their original author are also discussed separately – for example, Arthur **Brooke**, whose version of the Romeo and Juliet story is a loose adaptation of a French text definitely not known to Shakespeare, and the very different versions by **Caxton** and **Lydgate** of Guido delle Colonne's *Historia Troiana*. In considering the writing to which this volume is a guide, one is of course dealing all the time with somewhat arbitrarily selected points in a continuum of literary reworkings. But cross-references are provided in abundance in such cases, as well as in those of writers and works subsumed under headings (such as **Chronicle History Plays**) which collect a range of different minor figures or texts together. Cross-references are intended to help locate writers and texts discussed as part of Shakespeare's reading, and do not lead to mentions of them in other contexts. For these, and for occasional references to writers Shakespeare is not believed to have read, see the Index.

Within each main entry, the format for the series in which this compilation appears is followed, with necessary adjustments, and with flexibility in length and level of detail to allow for the variety of the writers treated and the ways in which Shakespeare used them. Section A is a brief, factual, biographical/historical description of the writer and/or work(s). Section B supplies information on the reputation, presentation, availability and use of the writer or work in Shakespeare's time, usually with an excerpt giving either a representative sample, particular Shakespearean source-material, or both at once. The aim is to indicate how the writer or work would have appeared to Shakespeare's eyes, and the dominant ways in which it was being represented. Section C is a detailed, though not exhaustive, discussion of the relationship to Shakespeare's plays and poems, with some reference to the scholarly literature and, where immediate comparisons seem illuminating, quotation of the Shakespeare work(s) in question. Finally, Section D contains a bibliography, prefaced by a headnote for quick guidance if there are more than a few items involved. These bibliographies go with Section C, that is, they are bibliographies on Shakespeare's use of the writer or text, though they also include any item cited in Section A or B. They are not intended to be fully comprehensive, particularly for much-discussed sources and on older publications.[4] The bibliographies will locate much

5

of the most significant material of recent decades, in which further references will be found, and give chapter and verse for items cited and/or quoted. Purely comparative studies and works which merely summarize previous ones are not included here. Some help is given to those who use smaller libraries by indications of more than one possible source, including for example reprints, of the same text. Unlike other volumes in this series, this one does not contain a comprehensive bibliography at the end, because it is in the case of this extremely extensively-researched field much more convenient for the reader to consult the Section D bibliographies under the individual headings.

It will be understood that absolutely complete coverage of the territory on which this volume gives guidance is not possible. In any case, entries supplying full information (biography, contemporary reputation, and so on) on the writers of works which figure in only brief and superficial ways in Shakespeare would be largely redundant. A shorter form of entry is therefore employed for many subjects with a slighter or more doubtful importance for Shakespeare. This consists solely of a sentence-long summary and a maximum of three bibliographical items, together with cross-references to any other relevant entry/ies, indicating where more information can be found on the subject. Some such entries are on writers and texts whose pertinence to Shakespeare has been disproved, information to which effect is assumed to be potentially useful. There are of course many cases in which it is a matter of opinion whether a given work is of slight importance for Shakespeare or not; but there are limits to how large such a compilation as this can be allowed to become. Hence the existence of, say, a single speculative article proposing a given writer as an influence on Shakespeare may not result in an entry for that writer, particularly where such a speculation has been made public some years ago and gone unsupported since then.

Quotations

Since works Shakespeare knew are usually quoted in order to show what he may have read, a version (text, translation, edition), or where possible *the* version, available to him is often drawn on – though the quotation of long stretches of foreign-language texts is avoided. For similar reasons, and also because evidence about Shakespeare's reading turns not seldom on small details of phrasing, and even on occasion of spelling, excerpts from such texts, whether taken directly from early editions or quoted from modern ones, involve minimal modernization.

(Very few special cases include **Mystery Plays**, which in their original form are rebarbatively difficult for some readers today, and which in any case Shakespeare is much more likely to have seen performed than to have read.) However, in all quotations, contractions, typographical ligatures and ampersands are expanded, ∫ is replaced by 's' and VV/vv by W/w, usage of u/v and i/j is regularized, and black letter, decorative or multiple initial capitals and superscript are ignored. Slight and obvious printing errors are corrected, silently where they make no difference to issues of borrowing and influence. No collation of press variants has been attempted; the copy used is from the Glasgow University Library collections where one is available, otherwise almost always the British Library or Cambridge University Library.

There seemed no corresponding necessity to quote Shakespeare himself from the (to most readers less than familiar) old-spelling texts, and I use instead Peter Alexander's modernized one in the form of *Complete Works of William Shakespeare* (reprint Glasgow, 1994), supplemented for the apocrypha by Stanley Wells and Gary Taylor, eds, *William Shakespeare: The Complete Works*, compact edition (Oxford, 1994), and by other texts individually referenced. Obvious misprints are also silently corrected in these texts. Layout of all play quotations is standardized for speakers' names, stage directions, etc.

Conventions Used

Titles of frequently cited works and standard journals are abbreviated as shown in the List of Abbreviations. To save space, frequently cited works are grouped together on a single line at the start of the bibliographical listing (Section D) in each entry if more than one figures in that list. Where a writer or topic which has an independent entry is referred to within another entry, attention is drawn to the existence of the independent entry by printing in bold the heading under which it appears on the first occasion it is mentioned in an entry, as in this introduction.

Notes

1 Bold print signals the heading of an entry in the body of this dictionary.
2 *TLS*, 5 February 1999, p. 19.
3 Robert S. Miola, 'Shakespeare and his Sources: Observations on the Critical History of "Julius Caesar"', *ShSu* 40 (1987), 69–76 (p. 71). See the full article.
4 For earlier publications see especially the bibliographies by John W. Velz,

Shakespeare and the Classical Tradition: A Critical Guide to Commentary, 1660–1960 (Minneapolis, 1968, currently being updated) and Selma Guttmann, *The Foreign Sources of Shakespeare's Works: An Annotated Bibliography* (New York, 1947).

A

Accolti, Bernardo (1458–1535), Italian Dramatist
Accolti's *Virginia* (first printed 1513) is based on the **Boccaccio** story used for *All's Well*; its few parallels in Shakespeare do not outweigh the unlikelihood of his direct acquaintance with the play, but it forms part of the tradition of the *All's Well* story.

Cole, Howard C. (1981). *The 'All's Well' Story from Boccaccio to Shakespeare*, pp. 114–37. Urbana, IL.

Achilles Tatius See **Greek Romance**.

Aeschylus (525–456 BC), Greek Tragedian Schleiner's notion that the graveyard scenes of the *Choephoroe* affected *Hamlet* prompts the further question of how Shakespeare would have known them: at one remove in Latin translation, or at several removes?

Schleiner, Louise (1990). 'Latinized Greek Drama in Shakespeare's Writing of *Hamlet*.' *ShQ* 41: 29–48.

Aesop (?6th Century BC), Greek Fabulist
(A) Traditional accounts, deriving largely from Aristotle and his circle,

represent Aesop as a slave in sixth-century Samos. There is no contemporary evidence on the authorship of the large collection of fables
ascribed to him (but certainly the work of several different writers), a
series of anecdotal stories using animal and, in perhaps the most
authentic ones, mythological characters to illustrate moral or satirical
points. They were popularized in the form of verse renderings by the
Roman poet Phaedrus about AD 40. This and a Greek version made by
Babrius soon afterwards are the principal manuscript sources. About
AD 400 the Roman Arianus used Babrius as the main basis of his forty-
two fables in Latin verse; the Aesopic material was particularly widely
diffused in this badly diluted form over many centuries. The fables,
numbering about eighty in typical Renaissance editions but through
various kinds of accretion now reaching over 350 in the largest collections, have for long been most familiar as texts for the young, but this at
least partly reflects the priorities of modern selection.

(B) Aesop was first printed in Latin in *c.* 1470, in Greek *c.* 1480. At
least thirty-five more editions followed before 1500, and the explosion
of interest was quickly reflected in such late medieval writers as
Henryson. Easily Henryson's longest poetic work is his *Morall Fabillis
of Esope the Phrygian* (1490s?), a collection of thirteen fairly elaborate
retellings of stories, half of which derive from the Latin Aesop and half
of which come from a separate tradition. They are made all the more
attractive by their 'hamelie language' and 'termis rude', and the narrative is developed strongly with the 'moralitas' separated into a discrete
section at the end. Henryson, like **Lydgate** and other medieval writers,
thought of Aesop as a poet, and Aesop descended to them either
through the twelfth-century Latin elegiacs of Gualterus Anglicus (the
most popular medieval collection) or the Old French verse of Marie
de France's *Ysopets Fabulae*. But from 1484, when **Caxton**'s version
included a translation of the spurious life of Aesop to which Maximus
Planudes, a fourteenth-century Byzantine monk, had given currency by
attaching it to his collection of fables, writers tended to imagine Aesop
in a very different role, and the fables were approached as works of
prose. The figure now (and until Bentley exploded the fiction in 1697)
imagined as Aesop was a gargoyle, deformed and of dubious moral
character; given wit by a goddess for an act of kindness, he was said to
have become a gadfly to discomfort the powerful. This Aesop figure for
a time assumed an independent literary life, pointing a moral in person

in a wide range of writers including in the Elizabethan era Francis Bacon, Sir Edward Dyer, Gabriel **Harvey** and **Nashe** (see Smith 1931). But this popular myth had little effect on those disposed to regard Aesop as the moral teacher he had already become for Henryson, and most of the early English versions of Aesop are intended for pedagogical purposes. As well as finding favour for its ethically improving effects, it has been proposed, Aesop's moralized view of nature may have been responsible for this tendency in much early modern natural history – indeed Baldwin claims, somewhat rashly, that 'there was no other literary view' (1944: 1, 638).

What early modern readers were actually reading was at several removes from the Greek or early Latin forms of Aesop's tales. There is so much rearrangement of the texts, with additions, subtractions and modifications to the original fables, that 'the "Aesop" of the late middle ages . . . is indeed no classical work, but a creation of the medieval period itself, though resting on a solid ancient basis' (Lathrop 1933: 18–19). Caxton's 'Aesop' was translated from Machault's French version of a German rendering of a Latin recension. Caxton's was the best-known English version, going through many editions, and apparently the only one available in Shakespeare's youth – though several others were made during Shakespeare's lifetime (for which see Baldwin 1944: 1, 607–40). Caxton's account of the well-known fable of the fox and the grapes (or here raisins; Chambry no. 32) is the kind of text sixteenth-century readers would have found if they had wanted Aesop in English (as Shakespeare apparently did not – see (C), below). Fig. 1 shows the text as it appeared with Caxton's woodcut illustration.

> He is not wyse / that desyreth to havre a thynge whiche he may not have / As reciteth this fable of a foxe / whiche loked and beheld the raysyns that grewe upon an hyghe vyne / the whiche raysyns he moche desyred for to ete them
> ¶ And whanne he sawe that none he myght gete / he torned his sorowe in to Joye / and sayd these raysyns ben sowre / and yf I had some I wold not ete them / And therfore this fable sheweth that he is wyse / which fayneth not to desyre that thynge the whiche he may not have /

> (Aesop 1976: sig. i3ʳ)

(C) The only direct mention of Aesop in the Shakespearean corpus

❡ The fyrst fable maketh mencyon of the foxe and of the rapsyns

He is not wyse/ that desyreth to haue a thynge whiche he may not haue/ As reciteth this fable Of a foxe/whiche loked and behelde the rapsyns that grewe vpon an hyghe vyne/the whiche rapsyns he moche desyred for to ete them ❡ And whanne he sawe that none he myght gete/ he torned his sorowe in to Joye/and sayd these rapsyns ben sowre/and yf I had some I wold not ete them/ And therfor this fable sheweth that he is wyse / whiche fayneth not to desyre that thynge the whiche he may not haue/

❡ The second fable is of the auncyent wesel and of the rat/

Figure 1 William Caxton, *The History and Fables of Aesop* (London, 1484), sig. i3ʳ.

gives the defeated Prince Edward in *3 Henry VI* a dismissive attitude towards his fables:

QUEEN MARGARET   Ah, that thy father had been so resolv'd!
GLOUCESTER   That you might still have worn the petticoat
                       And ne'er have stol'n the breech from Lancaster.
PRINCE   Let Aesop fable in a winter's night;
                       His currish riddles sorts not with this place.

(5.5.25–6)

(where 'currish' = 'base', 'ignoble', probably with a pun on 'dog-like', i.e. concerned with animals). Whether or not Shakespeare wrote these lines, it is doubtful whether he shared the attitude, for, if the Shakespeare apocrypha is included, some twenty or more of the Aesopic fables are fairly definitely referred to in the corpus, some more than once (Baldwin 1944: I, 617–37 gives a complete catalogue).

On the other hand, Shakespeare would not have associated all, or perhaps even many, of these twenty fables with Aesop. So heavily diffused were the fables in different kinds of compilation, including for example collections of **Emblems** and **Erasmus**' *Adagia*, that Shakespeare would probably have thought of 'Aesop' as a type of story rather than a fixed corpus of tales. Some of the tales had evidently become proverbial. For the same reasons it is probably an unreliable procedure to identify from variants of the tales used by him a single text of Aesop which Shakespeare could have relied upon (though Baldwin 1944: I, 615ff., thinks it must have been an edition, perhaps 1573, of the popular Latin compilation *Fabellae Aesopicae* made for use in schools by Camerarius, and points to some apparent verbal echoes of it).

Aesopic material is spread in no obvious pattern over Shakespeare's plays. Although his use of Aesop is sometimes said to constitute one of Shakespeare's ways of expressing similarities between human beings and animals, many instances support this vaguely at best. A typically Shakespearean use might be the story of the fox and the grapes ((B), above) as mentioned by Lafeu in *All's Well*:

O, will you eat
No grapes, my royal fox? Yes, but you will
My noble grapes, an if my royal fox
Could reach them.

(2.1.68–71)

Other fables used by Shakespeare are not in fact concerned with the animal world, but with natural features such as plants and rivers.

What is clear, however, is that Shakespeare alludes again and again to two or three Aesopic fables which can be used to express an idea particularly effectively or economically, and/or which strike his imagination especially strongly. Their effectiveness had led to their becoming proverbial. One is the story of the hawk and the dove, used to illustrate reversal of natural hierarchy in, for instance, *A Midsummer Night's Dream* 2.1.232, *Antony and Cleopatra* 3.13.195–7, and *Coriolanus* 5.6.115. Another is the story of the countryman and the snake he warms in his bosom only to have it bite him (Chambry no. 82), used still more often and 'regularly given . . . its proper moral application' by Shakespeare (Baldwin 1944: I, 618):

> I fear me you but warm the starved snake,
> Who, cherish'd in your breasts, will sting your hearts.
> > (*2 Henry VI*, 3.1.343–4)

> O villains, vipers, damn'd without redemption!
> Dogs, easily won to fawn on any man!
> Snakes, in my heart-blood warm'd, that sting my heart!
> > (*Richard II*, 3.2.129–31)

> I tore it from the traitor's bosom, King;
> Fear, and not love, begets his penitence.
> Forget to pity him, lest thy pity prove
> A serpent that will sting thee to the heart.
> > (*Richard II*, 5.3.55–8)

> help me; do thy best
> To pluck this crawling serpent from my breast! . . .
> Methought a serpent eat my heart away,
> And you sat smiling at his cruel prey.
> > (*A Midsummer Night's Dream*, 2.2.145–50)

(D)

Aesop, translated by William Caxton (1976). *The History and Fables of Aesop, Translated and Printed by William Caxton, 1484. Reproduced in facsimile from the copy in the Royal Library, Windsor Castle, with an introduction by Edward Hodnett*. London.

Baldwin (1944).

Chambry, Emile, ed. (1927). *Esope Fables, Texte Etabli par Emile Chambry*. Paris.

Crundell, H. W. (1935). 'Shakespeare, Lyly, and "Aesop".' *N&Q* 168: 312.

Lathrop, H. B. (1933). *Translations from the Classics into English from Caxton to Chapman*. Madison, WI.

Smith, M. Ellwood (1931). 'Aesop, A Decayed Celebrity: Changing Conception as to Aesop's Personality in English Writers before Gray.' *PMLA* 46: 225–36.

Africanus, Leo (Leo Joannes Africanus) (*c.* 1495–1552), Travel Writer Africanus, available in John Pory's 1600 translation *A Geographical Historie of Africa*, may have contributed details to Shakespeare's conception and portrayal of Othello.

Bullough, vii, 208–11.

Whitney, Lois (1922). 'Did Shakespeare know Leo Africanus?' *PMLA* 37: 470–83.

***Amadis de Gaule* (Spanish Romance)** This romance, especially in the version of 1542 by Feliciano de Silva (available in French from 1551), is notable for containing more than one story of a statue returned to life, in one case involving some other similarities to *The Winter's Tale*.

Bullough, viii, 133.

Honigmann, E. A. J. (1955). 'Secondary Sources of *The Winter's Tale*.' *PQ* 34: 27–38.

***Apollonius of Tyre* (Anon. Romance)** See **Greek Romance**.

Appian, of Alexandria (*fl. c.* AD 160), Greek Historian
(A) Appian was a barrister in the Roman civil service under Trajan and

Hadrian. His History (*Roman History, Historiae Romanae*) was written in Greek, organized geographically, and described Rome's conquests in different parts of the globe, from the arrival of Aeneas in Italy to the Battle of Actium of 31 BC, in twenty-four Books. Only ten Books survive in full, including those dealing with the Punic Wars and the Civil Wars; the contents of others are known through medieval summaries.

Appian follows different sources in different parts of his History, sometimes using poor authorities and sometimes distorting good ones. On the Civil Wars he shows himself a cautious writer, part of a 'long tradition of a complex and divided response to the Caesar story' (Schanzer 1956: xvii), mixing admiration for Brutus and Cassius with horror at the murder, and refusing to commit himself on their motives. Perhaps his major contribution to the history of this period is his portrayal of Antony as a schemer given to histrionics, but he also develops oratorical material, especially Brutus' and Antony's, considerably.

(B) A Latin version of Appian's History was made by Pietro Candido for Pope Nicholas V in 1452. The text was first printed in Greek at Paris in 1551. The earliest English translation, *An Auncient Historie and Exquisite Chronicle of the Romanes Warres, both Civile and Foren*, was made by 'W. B.' (perhaps William Barker, *fl.* 1570, translator of **Xenophon**) and issued in 1578. It is a scholarly piece of work, accurately reflecting the several versions of Appian's text in French, Latin and Greek on which it draws. Its printer's dedication, by Henry Bynneman, presents Appian's purpose very wrongly (but probably merely reflecting a standard Elizabethan attitude to Caesar's story) as being 'to extoll the princely rule', showing 'how God plagueth them that conspire against theyr Prince' (Appian 1578: sig. A2^{r-v}). Appian does indeed see the hand of God in the defeat of Brutus and Cassius, not, however, 'in pursuit of the providential plan for the establishment of imperial rule', like **Plutarch**, but 'in punishment of the multiple crime which they committed in slaying Caesar' (Schanzer 1963: 15–16).

Appian seems to have been well enough known among educated Elizabethans. Lawrence Humphrey in *The Nobles, or of Nobilitye* (1563) remarks that in '*Historical* knowledge', 'emongs the Grekes, *Plutarke, Appian, Thucydides*, are of greatest name'. **Lodge** based his play *The Wounds of Civil War* (published 1594) largely on Appian's History, and the anonymous play *Caesar's Revenge* (**Caesar and Pompey**), apparently an influence on *Julius Caesar*, derives both material and attitudes from him. The History was also consulted by Robert **Garnier** for his play *Marc-Antoine* (1578).

The excerpt from W. B.'s version given here contains the climax of Antony's funeral speech for Caesar in Book II.

When he had saide thus, he pulled up his gowne lyke a man beside hymselfe, and gyrded it, that he might the better stirre his handes: he stoode over the Litter, as from a Tabernacle, looking into it, and opening it, and firste sang his Himne, as to a God in heaven. And to confirme he was a God, he held up his hands, and with a swift voice, he rehearsed the warres, the fights, the victories, the nations that he had subdued to his Countrey, and the great booties that he had sent, making every one to be a marvell. Then with a continuall crie,

This is the only unconquered of all that ever came to hands with him. Thou (quoth he) alone diddest revenge thy countrey being injured .300. years, and those fierce nations that onely invaded *Rome*, and only burned it, thou broughtest them on their knees.

And when he had made these and many other invocations, he tourned hys voice from triumphe to mourning matter, and began to lament and mone him as a friend that had bin unjustly used, and did desire that he might give hys soule for *Caesars*. Then falling into moste vehement affections, uncovered *Caesars* body, holding up his vesture with a speare, cut with the woundes, and redde with the bloude of the chiefe Ruler, by the which the people lyke a Quire, did sing lamentation unto him, and by this passion were againe repleate with ire. And after these speeches, other lamentations wyth voice after the Country custome, were sung of the Quires, and they rehearsed again his acts and his hap.

Then made he *Caesar* hymselfe to speake as it were in a lamentable sort, to howe many of his enimies he hadde done good by name, and of the killers themselves to say as in an admiration, *Did I save them that have killed me?* This the people could not abide, calling to remembraunce, that all the kyllers (only *Decimus* except) were of *Pompeys* faction, and subdued by hym, to whom, in stead of punishment, he had given promotion of offices, governments of provinces and armies, and thought *Decimus* worthy to be made his heyre and son by adoption, and yet conspired hys death. While the matter was thus handled, and like to have come to a fray, one shewed out of the Litter

17

the Image of *Caesar*, made of waxe, for hys body it selfe lying flat in the Litter, could not be seene. Hys picture was by a devise turned about, and .xxiii. wounds wer showed over al his body, and his face horrible to behold. The people seeing this pittifull picture, coulde beare the dolour no longer, but thronged togyther, and beset the Senate house, wherein *Caesar* was kylled, and set it a fyre, and the kyllers that fledde for their lives, they ranne and sought in every place, and that so outragiouslye both in anger and dolour, as they kylled *Cynna* the Tribune being in name lyke to *Cynna* the Pretor that spake evill of *Caesar*, and wold not tarry to heare the declaration of his name, but cruelly tore him a peeces, and lefte not one parte to be put in grave. They caried fire against other mens houses, who manlye defending themselves, and the neighbours entreating them, they refrayned from fyre, but threatned to be in armes the next day.

(Appian 1578: sigs X3ᵛ–X4ʳ)

(C) *Julius Caesar* and *Antony and Cleopatra* seem to reflect knowledge of Appian. In both cases Appian supplements Plutarch with details not readily available to Shakespeare elsewhere. *Julius Caesar* uses him principally for the portrayal of Antony, in particular for Antony's funeral oration on Caesar, which has similarly theatrical, almost operatic, qualities in both writers. There are only a few verbal and formal resemblances between the scenes, however, and 'Appian's Antony differs from Shakespeare's Antony in his attitude to his audience, in the arrangement of his material, and to a considerable extent in the material itself . . . Nevertheless, in some of the details the speeches correspond' (MacCallum 1967: 647). Perhaps the strongest link is in the overall manner:

ANTONY   Good friends, sweet friends, let me not stir you up
          To such a sudden flood of mutiny.
          They that have done this deed are honourable.
          What private griefs they have, alas, I know not,
          That made them do it; they are wise and honourable,
          And will, no doubt, with reasons answer you.
          I come not, friends, to steal away your hearts;
          But, as you know me all, a plain blunt man,
          That love my friend; and that they know full well
          That gave me public leave to speak of him.

> For I have neither wit, nor words, nor worth,
> Action, nor utterance, nor the power of speech,
> To stir men's blood; I only speak right on.
> I tell you that which you yourselves do know;
> Show you sweet Caesar's wounds, poor poor dumb
>   mouths,
> And bid them speak for me. But were I Brutus,
> And Brutus Antony, there were an Antony
> Would ruffle up your spirits, and put a tongue
> In every wound of Caesar, that should move
> The stones of Rome to rise and mutiny.

ALL	We'll mutiny.
1 PLEBEIAN	We'll burn the house of Brutus.
3 PLEBEIAN	Away, then! Come seek the conspirators.

(3.2.210–33)

Antony and Cleopatra's material from Appian is more minor. Shakespeare seems to have consulted W. B.'s translation out of dissatisfaction with Plutarch's discussion of Pompey's rebellion and death and the uprisings of Fulvia and Lucius Antonius. Some of the obscurities in Plutarch's accounts of these matters are cleared up by Appian. MacCallum (1967: 648–52) lists verbal parallels, some more convincing than others, for Shakespeare's presentation of Pompey. Schanzer adds more for Pompey and the motives of Lucius Antonius. He concludes with the separate point that Enobarbus is 'Domitius' or 'Domitius Aenobarbus' in Plutarch but 'in Appian, where he plays a much more prominent part, he is always called simply "Aenobarbus" or "Oenobarbus"' (1956: xxvii). All this would indicate that, in *Antony and Cleopatra* as often elsewhere, Shakespeare supplemented his main source with additional material.

(D)

Appian, translated by W. B. (1578). *An Auncient Historie and Exquisite Chronicle of the Romanes Warres, both Civile and Foren.* London.

Bullough, v.

MacCallum, M. W. (1967). *Shakespeare's Roman Plays and their Background.* London (first published 1910).

Schanzer, Ernest (1956). *Shakespeare's Appian: A Selection from the Tudor Translation of Appian's 'Civil Wars'.* Liverpool.

19

Schanzer, Ernest (1963). *The Problem Plays of Shakespeare: A Study of Julius Caesar, Measure for Measure and Antony and Cleopatra.* London.

Apuleius, Lucius (b. *c.* AD 123), Latin Prose Writer

(A) Apuleius, Platonic Roman philosopher, was born in Numidia. He is popularly known for his long story, sometimes described as an early novel, *The Golden Ass* (*Asinus Aureius*), or *Metamorphoses* – the variant titles reflecting early readers' confusion about its intentions. It is a first-person adventure containing elements of horror story, satire, bawdy, neo-Platonism and romance built around a central narrative in which the transformation of the narrator into an ass is exploited to mostly comic effect. It includes an inset story, often translated and adapted (and therefore read) separately, constituting the oldest extant version of the legend of Cupid and Psyche. Apuleius' learned and luscious prose style, especially extreme in scenes describing the mysteries of Isis, is without a parallel in ancient literature.

(B) Sixteenth-century humanists such as **Erasmus** and Vives promoted Apuleius as a stylistic curiosity. Erasmus' and **More**'s reading of him is reflected in their own works in the Lucianic tradition to which he partly belongs, for example More's *Utopia*. Sir Philip **Sidney** cites *The Golden Ass* in the *Apology for Poetry* and alludes to the Cupid and Psyche story in the *Arcadia*; **Spenser** takes other elements as materials for *The Faerie Queene*, as does **Marlowe** in *Hero and Leander*. In the drama, **Dekker**, **Jonson**, **Marston** and Thomas Heywood are among those known to use Apuleius. There is also non-literary interest in *The Golden Ass* as a source of information on everyday life in ancient times.

Some (probably large) part of this popularity is owing to the appearance of the first, and until the eighteenth century only, complete English translation of *The Golden Ass* by William Adlington in 1566. The sober Adlington had little relish for Apuleius' flamboyance, and registers his difficulty with the tale's mixture of qualities and its sometimes 'dark and high' style for which 'new invented phrases' were needed. However, the idiom in direct narrative is straightforward enough, indeed fresh and vigorous, as in the central 'metamorphosis', the transformation of the narrator, Lucius, into an ass after using an ointment he is given by the servant-girl Fotis. The narrator's usual ill-founded optimism and the mismatch of human mind with animal

20

body, the core qualities in his asininity, are among the features on display here:

> Thus Fotis lamented in pittifull sort, but I that was now a perfect asse, and for Lucius a brute beast, did yet retaine the sence and understanding of a man. And did devise a good space with my selfe, whether it were best for me to teare this mischievous and wicked harlot with my mouth, or to kicke and kill her with my heels. But a better thought reduced me from so rash a purpose: for I feared lest by the death of Fotis I should be deprived of all remedy and help. Then shaking myne head, and dissembling myne ire, and taking my adversity in good part, I went into the stable to my own horse, where I found another Asse of Miloes, somtime my host, and I did verily think that mine owne horse (if there were any natural conscience or knowledge in brute beasts) would take pitty upon me, and profer me lodging for that night: but it chanced far otherwise. For see, my horse and the asse as it were consented together to work my harm, and fearing lest I should eat up their provender, would in no wise suffer me to come nigh the manger, but kicked me with their heeles from their meat, which I my self gave them the night before. Then I being thus handled by them, and driven away, got me into a corner of the stable, where while I remembred their uncurtesie, and how on the morrow I should return to Lucius by the help of a Rose, when as I thought to revenge my self of myne owne horse, I fortuned to espy in the middle of a pillar sustaining the rafters of the stable the image of the goddesse Hippone, which was garnished and decked round about with faire and fresh roses: then in hope of present remedy, I leaped up with my fore feet as high as I could, stretching out my neck, and with my lips coveting to snatch some roses.
>
> (Adlington 1639: III, 17)

(C) There are possible links to *The Golden Ass* in *Venus and Adonis* (diffusely; see Starnes 1945: 1025–30) and in a number of later Shakespeare plays, in particular. These include *Antony and Cleopatra* (for Cleopatra as Isis: see Lloyd 1959); *Macbeth* (for the Witches' incantations in 4.1); *The Tempest* (for Prospero's masque: see Starnes 1945: 1048–50); and *Cymbeline* (for the Cupid and Psyche story as a paradigm for the Platonic theme of 'gazing on beauty bare' in the Imogen plot; see Simonds 1992: 78–92). But asininity of one kind or another is the basis

21

on which most claims for Apuleius' presence in Shakespeare must be made. References to metamorphosis into an ass, not conclusively Apuleian in themselves, are found in *The Comedy of Errors*, but it is Bottom's transformation in *A Midsummer Night's Dream* that has the strongest claim in Shakespeare's work to be regarded as an Apuleian moment.

The case is not conclusive, and, because this episode has an alternative source in Reginald **Scot**'s *Discovery of Witchcraft*, it tends to rely on supporting material derived from other parts of the play. As far as the man/ass transformation is concerned, the play and the story have two unusual features: a man takes on the form of an ass, and a woman is captivated by this new form – so much so that they ludicrously spend a night of pleasure together (in Book XVI of *The Golden Ass*). The first element is found – together with very specific Shakespearean items such as the name 'Robin Goodfellow' – in Scot, but the second is not. There is a further parallel in Apuleius' story of Cupid and Psyche, in which Venus asks Cupid to avenge her by making her rival Psyche fall in love with some base object – though such an ingredient is common in folk tales. These connections are reinforced by a number of others in the *Dream* involving the Cupid and Psyche narrative (enumerated by Tobin 1984: 35–7), connections which have encouraged abstruse or 'philosophical' readings of the play along lines suggested by Kermode (1967: 28): 'On this narrative of Apuleius . . . great superstructures of platonic and Christian allegory had been raised; and there is every reason to suppose that these mysteries are part of the flesh and bone of *A Midsummer Night's Dream*.' McPeek (1972: 69) draws these conclusions about this process of incorporation:

> the fundamental pattern of the myth and the patterns of the main stories in the play are similar in several interlocking ways, and . . . if Shakespeare did not consciously recall the Psyche tale as he wrote, he nevertheless had in mind many of its archetypal features . . . The general impression is not that of an ordering of the play to correspond to the structure of the myth, but rather as if the mosaic of the myth had been shattered into its original *tesserae*, which Shakespeare has picked up and arranged to suit his own design.

(D) Starnes' (1945) article was pioneering and is still a useful short treatment, but the Shakespeare-Apuleius connections noted are sometimes more tenuous than it allows. Easily the most comprehensive

modern study is Tobin (1984), with full reference to previous literature. Tobin tends to discover Apuleius everywhere in Shakespeare; his
findings require careful evaluation where uncorroborated by other
commentators. For *Midsummer Night's Dream*, Generosa (1945), Wilson
(1962) and McPeek (1972), whose findings Tobin synthesizes, provide
some of the requisite corroboration, while Brooks (1979) has a judicious
summary and in an appendix adds new passages to Bullough.
Doody (1998) gives a lively account of Renaissance presentations and
adaptations of *The Golden Ass* outside England.

Adlington, William (1639). *The XI Bookes of the Golden Asse, Conteining the
    Metamorphosie of Lucius Apuleius.* London (first published 1566).
Brooks, Harold F., ed. (1979). *A Midsummer Night's Dream* (Arden
    Shakespeare). London.
Bullough, I.
Doody, Margaret Anne (1998). *The True Story of the Novel.* London (first
    published 1997).
Generosa, Sister M. (1945). 'Apuleius and *A Midsummer Night's Dream*:
    Analogue or Source, Which?' *SP* 42: 198–204.
Kermode, Frank (1967). 'The Mature Comedies', pp. 211–27 in John
    Russell Brown and Bernard Harris, eds, *Early Shakespeare* (Stratford-
    upon-Avon Studies, 3). London (first published 1961).
Lloyd, Michael (1959). 'Cleopatra and Isis.' *ShSu* 12: 88–94.
McPeek, James A. S. (1972). 'The Psyche Myth and *A Midsummer Night's
    Dream.*' *ShQ* 23: 69–79.
Simonds, Peggy Muñoz (1992). *Myth, Emblem and Music in Shakespeare's
    'Cymbeline': An Iconographic Reconstruction.* Newark, DE.
Starnes, D. T. (1945). 'Shakespeare and Apuleius.' *PMLA* 60: 1021–50.
Tobin, J. J. M. (1984). *Shakespeare's Favorite Novel: A Study of The Golden
    Asse as Prime Source.* Lanham (supersedes several previous short articles
    by Tobin in various journals).
Wilson, J. Dover (1962). *Shakespeare's Happy Comedies.* Evanston, IL.
Wyrick, Deborah Baker (1982). 'The Ass Motif in *The Comedy of Errors*
    and *A Midsummer Night's Dream.*' *ShQ* 33: 432–48.

**Aretino, Pietro (1492–1557), Italian Poet and Play-
wright** Cairns (1991) finds 'threads' from Aretino's comedies in
Love's Labour's Lost, Twelfth Night and *The Comedy of Errors*.

Cairns, Christopher (1991). 'Aretino's Comedies and the Italian "Erasmian" Connection in Shakespeare and Jonson', pp. 113–37 in J. R. Mulryne and Margaret Shewring, eds, *Theatre of the English and Italian Renaissance*. Basingstoke.

Ariosto, Ludovico (1474–1533), Italian Poet and Playwright (Excluding *I Suppositi*: see **Gascoigne, George**)
(A) Ariosto was born in Reggio Emilia, but his family quickly moved to the ducal capital of Ferrara, the father advancing as an officer in the service of Duke Ercole I. Having first attempted the study of law, Ludovico devoted himself to letters; but a lifetime's service as a courtier was to be imposed on him by financial pressures. In 1503 he was introduced to the Ferrarese court and employed as a diplomat by the Duke's son, Cardinal Ippolito d'Este, who rewarded him meanly. In about 1505, Ariosto began his capacious poem the *Orlando Furioso*, an epic or 'romance epic' on the adventures of the French hero Roland, a knight pursuing a ludicrous, distorted passion. Three versions of it appeared over the years 1516–32. When the Cardinal left Italy in 1518, his brother, Duke Alfonso, took the poet into his service, making him in the 1520s regional governor of the wild mountain district of Garfagnana. Following his return to Ferrara, Ariosto wrote five dramatic comedies including *I Suppositi*, works which were of some significance in the evolution of European comedy as vernacular imitations of Latin models, and completed the final version of his epic. He was also the author of sonnets, satires and Latin poems.

(B) The first English version of any substance from the *Orlando* was of the episode (an unusually self-contained one for the poem) which was to be most significant for Shakespeare, but the rude disguise in which it appeared makes Ariosto's original barely recognizable. This was the *Historie of Ariodanto and Jenevra, Daughter to the King of Scottes*, put into rugged English verse not dissimilar in character from that of Arthur **Brooke**'s *Tragicall Historye of Romeus and Juliet* by Peter Beverley, and printed about 1566 (see Prouty 1950). The response to Ariosto evinced here is very largely to a storyteller, and the first complete English version of 1591, by Sir John Harington, a courtier and sometime favourite of Queen Elizabeth, is not wholly different in this regard. This well-known Elizabethan translation is a work of great energy and occasional inspiration which is, however, a cruder product than its original. It freely omits and adapts its material in ways inspired largely by the high-minded attitude to epic that poets had acquired since Ariosto's time, prioritizing gravity and decorum. Some of Ariosto's minor works were also imitated or translated soon after this date, the satires by Joseph Hall (in *Virgidemiae*, 1598) and Gervase Markham (*Ariosto's Satyres*, 1608), and the sonnets earlier and more widely, by such as Wyatt, Surrey, **Spenser** and **Lodge**.

Harington's well-received English version may have stimulated Robert **Greene** to write his romantic comedy *Orlando Furioso* (1594), though this has a limited connection with the Italian work. In any event, Ariosto's epic was already well known in Britain before Harington's translation appeared. George **Gascoigne** had Englished parts of Canto xxxiii in 1572, followed in the next decade by John Stewart of Baldynnis' curious *Abregement of Roland Furious*, using Desportes' *Imitations de l'Arioste*. Harington himself speaks of an apparently lost version of the same Ginevra story that Beverley had translated, and a play on it is recorded at court in 1582/3 (Prouty 1950: 13) – this was evidently a familiar episode. In fact, the *Orlando Furioso* quickly became one of the most popular literary works of the sixteenth and seventeenth centuries. Several new terms it gave the English language, such as 'rodomont' and 'paladin', are documented around 1600. As with love lyrics and the novella, Italian epics lay behind the English attempt to establish native production, and, together with Tasso's *Gerusalemme Liberata*, Ariosto's was one of the two works often seen as central, as in the case of Spenser. Harington, conceiving of the *Furioso* as a moral and religious work with 'infinit places full of Christian exortation', had offered his readers an Ariosto who was as didactic as he was entertaining – this is partly a matter of the allegorical interpretation supplied in his notes – and such was the Ariosto adopted and acknowledged as a model for *The Faerie Queene*. But his effect on Spenser's poem remains in the end fairly superficial, even if 'conspicuous and fascinating' (Praz 1958: 300).

Though not one of the very popular English Renaissance translations, and indeed at times thoroughly disliked, Harington's Ariosto has been reprinted consistently up to the present. The following not otherwise remarkable passage gives the central part of the Don John/Borachio/Hero plot in *Much Ado*; for the context see (C), below.

When *Polynesso* (so the duke we call)
This tale unpleasant oftentime had hard,
Finding himselfe his likel'hood verie small,
When with my words her deeds he had compard,
Greev'd with repulse, and greeved therewithall,
To see this stranger thus to be prefard,
The love that late his heart so sore had burned,
Was cooled all and into hatred turned.

Entending by some vile and subtill traine,
To part *Genevra* from her faithfull lover,
And plant so great mislike betweene them twaine
Yet with so cunning show the same to cover,
That her good name he will so foule distaine,
Dead nor alive she never shall recover.
But lest he might in this attempt be thwarted,
To none at all his secret he imparted.

Now thus resolv'd (*Dalinda* faire) quoth he,
(So am I cald) you know though trees be topt,
And shrowded low, yet sprout yong shoots we see,
And issue of the head so lately lopt,
So in my love it fareth now with me.
Though by repulse cut short and shrewdly cropt,
The pared tops such buds of love do render,
That still I proove new passions do engender.

Ne do I deeme so deare the great delight,
As I disdain I should be so reject,
And lest this griefe should overcome me quight,
Because I faile to bring it to effect,
To please my fond conceipt this verie night,
Pray thee my deare to do as I direct.
When fair *Genevra* to her bed is gone,
Take thou the cloths she ware and put them on:

26

As she is wont her golden haire to dresse,
In stately sort to wynd it on her wyre,
So you her person lively to expresse,
May dresse your owne, and weare her head attire:
Her gorgets and her jewels rich no lesse,
You may put on t'accomplish my desire,
And when unto the window I ascend,
I will my comming there you do attend.

Thus I may passe my fancies foolish fit,
And thus (quoth he) my selfe I would deceave.
And I that had no reason, nor no wit,
His shamefull drift (though open) to perceave:
Wearing my Mistresse robes, that serv'd me fit,
Stood at the window, there him to receave.
And of the fraud I was no whit aware,
Till that fell out that caused all my care.

(Harington 1591: 33–4; v.21–6)

(C) Shakespeare may have known the *Orlando Furioso* in both the Italian form and in Harington's English translation (the assumption that he could not read Italian has been weakening in recent years). If he did not need to read Harington's English rendering, that is, however, no indication that he failed to do so – but verbal echoes from it seem not to be in evidence. A set of prints used in one of the handsome early Italian editions was later recycled in editions of Harington; Fig. 2 thus shows an illustration to Canto v which Shakespeare might have seen whichever language he read Ariosto in.

The Canto v story of Ariodante and Ginevra is recognized as a direct or indirect source for the plot involving Margaret's impersonation of Hero, and perhaps a few associated elements, in *Much Ado about Nothing*. The episode is set in Scotland, so had at least a measure of particular interest for British readers. Rinaldo travels to St Andrews to champion the Princess Ginevra in the face of an accusation of unchastity which would otherwise result in her being condemned to death. On the way he rescues Dalinda, Ginevra's maid, who reveals that Polynesso, a suitor of Ginevra's with whom the maid was in love, treacherously persuaded her to dress as her mistress, inviting Ginevra's true love Ariodante to witness Polynesso's entry to Ginevra's window by

Figure 2 Orlando Furioso in English Heroical Verse (London, 1591), p. [31]
(actual size 202 × 136mm).

night. Polynesso then planned the murder of Dalinda, from which Rinaldo has saved her. Rinaldo is anticipated at St Andrews by Ariodante, who after a number of complications in the lists kills the villain in single combat. The central figures in Ariosto's version of the story are Polynesso and Dalinda. Other versions, involving various other emphases, include **Bandello**'s, **Belleforest**'s and Spenser's (some fifteen further treatments down to 1601, including translations, plays, etc, are listed in Bullough, II, 533–4; Prouty 1950 seeks to explain the reasons for the story's popularity). Of these, Bandello's is particularly important for Shakespeare.

The main similarities to Shakespeare's plot, then, are the villain's jealousy, his (or his agent's) affair with the maid, her impersonation of the mistress, and her ignorance of its likely effects, including the witnessing of it by the lover. Rinaldo's challenge and the duel with the villain are apparently left aside by Shakespeare as unsuitable for comedy. Though Beatrice enjoins Benedick to 'Kill Claudio', and Claudio is also challenged by Leonato and Antonio, no combat takes place; and this has been thought, in a way, Shakespeare's point: 'romance has a vocation for cruelty but comedy can cure it' (Traugott 1982: 163). Shakespeare's presentation of domestic love and everyday affection, in distinction from romantic or chivalric devotion, has been the central concern of most discussions of *Much Ado*'s Ariostan source, whether or not involving considerations of generic contrast and contamination. Prouty sees in Beatrice and Benedick the 'realistic' rejection of 'dreary conventions' (1950: 62), though unlike some other commentators he also stresses Shakespeare's development of Hero and Claudio away from the impossible romance figures of Ariosto. Others note the combination of 'narrative' and 'theatre' in the elements freshly introduced by Shakespeare – Dogberry, the Friar, Leonato – and suggest his principal interest in the sources lay in 'their representation of the dangerous powers of dramatic play – staging scenes, acting roles, and creating spectacle' (Osborne 1990: 168).

Three other Shakespeare plays are insecurely related to Ariosto. Perhaps the romantic lead in *As You Like It* bears the name of Ariosto's hero because it calls up associations with the lush enchantment of the poem – or perhaps there is no connection. More concretely, several verbal echoes from the same area (Cantos IV–VI) of the *Orlando Furioso* that affected *Much Ado* are claimed in *Othello*, together with one more convincing instance, the expression 'prophetic fury' (3.4.72) in Othello's account of the manufacture of his mother's handkerchief, perhaps from Ariosto's description of Cassandra's 'furor profetico' in his final Canto (XLVI, 80). The expression is not the sole significant item: this 'might have come from another source, and the handkerchief is already in Cinthio; but the sibyl and the magic come from Ariosto alone' (Cairncross 1976: 181). Finally, a general relationship has been remarked between the *Furioso* and *A Midsummer Night's Dream*, for example by Croce, who observed that the play's changing vicissitudes of love and hate recall the complications arising 'in Italian chivalric romances thanks to the two famous neighbouring fountains, one of which filled the heart with amorous desire and the other turned the original ardour into iciness' (quoted Praz 1958: 304). Resemblances in specific details are weak, however, and even if it is agreed that 'without speaking of an actual source, one cannot help noticing a deeper affinity than with any other work of the same period in English literature' (Praz 1958: 305), the likelihood would be that the affinity arises from the interposition of intermediary Italian pastoral playwrights (Della Valle, Pasqualigo, Guazzoni, and others) to whom Ariostan atmospheres came naturally, even if they were not read at first hand by Shakespeare.

(D) Praz (1958) is interesting, if sometimes over-opinionated, on the early English response to Ariosto down to the time of Shakespeare, whereas Gibaldi (1974) begins in this era and continues to the present. Cairncross (1976) provides the basic facts on the Shakespearean relationships in short compass (together with a speculation about *Lear* which has gone unfollowed). Humphreys (1981) does so at slightly more length for *Much Ado* alone. The fullest treatment of this play's Ariostan links is Prouty (1950); Traugott (1982), Osborne (1990) and Rhu (1993) try a variety of new angles.

Cairncross, Andrew S. (1976). 'Shakespeare and Ariosto: *Much Ado about Nothing, King Lear*, and *Othello*.' *RenQ* 29: 178–82.

Gibaldi, Joseph (1974). 'The Fortunes of Ariosto in England and America', pp. 136–58 in Aldo Scaglione, ed., *Ariosto in 1974 in America: Atti del Congresso Ariostesco – Dicembre 1974, Columbia University*. Ravenna.

Harington, Sir John (1591). *Orlando Furioso in English Heroical Verse*. London.

Humphreys, A. R., ed. (1981). *Much Ado about Nothing* (Arden Shakespeare). London.

Osborne, Laurie E. (1990). 'Dramatic Play in *Much Ado about Nothing*: Wedding the Italian *Novella* and English Comedy.' *PQ* 69: 167–88.

Praz, Mario (1958). 'Ariosto in England', pp. 287–307 in Praz, *The Flaming Heart: Essays on Crashaw, Machiavelli, and other Studies in the Relations between Italian and English Literature from Chaucer to T. S. Eliot*. New York.

Prouty, C. T. (1950). *The Sources of Much Ado about Nothing: A Critical Study, Together with the Text of Peter Beverley's 'Ariodanto and Ieneura'*. New Haven.

Rhu, Lawrence (1993). 'Agons of Interpretation: Ariostan Source and Elizabethan Meaning in Spenser, Harington, and Shakespeare.' *RenD* 24: 171–88.

Traugott, John (1982). 'Creating a Rational Rinaldo: A Study in the Mixture of the Genres of Comedy and Romance in *Much Ado about Nothing*.' *Genre* 15: 157–81.

Augustine, of Hippo (Aurelius Augustinus) (354–430)

Claudius' 'limed soul' (*Hamlet* 3.3.68) and Iago's imagery in discussing the freedom of the will (*Othello* 1.3.321ff.) can both be paralleled in St Augustine's writings.

Battenhouse, Roy W. (1969). *Shakespearean Tragedy: Its Art and its Christian Premises*, esp. Appendix I. Bloomington.

Averell, William (*fl.* 1578–1590), Prose Writer

Averell's *Marvailous Combat of Contrarieties* (1588) used the fable of the Body's Members which appears in *Coriolanus* as a warning against sedition at the time of the Spanish Armada; but likelier sources include **Plutarch** and **Livy**.

Muir (1977), 238.

Bade (Badius), Josse See **Mantuan** (Giovanni Baptista Spagnuoli).

Baldwin, William (*fl.* 1547), editor of *A Mirror for Magistrates* See *Mirror for Magistrates, A*.

Bale, John (1495–1563), Bishop and Playwright Bale's *King John* (before 1560) offers a closer dramatic parallel to Shakespeare's death of King John than other known sources.

Morey, James H. (1994). 'The Death of King John in Shakespeare and Bale.' *ShQ* 45: 327–31.

Bandello, Matteo (1485–1561), Italian Novelist See also **Belleforest, François de**; **Brooke, Arthur**; *Gl'Ingannati*.
(A) Born into an aristocratic Lombardian family, Bandello joined the Dominican order as a youth and travelled to monasteries throughout Europe. He left the Church to follow a career as a courtier and court poet, initially at Mantua. He settled in Milan, but political intrigues forced him to flee the city in 1526 leaving his manuscript work behind. After a period of wandering in the service of various courtly patrons he

became an adviser to a pro-French Venetian general. Following the battle of Pavia in 1542 he fled to France, where he was granted a bishop's income, and where he was finally able to assemble the collection of novellas he had been writing for nearly fifty years.

His 214 *Novelle* were published in three volumes in 1554, to immediate acclaim throughout Europe (a fourth part followed posthumously in 1573). The stories, Bandello tells his readers, 'do not constitute a connected history but are a miscellany of diverse events'; they have no Boccaccian *cornice* or framework, though they are accompanied by epistles in which Bandello explains how he came across them, insisting on their authenticity even in some of the most far-fetched cases. Most are romantic, nearly a hundred of them being tales of illicit love. They are told in a racy, emphatically simple style meant to appeal to a courtly rather than popular readership. Bandello's moral stance is much less definite than in the case of **Cinthio**, indeed a cultivated ethical ambiguity is characteristic.

(B) The influence of Bandello's *Novelle* was widespread through Italy, Spain, France and England. Arthur **Brooke**, William **Painter** and especially Geoffrey **Fenton** (in his *Certain Tragicall Discourses of Bandello*, 1567) between them adapted into English a fairly large part of the collection from the 1560s onwards (bibliographical details in Scott 1916), though no complete Elizabethan English translation of Bandello is known. As with translators of other *novellieri*, one characteristic of these English writers is that 'while tending to concentrate on tragic tales from the Italian, they also maintain a moral and didactic purpose which dissipates the tragic complexities of the original text' (Kirkpatrick 1995: 239). Sometimes, especially with Fenton, Bandello's undecorated prose turns into a rhetorical display, largely because the translators were attracted by the pseudo-classical overlay imposed in the French versions of the stories in **Belleforest**'s *Histoires Tragiques* (1559–82), which they often worked from. English dramatists regularly used the translations: Painter's version of the history of the Duchess of Malfi (in part at least a true story), from Bandello via Belleforest, lies behind Webster's play of 1612; other Bandello-inspired playwrights include Beaumont, Fletcher and Massinger.

(C) Bandello was once considered one of the likely sources for *The Rape of Lucrece*, but this possibility is no longer accepted (see Baldwin 1950:

106, 150–1). There is a slight resemblance to his novella III.21, offering a Moor with an Aaron-like character, in the plot of *Titus Andronicus*, but even if Shakespeare knew the story it may have been in an English ballad version instead (see Maxwell 1968: xxxi). Otherwise, apart from his indirect influence on Shakespeare via Belleforest/Fenton (uncertain), Brooke, and Riche (see **Gl'Ingannati**), Bandello may have been useful for the murder scene in *Othello*, and, with **Ariosto**, is one of the two earliest and most important sources for the Hero plot of *Much Ado*.

Bandello's version of the Othello story was reworked by Belleforest and further debased by Fenton, and Shakespeare has been thought likelier to have used these French and English treatments than the original. But, leaving aside preconceptions about his knowledge of Italian, the use of one does not rule out use of another, and it is possible he went back to the Bandello volume he had taken up at the time of *Much Ado*. The murder scene in *Othello* (5.2) is, in fact, 'the strongest evidence that Shakespeare read Bandello in the original Italian': 'the sensational device of having Desdemona momentarily revive and exonerate Othello after having been apparently killed by him . . . is to be found only in Bandello' among known versions of this story (Shaheen 1994: 165), as are the maid's cry for help and the neighbours breaking in to find the dead husband lying prone on top of his expiring wife. Nor does Cinthio's account, which Shakespeare follows up to the murder scene, include a revival after apparent death. (Bullough, VII, 253–62, gives Fenton and his own literal English version of Bandello for comparison.) There is, however, a quite different English work of these years, the play *A Warning for Fair Women* (*c.* 1598–9), performed by Shakespeare's own company, which affords two scenes in which murder-victims are left for dead but regain consciousness and speech before they die.

With the Hero plot of *Much Ado* the case is more substantial. It seems that Bandello was indebted in his twenty-second novella to Ariosto's tale of Polynesso and Ariodante for one or two aspects of his story, but it is otherwise a separate entity (summarized by Prouty 1950: 27–9 and Bullough, II, 64–5). It tells how the knightly Sir Timbreo di Cardona falls in love with Fenicia, daughter of 'a poor gentleman and not his equal'. A rival informs him via an agent that he will see Fenicia betraying him if he hides in the garden. Her consequential 'death' eventually allows for her marriage to a repentant Sir Timbreo years later, unrecognized by him, and diverse joyful reunions. It is one of

Bandello's most successful tales, replete with varied passions and clever twists in the plot.

Shakespeare's combination of Ariosto's and Bandello's stories is remarkable: it 'shows a mind ranging over elements loosely similar but so markedly variant in tone and incidents that only the shrewdest of judgements could co-ordinate them into a theme of such tragi-comic force' (Humphreys 1981: 13). The overall significance of Bandello's story for *Much Ado* is that it takes place 'in the region where tragedy and comedy are cut out of the same cloth' (Doran 1954: 137): the rival's malicious plot for the heroine's affections leads only to mishap, so that a happy outcome is not precluded. But the release of potentially tragic energies is managed in different ways: in Bandello, Fenicia's family is sure God will reveal the truth, whereas in Shakespeare the Watch discovers it in advance. Shakespeare makes significant changes to heighten the dramatic effect in other directions too. The evidence of Hero's infidelity is made to seem much clearer; Claudio's conduct is more disturbing than Sir Timbreo's because more self-assured; the church scene is hence far more powerful; and the equalizing of rank between the families finally 'results in social cordiality all round and eliminates any intrusive considerations of status' (Humphreys 1981: 11). Overall, of course, the Hero plot is subordinated in a larger context, so Hero 'cannot show the fighting qualities of her modesty as does Fenicia in Bandello', because 'Shakespeare deliberately plays her down as compared with Beatrice' (Bullough, II, 77).

A modern English translation of Bandello's twenty-second novella is given by Bullough (II, 112–34). The sententious and rhetorical version by Belleforest, though sometimes proposed as Shakespeare's source, is on balance less likely to have been used than its original (see Humphreys 1981: 14).

(D) Kirkpatrick's (1995) reading of Bandello's work contains some factual inaccuracies. For some English and French translators and adapters, see Levenson (1984); for bibliographical details of English translators, see Scott (1916). Prouty's (1950) is the fullest account of the origins of *Much Ado*; Humphreys (1981) and Bullough summarize the matter with admirable precision. Osborne (1990) proposes 'spectacle' as the key to the play's treatment of its sources. Bullough (VII) and Shaheen (1994) together provide a good case for Bandello's impact on *Othello* 5.2.

Baldwin (1950); Bullough, II, VII.

Doran, Madeleine (1954). *Endeavors of Art: A Study of Form in Elizabethan Drama*. Madison, WI.

Humphreys, A. R., ed. (1981). *Much Ado about Nothing* (Arden Shakespeare). London.

Kirkpatrick, Robin (1995). *English and Italian Literature from Dante to Shakespeare: A Study of Source, Analogue and Divergence*. London.

Levenson, Jill L. (1984). 'Romeo and Juliet before Shakespeare.' *SP* 81: 325–47.

Maxwell, J. C., ed. (1968). *Titus Andronicus* (Arden Shakespeare). London (first published 1953).

Osborne, Laurie E. (1990). 'Dramatic Play in *Much Ado about Nothing*: Wedding the Italian Novella and English Comedy.' *PQ* 69: 167–88.

Prouty, Charles T. (1950). *The Sources of 'Much Ado about Nothing': A Critical Study, Together with the Text of Peter Beverley's 'Ariodanto and Ieneura'*. New Haven.

Scott, Mary Augusta (1916). *Elizabethan Translations from the Italian*. Boston.

Shaheen, Naseeb (1994). 'Shakespeare's Knowledge of Italian.' *ShSu* 47: 161–9.

Bassett, Robert (*fl.* 1599), Historical Writer Bassett is thought to be the author of one of the five Lives of **More** which are considered possible sources for *Sir Thomas More*.

Metz, G. Harold, ed. (1989). *Sources of Four Plays Ascribed to Shakespeare*. Columbia, MI.

Belleforest, François de (1530–1583), French Novelist See also **Bandello, Matteo**; **Brooke, Arthur**; *Gl'Ingannati*.
(A) In his youth a favourite of Marguerite of Navarre, at whose charge he is said to have been educated, the aristocratic Belleforest may have been inspired by her *Heptameron* to compile his own collection of tales. A minor follower of the Pléiade in poetry, and a compiler of chronicles, Belleforest is mainly known for his *Histoires Tragiques extraictes des Oeuvres Italien de Bandel* (in seven volumes, 1559–82), a project he took over from Pierre Boiastuau, who abandoned it after completing only six stories.

These 101 translations or 'retellings' did begin with **Bandello**'s work, but as the volumes went on their scope extended to stories from other classical and medieval writers, notably chroniclers. Belleforest's versions add to the original narrative materials moralistic diatribes and discourses, anticlerical animadversions, letters, and poems, and they effect alterations in emphasis and sometimes in plot which tend to sensationalize, sentimentalize, and reflect the translator's attachment to the notions of courtly love.

(B) The complicated publication history of the *Histoires tragiques* shows that even after a collected edition of 1580, each of the seven volumes was being reprinted separately, with some issued as many as eight times before the end of the sixteenth century. The British Library holds five separate editions of the fifth volume (the earliest of them dated 1576), containing the Hamlet story. There was no complete English translation, but Geoffrey **Fenton** (*c.* 1540–1608) worked extensively from Belleforest when translating thirteen Bandello tales for his *Certaine Tragicall Discourses*, published in 1566, before Belleforest's full collection became available in French. Similarly, William **Painter** drew on Belleforest for the Bandello stories in his influential *Palace of Pleasure* (1566–75). Among English versions of single Belleforest stories, the anonymous *Historie of Hamblet* (1608) is an unacknowledged and sometimes (designedly) inaccurate translation which appears at one or two points to draw on Shakespeare's play, and was presumably published to capitalize on its popularity.

Belleforest's own work nudges the stories in the direction of drama. He adapts 'loosely and in poor proportion perhaps, but with a bustle that points toward the stage. He also adds these techniques and stylistic qualities of his own: moral and psychological observations, . . . inflated dialogue, . . . and action-stopping asides, which point toward soliloquies' (Satin 1966: 382). Most of these features are displayed in this excerpt from the closet scene in the English *Historie of Hamblet* of 1608 (this passage of the translation involves no departures from Belleforest's text affecting the comparison with Shakespeare at this point; a few touches also seem to recall other passages in *Hamlet*).

To conclude, weepe not (madame) to see my folly, but rather sigh and lament your owne offence, tormenting your conscience in regard of the infamie that hath so defiled the ancient renowne and glorie that

37

(in times past) honoured queene Geruth; for wee are not to sorrowe and grieve at other mens vices, but for our owne misdeedes, and great folloyes. Desiring you, for the surplus of my proceedings, above all things (as you love your owne life and welfare) that neither the king nor any other may by any meanes know mine intent; and let me alone with the rest, for I hope in the ende to bring my purpose to effect.

Although the queene perceived herselfe neerly touched, and that Hamlet mooved her to the quicke, where she felt herselfe interested, neverthelesse shee forgot all disdaine and wrath, which thereby she might as then have had, hearing her selfe so sharply chiden and reprooved, for the joy she then conceaved, to behold the gallant spirit of her sonne, and to thinke what she might hope, and the easier expect of his so great policie and wisdome. But on the one side she durst not lift up her eyes to beholde him, remembering her offence, and on the other side she would gladly have imbraced her son, in regard of the wise admonitions by him given unto her, which as then quenched the flames of unbridled desire that before had moved her to affect K[ing] Fengon, to ingraff in her heart the vertuous actions of her lawfull spouse, whom inwardly she much lamented, when she beheld the lively image and portraiture of his vertue and great wise-dome in her childe, representing his fathers haughtie and valiant heart: and so, overcome and vanquished with this honest passion, and weeping most bitterly, having long time fixed her eyes upon Hamlet, as beeing ravished into some great and deepe contemplation, and as it were wholy amazed, at the last imbracing him in her armes (with the like love that a vertuous mother may or can use to kisse and entertaine her owne childe), shee spake unto him in this manner.

I know well (my sonne) that I have done thee great wrong in marrying with Fengon, the cruell tyrant and murtherer of thy father, and my loyall spouse: but when thou shalt consider the small meanes of resistance, and the treason of the palace, with the little cause of confidence we are to expect or hope for of the courtiers, all wrought to his will, as also the power hee made ready, if I should have refused to like of him, thou wouldest rather excuse then accuse me of lascivi-ousnes or inconstancy, much lesse offer me that wrong to suspect that ever thy mother Geruthe once consented to the death and murther of her husband.

(1608 text, ed. Gollancz 1926: 217–21)

(C) Belleforest's *Histoires Tragiques* were the route by which the saga of Amleth or Hamlet entered Elizabethan drama, drawn by the Frenchman from the Danish chronicler Saxo Grammaticus' Latin *Historia Danica*. Numerous parallels between Shakespeare's play and Belleforest's version which are not duplicated in Saxo mean that it must be either a direct source for the play, or an indirect one through the Ur-*Hamlet*, the lost pre-Shakespearean play sometimes supposed to have been written by **Kyd**. (The Ur-*Hamlet* must have been known to Shakespeare, as a play acted at his own theatre; but, as Stabler 1964 shows, there is no good evidence that he knew Saxo.) Some apparent verbal echoes of the French in Shakespeare noted by Jenkins (1982: 94–5) do not settle the question because they may have been present in the Ur-*Hamlet*, which as Jenkins points out could hardly have avoided drawing on Belleforest. The unusual Q1 and Q2 description of *Hamlet* as a 'Tragicall Historie' (recalling Belleforest's title) could also be explained away. But if Shakespeare did use Belleforest, he must have had the French text: the English translation came too late for *Hamlet*.

Whether directly or not, Belleforest is, so far as we can tell, responsible for some crucial elements of *Hamlet*. His main overall emphasis is on the 'great and gallant occurrences' involved in Amleth's carefully planned revenge, in particular the originality and cleverness of the method. This is not reflected in Shakespeare, where Hamlet's revenge is improvised and opportunistic, though Shakespeare may have picked up something of Belleforest's moralistic stress on the anti-Christian nature of revenge and regicide. However, Belleforest's local elaborations of plot, usually in the service of his attempts to sensationalize the story or add circumstantial detail, sometimes have far-reaching consequences for Shakespeare. He adds to Saxo the detail that the Claudius-figure had incestuously seduced his sister-in-law – 'incestueusement souillé la couche fraternelle' – before resorting to parricide, and comments that her subsequent remarriage may have led many to feel the murder was carried out partly to allow this relationship to continue. Belleforest's Queen begs Amleth on his mentioning this suspicion never to believe she consented to the murder (see (B)). The French tale also introduces an agreement that the loser of the combat between the old Hamlet and the King of Norway must pay a forfeiture, which may have suggested the recovery of Norway's lands by the young Fortinbras, who does not figure in Saxo or Belleforest himself. Since he seems to originate the episode of the Prince's sweetheart acting as the king's stalking-horse, Belleforest may even have hinted at the 'equivocal role as both temptress and lover' played by Ophelia (Jenkins 1982: 93–4; Belleforest's account is generally more misogynistic than Saxo's). Finally, whereas Saxo had referred to Hamlet's 'stoliditas' ('dulness') and 'inertia' ('lethargy'), Belleforest mentions 'la vehemence de la melancholie' in Amleth as a reason for his sensitivity to external impressions, including those from the spirit world. As outlined by Stabler (1966), this is possibly the germ of Hamlet's melancholy temper, since Shakespeare makes him say:

> The spirit that I have seen
> May be a devil; and the devil hath power
> T' assume a pleasing shape; yea, and perhaps
> Out of my weakness and my melancholy,
> As he is very potent with such spirits,
> Abuses me to damn me.
>
> (2.2.594–9)

Belleforest's version of the story seems, then, to have been decisive for at least some important features of *Hamlet*, whether or not Shakespeare knew it directly. (It has many other elements of the main plot in common with Saxo, of course, but the Ur-*Hamlet* need not have derived these from the French version.) The evident differences between Belleforest's and Shakespeare's handlings are explored in the service of a case about Kyd and the Ur-*Hamlet* by Law (1948), and summarized by Hibbard (1987: 11–12).

Among other Shakespeare plays, *Twelfth Night* may derive the occasional detail of phrasing from Belleforest's version of the **Gl'Ingannati** story that forms one of its sources, but even if the dramatist knew Belleforest's treatment its effect on his work was marginal. Belleforest's relationship to Shakespeare elsewhere is probably only indirect at most: for *Much Ado about Nothing* see **Bandello**; for *Romeo and Juliet* see **Brooke**.

(D) Both French and English texts of Belleforest's Hamlet story are widely supplied by Shakespeare authorities; they are given *en face* by Gollancz (1926). All the English texts are based on the sole known copy of *The Historie of Hamblet*, 1608, in Trinity College, Cambridge.

Small but numerous and often significant differences between various revisions of Belleforest over time make some early texts more authentic than others, but this does not mean the more authentic are the ones Shakespeare used (see the summary in Gollancz 1926: 318–19). A thorough comparison of Belleforest, Saxo and Shakespeare is carried out by Bullough.

Bullough, vɪɪ; Satin (1966).

Gollancz, Sir Israel, ed. (1926). *The Sources of 'Hamlet': With Essay on the Legend*. London.

Hibbard, G. R., ed. (1987). *Hamlet* (Oxford Shakespeare). Oxford.

Jenkins, Harold, ed. (1982). *Hamlet* (Arden Shakespeare). London.

Law, Robert Adger (1948). 'Belleforest, Shakespeare, and Kyd', pp. 279–94 in James G. McManaway *et al.*, eds, *Joseph Quincy Adams Memorial Studies*. Washington.

Ormsby-Lennon, Theresa Suriano (1977). ' "Piccolo, ma con gran vagghezza": A New Source for *Hamlet*.' *Library Chronicle* (Philadelphia) 41: 119–48.

Stabler, A. P. (1964). 'The Sources of Hamlet: Some Corrections of the Record.' *Research Studies* 33: 207–16.

—— (1966). 'Melancholy, Ambition, and Revenge in Belleforest's Hamlet.' *PMLA* 81: 207–13.

Bellenden (Ballantyne) See Boece (Boethius), Hector.

Bermuda Pamphlets (Jourdain, Strachey, *The True Declaration*, etc.)

Bermuda Pamphlets (Jourdain, Strachey, *The True Declaration*, etc.) These contemporary narratives of New World voyaging offer verbal parallels to certain points in *The Tempest* in the course of their presentation of stories of shipwreck and providential deliverance.

Cawley, Robert Ralston (1926). 'Shakespeare's Use of the Voyagers in *The Tempest*.' *PMLA* 41: 688–726.

Kermode, Frank, ed. (1964). *The Tempest* (Arden Shakespeare), pp. xxvi–xxx and Appendix A. London (first published 1954).

Vaughan, Virginia Mason, and Alden T. Vaughan, eds (1999). *The Tempest* (Arden Shakespeare). London.

Berners, John Bourchier, Lord (1467–1533), English Statesman and Author See **Chaucer, Geoffrey**; **Froissart, Jean**; *Huon of Burdeux*.

Bible, The See also **Book of Common Prayer**; **Homilies**.
(A) The wide availability of the Bible in English was in the later six-teenth century a recent innovation. Although printed Bibles in other European vernaculars had appeared previously, no complete English one existed until 1535. The late fourteenth-century 'Lollard' versions from the Vulgate (St Jerome's Latin Bible), associated with John Wycliffe, went unprinted, and had little or no influence on subsequent English renderings. A fresh start was made in the early sixteenth cen-tury, when zealous Protestants set out to put the Bible into the hands of a laity which increasingly demanded direct access to the text, in the teeth of often fierce opposition from the church and sometimes from the state – institutions which sought to control interpretation and use of the Bible. The process was complete by the time Shakespeare was born, though the reign of the Catholic Mary I (1553–8) temporarily saw a sudden reversal of the tide, with the burning of large numbers both of 'heretics' (see **Foxe**) and of English Bibles.

In 1525 the Lutheran William Tyndale, the first and greatest of the sixteenth-century Bible translators, published his New Testament, cop-ies of which were smuggled into England from the European continent. Tyndale took his text largely from **Erasmus**' Greek Testament, translating it into richly expressive English. He later published his Pentateuch and other segments of the Old Testament from the exile in Antwerp which his radicalism and Lutheranism had made neces-sary. The first complete English printed Bible, however, was Miles Coverdale's of 1535. Coverdale was an associate of Tyndale's and drew heavily on his work; his Bible too was imported from abroad. Coverdale's renderings of the Psalms proved particularly influential, but his Bible is throughout full of melody, essentially a text to be spoken.

Material from Tyndale and Coverdale's versions remained at the core of the English Bible through the later revisions of lesser figures. Such attempts at amalgamation and revision, though not fresh transla-tion, included the pseudonymous Thomas Matthew's of 1537 and the Great Bible of 1539–41, the first officially authorized English Bible, ordered to be placed in all churches. But their influence was also strong on the Geneva Bible of 1560, corporately retranslated from the original languages by Protestant exiles from the Marian regime in Calvin's Geneva. Any version of the Bible could be printed and owned from 1558 under Elizabeth (though possession of the Catholic Rheims Bible was seen as suspicious in later decades), and the Geneva version, though not singled out for official approval, soon became standard, and readily available to relatively ordinary people (it was also the first English Bible to be published in Scotland). The Geneva was printed in small quartos in Roman type, not the heavy black letter of previous, and some subsequent, Bibles. Textual and exegetical points were extensively discussed in its often fiercely polemical marginal notes which did not fail to stir up the controversy they often aimed at. The Geneva was incontrovertibly better than previous English editions, and was preferred over the authorized translations not only by Puritans but by many Anglicans.

The Geneva held its own after 1568 against the Bishops' Bible, an official revision of the Great Bible issued in that year, with the aim of diluting the Geneva's radical Calvinism. The Bishops' work, as a revision uneven and sometimes superficial, aspired to a dignity appropriate to public worship, but tended towards over-elaboration and solemnity. One of the sophisticated woodcuts from the first edition is shown in Fig. 3. It was by no means as popular as Lawrence Tomson's revision of the Geneva New Testament of a few years later, in 1576 (particularly valued for its notes); it was not reissued in less bulky quarto editions after 1584; and it was finally eclipsed by the 1611 Authorized Version. One more English translation is relevant here: the Rheims New Testament of 1582 was part of a Catholic equivalent to the Geneva Bible completed in 1610 by members of the English Catholic college founded at Douai; its publication was part of a systematic plan to win back the English to Rome.

(B) Biblical material was prescribed in later sixteenth-century grammar school curricula (see Baldwin 1944: I, 682ff.; Shaheen 1988), though less was taught in the decades of Shakespeare's childhood than might be assumed. Most religious instruction was carried out through texts such as catechisms, which, though based on Scripture, contained few quotations from it of any length. The Primer, taught at petty school, contained no extensive biblical excerpts other than the Seven Penitential Psalms. But the Bible which had now become available in the vernacular was, needless to say, the commonest book in the England

43

Figure 3 Job's Comforters, from the first edition of the Bishops' Bible (London, 1568; STC 2099), sig. X8ᵛ.

of Shakespeare's time, as in all eras since then; it is estimated that in the second half of the sixteenth century half a million English Bibles were purchased by an English population of six million. 'The Bible, the Word, was now central, not the drama of the mass in a language not understood'; and it was 'known with a thoroughness that is, simply, astonishing' (Daniell 1999: 169–70). It was also, for even the secular literature of this era, of seminal importance as a framework of shared knowledge, a potent influence on ways of thinking and perceiving, and· for writers and artists of all kinds a source of themes, subject-matter, imagery, typology and stylistic example.

One very clear biblical allusion in Shakespeare is Bottom's burlesque of St Paul in 1 Corinthians 2: 9, in his *recusatio* on recovering from his dream – 'the eye of man hath not heard ... what my dream was' (4.1.208–12). The Pauline text, linked as it is to other *loci classici* in texts both sacred and secular on the nature of true wisdom and folly, is one which evidently made a strong impression on Shakespeare. It is impossible to say exactly which version of the Bible was uppermost in his mind for Bottom's parodic treatment of this passage. But there is an intriguing link to Bottom's not otherwise easily explained name in the immediately following verses of the Tyndale translation which was the basis at this point for the Great Bible and the Matthew Bible texts (see Stroup 1978; Peters 1988; and *per contra* Willson 1979), the latter of which is quoted here primarily to display the distance between the directly Tyndale-based Bibles of the mid-sixteenth century and more familiar later revisions:

> That we speak of / is wysdome amonge them that are perfecte: not the wysdom of thys worlde / nether of the rulars of thys world (which go to nought) but we speke the wysdome of God / which is in secret and lyeth hyd / which God ordeyned before the world / unto our glory: which wysdoom none of ye rulars of this worlde knewe. For had they knowen it / they wolde not have crucified the Lord of glory. But as it is written: The eye hath not sene / and the eare hath not hearde / nether have entred into the heart of man / the thinges which God hath prepared for them that love him.
>
> But God hath opened them unto us by hys sprete. For the sprete searcheth all thynges / ye the botome of Goddes secrets. For what man knoweth the thynges of a man: save the sprete of a men which is with in hym.

> (1 Cor. 2: 6–11)

(C) There is no evidence Shakespeare knew the Vulgate (Noble 1935: 87), or the Wycliffite translation of the Vulgate (1380–1400), or **Caxton**'s *Golden Legend*, containing portions of scriptural narrative. He once copies out a passage from a French Bible, the Olivetan (*Henry V* 3.7.63–4), but this is clearly a special case. Indications of acquaintance with the Rheims are never clear (Shaheen 1999: 35–6), and the King James ('Authorized') version issued in 1611, five years before his death, leaves no discernible traces. Shakespeare's Bible is primarily the Geneva and Bishops' Bible; he also uses arrangements of biblical material in the **Book of Common Prayer** and the Psalter (the texts for the Psalter printed at the back of many Bibles were drawn from the Great Bible; Shakespeare also draws on the versions in the Prayer Book). There are echoes specifically of the Bishops' Bible (printed until the late sixteenth century) in the earlier plays and in references to biblical material in which he might have been drilled at school, whereas in later years, from the time of *2 Henry IV*, he seems to turn to the Geneva (Noble 1935: 75–6; Baldwin 1944: I, 687). There is evidence that for the Geneva he routinely used an edition with the standard contents of a Genevan Old Testament and Apocrypha bound together with the Tomson revision of the Genevan New Testament (see Noble 1935: 58ff.; Shaheen 1995). There is no doubt he is influenced by Geneva glosses (see for example Burnet 1979, 1980, 1981). In the great majority of individual cases it is impossible to associate his biblical references with a specific text because the many Tudor Bibles are too similar to each other, and Shakespeare's verbal echoes too slight, but Shaheen (1999: 39–40) claims to identify some thirty passages in which he 'clearly refers to the Geneva'. A Geneva Bible with Tomson New Testament (STC 2175) is quoted below except where stated.

Shakespeare's biblical knowledge is usually thought if anything more extensive than average for a writer of his era, and he makes fewer mistakes in his biblical allusions than, say, Bacon. It probably derived from a mixture of school, home, private study and attendance at church – which was compulsory, and where the Psalter, the Book of Common Prayer and the thirty-three **Homilies**, set texts created for delivery by the many preachers unlicensed to compose their own sermons, and interlaced with biblical quotations, were important additional vehicles for biblical material. Shaheen (1988) rejects Baldwin's (1944) claims for the effect of school work, considers home influences improbable on the grounds of Shakespeare's parents' presumed illiteracy, and

46

stresses the alternative of private study. But it is not reasonable to discount any of these sources entirely.

The sole mention of the Bible as such in Shakespeare is in *The Merry Wives of Windsor*, where the comically murderous Caius concludes that Hugh Evans in failing to keep his assignation 'has pray his Pible well dat he is no come' (2.3.7). And Shakespeare's explicit allusions to biblical material, though they range widely in the Bible, are not especially frequent. Perhaps it is true that 'there is hardly a book of the Old or the New Testament which is not represented at least by some chance word or phrase in one or other of his plays' (Milward 1973: 87), but it is often a moot point how directly biblical (as opposed to proverbial, or via other writers and texts) these words and phrases are. For example, the habit Shakespeare's characters have of referring to life as a pilgrimage has probably been acquired from **Lyly**'s *Euphues*, and some of the memorable Psalm-related phrases in Macbeth's last soliloquy must have been common currency – 'dusty death', 'a walking shadow'. On the other hand, because Shakespeare's was only the second or third generation to which an English Bible was readily available, everyday language had far fewer set phrases deriving from it than did, say, nineteenth-century English. The subject of biblical influence on Shakespeare's language itself, at the level of vocabulary, lexis, syntax, and so on, is not treated here.

All the indications are that Shakespeare knew best the biblical material he might be expected to have known best: Genesis, Job, Psalms, the Gospels, Acts, Romans, and Ecclesiasticus from the Apocrypha. Of these, he seems to draw on Job and Ecclesiasticus 'in a much more direct way than is usual with his biblical echoes'. The interest in Job and perhaps the Psalms too 'could be explained as a poet's gravitation toward some of the finest poetry available to him . . . But the familiarity with the wisdom literature does seem to indicate a natural affinity for the solidly secular, moral sanity of these works' rather than with more theologically engaged material (Sanders 1980: 330). Examples of his most frequently used texts are St Paul's warning against Satan in the form of an angel of light (2 Cor. 11: 14); St Matthew's 'Love thine enemies' (Matt. 5: 44); and the Burial service text 'In the sweat of thy face thou shalt eat bread till thou returne to the earth: for out of it wast thou taken, because thou art dust, and to dust shalt thou returne' (Gen. 3: 19) (see Appendix A in Shaheen 1999 for play references for these texts).

47

The claim that Shakespeare derives from the Bible 'the central ideas and images that run through all his plays' (Milward 1973: 87) can hardly be proved or disproved. The presence of decidedly more than occasional or local borrowings must be conceded, however, since it can often be inferred from such local echoes in phraseology that Shakespeare has biblical materials in mind at a more fundamental level. There is, for instance, the moment in *Macbeth* at which the wider significance of Duncan's murder is driven home by Macduff's 'Most sacrilegious murder hath broke ope / The Lord's anointed temple' (2.3.65–6). This summons up both the references to the king as the Lord's anointed in 1 Samuel, particularly David's repeated refusal to harm Saul despite having opportunity and justification (24: 6, 26: 9, 27: 23), and St Paul's conception of the sacredness of God's people, 'the Temple of the living God' (1 Cor. 3: 16) – relevantly in this context, a conception spread across the New Testament, usually with a corporate rather than individual reference. In a more diffused way, the parable of the Prodigal Son evidently lies behind the *Lear* story, though with Lear cast as the child and Cordelia as the parent. To this use of the Bible as paradigm in *Lear* may be added other kinds of reference. The apocalyptic biblical texts drawn upon elsewhere in the play (Revelation, the eschatological discourse of Christ, some apostolic writings) do not supply narrative material, but are not drawn upon merely for the adornment of an unconnected story or theme (see Wittreich 1984). The same can be said of the undertones of the wisdom Books, of Job's patience (see especially Marx 2000: 59–78), or the endurance enjoined in Ecclesiastes and the Psalms. Verbal echoes in these areas seem only signs of a fundamental empathy – 'the point of *King Lear*', says Rosalie Colie (1974: 136), is 'surely, that, as the Psalmist proclaims, man is inexorably and inextricably bound in with other men, brought to trial whether or not he deserves it. Man has no choice but to endure his life with such strengths as he can muster, and in his endurance lies his value as a man.' Colie also notes *Lear*'s important use of the Pauline view of wisdom and folly (as in (B)), played off by Shakespeare against the play's condemnation of the folly proscribed in Proverbs (for *Lear* see also Milward 1975).

As well as deep and diffused imaginative use of biblical material, dense local combinations of it also occur. Many soliloquies can be described in this way, such as Portia's 'The quality of mercy' (*Merchant of Venice* 4.1.180–200), Claudius' 'Oh, my offence is rank' (*Hamlet* 3.3.

35–72), and Macbeth's 'If it were done' (1.7.1–28). A less familiar case in point is this speech of Helena's to the king she hopes to cure:

> He that of greatest works is finisher
> Oft does them by the weakest minister.
> So holy writ in babes hath judgement shown,
> When judges have been babes. Great floods have flown
> From simple sources, and great seas have dried
> When miracles have by the greatest been denied.
>
> (*All's Well* 2.1.135–41)

Here are more or less explicit references to three Old Testament episodes: the righteous judgement of young Daniel which saves Susanna when condemned by all the elders (Susanna 45–50, though the word 'babes' is probably inflected by Matt. 21: 16 on right judgement proceeding from 'the mouth of babes and sucklings'); Moses striking the rock at Horeb (Exod. 17: 6); and the crossing of the Red Sea (Exod. 14; 'the greatest' is Pharaoh, who in Exod. 14: 4 has had his heart 'hardened' to pursue the Israelites). Beyond this, there are also overtones of Mary's canticle, the Magnificat (Luke 1: 46–55), in the notion of a weak vessel chosen for divine purpose, which coalesce with associations elsewhere in *All's Well* between Helena and the Virgin. And the whole passage is fully in tune with the general principle of St Paul on wisdom and folly (in (B)). A dual process seems to be at work, then: Shakespeare's presentation of Helena is vivified by his deliberate use of biblical material, while at the same time his very conception of the character is affected by memories of the same – and probably additional – biblical texts.

The range of ways in which Shakespeare uses the Bible is wide: only a few examples can be given here by way of conclusion. At the level of individual allusion, a notably bold comparison between Joan of Arc and the invincible prophetess Deborah of Judges 4–5, for whom even the stars in their courses fought, and to whom all Israel rallied to defeat the Canaanites, figures in *1 Henry VI* (1.2.104–5). An important element in the presentation of Richard III – with Henry VI one of the two Shakespeare characters who most frequently quote the Bible – is his way of 'positively impersonating, with mischievous exhilaration, the unscrupulous Apostle [Paul] of the Gentiles', a feature developed from a single episode in **More**'s *History of King Richard III* (Carnall 1963:

188). *Measure for Measure* is titled, and in some sense conceived, through Matthew 7: 2, 'with what measure ye mete, it shalbe measured unto you againe' (though the phrase was proverbial, its biblical origins are made clearly relevant to the play, including the Old Testament ideas it echoes, of just retribution and the virtue of moderation). The tradition of drama on the Prodigal Son theme which underlies the relationship of Hal and Falstaff was already old by the 1590s, and it might therefore be thought unnecessary to invoke the Bible directly to explain what Shakespeare is doing there; but the terminology of 'reformation' and 'redeeming' in Hal's soliloquy at the end of 1.2 (with his 'Redeeming time' compare especially Eph. 5: 16 and Col. 4: 5, 'Redeeming/redeeme the season' in Tomson, 'tyme' in some other Tudor Bibles) clearly plays its part in Hal's adoption of this scriptural role. So it is that 'Hal's success in persuading his subjects of his transformation . . . depends upon the conscious manipulation of the religious convictions of his age' (Scragg 1996: 23).

Finally at the level of the complete play, *The Merchant of Venice* is in the Shakespeare canon the most thoroughgoing use of the Bible – a work in which Shakespeare 'very evidently taxed his Scriptural knowledge' (Noble 1935: 96). Not only does the main plot revolve around the confrontation of the Old Law and the New – with some vexed interpretative issues carefully explored in Antonio's debate with Shylock over the episode, obscure for most modern readers but evidently not for Shakespeare's audience, 'when Jacob grazed his uncle Laban's sheep' in Genesis 30 (1.3.63–86); the narrative proceeds through biblical allusions of many other kinds which can only be glancingly illustrated here. The main plot itself can be said to generate oppositions in the play at what medieval theologians would have called an allegorical level, 'symboliz[ing] the confrontation of Judaism and Christianity as theological systems . . . and also as historic societies' (Lewalski 1962: 331) – though it is debatable how much of this would have been perceptible to Shakespeare's audience. The Launcelot-Gobbo exchange in 2.2 sees Launcelot unwittingly re-enacting two popular Bible stories, Jacob's deception of his blind father Isaac, and the deception practised by Joseph's brothers (Gen. 27, 37). And the biblical connotations of Portia as both Shylock and Gratiano imagine her, 'a Daniel' (4.1.218), 'a second Daniel' (4.1.329), are several. A Daniel was a wise and upright person in reference to the Apocryphal Book of Susanna. But in the Book of the Prophet Daniel, the name was glossed in Tudor Bibles as 'the Judgement of God', and, according to both the Geneva and the Bishops' Bible, Daniel's prayer (Daniel 9: 18) shows how 'the godly flee unto gods mercies . . . when they seeke for remission of their sinnes'. Even Portia's disguise as 'Balthasar' is probably owing to the name 'Baltassar' under which Daniel goes in the same Book (see Lewalski 1962: 340–1).

(D) There are many accounts of the English Bible's development to Shakespeare's time, including Hammond (1982), Daniell (1999), and the short treatments in Noble (1935), Shaheen (1999) and, with diversely literary emphases, Norton (1993). On Shakespeare himself, Noble (1935) raises a variety of important general issues in his early chapters, then assembles an admirably restrained listing of echoes play by play and scene by scene. Milward (1987) covers the four Bradleyan tragedies in similar fashion, but adding summaries for each play and consistently claiming more biblical influence than Noble. Shaheen (1999) is at bottom an expansion of Noble at a length of nearly 900 pages, its bulk a comprehensive play-by-play treatment (involving some 1,040 biblical references), distinguished by efforts to take into account other possible sources of what appears to be biblical material in each play, and by what for at least some purposes is an over-generous interpretation of 'biblical' – to include, for example, phraseology based ultimately on a biblical passage. Both Noble and Shaheen provide an index of biblical texts and a discussion of Shakespeare's use of different versions of the Bible. Frye (1963) is not strictly concerned with the Bible, but with commonplace theological themes such as Atonement, Death, the Devil, and the Parliament of Heaven at which man is judged, which, however, are often expressed most notably for Shakespeare in biblical passages. Marx (2000), on a selection of five major plays, develops new, often highly speculative suggestions on matters of patterning, at many different levels (for example with *The Tempest*, Prospero as the Joseph of Genesis, the masque as revelatory vision, the play's First Folio positioning paralleling the storm with the Creation). Many more short articles and notes tracing echoes of biblical phraseology, etc., can be found in journals such as *N&Q*.

Anderson, Douglas (1985). 'The Old Testament Presence in *The Merchant of Venice*.' *ELH* 52: 119–32.
Baldwin (1944).

Boose, Lynda E. (1981). 'Othello's "Chrysolite" and the Song of Songs Tradition.' *PQ* 60: 427–37.

Burnet, R. A. L. (1979). 'Shakespeare and the Marginalia of the Geneva Bible.' *N&Q* 224: 113–14.

—— (1980). 'Some Echoes of the Genevan Bible in Shakespeare and Milton.' *N&Q* 225: 179–81.

—— (1981). 'Two Further Echoes of the Genevan Margin in Shakespeare and Milton.' *N&Q* 226: 129.

Carnall, Geoffrey (1963). 'Shakespeare's Richard III and St. Paul.' *ShQ* 14: 186–8.

Colie, Rosalie L. (1974). 'The Energies of Endurance: Biblical Echo in *King Lear*', pp. 117–44 in Rosalie L. Colie and F. T. Flahiff, eds, *Some Facets of King Lear: Essays in Prismatic Criticism*. London.

Daniell, David (1999). 'The Bible', pp. 158–71 in David Scott Kastan, ed., *A Companion to Shakespeare*. Oxford.

Fraser, Russell (1991). 'Shakespeare's Book of Genesis.' *CompD* 25.ii: 121–9.

Frye, Roland Mushat (1963). *Shakespeare and Christian Doctrine*. Princeton.

Hammond, Gerald (1982). *The Making of the English Bible*. Manchester.

Hassell, Chris, Jr (1986). 'Last Words and Last Things: St. John, Apocalypse, and Eschatology in *Richard III*.' *ShSt* 18: 25–40.

Lewalski, Barbara K. (1962). 'Biblical Allusion and Allegory in *The Merchant of Venice*.' *ShQ* 13: 327–43.

Marx, Steven (2000). *Shakespeare and the Bible*. Oxford.

Milward, Peter (1973). *Shakespeare's Religious Background*. London.

—— (1975). *Biblical Themes in Shakespeare – Centering on King Lear*. Tokyo.

—— (1987). *Biblical Influences in Shakespeare's Great Tragedies*. Bloomington.

Noble, Richmond (1935). *Shakespeare's Biblical Knowledge and Use of the Book of Common Prayer as Exemplified in the Plays of the First Folio*. London.

Norton, David (1993). *A History of the Bible as Literature*, 2 vols; Vol. 1: *From Antiquity to 1700*. Cambridge.

Peters, Helen (1988). 'Bottom: Making Sense of Sense and Scripture.' *N&Q* 233: 45–7.

Sanders, Wilbur (1980). *The Dramatist and the Received Idea: Studies in the Plays of Marlowe and Shakespeare*. Cambridge (first published 1968).

Scragg, Leah (1996). *Shakespeare's Alternative Tales*. London.

Shaheen, Naseeb (1988). 'Shakespeare's Knowledge of the Bible – How Acquired.' *ShSt* 20: 201–14.

—— (1992). 'Shakespeare, the Psalter, and the Vulgate in *Henry V.*' *ShQ* 43: 71–2.

—— (1995). 'Shakespeare and the Tomson New Testament.' *N&Q* 240: 290–1.

—— (1999). *Biblical References in Shakespeare's Plays*. Newark, DE (supersedes Shaheen's three previous books *Biblical References in Shakespeare's Comedies, . . . Histories, . . . Tragedies*).

Stroup, Thomas B. (1978). 'Bottom's Name and His Epiphany.' *ShQ* 29: 79–81.

Velz, Sarah (1972). 'Man's Need and God's Plan in *Measure for Measure* and Mark IV.' *ShSu* 25: 37–44.

Willson, Robert F., Jr (1979). 'God's Secrets and Bottom's Name: A Reply.' *ShQ* 30: 407–8.

Wittreich, Joseph (1984). ' "Image of that Horror": The Apocalypse in *King Lear*', pp. 175–206 in C. A. Patrides and Joseph Wittreich, eds, *The Apocalypse in English Renaissance Thought and Literature: Patterns, Antecedents, and Repercussions*. Ithaca.

Boccaccio, Giovanni (1313–1375), Italian Poet, Prose Writer, and Scholar See also Cinthio, Giovanni Baptista Giraldi; Lydgate, John.

(A) Boccaccio was born illegitimately either in Florence or in Certaldo, Val d'Elsa, moving at fourteen to Naples with his father. His father's position as representative of the great Bardi banking family of Florence gave him entrée to the courtly circles whose culture informs much of his literary work. To this work he dedicated himself fully after first trying banking and the law. Boccaccio's Neapolitan writings include the prose romances *Il Filocolo* and *Il Filostrato* (on the Troilus and Criseyde story), and the first epic poem in Italian, *Il Teseida* ('The Book of Theseus'). Following his return to Florence in about 1340 he tried a range of other poetic genres before writing *Il Decamerone* (*c.* 1348–51), a collection of one hundred stories in a variety of kinds (bawdy, satirical, pathetic) and from a wide range of sources (classical, folk, romance). He also held various minor public offices and represented the commune of Florence on missions in northern Italy. To his later years belong a number of mainly compilatory Latin works, often connected with the influence of his friend **Petrarch**, including *De Casibus Virorum Illustrium* ('On the fate of illustrious men'), *De Claris Mulieribus* ('Of famous women'), and *De Genealogiis Deorum Gentilium*, an encyclopedic guide to the genealogies of the gods. He lectured in Florence on, and published a commentary to, **Dante**'s *Divina Commedia* in 1373–4, and died at Certaldo in 1375.

(B) Reading, translation and adaptation of Boccaccio in Britain began early, most notably with **Chaucer**'s use of the *Teseida* in his *Knight's Tale* and of the *Filostrato* for *Troilus and Criseyde*. Boccaccio's early reputation was that of a great moralist, comparable to **Boethius** and the Younger **Seneca**, and his Latin writings the most commonly read. The *Decameron*, today considered his masterpiece, was slow to become well known. Three of its stories found their way into English via French or Latin versions in the fifteenth century, and others followed in the next, but the first English version of the collection as a whole did not appear until 1620. This contrasts with the situation in nearby countries, such as Spain, Germany and France. A full French translation had been produced as early as 1414, followed by the racy and accurate version of Antoine Le Maçon in 1545. In England, responses were sometimes confused. Many of the *Decameron* tales were regarded as examples of the caprices of Fortune, and so in keeping with those afforded by *A Mirror for Magistrates*, a work from which one adapter of a tale from the *Decameron* saw nothing incongruous in borrowing a stanza (see Wright 1957: 480). Again, an early English tragedy, *Gismond of Salerne* (by members of the Inner Temple, 1567/8), which is modelled directly on the story of Sigismonda and Guiscardo (*Decameron* IV, 1), perversely makes Boccaccio's tale into a warning against those who 'suppress not their unruly affections'.

The most important English translator of the *Decameron* in Shakespeare's lifetime was William **Painter**, whose sixteen tales from it were included in his popular compendium of stories *The Palace of Pleasure* (1566–75). Painter complains of the tales' immodesty – 'the best to be followed, and the worst to be avoyded . . . some (in my judgement) that be worthy to be condempned to perpetual prison' – but considers that 'Boccaccio for his stile, order of writing, gravitie, and sententious discourse, is worthy of intire provulgation' (Painter 1575: I, 11). Painter can be incoherent or over-didactic, but his lively work is not usually seriously unfaithful to Boccaccio, thanks in large measure to his use of Le Maçon. It is far removed from the complete 1620 *Decameron* in

English, anonymous but now usually ascribed to John **Florio**, 'by far the most earnest of Boccaccio's editors and translators', whose work is 'uniquely solemn and decorous' (Cole 1981: 80).

The form or forms in which Shakespeare knew Boccaccio's text cannot be established for certain. The possibilities are: Boccaccio's original Italian; Le Maçon's French; and, for the sixteen tales he translated, Painter's contemporary English. Painter is the likely source for at least the material used in *All's Well that Ends Well* and *Romeo and Juliet* (see (C), below), and is responsible for the version given here of a passage from the end of the *All's Well* story.

> The countesse knowinge that her husbande was goone from Florence and retourned home, was verye gladde, continuing in Florence till the time of her childbedde, being brought a bedde of twoo sonnes, whiche were very like unto their father, and caused them carefully to be noursed and brought up, and when she sawe time, she toke her journey (unknowen to anie) and arrived at Monpellier, and resting her selfe there for certayne dayes, hearing newes of the counte, and where he was, and that upon the daye of Al Sainctes, he purposed to make a great feaste and assembly of ladies and knightes, in her pilgrimes weede she repaired thither. And knowing that they were all assembled, at the palace of the counte, readie to sitte downe at the table, she passed through the people without chaunge of apparell, with her twoo sonnes in her armes: and when shee was come up into the hall, even to the place where the counte sat, falling downe prostrate at his feete, weeping, saying unto hym: My lorde, I am thy poore infortunate wyfe, who to th'intent thou mightest retourne and dwel in thine owne house, have bene a great whyle begging aboute the worlde. Therefore I nowe beseche thee, for the honoure of God, that thou wilt observe the conditions, which the twoo (knightes that I sent unto thee) did commaunde me to doe: for beholde, here in myne armes, not onely one sonne begotten by thee, but twayne, and likwyse thy ryng. It is nowe time then (if thou keep promise) that I should be received as thy wyfe. The counte hearing this, was greatly astonned, and knewe the ryng, and the children also, they were so like hym. But tell me (quod he) howe is this come to passe? The countesse to the great admiration of the counte, and of all those that were in presence, rehersed unto them in order all that, whiche had bene done, and the whole discourse thereof. For which cause the

counte knowing the thinges she had spoken to be true (and perceiving her constant minde and good witte, and the twoo faire young boyes to kepe his promise made, and to please his subjectes, and the ladies that made sute unto him, to accept her from that tyme foorth, as his lawefull wyfe, and to honour her), abjected his obstinate rigour, causing her to rise up, and imbraced and kissed her, acknowledging her againe for his lawefull wyfe. And after he had apparelled her according to her estate, to the great pleasure and contentation of those that were there, and of al his other frendes not onely that daye, but many others, he kept great chere, and from that time forth, hee loved and honoured her, as his dere spouse and wyfe.

(ɪ, 38; Painter 1575: sigs 91ᵛ–92ᵛ)

(C) Bawcutt (1984) suggests a very probably indirect source in the *Filostrato* for the close of Shakespeare's Sonnet 38. In Shakespeare's drama, there are some approximate parallels with the *Decameron* for *Romeo and Juliet* (see Zbierski 1971), and with the *Filostrato* (directly, as opposed to through the Chaucer poem it inspired) for *Troilus and Cressida* (see Donaldson 1979). Some situations in *The Merry Wives of Windsor* can be related to episodes in the *Decameron*, but a large element of coincidence must be allowed for here; most of the relevant tales would have been available only in French or Italian. The direct use of the *Teseide* by one or both of the playwrights responsible for *The Two Noble Kinsmen* cannot wholly be ruled out, though none of the possible effects seems important. Otherwise, Boccaccio's impact on Shakespeare is confined to *All's Well* and *Cymbeline*.

The main source of *All's Well* is the tale of Giletta de Nerbone, the thirty-eighth in Painter's *Palace of Pleasure* and the ninth story of the third day of Boccaccio's *Decameron*. Hunter (1962: xxv–xxvi) and Wright (1957: 214) suggest that the next-but-one story in Boccaccio and in Painter, that of Tancred of Salerne (ɪᴠ, 1), may also have influenced Shakespeare's play in its opposition of virtue and gentility generally and for the King's speech on this topic in 2.3, the latter point being strengthened by the fact that Ghismonda's speech on individual merit here is one of the most powerful in the whole *Decameron*. Where the Giletta story is concerned, a case was made for Shakespeare's use of Le Maçon's attractive and much-reprinted French *Decameron*, instead of Painter's English one, by Wright (1955). Though the evidence is too inconclusive to cancel out the probability that Shakespeare would use a popular English version in preference to a less widely available French one, it is supported by the possibility that he used Le Maçon for *Cymbeline* (see below). He may have used both; it is also possible that he used Boccaccio's Italian original. However, Painter's version is close to Boccaccio's, and all these versions of the story closer to each other than to Shakespeare's.

Shakespeare's adaptations move his story away from Boccaccio's relatively short and relatively light tale of an enterprising and well-connected heiress who uses clever devices to prove herself worthy of the Count of Rosillion, the Count eventually being brought to perceive a good bargain in her offer. Shakespeare imposes the pattern of the chivalric quest (with reversed genders) onto the two basic themes of this 'clever wench' story-type, 'the healing of the king' and 'the fulfilment of the task', as well as directly juxtaposing it with the seaminess of Parolles. This movement brings with it most of the problems conventionally discerned in *All's Well*, in that the very same actions that Boccaccio depicts are now 'handled so as to break down Boccaccio's neat closure and at several points to generate uneasy questioning', and the narrative's modality is complicated by 'admixtures of social realism, by disquieting inversions of the fairy-tale pattern, and by a more intimate view of the emotions and reactions of both Helen as pursuing maiden and Bertram as reluctant bridegroom' (Snyder 1993: 3).

All the same, the contrast is not entirely between an artless, undemanding Boccaccio and a difficult, sophisticated Shakespeare. Cole remarks, albeit with some exaggeration, that 'since Shakespeareans necessarily tend to examine what Boccaccio did mainly in terms of what was done to him, not what he was attempting in his own right, their comparisons usually leave us admiring Shakespeare's complexity and patronizing Boccaccio's simplicity' (1981: 12). Boccaccio's teasing suggestiveness as to the interpretation of Giletta's story may be one example of his sophistication: its context in the Third Day of the *Decameron* makes it an example of the achievement of one's goals through initiative, in Giletta's case apparently a matter of successful pursuit of her sexual prey, for whom her feelings are 'more than was meet for a maiden of her age'. Shakespeare's interest in the secret impulses of sexual attachment is not unprecedented in Boccaccio. 'Has Giletta thrown honesty to the winds in duping and bedding Beltrano? . . . Boccaccio's answers reside in his smile . . . he was there ahead of

Shakespeare, subduing an old piece of fabling with a fine curiosity and intelligence' (Layman 1972: 51).

But it can be said that Shakespeare brings to the surface the latent tensions of the tale of the clever wench in dramatizing it. The final episode underlines all the contrasts. Most obviously, there is in Boccaccio no counterpart to Bertram's lies and evasions, since his Beltramo, with his eye on expediency, is happy to accept Giletta now that he is impressed by her 'constant minde and good witte' (see (B)). In contrast to the situation depicted by Boccaccio/Painter, Shakespeare's Helena 'retains her ascendancy over Bertram, . . . holding out the promise of a new order', while 'Bertram's misconduct is at once recapitulated and augmented' (Scragg 1996: 126). On the other hand, for Stewart (1991: 338–9) there is another sense in which Shakespeare's resolutions and non-resolutions are ultimately dictated by his Italian source: 'the whole last scene, with its complicated imbroglio and bittersweet taste of suspended happiness, is . . . [Shakespeare's] response to the main difficulty posed by the continuation of two different themes in the basic plot he inherited from Boccaccio'.

Boccaccio's tale of Bernabo and Ambrogiuolo (*Decameron* II, 9) has a stronger claim than any other version of the story to be the source of the wager plot in *Cymbeline*, though differences have led to much speculation about the contributions of other texts (see Thrall 1931, Wright 1957: 220–1), and possibly no specific source need be posited for Shakespeare's handling of a story widespread for several centuries before he wrote. The Italian narrative of the deception of one merchant by another, who is carried in a chest into his wife's bedroom to note details and steal tokens, concludes with the punishment of Ambrogiuolo for his deception by being tied to a stake, his body smeared with honey, and left to be devoured by insects. Boccaccio's tale may be somewhat remote from the play in tone and setting, but as well as containing some specifics not paralleled elsewhere, it has, compared to other possible sources, a richness of detail and atmosphere that can well be imagined to have attracted Shakespeare. Further slight support for the connection is provided by Autolycus' reference to a punishment like Ambrogiuolo's (not of course found in *Cymbeline*, and not in alternative sources for *Cymbeline*) in *The Winter's Tale*, 4.4.773ff. Since this part of the *Decameron* was not Englished until 1620, Shakespeare's reading would have had to be either in the Italian or Le Maçon's French rendering; Wright (1957) argues for the latter.

(D) For Boccaccio's readers, translators and adapters in Europe and especially England, including analysis of the relevant Shakespeare texts, Wright (1957) is standard. Hunter (1962) offers a brief table of contrasts between *All's Well* and its Boccaccian source. Cole (1981), Layman (1972) and Snyder (1993) furnish more detailed analysis. Stewart (1991) and Scragg (1996) both stress the traditional elements in Boccaccio's tale and the gender implications of Shakespeare's manipulation of them. For *Cymbeline*, Thrall (1931) and Nosworthy (1969) are lucid accounts dealing with the range of possible alternatives as well as the Boccaccian story; Almansi (1975) is unhelpfully concerned to promote the merits of Boccaccio over Shakespeare.

Almansi, Guido (1975). *Il ciclo della scommessa: dal 'Decameron' al 'Cymbeline' di Shakespeare*. Rome.

Bawcutt, Priscilla (1984). 'A Note on Sonnet 38.' *ShQ* 35: 77–9.

Bullough, II.

Cole, Howard C. (1981). *The 'All's Well' Story from Boccaccio to Shakespeare*. Urbana, IL.

Donaldson, E. Talbot (1979). 'Briseis, Briseida, Criseyde, Cresseid, Cressid: Progress of a Heroine', pp. 3–12 in Edward Vasta *et al.*, eds, *Chaucerian Problems and Perspectives: Essays Presented to Paul E. Beichner, C. S. C.* Notre Dame.

Fleissner, Robert F. (1978). 'The Malleable Knight and the Unfettered Friar: *The Merry Wives of Windsor* and Boccaccio.' *ShSt* 11: 77–93.

Hunter, G. K., ed. (1962). *All's Well that Ends Well* (Arden Shakespeare). London (first published 1959).

Layman, B. J. (1972). 'Shakespeare's Helena, Boccaccio's Giletta, and the Riddles of Skill and Honesty.' *English Miscellany* 23: 39–53.

Marrapodi, Michele (1997). 'Da Boccaccio a Shakespeare: Il racconto dell'eros e la trasgressione della commedia', pp. 131–52 in Viola Papetti and Laura Visconti, eds, *Le forme del teatro*, V: *Eros e commedia sulla scena inglese dalle origini al primo seicento*. Rome.

Nosworthy, J. M., ed. (1969). *Cymbeline* (Arden Shakespeare). London.

Painter, William (1575). *The Palace of Pleasure Beautified, Adorned, and Well Furnished with Pleasaunt Histories and Excellent Novels*. London.

Potter, Lois, ed. (1997). *The Two Noble Kinsmen* (Arden Shakespeare). Walton-on-Thames.

Rodax, Yvonne (1968). *The Real and the Ideal in the Novella of Italy, France and England: Four Centuries of Change in the Boccaccian Tale*. Chapel Hill.

Scragg, Leah (1996). *Shakespeare's Alternative Tales*. London.

Snyder, Susan, ed. (1993). *All's Well that Ends Well* (Oxford Shakespeare). Oxford.

Stewart, Pamela D. (1991). 'How to Get a Happy Ending: *Decameron* III.9 and Shakespeare's *All's Well*.' *Studi sul Boccaccio* 20: 325–44.

Thrall, William Flint (1931). '*Cymbeline*, Boccaccio, and the Wager Story in England.' *SP* 28: 639–51.

Wright, H. G. (1955). 'How Did Shakespeare Come to Know the "Decameron"?' *MLR* 50: 45–8.

Wright, Herbert G. (1957). *Boccaccio in England from Chaucer to Tennyson*. London.

Zbierski, Henryk (1971). 'Possible Echoes of Boccaccio's *Decameron* in the Balcony Scene of *Romeo and Juliet*.' *Studia Anglica Posnaniensia* 3.i–ii: 131–8.

Boece (Boethius), Hector (1465?–1536), Scottish Historian Boece's Latin *Scotorum Historia* (1527), translated by John Bellenden, is one of the sources on which the compilers of the Scottish parts of **Holinshed**'s Chronicle drew; there are a few signs that Shakespeare might have consulted it independently.

Farrow, Kenneth D. (1994). 'The Historiographical Evolution of the Macbeth Narrative.' *Scottish Literary Journal* 21: 5–23.

Mapstone, Sally (1998). 'Shakespeare and Scottish Kingship: A Case History', pp. 158–89 in Sally Mapstone and Juliette Wood, eds, *The Rose and the Thistle: Essays on the Culture of Late Medieval and Renaissance Scotland*. East Linton.

Boethius, Anicius Manlius Severinus (*c.* AD 476–524), Roman Poet and Philosopher There are some scattered indications of direct acquaintance with Boethius' *De Consolatione Philosophiae* in Shakespeare, but the extremely wide and long diffusion of the poem almost inevitably compromises attempts to demonstrate it.

Asp, Carolyn (1978). 'Shakespeare's Paulina and the *Consolatio* Tradition.' *ShSt* 11: 145–58.

Marshall, Cynthia (1987). 'The Seven Ages of *Pericles.*' *Journal of the Rocky Mountain Medieval and Renaissance Association* 8: 147–62.

Presson, Robert K. (1965). 'Boethius, King Lear, and "Maystresse Philosophie".' *JEGP* 64: 406–24.

Boethius, Hector See **Boece (Boethius), Hector**.

Boiardo, Matteo Maria (1441?–1494), Italian Poet and Dramatist Bioardo's verse drama *Timone* (*c.* 1487) is largely a translation and expansion of the Timon dialogue by **Lucian**.

Bond, R. Warwick (1931). 'Lucian and Boiardo in "Timon of Athens".' *MLR* 26: 52–68.

Bullough, vi.

Boiastuau (Boisteau, etc.), Pierre See **Brooke, Arthur**.

Book of Common Prayer, The See also **Bible**.

(A) The origins of the Book of Common Prayer, the most cherished monument of the English Church, lie with the 1549 'book of the common prayer' of Edward VI, prior to which church services varied from one diocese to another, and the only printed service books were Latin ones for priests. The 1549 manual, for the contents of which Henry VIII's Archbishop Thomas Cranmer was largely responsible, adapted, simplified and translated into English the four main service books of the pre-Reformation Church into services of Matins and Evensong, Communion, Baptism, Matrimony, Burial, and a few lesser offices. It also introduced new theological ideas drawn from the continental Reformation. A heavily Protestant revision of 1552 (the 'second Edward VI' Prayer Book) was intended to counter criticism that the new liturgy was only a version of the Catholic Mass and hence, for instance, it removed the notions of purgatory and the invocation of saints. This version was proscribed under Mary, but lightly revised to form the Prayer Book of Elizabeth, adopted by the Act of Uniformity on her ascending the throne in 1558. A further revision in 1604 was slight, consisting largely of additional prayers of thanksgiving; today's Book of Common Prayer was finalized by a more substantial revision of 1662. The Prayer Book has always been routinely printed together with the Psalter.

Textually, though the Prayer Book drew the scriptural texts it included for daily readings from the Great Bible of 1539–41 (with variations), many briefer passages of Scripture occurring in the services were independent renderings, perhaps by Latimer. Hence, for example, the Ten Commandments do not exactly match any biblical version of Exodus 20, nor the Lord's Prayer the text in any other version of Matthew 6. Daily services specified in the Prayer Book provided for a systematic reading of specified Bible texts in an annual cycle of lessons, excerpted from the whole Bible apart from 'certaine Bookes and Chapters, which be least edifying'. For Sundays and holy days it specified a reading of one of the **Homilies**, or, if a licensed preacher was available, a sermon.

(B) All Shakespeare's contemporaries were exposed on at least a weekly basis to the liturgy of the Prayer Book: from 1559 onwards its prescribed offices, prayers, sacraments and readings were part of the fabric of life for English people. It was 'first and foremost "liturgy", that is "work", intended not so much to be read in a passive sense, but to be used, performed, experienced' (Maltby 1998: 3). Prominent in this respect were the responses, initially ridiculed by detractors as creating an effect like a tennis match but evidently helpful in creating a sense of communal activity. The Prayer Book was also an instrument of state control, for 'there was probably no other single element of the Reformation in England which touched more directly and fundamentally on the religious consciousness, or lack of it, of ordinary clergy and laity, than did the reform of rituals and liturgy' (Maltby 1998: 4). From the mid-sixteenth century, a minister using a non-prescribed form of worship was subject to a fine or imprisonment. Lay people were similarly obliged to attend church services on Sundays and holy days. By the Act of Uniformity of 1559, disrespectful references to the Prayer Book in interludes, plays, songs and rhymes were forbidden. Even libertine dramatists took care to conform to the law, thus restricting the amount of allusion to the Prayer Book found in Elizabethan plays (for two Shakespearean cases of possible self-censorship see Noble 1935: 82–3).

Cranmer was a fine scholar, and his work drew on wide reading in different traditions. But he avoided the pomposity and prolixity that

Greek and Latin learning were introducing into English, and his extraordinary ear for prose led to beauties sufficiently well known. The following brief sample is from what is now one of the less familiar texts, the Catechism laid down to be learned before Confirmation, a crucial part of the Prayer Book's new emphasis on instruction of the laity.

Question.

What is thy duetie towards thy neighbour?

Answer.

My duetie towards my neighbour is, to love him as my selfe, and to doe to all men, as I would they should doe unto me. To love, honour, and succour my father and mother. To honour and obey the Queene and her ministers. To submit my selfe to all my governours, teachers, spirituall Pastors, and Masters, to order my selfe lowly and reverently to all my betters. To hurt no body by worde nor deede. To be true and just in all my dealing. To beare no malice nor hatred in my heart. To keepe my hands from picking and stealing, and my tongue from evill speaking, lying, and slaundering. To keepe my body in temperance, sobernesse, and chastitie. Not to covet nor desire other mens goods, but to learne and labour truely to get myne owne living, and to doe my duetie in that state of life, unto the which it shall please God to call me.

Question.

My good childe know this, that thou art not able to doe these things of thy selfe, nor to walke in the commaundements of God, and to serve him, without his speciall grace, which thou must learne at all times to call for by diligent prayer. Let me heare therefore if thou canst say the Lords prayer.

(BCP 1583: sig. O5ᵛ)

(C) Almost all parts of the Prayer Book are mentioned or alluded to somewhere in Shakespeare, from the reference to Matins and Evensong ('Morning Prayer' and 'Evening Prayer' by 1552) in Mistress Quickly's commendation of Mistress Page as 'one . . . that will not miss you morning nor evening prayer, as any is in Windsor, whoe'er be the other' (*Merry Wives of Windsor* 2.2.90–1), to the echoes of the phrase 'dust to dust' from the Order for the Burial of the Dead in Hamlet's 'quintessence of dust' (2.2.307) or the refrain of the song in *Cymbeline*, 'come to dust' (4.2.264), to the form of response from the Commination against Sinners ('*Minister* Cursed is he that curseth his father, and mother. / *Answer* Amen.') invoked by Constance in *King John*:

> O, lawful let it be
> That I have room with Rome to curse awhile!
> Good father Cardinal, cry thou 'amen'
> To my keen curses
>
> (3.1.179–83)

For the most part, Shakespeare's allusions to Prayer Book material tend to be a way of appealing to shared cultural understandings and assumptions in his audience, and are not particularly unusual when compared with those of contemporary writers. The Marriage service is thus unsurprisingly the part of the Prayer Book most often called up, and it is invoked with some regularity in the romantic comedies in particular. The ceremony itself is presented, but broken off, at the crisis of *Much Ado About Nothing* (4.1 – though the characters are supposed to be Italians in Messina), and spoken over in pretence by Orlando and Rosalynde (*As You Like It* 4.1). Its concluding injunctions are echoed on numerous occasions, often to comic effect, as by the Clown in *All's Well*, who has in mind the exhortation to husbands, 'He that loveth his owne wife, loveth him selfe: For never did any man hate his owne fleshe' (BCP 1583: sig. P2ᵛ):

> He that comforts my wife is the cherisher of my flesh and blood; he that cherishes my flesh and blood loves my flesh and blood; he that loves my flesh and blood is my friend; ergo, he that kisses my wife is my friend.
>
> (1.3.47–8)

Elsewhere in the plays, a surprising dearth of echoes of the Communion, and none at all from the Order for Confirmation, contrasts with some more extensive ones from the Baptismal service (see Milward 1973: 108–9).

From the Catechism which precedes the Order for Confirmation ((B), above) Shakespeare draws phrases which would surely have summoned up the context of the Prayer Book for his audience, since, though the phrases may have become proverbial, English people would have memorized this catechism in their youth (see Shaheen 1999: 394; Maltby 1998: 69–70). The duty 'to keepe my hands from picking and stealing' is recalled in Hamlet's reply to Rosencrantz's complaint 'you once did love me' – 'And do so still, by these pickers and stealers' (3.2.327). The expression in the penultimate sentence of the passage quoted in (B), 'speciall grace', reappears in Berowne's lines (see Shaheen 1991 for other biblical echoes here):

> Necessity will make us all forsworn
> Three thousand times within this three years' space;
> For every man with his affects is born,
> Not by might mast'red, but by special grace.
> (*Love's Labour's Lost* 1.1. 147–50)

More significantly still, Cordelia's undertaking to Lear to 'Obey you, love you, and most honour you' (1.1.97), sometimes explained in terms of the Marriage service promise to 'love, honour, and serve', is at least as appropriately glossed by the Catechism's verbally no more distant and situationally much closer 'To love, honour, and succour my father and mother'.

A final point should be mentioned regarding the Psalms. Shakespeare refers more often to the Psalms than to any other part of the Bible. Since he can often be shown to use the versions of them given in the Psalter specifically, as opposed to those given in contemporary Bibles' versions of the Book of Psalms, all these cases might be thought of as uses of the 'Prayer Book' (with Psalter normally appended) in a wider but customary sense.

(D) For an attractive brief history of the English service book to 1661, with sample pages from each version, see Ratcliff (1949); for its place in sixteenth-century life (especially religious and political) and church history, Maltby (1998). Shaheen (1999: Appendix A) supplies a comprehensive, indeed over-generous, listing of Shakespeare references for all parts of the Book of Common Prayer.

BCP (Book of Common Prayer) (1583). *The Boke of Common Praier, and Administration of the Sacramentes, and Other Rites and Ceremonies of the Churche according to the Use of the United Churche of England and Ireland, together with the Psalter.* London.

Maltby, Judith D. (1998). *Prayer Book and People in Elizabethan and Early Stuart England*. Cambridge.

Milward, Peter (1973). *Shakespeare's Religious Background*. London.

Noble, Richmond (1935). *Shakespeare's Biblical Knowledge and Use of the Book of Common Prayer as Exemplified in the Plays of the First Folio*. London.

Ratcliff, Edward C. (1949). *The Booke of Common Prayer of the Churche of England: Its Making and Revisions M.D.XLIX–M.D.CLXI set forth in eighty illustrations*. London.

Shaheen, Naseeb (1991). 'Biblical References in *Love's Labour's Lost*.' *N&Q* 236: 55–6.

—— (1999). *Biblical References in Shakespeare's Plays*. Newark, DE.

Bourchier, John, Lord Berners See **Berners, John Bourchier, Lord**.

Bright, Timothy (1550–1615), Physician, Clergyman and Scientific Writer Bright's *Treatise of Melancholy* (1586) may be a subsidiary source for the depiction of Hamlet's humour, but the extent of its likely influence on Shakespeare's conception of the character has sometimes been overstated.

Jenkins, Harold, ed. (1982). *Hamlet* (Arden Shakespeare), pp. 106–8. London.

O'Sullivan, Mary Isabelle (1926). 'Hamlet and Dr Timothy Bright.' *PMLA* 41: 667–79.

Wilson, John Dover (1935). *What Happens in 'Hamlet'*, Appendix E. Cambridge.

Bromhall, Thomas See **Le Loyer, Pierre**.

Brooke, Arthur (d. 1563), Poet
(A) Brooke is an obscure figure whose biography tells little more than that he drowned as a young man on a military expedition to assist the Huguenots in France. He is known for *The Tragicall Historye of Romeus and Juliet* (1562), a loose translation of a French prose version by Pierre

Boiastuau of an Italian tale by Matteo **Bandello** (Boiastuau's work appeared as part of **Belleforest**'s 1559 *Histoires Tragiques extraictes . . . de Bandel*). Brooke's retelling of the Romeo and Juliet story consists of some 3,000 lines in poulter's measure (alternate twelve- and fourteen-syllable lines; sample in (C)). His poem is usually thought undistinguished, though its period charms have attracted a few admirers. The plot is summarized by Muir (1977: 39–40).

(B) It is clear that Brooke was working with a story already familiar to the English audience, since he writes in his address 'To the Reader' of having seen 'the same argument lately set foorth on stage'. This address also proposes a moral programme which is fortunately forgotten in the narrative itself – the story is one of '*lovers, thralling themselves to unhonest desire, neglecting the authoritie and advise of parents and frendes, conferring their principall conscels with dronken gossips, and superstitious friers (the naturally fitte instruments of unchastitie)*'. Brooke is actually sympathetic to the lovers (Shakespeare still more so), and his chief original contribution to the tale is an emphasis on the power of fortune over them which distinctly recalls **Chaucer**'s *Troilus and Criseyde*, the greatest romance narrative in Brooke's own language. Brooke's work was in its turn imitated by Bernard Garter in the 1565 poem *The Tragicall and true Historie which happened betwene two English Lovers*; this perhaps indicates the success of Brooke's work, as do its fresh editions in 1567 and 1587. In the former year appeared also William **Painter**'s prose version of the story, again taken from the French. Brooke's poem certainly contributed to the rise of the 'psychological novella' (such as **Lyly**'s *Euphues*) in England.

(C) Shakespeare takes some minor details from *The Tragicall Historye* in *3 Henry VI* and *Two Gentlemen of Verona* (for the latter see Allen 1938), but it is the principal source for *Romeo and Juliet*. It is clear that Brooke's poem and not the French or Italian tales from which it derives is Shakespeare's immediate source: some very specific incidents in the play (such as Juliet's asking the names of the masquers, with Romeo's coming last, 1.5.126–35) are found exclusively in Brooke.

In Shakespeare the action is condensed from nine months into a few days, throwing emphasis on the impulsiveness of the lovers and overshadowing their consummation with the necessity of immediate parting. Shakespeare 'absorbs from Brooke the vivid atmosphere and lively detail' but develops 'more intricate patterning' (Gibbons 1980: 38–9).

Brooke's sketchy characters are developed into more real and effective figures, Juliet being made even younger. Tybalt and Mercutio are worked out from the merest hints ('*Mercutio* . . . courteous of his speeche and pleasant of devise', 254–6), among other things so as to emphasize the unreasonableness and futility of the feud and to excuse Romeo's participation. Romeo's passion for Rosalind 'becomes the typical romantic love of the sonneteers for a cruel beauty, instead of the sexual pursuit of a virtuous maid . . . [and] a more effective contrast with Romeo's love for Juliet' (Muir 1977: 42). There are many verbal echoes of Brooke's poem in the play, but again, Shakespeare's development of Brooke's phraseology into poetry is much more significant than his indebtedness; 'the surprising thing is that Shakespeare preserved so much of his source in vitalizing its dead stuff' (Bullough, I, 278).

H. A. Mason places the emphasis on Shakespeare's poetic and dramatic exploitation of discrete moments in Brooke's material. Initial impressions may be that Shakespeare is only updating the idiom of a narrative which by the time of *Romeo and Juliet* was a generation old, 'but gradually he reaches out from narrative style towards true drama' (Mason 1970: 37). Juliet's reflections before drinking the poison, first here from Brooke and then Shakespeare, are transformed from a stiff, external, and poetically conventional picture into the words of a fully realized dramatic voice:

Shall not the fryer and my Romeus when they come,
Fynd me (if I awake before) ystyfled in the tombe?
    And whilst she in these thoughts doth dwell somwhat to long,
The force of her ymagining anon dyd waxe so strong,
That she surmisde she saw out of the hollow vaulte,
(A grisly thing to looke upon,) the carkas of Tybalt,
Right in the selfe same sort that she few dayes before
Had seene him in his blood embrewd, to death eke wounded sore.
And then, when she agayne within her selfe had wayde
That quicke she should be buried there, and by his side be layde
All comfortles, for she shall living feere have none
But many a rotten carkas, and full many a naked bone:
Her daynty tender partes gan shever all for dred,
Her golden heares did stand upright upon her chillish hed.
Then pressed with the feare that she there lived in,
A sweat as colde as mountayne yse, pearst through her tender skin,

That with the moysture hath wet every part of hers,
And more besides, she vainely thinkes, whilst vainly thus she feares,
A thousand bodies dead have compast her about,
And least they will dismember her, she greatly standes in doute,
But when she felt her strength began to weare away,
By little and little, and in her hart her feare increased ay:
Dreading that weakenes might or foolish cowardise
Hinder the execution of the purposde enterprise,
As she had frantike been, in hast the glasse she cought,
And up she drank the mixture quite, withouten farther thought.

                    (2375–2400; Brooke 1562: fos 66ᵛ–67ᵛ)

        How if, when I am laid into the tomb,
        I wake before the time that Romeo
        Come to redeem me? There's a fearful point.
        Shall I not then be stifled in the vault,
        To whose foul mouth no healthsome air breathes in,
        And there die strangled ere my Romeo comes?
        Or, if I live, is it not very like
        The horrible conceit of death and night,
        Together with the terror of the place –
        As in a vault, an ancient receptacle
        Where for this many hundred years the bones
        Of all my buried ancestors are pack'd;
        Where bloody Tybalt, yet but green in earth,
        Lies fest'ring in his shroud; where, as they say,
        At some hours in the night spirits resort –
        Alack, alack, is it not like that I,
        So early waking – what with loathsome smells,
        And shrieks like mandrakes' torn out of the earth,
        That living mortals, hearing them, run mad –
        O, if I wake, shall I not be distraught,
        Environed with all these hideous fears,
        And madly play with my forefathers' joints,
        And pluck the mangled Tybalt from his shroud,
        And, in this rage, with some great kinsman's bone,
        As with a club, dash out my desp'rate brains?
        O, look! methinks I see my cousin's ghost

> Seeking out Romeo, that did spit his body
> Upon a rapier's point. Stay, Tybalt, stay.
> Romeo, I come. This do I drink to thee.
>
> (4.3.30–58)

In his use of Brooke the early Shakespeare 'was already ... manipulating his source-material with a masterly sense of dramatic possibilities' (Muir 1977: 41). But this is a matter of taking local opportunities, not of overall direction: Shakespeare 'was for much of the time living through and filling out in stage terms what was essentially a narrative, a story, content to reap the full benefit from each incident, but ... not very much concerned with any total significance' (Mason 1970: 40).

(D) Muir (1977: 39–46) gives a useful brief résumé of the relationship between Brooke's poem and *Romeo and Juliet*; Law (1929) lists verbal echoes carefully. Bullough concentrates largely on plot, while Gibbons (1980) considers atmosphere and patterning at some length. Mason's more elaborate comparative exercise is an attempt to gauge Shakespeare's priorities in the play as a whole.

Bullough, i, 276–83 and viii, 386–7; Muir (1977).
Allen, Mozelle Scaff (1938). 'Brooke's *Romeus and Juliet* as a Source for the Valentine-Sylvia Plot in *The Two Gentlemen of Verona.*' *University of Texas Studies in English* 18: 25–46.
Br[ooke], Ar[thur] (1562). *The Tragicall Historye of Romeus and Juliet written first in Italian by Bandell.* London.
Gibbons, Brian, ed. (1980). *Romeo and Juliet* (Arden Shakespeare). London.
Law, Robert Adger (1929). 'On Shakespeare's Changes of his Source Material in *Romeo and Juliet.*' *University of Texas Studies in English* 9: 86–102.
Mason, H. A. (1970). *Shakespeare's Tragedies of Love: An Examination of the Possibility of Common Readings of 'Romeo and Juliet', 'Othello', 'King Lear', and 'Anthony and Cleopatra'.* London.

Bruto, Giovanni Michele (1517–1592), Italian Historian
A manual by Bruto translated in 1598 as *The Necessarie, Fit, and Convenient Education of a Yong Gentlewoman* is the only known English source to supply an account of Giulio Romano before the date of *The*

Winter's Tale; but if there is a requirement for a printed source, Vasari's Italian one was also available.

Ziegler, Georgianna (1985). 'Parents, Daughters, and "That Rare Italian Master": A New Source for *The Winter's Tale*.' *ShQ* 36: 204–12.

Buchanan, George (1506–1582), Scottish Poet and Historian See also **Holinshed, Raphael**.

(A) Scotland's leading sixteenth-century humanist was born into a farming family with connections to the local laird in the Blane Valley, near Glasgow. He took a degree from St Andrews in 1525, but received part of his higher education in France, including a spell at the Sorbonne during its time as a centre of radical political thought. Returning to Scotland about 1534, Buchanan gravitated towards the court, becoming tutor to the illegitimate son of James V and composing some dangerously satirical poems in Latin. Powerful enemies brought about an investigation into his religious conformity in 1539, but he escaped to Bordeaux. There he taught at the Collège de Guyenne in a period coinciding with the attendance of the young **Montaigne**, and in the next few years wrote poems, two Latin plays, and translations of two of **Euripides**' tragedies into Latin. He continued a continental scholar and teacher until 1560, his Latin writings, including his admired versions of the Psalms (composed as it happens in Portugal), belonging to the French rather than the Scottish or English Renaissance. He was converted to Calvinism following his return to Scotland as a distinguished scholar and poet about 1561, and, having written poems and masques in honour of Mary Queen of Scots in 1563–5, assisted in her prosecution for treason in 1568. He was an influential political and Church figure throughout these years, holding office as Keeper of the Privy Seal, Moderator of the Kirk, and in many other capacities, later as tutor to the young **James VI** (b. 1566). His two principal prose works (often printed together) were not completed until near the end of his life, though both his treatise on kingship, *De Jure Regni* (1579), and his greatest achievement, his posthumously published Latin history of Scotland, *Rerum Scoticarum Historia* (1582), were probably first drafted in the 1560s. The latter as much as the former is readable as an extended political treatise, with a much greater interest in constitutional and ideological issues than previous Scottish chronicles, and attempting in particular to justify the overthrow of Mary Queen of Scots. Both works were warmly received in certain Protestant circles, but their democratic, anti-absolutist emphases led to their condemnation from many quarters, including monarchist English and Roman Catholic ones (Buchanan's name had in fact been on the Papal Index since 1570).

(B) Buchanan's very considerable stature as a European thinker led to his publication in a number of countries in his lifetime and immediately afterwards, notably the Netherlands and Germany (Durkan 1994 gives full details). A flurry of printings of his works in England from 1577 to 1583, the year after his death, is largely attributable to the activities of a circle of admirers including Sir Philip **Sidney**, who in the *Apology for Poetry* writes that he views Buchanan's plays, together with *Gorboduc*, as the only good British drama written in his lifetime. Further editions of his work followed in the 1590s, but the next generation shows little activity; although there is 'firm interest in the poetry of the humanist', the rest of the corpus suffers 'varying political fortunes determined by the evolution of events in England' (McFarlane 1981: 481). In Scotland, 'it became acceptable at [James's] court to admire Buchanan's poetic skills while lamenting that he had been led astray by dubious political ideas' (Norbrook 1987: 92). A number of polemicists quickly took issue with Buchanan's democratic readings of Scottish history, and James himself tried to suppress his last works after his assumption of personal rule in 1584, then drastically revised Buchanan's political priorities in his own *True Law of Free Monarchies*, 1598. This official opposition seems to have combined with disapproving Presbyterian attitudes to his profane poetry to prevent publication of Buchanan's works in his native country after his death. Importantly, however, the *Historia* was used as a major source for the Scottish segment rewritten by Francis Thynne in the 1587 edition of **Holinshed**'s Chronicle.

(C) One Latin poem of Buchanan's, 'Pompa Deorum in nuptiis Mariae', may have lent a hint for the reference to the Platonic doctrine that Love keeps the world from chaos in *Venus and Adonis* 1017–20 (see Baldwin 1944: II, 650–8); this is the only plausible Shakespearean debt to Buchanan outside *Macbeth*. Buchanan's Latin poems were well known, but the status of his history was more equivocal. Though it cannot be proved that Shakespeare knew the *Historia* directly (as opposed to via Holinshed), it seems likely he did; this despite the facts that (1) Buchanan's book was until the later seventeenth century available only in its original Latin; (2) there is considerable overlap between the details Buchanan supplied for *Macbeth* and for the 1587 edition of Holinshed's Chronicle. The evidence for Shakespeare's use of Buchanan in *Macbeth* consists of a number of fairly strong parallels of narrative approach and narrative detail, indirectly supported by signs of the use of other relevant historians in the play which suggest some sort of effort to research the subject.

Six examples of apparent use of Buchanan are given by Paul (1950: 213–19), as follows:

1   The early Macbeth's excellent qualities, but lack of moderation, are mentioned by Buchanan whereas Holinshed only says that he was 'a valiant gentleman' though 'somewhat cruel'.
2   Buchanan is concerned to depict the workings of Macbeth's mind, whereas Holinshed is unsuggestive in this area.
3   Whereas Holinshed's Macbeth does not plan to obtain the kingdom until after he has met the weird sisters, in Buchanan the sisters only confirm a previous determination.
4   Shakespeare's depiction of Macbeth's remorse draws on the story of King Kenneth, Macbeth's great-grandfather, who killed his nephew. Buchanan's presentation of the murderer's feelings is much more detailed and much closer to Shakespeare's than Holinshed's.
5   The 'almost daily taunts' of Lady Macbeth, who 'shared all his plans', are mentioned exclusively by Buchanan; in Holinshed she only presses him to act through her great ambition.
6   Buchanan's depiction of Banquo as powerful and resourceful enough to imitate Macbeth's example, used by Shakespeare to provide a secondary motive for Banquo's murder, is not matched in Holinshed.

Paul concludes: 'The proper generalization is that upon the picturesque background of imaginary facts supplied by Holinshed, Shakespeare imposed ideas suggested by Buchanan; but they are ideas relating to the workings of the minds of the characters rather than to their acts' (1950: 219). Some minor additions and qualifications to these findings are given by Bullough and Muir (1977: 210–11). Norbrook's politically alert account takes up the fourth in more detail –

Shakespeare 'inverts the assumptions behind Buchanan's account of Kenneth III's grief, making the disruption, not the establishment, of a hereditary system the source of guilt' (1987: 102) – but also offers the new and intriguing suggestion that *Macbeth*'s 'Senecan' dramaturgical mode as a whole may reflect a certain 'anxiety of influence' in respect of Buchanan's plays.

(D)

Baldwin (1944); Bullough, vii, 438–40; Muir (1977).

Durkan, John (1994). *Bibliography of George Buchanan*. Glasgow.

McFarlane, I. D. (1981). *Buchanan*. London.

Norbrook, David (1987). '*Macbeth* and the Politics of Historiography', pp. 78–116 in Kevin Sharpe and Steven N. Zwicker, eds, *Politics of Discourse: The Literature and History of Seventeenth-Century England*. Berkeley.

Paul, Henry N. (1950). *The Royal Play of Macbeth: When, Why, and How it was Written by Shakespeare*. New York.

Sinfield, Alan (1988). '*Macbeth*: History, Ideology and Intellectuals', pp. 63–77 in Colin MacCabe, ed., *Futures for English*. Manchester.

Caesar and Pompey, or Caesar's Revenge (Anon. Play)

This academic tragedy of uncertain date (but probably Elizabethan) has been thought to lie behind the imagery and idiom of Antony's vision of civil war (3.1.259–75) and certain other features both general and local in *Antony and Cleopatra*, as well as influencing *Julius Caesar*.

Pearson, Jacqueline (1981). 'Shakespeare and *Caesar's Revenge*.' *ShQ* 32: 101–4.

Ronan, Clifford J. (1987). '*Caesar's Revenge* and the Roman Thoughts in *Antony and Cleopatra*.' *ShSt* 19: 171–82.

Schanzer, Ernest (1954). 'A Neglected Source of "Julius Caesar".' *N&Q* 199: 196–7.

Camden, William (1551–1623), Scholar, Teacher and Historian

(A) Camden, a product of Christ's Hospital School and St Paul's School in London, then Magdalen College and Christ Church, Oxford, was a noted educator, scholar and antiquarian. In the first of these roles he taught Ben **Jonson** and other well-known figures of the time at Westminster School, and became headmaster there in 1593. In the others he compiled his large Latin work on ancient and medieval English, Scottish and Irish history and topography, the *Britannia*, first published in 1586, the original aim of which was to collate the national topography with mainly Roman literary remains so as to reconstruct the pre-Roman British landscape. It was augmented by a vast collection of material of more recent import, such as genealogical and property records, until its sixth edition of 1607. Excerpts in English were published in Camden's 1605 *Remaines of a Greater Worke concerning Britain*, an assemblage arranged in sections with headings such as 'Surnames' (a list, with some explanations), 'Epitaphs', and 'Wise Speeches' (see (B)). In 1615 appeared the first part of his *Annales rerum Anglicarum et Hibernicarum regnante Elizabetha*, a Latin history of the reign of Elizabeth which has ever since then furnished details for students of Elizabethan Britain. He also wrote a history of the Gunpowder Plot.

As well as for his historical writings, Camden was noted as an expert on heraldry, the founder of a Chair of History at Oxford University, and the principal founder of the Society of Antiquaries, an important intellectual body of his day. He may have known Shakespeare personally through Ben Jonson, whose lifelong friend he became, or through others. He has been highly regarded by modern authorities on account of his impartial and scholarly procedures, though this is a matter of degree: like other sixteenth-century histories, his cannot be exempted from charges of embroidery or other manipulation, or of deploying ideologically suasive tactics.

(B) The importance of Camden's historical work was its foundation in classical as opposed to traditional sources, or more fundamentally its status as history and not the second-rate antiquarianism of his predecessors. It was readily taken up by such historical writers as John Clapham, Samuel **Daniel**, John Selden and John **Speed**, all of whom in the first twelve years of the seventeenth century were able to use Camden as an alternative to such authorities as **Geoffrey of Monmouth** (whose untruthfulness Camden often censures) and hence avoid the anachronistic conceptions of the ancient Britons as medieval kings and gentlemen that such writers had fostered. In the same way, Camden was directly or indirectly responsible for the new conception of the ancient Britons found in works such as **Drayton**'s English topographical poem *Poly-Olbion* (1613?) and Fletcher's play *Bonduca* (*c.* 1613). Camden's availability in English on the small scale of the *Remaines* of 1605 was supplemented by a full translation of the *Britannia* by Philemon Holland in 1610.

76

The following excerpt is one of the 'Wise Speeches' from the *Remaines*, and retells a fable readily recognizable to readers of *Coriolanus*.

Pope *Adrian* the fourth an English man borne, of the familie of *Breakespeare* in *Middlesex*, a man commended for converting *Norway* to christianity, before his Papacie, but noted in his Papacie, for using the Emperour *Fredericke* the second as his Page, in holding his stirroppe, demaunded of *John* of *Sarisbury* his countryman what opinion the world had of the Church of *Rome*, and of him, who answered: *The Church of Rome which should be a mother, is now a stepmother, wherein sit both Scribes and Pharises; and as for your selfe, whenas you are a father, why doe you exspect pensions from your children? &c.* Adrian smiled, and after some excuses tolde him this tale, which albeit it may seeme long, and is not unlike that of *Menenius Agrippa* in *Livie*, yet give it the reading, and happly you may learne somewhat by it. *All the members of the body conspired against the stomacke, as against the swallowing gulfe of all their labors; for whereas the eies beheld, the eares heard, the handes labored, the feete traveled, the tongue spake, and all partes performed their functions, onely the stomacke lay ydle and consumed all. Hereuppon they joyntly agreed al to forbeare their labors, and to pine away their lasie and publike enemy. One day passed over, the second followed very tedious, but the third day was so grievous to them all, that they called a common Counsel; The eyes waxed dimme, the feete could not support the body, the armes waxed lasie, the tongue faltered, and could not lay open the matter; Therefore they all with one accord desired the advise of the Heart. There Reason layd open before them, that hee against whome they had proclaimed warres, was the cause of all this their misery: For he as their common steward, when his allowances were withdrawne, of necessitie withdrew theirs fro them, as not receiving that he might allow. Therfore it were a farre better course to supply him, than that the limbs should faint with hunger. So by the perswasion of Reason, the stomacke was served, the limbes comforted, and peace re-established. Even so it fareth with the bodies of Common-weales; for albeit the Princes gather much, yet not so much for themselves, as for others: So that if they want, they cannot supply the want of others; therefore do not repine at Princes heerein, but respect the common good of the whole publike estate.*

(Camden 1605: sigs Cc3^v–Cc4^r)

(C) Camden's insistence on historical authenticity is in general unShakespearean. But the *Remaines* are sometimes thought to have been known to Shakespeare, as a minor source for *Coriolanus* and *King Lear*.

the book contains a short version of the Lear story and the fable of the Body's Members as given in (B), above. Menenius' speech, *Coriolanus* 1.1.94–144 (quoted in part under **Livy**), seems to fuse together recollections of several versions of this fable (notably those in Livy, **Plutarch** and **Sidney** – all printed in Bullough, v) which Shakespeare had read at various times, suggesting he must have pondered it deeply. Some three small parallels between Shakespeare and Camden are replicated in none of the other texts which contain the fable, the strongest of which is that the belly is called a 'gulf' (1.1.96). But this is a standard enough usage in the later sixteenth century, and the other parallel expressions could also have suggested themselves independently to the two writers.

It is possible that Camden's version of the Lear story lies behind Cordelia's remarks at 1.1.99–103 about her wifely affections supplanting some of her filial ones, and the Fool's jest about a peascod at 1.4.198, as well as several of the play's personal names and a few other details (see Perrett 1904; Muir 1972: xxxii–xxxiii; Musgrove 1956). So miscellaneous a series of links is generally weak evidence for Shakespeare's having read a text unless he is assumed to have engaged in the methodical study of a topic as preparation for his work.

(D)

Camden, William (1605). *Remaines of a Greater Worke, Concerning Britaine.* London.

Curran, John E., Jr (1997). 'Royalty Unlearned, Honor Untaught: British Savages and Historiographical Change in *Cymbeline.' CompD* 31: 277–303.

Herendeen, W. H. (1988). 'William Camden: Historian, Herald, and Antiquary.' *SP* 85: 192–210.

Muir, Kenneth, ed. (1972). *King Lear* (Arden Shakespeare). London.

Musgrove, S. (1956). 'The Nomenclature of *King Lear.' RES* 7: 294–8.

Perrett, Wilfred (1904). *The Story of King Lear from Geoffrey of Monmouth to Shakespeare.* Berlin.

Castiglione, Baldassare (1478–1529), Italian Courtier, Diplomat and Writer See also **Elyot, Sir Thomas**.

(A) Castiglione was born into a landed family in the Mantua region in 1478, and brought up at the court of Lodovico Sforza in Milan. He returned home in 1499, entering the service of Francesco Gonzaga, the Marquis of Mantua. In 1504 he moved to another small court at Urbino, where he composed elegant Latin verse, became for a period Duke Giudobaldo's ambassador to Rome, and in 1506 was accredited to Henry VII's court to receive the Order of the Garter on behalf of the Duke of Urbino. His time in Urbino was the basis of the volume he published two decades later, *Il Cortegiano* ('The Courtier'), written in the period 1513–18. He later became papal nuncio to Spain, and died in Toledo shortly after the publication of his book in Venice and his election as Bishop of Avila.

Il Cortegiano is both a source of information on the courtly arts and an illustration of courtly conversation. Its entertaining and notably dramatic dialogues involve over twenty historical figures in four imaginary discussions over four evenings at the ducal palace of Urbino. It also develops other topics, sometimes unexpected ones: a discussion of the ideal courtier's knowledge of the visual arts, for example, turns into a comparison of the relative merits of painting and sculpture. It is a significant channel for the transmission of Platonic love theory to the later Renaissance.

(B) Following its publication in 1528, translations of *The Courtier* into French and Spanish appeared within a decade. Some sixty editions of the text in translation had been issued by the time of Shakespeare's death, though in unexpurgated form it was placed on the international Catholic Index in 1590 owing to what the tribunal called its *mucha libertad*, including jokes at the expense of cardinals. It 'became an Englishman' through Sir Thomas Hoby (1530–1566, English ambassador to France), whose version was published in 1561 and reprinted in 1577, 1588 and 1603. Hoby's thoroughly sympathetic if not always accurate rendering has proved one of the most enduring Elizabethan translations from the Italian.

The book's currency in England begins to be especially striking in the decade following Hoby's translation, though original-language editions are also commonly owned after this date, by for example Mary Queen of Scots, William Drummond and Sir Thomas Tresham (Burke 1995: 58–61). John **Florio** in the dedication to his *Second Frutes* (1591) mentions 'Castilion's Courtier and Guazzo his dialogues' as the two books likeliest to be read by anyone wishing to acquire some Italian. Six editions of Bartholomew Clerke's extremely successful Latin version

(1571) also appeared by 1612. The pervasive influence of *The Courtier* on Elizabethan culture and on English writers came about partly directly and partly through Castiglione's primary place in the 'courtesy tradition' of writings by other authorities, such as Sir Thomas **Elyot**. Sir Philip **Sidney** went off to the wars with the volume in his baggage, and has been described as Castiglione's disciple. Gabriel **Harvey**, whose copious annotations to his copy survive, recommended the study of Castiglione to his students at Cambridge. As for playwrights, 'the forerunners of Shakespeare could have had at their disposal no dialogue more smooth, light and swiftly moving' (Matthiesson 1931: 16).

Examples of hostility are also available. **Marston** took what he called 'the absolute Castilio' as a type of the empty-headed fop in the first of his *Satyres*. Mixed or ambivalent responses in others, such as Roger Ascham, tend to mirror ambivalent attitudes towards the court itself. The book's fortunes declined in the seventeenth century, its successors concentrating more on the Christianity of the Christian prince than had Castiglione, but during an eighteenth-century revival it was recommended by Johnson (to Boswell) as 'the best book that ever was written upon good breeding'.

In this snippet from Hoby's 1561 translation, the courtiers are discussing the potential ruler's delegation of his authority; it is part of a passage which in obvious ways may lie behind *Measure for Measure* (see (C)):

> Therefore said Bias well, that promotions declare what men be: for even as vesselles while they are emptie, though they have some chinke in them, it can ill be perceived, but if they be filled with licour, they showe by and by on what side the fault is, so corrupt and il disposed mindes syldome discover their vices, but whan they be filled with authoritie. For then they are not able to carie the heavie burdien of poure, but forsake them selves and scatter on every side greedie desire, pride, wrath, solemnesse and such tiranicall fecions as they have within them. Wherupon without regard they persecute the good and wise, and promote the wicked ... [and] maintain spies, promoters, murtherers and cutthrotes to put men in feare and to make them become faintharted.
>
> (Castiglione 1561: sigs Pp2^v–Pp3^r)

(C) Speculation about Shakespeare's likely response to Castiglione has unearthed no incontrovertible evidence of direct use, and Barbara Johnson's is a typical approach: 'to take *The Courtier* as a grid on which to plot corresponding elements in *Hamlet* in order to perceive the problems and possibilities of being a Renaissance man, artist, and ruler as these are refracted in the play' (Johnson 1987: 35; for *Hamlet* see also Biswas 1984). Johnson's conclusion that *Hamlet* is 'haunted' by Castiglione's model courtier is not dependent on the similarity first noted in the nineteenth century between the real-life poisoning in Urbino in 1538 of Duke Francesco Marie I (the Lord General of *The Courtier*, I, and the nephew and successor of *Il Cortegiano*'s Duke Guidobaldi) by means of a lotion poured into the ear, and the method in *Hamlet*'s 'Murder of Gonzago' play. Similarly with *Henry V*, another play which must almost necessarily at some level show the influence of *The Courtier*. Sufficient local parallels exist to suggest it might have been in Shakespeare's mind in the process of composition, especially in points of convergence between Hal's and the Courtier's inner and outer characteristics (see Witt 1983). But these could be explained by indirect connections and coincidences, and what importance Castiglione may have for the play probably lies elsewhere, in his work's forming part of the overall context of Renaissance discussion of the princely virtues.

Some other supposed direct connections seem to be cases of wishful thinking. Bradbrook (1991) shows no direct use of Castiglione in *The Two Gentlemen of Verona*. Roe (1992: 19–20) speculates on no particular grounds that *Venus and Adonis* may draw from *Il Cortegiano* its maturity, sophistication and moderation or *mediocritas*, as well as its qualified 'vision of ideal love'. Again, some parallels between the combats of wit which occupy Beatrice and Benedick in *Much Ado about Nothing* and those indulged in by Lady Emilia Pia and Lord Gaspare Pallavicino in *The Courtier* have long been pointed out (Scott 1901), but are not especially close. Bullough classes Castiglione as only an analogue for this play, while noting that 'although Castiglione's couple are not lovers they are friends despite their wordy warfare, and Count Ludovico . . . makes remarks which read like a germ of the Beatrice-Benedick relationship when he is discussing indirect ways of wooing' in Book III (II, 79). But, since Shakespeare is likely to have had knowledge of *The Courtier*, some small parallels may be more than coincidences. In *Much Ado about Nothing* the name of Baltasar, Don Pedro's attendant (with an exaggerated 'courtly' modesty), is unlikely to be chosen at random. A sequence of small-scale links in *Love's Labour's Lost* has also been traced (Baldini 1997).

In the case of *Measure for Measure*, stronger connections can be found to one section of *The Courtier*, the discussion led by Lord Octavian in IV.1 on the conduct and qualities of the potential ruler (sampled in (B)). Octavian argues that the ruler may delegate his responsibilities but 'never credit nor trust any officer so much, as to give him the bridle wholly into his hands'. The prince's principal virtue is temperance, from which he acquires 'likewise Justice an undefiled virgin' (1561: sig. Oo3ᵛ). This hint of allegory, though the idea is an old one, may help explain Isabella's standing as the embodiment of a kind of justice. Other significant parallels also help to imply a specific connection between the two works, though there is no systematic correspondence.

(D) Burke (1995) is authoritative on the response to Castiglione in Europe, including England, and has an appendix comprehensively listing editions and translations. For Hoby and his reception see also Matthiesson (1931). There is no worthwhile synoptic treatment of Shakespeare and Castiglione: for individual plays see items below, especially Gent (1972) on *Measure for Measure*.

Baldini, Donatella (1997). 'The Play of the Courtier: Correspondences between Castiglione's *Il libro del Cortegiano* and Shakespeare's *Love's Labour's Lost.*' *Quaderni d'Italianistica* 18: 5–22.

Biswas, D. C. (1984). 'Shakespeare's Conception of a Courtier', pp. 44–52 in Visvanath Chatterjee, ed., *The Romantic Tradition*. Calcutta.

Bradbrook, M. C. (1991) 'Courtier and Courtesy: Castiglione, Lyly and Shakespeare's *Two Gentlemen of Verona*', pp. 161–78 in J. R. Mulryne and Margaret Shewring, eds, *Theatre of the English and Italian Renaissance*. Basingstoke.

Bullough, II, 78–80.

Burke, Peter (1995). *The Fortunes of the 'Courtier': The European Reception of Castiglione's 'Cortegiano'*. Cambridge.

Castiglione, Baldassare (1561). *The Courtyer of Count Baldessar Castilio . . . done into English by Thomas Hoby*. London.

Gent, C. L. (1972). '*Measure for Measure* and the Fourth Book of Castiglione's *Il Cortegiano.*' *MLR* 67: 252–6.

Johnson, Barbara A. (1987). 'The Fabric of the Universe Rent: *Hamlet* as an Inversion of *The Courtier.*' *Hamlet Studies* 9: 34–52.

Matthiesson, F. O. (1931). *Translation: An Elizabethan Art.* Cambridge, MA.

Roe, John, ed. (1992). *The Poems* (New Cambridge Shakespeare). Cambridge.

Scott, J. W. (1972). '*Measure for Measure* and Castiglione.' *N&Q* 217: 128.

Scott, Mary Augusta (1901). '*The Book of the Courtyer*: A Possible Source of Benedick and Beatrice.' *PMLA* 16: 475–502.

Witt, Robert W. (1983). 'Prince Hal and Castiglione.' *Ball State University Forum* 24.iv: 73–9.

Cavendish, George See **Stow, John**.

Caxton, William (*c.*1422–1491), Printer and Translator

(A) Caxton, the 'father of English printing', was born in Kent. He became involved in the textile industry, rising to an office as the representative of the Merchants' Guild in Bruges, eventually becoming governor of the English diplomatic and commercial colony in the Low Countries. As such he was sometimes employed as Edward IV's representative in negotiations, and in 1469, still in Bruges, he became adviser to Edward's sister Margaret, Duchess of Burgundy. He now began to learn the new craft of printing and to work on literary translations, starting with his *Recuyell* ['recoil', 'gathering'] *of the Historyes of Troye*, a version of Guido delle Colonne's thirteenth-century *Historia Troiana* via the French translation by Raoul Lefèvre, chaplain to Duke Philip of Burgundy. This was published in Bruges in 1474 or 1475 as the first book Caxton printed. He returned to England in 1476, producing in 1477 the first book to be printed there. Though not himself a scholar, he was shrewd enough to develop a 'list' of eventually over a hundred separate titles appealing to a wide range of customers, including the works of **Chaucer** and many first English versions of classics (such as **Aesop**'s fables), many in his own translations.

(B) Through his many and various publications Caxton exerted a major influence on English writing for a century and more, his longest-lasting contribution perhaps being his reshaping (in chapter and book divisions) and printing of Thomas Malory's Arthurian works (as *Le Morte d'Arthur*). But only the *Recuyell of the Historyes of Troye* is directly relevant to Shakespeare. A usually literal but error-prone translation, it was in steady demand from its first publication down to the eighteenth century. It was reprinted in 1502–3, 1553, 1596 (henceforth 'newly corrected, and the English much amended, by William Fiston'), 1607, 1617, and on further occasions to 1738. The explanation for its popularity lies largely in Guido's claim to historical authority. Well into the sixteenth century, **Homer** was thought of as an unsatisfactory source on the subject of the Trojan War: he was Greek and hence biased; he was born after the events he portrayed took place; and he mingled fact with fiction, such as the gods' part in the battles. Non-Homeric sources, such as Dares Phrygius and Dictys Cretensis (both supposedly participants in the Trojan War), and those, including Guido, who based their work on them, were for long accorded far higher authority; and the events they were supposed to have witnessed were, for the royal houses of western Europe, key elements in the pedigrees they traced back to Aeneas (a Trojan, like Dares). Caxton's version was one of two principal English treatments, the other being John **Lydgate**'s *Troy Book*. (For a comprehensive discussion of the relationships between these and other medieval Troy texts see Sommer 1894: I, xvii–xlvi.)

Shakespeare knew the earlier version of the Caxton text, hence probably not the late sixteenth-century sophistication of it by Fiston. This is established by his use of the word 'orgulous' in the second line of the Prologue of *Troilus and Cressida*: the word appears commonly in pre-1596 editions of Caxton but it was later considered old-fashioned and altered to 'proud'. This sample from the early version corresponds to Shakespeare's treatment of the combat between Hector and Ajax (*Troilus and Cressida* 4.5) in two details distinctive to Caxton among the sources: Hector embraces Ajax and calls him his 'cosyn germayn'.

In this day had the trojans had vittorye of alle the grekes yf fortune that is dyverse had wylle consentyd / For they myght have slayn hem alle And eschewyd the grete evyllys that after cam to them. Certes hit is not wysedom whan ony man fyndeth his enemye in grete perylle and fortune / to offre his power to delivere hym thereof / For hit happeth ofte tymes / that he shall never recovere to have his enemye in the same caas / but that fortune torne her backe Thus hit happend this day to the unhappy hector / that was at the above of his enemyes and myght have slayn hem alle yf he had wolde / for they soughte no thynge but for to flee / whan by grete mysaventure cam afore hym in an encountre thelamon Ayax that was sone of kynge thelamon and exione And was cosyn germayn of hector and of his brethern whiche was wyse and vayllyant / whiche adressid hym ayenst hector and deliveryd to hym a grete assault And hector to hym as they that were valyant bothe two / and as they were fightyng they spak to geder And therby hector knewe that he was his cosyn germaine sone of his aunte And than hector for curtoisye enbraced hym in his armes and made hym grete chiere And offryd to hym to do all his playsir yf he desired ony thynge of hym / And prayd hym that he wolde come to troye with hym for to see his lignage of hys moder syde / But the sayd Thelamon that entended no thynge but to his avauntage sayde that he wolde not goo at thys tyme / But prayd to hector sayng / that yf he lovyd hym so mocheas he sayde / that he wolde for his sake and at his Instance do cesse the battail for that day / and that the trojans shold leve the grekes in pees / The unhappy hector accorded to hym his requeste.

(1474/5 text; ed. Sommer 1894: ɪɪ, 589–90)

(C) There are large overlaps between the three main sources Shakespeare probably knew for the Troy legend (Chaucer's *Troilus and Criseyde*, Lydgate's *Troy Book*, and Caxton), but Shakespeare clearly prefers Caxton at some points (for details see especially Presson 1953, more briefly Palmer 1982). Caxton may be seen as anticipating Shakespeare in particularly emphasizing Diomedes' love for Cressida and Troilus' status as a warrior rather than a lover. Substantially the same story is told by all three Troy story sources, however, and in *Troilus and Cressida* the principal fact is usually Shakespeare's manipulation of what is common to them. Here, especially if we discount the possibility of Homer's having had a part in the play's construction, what is perhaps most notable is how far Shakespeare is under the influence of medieval presentations of the tale. G. K. Hunter suggests that the play 'may be seen as the product of a collision between the medieval versions . . . and the Renaissance handlings of the same material', taking the latter to include **Chapman**'s Homer, **Greene**'s *Euphues his Censure to Philautus*, and perhaps **Ovid**'s *Metamorphoses*, xɪɪɪ (Hunter 1971: 60). Lydgate's and the other medieval handlings should not, however, be thought of as precedents for a derogatory or satirical presentation of the story (see Sacharoff 1970).

One suggestion for Caxton's influence on Shakespeare outside

Troilus is Shulman's (1980) that in *As You Like It* Orlando's modesty is based on that of Hercules as mentioned (with similar phrasing) in the *Recuyell*.

(D)

Bullough, vi.

Caxton, William (1596). *The Auncient Historie, of the Destruction of Troy, Newly corrected, and the English much Amended, by William Fiston.* London.

Henderson, W. B. Drayton (1935). 'Shakespeare's *Troilus and Cressida*: Yet Deeper in its Tradition', pp. 127–56 in Hardin Craig, ed., *Essays in Dramatic Literature: The Parrott Presentation Volume.* Princeton (reprinted New York, 1967).

Hunter, G. K. (1971). 'Shakespeare's Reading', pp. 55–66 in Kenneth Muir and S. Schoenbaum, eds, *A New Companion to Shakespeare Studies.* Cambridge.

James, Heather (1997). *Shakespeare's Troy: Drama, Politics, and the Translation of Empire.* Cambridge.

Palmer, Kenneth, ed. (1982). *Troilus and Cressida* (Arden Shakespeare). London.

Presson, Robert K. (1953). *Shakespeare's 'Troilus and Cressida' and the Legends of Troy.* Madison, WI.

Sacharoff, Mark (1970). 'The Traditions of the Troy-Story Heroes and the problem of Satire in *Troilus and Cressida.' ShSt* 6: 125–35.

Shulman, Jeff (1980). ' "The Recuyell of the Historyes of Troye" and the Tongue-Tied Orlando.' *ShQ* 31: 390.

Sommer, H. Oskar, ed. (1894). *The Recuyell of the Historyes of Troye, Written in French by Raoul Lefèvre, Translated and Printed by William Caxton (about A.D. 1474), the First English Printed Book, now Faithfully Reproduced,* 2 vols. London.

Stein, Elizabeth (1930). 'Caxton's *Recuyell* and Shakespeare's *Troilus.' MLN* 45: 144–6.

Tillyard, E. M. W. (1965). *Shakespeare's Problem Plays.* Harmondsworth (first published 1950).

Cervantes, Miguel de (1547–1616), Spanish Novelist The lost play *The History of Cardenio* is derived from Cervantes' tale of Cardenio and Luscinda in *Don Quixote* (1605).

Metz, G. Harold, ed. (1989). *Sources of Four Plays Ascribed to Shakespeare*, pp. 284–9. Columbia, MI.

Chaloner, Sir Thomas See **Erasmus, Desiderius**.

Chapman, George (1559–1634), Poet and Dramatist See also **Homer**. Shakespeare shows only faint echoes of Chapman – a name here, a phrase there – in part, no doubt, because much of Chapman's work appeared too late to have any impact on him.

Lewalski, Barbara K. (1970). 'Hero's Name – and Namesake – in *Much Ado About Nothing*.' *ELN* 7: 175–9.
Walter, J. H. (1965). '"In a little room": Shakespeare and Chapman.' *N&Q* 210: 95–6.

Chariton, of Aphrodisia See **Greek Romance**.

Chaucer, Geoffrey (*c.* 1340–1400), Poet See also **Greene, Robert**.
(A) The son of a London vintner who was occasionally employed on service for the king, the young Chaucer soldiered in France in 1359. He then settled down to a career in the royal courts of Edward III and Richard II, mostly as a London customs comptroller but often travelling abroad on official business and diplomatic visits. Other than prose works, his writings consist of *The Canterbury Tales*, unfinished but still one of the largest and most varied collections of medieval verse narratives; *Troilus and Criseyde*, a poem in five Books based on **Boccaccio**'s romance *Il Filostrato*; the dream poems *The Book of the Duchess*, *The House of Fame* and *The Parliament of Fowls*; *The Legend of Good Women*, an incomplete collection of tales based on classical Latin sources; and many lesser works.

(B) Much eulogistic reference is made to Chaucer by early modern English writers: he is the father of English poetry, the English Homer.

This is not merely lip-service, but some of the praise is conventional, and the extent of his readership and influence do not fully tally with it. The Elizabethans evidently used Chaucer as a name on which to hang a native pantheon while finding his work in some ways rather remote. They sense a gap in literary history between the medieval classics and themselves, and this feeling becomes stronger after the end of the sixteenth century. Language and metre are a principal part of the problem. **Jonson** in *Timber* is against letting the young 'taste Gower, or Chaucer at first, lest falling too much in love with antiquity . . . they grow rough and bare in language'. As for Chaucer's versification, the ignorance of the sixteenth-century editors (William Thynne, 1532; John **Stow**, 1561; Thomas Speght, 1598, 1602) about changes in pronunciation since the fourteenth century produces catastrophic results when they attempt to 'correct' their texts; knowledge of the use of final 'e' in Middle English, in particular, is needed to understand Chaucer's prosody. 'Chaucer is hard even to our understanding', writes **Marston** in 1598.

Nevertheless, as the number of published editions (above) suggests, Chaucer was much read and much enjoyed by Shakespeare's contemporaries (for responses see Brewer 1978: 1). In general he was thought of as 'a serious romantic writer' (Thompson 1978: 216) of tales, particularly *Troilus* and *The Knight's Tale*, which were not regarded as impossibly old-fashioned. His 'moral' aspects tended to be made central: the sententiousness of *Troilus and Criseyde*, in particular, stood the poem in good stead. He was praised as a learned poet, both for his use of foreign authors and for his knowledge of 'astronomie, philosophie, and other parts of profound or cunning art' (Gabriel **Harvey**, *c.* 1585; see Brewer 1978: 1, 121). At a more popular level, the expression 'Canterbury tale' came to mean 'bawdy story', suggesting the racy reputation of the collection but also its lowly literary status, at least relative to the modern estimate. Chaucer was much pillaged by dramatists: over a dozen plays apparently based on Chaucerian materials (usually for plot only) appear between 1558 and 1625, excluding Shakespeare's but including two lost treatments of the Troilus and Cressida story (by Nicholas Grimald, 1559, and by Thomas **Dekker** *et al.*, 1599).

Troilus and Criseyde was Chaucer's best-known single work in the sixteenth century. One of the episodes which resurfaces in Shakespeare (see (C)) is Pandarus' interview with Criseyde after she has spent the night with Troilus. Its sinister undertones are a reminder of the complex texture of Chaucer's poem.

> Pandare a morowe, which that comen was
> Unto his nece, and gan her faire grete
> And saied, all this night so rained it alas
> That all my drede is, that ye nece swete
> Have little leiser had to slepe and mete
> Al this night (quod he) hath rain so do me wake
> That some of us I trowe her heddes ake.
>
> And nere he came and said, how stant it now
> This merie morow, nece how can ye fare
> Creseide answerd, never the bet for you
> Foxe that ye been, God yeve your hart care
> God helpe me so, ye caused all this fare
> Trowe I (quod she) for all your words white
> O who so seeth you, knoweth you full lite.
>
> With that she gan her face for to wrie
> With the shete and woxe for shame all redde
> And Pandarus gan under for to prie
> And saied nece, if that I shall been dedde
> Have here a sworde, and smiteth off my hedde
> With that his arme, all sodainly he thrist
> Under her necke, and at the last her kist.
>
> (III, 1555–75; ed. Speght 1598: fo. 174^{r-v})

One further passage underlines this point about the tone of *Troilus and Criseyde*. Near the end of the narrative Troilus becomes for a short while the Trojans' champion, seeking honour in war in recompense for his lost love. All medieval versions of the tale include this material, but Chaucer in particular (sadly mangled here in Speght, alas) emphasizes Troilus' new-found 'cruelty' – a quality Shakespeare will also stress in Troilus' altercations with Hector.

> In many cruell battaile out of drede
> Of Troylus, this ilke noble knight,
> (As men may in these old bokes rede)

> Was seen his knighthod, and his great might
> And dredelesse his ire day and night
> Ful cruelly the Grekes aie abought
> (And alway most this Diomede) he soughte
>
> And oft time (I find) that they mette
> With bloody strokes, and with words great
> Assaying how her speares were whette
> And God it wote, with many a cruel heat
> Gan Troylus upon his helme to beat
> But nathelesse, fortune naught ne would
> Of outher hond that either dien should
> (v, 1751–64; ed. Speght 1598: fo. 193ᵛ)

(C) There is much uncertainty about Shakespeare's reading of Chaucer, in part because Chaucer's materials are almost always found in other possible sources: for example, the story of the Siege of Troy in *Troilus and Criseyde* was available to Shakespeare in **Chapman**'s **Homer**, in **Lydgate**, in **Caxton**, and perhaps in one or two now lost plays (see Presson 1953). And the Fall of Troy was a widely understood emblem of betrayal, endlessly recycled – 'to the sixteenth century the highest secular symbol of Disaster' (Bradbrook 1958: 311–12). Moreover, 'Chaucer's linguistic remoteness must have discouraged direct quotation, and . . . to an exceptional degree, his characteristics vanish when he is paraphrased, and his work becomes almost unrecognizable at second-hand' (Thompson 1978: 10). Hence gauging Chaucer's part in Shakespeare's work is a matter of probabilities rather than certainties. Shakespeare would have read Chaucer either in Speght's 1598 edition (from which quotations here are taken) or the older Stow or Thynne ones. Coghill's (1959) list of twelve verbal and 'notional' parallels leads him to surmise that Shakespeare read or re-read Chaucer in the years of *Romeo and Juliet*, *A Midsummer Night's Dream* and *Richard III*.

In the conventional view of *Troilus and Cressida*, Chaucer's Criseyde, an amorous, warm-hearted young woman, is turned by Shakespeare into a shallow and selfish creature, while Troilus becomes 'the feverish lover of late romantic poetry', prone to 'deep-rooted doubt and uncertainty' (Pettet 1949: 144). But arguably he always was, and certainly this reading cannot be supported throughout. In Cressida's interview with Pandarus for which the corresponding Chaucerian passage is given in (B), for instance, Shakespeare clearly has no interest in exploiting the undertones present in Chaucer:

PANDARUS How now, How now! How go maidenheads? Here, you
          maid! Where's my cousin Cressid?
CRESSIDA Go hang yourself, you naughty mocking uncle,
          You bring me to do, and then you flout me too.
PANDARUS To do what? To do what? Let her say what. What have I
          brought you to do?
CRESSIDA Come, come, beshrew your heart! You'll ne'er be good,
          Nor suffer others.
PANDARUS Ha, ha! Alas, poor wretch! A poor capocchia! Hast not
          slept to-night? Would he not, a naughty man, let it sleep?
          A bugbear take him!
CRESSIDA Did not I tell you? Would he were knock'd i' th' head.
                                                      (4.2.23–34)

The simple contrast between positive Chaucerian portrayals and negative Shakespearean ones of the principals in *Troilus and Cressida* is probably based on selective interpretation of Chaucer's poem, and it may have been rather the ambiguities of his source that attracted Shakespeare – whose own ambiguities are not the same. So Smith (1982: 65–9), and Donaldson (1985: 3–5) sums up this position:

> Shakespeare understood Chaucer's poem for what it is, a marvelous celebration of romantic love containing a sad recognition of its fragility, a work full of ironic contradictions and yet ringing true in a way that far more realistic literature fails to do. But the poem one meets in the criticism of Shakespeare's play is one with a relatively straightforward, oversimplified meaning ... Shakespeare naturally understood the ambiguity with which the poem had treated Criseyde, and ... implanted in Cressida a complex ambiguity of her own.

One may speculate that in other respects Shakespeare's response to Chaucer's work was mainly to do otherwise. In the handling of narrative time, Chaucer's deliberate sluggishness may have encouraged Shakespeare to speed up Criseyde's departure from Troy and her surrender to Diomedes, and the very potent sense of temporal distancing

91

that Chaucer can deploy, especially in Book v, may have given Shakespeare an impulse towards the sudden concentration of temporal distance at the end of 3.2. Again, the elaborate withdrawal of the Chaucerian narrator in the last stretch of the poem might have done something to prompt Shakespeare's very different multiple detachments of the play's triple ending.

The Chaucerian debt of *The Two Noble Kinsmen* is acknowledged in the Preface: the play

> has a noble breeder and a pure,
> A learnèd, and a poet never went
> More famous yet 'twixt Po and silver Trent.
> Chaucer, of all admir'd, the story gives,
> There constant to eternity it lives.
>
> (10–14)

This image of Chaucer is conventional for the time; and the source for this play, *The Knight's Tale*, was the second most famous Chaucerian work after *Troilus and Criseyde*. The relationship of poem to play is again complex. Again, the narrative is not adhered to closely; again, apparently Chaucerian ideas and details are widely scattered; and there is the additional complication in this case that in their collaboration Shakespeare and Fletcher may have seen different things in *The Knight's Tale* and hence used it in different ways. Thompson (1978: 214) has it that Fletcher's parts (not securely identified) seem to stay closer to the Chaucerian material whereas Shakespeare apparently takes greater freedoms, but such conclusions are apt to be influenced by preconceptions. The 'almost gratuitous preoccupation with horrors' in Shakespeare's play as a whole may be 'adopt[ed] from the starker side of his Chaucerian source', though the 'harsher, more remote, more prideful, more bullheaded Theseus' is Shakespeare's invention (Donaldson 1985: 56, 66). The horrors are part of a vision of human life under the sway of cosmic forces which Shakespeare/Fletcher perhaps acquired from *The Knight's Tale*, where it is concentrated in the descriptions of the temples of the gods (echoed in the prayers of Arcite, Palamon and Emilia in Act 5), and the quality of which may be thought of as Lucretian even though Lucretius was unknown to Chaucer.

The Emilia of *The Two Noble Kinsmen* is more fully developed and more interesting than Chaucer's figure. Her prayer to Diana in Act 5

shows both departures from Chaucer (Diana has no 'vengeance' or 'ire')
and similarities (her request is precisely identical). However, although
all of Act 5 is usually attributed to Shakespeare, this passage looks
distinctly unlike his work. Emily's speech is followed by Emilia's here:

> O chaste goddesse of the woddes grene
> To whom bothe heven and yearth and see is sene
> Quene of the reigne of Pluto, derke and low
> Goddesse of maidens, that myn hert hath know
> Ful many a yere, and woste what I desire
> As kepe me fro the vengeaunce of thyn yre
> That Acteon abought cruelly
> Chaste goddesse, well woste thou that I
> Desyre to ben a mayde al my life
> Ne never woll I be love ne wife
> I am (thow woste well) of thy company
> A maide, and love hunting and venery
> And for to walken in the woddes wilde
> And not for to ben a wife, and ben with childe
> Nought will I know company of man
> Now helpe me lady sith you may and can
> For tho thre formes that thou hast in the
> And Palamon, that hath such a love to me
> And eke Arcite, that loveth me so sore
> This grace I pray the withouten more
> And send love and peace betwixt hem two
> And fro me turne away her hertes so
> That all her hotte love, and her desire
> And all her busy turment, and all her fire
> Be queint, or turned in another place
> And if so be thou wolte not do me that grace
> Or if so be my destinie be shapen so
> That I shall nedes have one of hem two
> As sende me him that most desireth me
>   (2297–2325; Speght 1598: fo. 7ʳ)

> O sacred, shadowy, cold, and constant queen,
> Abandoner of revels, mute contemplative,

93

> Sweet, solitary, white as chaste, and pure
> As wind-fanned snow, who to thy female knights
> Allow'st no more blood than will make a blush,
> Which is their order's robe: I here, thy priest,
> Am humbled fore thine altar. O, vouchsafe
> With that thy rare green eye, which never yet
> Beheld thing maculate, look on thy virgin;
> And, sacred silver mistress, lend thine ear –
> Which ne'er heard scurril term, into whose port
> Ne'er entered wanton sound – to my petition,
> Seasoned with holy fear. This is my last
> Of vestal office. I am bride-habited,
> But maiden-hearted. A husband I have 'pointed,
> But do not know him. Out of two, I should
> Choose one and pray for his success, but I
> Am guiltless of election. Of mine eyes
> Were I to lose one, they are equal precious –
> I could doom neither: that which perished should
> Go to't unsentenced. Therefore, most modest queen,
> He of the two pretenders that best loves me
> And has the truest title in't, let him
> Take off my wheaten garland, or else grant
> That file and quality I hold I may
> Continue in thy band.
>
> (5.3.1–26)

Other than in *Troilus and Cressida* and *The Two Noble Kinsmen*, the most substantial claims for Chaucerian influence on Shakespeare come with *A Midsummer Night's Dream*. This play apparently reflects three or more of Chaucer's works. Brooks (1979) catalogues local correspondences with *The Knight's Tale*, especially for the framing action and for plot elements, and with *The Merchant's Tale* for Oberon and Titania's quarrel. *The Legend of Good Women* is used for the Pyramus and Thisbe story, which because of certain correspondences in the details of the respective parodies is also held by Donaldson (1985: 9) to be 'the moral equivalent – an inspired recreation – of Chaucer's *Tale of Sir Thopas*'. Theseus is by no means simply taken over from *The Knight's Tale*. He is closer to the condition of the lovers by virtue of his unmarried state, and Shakespeare acknowledges – as Chaucer does not – his womanizing past. The near-interchangeableness of Demetrius and Lysander may be an idea borrowed from the same poem, with their triangular love-relationship squared 'to convert the plot from tragicomedy ... to comedy' (Donaldson 1985: 36). Pluto and Proserpina from *The Merchant's Tale* have long been recognized as the models for Oberon and Titania, though there are complicating factors such as the Shakespearean names (from **Huon of Burdeux** and **Ovid** respectively). Some of the overall scepticism of *A Midsummer Night's Dream* about young love may be caught from the same Chaucerian work.

A few more tenuous links have been drawn between Shakespeare and Chaucer. *Romeo and Juliet* perhaps appropriates elements from the presentation of the lovers in *Troilus and Criseyde* (see Mehl 1984), though the picture is complicated by the undoubted use of Chaucer's poem by Arthur **Brooke** in Shakespeare's principal source, *The Tragicall Historye of Troilus and Criseyde* (see Gibbons 1980: 36–42). *The Franklin's Tale* has been linked with Prospero's magic (Hillman 1983). *The Legend of Good Women* may have suggested details for *The Rape of Lucrece* (see Bush 1932: 150), and the plot of *The Knight's Tale* has one element in common with *The Two Gentlemen of Verona* (see Leech 1969: xxxvi). A number of interesting Chaucerian details in *The Merry Wives of Windsor*, especially concerning Falstaff, and in the figure of Falstaff in other plays, especially via the Wife of Bath, have been suggested (by Judith Kollmann in Donaldson and Kollmann 1983, and by Donaldson 1985).

(D) Coghill (1959) supplies a résumé of earlier discussion. Thompson (1978) was the first book-length study of the subject and contains a full bibliography up to 1978; only major items and cited items up to that date are listed below. A substantial recent discussion of *The Two Noble Kinsmen* which develops from Thompson's conclusions is Metz (1989: 409–18). The subtly worked arguments of Donaldson (1985), not universally accepted, extend and elaborate Chaucerian connections for *A Midsummer Night's Dream, The Two Noble Kinsmen, Troilus and Cressida* and, more conjecturally, *Romeo and Juliet* and the figure of Falstaff. Donaldson and Kellmann's edited essay collection (1983) overlaps but moves also to *The Taming of the Shrew* and other Shakespearean contexts with no particular Chaucerian background.

Bergeron, D. M. (1969). 'The Wife of Bath and Shakespeare's *Taming of the Shrew.*' *University Review* 35: 279–86.

Bradbrook. M. C. (1958). 'What Shakespeare did to Chaucer's *Troilus and Criseyde.*' *ShQ* 9: 311–19.

Brewer, Derek, ed. (1978). *Chaucer: The Critical Heritage*, 2 vols. London.

Brooks, Harold F., ed. (1979). *A Midsummer Night's Dream* (Arden Shakespeare). London.

Bush, Douglas (1932). *Mythology and the Renaissance Tradition in English Poetry.* London.

Coghill, Nevill (1959). 'Shakespeare's Reading in Chaucer', pp. 86–99 in *Elizabethan and Jacobean Studies Presented to Frank Percy Wilson.* Oxford.

Donaldson, E. Talbot (1985). *The Swan at the Well: Shakespeare Reading Chaucer.* New Haven.

Donaldson, E. Talbot, and Judith J. Kollmann, eds (1983). *Chaucerian Shakespeare: Adaptation and Transformation.* Detroit.

Gibbons, Brian, ed. (1980). *Romeo and Juliet* (Arden Shakespeare). London.

Hale, David G. (1985). 'Bottom's Dream and Chaucer.' *ShQ* 36: 219–20.

Hillman, Richard (1983). 'Chaucer's Franklin's Magician and *The Tempest*: An Influence Beyond Appearances?' *ShQ* 34: 426–32.

James, Heather (1997). *Shakespeare's Troy: Drama, Politics, and the Translation of Empire.* Cambridge.

Leech, Clifford, ed. (1969). *The Two Gentlemen of Verona* (Arden Shakespeare). London.

Lehnert, Martin (1967). 'Shakespeare und Chaucer.' *ShJ* 103: 7–39.

Mehl, Dieter (1984). 'Chaucerian Comedy and Shakespearean Tragedy.' *ShJ* 120: 111–27.

Metz, G. Harold, ed. (1989). *Sources of Four Plays Ascribed to Shakespeare.* Columbia, MI.

Pettet, E. C. (1949). *Shakespeare and the Romance Tradition.* London.

Presson, Robert K. (1953). *Shakespeare's 'Troilus and Cressida' and the Legends of Troy.* Madison, WI.

Smith, Valerie (1982). 'The History of Cressida', pp. 61–79 in J. A. Jowitt and R. K. S. Taylor, eds, *Self and Society in Shakespeare's 'Troilus and Cressida' and 'Measure for Measure'* (Bradford Centre Occasional Papers, 4). Bradford.

Speght, Thomas, ed. (1598). *The Workes of our Antient and Learned English Poet, Geffrey Chaucer.* London.

Thompson, Ann (1978). *Shakespeare's Chaucer: A Study in Literary Origins.* Liverpool.

Turner, Robert K., Jr (1980). '*The Two Noble Kinsmen* and Speght's Chaucer.' *N&Q* 225: 175–6.

Chester, Robert (*c.* 1566–1640), Poet The 1601 edition of Chester's peculiar poem *Loves Martyr* included Shakespeare's *The Phoenix and the Turtle* as one of several responses to it; Shakespeare had evidently studied Chester's work for the occasion and appropriated its allusive, mystical manner.

Buxton, John (1980). 'Two Dead Birds: A Note on *The Phoenix and Turtle*', pp. 44–55 in [John Carey, ed.,] *English Renaissance Studies Presented to Dame Helen Gardner in Honour of her Seventieth Birthday*. Oxford.
Prince, F. T., ed. (1969). *The Poems* (Arden Shakespeare), xxviii–xlvi. London (first published 1960).

Chronicle History Plays (Including *The Famous Victories of Henry V*, *The True Tragedie of Richard III*, *The Troublesome Raigne of King John*, *The True Chronicle History of King Leir*, *Woodstock*) See also **Morality Tradition.**
(A) The English history play which emerged as a distinct type by the late 1580s was in one sense 'built on the foundations of morality structure' (Potter 1975: 113). But these plays, unlike the historical dramas of the immediately preceding decades, moved decisively away from the figurative and earnestly moralistic modes of the **Morality Tradition** to become fully historical in content, though typically they have contemporary political implications. In general, chronicle history plays are plays of the 1580s and 1590s based on historical authorities such as **Hall**, **Holinshed**, **Foxe** and **Stow** (Holinshed is usually the immediate source, but the material involved is often drawn ultimately from Hall), using the history for a didactic purpose (like *Henry V*) and not merely for the sake of the story or its historical trappings (like *Cymbeline*).
   With the exception of *Woodstock*, all the chronicle histories which may have been used by Shakespeare (see heading, above) belonged to the repertory of the Queen's Men (founded 1583). They were acted in the years of the company's greatest prestige in the mid-1580s, but were not printed until after its collapse in 1594 (see Gurr 1996: 210). Most are

examples of the 'large play' type, with fifteen or more speaking parts, pioneered and made fashionable by the Queen's Men (see Gurr 1996: 58–61), and are notable for moral and particularly patriotic conformism, the latter 'prepared for by a revival of interest in wars of long ago' during the 'Armada period' (*c.* 1583–96) in which 'Englishmen were exhorted to defend their country . . . by means of plentiful citations of famous English exploits' (Honigmann 1954b: xxvi). More recent claims that 'the chronicle plays are framed to permit – indeed to encourage – . . . responses that . . . accommodate and stimulate the divergent political views of a socially heterogeneous audience' (Champion 1990: 13) are often only doubtfully sustainable. *The Famous Victories of Henry V* celebrated what the Tudors saw as England's finest hour, Agincourt; *The Troublesome Raigne of King John* was apparently written immediately after the near-invasion of the Armada, and is strongly anti-Catholic, depicting for example the Bastard's discovery of clerical lust and avarice in the course of sacking a monastery (an episode which ends in the arrest of 'Peter, a Prophet'). Another of the notable features of these plays is their development away from rhetorical modes towards the spontaneous and modulated manner of speech (whether in prose or verse) that will typify later Elizabethan drama (see Clemen 1961).

Chronicle histories tended to be published anonymously, and have been severally and uncertainly ascribed over the years to a wide range of Elizabethan playwrights including **Greene**, **Lodge**, Peele and **Rowley**. Some must have been written by several hands. It is important to appreciate that they were not always static texts which stayed in the repertory for a shorter or longer period and then disappeared from it: they were subject to revision or adaptation for revivals, either by a new hand within the company they belonged to, or when the rights to them passed from one company to another (though there is rarely any evidence of more than one such revision of a single play). A well-known example of this practice from a later decade is the 1602 revision of **Kyd**'s *Spanish Tragedy*, involving five passages of fresh material totalling some 320 lines. Such revision should be distinguished from the wholesale reworking of a play – *King Lear*, for example (labelled a 'true chronicle history' on its first appearance in quarto in 1608), has a far more distant relationship to the *True Chronicle History of King Leir* (see (C)). In the case of *The Spanish Tragedy* the different versions are both extant, but with the chronicle histories the printed versions show only some eventual state of the text, which may therefore not reflect what was available when Shakespeare is likely to have seen or read them.

(B) Writing in defence of stage plays in 1592, **Nashe** says:

> First, for the subject of them (for the most part) it is borrowed out of our English Chronicles, wherein our forefathers valiant actes (that have lyne long buried in rustie brasse and worme-eaten bookes) are revived, and they them selves raysed from the Grave of Oblivion, and brought to pleade their aged Honours in open presence: than which, what can bee a sharper reproofe, to these desperate effeminate dayes of ours?
>
> (Nashe 1969: 26)

Though perhaps tongue-in-cheek, this passage from *Pierce Penilesse* leaves no room for doubt of the extreme popularity of the chronicle play during the early phases of Shakespeare's dramatic career.

The Famous Victories of Henry V contains several scenes which look familiar to readers of Shakespeare. In comparison with the following passage, 'the play-acting that goes on between Hal and Falstaff in 2.4 of Shakespeare's play is incomparably richer, and yet it, too, connects the comic tavern world with the political scene at court through mimicry and role-playing' (Bevington 1987: 22). Derick is a carrier, John Cobler an innkeeper, and they here act over again what has just happened, the Lord Chief Justice committing the Prince to the Fleet for boxing him on the ear. One can imagine good actors making it tolerably entertaining:

DER.   Faith John, Ile tel thee what, thou shalt be my
      Lord chiefe Justice, and thou shalt sit in the chaire,
      And ile be the yong prince, and hit thee a boxe on the eare,
      And then thou shalt say, to teach you what prerogatives
      Meane, I commit you to the Fleete.
JOHN   Come on, Ile be your Judge,
      But thou shalt not hit me hard.
DER.   No, no.
JOHN.   What hath he done?
DER.   Marry he hath robd Dericke.
JOHN.   Why then I cannot let him go.
DER.   I must needs have my man.

JOHN.   You shall not have him.

DER.   Shall I not have my man, say no and you dare:
        How say you, shall I not have my man?

JOHN.   No marry shall you not.

DER.   Shall I not John?

JOHN.   No Dericke.

DER.   Why then take you that till more come,
        Sownes, shall I not have him?

JOHN.   Well I am content to take this at your hand,
        But I pray you, who am I?

DER.   Who art thou, Sownds, doost not know thy self?

JOHN.   No.

DER.   Now away simple fellow,
        Why man, thou art John the Cobler.

JOHN.   No, I am my Lord chiefe Justice of England.

DER.   Oh John, Masse thou saist true, thou art indeed.

JOHN.   Why then to teach you what prerogatives mean
        I commit you to the Fleete.

                    (Anon. 1598: sig. B4^{r-v})

(C) A strikingly large number of non-Shakespearean chronicle plays have Shakespearean associations or affinities, and the reasons for this have never been fully explained. Among Shakespeare's works the Histories are naturally the ones in which influences from chronicle plays would be expected to be strongest. Largely because of the difficulty of establishing even basic facts such as the sequence of composition and revision for chronicle plays and related Shakespearean texts, it is an open question how far Shakespeare might be said to have invented a kind of history play distinct from what the English stage could already show. F. P. Wilson's famous (and strictly true) remark that 'there is no certain evidence that any popular dramatist before Shakespeare wrote a play based on English history' (Wilson 1953: 106) runs directly counter to David Riggs' attempt to show that Shakespeare 'set out to imitate a kind of heroical history play that Greene and his contemporaries had already brought to fruition' (1971: 2).

Uncertainties about chronology are the main sticking-point in establishing the relationships in the cases of *Richard III* and *King John*. The crude but in some ways powerful *True Tragedie of Richard III* (published 1594) covers much of the same ground as *Richard III*, and there are occasional verbal resemblances including, for example, the *True Tragedie* Richard's call for a new mount at Bosworth, 'A horse, a horse, a fresh horse!' But these similarities can be explained variously, especially since only a corrupt text of the chronicle play survives: 'there must have been a textually sound *True Tragedy* . . . which may have ante-dated *Richard III* and influenced Shakespeare', and it is 'likely' that the extant version conflates and garbles both this and the Shakespeare play (Honigmann 1968: 14). And, though Shakespeare must at some point have read or heard this earlier version, there are arguments for both Shakespeare's influence on it (Honigmann 1954a) and the converse (Wilson 1952). *The Troublesome Raigne of King John*, a clumsy work published in 1591 (ed. Sider 1979), is so obscurely related to Shakespeare's play that it has sometimes been dubbed 'The Troublesome Play of King John'. The relationship has deeply influenced critical discussion of *King John*. The *Troublesome Raigne* was printed as Shakespeare's own in 1611 and 1622. It contains lines and phrases identical and near-identical with ones in Shakespeare's play (as well as material purloined from **Marlowe** and other dramatists), and 'the selection and compression of historical material and the sequence of events are sometimes extremely close' (Braunmuller 1989: 5; for a running comparison see Bullough, IV, 9–15). Again, dating of the Shakespeare play is difficult. On balance of probabilities it post-dates the *Troublesome Raigne*, but the similarities still need not reflect the direct influence of the *Raigne* on Shakespeare, though this is the current consensus (for example, Bullough, IV, 5; Smallwood 1974: 365–74 – for other hypotheses see Braunmuller 1989: 10–11).

Richard II has a major source in *Woodstock* (*c.* 1591–4; also called *Thomas of Woodstock* and *The First Part of the Reign of King Richard the Second*; ed. Rossiter 1946). This play deals with the reign of Richard II from the time of his marriage to Anne of Bohemia in 1382 to the murder of his uncle Thomas of Woodstock, Duke of Gloucester, in 1397. Itself apparently dependent on Shakespeare's *2 Henry VI*, it is a high-quality play combining good comedy with serious presentation of the conflict between upstarts and established nobility. Though it covers events historically prior to those of Shakespeare's play, Shakespeare's cannot be regarded as a sequel to it: for one thing, its central figure is not Richard but Gloucester. But Shakespeare does allude to it some twelve times in *Richard II* 1.2, as well as elsewhere in his work, and seems to assume, or even to be 'peculiarly dependent' on, his audience's memory of it to explain elements in his own Richard II play (Rossiter 1961: 29). In particular, the question of who was responsible for Woodstock's death lurks behind *Richard II*. Though it may be argued that Shakespeare deliberately clouds the issue as part of his play's 'political agnosticism' (so Sanders 1968: 158–65), it is the case that if the audience assumes Richard's culpability (as shown in *Woodstock*), then 'his confused actions throughout Acts I and II' can be viewed as deriving 'from a guilt, or guilts, out of which there is no clear path' (Rossiter 1961: 36). Apart from this special link to Shakespeare's play, *Woodstock* is sometimes thought to have been significant for *Richard II* dramaturgically or stylistically, and sometimes merely as one of several sources for the historical events of the reign. The first of these positions involves ascribing a morality 'shape' to Richard's career:

> Poised between grave counselors (John of Gaunt) and flattering vices (Bushy, Green, Bagot) Richard makes the traditional wrong choices and suffers the chastening results . . . The instrument of Richard's correction, Henry Bolingbroke, becomes in his own turn a figure of royal morality . . . The moment of contrition which in the traditional morality sequence leads directly on to repentance is employed by Shakespeare as a superbly ironic ending, pointing forward to 'the unquiet time of King Henry the Fourth'. (Potter 1975: 130)

Shakespeare's *1 Henry IV* also seems to have been affected by *Woodstock*: there are close verbal similarities in one passage and, more debatably, a villain with some resemblances to Falstaff and an integration of low comedy with court drama (see Elson 1935; Humphreys 1974: xxxvi–xxxvii).

The Famous Victories of Henry the Fifth: Containing the Honourable Battell of Agin-court deals with the hero's exploits not only at Agincourt but in London as Prince of Wales. Hence it – or some other version very like it – was a source for both *Henry IV* and *Henry V*. It was entered in the Stationers' Register in 1594 but is not known to have been printed until 1598. *1 Henry IV* shares its overall narrative outline, several scenes or incidents such as the tavern play-acting in (B), above, and details such as names and expressions. As for *Henry V*, 'on the available evidence, Holinshed and *The Famous Victories* between them provided all the material from which [Shakespeare] created the dramatic action' (Craik 1995: 10). But there were other, non-extant, plays about Henry V as well as this one. If the full picture could be seen, 'a flood of light might be thrown on Shakespeare's use of this material . . . That he used some form of *The Famous Victories* the resemblances show: that it was not the existing patchwork is suggested by, first, *The Famous Victories'* almost imbecile nature . . . and, second, the fact that Oldcastle must have been more familiar to Elizabethan audiences when Shakespeare took him up than he could possibly be from *The Famous Victories'* (Humphreys 1974). A particularly full canvassing of the various possibilities is Melchiori (1989).

One other chronicle play-source pertains principally to *King Lear*, though earlier echoes of it can also be found, for instance in *Richard II*. The anonymous *True Chronicle History of King Leir and his Three Daughters* (published 1605, but probably dating from the sixteenth century) is an inept play, notwithstanding Tolstoy's notorious preference for it over Shakespeare's. It gave Shakespeare an outline of one possible route through the story (for a summary of the play see Muir 1972: xxv–xxvi). But after the opening scene of *King Lear*, where the overall plot motivation is taken from the *Chronicle History*, the divergences are in most ways greater than the parallels: there is in *Leir* no fool, no storm, no madness, no Poor Tom, no banished or disguised Kent, and no death for Lear or Cordelia (who are restored to power and happiness). Hence it may be argued that Shakespeare handled the source with complete freedom. Accounts stressing the importance of *Leir* include Law (1958), Lynch (1986 and 1998) and Nameri (1976: i). Pauls (1984) provides a careful and conservative review, concluding that the closest similarities between the two plays lie in numerous verbal echoes and the structure of some of the longer speeches.

(D) Excerpts from the chronicle histories are liberally provided in Bullough, iii–iv, and Satin (1966), but for full texts see the complete editions below or those in series such as the Malone Society Reprints. Almost all the published scholarship on these works as Shakespeare sources is on single plays, often in editions of Shakespeare, and there is no good synoptic discussion of the area. The nearest things are Tillyard (1944) and Champion (1990), both of which deal with the chronicle histories *in extenso* but neither of which engages closely with their Shakespearean connections. The groundwork on Shakespeare was mainly done in the literature on individual plays in the first half of the twentieth century; see the recent articles and editions listed for refinements and reassessments.

Bullough, III–IV; Jones (1977); Satin (1966); Tillyard (1944).

Anon. (1598). *The Famous Victories of Henry the Fifth: Containing the Honourable Battell of Agin-court.* London.

Bevington, David, ed. (1987). *Henry IV, Part 1* (Oxford Shakespeare). Oxford.

Boyd, Brian (1995). '*King John* and *The Troublesome Raigne*: Sources, Structure, Sequence.' *PQ* 74: 37–56.

Braunmuller, A. R., ed. (1989). *King John* (Oxford Shakespeare). Oxford.

Brooks, Harold F. (1980). '*Richard III*: Unhistorical Amplifications: The Women's Scenes and Seneca.' *MLR* 75: 721–37.

Campbell, Lily B. (1947). *Shakespeare's "Histories": Mirrors of Elizabethan Policy.* San Marino, CA.

Champion, Larry S. (1990). '*The Noise of Threatening Drum*': *Dramatic Strategy and Political Ideology in Shakespeare and the English Chronicle Plays.* Newark, DE.

Clemen, Wolfgang (1961). *English Tragedy before Shakespeare: The Development of Dramatic Speech.* London.

Craik, T. W., ed. (1995). *King Henry V* (Arden Shakespeare). London.

Elson, John James (1935). 'The Non-Shakespearean *Richard II* and Shakespeare's *Henry IV, Part 1*.' *SP* 32: 177–88.

Gurr, Andrew (1996). *The Shakespearian Playing Companies.* Oxford.

Hamilton, Donna B. (1983). 'The State of Law in *Richard II*.' *ShQ* 34: 5–17.

Hammond, Antony, ed. (1981). *King Richard III* (Arden Shakespeare). London.

Honigmann, E. A. J. (1954a). 'Shakespeare's "Lost Source-Plays".' *MLR* 49: 293–307.

—— ed. (1954b). *King John* (Arden Shakespeare). London.

—— ed. (1968). *Richard III* (New Penguin Shakespeare). Harmondsworth.

Humphreys, A. R., ed. (1974). *The First Part of King Henry IV* (Arden Shakespeare). London (first published 1960).

Law, Robert Adger (1958). '*King Leir* and *King Lear*: An Examination of the Two Plays', pp. 112–24 in Don Cameron Allen, ed., *Studies in Honor of T. W. Baldwin.* Urbana, IL.

Lynch, Stephen J. (1986). 'Sin, Suffering and Redemption in *Leir* and *Lear*.' *ShSt* 18: 161–74.

—— (1998). *Shakespearean Intertextuality: Studies in Selected Sources and Plays.* Westport, CT.

Melchiori, Giorgio, ed. (1989). *The Second Part of King Henry IV* (New Cambridge Shakespeare). Cambridge.

Muir, Kenneth, ed. (1972). *King Lear* (Arden Shakespeare). London.

Nameri, Dorothy E. (1976). *Three Versions of the Story of King Lear Studied in Relation to One Another*, 2 vols. Salzburg.

Nashe, Thomas (1969). *Pierce Peniless 1592*. Menston (facsimile reprint of first edition).

Pauls, Peter (1984). '*The True Chronicle History of King Leir* and Shakespeare's *King Lear*: A Reconsideration.' *Upstart Crow* 5: 93–107.

Perrett, Wilfrid (1904). *The Story of King Lear from Geoffrey of Monmouth to Shakespeare*. Berlin.

Potter, Robert (1975). *The English Morality Play: Origins, History and Influence of a Dramatic Tradition*. London.

Riggs, David (1971). *Shakespeare's Heroical Histories: 'Henry VI' and its Literary Tradition*. Cambridge, MA.

Rossiter, A. P., ed. (1946). *Woodstock: A Moral History*. London.

Rossiter, A. P. (1961). *Angel with Horns: Fifteen Lectures on Shakespeare*. London.

Sanders, Wilbur (1968). *The Dramatist and the Received Idea: Studies in the Plays of Marlowe and Shakespeare*. Cambridge.

Sider, J. W., ed. (1979). *The Troublesome Raigne of John, King of England*. New York.

Simmons, J. L. (1969). 'Shakespeare's *King John* and its Source: Coherence, Pattern, and Vision.' *Tulane Studies in English* 17: 53–72.

Smallwood, Robert, ed. (1974). *King John* (New Penguin Shakespeare). Harmondsworth.

Thomas, Sidney (1986). '"*Enter a Sheriffe*": Shakespeare's *King John* and *The Troublesome Raigne*.' *ShQ* 37: 98–100 (and correspondence, 38: 124–30).

Wilson, F. P. (1953). *Marlowe and the Early Shakespeare*. Oxford.

Wilson, J. Dover (1952). 'Shakespeare's *Richard III* and *The True Tragedy of Richard the Third*, 1594.' *ShQ* 3: 299–306.

Chronicque de la Traïson et Mort de Richard Deux (Anon.)

The *Traïson* is an eye-witness account of the fall of Richard II, available only in manuscript in Shakespeare's time. Some commentators detect echoes of its phrasing in *Richard II*; if they are right to do so, it could have been 'a source of creative inspiration or "invention"' (Ure 1961: xlvi) for important aspects of the play.

Ure, Peter, ed. (1961). *Richard II* (Arden Shakespeare), pp. xliv–xlix. London.

Cicero, Marcus Tullius (106–43 BC), Roman Orator, Statesman and Writer

(A) Cicero was born into a wealthy but not high-ranking family in Latium, studied law, oratory and Greek at Rome, and served in the Roman army in 90–88 BC. His first important speeches were as a pleader in the forum when he was in his twenties. He held a succession of public offices, first abroad, then, after recommencing with great distinction his career as an orator in the forum, in Rome, as praetor and subsequently consul. In this capacity in 63 he foiled Catiline's conspiracy by securing the execution of five conspirators. At first seen as a hero, he was shortly condemned to exile on account of this (illegal) action, but was recalled to Rome in 55 BC. During the Civil War he first supported Pompey, then Caesar. His *Philippics*, speeches against Mark Antony delivered in 43, cost him his life, for the triumvirate formed by Antony, Octavian and Lepidus proscribed him; fleeing to his villa, he was overtaken and killed by Antony's soldiers.

Cicero's works include seven treatises on rhetoric; political philosophy, notably the only partly surviving *De Republica*; philosophical and ethical treatises including the *Tusculanae Disputationes*, *De Senectute* (*On Old Age*), *De Amicitia* (*On Friendship*), *De Officiis* (*On Duties*) and *De Beneficiis* (*On Benefits*); fifty-six orations; and over 800 epistles.

(B) It would be hard to overstate Cicero's importance to early modern writers and readers, of many different persuasions. Martin Luther ranked him above Aristotle, thinking of his philosopho-theological works in declaring that he treated the finest and best of questions. Cicero was also the Humanists' hero: for completely different reasons, **Erasmus** promoted him as a teacher of ethics closer to Christ than the scholastic theologians. As politician, orator and moralist he united the active and the contemplative life; his style was (often) the ultimate model of eloquence; his ethical writings were unquestioned authorities; his rhetorical works were the source of the Humanists' educational theory. Cicero was probably read more often and by a wider range of people than any other classical author in the sixteenth century. **Jonson**, who in *Catiline* presented him as a dramatic figure and translated him, noted in *Timber* that Cicero was 'said to be the only wit, that the people of Rome had [whose greatness] equalled to their empire'.

Cicero was Englished from the mid-fifteenth century, as early as almost any classical author. By 1600 many of his writings were available in English, the more popular sometimes in a choice of renderings. His sixteenth-century translators, whose work often ran to many editions, included Nicholas Grimald (1555), John Dolman (1561), John Harington (father of the Elizabethan poet, 1562) and Thomas **Newton** (1569, 1577).

The following samples are from the Dolman translation of Cicero's *Tusculan Disputations*, an immensely popular set of five discourses on philosophical questions set at Cicero's villa in Tusculanum. The first passage, from Book I on the nature of the soul, exhibits the more speculative side of this famous work; the next excerpts, from Book V, show a more down-to-earth element:

So the soule (whych if it be of any of those .iiii. bodyes, whereof all thinges are made, doth undoubtedly consist of fyer, whiche opinion Panetius also liketh best) must nedes flie to the higher regions: For those .ii. elementes, namelye fyer and aer, have no fallynge, but go always upwardes. So it comes to passe, that whether they are scattered farre from the earth, or els do abide and always kepe theyr own nature, by all these reasons it must necessarilye folowe, that our soules ascend unto heaven deviding thys grosse and compound aer, which is next to the earth. For our soule is more whote, or rather more fyerye, than this aer, which I termed whilome grosse and compound. And that hereby we may wel perceive: because our dumpishe earthly bodies do waxe whote, with the heate of our mindes. Furthermore, it must nedes be, that the soule must lightly passe through this aer (whiche I doe often terme grosse) because there is nothinge more swifte then it, neyther anye such quickenesse, as may by anye meanes be compared with the quicknes of the same. Whiche if he remayne unwasted, and like to his former being he muste needes so move, that he, shall pearce and cut all this lower aer, in the which, cloudes, wyndes, and showers, are gathered. Which is both moist and cloudye with the exhaltacions of the earth.

(Cicero 1561: sig. D4^{r–v})

But he sayeth, he is contented onely with the remembraunce of his former pleasures. As if, a man well nye parched with heate, so that, he is no longer able to abide the sonne should comfort him selfe with the remembraunce, that once heretofore, he had bathed him selfe in the cold ryvers of Arpynas. For truly, I see not, howe the pleasures that are past, may ease the greyeves that are present . . .

What is there, that a man should feare? Exile perhaps, which is counted one of the greatest evels. Yet, if you count it to be evell, because of the pleasure and grudge of the people, then howe litle we ought to esteeme it, I have spoken afore. But if you counte it a misery, to be from your countrey: then trulye is every province ful of wretched men, of whom very fewe retourne home againe into theyr countrey. But all banyshed men lose their goods. What then have we shewed nothing howe men ought to beare povertye? And truly, exyle and banishement, if we weygh the nature of the thinge, and not the shame of the name, howe much differeth it from that continuall wanderinge, in the whyche these most notable philosophers . . . have spent their whole age, and the course of their life? Who, after they once departed from theyr countreyes, never came thither agayne.

And truly, it could put a wyse man (of whom only our talke is at this present) to no shame at all. Because, no suche thing, can rightfully come unto him. For such a one, as is ryghtfully banyshed, we ought not to comfort. To conclude, to prove this, we may easely applie their opinion, who referre al thinges in this life to pleasure. For in what soever place we have such thynges, there we may live well and happelye. And therfore, hereunto, that sayeng of Teucer may well be applyed.

My countrey (quod he) is, wheresoever I live well. And Socrates, when one asked of him whence he was: He aunswered of the worlde.

(Cicero 1561: sigs ²C6^r, ²E1^r–²E2^r)

(C) Shakespeare, like all educated Elizabethans, would have encountered Ciceronian texts almost continuously through his school years, at least for rhetoric (especially the *Topica* and the pseudo-Ciceronian *Ad Herennium*) and moral philosophy (especially *De Officiis*). Though the character of Cicero in *Julius Caesar* probably reflects Shakespeare's reading of **Plutarch** in the *Life of Cicero* rather than of Cicero himself (*pace* Vawter 1976, who argues it is based on Cicero's *De Divinatione*), Shakespeare does refer directly to Cicero (as 'Tully') more than once. The *Treatise on Eloquence* addressed to Brutus (*Orator*), one of the most often quoted of Cicero's rhetorical works, is alluded to in *Titus Andronicus*, where Titus remarks to young Lucius of Lavinia:

> Ah, boy, Cornelia never with more care
> Read to her sons than she hath read to thee
> Sweet poetry and Tully's Orator.
>
> (4.1.12–14)

And the well-known circumstances of Cicero's death are made a paradigm by the soon-to-be-executed Suffolk in *2 Henry VI*:

> Come, soldiers, show what cruelty ye can,
> That this my death may never be forgot –
> Great men oft die by vile bezonians:
> A Roman sworder and banditto slave
> Murder'd sweet Tully
>
> (4.1.132–6)

Rather less obvious is that the book Hamlet is reading immediately before his 'To be or not to be' soliloquy (3.1.56) seems to have been Cicero's *Tusculan Disputations* (see Baldwin 1944: II, 603–8) – though there are one or two other candidates.

Because Cicero's were for the Renaissance the archetypal formulations of many principles of ethical and intellectual conduct, it is unsurprising that the behaviour of Shakespeare's characters sometimes reflects them closely (for one example see Adams 1968). Shakespeare obviously learned directly or indirectly from Cicero's rhetorical works too, especially *Ad Herennium*, an elementary grammar school text which the playwright uses variously. For example, Holofernes in *Love's Labour's Lost* uses Cicero's technical terms for letter-writing in Book IV, and in *Romeo and Juliet* 5.3 the inquiry involving the Prince, the Watch and the Friar closely follows Cicero's explanation of a conjectural cause judicial (see Baldwin 1944: II, 76–107). This knowledge is more than theoretical for Shakespeare: the general manner of Ciceronian oratory is readily identifiable in speeches in many Shakespeare works. For example, in Marullus' speech to the people in *Julius Caesar* Shakespeare employs 'the syntactical and rhetorical control, the fire and variety of movement, which we find in Cicero's speeches' (Martindale 1990: 139). There are also many quite specific rhetorical features more likely to have been learned from Ciceronian texts than from any others in Shakespeare's time – plain diction, rhetorical questions, apostrophes and exclamations, personification, variation in sentence-length, even the *tricolon crescendo* of the fourth line. 'This, we may feel, is how a Roman orator might speak if he spoke in English' (Martindale 1990: 139):

> Wherefore rejoice? What conquest brings he home?
> What tributaries follow him to Rome,
> To grace in captive bonds his chariot wheels?
> You blocks, you stones, you worse than senseless things!
> O you hard hearts, you cruel men of Rome,
> Knew you not Pompey? Many a time and oft
> Have you climb'd up to walls and battlements,
> To tow'rs and windows, yea, to chimney-tops,
> Your infants in your arms, and there have sat
> The livelong day, with patient expectation,
> To see great Pompey pass the streets of Rome.
> And when you saw his chariot but appear,
> Have you not made an universal shout,
> That Tiber trembled underneath her banks,
> To hear the replication of your sounds
> Made in her concave shores?
> And do you now put on your best attire?
> And do you now cull out a holiday?
> And do you now strew flowers in his way
> That comes in triumph over Pompey's blood?
> Be gone!
> Run to your houses, fall upon your knees,
> Pray to the gods to intermit the plague
> That needs must light on this ingratitude.
>
> (1.1.33–56)

As well as having this general impact, directly or indirectly, on the style and structure of Shakespeare's more rhetorical writing, Cicero lies behind the content of several other parts of his work. Sometimes this appears to take the form of an acquaintance with a complete text, sometimes only with the *sententiae* that were abstracted from Cicero in *florilegia* and other compilations. For example, a passage in the *Tusculan Disputations* observing that sleep is the image of death seems to give the structure as well as the idea to the Duke's consolation of Claudio (*Measure for Measure*, 3.1.17–19), but this is an 'imitation' of something 'recognized as a *sententia* long before Shakespeare' (Baldwin 1944: ii, 603). However, the quantity of reference in Shakespeare to this particular Ciceronian text, including associations between consecutive passages, indicates that he must have known it in full form, either in Latin or John Dolman's English translation.

Two examples of Shakespeare's proximity to parts of the *Tusculans* are given here. The passage quoted in (B), above, from Book i can be associated with Sonnet 44 (printed below) and its companion-piece Sonnet 45 (more strongly so if we take into account the references to **Ovid** and Lactantius provided in the standard edition of Cicero – see Baldwin 1950: 249):

> If the dull substance of my flesh were thought,
> Injurious distance should not stop my way;
> For then, despite of space, I would be brought
> From limits far remote, where thou dost stay.
> No matter then, although my foot did stand
> Upon the farthest earth remov'd from thee,
> For nimble thought can jump both sea and land
> As soon as think the place where he would be.
> But ah! thought kills me that I am not thought,
> To leap large lengths of miles when thou art gone,
> But that, so much of earth and water wrought,
> I must attend time's leisure with my moan,
> > Receiving nought by elements so slow
> > But heavy tears, badges of either's woe.

Second, the passage quoted in (B) from *Tusculan Disputations* v appears, notwithstanding parallels in other texts, to be connected with Bolingbroke's complaint on his impending exile in *Richard II* (see Muir 1977: 57–8):

> O, who can hold a fire in his hand
> By thinking on the frosty Caucasus?
> Or cloy the hungry edge of appetite
> By bare imagination of a feast?
> Or wallow naked in December snow

> By thinking on fantastic summer's heat?
> O, no! the apprehension of the good
> Gives but the greater feeling to the worse.
> Fell sorrow's tooth doth never rankle more
> Than when he bites, but lanceth not the sore . . .
> Then, England's ground, farewell; sweet soil, adieu;
> My mother, and my nurse, that bears me yet!
> Where'er I wander, boast of this I can:
> Though banish'd, yet a trueborn English man.
>   (1.3.294–303, 306–9)

(D) Jones 1998 is a thorough account of Cicero's place in Tudor culture in a broad sense. Baldwin 1944 provides the fullest treatment of Shakespeare's use of Cicero, but it is scattered throughout the volume.

Baldwin (1944); Baldwin (1950); Martindale (1990).

Adams, Barry B. (1968). 'The Prudence of Prince Escalus.' *ELH* 35: 32–50.

Anderson, Colleen (1992). 'Ciceronian Rhetoric Evidenced in Selected Trial Scenes in Shakespeare Plays.' PhD diss. Catholic University of America.

Cicero, translated by John Dolman (1561). *Those Fyve Questions, which Marke Tullye Cicero Disputed in his Manor of Tusculanum*. London.

Jones, Howard (1998). *Master Tully: Cicero in Tudor England*. Nieuwkoop.

Sohmer, Steve (1997). 'What Cicero Said.' *N&Q* 242: 56–8.

Vawter, Marvin L. (1974). '"Division 'tween Our Souls": Shakespeare's Stoic Brutus.' *ShSt* 7: 173–95.

—— (1976). ' "After Their Fashion": Cicero and Brutus in *Julius Caesar*.' *ShSt* 9: 205–19.

Cinthio, Giovanni Baptista Giraldi (1504–1573), Italian Scholar, Poet, Playwright, and Novelist

(A) Cinthio (the self-styled 'Il Cinzio', in which fashion the name is pronounced) was born and educated in Ferrara. He became renowned as a professor at Ferrara University, 1541–62, then at Pavia, in philosophy and rhetoric. He was a prolific story writer, gathering a collection under the title *Gli Hecatommithi* ('The Hundred Stories') in 1565. This book's structure is similar to that of **Boccaccio**'s *Decameron*, but its emphasis is more moralistic and the material more miscellaneous: some tales concern brutal or squalid crimes, others are love stories varying in tone from the extremely romantic to the obscene or comic. It includes several tales which Cinthio used as material for his plays, noted in their time as efforts to move tragic drama away from its classical roots to reflect modern life and the tenets of Christian humanism. His *Discorso sulle Comedie e sulle Tragedie* (1554) sets out his theoretical views: he argues in support of *tragedia mista* ('mixed tragedy'), in which a happy ending or a double ending shows justice meted out to good as well as bad characters (as in *Epitia*, his *tragedia di fin lieto* – see (C)), and promotes romance as a form of epic, its best model **Ariosto**'s *Orlando Furioso*. He also wrote an epic poem, *Ercole*, and three dialogues on the moral education of children.

(B) No sixteenth-century English translation of the *Hecatommithi* is known, but the book was familiar enough to English readers. There were at least six Italian editions between 1565 and 1600, and a French rendering by Gabriel Chappuys in two volumes as *Cent Excellentes Nouvelles*, 1583–4, as well as versions of individual tales made by such writers as William **Painter** in his *Palace of Pleasure* (1566–75), Barnaby Riche in *Riche his Farewell to Militarie Profession* (1581) and Robert **Greene** in his play *James the Fourth* (1590). Other dramatists also relished Cinthio's portrayals of intrigue and secret love, laced with revengeful violence and gore: his play *Orbecche*, in particular, from a story in the *Hecatommithi*, was influential in Italy during the rise of Renaissance Senecanism. Ludowick Bryskett in his 1606 *Discourse of Civil Life* describes Cinthio as one of several 'late writers' who had popularized moral philosophy: his dialogues on the training of youth were widely known to Elizabethan readers of Italian because they were published with the novelle of the *Hecatommithi*, all these works being described on the collective title-page as aids to good conduct.

George Whetstone produced both a dramatic and a prose narrative version of Cinthio's story of Promos and Cassandra in 1578 and 1582 respectively, neatly paralleling (in reverse order) Cinthio's own practice of casting some of his stories into both forms. Shakespeare may have known both of Whetstone's treatments (see (C)). The following is the argument prefixed to Whetstone's play *The Right Excellent and Famous Historye, of Promos and Cassandra, Devided into two Commicall Discourses*, 1578:

In the Cyttie of *Julio* (sometimes under the dominion of *Corvinus* Kinge of *Hungarie*, and *Boemia*) there was a law, that what man so ever commited Adultery, should lose his head, and the woman offender, should weare some disguised apparrel, during her life, to make her infamouslye noted. This severe lawe, by the favour of some mercifull magistrate, became little regarded, untill the time of Lord *Promos* auctority: who convicting a yong Gentleman named *Andrugio* of incontinency, condemned, both him, and his minion to the execution of this statute. *Andrugio* had a very vertuous, and beawtiful Gentlewoman to his Sister, named *Cassandra*: *Cassandra* to enlarge her brothers life, submitted an humble petition to the Lord *Promos*: *Promos* regarding her good behaviours, and fantasyng her great beawtie, was much delighted with the sweete order of her talke: and doyng good, that evill might come thereof: for a time, he repryv'd her brother: but wicked man, tourning his liking unto unlawfull lust, he set downe the spoile of her honour, raunsome for her Brothers life: Chaste *Cassandra*, abhorring both him and his sute, by no perswasion would yeald to this raunsome. But in fine, wonne with the importunitye of hir brother (pleading for life:) upon these conditions, she agreede to *Promos*. First that he shoulde pardon her brother, and after marry her. *Promos* as fearles in promisse, as carelesse in performance, with sollemne vowe, sygned her conditions: but worse then any Infydel, his will satisfyed, he performed neither the one nor the other: for to keepe his aucthoritye, unspotted with favour, and to prevent *Cassandraes* clamors, he commaunded the Gayler secretly, to present *Cassandra* with her brothers head. The Gayler, with the outcryes of *Andrugio*, abhorryng *Promos* lewdenes, by the providence of God, provided thus for his safety. He presented *Cassandra* with a Felons head newlie executed, who (being mangled, knew it not from her brothers, by the Gayler, who was set at libertie) was so agreeved at this trecherye, that at the pointe to kyl her selfe, she spared that stroke, to be avenged of *Promos*. And devisyng a way, she concluded, to make her fortunes knowne unto the King, that forthwith he hasted to do Justice on *Promos*: whose judgement was, to marrye *Cassandra*, to repaire her crased Honour: which donne, for his hainous offence he should lose his head. This maryage solemnised, *Cassandra* tyed in the greatest bondes of affection to her husband, became an earnest suter for his life: the Kinge (tenderinge the generall benefit of the common weale, before her special ease, although he favoured her much) would not graunt her sute. *Andrugio* (disguised amonge the company) sorrowing the griefe of his sister, bewrayde his safetye, and craved pardon. The Kinge, to renowne the vertues of *Cassandra*, pardoned both him and *Promos*.

(Whetstone 1578: sig. A4$^{\mathrm{r-v}}$; roman for italic)

(C) Novel iii.7 of the *Hecatommithi* is the principal source for *Othello*, while Novel viii.5, the story of Promos and Cassandra, is related to *Measure for Measure*. This may indicate that Shakespeare came into contact with Cinthio's work, or at least discovered its dramatic possibilities, about 1604. Bullough (vii, 221–2) speculates that Shakespeare may have read further tales in the book, and Richmond (1985, 1991) notes some structural and thematic similarities between Novel ii.9 and *A Midsummer Night's Dream*. It is not clear whether Shakespeare would have used Cinthio's Italian text, but there are definite signs that he looked at Chappuys' French translation. It is agreed that Cinthio provided only very limited starting-points for Shakespeare – Muir (1977: 182–6) even suggests he was specifically inspired by the challenge of using such unpromising material in *Measure for Measure*. But why use it at all? Everett, proposing almost the same thing as Muir of *Othello*, surmises: 'the value to Shakespeare of a story like Cinthio's . . . may have lain essentially in its relative unlikelihood – its thinness, its simplicity, its functionalism', its capacity to activate dormant experiences and ideas and 'by its lack of other merit not to obtrude on this activity once it was well begun'. Most of all, Shakespeare's 'imagination was compelled . . . by the random premise of Cinthio's opening phrase, "Fu già in Venezia un Moro"' (Everett 1982: 101–2).

The *Measure for Measure* story is a very old one, but Cinthio altered it in distinctive ways. Complicating the question of what sources Shakespeare knew, so did Whetstone; what makes it truly vexed is that both Cinthio and Whetstone produced both narrative and dramatic versions of their story, and did so in time for Shakespeare to have known all four treatments. The place to begin is obviously with Cinthio's prose one of 1565, which occurs within a sequence of tales in the *Hecatommithi* about ingratitude. Cinthio's changes to the story as he found it in previous versions include making the Isabella figure the sister and not the wife of the condemned man, and having the Angelo figure appointed by the overlord. At some date before his death in 1573, Cinthio turned this story into a five-act tragicomedy, *Epitia*, a neoclassical drama set within the single day after Epitia has given herself to the official. It went unacted, but was published by Cinthio's son in 1583. This dramatic recasting develops the plot in some ways that distance it further from *Measure for Measure*, but introduces some verbal similarities to Shakespeare's play. Next, the original novella was used, perhaps together with *Epitia*, by George Whetstone (1551–87) as the basis of his play *Promos and Cassandra*, which, like Cinthio's, was never staged, but was published in 1578. This is in clumsy verse and is dramaturgically crude, but has a strong vein of coarse humour. It lacks the preliminary interview between officer and overlord figure (one of the features which suggests Shakespeare knew Cinthio's original prose treatment), but its innovations include the revival of a harsh old law, the brother's request to the sister to plead for him, and the lord's initial pretence of ignorance of the Angelo figure's crimes on his final appearance. Perhaps most significantly, it is a work which 'gives a much fuller picture of society than Cinthio had done'; 'Whetstone was interested in justice as applied to the poor as well as the rich' (Bullough, ii, 413). Finally, in 1582 Whetstone published his non-dramatic version of the story, using his own play as his source, in his *Heptameron of Civil Discourses* (a collection which is modelled on but does not translate Cinthio's). This version is only a few pages in length, omitting much of the material found in the dramatic one.

Shakespeare's awareness of all four treatments is suggested by textual similarities. *Epitia* would have been much the most difficult version to obtain – it was printed only once, whereas the *Hecatommithi* was reissued at least five times before 1600 – but *Measure for Measure* shows what seem to be significant resemblances, both of plot (Doran 1954: 387–9) and verbal (Shaheen 1994: 167–9). Similarly, Whetstone's prose narrative seems to be the only possible source of the name of Isabella (the narrator). But it is fairly clear that Whetstone's dramatic version is the primary narrative source, except for the bed-trick episode which Shakespeare derived from Boccaccio and had already used in *All's Well that Ends Well*. Whetstone provided both a coherent main plot and a realistic background of moral corruption (see especially Prouty 1964); Shakespeare 'let the main plot serve as a spur to his imagination, abandoning much of his source once he had got under way and freely developing the background'. Thus *Measure for Measure* 'makes deliberate use of its prototype's . . . main components, and there is a marked similarity of basic structural pattern, though this is something which is perhaps

116

obscured by the very manner in which the work of an honest plodder is transmuted' (Nosworthy 1969: 16).

As Nosworthy says, Whetstone's work is only barely detectable behind Shakespeare's, though this may be partly a matter of differing aims as well as differing quality. Whetstone is at his strongest in depicting Promos' internal debates, which can have a strangely Ovidian manner; but comparison with *Measure for Measure* here does expose a number of limitations:

> Do what I can, no reason cooles desire,
> The more I strive, my fonde affectes to tame:
> The hotter (oh) I feele, a burning fire
> Within my breast, vaine thoughts to forge and frame.
> O straying effectes, of blinde affected Love,
> From wisdomes pathes, which doth astraye our wittes:
> Which makes us haunt, that which our harmes doth move,
> A sicknesse lyke, the Fever Etticke fittes:
> Which shakes with colde, when we do burne like fire.
> Even so in Love, we freese, through chilling feare,
> When as our hartes, doth frye with hote desire:
> What saide I? lyke to Etticke fittes, nothing neare:
> In sowrest Love, some sweete is ever suckt.
> The Lover findeth peace, in wrangling strife,
> So that if paine, were from his pleasure pluckt,
> There were no Heaven, like to the Lovers life.
> But why stande I to pleade, their joye or woe
> And rest unsure, of hir I wish to have.
>
> (Whetstone 1578: sig. C4ʳ)

Whetstone's emphasis on morality both at the level of individual human relationships and of the state may be particularly relevant to *Measure for Measure*, and is not Shakespeare's invention: it can be argued that 'in *Promos and Cassandra*, he . . . found a model which expounded those ideas which, at the time, he was himself intent on expounding' (Nosworthy 1969: 19).

The *Othello* connection is evidenced by a small number of tiny but decisive verbal links to both French and (particularly) Italian versions of Novel III.7 (enumerated by Honigmann 1966 and Sanders 1984: 3). Unless a now lost English translation reached Shakespeare, he must

117

have adopted the easily recognized French or Italian vocabulary behind such unusual words and expressions as 'acerb', 'molestation' and 'ocular proof'. Cinthio's characters, who apart from 'Disdemona' are named only as 'the Moor', 'the Ensign', etc., are flat, stock types; for example, Emilia is a traditional servant figure (*servetta*) to the *inamorata* role of Desdemona. They participate only in a sordid Italian intrigue, or at best a story of domestic woe, which culminates in trials, imprisonments and tortures. Shakespeare nevertheless owes many of the basic data to Cinthio/Chappuys: the two geographical locations, Venice and Cyprus; the well-concealed yet extreme evil of the Iago figure, and his cashiering of the 'Captain'; the crucial false evidence of the handkerchief. The playwright's telling manipulations of these givens, and especially of the character types, reflect characteristic abilities. In addition, there are everywhere in Cinthio's narrative 'small details, words and ideas which are the germs of so many aspects of the play's totality' (Sanders 1984: 8). For example, a single sentence in Cinthio to the effect that Disdemona's family wanted her to marry another man appears to lie behind her noble birth, her elopement, and the character of her angry, hostile father. Cinthio is followed more closely in Acts 3–5, where indeed Shakespeare might have tried harder to break away from the Italian tale, but in Acts 1–2 new characters (Roderigo, Montano, Ludovico) and new emphases are developed.

(D) Orr (1970) supplies a full review of the literature on this subject to that date. Doran (1954: Appendix 3) summarizes schematically the relationships between *Measure for Measure* and the Cinthio novella/play, including the versions by Whetstone; Bawcutt (1991) is the fullest recent analysis of the issues here. For *Othello*, modern English texts of the *Hecatommithi* narrative are given by Satin (1966) and Bullough (vii, reprinted Honigmann 1997); Bullough (vii, 214–38) also makes a detailed comparison of play with story.

Bullough; Muir (1977), 182–6; Satin (1966).

Ball, Robert H. (1945). 'Cinthio's *Epitia* and *Measure for Measure*', pp. 132–46 in *Elizabethan Studies and Other Essays in Honor of George F. Reynolds*. Boulder, CO.

Bawcutt, N. W., ed. (1991). *Measure for Measure* (Oxford Shakespeare). Oxford.

Doran, Madeleine (1954). *Endeavors of Art: A Study of Form in Elizabethan Drama*. Madison, WI.

Everett, Barbara (1982). '"Spanish" Othello: The Making of Shakespeare's Moor.' *ShSu* 35: 101–12 (reprinted in Everett, *Young Hamlet: Essays on Shakespeare's Tragedies*, Oxford, 1989).

Honigmann, E. A. J. (1966). '*Othello*, Chappuys, and Cinthio.' *N&Q* 211: 136–7.

—— ed. (1997). *Othello* (Arden Shakespeare). Walton-on-Thames.

Nosworthy, J. M., ed. (1969). *Measure for Measure* (New Penguin Shakespeare). Harmondsworth.

Orr, David (1970). *Italian Renaissance Drama in England before 1625: The Influence of 'Erudita' Tragedy, Comedy, and Pastoral on Elizabethan and Jacobean Drama*. Chapel Hill.

Pope, Elizabeth Marie (1949). 'The Renaissance Background of *Measure for Measure*.' *ShSu* 2: 66–82.

Prouty, Charles T. (1964). 'George Whetstone and the Sources of *Measure for Measure*.' *ShQ* 15.ii: 131–45.

Richmond, Hugh M. (1985). 'Shaping a Dream.' *ShSt* 17: 49–60.

—— (1991). 'Shakespeare's Verisimo and the Italian Popular Tradition', pp. 179–203 in J. R. Mulryne and Margaret Shewring, eds, *Theatre of the English and Italian Renaissance*. Basingstoke.

Sanders, Norman, ed. (1984). *Othello* (New Cambridge Shakespeare). Cambridge.

Shaheen, Naseeb (1994). 'Shakespeare's Knowledge of Italian.' *ShSu* 47: 161–9.

Whetstone, George (1578). *The Right Excellent and Famous Historye, of Promos and Cassandra, Devided into two Commicall Discourses*. London.

Coggleshall, Ralph of (d. after 1227), Chronicler Shakespeare may have known Coggleshall's account of the attempted blinding and killing of Prince Arthur; Honigmann (1954: 163–7) reprints it.

Honigmann, E. A. J., ed. (1954). *King John* (Arden Shakespeare), pp. 163–7. London.

Colonne, Guido delle See **Guido delle Colonne**.

Commedia dell'Arte The Italian *commedia dell'arte* tradition was exported to England by travelling players towards the end of the sixteenth century. If Shakespeare owes direct debts to it, they may be of the general kind outlined by Clubb (1989), or may involve specific elements in specific plays: Mendonça (1968), for example, pursues comparisons between Iago and a *commedia dell'arte* character.

Campbell, O. J. (1925). *Love's Labour's Lost Restudied*. Ann Arbor.
Clubb, Louise George (1989). *Italian Drama in Shakespeare's Time*, pp. 249–80. New Haven.
Mendonça, Barbara Heliodora C. de (1968). ' "Othello": A Tragedy Built on a Comic Structure.' *ShSu* 21: 31–8.

Constable, Henry (1562–1613), Poet Sonnet 99 seems to take its departure from a sonnet ('Sonetto decisette') in Constable's *Diana* (1592), a unique case in Shakespeare's sequence of his direct reliance on a single contemporary source.

Baldwin (1950), 302–3.

Contarini, Gasparo See **Lewkenor**, **Sir Lewis**.

Cooper, Thomas (1517?–1594), Latinist and Clergyman See also **Virgil**. Cooper's *Thesaurus Linguae Romanae et Brittanicae*, a standard Latin dictionary, contains glosses which Shakespeare's interpretations of **Virgil** sometimes seem to reflect, and a description of Midas which may be either an analogue or a source for Shakespeare's reference to the story in *A Midsummer Night's Dream*.

Baldwin (1944); Bullough, I, 397–8.

Coverdale, Miles See **Bible**.

Créton, Jean (*fl.* 1398), French Chronicler and Poet Créton wrote a French eye-witness account of the death of Richard II, drawn

120

upon by **Stow** and **Holinshed** and possibly consulted independently by Shakespeare.

Ure, Peter, ed. (1961). *Richard II* (Arden Shakespeare), pp. xliv–xlix. London.

Crompton, Richard (*fl.* 1573–1599), Legal and Historical Writer Crompton's *Mirror of Magnamitie* (1599), a historical work printed by Shakespeare's associate or friend Richard Field, has a passage defending Henry V's slaughter of prisoners; though he draws on **Holinshed**, Crompton's emphases fall differently. There is no clear evidence that Shakespeare knew the work.

Gurr, Andrew, ed. (1992). *King Henry V* (New Cambridge Shakespeare), pp. 27–8 and Appendix 3. London.

Culmann, Leonhard (1497/8–1562), German Educator Culmann's *Sententiae Pueriles*, a collection of Latin maxims and proverbs from diverse authors which was widely used in sixteenth-century schools, is very likely to be the direct source of some part of Shakespeare's knowledge of such sayings, though the suggestion (Baldwin 1944; Smith 1963) that he memorized it wholesale seems unnecessary.

Baldwin (1944), i, 592–3.
Monitto, Gary V. (1985). 'Shakespeare and Culmann's *Sententiae pueriles.*' *N&Q* 230: 30–1.
Smith, Charles George (1963). *Shakespeare's Proverb Lore: His Use of the Sententiae of Leonard Culman and Publilius Syrus.* Cambridge, MA.

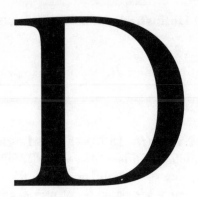

Daniel, Samuel (1562–1619), Poet and Dramatist

(A) Daniel was born in Somerset and educated at Oxford. He became tutor to William Herbert, son of Mary Sidney (Herbert) and later Shakespeare's patron, and then to Anne Clifford, daughter of the Earl of Cumberland. He published a translation from the Italian constituting the first treatise in English on *imprese* (see **Emblems**) in 1585. Some of his sonnets were printed in the surreptitious 1591 edition of **Sidney**'s *Astrophil and Stella*. Then in 1592 Daniel published his sonnet sequence *Delia* together with *The Complaint of Rosamond* (title page shown in Fig. 4). In 1594 came his tragedy *Cleopatra* and in 1599 *Musophilus, or Defence of all Learning*, a colloquium in stanzaic verse in which two characters debate the merits of knowledge and virtue against worldly arts. Daniel wrote pastoral tragicomedies; *Philotas*, another Senecan tragedy; several court masques; a prose *History of England*; and a treatise in *Defence of Ryme*, affirming the fitness of English for rhymed verse. His most extensive work is his epic poem in eight Books, *A History of the Civil Wars between the two Houses of York and Lancaster*, published 1595–1609.

He was appointed licenser of new plays of the Queen's Revels in 1604, becoming one of the Queen's Grooms of the Privy Chamber in 1607 and remaining in the service of Queen Anne for almost the rest of his life. He was a member of literary circles around Mary Sidney and Lucy, Countess of Bedford. In later years he lived 'retiredly to enjoy the company of the Muses', and Shakespeare is said to have been one of his few visitors. Shakespeare and Daniel are mentioned together in the

122

ΔΙΟΣ ΑΓΙΟΧΙΟΝ

DELIA.

Containing
certaine Son-
nets : with the
complaynt of *Ro-
samond.*

Ætas prima ca-
nat Veneres postre-
ma tumul-
tus.

1592.

AT LONDON,
Printed by *J. C.* for *S.*
Waterſonne.

Figure 4 Title Page of Daniel's *Delia . . . with the complaynt of Rosamond*

123

play *The Second Part of the Return from Parnassus* of 1603, and, if 'Mr W. H.' is William Herbert, Daniel may be the rival poet in Shakespeare's *Sonnets*.

(B) As well as being prolific, Daniel's writing is correct and genteel beyond the Elizabethan norms. He was, in fact, a self-conscious *littérateur*, with aesthetic inclinations the opposite of populist. His three works with strongest Shakespearean connections are characterized here.

The *Complaint of Rosamond* is in the manner of the **Mirror for Magistrates**, turned into a mirror for ladies. It is an account of the seduction and death of 'Fair Rosamond', the young mistress of Henry II. Daniel uses the familiar device of having the ghostly visitant bewailing in rhyme royal, but gives his damned lady a refined sensibility. As well as the strong relationship posited between *Rosamond* and *A Lover's Complaint* (see (C)), some of the concluding stanzas, below, are generally accepted to lie behind Romeo's final speech in *Romeo and Juliet* (5.3.88–120):

> The poyson soone disperc'd through all my vaines,
> Had dispossess'd my living sences quite:
> When naught respecting, death the last of paynes,
> Plac'd his pale collours, th'nsigne of his might,
> Upon his new-got spoyle before his right;
>   Thence chac'd my soule, setting my day ere noone,
>   When I least thought my joyes could end so soone . . .
>
> Pittifull mouth (quoth he) that living gavest,
> The sweetest comfort that my soule could wish:
> O be it lawful now, that dead thou havest,
> Thys sorrowing farewell of a dying kisse.
> And you faire eyes, containers of my blisse,
>   Motives of love, borne to be matched never:
>   Entomb'd in your sweet circles sleepe for ever.
>
> Ah how me thinks I see death dallying seekes,
> To entertain it selfe in loves sweet place:
> Decayed Roses of discoloured cheekes,
> Doe yet retaine deere notes of former grace:

And ougly death sits faire within her face;
  Sweet remnants resting of vermilion red,
  That death it selfe, doubts whether she be dead.
        (603–9, 666–79; Daniel 1592: fos 85ʳ, 88ᵛ–89ʳ)

Daniel tells us he designed his closet drama *Cleopatra* as a companion-piece to his patroness Mary Sidney's *Antonie*, her translation from Robert **Garnier**'s play, and it was dedicated to her. It is arguably one of the best original Senecan tragedies the Elizabethans produced. Not being theatrical (revised versions have more animation, but are still not plausibly stage spectacles), it depends for its effect on the elegiac and rhetorical qualities of its genre. The chorus, nuntius and use of rhyming verse are generically standard. Daniel takes up the story of Cleopatra from **Plutarch** after the death of Antony, and the play is devoted largely to her feelings as she contemplates suicide. This sample comes from the first scene, Cleopatra's opening soliloquy (of almost 200 lines):

              Of all, see what remaines,
    This monument, two maides, and wretched I.
    And I, t'adorne their triumphs am reserv'd
    A captive, kept to honour others spoiles,
    Whom *Caesar* labors so to have preserv'd,
    And seekes to entertaine my life with wiles.
    But *Caesar*, it is more then thou canst do,
    Promise, flatter, threaten extreamitie,
    Imploy thy wits and all thy force thereto,
    I have both hands, and will, and I can die.
    Though thou, of both my country and my crowne,
    Of powre, of meanes and all dost quite bereave me;
    Though thou hast wholy Egypt made thine owne,
    Yet hast thou left me that which will deceive thee.
    That courage with my bloud and birth innated,
    Admir'd of all the earth as thou art now,
    Can never be so abjectly abated
    To be thy slave that rul'd as good as thou.
    Thinke *Caesar*, I that liv'd and raign'd a Queene,
    Doe scorne to buy my life at such a rate,
    That I should underneath my selfe be seene,
    Basely induring to survive my state:

> That Rome should see my scepter-bearing hands
> Behind me bound, and glory in my teares,
> That I should passe whereas *Octavia* stands,
> To view my miserie that purchas'd hers.
>   (1599 text, 45–70; ed. Bullough, v, 409)

The Civile Wars of 1595 onwards is an unfinished epic poem in *ottava rima* in which 'the scholarly follower of the Countess of Pembroke tried to apply Lucan's methods to a British theme, but in a plain clear style which at times dropped into the prosy and at others rose to a restrained eloquence' (Bullough, III, 373). Daniel was an inveterate reviser, and the poem has a complicated textual history; suffice it here to say that by the date of Shakespeare's supposed use of it, only the first half of an eventual eight Books had been published (*The First Fowre Bookes of the Civile* Wars, 1595); Daniel's intended finishing-point, the death of Richard III, was not reached even when the poem was substantially complete, in 1609, when it ended with the marriage of Edward IV. Its elegiac gentleness gives a slow-motion effect to the storms portrayed, as when the imprisoned Richard II compares his condition to that of a peasant he sees through a grate:

> The morning of that day, which was his last,
> After a weary rest rysing to paine
> Out at a little grate his eyes he cast
> Uppon those bordering hils, and open plaine,
> And viewes the towne, and sees how people past,
> Where others libertie makes him complaine
> The more his owne, and greeves his soule the more
> Conferring captive-Crownes with freedome pore.
>
> O happie man, saith hee, that lo I see
> Grazing his cattel in those pleasant fieldes!
> O if he knew his good, how blessed hee
> That feeles not what affliction greatnes yeeldes,
> Other then what he is he would not bee,
> Nor chaung his state with him that Scepters weildes:
> O thine is that true life, that is to live,
> To rest secure, and not rise up to grieve.

126

Thou sit'st at home safe by thy quiet fire
And hear'st of others harmes, but feelest none;
And there thou telst of kinges and who aspire,
Who fall, who rise, who triumphes, who do mone:
Perhappes thou talkst of mee, and dost inquire
Of my restraint, why here I live alone,
O know tis others sin not my desart,
And I could wish I were but as thou art.
                    (iii, 63–5; Daniel 1595: fos 55^v–56^r)

(C) Unsurprisingly, since Daniel was one of the leading literary figures of his day, Shakespeare may have known almost all of Daniel's work. Attention has been drawn to apparent echoes from many individual texts, including *The Worthy Tract of Paulus Jovius* (on *imprese*), *Delia*, *The Complaint of Rosamond*, *Cleopatra*, *Musophilus*, *The Civil Wars*, several shorter poems and *The Queen's Arcadia*. In most of these cases the connections are slight, for example with Taylor's (1984) enumeration of some four small similarities between *Julius Caesar* and *Musophilus*. In others they are unreliable: on Kau's (1975) suggestion of the *Worthy Tract* as the source for an image of a down-turned torch in *Pericles* and Sonnet 73, see Young's (1985: 455) confutation. The most substantial links for Shakespeare's plays are with Daniel's *Cleopatra* and *The Civil Wars*; for Shakespeare's poems, with *Delia* and *The Complaint of Rosamond*.

Norman (1958), Muir (1977: 229–36) and Bullough (v, 231–8) list relevant Daniel parallels for *Antony and Cleopatra*. As well as *Cleopatra* itself, Daniel's Ovidian verse epistle *A Letter from Octavia to Marcus Antonius*, which preceded the tragedy in his 1599 volume *Poeticall Essayes*, may have supplied several local ideas for Shakespeare's drama, in the portrayal of Octavia. Vexed questions arise about the different versions of the Daniel play: after its first appearances in print from 1594 on, Daniel remodelled it in 1607, the title page describing it as 'newly altred'. In the revision Daniel moved towards a more dramatic form and has been shown to use new material derived from Mary Sidney's *Antonie* (1590). It is not clear that Shakespeare knew the 1607 as well as the earlier version of the play, but it seems certain he did know Daniel's tragedy in some form, and though the quantity of material demonstrably involved in the several echoes (mainly, for obvious reasons, in his Act 5) is small, it sometimes suggested significant touches, if not more, for Shakespeare. For example, Shakespeare's Cleopatra, like Daniel's, gives among her motives for suicide her fear of being triumphed over by the Roman rabble and by Octavia (see (B), above, and *Antony and Cleopatra* 5.2.52–6, famously elaborated in 206–19). This is 'an idea not much developed by Plutarch but repeated several times by Shakespeare' (Wilders 1995: 63). Looser but larger parallels imply to some commentators more far-reaching effects. Perhaps it was Daniel who suggested Shakespeare's elaboration of the Seleucus episode (though Stirling 1964 stresses differences), the figure of Dolabella, and Shakespeare's 'treatment of the perplexing contradictions of Plutarch's Octavius Caesar' (Neill 1994: 17). More decisively still, but no less difficult of proof, Daniel's self-consciously theatrical queen could have suggested Shakespeare's Cleopatra much more strongly than could Garnier's, and her rhetorical attempt to transform the past after Antony's death could have been 'the factor that impelled Shakespeare towards the one use, in all his tragedies, of the divided catastrophe' (Barton 1994: 125).

Considerable disagreement has existed (for the older literature see Logan 1976: 121) about the direction of the borrowing between *The Civil Wars* on the one hand and the histories *Richard II*, *Henry IV* and *3 Henry VI* on the other. The difficulties arise, once again, from dating and revision of Daniel's texts, and from the two writers' common sources in the chronicles (to which Daniel adheres more closely than Shakespeare). The consensus is now for Daniel's influence on Shakespeare – so Michel (1958) and Bullough (III), with a case specifically mounted by Logan (1976).

For *Richard II*, Shakespeare apparently used Daniel in, among other passages, Gaunt's panegyric on England; the Bishop of Carlyle's protest (4.1.114–49); Richard's speech of reproach to Northumberland (5.1.55–68); the entry of Bolingbroke and Richard into London (5.2); and the hints given by Henry IV for the murder of Richard to Sir Piers of Exton (5.4.1–7). Additionally there are some more general parallels of possible significance: both Shakespeare and Daniel take up the story at the same point in Richard's reign; both present Queen Isabel as a mature woman, with understanding well beyond that of the eleven-year-old presented in the chronicles; the political philosophy underlying each play is very similar; and both present the miseries of the reign as a prelude to the glories of the Tudors. Perhaps the closest and most sustained single parallel is that between Richard's melancholy prognostication of the stories Isabel will tell about him and the passage quoted from *The Civil Wars* Book III in (B), above. The passages share 'verbal details, an atmosphere of wistful self-pity, and the general situation of comfortable small people gossiping about the misfortunes of the great' (Logan 1976: 124). The comparison also shows major differences of kind between the two passages:

> Good sometimes queen, prepare thee hence for France.
> Think I am dead, and that even here thou takest,
> As from my death-bed, thy last living leave.
> In winter's tedious nights sit by the fire
> With good old folks, and let them tell thee tales
> Of woeful ages long ago betid;
> And ere thou bid good night, to quit their griefs
> Tell thou the lamentable tale of me,
> And send the hearers weeping to their beds;
> For why, the senseless brands will sympathize
> The heavy accent of thy moving tongue,
> And in compassion weep the fire out;
> And some will mourn in ashes, some coal-black,
> For the deposing of a rightful king.
>
> > (5.1.37–50)

Two scenes in particular in *3 Henry VI* show resemblances to *The Civil Wars* not accounted for by common material in the chronicles: the wooing of Lady Grey by Edward IV (3.2), and King Henry on the molehill at Towton (2.5.20–54) (see Michel 1958: 27–8). The latter harks back to Richard's soliloquy in Daniel's Book III already quoted. With *Henry IV* the picture is complicated by Daniel's apparent following of Shakespeare's play in his 1609 revision of *The Civil Wars*. Michel (1958: 21–6) and others disentangle the matter, leaving Shakespeare owing to Daniel a substantial number of pieces of diction and imagery, plays on words, incidents including the failure of the Welsh to appear at the Battle of Shrewsbury, plot elements such as Hotspur's being made a contemporary of Prince Henry, the emphatically sad and remorseful character of Henry IV (Bullough, IV, 254–6), and an overall development of the idea of Nemesis as 'a kind of retributive justice working through all the political action and forcing Henry to express remorse over his past conduct' (Michel 1958: 21).

129

Daniel's 1592 *Delia* volume has been seen as a decisive structural influence on Shakespeare's *Sonnets* and *A Lover's Complaint*. The book contained fifty sonnets, a short ode in anacreontic metre, and *The Complaint of Rosamond*. As Duncan-Jones (1983) shows, *Delia* spawned a series of publications in the 1590s containing a sonnet sequence, a lyric interlude, then a long poem (Spenser's *Amoretti* is one example). The structure may be said to be followed also in the first (1609) printing of Shakespeare's *Sonnets*, which closes with the text of *A Lover's Complaint* (though this was not mentioned on the title page), and in which the last two Sonnets (Sonnets 153–4), on Cupid, are anacreontics (in trochaic tetrameter). Kerrigan places the Shakespeare collection firmly within a 'Delian tradition': 'modern critics may be baffled by the heterogeneity of the volume; Shakespeare's audience had a framework for reading it' (Kerrigan 1986: 14). Read thus, the *Sonnets* and *A Lover's Complaint* can also be supposed to have strong connections, the latter 'not merely a formal pendant to the sonnets, but a carefully balanced thematic counterpart to them' (Duncan-Jones 1997: 92), corresponding to the arrangement in the *Delia* volume:

> the Sonnets and the complaint [in Daniel] illuminated each other by inversion. Something similar happens in Shakespeare's 1609 collection, because the poet of the complaint, detached from his tale by double rewording, stands by in appalled fascination as he hears how the unscrupulous young man seduced the 'fickle maid full pale', just as, in later sonnets, he watches helplessly while the dark lady seduced his fickle young friend.
>
> (Kerrigan 1986: 17)

This argument, if accepted, has considerable implications for criticism of the Shakespeare texts involved, particularly *A Lover's Complaint* (some are mentioned in Duncan-Jones 1997, especially 88–95).

(D) Any of Norman (1958), Muir (1977), or Bullough (v, 231–8) will serve as a starting-point on Shakespeare's use of *Cleopatra*. For Shakespeare and *The Civil Wars*, the introduction to Michel's edition (1958) gives a full overview, but is now largely superseded by more recent literature, among which Logan (1976) and Bullough, iii, are especially useful. Links between the *Delia* volume and Shakespeare's *Sonnets* volume were first suggested by Malone, more fully explained by

130

Duncan-Jones (1983), then Kerrigan (1986), and consolidated in editorial form in Duncan-Jones' 1997 edition of the *Sonnets*.

Bullough, III, IV, V; Muir (1977).

Barton, Anne (1994). *Essays, Mainly Shakespearean.* Cambridge.

Daniel, Samuel (1592). *Delia, Contayning Certayne Sonnets: with The Complaynt of Rosamond.* London.

—— (1595). *The First Fowre Bookes of the Civile Wars between the Two Houses of Lancaster and Yorke.* London.

Duncan-Jones, Katherine (1983). 'Was the 1609 *Shak-speares Sonnets* really Unauthorized?' *RES* 34: 151–71.

—— ed. (1997). *Shakespeare's Sonnets* (Arden Shakespeare). Walton-on-Thames.

Hiller, Geoffrey G. (1997). ' "What's in a Name?": Shakespeare's *Romeo and Juliet*, Samuel Daniel, and the Epitaph of "Fair Rosamund".' *N&Q* 242: 495–6.

Kau, Joseph (1975). 'Daniel's Influence on an Image in *Pericles* and Sonnet 73: An *Impresa* of Destruction.' *ShQ* 26: 51–3.

Kerrigan, John, ed. (1986). *William Shakespeare: The Sonnets and A Lover's Complaint.* Harmondsworth.

Law, Robert Adger (1947). 'Daniel's *Rosamond* and Shakespeare.' *University of Texas Studies in English* 26: 42–8.

Logan, George M. (1976). 'Lucan – Daniel – Shakespeare: New Light on the Relation between *The Civil Wars* and *Richard II*.' *ShSt* 9: 121–40.

Maxwell, J. C. (1967). ' "Rebel Powers": Shakespeare and Daniel.' *N&Q* 212: 139.

Michel, Laurence, ed. (1958). *The Civil Wars by Samuel Daniel.* New Haven.

Michel, Laurence, and Cecil C. Seronsy (1955). 'Shakespeare's History Plays and Daniel – an Assessment.' *SP* 52: 549–77.

Neill, Michael, ed. (1994). *The Tragedy of Anthony and Cleopatra* (Oxford Shakespeare). Oxford.

Norgaard, Holger (1955). 'Shakespeare and Daniel's "Letter from Octavia".' *N&Q* 200: 56–7.

Norman, Arthur M. Z. (1958). 'Daniel's *The Tragedie of Cleopatra* and *Antony and Cleopatra*.' *ShQ* 9: 11–18.

Ronan, Clifford J. (1985). 'Daniel, Rainolde, Demosthenes, and the Degree Speech of Shakespeare's Ulysses.' *Renaissance and Reformation* 9: 111–18.

Schaar, Claes (1960). *An Elizabethan Sonnet Problem: Shakespeare's Sonnets, Samuel Daniel's 'Delia', and their Literary Background* (Lund Studies in English, 28). Lund.

Schanzer, Ernest (1957). 'Daniel's Revision of his *Cleopatra*.' *RES* 8: 375–81.

Stirling, Brents (1964). 'Cleopatra's Scene with Seleucus: Plutarch, Daniel, and Shakespeare.' *ShQ* 15: 299–311.

Taylor, Gary (1984). '*Musophilus, Nosce Teipsum*, and *Julius Caesar*.' *N&Q* 229: 191–5.

Wilders, John (1995). *Antony and Cleopatra* (Arden Shakespeare). London.

Young, Alan R. (1985). 'A Note on the Tournament Impresas in *Pericles*.' *ShQ* 36: 453–6.

Dante Alighieri (1265–1321), Italian Poet Asp (1978) relates the consolations Paulina offers Hermione in *The Winter's Tale* to some of the words of Dante's Beatrice in the *Divina Commedia* (begun *c.* 1307); Muir (1949) discerns some small-scale affinities between the *Inferno* and *Macbeth*. Dante was virtually unknown in early modern England: the snippets in **Florio**'s Italian–English dictionary, uninspiring enough in themselves, are the only plausible route suggested to Shakespeare.

Asp, Carolyn (1978). 'Shakespeare's Paulina and the *Consolatio* Tradition.' *ShSt* 11: 145–58.

Muir, Kenneth (1949). '*Macbeth* and Dante.' *N&Q* 194: 333.

Davies, Sir John (1569–1626), Poet and Statesman Three or four parallels in detail link *Julius Caesar*, by no means securely, with Davies' long didactic poem on the immortality of the soul, *Nosce Teipsum* (1599).

Taylor, Gary (1984). 'Musophilus, *Nosce Teipsum*, and *Julius Caesar*.' *N&Q* 229: 191–5.

Dekker, Thomas (1570?–1632), Playwright See also **Euripides**. A bawdy line in *Julius Caesar* may allude to or be indebted to Dekker's *Shoemaker's Holiday*, first performed in the same year as Shakespeare's play.

Bate, Jonathan (1984). 'The Cobbler's Awl: *Julius Caesar*, I.i.21–24.' *ShQ* 35: 461–2.

Digges, Sir Dudley (1583–1639), Diplomat and Judge

One of Digges' essays in the 1604 volume *Foure Paradoxes, or Politique Discourses* makes reference to Coriolanus in ways that anticipate Shakespeare.

Muir (1977), 239–41.

Diogenes the Cynic (*c.* 400–325 BC), Greek Philosopher

None of Diogenes' authentic writings, if there ever were any, survived into Shakespeare's time, but Renaissance collections of *sententiae* often included apophthegms attributed to him. Shakespeare may well have encountered them, but specific influence is hardly possible to demonstrate.

Donawerth, Jane (1977). 'Diogenes the Cynic and Lear's Definition of Man, *Lear* III,4, 101–109.' *ELN* 15: 10–14.
Pauls, Peter (1980). 'Shakespeare's *Timon of Athens* and Renaissance Diogeniana.' *Upstart Crow* 3: 54–66.

Dolman, John See Cicero, Marcus Tullius.

Donatus, Aelius See Terence (Publius Terentius Afer).

Donne, John (1572?–1631), Poet and Divine
A sentence in the eighth of Donne's *Devotions* (1624) on the paradox of the vulnerability of royalty has some similarity of phrase and imagery with a passage in the deposition scene of *Richard II*.

Barbieri, Richard E. (1975). 'John Donne and *Richard II*: An Influence?' *ShQ* 26: 57–62.

Douglas, Gavin (1475?–1522), Scottish Bishop and Poet

The *Hamlet* passage on 'the morn in russet mantle clad' (1.1.170–2) has a source in Douglas' *The Palis of Honoure*, a sufficiently well-known work in 1601.

Fowler, Alastair (1994). 'Two Notes on *Hamlet*', pp. 3–10 in Mark Thornton Burnett and John Manning, eds, *New Essays on 'Hamlet'*. New York.

Drant, Thomas See Horace (Quintus Horatius Flaccus).

Drayton, Michael (1563–1631), English Poet

Leishman identifies some Drayton parallels in Shakespeare's *Sonnets*, Fowler a possible model in Drayton's 'Mortimeriados' (1596) for the style of *The Murder of Gonzago*; but it is surprising that so few even adequately plausible Drayton echoes have been isolated in Shakespeare.

Fowler, Alastair (1994). 'Two Notes on *Hamlet*', pp. 3–10 in Mark Thornton Burnett and John Manning, eds, *New Essays on 'Hamlet'*. New York.
Leishman, J. B. (1961). *Themes and Variations in Shakespeare's Sonnets*. London.

Eden, Richard (1521?–1576), Translator Eden's *History of Travaille*, 1577, a voyager narrative, seems to have contributed the name 'Setebos' and perhaps other local colour to *The Tempest*.

Kermode, Frank, ed. (1964). *The Tempest* (Arden Shakespeare), pp. xxxii–xxxiii. London (first published 1954).

Edwards, Richard (1523?–1566), Poet and Playwright Edwards' *Palamon and Arcite* (1566) was the best-known Chaucerian dramatization of its era. Since it went unprinted it is normally assumed it was unavailable to Shakespeare, but Potter (1997: 46–7) suggests it might have been remembered as late as the 1610s, and may help explain one or two minor anomalies in *The Two Noble Kinsmen*.

Potter, Lois, ed. (1997). *The Two Noble Kinsmen* (Arden Shakespeare). Walton-on-Thames.

Eliot, John (b. 1562), Teacher of French
(A) A Warwickshire man, Eliot attended Brasenose College, Oxford, subsequently leading a roaming life in France, Italy and Spain as a schoolmaster, a hack journalist and at one point a novice monk. He became involved in French politics, possibly as a secret agent, but on the

assassination of Henri III in 1589 made his way back to London. Here he worked as a French language teacher and as a translator of French political tracts for the printer Reginald Wolfe. He must have known Robert **Greene**, for whom he wrote a commendatory sonnet in 1588. In 1593 he published his *Survay, or Topographical Description of France* (anonymously), and *Ortho-epia Gallica*. The latter is a French language textbook consisting of a series of parallel-text dialogues on contemporary life and manners, but it also works on other levels. It contains allusions to and parodies of the rival primers of **Florio** and Vives, and ultimately, perhaps, the entire class of dialogues and colloquies used for language-learning, as well as animadversions on the Huguenot refugees who as French teachers in London had begun to threaten Eliot's livelihood. The whole is done with a wealth of (often **Rabelais**-inspired) wit and eloquence, and it abounds in fragments of sixteenth-century French literature, with borrowings of phraseology and of larger-scale material from such writers as Boiastuau and Du Bartas.

At the age of thirty-one Eliot disappeared from the London scene and no more is heard of him.

(B) Though it has been called 'a minor Elizabethan classic' (Lever 1953: 79), *Ortho-epia Gallica* was not reprinted in its own time. Something of its flavour, at times burlesque or surreal, at others tongue-in-cheek or sardonic, is indicated by the following excerpt, in which the speakers are examining a map in a painter's shop (the *en face* French is omitted):

See you this Mappe of the world? I see it well. Whats this a Sea? I see but a litle water, which is not greater then the Thames. I marvell the French King doth not make a fine bridge to passe from one country to another. The Sea betweene France and England is it no broader then that? By my faith I will then easily shoote an arrow from Dover Castle to the white sandes of Cales. See here the huge Ocean Sea. Is that the ocean Sea? That. Is this the earth? They say that Sir Francis Drake, maister Candish, And Magellanes, have bene almost three yeares in compassing the earth and the Sea. By my troth to win a good pinte of claret wine, in lesse then a daies journy, in a faire afternoone, I will go round about them on foote without Horse, Asse, Mule, Ship-boat or Brygandine. Thy fevers quartanes thou wilt not. Looke here Cullion! See Asia. Here are Tygris and Euphrates. See here Quinzay, a Citie so famous amongst the Azians: and hath xii.

thousand stonebridges, under which the ships passe with full saile, and never pull downe their masts. See Affrick! Here is the mountayn of the Moone! Seest thou the Fennes of Nyle? Lo here the red Sea. Looke upon the great Caire! On this side is Europe. This top here all white, are the Hyperborean mountains. Here are the Alpes, over which we go downe into Italie. There are the Appenines: and here are the Pyrenaean hilles, by which you may go directly into Spaine. See here where is the Citie of London.

(Eliot 1968: 79; roman for italic, lineation ignored)

(C) Shakespeare and Eliot had common acquaintances and were near-contemporaries from Warwickshire. They may thus have known each other in London; there is no external evidence on the point, though a complex set of interrelations seems to link Eliot's language manual to the **Harvey–Nashe** polemic in the background of *Love's Labour's Lost* (with possible verbal echoes in the play: see Yates 1936: 50–72; Schrickx 1956; David 1968: xxxix–xlii). But *Ortho-epia* does seem, in any case, exactly the type of book Shakespeare could have used to teach himself French. Shakespeare's French is usually thought to be not quite of a standard commensurate with professional (or native-speaker) help; and Eliot's book is by some distance the liveliest work of its kind that might have been available to him. His apparent recall of scraps from the book over the course of his career is consistent with the type of enduring, though inconsequential, memories often created by drilling (including self-drilling) in the course of language-learning.

A peculiarity of the text of *Henry V* in the First Folio is the line in which Pistol has his boy translate his words into French to threaten Monsieur le Fer, his prisoner: '*Il me commande a vous dire que vous faite vous prest, car ce soldat icy est disposee tout asture de couppes vostre gorge*' (Shakespeare 1866: *Henry the Fift*, p. 87; 4.4.37–9). The word 'asture', emended by Rowe and all subsequent editors to 'à cette heure', is given several times in *Ortho-epia* with this sense. According to Lever (1953: 81) it is unique to Eliot. If so this would be one of the strongest single indications of a knowledge of Eliot on Shakespeare's part; but it is in fact frequently encountered in sixteenth-century French. There may however be reverberations in the Pistol episode of a dialogue on a thief which makes up Eliot's Chapter 14 (Lever 1953: 85).

There are apparent echoes in several other plays, notably Histories, mostly at the level of phraseology and usually of little further significance. A more general response to Eliot (probably), and/or to books like his (certainly), is found in the Bastard's first soliloquy in *King John*:

> Now your traveller,
> He and his toothpick at my worship's mess –
> And when my knightly stomach is suffic'd,
> Why then I suck my teeth and catechize
> My picked man of countries: 'My dear sir,'
> Thus leaning on mine elbow I begin
> 'I shall beseech you' – That is question now;
> And then comes answer like an Absey book:
> 'O sir,' says answer 'at your best command,
> At your employment, at your service, sir!'
> 'No, sir,' says question, 'I, sweet sir, at yours.'
> And so, ere answer knows what question would,
> Saving in dialogue of compliment,
> And talking of the Alps and Apennines,
> The Pyrenean and the river Po –
> It draws toward supper in conclusion so.
>
> (1.1.189–204)

Here 'Absey book' is a corruption of 'ABC-book', a primer 'often in catechism or dialogue form' (*OED*), that is, such a work as *Ortho-epia*, and there is a possible relationship specifically with the passage given in (B), above (first pointed out by Yates 1936: 51ff.).

Even if only some of the dozen or so putative echoes of Eliot's textbook recorded by Lever and Porter are genuine, they span an unusually large stretch of time in Shakespeare's career. Lever (1953: 84) speculates that after first using the book at an earlier date, Shakespeare had a second phase of interest in the French language around 1598 (reflected in the French dialogue in *Henry V* and *The Merry Wives of Windsor*). More widely, the tenacity of Shakespeare's memories of the manual may have been owing to a combination of the strong impressions often made on a student by a primer with the particular format of the dialogues, which have 'the vigorous unpredictability of good drama', and read 'like playlets without speech headings or stage directions' (Porter 1986: 488).

138

(D)

David, Richard, ed. (1968). *Love's Labour's Lost* (Arden Shakespeare). London.

Eliot, John (1968). *Ortho-Epia Gallica: Eliots Fruits for the French, 1593*, facsimile reprint. Menston.

Lever, J. W. (1953). 'Shakespeare's French Fruits.' *ShSu* 6: 79–90.

Porter, Joseph A. (1986). 'More Echoes from Eliot's *Ortho-epia Gallica*, in *King Lear* and *Henry V.*' *ShQ* 37: 486–8.

Schrickx, W. (1956). *Shakespeare's Early Contemporaries: The Background of the Harvey–Nashe Polemic and 'Love's Labours Lost'*. Antwerp.

Shakespeare, William (1866). *The First Collected Edition of the Dramatic Works . . . A Reproduction in Exact Fac-simile*. London.

Yates, Frances A. (1931). 'The Importance of John Eliot's *Ortho-epia Gallica.*' *RES* 7: 419–30.

—— (1936). *A Study of 'Love's Labours Lost'*. Cambridge.

Elyot, Sir Thomas (*c.* 1490–1546), Administrator, Lexicographer and Writer

(A) The son of an attorney and serjeant-at-law, Elyot was educated at the Inns of Court during the time when they were rapidly becoming centres of humanist study. He practised as a lawyer, becoming a Clerk of Assize and then Clerk of the Council under Wolsey, but spent most of his life on the fringes of Henry VIII's court, at one stage being sent on an unsuccessful diplomatic mission to enlist the support of the Holy Roman Emperor for Henry's divorce of Katherine of Aragon. Between 1531 and 1545 he published some twelve works of didactic prose, an ambitious range of writings aimed at promoting the training both inward and outward of the Christian humanist. These much-reprinted texts included translations of **Lucian** and of opuscula by Isocrates, **Plutarch** and Pico della Mirandola; the first English–Latin dictionary of any size; an edifying life of the Emperor Severus Alexander; and a sermon on the 'last things'. Easily his most famous work is *The Boke Named the Governour* (1531), an extended essay on political ethics and the education of the prince and statesman. Sometimes described as the earliest treatise on moral philosophy in English, it is also a milestone in the evolution of English prose. Though addressed to magistrates and deputies, it was also intended for the eyes of Henry VIII, and propounded the sort of monarchical theories he was anxious to encourage.

Since Elyot held the optimistic, non-Machiavellian view that the same qualities that make a good king make a good man, the chapters on government are strongly related to the discussions of training in knowledge, manners and virtue.

(B) *The Governour* quickly became one of the most popular books of its age. It was reprinted three times during Elyot's life and frequently after his death, running through nine or ten editions in fifty years (some editions remove passages not conforming with later religious ortho- doxy). It was imitated in title and subject, borrowed from both with and without acknowledgement, quoted, and 'used by other writers as a compendium of illustrative materials on subjects as widely differing as shooting a long bow and ruling a commonwealth' (Starnes 1927: 112). Its influence extended to such works as Ascham's *Toxophilus* (1546) and *The Schoolmaster* (1570), and a century after its publication it is still part of the background of such a book as Peacham's *Compleat Gentleman* (1622). After an edition of 1580, however, no further printings took place until the nineteenth century.

Almost at the very start of *The Governour*, Elyot undertakes to show 'of what estimation ordre is' in society. (His ardent, even religious devotion to the same principle also informs his courtly account of dancing else- where in the book, celebrated by his distant relation T. S. Eliot in *East Coker*.) These excerpts come from Book I, Chapters 1–2:

> Beholde also the ordre that god hath put generally in al his creatures, begynnyng at the moste inferior or base, and assendynge upwarde: he made not only herbes to garnisshe the erthe, but also trees of a more eminent stature than herbes, and yet in the one and the other be degrees of qualitees; some pleasant to beholde, some delicate or good in taste, other holsome and medicinable, some commodious and necessary . . . so that in every thyng is ordre, and without ordre may be nothing stable or permanent; and it may nat be called ordre, except it do contayne in it degrees, high and base, accordynge to the merite or estimatioun of the thyng that is ordred . . .

> The popular astate, if any thing do varie from equalitie of substance or estimation, or that the multitude of people have over moche liberte, of necessite one of these inconveniences muste happen: either tiranny, where he that is to moche in favour wolde be elevate

and suffre none equalite, orels in to the rage of a communaltie, whiche of all rules is moste to be feared . . . For who can denie but that all thynge in heven and erthe is governed by one god, by one perpetuall ordre, by one providence? One Sonne ruleth over the day, and one Moone over the nyghte; and to descende downe to the erthe, in a litell beest, whiche of all other is moste to be marvayled at, I meane the Bee, is lefte to man by nature, as it semeth, a perpetuall figure of a juste governaunce or rule: who hath amonge them one principall Bee for theyr governour, who excelleth all other in greatnes, yet hath he no pricke or stinge, but in hym is more know-ledge than in the residue . . .

The capitayne hym selfe laboureth nat for his sustinance, but all the other for hym; he onely seeth that if any drane or other unprofit-able bee entreth in to the hyve, and consumethe the hony, gathered by other, that he be immediately expelled from that company . . .

The Grekes, which were assembled to revenge the reproche of Menelaus, that he toke of the Trojans by the ravisshing of Helene, his wyfe, dyd nat they by one assent electe Agamemnon to be their emperour or capitain?   (1531 text, ed. Croft 1883: I, 4–5, 10–16)

(C) Though perhaps no individual echo of Elyot in Shakespeare is fully conclusive, the popularity of *The Governour* during Shakespeare's life-time, the number of more or less plausible affinities in the plays, and the clustering together of apparent Elyot source-material for several of the plays within one or two short sections of the book, combine to make some kind of direct connection seem highly probable.

To summarize: Elyot is the likeliest source for the main plot of *The Two Gentlemen of Verona*, though the story in question was also available elsewhere. There are strong echoes or apparent echoes of the first two chapters of *The Governour* in *Henry V* and *Troilus and Cressida*. Further material apparently echoed in *2 Henry IV* may have come to Shake-speare via the chronicler **Stow**. Fainter connections with *The Governour* have been discerned in a number of other plays including *Coriolanus*, and, largely at the level of local phraseology, *Julius Caesar*, *Richard II* and *Sir Thomas More* (for these see the references in (D)).

Elyot's Chapter II, 12 is headed 'The wonderfull history of Titus and Gisippus, and whereby is fully declared the figure of perfet amitie'. It is the story of an ideal friendship between two aristocratic Athenian stu-dents, one Greek and the other Roman. The Greek praises his fiancée to his friend, who falls in love with her; his struggles against his passion proving vain, the girl is offered to the friend in terms very similar to those used by Shakespeare's Valentine: 'Here I renounce to you clerely all my title and interest that I nowe have or mought have in that faire mayden' (ed. Croft 1883: II, 141–2; compare Valentine's 'And, that my love may appear plain and free, / All that was mine in Silvia I give thee', *Two Gentlemen of Verona* 5.4.82–3). The story of Titus and Gisippus had been popular at least since **Boccaccio**'s treatment in the *Decameron*, and other sixteenth-century English versions both poetic and dramatic are extant (see Sargent 1950). Elyot's version, however, matches Shakespeare's at some of the crucial points of divergence between the different versions – though, once again, Shakespeare's is itself in other respects divergent from Elyot's.

As strong a case can be made for Shakespeare's familiarity with the early discussions in *The Governour* (I, 1–2, but the basic ideas are often repeated later) of order and degree in society. Elyot's figure of the beehive and his presentation of Platonic ideas of harmony and degree as a law of nature and of God (see (B)) are met with in *Henry V* and *Troilus and Cressida*. In the former, the Archbishop of Canterbury famously discusses how the honey bee teaches 'the act of order to a peopled kingdom' (1.2.189). These lines have parallels in **Lyly**'s *Euphues* and in Lyly's own sources, **Pliny** and **Virgil**, but none of these could have supplied the Platonic or neo-Platonic ideas of order, degree and harmony (though the 'agreements in phraseology and arrangement' discerned by Starnes 1927 are not remarkable). A speech in *Troilus and Cressida* has a definite relationship with Canterbury's: that of the Machiavellian Ulysses on order (1.3.78–137), in which he attempts to make Achilles return to the battle. Other possible sources in this case include **Hooker**, but 'there is in Ulysses' speech . . . much in common with the first two chapters in *The Governour*, and lacking in the *Ecclesiastical Polity*' (Starnes 1927: 124), including once more the beehive image itself, and the conclusion that one man should be the chief ruler – in Ulysses' formulation, 'The specialty of rule hath been neglected' (1.3.78). The presence of nearby material on the Greek leaders in *The Governour* is surely fortuitous, and hardly likely to have suggested the action of *Troilus and Cressida*.

Finally, *The Governour* contains (II, 6) the earliest known version of the probably unhistorical episode referred to in *2 Henry IV* of the sentencing of Prince Hal to prison by the Lord Chief Justice. Elyot recounts it picturesquely and dramatically. The King on hearing of the incident, Elyot writes,

> a whiles studyienge, after as a man all ravisshed with gladness, holdyng his eien and handes up towarde heven, abrayded, sayinge with a loude voice, O mercifull god, howe moche am I, above all other men, bounde to your infinite goodnes; specially for that ye have gyven me a juge, who feareth nat to ministre justice, and also a sonne who can suffre semblably and obey justice?
>
> (1531 text, ed. Croft 1883: ii, 72)

This speech is a part of the story paralleled in Shakespeare (*2 Henry IV* 5.2.108–12) but omitted in the later versions given by **Hall** and **Holinshed**. Stow supplies it in his *Annals*, however, placing the whole passage in quotation marks and attributing it to Elyot. If Shakespeare knew the *Governour* text of it, 'it is noteworthy that the narrative . . . appears in Elyot's exposition of the nature of Majesty and of the virtues which a king should possess' (Starnes 1927: 116).

(D) Starnes (1927) lays out the strongest and most extensive cases of apparent echoes, in *2 Henry IV*, *Henry V*, *Troilus and Cressida* and *Coriolanus*, with useful parallel passages. Sargent (1950) makes the fullest case in respect of *The Two Gentlemen of Verona*.

Brooks, Harold F. (1963). 'Shakespeare and *The Gouernour*, Bk. II, ch. xiii. Parallels with *Richard II* and the *More* Addition.' *ShQ* 14: 195–9.

Bullough, i.

Bush, Douglas (1937). '*Julius Caesar* and Elyot's *Governour*.' *MLN* 52: 407–8.

Croft, Henry Herbert Stephen, ed. (1883). *The Boke Named the Governour, Devised by Sir Thomas Elyot, Knight, Edited from the First Edition of 1531*, 2 vols. London.

Maxwell, J. C. (1956). ' "Julius Caesar" and Elyot's "Governour".' *N&Q* 201: 147.

Sargent, Ralph M. (1950). 'Sir Thomas Elyot and the Integrity of *The Two Gentlemen of Verona*.' *PMLA* 65: 1166–80.

Starnes, D. T. (1927). 'Shakespeare and Elyot's *Governor*.' *University of Texas Studies in English* 7: 112–32.

Emblems (Including *Imprese*)

(A) In the sense used here, the emblem as known in Shakespeare's time was a combination of a motto (usually in a foreign language) and a short poem (or sometimes prose text) with a picture, used together to expound some moral or ethical truth (see the example in Fig. 5). Much of the subject-matter employed – phoenix, pelican, vine and elm – is drawn from literary topoi familiar long before emblems came into vogue. Emblem books were a largely continental European phenomenon of the sixteenth and seventeenth centuries, during which time two thousand or more (depending on the definition adopted) were printed, beginning with Andrea Alciati's *Emblematum Liber* (Augsburg, 1531). Successive editions of Alciati spread the fashion from Italy to France, where, around 1540, works by Guillaume de la Perrière and Gilles Corrozet included collections of historical apologues, proverbs, maxims of love, wonderful adventures and fables, all developed from Alciati's

DEVISES
Sic ſpeĉtanda fides.

Si pour eſprouuer le fin Or, ou autres metaus, lon les raporte ſus la Touche, ſans qu'on ſe confie de leurs tintemens, ou de leurs ſons, auſſi pour connoitre les gens de bien, et vertueus perſonnages, ſe faut prendre garde à la ſplendeur de leurs œuures, ſans s'arreſter au babil.

ſic

Figure 5 Claude Paradin, *Les Devices Heroiques* (Anvers, 1562), fo. 100ᵛ.

model. A considerable body of theoretical discussion of the subject also emerged in the later sixteenth century, and emblems began to figure, in Europe generally, in decorative schemes in other media, including plaster, tapestry and paintings. Drama is sometimes said to be intrinsically allied to the emblem because it combines the verbal and the visual. Regular contexts for the use of emblems in England in the later sixteenth century and beyond also include civic pageantry, royal entrances, masques and chivalric ceremonial. The last was the home of a special type of emblem, the *imprese* which were presented to the presiding lord or monarch by each knight participating in a tournament. As in the fictional examples in **Sidney**'s *Arcadia* or **Spenser**'s *Faerie Queene*, a knight's *impresa* consisted of a personal motto and emblematic representation of his hopes and intentions on the occasion, painted onto a pasteboard shield (for a full study see Young 1987). In 1613 Shakespeare was paid to compose an *impresa* for the Earl of Rutland.

(B) Geoffrey Whitney's *A Choice of Emblemes, and Other Devises*, 1586, is often described as the first printed emblem book in England. This is in some sense an anthology: Green (1870: 252) showed that of the 248 woodcuts, 202 are printed from blocks previously used by the printer Plantin for books by Alciati, Hadrian Junius, Claude Paradin and Joannes Sambucus. The cultured English-speaking reader also had direct access to the work of such writers as these through the enormously larger output of emblem material from continental presses; there is ample evidence of the diffusion in Britain of French, Italian and Dutch emblem books, as well as many Latin examples. The first printed emblem book of wholly English origin was Andrew Willet's *Century of Sacred Emblems* of 1598.

Within three years of Whitney's 1586 volume, **Puttenham**'s *Arte of English Poesie* devotes a whole chapter to emblems: the growth in their popularity in England is rapid. Whitney was also used by William Byrd, who set five of his emblems as madrigals in his *Psalms, Songs and Sonnets* (1586), and elsewhere in the 1580s and 1590s in decorative applications in silverware and painting (see Bath 1994: 86–9). To the later Elizabethans, 'emblem writing was a gentlemanly accomplishment of the same type as the ability to play the lute or to dance the lavolta' (Freeman 1967: 3). For the poet or playwright, their presence in everyday life made it impossible to ignore them. Sometimes this means a playwright alludes to individual emblems he knows: **Marston**'s *The Malcontent*

(1603) makes reference to a device of a bear licking her young into shape found in Horapollo's *Hieroglyphica* and elsewhere, to an emblem of the eagle and the tortoise (perhaps derived from Sidney's *Arcadia*), and to the ivy destroying the tree which has helped it to mount (found emblematically in several sources; references for all three items in Praz 1964: 216–17). At other times it means a playwright draws more or less directly on the emblem convention: **Chapman**'s tragedies, for example, use it directly for elaborate emblematical descriptions which include 'speaking picture', interpretation and moral lesson. Earlier plays had anticipated his manner in cruder forms – the anonymous *Locrine* (1590s), for instance, provided an emblem, with motto, to precede each Act. Less direct appropriations of the convention shade off into the use of 'emblematic' forms such as dumb shows (see Mehl 1969), and various kinds of what is sometimes unsatisfactorily called an 'emblematic style'. *Imprese* devices also found their way into plays: **Middleton** uses some elaborately in *Your Five Gallants*.

Jonson was happy to refer to emblem mottos in his plays as well as masques, but he parodies the convention in *Cynthia's Revels*, in the burlesque episode in which prizes are awarded for courtly compliments:

> For the bare Accost, two Wall-eyes, in a face forced: For the better Reguard, a Face favorably simpring, with a Fanne waving: For the solemne Addresse, two Lips wagging, and never a wise word: For the perfect Close, a Wring by the hand, with a Banquet in a corner.
>
> (5.3.106–10; ed. Herford and Simpson 1925–51: iv, 138)

Marston's madcap character Balurdo in *Antonio and Mellida* (1599 or 1600) also pokes fun at the vogue for *imprese*. Emblems in general often cultivate esotericism; *imprese* and the books which depicted them were intended to summon up a world of feudal patronage, and their exclusivity is reflected in literature: only the princess understands Musidorus' jewel 'made in the figure of crab-fish' in Sidney's *Arcadia*, and only Maecenas, not the foolish Lupus, understands Horace's *impresa* in Jonson's *Poetaster*.

(C) It is often claimed that Shakespeare's work is influenced formally or structurally by emblem writers: elements of his imagery, iconography, stage presentation and stage properties have been approached in this way. Such influence is perfectly possible, though there is little consensus about it. But these phenomena do not lead back to any *particular* emblem book or author, even on some occasions when Shakespeare makes reference to a particular (but widely known) emblem (one example is the weeping stag which the melancholy Jacques watched, *As You Like It* 2.1.33ff.: see Bath 1986). Thus they may be attributable more to the effect of widespread ways of thinking and writing – described by such terms as 'Renaissance iconography' – than to the direct reading of emblem literature on Shakespeare's part. The present discussion is therefore oriented in other directions.

A direct, light-hearted reference to the emblem convention generally occurs in *The Two Noble Kinsmen*: Emilia contends that a rose is

>   the very emblem of a maid –
> For when the west wind courts her gently,
> How modestly she blows, and paints the sun
> With her chaste blushes! When the north comes near her,
> Rude and impatient, then, like chastity,
> She locks her beauties in her bud again,
> And leaves him to base briers.

WOMAN   Yet, good madam,
> Sometimes her modesty will blow so far
> She falls for't – a maid,
> If she have any honor, would be loath
> To take example by her.

>   (2.2.137–47)

Surprisingly, this is the only metaphorical use of the word 'emblem' in the Shakespeare canon (the only two other examples refer to actual, physical emblems). As often in other writers, the term is applied here to the pictorial element alone, except that Emilia is also thinking of the type of fable which the pictures illustrated. There is no call to seek a particular emblematic source for Emilia's suggestion.

As has almost always been recognized, Shakespeare rarely borrows directly from emblem writers, but a passage in which multiple borrowings of *impresa* mottos occur is the tournament scene in *Pericles*:

SIMONIDES   'Tis now your honour, daughter, to entertain
>   The labour of each knight in his device.
THAISA   Which, to preserve mine honour, I'll perform.

147

Emblems

Enter a Knight; he passes over, and his Squire presents his shield to the Princess.

SIMONIDES   Who is the first that doth prefer himself?
THAISA   A Knight of Sparta, my renowned father;
             And the device he bears upon his shield
             Is a black Ethiope reaching at the Sun;
             The word, 'Lux tua vita mihi'.
SIMONIDES   He loves you well that holds his life of you.

The Second Knight passes by.

             Who is the second that presents himself?
THAISA   A Prince of Macedon, my royal father;
             And the device he bears upon his shield
             Is an arm'd knight that's conquer'd by a lady;
             The motto thus, in Spanish, 'Piu por dulzura que por fuerza'.

The Third Knight passes by.

SIMONIDES   And what's the third?
THAISA   The third of Antioch;
             And his device a wreath of chivalry;
             The word, 'Me pompae provexit apex'.

The Fourth Knight passes by.

SIMONIDES   What is the fourth?
THAISA   A burning torch that's turned up-side down;
             The word, 'Quod me alit, me extinguit'.
SIMONIDES   Which shows that beauty hath his power and will,
             Which can as well inflame as it can kill.

The Fifth Knight passes by.

THAISA   The fifth, an hand environed with clouds,
             Holding out gold that's by the touchstone tried;
             The motto thus, 'Sic spectanda fides'.

PERICLES as Sixth Knight passes by.

148

SIMONIDES   And what's the sixth and last, the which the knight himself
            With such a graceful courtesy deliver'd?
THAISA   He seems to be a stranger; but his present is
            A withered branch, that's only green at top;
            The motto, 'In hac spe vivo'.

                                                          (2.2.14–44)

Real-life sources for these *imprese* have been found. The first knight's
motto was that of the Blount family of Worcestershire, and would have
been accompanied by a visual device (of unknown form) in some
contexts; Pericles' *impresa* has been identified with one composed by
Sir Philip **Sidney**, and so on. This leads Young (1985) to conclude that
Shakespeare was familiar with at least one printed collection of *imprese*,
perhaps *The Heroicall Devices of M. Claudius Paradin* Englished in 1592 by
'P. S.'. Fig. 5 shows the version of the Fifth Knight's emblem found in
the 1562 French version of Paradin's *Devises Heroiques* (for the range of
possible Shakespearean sources here see Young 1985: 455).

On many occasions of possible reference to emblems, however, it is
much less clear how far Shakespeare is alluding to particular examples.
When, for instance, Hamlet's comparison of Rosencrantz and courtiers
in general to a sponge (4.2.12–16) is related to Alciati or Whitney's
emblem of a king squeezing out a sponge and the courtiers who suck
their sustenance from him, the similarity is too limited to give evidence
of Shakespeare's reading – the analogy was commonplace, and not
original with Alciati or Whitney. The fact that Hamlet himself spells
out his meaning in using it also makes the passage work independently
of any emblem the audience might or might not call to mind. With
Othello's words on entering the room to murder Desdemona, light in
hand – 'Put out the light, and then put out the light' (5.2.7) – the case is
slightly different. Horapollo's *Hieroglyphica* had included an emblem of a
lighted lamp as symbolizing life, but more specifically relevant are the
many emblematic instances of the motif of a torch bring quenched,
and the frequent association, as in the Fourth Knight's emblem in the
Pericles scene, above, with the power of love and beauty to induce either
joy or despair. Thus in Shakespeare's scene 'we are presented not only
with an emblem of the fragility of the transience of human life but also
with an emblem of the paradoxical powers of love' (Young 1976: 6).
Yet, while this may be taken as an indication of the associations some
members of an early seventeenth-century audience might have brought

to this moment in the play, once again this information does not necessarily reveal that Shakespeare was acquainted with this particular
emblem tradition.

Attempts to discover instances of Shakespeare working from particular emblems are almost always dogged by uncertainty. An image in an
emblem book reminds a commentator of a scene in Shakespeare; the
commentator then does his or her best to discover reasons why Shakespeare might have known the emblem – this is not a promising
procedure, though some such arguments (e.g. Butler 1984) are better
than others. Elsewhere, the likely availability of an emblem book to
Shakespeare prompts the reverse process; neither Richards (1980) nor
Waddington (1976) is convincing as to the effect of individual Whitney
emblems on the *Sonnets* and *The Merchant of Venice*. With Shakespeare as
with other writers, then, 'except in rare instances the attempt to establish specific literary or iconographical indebtedness [to an emblem] can
be misleading. In most cases the parallels are valuable chiefly as
parallels and nothing more; the commonplaces as commonplaces, and
precisely because they *are* such' (Steadman 1979: 32).

(D) Praz (1964) provides a broad study of emblem writing as such (with
full primary bibliography), and of emblematic imagery as found in
early modern European and English literature. Bath (1994) is a full
recent study of the English emblem tradition. On Shakespeare, Green
(1870) was pioneering, but his over-enthusiasm leads to arbitrariness in
claiming emblem influence, and to the plays being treated merely as
arenas for source-hunting. Some problems and pitfalls of identifying
emblematic material in Shakespeare are usefully discussed by Peter
Daly in Fabiny 1984: 156–75. The bibliography below includes a few
examples of critical literature on the formal or structural use of
emblems in Shakespeare, not related to any particular emblem book he
may have known (such as Manning 1994), and on emblems as
analogues for Shakespeare (Simonds 1992 is unusual among them in
dealing with emblematic and related aspects of a single play at book
length). A more comprehensive bibliography can be found in Daly
1993, in five sections: Bibliographies; General Articles on the Emblem;
The Emblem as Genre and Form; Shakespeare, Imagery and the
Visual Arts; Specialized Studies of Shakespeare.

Andresen, Martha (1974). ' "Ripeness is all": Sententiae and Commonplaces in *King Lear*', pp. 145–68 in Rosalie L. Colie and F. T. Flahiff, eds, *Some Facets of King Lear: Essays in Prismatic Criticism*. London.

Bath, Michael (1986). 'Weeping Stags and Melancholy Lovers: The Iconography of *As You Like It* II.i' *Emblematica* 1: 13–52.

—— (1994). *Speaking Pictures: English Emblem Books and Renaissance Culture*. London.

Butler, Guy (1984). 'Shakespeare's Cliff at Dover and an Emblem Illustration.' *HLQ* 47: 226–31.

Daly, Peter M. (1993). *Teaching Shakespeare and the Emblem: A Lecture and a Bibliography*. Acadia.

Dundas, Judith (1983). 'Shakespeare's Imagery: Emblem and the Imitation of Nature.' *ShSt* 16: 45–56.

Fabiny, Tibor, ed. (1984). *Shakespeare and the Emblem: Studies in Renaissance Iconography and Iconology*. Szeged, Hungary.

Freeman, Rosemary (1967). *English Emblem Books*. London (first published 1948).

Green, Henry (1870). *Shakespeare and the Emblem Writers*. London.

Herford, C. H., Percy and Evelyn Simpson, eds (1925–51). *Ben Jonson*, 8 vols. Oxford.

Hoyle, James (1971). 'Some Emblems in Shakespeare's *Henry IV* Plays.' *ELH* 38: 512–27.

Iwasaki, Soji (1973). '*Veritas filia temporis* and Shakespeare.' *ELR* 3: 249–63.

Manning, John (1994). '*Symbola* and *Emblemata* in *Hamlet*', pp. 11–18 in Mark Thornton Burnett and John Manning, eds, *New Essays on 'Hamlet'*. New York.

Mehl, Dieter (1969). 'Emblems in English Renaissance Drama.' *RenD* 2: 39–57.

Pellegrini, G. (1964). 'Symbols and Significances: "All such emblems".' *ShSu* 17: 180–7.

Praz, Mario (1964). *Studies in Seventeenth-Century Imagery*. London (first published 1939, expanded 1947).

Richards, Bernard (1980). 'Whitney's Influence on Shakespeare's Sonnets 111 and 112, and on Donne's Third Satire.' *N&Q* 225: 160–1.

Rosenblum, Joseph (1981). 'Why an Ass?: Cesare Ripa's *Iconologia* as a Source for Bottom's Translation.' *ShQ* 32: 357–9.

Simonds, Peggy Muñoz (1992). *Myth, Emblem and Music in Shakespeare's 'Cymbeline': An Iconographic Reconstruction*. Newark, DE.

Steadman, John M. (1979). *Nature into Myth: Medieval and Renaissance Moral Symbols*. Pittsburgh.

Waddington, Raymond B. (1976). '*The Merchant of Venice* III.i.108–113: Transforming an Emblem.' *ELN* 14: 92–8.

Young, Alan R. (1976). 'Othello's "Flaming Minister" and Renaissance Emblem Literature.' *English Studies in Canada* 2: 1–7.

—— (1985). 'A Note on the Tournament Impresas in *Pericles*.' *ShQ* 36: 453–6.

—— (1987). *Tudor and Jacobean Tournaments*. London.

Erasmus, Desiderius (*c.* 1466–1536), Dutch Humanist, Biblical Scholar and Writer

(A) The natural son of a cleric, Erasmus became an Augustinian canon and a priest, ordained in 1492. He studied and taught in Paris and later in several other European centres of learning, including Oxford (1499) and as a professor at Cambridge (1509–14). He settled in Basle in 1521, later leaving its atmosphere of religious dissent for Freiburg. He was for much of his lifetime the pre-eminent scholar and controversialist of Europe, welcomed by princes, protected by emperors, and in later years offered a cardinal's hat. Broadly, he saw his life's work as being to present the intellectual and moral ideas of Greek and Roman antiquity to his contemporaries as a direct means of enriching the civilization of his time. This took many forms, including school textbooks, manuals and examples of good style, translations, editorial work, specialist treatises, literary entertainments, and often a combination of several of these things at once, as for example in his *Collectanea Adagiorum Veterum*, 1500. This was an anthology of (eventually) over 5,000 adages taken from Greek and Latin literature, in expounding which Erasmus sets out the principles of right thinking and right conduct as he conceived them, in his usual stylistic combination of the lapidary and epigrammatic qualities of Latin with personal élan. His *Enchiridion Militis Christiani* ('Handbook of the Militant Christian', or in its earliest translation 'Manual of a Christian Knight', 1503) and *Instituto Principis Christiani* ('The Education of the Christian Prince', 1516) stressed the importance of learning to the Christian life. The *Moriae Encomium* ('Praise of Folly', 1511, written for Sir Thomas **More**) is a satire on the Church but also on human pretensions at large. Erasmus' supreme talents as an educator are evident in the *Colloquia Familiaria* ('Familiar Conversations', 1518 onwards), a collection of dialogues which teach both good Latin expression and a humane way of life. His 1516 edition and translation of the Greek New Testament was epoch-making in bringing the original texts to bear on traditional biblical interpretation; but his free-thinking humanism frequently brought him into confrontation with the Church whose unity he nevertheless cherished.

(B) Erasmus was the most extensively influential writer of the Northern Renaissance, in many quarters and at many levels, at the centre of which was the humanist enterprise in its educational, religious and political aspects. Especially important in England was the adoption of his educational and literary principles at St Paul's School, with whose founding by Colet he was closely connected, since St Paul's became a prototype for Tudor grammar schools, including Stratford's (see Baldwin 1944: I, 118–84). But a full account of Erasmus' place in sixteenth-century English culture would require many words (for English translations see Devereux's 1983 bibliography). Some illustrations are instead given here of English-language renderings of his three works most strongly associated with Shakespeare.

The *Praise of Folly* was first Englished by Sir Thomas Chaloner (1520–1565), a well-known diplomat and solder as well as translator, in 1549; his version was reissued in ?1560, 1576, and in the later seventeenth century. Chaloner's tangy English here renders Folly's complaints of life's sufferings and, second, her promotion of foolishness as a remedy, notions easily paralleled in the tragedies (perhaps especially *Hamlet*) and elsewhere in Shakespeare:

> Admitte than, some one, (as the *Poetes* feigne by *Jupiter*) shulde out of an high high place behold and see in how many miseries mans life is wrapped, how wretched and vile his byrthe is, how harde his bring-yng up, how weake and pewlyng his childhode, how travailsome his youthe, how heavy his age, and last how feareful his death were. Further, duryng all his lyfe, what bandes of sickenesses doe assaile hym, what narow chaunces hange over his head, what displeasures come upon hym, how in all thynges he fyndeth more galle than hony, besydes the injuries whiche one of you scourgeth an other withall, as povertee, enprisonment, worldely shame, rebukyng, rackyng, gyle, treason, sklaunder, discencion, disceite (but now *I goe about to tell the gravell of the sea*) that for what offences men deserved suche miseries,

or what god beyng theyr heavie lorde, condemned theim to leade their lyves so pestred and plonged in the same, ye shall perdon me, from expressing, as not leeful for me at this present to utter unto you.

... suche ideotes are free, and exempt from all feare of death, whiche feare is no small corrosive, to a mind that mindeth it I warrant you. Lyke as they fele not what a twitching turment it is, to have a grudged conscience, and shrinke as little at these oldwives tales of sprites, of divelles, of hobgoblyne and the fayries, neither mournyng to theim selves for feare of evilles and adversitees impendyng, nor braggyng overmuche upon hope of any good lucke commyng. To be briefe, they are not tawed, nor pluckt a sunder with a thousande thousand cares, wherwith other men are oppressed. Thei blushe at nothyng, they doubt nothyng, they coveite no dignitee, they envie no mans fortune, they love not peramours: and lastly if they be veraie brute *Naturalles*, now they sinne not, as doctours doe affirme.

(1549 text, ed. Miller 1965: 40–1, 48; italic for bold)

Richard Taverner (1501?–1575) was the first translator of some of Erasmus' *Adages* in 1569 (over a hundred editions of the original had been published by this date, and Sir Thomas **Elyot**'s Latin dictionary, 1538 and 1559, had already included a good number of the proverbs, as did later sixteenth-century dictionaries and collections of proverbs by such writers as John **Florio**). This exposition of the proverb 'Nosce tempus' has been thought to lie behind Lucrece's lament in *The Rape of Lucrece* (see (C)):

Nosce tempus.

Know time. Oportunitie is of such force, that of honest it maketh unhonest, of dammage avauntage, of pleasure, grevaunce, of a good turne a shrewed turne, and contrariwise of unhonest honest, of avauntage dammage, and brieflie to conclude it cleane chaungeth the nature of thinges. This oportunitie or occasion (for so also ye maye call it in aventuringe and finishinge a busines) doubtles beareth the chiefe stroke, so that not without good skill the painims of old time counted it a divine thinge.

And in this wise they painted her. They made her a goddesse standing with fethered feete uppon a whele, and turning her self about the circle therof most swiftely, beinge on the former part of her

head more hearie and on the hinder part balde, so that by the fore
parte she may easely be caught, but by the hinder part not so.

(1569 text, ed. Starnes 1956: fo. 23^{r-v})

Finally, the volume of *Colloquies*, though initially designed to teach
good Latin to beginners, became in its gradually augmented forms a
vehicle for Erasmus' views on the most serious of subjects (for example,
philosophical and religious), presented with a lightness and grace that
made them an entertainment too. 'Proci et puellae' is a dialogue
between a girl, Maria, and a suitor, Pamphilus, which includes among
other things a wittily developed case against the over-valuation of
virginity. Nicholas Leigh's translation appeared in 1568:

Pam. . . . Tell me if you had a goodly orchyarde plat, whether
woulde you wish nothing should therein grow but blossomes, or else
had you rather (the blossomes fallen away) beholde your trees fraught
and laden with pleasaunt fruite?

Maria. Howe sliely he reasoneth.

Pam. At the least aunswere me to this: whether is it a better sight
for a Vine to lye uppon the grounde and rot, or the same to embrace
a poale, or an elme, and lode it full with purple grapes?

Maria. Now sir aunswere me to this againe, whether is it a more
pleasant sight a Rose trim and milke white, yet growing on his stalk,
or the same plucked with the hande and by little and little withering
awaye?

Pam. Certes in mine opinion the rose is the happiest, and commeth
to the better ende which withereth and dieth in the hande of man,
delighting in the meane while both the eies and nosethrils, than
thother which withereth on the bush, for there muste it needes wither
also at length, even as that wine hath better luck which is drunken,
than that which standeth still, and is turned into vinigar. And yet the
flowring beautie of a woman doth not decay forthwith as soone as
she is maried, for I know some my selfe, who before they were
maried, were pale colored, faint, and as it were pined away, who by
the friendly felowship of an husband, have waxed so faire and welfa-
voured, that you would think they never came to the flower of their
beautie till then.

Ma. But for all your saying, virginity is a thing much beloved and
liked with all men.

155

> *Pam.* I graunt you, a yong woman, a virgine, is a fayre, and goodly thing, but what by course of kind is more unseemly than an old wrinkled maide: Had not your mother bene contented to lose the flower of hir virginitie, surely we had not had this flower of your beautie. So that in case (as I hope) our mariage be not barren, for the losse of one virgine we shall paye God manye.
>
> (Leigh 1568: sig. B7^{r-v}, paragraphing added)

(C) That the Erasmian spirit seems generally to echo through Shakespeare's plays would be widely agreed. The principal works to have been connected with them are the *Colloquies*, *Praise of Folly* and *Adagia*. But it is on many occasions of resemblance between the two writers impossible to determine whether Shakespeare's reading was in Erasmus or one of the many possible intermediaries. The extremely wide diffusion of Erasmian ideas as well as writings in the sixteenth century means that it goes almost without saying, for example, that the *Instituto Principis Christiani* lies somewhere in the background of *Henry V*, but a tabulation of 'parallels' (such as Walter 1954) may look very inconclusive.

At other times, however, more substantial or cumulative evidence can indicate direct use fairly clearly. For example, the colloquy 'Proci et puellae' contains the sentence 'Ego rosam existimo feliciorem, quae marescit in hominis manu, delectans interim et oculos et nares, quam quae senescit in fruitice' (see (B) for Leigh's translation). There is a resemblance here to a number of passages in the poems and plays, such as the following lines of *A Midsummer Night's Dream* (as was pointed out by Malone):

> But earthlier happy is the rose distill'd
> Than that which withering on the virgin thorn
> Grows, lives, and dies, in single blessedness.
>
> (1.1.76–8)

Of course, the commonness of the idea, and the fact that the *Colloquies* were so pervasively used as an elementary text, seem to rule out a secure connection. However, this colloquy is echoed elsewhere in Shakespeare. Possible reminiscences of it in *Much Ado*, the *Sonnets*, *The Comedy of Errors* and *All's Well that Ends Well* (see Baldwin 1944: I, 737–8) are proposed by more commentators than one, and the verbal echoes especially in Act I of *All's Well* (noted by Hunter 1962 and Simonds 1989), though of limited importance in themselves, support the hypothesis that other features of the dialogue helped suggest the play's incidental use of the archetypes of marital myth, Venus, Mars and Cupid (see Snyder 1993: 7–8). Woodbridge (1983) proposes another use of 'Proci et puellae' as the 'germ' of *As You Like It*'s scepticism and mockery of the Petrarchan conventions, and finds echoes of the other colloquy translated in Leigh's little 1568 volume (see (B)), 'Adolescens et scorti', in several other plays. And Shakespeare's use of one or two colloquies may further suggest he knew others. Hosley (1963–4: 299–300) proposes 'Conjugium', in English translation, for *The Taming of the Shrew*, Miller (1986) two others for a line in *Hamlet*, and Muir (1956) the 'Funus' for *Measure for Measure*, a context coupling the names of Barnadine and Vincentio with a story involving a friar. But 'one is likely to be more impressed with coincidences in spirit between Erasmus and Shakespeare than in mere . . . information' (Baldwin 1944: I, 741) – coincidences in, for instance, the *Colloquies'* word-play and other forms of wit.

Baldwin's observation applies still more strongly to the *Praise of Folly*, which has very frequently been offered as a source for Shakespeare, especially for his interest in the figure of the wise, critical fool (for general accounts of the relationship see Welsford 1935: 236ff.; Goldsmith 1955; Kaiser 1964; and Corti 1998: 13–40). Erasmus' Folly makes points similar to Lear's Fool about sane lunatics in a mad world, and Erasmus' presentation of Christian 'folly' can be linked with Cordelia's – 'the similarities between Cordelia's foolish conduct and Christ's are unmistakable, particularly when one sees the imagery refracted through *The Praise of Folly*' (Evans 1990: 15). Some of what Jacques and other characters in *As You Like It* say about folly and wisdom is also to be found in Erasmus (Rea 1919; Aoki 1979), as likewise are analogues for the passion/madness themes of *A Midsummer Night's Dream* (Birkinshaw 1992) and an intermediate source for Bottom's mock-Pauline description of his dream (Palmer 1987). Possibly the qualities of Thersites, and the large number of references to folly in *Troilus and Cressida*, can also be ascribed to its influence (so Henderson 1935). And in general, the Lucianic temper of the *Praise of Folly* has often struck readers as Shakespearean (see especially Sacton 1949; Aoki 1979). A detailed case has been mounted for this work's pervasive effect on *Hamlet* (McCombie 1974), though one can grant a sometimes remarkably similar quality of

157

thought in the play's hero without either taking it as evidence of Shakespeare's close and immediate use of Erasmus or accepting other claimed parallels, on such notoriously common topoi as madness, the court, Fortune and the deceptiveness of appearances.

Erasmus' *Adagia*, in its various incarnations (especially the Taverner translation) through the sixteenth century and beyond, was an easier and, to judge by the number of editions, far more widely read text than the *Praise of Folly*, partly because of school use. As elsewhere, this diffusion must tend to cover up Erasmus' tracks, when proximate sources offer closer resemblances. And, like several of Erasmus' other works, this is a text in which Shakespeare could easily have drawn suggestions from the authors cited rather than from Erasmus' own words. For example, Baldwin (1950: 134–6) and Muir (1956) show how his combination of two quotations from **Horace** could have been the origin of a stanza in *The Rape of Lucrece* (855–61). Hence Shakespeare might be drawing on the *Adages* when he may appear to be using other sources. Again, Erasmus' presentation here and in the *Praise of Folly* of the Silenic Socrates is a more likely source for the Socratic Falstaff than the dialogues of **Plato** (Tiffany 1999). More straightforwardly, it is very likely that Taverner's 1569 *Adages*, the earliest English version of some proverbs, is connected with Shakespeare's use of several sayings. Three examples must suffice here. The best explanation of 'good wine needs no bush' in the Epilogue of *As You Like It* is in Taverner's exposition of the adage 'Vino vendibili suspense hedera nihil opus': 'Wyne that is saleable and good needeth no bushe or garlande of yvie to be hanged before' (ed. Starnes 1956: fo. 39ᵛ). Ulysses' 'wallet of oblivion' (*Troilus and Cressida* 3.3.145–6) is glossed by Taverner's disquisition on 'Non videmus manticae quod in tergo est': 'We loke not what is in the wallet behynde' (ed. Starnes 1956: fo. 57ʳ). And Taverner's comment on 'Nosce tempus' (in (B)) has been thought to stand behind Lucrece's diatribe on opportunity in *The Rape of Lucrece* 876–924 (Bush 1927: 301–2).

Finally, Erasmus' *De Parabolis Sive Similia*, a collection of wise sayings designed to instil ethical values, is connected with details of *The Two Gentlemen of Verona* by Baldwin (1944: II, 350); with Sonnet 60 by Stanivukovic (1990); and with Shakespeare's twice-repeated comparison of a troubled mind to a fountain by Soellner (1956).

(D) The literature on Erasmus and Shakespeare is very miscellaneous. Baldwin (1944) is a solid starting-point, but perhaps also a stolid one:

Jones (1977: 9–13) has a lighter touch. Despite their title, the essays in Corti (1998) are largely on Shakespeare, and so constitute the most recent gathering of such work. For the influence, doubtless indirect, of Erasmus' *De copia* on Shakespeare's way of writing in general, see Trousdale (1982: 39ff.).

Baldwin (1944); Baldwin (1950); Jones (1977).

Andrews, Michael Cameron (1987). 'Erasmus and *Macbeth*: "Making the green one red".' *Erasmus in English* 15.viii: 30–1.

Aoki, Kazuo (1979). '*The Praise of Folly* and Shakespeare's Early and Middle Comedies.' *Shakespeare Studies* (Japan) 18: 1–27.

Baines, Barbara J. (1982). 'Shakespeare's Plays and the Erasmian Box.' *Renaissance Papers*, 1981: 33–44.

Battenhouse, Roy (1985). '*Henry V* in the Light of Erasmus.' *ShSt* 17: 77–88.

Birkinshaw, Catharine (1992). '"Past the Wit of Man": *A Midsummer Night's Dream*'s Debt to *Praise of Folly*.' *Shakespeare in Southern Africa: Journal of the Shakespeare Society of Southern Africa* 5: 43–58.

Bush, Douglas (1927). 'Notes on Shakespeare's Classical Mythology.' *PQ* 6: 295–302.

Corti, Claudia, ed. (1998). *Silenos: Erasmus in Elizabethan Literature*. Ospedaletto.

Devereux, E. J. (1983). *Renaissance English Translations of Erasmus: A Bibliography to 1700*. Toronto (first published as *A Checklist of English Translations of Erasmus to 1700*, London, 1968).

Evans, John X. (1990). 'Erasmian Folly and Shakespeare's *King Lear*: A Study in Humanist Intertextuality.' *Moreana: Bulletin Thomas More* 103 (series 27): 3–23.

Goldsmith, Robert H. (1955). *Wise Fools in Shakespeare*. East Lansing.

Henderson, W. B. Drayton (1935). 'Shakespeare's *Troilus and Cressida*: Yet Deeper in its Tradition', pp. 127–56 in Hardin Craig, ed., *Essays in Dramatic Literature: The Parrott Presentation Volume*. Princeton (reprinted New York, 1967).

Hosley, Richard (1963–4). 'Sources and Analogues of *The Taming of the Shrew*.' *HLQ* 27: 289–308.

Hunter, G. K. ed. (1962). *All's Well that Ends Well* (Arden Shakespeare). London (first published 1959).

Kaiser, Walter (1964). *Praisers of Folly: Erasmus, Rabelais, Shakespeare*. London.

L[eigh], N[icholas] (1568). *A Modest Meane to Mariage, pleasauntly set foorth by that Famous Clarke Erasmus Roterodamus, and translated into Englishe.* London.

McCombie, Frank (1974). '*Hamlet* and the *Moriae Encomium*.' *ShSu* 27: 59–69.

Miller, Anthony (1986). 'A Reminiscence of Erasmus in *Hamlet*, III.ii. 92–95.' *ELN* 24: 19–22.

Miller, Clarence H., ed. (1965). *The praise of folie; [translated] by Sir Thomas Chaloner* (Early English Text Society 257). London.

Muir, Kenneth (1956). 'Shakespeare and Erasmus.' *N&Q* 201: 424–5.

Palmer, D. J. (1987). 'Bottom, St. Paul, and Erasmus' *Praise of Folly*', pp. 112–13 in *KM 80: A Birthday Album for Kenneth Muir*. Liverpool.

Rea, John D. (1919). 'Jacques in Praise of Folly.' *MP* 17: 465–9.

Sacton, Alexander H. (1949). 'The Paradoxical Encomium in Elizabethan Drama.' *University of Texas Studies in English* 28: 83–104.

Simonds, Peggy Muñoz (1989). 'Sacred and Sexual Motifs in *All's Well that Ends Well*.' *RenQ* 42: 33–59.

Snyder, Susan, ed. (1993). *All's Well that Ends Well* (Oxford Shakespeare). Oxford.

Soellner, Rolf (1956). 'The Troubled Fountain: Erasmus Formulates a Shakespearean Simile.' *JEGP* 55: 70–4.

Stanivukovic, Goran (1990). 'The Erasmian Echo in Shakespeare's Sonnet 60.' *N&Q* 235: 173–5.

Starnes, DeWitt T., ed. (1956). *Proverbs or Adages by Desiderius Erasmus . . . Englished (1569) by Richard Taverner*. Delmar, N.Y.

Tiffany, Grace (1999). 'Shakespeare's Dionysian Prince: Drama, Politics, and the "Athenian" History Play.' *RenQ* 52: 366–83.

Trousdale, Marion (1982). *Shakespeare and the Rhetoricians*. London.

Walter, J. H., ed. (1954). *King Henry V* (Arden Shakespeare). London.

Welsford, Enid (1935). *The Fool: His Social and Literary History*. London.

Woodbridge, L. T. (1983). 'Shakespeare's Use of Two Erasmian Colloquies.' *N&Q* 228: 122–3.

Euripides (*c.* 484–?406 BC), Greek Tragedian

(A) The last of the three Greek tragedians, the younger rival of **Aeschylus** and **Sophocles**, Euripides is said to have lived mostly in seclusion in Salamis, moving late in life to the Macedonian court. He wrote in all some ninety plays, of which eighteen tragedies and one satyr play survive in full – a higher proportion than for his elder contemporaries, reflecting his greater popularity in ancient times. His plays are often regarded as focusing especially strongly on individuals, notably women. Such is the case with what are today his best-known tragedies, which include *Medea*, *Hippolytus*, *The Trojan Women* and *The Bacchae*. He is usually thought of as the 'modernist' among Greek tragedians, reflecting the rationalist priorities of his generation and hence interested much more in man than in the gods whom he seems almost to make into natural forces. Formally, Euripides is known for his use of naturalistic dialogue, prologues and epilogues, and recognition scenes.

(B) Like the other Greek tragedians, Euripides was not often a curricular author in the age of Shakespeare, and sixteenth-century editions tended to be expensive and philologically oriented. Latin translations existed, including the more than merely functional ones by the Scottish humanist George **Buchanan**, though, again, the standard *en face* versions were not designed for the Greekless. But Euripides was more frequently translated, and imitated, than the supposedly more difficult Aeschylus and Sophocles; his emphasis on depicting human emotions, his realistic style, prominent use of rhetoric, and *sententiae* made him more congenial. A translation by Jane, Lady Lumley, of the *Iphigenia in Aulis* (1550s) is credited as the first Englishing of a Greek tragedy. In several cases, however, Euripides' works were overshadowed by the more familiar Senecan texts based on Euripidean subjects. The existence of the well-known plays by **Seneca** on the Medea and Hippolytus stories tended to deter readers from delving into the little-known Euripidean ones. This was probably less on account of their inaccessibility (see below for editions and translations) than of the greater compatibility of Senecan drama with the indigenous products of the *De Casibus* tradition and the English tastes deriving from it. The Greek tragedians were sometimes promoted by the learned, as in Ascham's oft-quoted verdict of 1570 (in *The Schoolmaster*) that 'the Grecians Sophocles and Euripides far over match our Seneca in Latin, namely in *Oikonomia et Decoro* [structure and ornament], although Senecas elocution and verse be verie commendable for his time'. On other occasions they were not, as when J. C. Scaliger declared the majesty of Seneca no less than Euripides', and his cultivation greater (*Poetices Libri Septem*, v, 16).

Priorities within the Euripidean corpus were not those of today. The *Hecuba*, *Iphigenia in Aulis* and *Phoenician Women* were admired in the

Renaissance as in the Byzantine schools. The first and second were translated into Latin by **Erasmus**. The last, singled out by Renaissance commentators such as Neander for its ethical teaching, was the subject of one of the three fully documented sixteenth-century performances of Greek tragedy in England, at Gray's Inn in 1566. But the English play performed, with spectacular stage effects, under the title *Jocasta* (by George **Gascoigne** and Francis Kinwelmersh) is at three removes from Euripides, being based on Ludovico Dolce's partly Senecanized Italian version *Giocasta*, in turn drawing on a Latin translation of the Greek text. The Gray's Inn play, the staging plans for which survive in a British Library manuscript, transposes Euripides' delicately balanced ironies to 'a dramatic universe where good and evil are clearly demarcated' (Smith 1988: 221). A sturdy moral framework in the dialogue itself is underpinned by the presentation of emblematic figures and dumbshows on stage before each act, harking back to the **Morality tradition**, and Senecan choruses moralizing on ambition and Fortune, with no counterpart in Euripides. Such a concern is also evident in Oedipus' final speech, which adapts Euripides to turn the protagonist into a victim of Fortune, and the first lines of which are accompanied in the first edition by the marginal note 'A mirror for Magistrates':

> Deare citizens, beholde your Lord and King
> That Thebes set in quiet government,
> Now as you see, neglected of you all,
> And in these ragged ruthfull weedes bewrapt,
> Ychased from his native countrey soyle,
> Betakes himself (for so this tirant will)
> To everlasting banishment: but why
> Do I lament my lucklesse lot in vaine?
> 'Since every man must beare with quiet minde,
> The fate that heavens have earst to him assignde'.
> (1566 text; ed. Cunliffe 1907: 1, 324)

(C) The traditional position on Shakespeare's knowledge of Euripides is as with other Greek tragedy: it is non-existent, or only arrived at through the extensive filtration provided by Seneca. Though this has been challenged in recent years, it is still orthodox. Where there is no Senecan version of a Euripidean play, other intermediary sources are sometimes proposed, as in the notion that Hamlet's similarities to Euripides' Orestes (conflict with the avenging Furies resulting in madness but not matricide) derive from a lost play associated with **Dekker** and Henry Chettle, *Orestes Furious* or *Orestes' Furies* (Schleiner 1990). Nuttall (1989: 8–9), speaking particularly of *The Winter's Tale*, offers an alternative suggestion, that Shakespeare 'instinctively' recognized the Greek tragedy outlines behind **Plautus**, in order to reconcile his claims for the strongest 'similarity' or 'congruity' ('if we read, not as source-hunters but as critics, we shall see that late Euripides is *like* late Shakespeare as no other dramatist is') with the acceptance that 'there is only the most tenuous and speculative historical connection'. Or Shakespeare is on occasion imagined as having imbibed Euripidean qualities from the atmosphere more generally – but one may accept that a play such as *Troilus and Cressida* has Euripidean features without Euripides' actually constituting a source (see Arnold 1984).

More verifiable are the specific cases of Shakespeare's possible use of *Hecuba* in *Titus Andronicus* and *Iphigenia in Aulis* in *Julius Caesar*. Jones (1977: 118) was the first to propose them, stopping short of categorical claims. In the first case the principal bases are the structural similarities of dual suffering and revenge, the 'posture which Hecuba assumes as the protagonist of a drama, and . . . the degree of identification she elicits', and 'the superb swing of the action' (Jones 1977: 103). This is vague. In any event, since the story of Hecuba appears also in *Metamorphoses* XIII, the choice of influences 'is between Ovid alone and Ovid together with Euripides' (Jones 1977: 102). With *Julius Caesar* the case is limited to one scene, the quarrel between Brutus and Cassius (4.3). This scene is based primarily on **Plutarch**, but may owe something to the confrontation between Agamemnon and Menelaus near the start of the *Iphigenia in Aulis* (one of the plays translated by the prestigious hand of Erasmus): in both cases a bitter quarrel is unexpectedly followed by an undertaking of renewed friendship.

Overall, not enough has been done by proponents of Euripides as a Shakespeare source to convert these resemblances into positive evidences of influence, or to overturn the view that 'Seneca was the closest Shakespeare ever came to Greek tragedy, but . . . that was quite close enough' (Martindale 1990: 44).

(D) Jones (1977) is the basis of most of the subsequent discussion, and later literature makes less concrete (or, like for example Bryant, mainly comparative) claims. Schleiner provides a brief account of how Euripides was read in Shakespeare's time, with some suggestions on the transmission of *Alcestis* to Shakespeare via Latin renderings, and Smith a fuller one of the sixteenth-century staging of Greek tragedies.

Baldwin (1944); Jones (1977); Martindale (1990).

Arnold, Margaret J. (1984). ' "Monsters in Love's Train": Euripides and Shakespeare's *Troilus and Cressida*.' *CompD* 18: 38–53.

Bryant, A. J., Jr (1982). '*Julius Caesar* from a Euripidean Perspective.' *CompD* 16: 97–111 (reprinted pp. 144–58 in Clifford Davidson, Rand Johnson and John H. Stroupe, eds, *Drama and the Classical Heritage: Comparative and Critical Essays*, New York, 1993.)

Cunliffe, John W., ed. (1907). *The Complete Works of George Gascoigne*, 2 vols. Cambridge.

Nuttall, A. D. (1989). *The Stoic in Love: Selected Essays on Literature and Ideas*. London.

Schleiner, Louise (1990). 'Latinized Greek Drama in Shakespeare's Writing of *Hamlet*.' *ShQ* 41: 29–48.

Smith, Bruce R. (1988). *Ancient Scripts and Modern Experience on the English Stage 1500–1700*. Princeton.

Sohmer, Steve (1997). 'What Cicero Said.' *N&Q* 242: 56–8.

Stump, Donald V. (1983). 'Greek and Shakespearean Tragedy: Four Indirect Routes from Athens to London', pp. 211–46 in Stump *et al.*, eds, *Hamartia: The Concept of Error in the Western Tradition: Essays in Honor of John M. Crossett*. New York.

Wilson, Douglas B. (1984). 'Euripides' *Alcestis* and the Ending of Shakespeare's *The Winter's Tale*.' *Iowa State Journal of Research* 58: 345–55.

Eustachio (Eustachius), Bartolommeo (*c.* 1507–1574), Medical Writer Gross (1984) disposes of previous claims that the method of poisoning in *Hamlet* indicates Shakespeare's familiarity with Eustacius' *De Auditus Organis*.

Gross, Dalton, and Mary Jean Gross (1984). 'Shakespeare, Eustachio, Marlowe, and Hamlet.' *N&Q* 229: 199–200.

Evanthius See **Terence (Publius Terentius Afer)**.

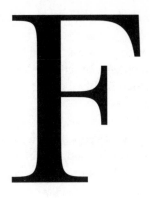

Fabyan, Robert (d. 1513), Chronicler

(A) Fabyan was a wealthy merchant, a member of the Draper's Company, and in 1493–4 Sheriff of London. He resigned as an alderman in 1502 to avoid the expense of becoming mayor. An amateur historian, he expanded his diary into a full-blown history of England, completed according to the author in 1504 and published posthumously in 1516. It was edited by Richard Pynson, and covered the years to 1485. A second edition by William Rastell (1533) brought the narrative down through the reign of Henry VII, a later one still (1559) down to Elizabeth. By this time it was titled and referred to as *Fabyan's Chronicle*. Like other sixteenth-century chronicles, Fabyan's is often an assemblage of work by earlier writers, but he also uses such testimony (oral or archival) as lay to hand for a member of the London city government. It is this feature that has proved of special interest to students of Tudor England, allowing as it does the view of the city, not merely of other chroniclers or propagandists, to be discerned. Otherwise, 'Fabyan wrote in the owlish spirit of a medieval chronicler, gathering his facts largely for their own sake and presenting them from a naïvely providential point of view' (Reese 1961: 49).

(B) Fabyan's work was aptly described in the ***Mirror for Magistrates***: 'Unfruitful Fabyan followed the face / Of time and deeds but let the causes slip.' Since his work provided data for subsequent writers (initially other chroniclers) it was not wholly unfruitful, however, and his uncritical style of history was not superseded until much later in the sixteenth century.

Fabyan recounts in this sample section the failed invasion by Margaret, the French Queen of Henry VI, following Edward IV's reassumption of the throne in 1471. The lacunae reflect the imperfect state of his information.

Repossessio Edwardi Quarti.

Edwarde the. iiii. before named, began agayne his domynyon over the realme of Englande the. xiiii. daye of Apryll, in the begynnynge of the yere of our Lorde. M.CCCC.lxxi. and the. xii. yere of Lowys the Frenshe kynge, and repossedyd all thynges as he before had done. And when the said. ii. corps hadde lyen in Paulys openly from the Sondaye tyll the Tuysdaye, they were hadde from thens and buryed where the kynge wolde assygne them.

The kynge thanne beynge in auctorytie, made provycion for the defence of landynge of quene Margarete and [her] sone, the whiche all this whyle laye at the see syde taryinge the wynde, and soo lastly landyd at   , and came with a strength of Frenshmen and other, as far within the lande as to a vyllage in   called Tewkysbury, where the kynge mette with her and [her] distressyd, and chasyd her company and slewe many of theym. In the whiche batayll she was taken, and sir Edwarde her sone, and so brought unto the kynge. But after the kynge hadde questyoned with the sayd sir Edwarde, and he had answeryd unto hym contrarye his pleasure, he thenne strake hym with his gauntelet upon the face: after whiche stroke so by hym receyved, he was by the kynges servauntes incontynently slayne upon the. iiii. day of the moneth of May.

Whan kynge Edwarde hadde thus subduyd his enemyes, anone he sent quene Margarete unto London, where she restyd a season, and fynally she was sent home into her countre.

(Fabyan 1811: 661–2)

(C) The largely unadorned blow-by-blow narrative of Fabyan's Chronicle is a somewhat unpromising source for a dramatist, but it is accepted that Shakespeare used it here and there in *Henry VI* and *Richard III*, perhaps having gone to it merely in search of information. The uncertainties of the matter have to do, as usually with chronicle sources, with the recycling of one compiler's material by others, for example

Fabyan being drawn upon by **Stow**. However, Boswell-Stone (1907: 213, 221, 225) was able to demonstrate Fabyan's contribution of details in two or three scenes of *1 Henry VI*. The two strongest cases, at 1.3.57–78 and 3.1.76–103, are scenes set in London and involving the Lord Mayor, the type of details about which Fabyan is especially informative (see also for comment Wilson 1952: xxxv–xxxviii). Where *Richard III* is concerned, Churchill summarizes Fabyan's account of Richard, stressing the special interest of his details on Prince Edward's death (in (B)): 'Here for the first time, thirty years after the event, do we meet with the statement that the prince was captured in the battle and brought to the king' (1900: 74).

(D)
Boswell-Stone, W. G. (1907). *Shakespeare's Holinshed: The Chronicle and the Plays Compared.* London.

Churchill, George B. (1900). *Richard the Third up to Shakespeare.* Berlin.

Fabyan, Robert (1811). *The New Chronicles of England and France, in Two Parts; named . . . the Concordance of Histories. Reprinted from Pynson's Edition of 1516.* London.

Reese, M. M. (1961). *The Cease of Majesty: A Study of Shakespeare's History Plays.* London.

Wilson, John Dover, ed. (1952). *King John* (New Shakespeare). Cambridge.

Famous Victories of Henry V, The See **Chronicle History Plays**.

Fenton, Sir Geoffrey (Geffraie) See **Bandello**, **Matteo**; **Belleforest**, **François de**.

Ferrers, George See *Mirror for Magistrates, A*.

Fiorentino, Giovanni (14th Century), Italian Novelist
(A) Almost nothing is known of the life of Fiorentino ('Ser Giovanni'), whose real name appears to have been Giovanni Antonio degli Antonii,

167

except that he was a notary. His collection of stories *Il Pecorone* ('The Big Sheep', i.e. 'The Big Fool') was written about 1378 and eventually published in Milan in 1558. The fifty novellas are intended to emulate **Boccaccio**'s, but, unlike those in the *Decameron*, they are often awkwardly written and have no overall unity. In the framing story the narrators are two lovers, a monk and a nun, conversing in the parlour of the monastery at Forlì.

(B) There is no known sixteenth-century English translation of the complete *Pecorone*, but Fiorentino was adapted and discussed at this time, although it is unlikely he was 'almost as well known as Boccaccio' (Scott 1916: xli) to the Elizabethans. The ninety-fifth debate or declamation in **Silvayn**'s *Orator* (1581; English translation 1596), for example, deals with the moral issues raised by Fiorentino's tale of Giannetto of Venice (see (C)). Two works associated with Richard Tarlton in 1580–90, *News out of Purgatorie* and *Cobbler of Canterburie*, also respond to Fiorentino's book.

(C) Shakespeare clearly used Fiorentino's story of Giannetto of Venice and the Lady of Belmont, the first story of the fourth day, for *The Merchant of Venice*, and gives every appearance of knowing it directly, in the Italian. (Modern translations of the Italian text are given in Brown 1964; Satin 1966; and Bullough.) The plots resemble each other closely, despite no known English translation having been available, and there are, moreover, verbal parallels with the original. Though it is not possible to rule out the existence in the 1590s of a translation (printed or manuscript) which has not survived, these facts constitute some of the strongest evidence available that Shakespeare had a reading knowledge of Italian (for other evidence see Shaheen 1994).

The stories match especially well for the latter half, corresponding to Shakespeare's Acts 3–5, but the casket plot is not part of the Italian narrative. In Fiorentino, the Bassanio figure, Giannetto, is sent to seek his fortune by his godfather, and his task is much more basically sexual – he must simply succeed in sleeping with the Lady of Belmont, which will mean he becomes lord of the land; if he fails he will forfeit all he possesses (this all-or-nothing absoluteness probably lies behind the parallel, and unexplained, condition of the test in Shakespeare). Giannetto bankrupts his godfather because the Lady drugs him and seizes his riches on the first two attempts, but on the third, for which his godfather borrows money from a Jew, her maid warns him to avoid the spiked wine he is being given. Leaving aside this different treatment of the wooing of the lady, however, Fiorentino's tale corresponds much better to the play than any other earlier version of the flesh-bond narrative (though Shakespeare seems to have used others as supplements to it – see **Munday**; **Silvayn**). The lady-judge resolving the merchant's dilemma at the Jew's expense, and the ring demanded as a fee, for instance, are both present in Fiorentino.

As with the plot structure, so with some of the finer points. The playwright

> seizes upon all the vivid details of the Lady's intervention to save Ansaldo – her taking the bond and reading it, her conceding its validity so firmly that the Jew approaches the merchant with his razor bared, her dramatic last-minute halt to the proceedings. Generations of actors who have never read *Il Pecorone* have instinctively felt it right for the thwarted Shylock to tear up his bond.
>
> (Mahood 1987: 2)

There are the verbal parallels too (see Grebanier 1962: 136–45). The notion that a reference in a play of 1579 to a drama called *The Jew* indicates the existence of an intermediate version used directly by Shakespeare has been generally discounted (see Brown 1961: xxix–xxx; Mahood 1987: 5). On the other hand, the Fiorentino novella is a work of no great subtlety, and if it was a direct source for Shakespeare it required development in substantial ways. For example, Fiorentino's thinly delineated and straightforwardly comic Jew is given stronger features, including a more serious point of view, and his punishment in the courtroom is no longer merely that his suit is frustrated. Shakespeare's 'cultivation of the problematic and the probing . . . multiplies both his cast-list and the story's complications' and explains why Fiorentino's test of virility and seduction was displaced by the decorous formality of the casket plot; 'the trickery of the trial scene and the sexual trickery in Belmonte in *Il Pecorone* . . . belong to a coarser and simpler comic world . . . [which] gets pushed to the side of the drama and is expressed through the figures of Gratiano and Nerissa' (Lyon 1988: 22–4). The contention that Shakespeare was the first teller of this tale to splice together the casket and the flesh-bond plots is supported by what seem to be remaining traces of Fiorentino's tale of the drugged wine (see

Levy 1960). For example, Bassanio's 'great debts' at the start of the play are not strictly necessary for Shakespeare's story, since Antonio could be made to stand surety for his friend in any case, but may recall the forfeiture of Giannetto's property after his two failed attempts at the test at the beginning of the Italian tale.

If Shakespeare used *Il Pecorone* at all, as he did, he might well have looked at the second story (1.2), of the Bolognese student who asks his tutor for instruction in the art of love. The student reports back on his progress until he makes the assignation with the lady, who, unbeknown to the student, is the tutor's wife. This tale is either a source or a close analogue for *The Merry Wives of Windsor*. The husband's attempts to catch the lovers involve hiding in damp washing and stabbing the laundry pile. No English translation of this story is known to have been available to Shakespeare.

(D)

Bullough, 1; Muir (1977); Satin (1966).

Brown, John Russell, ed. (1961). *The Merchant of Venice* (Arden Shakespeare). London.

Grebanier, Bernard (1962). *The Truth about Shylock*. New York.

Levy, Milton A. (1960). 'Did Shakespeare Join the Casket and Bond Plots in *The Merchant of Venice*?' *ShQ* 11: 388–91.

Lyon, John (1988). *The Merchant of Venice*. Hemel Hempstead.

Mahood, M. M., ed. (1987). *The Merchant of Venice* (New Cambridge Shakespeare). Cambridge.

Oliver, H. J., ed. (1971). *The Merry Wives of Windsor* (Arden Shakespeare). London.

Scott, Mary Augusta (1916). *Elizabethan Translations from the Italian*. Boston, MA.

Shaheen, Naseeb (1994). 'Shakespeare's Knowledge of Italian.' *ShSu* 47: 161–9.

Fiorentino, Remigio See **Nannini, Remigio**.

First Part of the Reign of King Richard the Second See **Chronicle History Plays**.

Fleming, Abraham See **Holinshed, Raphael**; **Virgil (Publius Vergilius Maro)**.

Florio, John (Giovanni) (*c.* **1553–1625), Italian–English Linguist and Translator** See also **Montaigne, Michel Eyquem de**. Occasional lines in *Hamlet, Othello* and *The Taming of the Shrew* resemble (English) ones in Florio's Italian language manuals *Firste Fruits* (1578) and *Second Frutes* (1591).

Shaheen, Naseeb (1994). 'Shakespeare's Knowledge of Italian.' *ShSu* 47: 161–9.

Florus, ?Lucius Annaeus (2nd Century AD), Roman Historian Florus' abridgement of Roman history, well known to English schoolboys in Latin form, refers to Coriolanus briefly in his Book I, and gives a version of the fable of the Body's Members.

Baldwin (1944), II, 576; Bullough, V, 473–4.

Forde, Emanuel (*fl.* 1607), Romance Writer Forde's romance *Parismus* (1598) and its sequel *Parismenos* (1599) perhaps gave hints towards two names, and some suggestion of romantic mood, for *Twelfth Night*.

Bullough, II, 276–7.

***Four Foster Children of Desire, The* (Anon. Play, 1581)** Close structural, character and other parallels have been discerned between this otherwise unconnected Court play and *Love's Labour's Lost*, but among other difficulties the large time lag between it and Shakespeare's work does not tend to support the case.

Wickham, Glynne (1985). '*Love's Labor's Lost* and *The Four Foster Children of Desire*, 1581.' *ShQ* 36: 49–55.

Foxe, John (1516–1587), Martyrologist and Historian

(A) Foxe was born in Boston, Lincolnshire, and educated at Magdalen College, Oxford. He resigned his fellowship there in 1545 and worked first as a tutor in the family of the Lucys at Charlecote, near Stratford, later as tutor to three children of the executed Henry Howard, Earl of Surrey. He lived in exile in Germany during the Catholic Marian regime of 1553–8 and there completed the Latin text of his *Actes and Monuments* or *Book of Martyrs*, a massive history of Protestantism focusing on those English Protestants who suffered under Queen Mary. Its militant Protestantism combines with nationalism: God's favour is bestowed on England in Foxe's account because of her fidelity to the true Gospel. Two editions were published: in Strasbourg, 1552, and Basle, 1559. Foxe returned to England in 1559 to translate and edit the work for the printer John Day, who published the expanded English version in 1563. Of his other published works, the Latin play *Titus et Gesippus* (written 1544) is an early specimen of English romantic comedy, with important Terentian additions, from a source in **Elyot**'s *Governour* and ultimately in **Boccaccio**.

(B) The *Book of Martyrs* was an immediately popular and influential work, though Foxe's obvious religious and national partisanship meant that his probity as a historian was questioned from an early date. The enlarged 1570 edition was legally required to be made available in all English cathedrals. It was reprinted frequently, becoming for many readers a kind of supplement to the Bible. The high-quality illustrations of many editions graphically depict the martyrs' sufferings, usually at the stake (see Fig. 6).

This passage, with a very close parallel in Shakespeare, is from a report of Thomas Cranmer's life which appears among the lives of martyrs of Queen Mary's reign. A previous passage concerns Henry VIII's personal notification to Cranmer of his committal to the Tower at the instigation of the Bishop of Winchester 'and other of the same sect'.

When the king had sayde his minde, the Archbishop kneeled downe and sayd: I am content if it please your grace, with all my heart, to goe thither at your highnesse commandement, and I most humbly thanke your Majesty that I may come to my trial, for there be that have many wayes slandered me, and now this way I hope to try my selfe not worthy of such report.

Figure 6 John Foxe, *Actes and Monuments* (London, 1583), p. 1944
(Actual size 132 × 180mm).

The king perceivyng the mans uprightnesse, joyned with such simplicitie, sayd: Oh Lorde, what maner a man be you? What simplicitie is in you? I had thought that you would rather have sued to us to have taken the paynes to have heard you, and your accusers together for your trial, without any such indurance. Do not you know, what state you be in with the whole world, and how many great enemies you have? Do you not consider what an easy thing it is, to procure three or foure false knaves to witnesse agaynst you? Thinke you to have better lucke that way, then your maister Christ had? I see by it, you will run hedlong to your undoyng, if I would suffer you. Your enemies shall not so prevayle against you, for I have otherwyse devised with my selfe to keepe you out of their handes. Yet notwithstanding to morrow when the Counsaile shal sit, and send for you, resort unto them, and if in chargyng you with this matter, they do commit you to the Tower, require of them, because you are one of them, a Counsailor, that you may have your accusers brought before them without any further indurance, and use for your selfe as good perswasions that way as you may devise, and if no intreatie or reasonable request will serve, then deliver unto them this my ring, (which [t]hen the king delivered unto the Archbishop) and say unto them, if there by no remedy my Lordes, but that I must needes go to the Tower, then I revoke my cause from you, and appeale to the kings owne person by this his token unto you all, for (sayd the King then unto the Archbishop) so soone as they shall see this my ryng, they know it so well that they shall understande that I have resumed the whole cause into myne owne handes and determination, and that I have discharged them thereof.

The Archbishop perceivyng the Kinges benignitie so muche to hym wardes, had much adoe to forbeare teares. Well, sayde the Kyng, go your wayes my Lorde, and doe as I have bidden you. My Lord humblyng himselfe with thankes, tooke hys leave of the Kynges highnesse for that nyght.

(Foxe 1583: 1866)

(C) Shakespeare would most likely have used the fourth edition of the *Book of Martyrs*, 1583, on the first occasions when he probably drew upon it, in the 1590s for *2 Henry VI* and *King John*. On a later occasion, for *Henry VIII*, the 1597 edition was also a possibility, but in any case the passages involved do not vary much between these two editions.

The use of Foxe for *2 Henry VI* is not certain, *pace* Pearlman (1999). The entertaining story of the false miracle of Simpcox (2.1.68ff.), originally told in Sir Thomas **More**'s *Dialogue of the Veneration and Worship of Images* (1529), is repeated in **Grafton**. But the editors of **Holinshed** directed readers to Foxe for more information on Duke Humphrey – 'sith the praise of this noble man deserveth a large discourse', they write, 'I refer the readers unto maister Foxe's booke of Acts and Monuments' – and it is not unlikely Shakespeare followed the direction. The parallel with Foxe (texts in Bullough, III, 126–8 and Cairncross 1957: 178–9), though close, cannot confirm indebtedness because the details of the story are similar in all versions. The case of *King John* is not dissimilar. It would be unsurprising if Shakespeare had turned in writing this work, a play impinging heavily on religious issues, to the leading English Church historian, as a number of otherwise inconsequential details suggest he may have done. The point could be confirmed if it were possible to discount many overlapping details in *The Troublesome Raigne of King John* (see **Chronicle History Plays**) on the grounds that it did not precede Shakespeare's play (see Honigmann 1954: xx).

A further tentative connection with Foxe may be made for *Henry IV*. Shakespeare's motives for presenting on stage a burlesque version of the historical Sir John Oldcastle remain a matter of speculation. It is possible he 'unwittingly took the name from *Famous Victories* which had provoked no objection from the Cobhams, perhaps because Oldcastle is a minor character' (Corbin and Sedge 1991: 12). Yet Foxe is not only the most likely source for the dramatists of *1 & 2 Sir John Oldcastle*: his account of Oldcastle's 'martyrdom' may well have been known directly to Shakespeare, simply as a reader of the *Book of Martyrs*. If Shakespeare's dissolute figure of Oldcastle-Falstaff is a deliberate departure from Foxe's presentation, several interpretations are possible, from the political – 'the family name of Oldcastle symbolized reforming zeal to many who were pressing for changes in the established Protestant church in the 1590s' (Bevington 1987: 4) – to the personal, since Oldcastle's descendant the seventh Lord Cobham, as Lord Chamberlain from 1596–7, oversaw the office of Master of the Revels and the licensing of plays.

The use of Foxe in *Henry VIII* is easier to establish. The Cranmer story in 5.1–3 was certainly taken from *The Book of Martyrs*: 'neither Hall nor Holinshed records the attempt to arrest Cranmer for heresy, his being kept waiting outside the council-chamber, or the King's protection of him' (Muir 1977: 285). Other significant elements from Foxe are connected with Katherine: Gardiner's plot on her life, her interview with him, and the King's displeasure at the plan to arrest her at Hampton Court. Shakespeare and/or his presumed collaborator Fletcher may also have used Foxe more miscellaneously, transferring episodes or expressions in the *Book of Martyrs* freely from one context to another (see Foakes 1968: xxxvi). But in the Cranmer episodes Shakespeare is at his closest to Foxe; indeed, the following passage is effectively a versification of the one quoted in (B), above.

CRANMER   Most dread liege,
            The good I stand on is my truth and honesty;

If they shall fail, I with mine enemies
Will triumph o'er my person; which I weigh not,
Being of those virtues vacant. I fear nothing
What can be said against me.

KING   Know you not
How your state stands i' th' world, with the whole world?
Your enemies are many, and not small; their practices
Must bear the same proportion; and not ever
The justice and the truth o' th' question carries
The due o' th' verdict with it; at what ease
Might corrupt minds procure knaves as corrupt
To swear against you? Such things have been done.
You are potently oppos'd, and with a malice
Of as great size. Ween you of better luck,
I mean in perjur'd witness, than your Master,
Whose minister you are, whiles here He liv'd
Upon this naughty earth? Go to, go to;
You take a precipice for no leap of danger,
And woo your own destruction.

CRANMER   God and your Majesty
Protect mine innocence, or I fall into
The trap is laid for me!

KING   Be of good cheer;
They shall no more prevail than we give way to.
Keep comfort to you, and this morning see
You do appear before them; if they shall chance,
In charging you with matters, to commit you,
The best persuasions to the contrary
Fail not to use, and with what vehemency
Th' occasion shall instruct you. If entreaties
Will render you no remedy, this ring
Deliver them, and your appeal to us
There make before them. Look, the good man weeps!
He's honest, on mine honour. God's blest Mother!
I swear he is true-hearted, and a soul
None better in my kingdom. Get you gone,
And do as I have bid you.   [*Exit Cranmer.*
He has strangled his language in his tears.

                                                    (5.1.121–57)

(D)

Bullough, iii, iv; Muir (1977).

Bevington, David, ed. (1987). *Henry IV, Part 1* (Oxford Shakespeare). Oxford.

Cairncross, Andrew S., ed. (1957). *The Second Part of King Henry VI* (Arden Shakespeare). London.

Corbin, Peter, and Douglas Sedge, eds (1991). *The Oldcastle Controversy: 'Sir John Oldcastle, Part 1' and 'The Famous Victories of Henry V'.* Manchester.

Foakes, R. A., ed. (1968). *Henry VIII* (Arden Shakespeare). London (first published 1957).

Foxe, John (1583). *Actes and Monuments of Matters most Speciall and Memorable, happenying in the Church . . . Newly revised and recognised, partly also augmented*, 3 vols. London.

Honigmann, E. A. J., ed. (1954). *King John* (Arden Shakespeare). London.

Pearlman, E. (1999). 'The Duke and the Beggar in Shakespeare's *2 Henry VI.*' *Criticism* 41: 309–21.

***Frederyke of Jennen* (Anon. Tale, 1560)** This version of the wager story found in *Cymbeline* might have been as familiar to Shakespeare as **Boccaccio**'s, but many different treatments of it were available.

Bullough, viii, 15–19.

Nosworthy, J. M., ed. (1969). *Cymbeline* (Arden Shakespeare), pp. xxii–xxv. London.

Froissart, Jean (1338–1410), French Chronicler and Poet

(A) A native of Hainaut, Froissart visited England in 1361 and was, he tells us, 'brought up in the court of the noble king Edward III, and of Queen Philippa his wife', travelling extensively under their protection. He returned to France in 1369 to begin work on the first Book of his *Chroniques*, his colourful account of the chivalry of western Europe during the first half of the Hundred Years' War. He crossed the English Channel again in 1395 to present his poems to Richard II, and followed subsequent events in England with much interest, pitying the man who had received him kindly and his French Queen. The four-volume Chronicle, for which Froissart interviewed many of the participants and observed some events at first hand, ends with the deposition and death of Richard II at the close of the fourteenth century. One of the last great medieval writers, Froissart aims to record a world that was quickly passing away, so that its deeds of chivalry might be remembered and serve as examples. But he is much interested too in the motives of actions and the mental workings of the figures involved, and the Chronicle's techniques are in important respects dramatic. Froissart was also responsible for a number of accomplished poems and several verse romances in the courtly love tradition.

(B) Froissart's Chronicle was made English by John Bourchier, Lord Berners (1469–1533), a considerable political figure who became Lord Chancellor under Henry VIII, in a translation undertaken at Henry VIII's bidding and published in two volumes in 1523–5. Froissart thus became one of the recognized authorities for the reigns of Edward III and Richard II.

The following passage from the narrative of the reign of Richard II is one of the descriptions of John of Gaunt:

> The duke of Lancastre was sore dyspleased in his mynde to se the kynge his nephewe mysse use hymselfe in dvyers thynges as he dyd. He consydred the tyme to come lyke a sage prince, and somtyme sayd to suche as he trusted best: Our nephue the kynge of Englande wyll shame all or he cease: he beleveth to lyghtly yvell counsayle who shall distroy hym; and symply, if he lyve longe, he wyll lese his realme, and that hath been goten with moche coste and travayle by our predecessours and by us; he suffreth to engendre in this realme bytwene the noble men hate and dyscorde, by whom he shulde be served and honoured, and this lande kepte and douted. He hath caused my brother to dye, whiche is one thynge to be noted, and the erle of Arundell, bycause they shewed hym trouthe: but he wolde nat here them nor none other that wolde counsayle hym agaynst his appetyte. He canne nat better dystroye his realme than to put trouble and hatred bytwene the noble men and good townes. The Frenchemen are right subtyle; for one myschiefe that falleth amonge us, they wolde it were ten, for otherwyse they canne nat recover their dommages, nor come to their ententes, but by our owne meanes and

dyscorde betwene ourselfe. And we se dayly that all realmes devyded are dystroyed; it hath bene sene by the realme of Fraunce, Spayne, Naples, and by landes of the churche, as we maye se dayly by the two Popes, whiche is and shall be to their dystructyon; also it hath been sene by the countrey of Flaunders, howe by their owne meanes they are distroyed; also presently it is sene by the lande of Frece, with whome our cosyns of Haynalt are in warre, and how the Frenchemen amonge theymselfe are dystroyed; in lykewise amonge ourselfe, without God provyde for us, we shall dystroy our selfe; the apparaunce therof sheweth greatly.

(1523–5 text, Ch. 224; ed. Ker 1901–3: vi, 311)

(C) Shakespeare would have been acquainted with the Berners transla-tion of Froissart, or at least 'it would be strange if he did not look into . . . the translation' (Bullough, iii, 367), since it was so well known and, compared with alternative sources for the historical material it embraced, such as the ***Mirror for Magistrates*** and other chronicles, so lively. Prior (1994) argues that the author, or one of the authors, of *Edward III* used the copy of the 1513 French edition owned and annotated by Henry Cary, Lord Hunsdon, patron of Shakespeare's company at the time of that play's production. This figure need not have been Shakespeare, and his use of it need not preclude the use of Berners. Froissart's status as a source for *Edward III* was first established by Smith (1911).

More importantly, the Chronicle is a source for *Richard II*. The figure of Gaunt is not fully anticipated in other sources, though Shakespeare could have imagined or inferred many of his characteristics and atti-tudes from **Holinshed** (so Ure 1961: xxxv–xxxvi), or based him on Thomas of Woodstock, Duke of Gloucester, the hero of *Woodstock* (see **Chronicle History Plays**). But he may well have drawn from Froissart the Duke's refusal to avenge Gloucester's death and some of Gaunt's complaints about his nephew in 2.1, even if in the second case Froissart's figure warns against allowing discord among the nobility rather than against farming the kingdom, like Shakespeare's. (This speech, in (B), may also have been recalled for the Bastard's injunctions against disunity in the face of French envy in *King John*.) Some other parallels with *Richard II* are found in Richard's reasons for banishing Bolingbroke and Mowbray, either derived from the *Chroniques* or merely showing Shakespeare 'filling up some gaps in Holinshed with invented

179

matter' (Ure 1961: 28); and Froissart's story of a favourite greyhound that deserted Richard to fawn upon Bolingbroke may have helped suggest the complaint Shakespeare's Richard makes of 'roan Barbary' being ridden by his rival (see Wilson 1939). More minor or more inconclusive connections (for which see Reyher 1924 and Bullough, III, 368–9) can be added. Shakespeare's particular debts to Froissart in *Richard II*, then, are few, the likeliest being the hints for the treatment of Gaunt. But a reading of Froissart's work could also have encouraged important overall emphases, including the sympathetic presentation of Richard in his fall and of the Queen as a figure of pathos – even though these features are not unique to the Frenchman's account of the reign.

(D)
Bullough, III; Muir (1977), 51–2.

Ker, W. P., ed. (1901–3). *The Chronicle of Froissart. Translated out of French by Sir John Bourchier, Lord Berners, annis 1523–25*, 6 vols. London.

Prior, Roger (1994). 'Was *The Raigne of King Edward III* A Compliment to Lord Hunsdon?' *Connotations* 3: 243–64.

Reyher, Paul (1924). 'Notes sur les Sources de Richard II.' *Revue de l'Enseignement des Langues Vivantes*, 1–13, 54–64, 106–14, 158–68.

Smith, Robert Metcalf (1911). '*Edward III* (A Study of the Authorship of the Drama in the Light of a New Source).' *JEGP* 10: 90–104.

Ure, Peter, ed. (1961). *King Richard II* (Arden Shakespeare). London.

Wilson, John Dover, ed. (1939). *King Richard II* (New Shakespeare). Cambridge.

Garnier, Robert (1544/5–1590), French Dramatist

(A) Born in Maine, Garnier studied law at Toulouse and followed a legal career, holding high offices through the French Wars of Religion, in Paris and later Le Mans. His literary interests led to lyric verse and to eight plays, thanks to which he is acknowledged as the leading French tragedian of his time. Three are tragedies on Roman subjects, *Porcie* (1568), *Cornélie* (1574) and *Marc-Antoine* (1578); three are on Greek ones, *Hippolyte* (1573), *La Troade* (1579) and *Antigone* (1580). Garnier's style is inspired by **Seneca** for declamatory speeches, stichomythic exchanges and *sentences*, and by **Ronsard** and the Pléiade (though he was not a member) for such features as Petrarchism, mythological allusion and euphony. His plays were performed to the end of the sixteenth century and in some cases beyond.

(B) Mary Sidney Herbert translated *Marc-Antoine* in 1590, by which time Garnier was a celebrated writer in the French theatrical avant-garde. In this translation (published 1592, again in 1595) she initiated a courtly Senecan movement which led several members of her circle to compose Roman tragedies within the next fifteen years. (**Kyd**'s 1594 version of *Cornélie*, the only other direct English translation of Garnier to be published in the period, was apparently an attempt on his part to gain acceptance in her circle.) This movement produced plays strikingly unlike other English drama of these years, and had far-reaching consequences for English drama more generally.

Mary Sidney's *Antonius*, a careful, line-by-line blank verse rendering from the 1585 edition of *Marc-Antoine*, as well as being historically important, is increasingly recognized as a substantial literary achievement creating 'a distinctive style of English verse' (Hannay *et al.* 1998: I, 151), and not merely a collection of 'sluggish Senecan monologues' (as Satin 1966: 573 has it). The Garnier play's remarkably sympathetic treatment of Cleopatra may have had special appeal for Mary Sidney. In Act 1 Antony, in soliloquy, laments his thraldom to Cleopatra, which has made him neglect the Pythian Wars. In Act 2 Cleopatra justifies herself:

Cleopatra. Eras. Charmian. Diomede.

CLEOPATRA   That I have thee betraid, deare *Antonie*,
My life, my soule, my Sunne? I had such thought? . . .
Rather, ô rather let our *Nilus* send,
To swallow me quicke, some weeping *Crocodile.*
   And didst thou then suppose my royall hart
Had hatcht, thee to ensnare, a faithles love?
And changing minde, as Fortune changed cheare,
I would weake thee, to winne the stronger, loose?
O wretch! ô caitive! ô too cruell happe!
And did not I sufficient losse sustaine
Loosing my Realme, loosing my liberty,
My tender of-spring, and the joyfull light
Of beamy Sunne, and yet, yet loosing more
Thee *Antony* my care, if I loose not
What yet remain'd? thy love alas! thy love,
More deare then Scepter, children, freedome, light.
   So ready I to row in *Charons* barge,
Shall leese the joy of dying in thy love:
So the sole comfort of my miserie
To have one tombe with thee is me bereft.
So I in shady plaines shall plaine alone,
Not (as I hop'd) companion of thy mone,
O height of griefe!

ERAS.   Why with continuall cries
Your griefull harmes doo you exasperate?
Torment your selfe with murthering complaints?
Straine your weake breast so oft, so vehemently?

> Water with teares this faire alabaster?
> With sorrowes sting so many beauties wound?
> Come of so many Kings want you the hart
> Bravely, stoutly, this tempest to resist?

CL.   My ev'lls are wholy unsupportable,
            No humain force can them withstand, but death.
            (1592 text, 394–5, 404–33; ed. Hannay *et al.* 1998: I, 164–5)

(C) Shakespeare's *Antony and Cleopatra* contains 'enough verbal similarities to show that the countess's tragedy lingered in Shakespeare's mind' (Wilders 1995: 62), but all are small-scale. (Eras' phrase 'come of so many Kings', above, is not necessarily significant for Shakespeare's 'Descended of so many royal kings' (5.2.325), since it is paralleled in **Plutarch**'s death-scene.) These verbal similarities are listed by Schanzer (1956) and Muir (1977: 225–7). Bullough sees them as 'quite in accord with Shakespeare's habit of floating to the surface of his memory details from works read sometimes years before' (v, 231), while Schanzer imagines Shakespeare reading the translation 'shortly before or during the composition of *Antony and Cleopatra*'. But the presence of *Marc-Antoine* behind Shakespeare's play may well be more substantial in the presentation of Cleopatra, and of the idealizing-romantic aspects of her love which her Act 2 speech (above) evokes. This is to say that the Cleopatra of *Marc-Antoine/Antonius*, who is much more sympathetic than Plutarch's, is of special interest for the Cleopatra of Shakespeare's Act 5. Although Garnier/Sidney's figure is 'more simple and less vital, she is basically Shakespeare's Cleopatra of Act V . . . Her love for Antonius has been deep and true from the first.' Antonius' part in the relationship, on the other hand, is severely condemned by various speakers, so that 'In *Antonius* . . . as in Shakespeare's play, we find side by side both condemnation and glorification of the love of Antony and Cleopatra' (Schanzer 1963: 151).

Some general similarities of emphasis and patterning between Garnier's 'heroine tragedies' *Marc-Antoine* and *Cornélie* and Shakespeare's presentation of his heroine in *The Rape of Lucrece* have been noted (Soellner 1982). But there are no apparent verbal echoes of either the French texts or the English reworkings of **Daniel** and Kyd (respectively *The Tragedy of Cleopatra* and *Cornelia*) which were published only very shortly before Shakespeare's poem.

(D) For an account of Garnier's influence in England via Mary Sidney and her circle, see Witherspoon's still useful but little-known 1924 study.

Bullough, v; Muir (1977); Satin (1966).

Hannay, Margaret P., Noel J. Kinnamon and Michael G. Brennan, eds (1998). *The Collected Works of Mary Sidney Herbert, Countess of Pembroke*, 2 vols. Oxford.

Schanzer, Ernest (1956). '*Antony and Cleopatra* and the Countess of Pembroke's *Antonius*.' *N&Q* 201: 152–4.

—— (1963). *The Problem Plays of Shakespeare: A Study of Julius Caesar, Measure for Measure and Antony and Cleopatra*. London.

Soellner, Rolf (1982). 'Shakespeare's *Lucrece* and the Garnier–Pembroke Connection.' *ShSt* 15: 1–20.

Steppat, Michael (1987). 'Shakespeare's Response to Dramatic Tradition in *Anthony and Cleopatra*', pp. 254–79 in Bernhard Fabian and Kurt Tetzeli von Rosador, eds, *Shakespeare: Text, Language, Criticism: Essays in Honour of Marvin Spevack*. Hildesheim.

Wilders, John, ed. (1995). *Antony and Cleopatra* (Arden Shakespeare). London.

Witherspoon, Alexander McLaren (1924). *The Influence of Robert Garnier on Elizabethan Drama*. New Haven.

Gascoigne (Gascoine), George (1535?–1577), Poet and Translator

(A) The son of a wealthy Bedfordshire knight, Gascoigne passed a riotous youth as 'a notorious ruffiane', studying 'such lattyn as I forgat' at Cambridge, and enrolling at Gray's Inn in 1555. He sat as a Member of Parliament for Bedford under both Mary and Elizabeth, but given his extravagance never remained respectable for long, and was at one time branded an atheist, murderer, bankrupt and 'common rymer'. His diverse and innovative writings, which often domesticated foreign forms for the first time, include the *Notes Concerning the Making of Verse* (1575), one of the first specimens of English literary criticism; *The Stele Glas* (1576), sometimes called the first regular English satire and a very early example of non-dramatic blank verse; and *Jocasta* (with Francis Kinwelmersh, 1566), only the second blank verse English tragedy (see **Euripides**). A major collection of his verse was first published, supposedly without his permission, as *A Hundreth Sundrie Flowers* (1573), and revised as *The Posies of George Gascoigne Esquire* (1575). *Supposes*, Gascoigne's vivid and accurate translation of **Ariosto**'s play *I Suppositi* (1509 in prose, later versified), seems to have been presented for the first time at Gray's Inn in 1566. He further composed closet drama, war journalism and other translations, as well as more work as a courtier-poet – a masque, and entertainment on two royal progresses.

(B) Shakespeare's use of Gascoigne's work is more or less confined to *Supposes*, the 'hard, dry, classical comedy of subterfuge and misunder-standing' (Bullough, I, 66) which introduced the essential formulae of Italian comic drama to the English stage (for the special appeal of Ariosto's original, see Clubb 1989: 9–10, 33). After its production in 1566 it was first printed in 1573 (unauthorized), in 1575 in *The Posies of George Gascoigne*, and again in the posthumous *Whole Works of George Gascoigne* (1587). It seems to have been revived in Oxford in 1582. But as an example of an early Italian play adapted for the English stage it remained for some time a rarity: 'after the first minor outburst at the Inns in the sixties, most of which is credited to only one man, Gascoigne, there are no known instances of Italian drama in England until well after the forms of English drama had crystallized' (Orr 1970: 106). Bullough supplies a complete text.

The theatrical possibilities of some episodes in *Supposes* clearly struck Shakespeare strongly. One such is a sequence of mistaken identities which develops at the window of an inn in Gascoigne's scenes 4.4–7, borrowed for 5.1 of *The Taming of the Shrew*. The first of these short scenes in *Supposes* is printed here; Litio's last lines in it give a glimpse of the topsy-turvy world Shakespeare was to create:

DALIO the cooke. FERARESE the inholder.
PHILOGANO. LITIO his man.

[DA.] What devill of hell is there? I thinke hee will breake the gates in peeces.

LI. Marie sir, we had thoughte you had beene on sleepe within, and therefore we thought best to wake you: what doth *Erostrato*?

DA. He is not within.

PHI. Open the dore good fellow I pray thee.

DA. If you thinke to lodge here, you are deceived I tell you, for here are guestes enowe already.

PHI. A good fellow, and much for thy maister honesty by our Ladie: and what guestes I pray thee?

DA. Here is *Philogano* my masters father, lately come out of *Sicilia*.

PHI. Thou speakest truer than thou arte aware of, he wil be, by that time thou hast opened the dore: open I pray thee hartily.

DA. It is a small matter for me to open the dore, but here is no lodging for you, I tell you plaine, the house is full.

PHI. Of whome?

DA. I tolde you: here is *Philogano* my maisters father come from *Cathenea*.

PHI. And when came he?

DA. He came three houres since, or more, he alighted at the Aungell, and left his horses there: afterwarde my maister brought him hither.

PHI. Good fellow, I thinke thou hast good sport to mocke mee.

DA. Nay, I thinke you have good spor[te] to make me tary here, as though I have nothing else to doe: I am matched with an unrulye mate in the kitchin. I will goe looke to him another while.

PHI. I thinke he be drunken.

FER. Sure he semes so: see you not how redde he is about the gilles?

PHI. Abide fellow, what *Philogano* is it whome thou talkest of?

DA. An honest gentleman, father to *Erostrato* my maister.

PHI. And where is he?

DA. Here within.

PHI. May we see him?

DA. I thinke you may if you be not blind.

PHI. Go to, tel him here is one wold speake with him.

DA. Mary that I will willingly doe.

PHI. I can not tell what I shoulde say to this geere, *Litio*, what thinkest thou of it?

LI. I cannot tell you what I shoulde say sir, the worlde is large and long, there maye be moe *Philoganos* and moe *Erastratos* than one, yea and moe *Ferraras*, moe *Sicilias*, and moe *Cathaneas*: peradventure this is not that *Ferrara* whiche you sent your sonne unto.

PHI. Peradventure thou arte a foole, and he was another that answered us even now. But be you sure honest man, that you mistake not the house?

FER. Nay, then god helpe, thinke you I knowe not *Erostratos* house? yes, and himselfe also: I sawe him here no longer since than yesterday. But

186

here comes one that wil tell us tidyngs of him, I like his countenaunce
better than the others that answered at the windowe erewhile.

> *Dalio draweth his hed in at the wyndowe, the Scenese commeth out.*
> (1566 text, ed. Cunliffe 1907: I, 221–3)

(C) A 'suppose', according to Gascoigne's Prologue, was 'nothing else
but a mystaking or imagination of one thing for another', i.e. what in
French is still called a *quiproquo* (though Ariosto occasionally puns scato-
logically on 'suppositories' too). In the 1575 edition, each of some
twenty-four instances is pointed out in a marginal note. The play may
hence have suggested the overall idea of the 'errors' in *The Comedy of
Errors*. It may also underlie Shakespeare's double plot structure, since,
although **Plautus** is the source of the material itself, the formal principle was elaborated by the Italians, and the likelihood that Gascoigne's
influential work stimulated Shakespeare's more than classically complicated plot is increased by some more specific resemblances between
Errors and *Supposes*. These are summarized by Salingar (1974: 207–8),
who notes for example that 'the scene (III.i) where Antipholus of
Ephesus first comes on the stage, to be shut out of his own house, is
largely borrowed from *Amphitryon*, but the indirect way it arises recalls
the scene of doubled identities where the father is refused admission to
his son's lodging in *Supposes*'.

The use of Gascoigne's play for *The Taming of the Shrew* is much
clearer, necessarily so if, as is likely, Shakespeare aimed here to exploit
the contemporary prestige of foreign dramatic models and of all things
Italian. It has been speculated that even the problematic Sly induction
may be illuminated by *Supposes*, if we imagine the playwright began with
a shrew-taming story but opted later to extend the 'supposes' theme,
'carr[ying] its implications into the shrew plot and into as much of the
induction as would bear the changed emphasis' (Seronsy 1963: 29).
Otherwise, he takes from it both large and small things, expanding, for
instance, a summarized 'prehistory' to form most of 1.1, and recycling
some characters' names. But the main structures and emphases of
the later play are independently worked out, and bring into service
elements from *Supposes* only when they are useful. The new character
of Hortensio, in particular, joining Lucentio in the disguise of a tutor,
increases the narrative complications appreciably; Lucentio is much
altered from his model too; and Bianca is unlike hers in being a virgin
and in having a sister. Even Baptista is 'subdued to the new emphasis':

in *Supposes* he airs his opinions at length on the ingratitude of off-
spring to parents in a long speech (III.iii) which is one of Gascoigne's
additions to Ariosto, and goes so far as to imprison the feigned
Erostrato, threatening him with dire penalties for seducing his daughter. There is nothing of this in Shakespeare's Baptista. He is a father
and a merchant, and we learn little more about him than that.

(Morris 1981: 82–3)

This is a reminder that Gascoigne's play was also attractively different
in its emphases from the New Comedy tradition it issues from, a play of
love and matrimony rather than of sex – though this is not necessarily
to say that Shakespeare aims to 'renovate' Gascoigne's 'endorsement of
romantic passion' as support for 'Protestant marriage ideology'
(Mikesell 1989: 150).

Since Shakespeare is known to have looked closely at *Supposes*, elements from it may resurface in later plays. But there is no special reason to
connect, for example, Gascoigne's bribeable nurse, Balia (suppressed
completely in the *Shrew*), with Juliet's (as does Bullough, speculatively, 1,
66). One other Gascoigne work to have been associated with Shakespeare is his *Adventures Passed by Master F. J.*, a risqué story in the *Hundreth
Sundrie Flowres*, 1573, and a very early example of an original English
Renaissance prose narrative. Velz thinks it may have furnished a
model for Bianca's wooing by the fake instructors Hortensio/Litio
and Lucentio/Cambio, but is forced to concede that 'the differences
between the scenes are as significant as the similarities' (1973: 131).

(D)

Bullough, 1.

Baldwin, T. W. (1947). *Shakspere's Five-Act Structure: Shakspere's Early Plays
    on the Background of Renaissance Theories of Five-Act Structure from 1470.*
    Urbana, IL.

Cole, Howard C. (1981). *The All's Well Story from Boccaccio to Shakespeare.*
    Urbana, IL.

Clubb, Louise George (1989). *Italian Drama in Shakespeare's Time.* New
    Haven.

Cunliffe, John W., ed. (1907). *The Complete Works of George Gascoigne*, 2
    vols. Cambridge.

Hosley, Richard (1963–4). 'Sources and Analogues of *The Taming of the
    Shrew.*' *HLQ* 27: 289–308.

Mikesell, Margaret Lael (1989). '"Love Wrought these Miracles": Marriage and Genre in *The Taming of the Shrew*.' *RenD* 20: 141–67.

Morris, Brian, ed. (1981). *The Taming of the Shrew* (Arden Shakespeare). London.

Orr, David (1970). *Italian Renaissance Drama in England before 1625: The Influence of 'Erudita' Tragedy, Comedy, and Pastoral on Elizabethan and Jacobean Drama*. Chapel Hill.

Salingar, Leo (1974). *Shakespeare and the Traditions of Comedy*. Cambridge.

Seronsy, Cecil C. (1963). '"Supposes" as the Unifying Theme in *The Taming of the Shrew*.' *ShQ* 14: 15–30.

Velz, John W. (1973). 'Gascoigne, Lyly, and the Wooing of Bianca.' *N&Q* 218: 130–3.

Geoffrey of Monmouth (*c.* 1100–1154), English Historical Writer

(A) Born into a clerical family, Geoffrey was educated at Monmouth's Benedictine abbey, probably becoming a monk but remaining primarily a scholar, and living in Oxford. In his old age he was made Bishop of St Asaph. His *Historia Regum Brittaniae* (*c.* 1140) claims to be a Latin translation of a 'very old book in the British tongue' recounting the history of Britain down to King Arthur. In fact, it seems to mix together various chronicle sources with biblical, classical and traditional stories, and perhaps Geoffrey's own fictions, to create the story of a British kingdom, to some extent paralleling that of Israel. It was intended to appeal to a fashion for courtly tales. In describing the rise of the British people to glory in the reigns of Uther Pendragon and Arthur, Geoffrey established the Arthurian legend; other well-known British historical myths also have their origins here, in what has been called the most important literary work of its century.

(B) Geoffrey's History was widely diffused in England and in continental Europe: some 170 manuscript versions still survive, of which 27 are thought to date from the twelfth century. It was found especially useful when Henry VII appointed a commission to trace the Tudors' British ancestors, and sections, at least, were consulted and reworked around this time by many English chroniclers (notably **Holinshed**), in whose work the material often retains a slightly alien air. Geoffrey's mythical and semi-mythical material was also drawn upon more widely and variously in the sixteenth century and well beyond, in particular the story of the New Troy, the founding of Albion by Aeneas' great-grandson Brute. 'Not only had the legends become a conspicuous part of the Tudor myth, but they also carried substantial weight regarding Britain's own ancient past' (Curran 1999: 3). Direct use was made of them by **Drayton**, **Spenser** and later Milton, who described the stories as 'defended by many, deny'd utterly by few' and followed them only cautiously in his own *History of Britain*; as early as the first half of the sixteenth century there had been a wave of scepticism about Geoffrey's reliability from such writers as Polydore Vergil and William **Camden** (see Ferguson 1993: 85–105).

For the stage, there are four surviving Galfridian chronicle plays on pre-Roman English history near the end of the sixteenth century: *Gorboduc*, and the anonymous *Locrine, Nobody and Somebody*, and *The True Chronicle History of King Leir* (see **Chronicle History Plays**), as well as others now lost but recorded by Philip Henslowe. All the known examples follow Geoffrey's outline with some strictness, probably at least partly because of a lingering suspicion that the material is really historical; this distinguishes them from *King Lear* (see Curran 1999). There is no known English translation of Geoffrey's Latin in or before the Tudor period, but there were at least three French ones as early as the twelfth century.

(C) As well as furnishing much of Holinshed's material and hence con-stituting an indirect source for *King Lear* (of which story it is the earliest known version) and *Cymbeline*, Geoffrey's work may have been consulted directly by Shakespeare. Perrett (1904: 283–4) argues that he may have been led to it by a marginal reference in Holinshed to 'Gal. Mon.', a name which, if Shakespeare did not already recognize it as that of the chief authority for this period of British history, he could have looked up in Holinshed's list of 'authors from whome this Historie . . . is collected'. He would have had no trouble obtaining a copy of one version or another of Geoffrey's work (from, for example, his friend Drayton). Shakespeare may have read the Latin, or used some no longer extant translation. Conceivably he might have taken details from more recent writers who had paraphrased Geoffrey in the course of historical works in English.

The main textual evidence to support this hypothesis of such direct or near-direct acquaintance is as follows (based on Perrett 1904: 280–1):

1   Among authorities available to Shakespeare, only Geoffrey and *Perceforest*, a less likely source, mention the unequal division of the kingdom intended by Leir.

2   Geoffrey alone among authorities available to Shakespeare supplies the pretexts Goneril and Regan use in the play for reducing Lear's retinue.

3   The figures of Kent, and in the Folio text the Gentleman who nurses Lear, are anticipated by a character in Geoffrey, a knight who is the last remnant of Leir's retinue.

4   Leir's character as presented by Geoffrey corresponds more closely to Shakespeare's figure than to those in other possible sources in respect of 'his virility, his violent indignation, his intense grief at the loss of his power, his longing for vengeance' (Perrett 1904: 281).

5   There are also some three possible verbal echoes of Geoffrey's Latin in *Lear*'s first two scenes, all very small in scale (Perrett 1904: 213, 229).

Muir (1977: xxxiii), while not dismissing this evidence, counters that Shakespeare could have arrived at all these details independently.

If Shakespeare knew Geoffrey's narrative of the reign of Leir then it may, of course, have been from Geoffrey that many other elements of his story were derived. Since these features are also found in many of the other possible *Lear* sources, such as Holinshed and the **Mirror for Magistrates**, this cannot be demonstrated.

(D)
Bullough, VII.
Curran, John E., Jr (1999). 'Geoffrey of Monmouth in Renaissance Drama: Imagining Non-History.' *MP* 97: 1–20.
Ferguson, Arthur B. (1993). *Utter Antiquity: Perceptions of Prehistory in Renaissance England.* Durham, N.C.
Muir, Kenneth, ed. (1972). *King Lear* (Arden Shakespeare). London.
Perrett, Wilfrid (1904). *The Story of King Lear from Geoffrey of Monmouth to Shakespeare.* Berlin.

Gernutus, The Jew of Venice (Anon. Ballad) One or two unusual minor details of *The Merchant of Venice* can be found in this

191

ballad, which however may not precede the play in time – it has not been dated certainly.

Brown, John Russell, ed. (1961). *The Merchant of Venice* (Arden Shakespeare), pp. xxx–xxxi, Appendix ii. London.

Gesta Romanorum See also **Twine, Lawrence**. This collection of medieval Latin prose tales on classical figures, Christian saints and Eastern material contains a likely source for the casket story in *The Merchant of Venice*. It was translated by Wynkyn de Worde in *c.* 1512 and by Richard Robinson in 1577.

Brown, John Russell, ed. (1961). *The Merchant of Venice* (Arden Shakespeare), pp. xxxii, 172–3. London (first published 1955).
Muir (1977), 89.

Giovanni, Ser See **Fiorentino, Giovanni**.

Gl'Ingannati

(A) *Gl'Ingannati* ('The Deceived Ones') is an Italian comedy produced by a Sienese literary society, the Academy of the Intronati ('the Thunderstruck [by love]'), in 1531. The Intronati translated from classical poetry, performed drama by the Italian masters, and wrote numerous original comedies. This one depicts the amorous adventures of Lelia, a young woman of contemporary Modena who has been betrothed by her father, Virginio, to old Gherardo. She runs away from the convent of ill repute in which her father has lodged her and enters the service of her old flame Flamminio disguised as a page. Acting as Flamminio's intermediary, she finds her male self admired by Isabella, the lady he now wishes to marry, who happens to be Gherardo's daughter. Lelia is extricated from the triangle by the appearance of her long-lost brother, who eventually pairs off with Isabella. *Gl'Ingannati* is a fast, satirical, by no means deep play loosely within the ***commedia dell'arte*** tradition, full of slapstick, colloquial insults and salaciousness, especially from the chorus of clownish servants; it ends with Lelia and Flamminio in bed offstage while the nurse's daughter reports to the audience the words and sounds she can hear. The prologue plausibly claims that it was composed in only three days. For its Italian comedy context see Clubb (1989).

(B) By 1600 the play had been translated and imitated in various dramatic and fictional forms, in French, Spanish, Italian, Latin and English: at least six major dramatic versions such as Nicolò **Secchi**'s, and a long line of derivative prose stories, are extant. The sole English version was by Barnaby Riche, an army captain who had seen long service in Ireland, and friend of Churchyard, **Gascoigne** and **Lodge**. Riche's prose tale or novella *Of Apolonius and Silla* was the second of eight stories in his collection *Riche his Farewell to Militarie Profession*, 1581 (perhaps also reprinted later, since entered in the Stationers' Register in 1591). This derives from the play via a narrative version in François de **Belleforest**'s *Histoires Tragiques*, IV, itself taken from the earlier Italian prose adaptation in Matteo **Bandello**'s *Novelle* (1554), II.36. Clearly, the great innovation of *Gl'Ingannati*, and the cause of the profusion of imitations and translations, was the exciting gender confusion of girl dressed as boy, then fancied by a girl.

A full text of *Gl'Ingannati* in modern translation is given by Bullough (II, 286–339) and Satin (1966). The Italian play itself was only possibly known to Shakespeare, but an excerpt from the Riche reworking which he certainly read is given below (a full text of the rare 1581 edition of Riche is given in Lothian and Craik 1975 and in Benson 1996; in modernized form in Satin 1966).

> there was remainyng in the Citie a noble Dame a widowe, whose housebande was but lately deceased, one of the noblest men that were in the partes of *Grecia*, who left his Lady and wife large possessions and greate livinges. This Ladies name was called *Julina*, who besides the aboundance of her wealth, and the greatnesse of her revenues, had likewise the soveraigntie of all the Dames of *Constantinople* for her beautie. To this Ladie *Julina*, *Apolonius* became an earnest suter, and accordyng to the maner of woers, besides faire woordes, sorrowfull sighes, and piteous countenaunces, there must bee sendyng of lovyng letters, Chaines, Bracelettes, Brouches, Rynges, Tablets, Gemmes, Juels, and presentes I knowe not what: So my Duke, who in the tyme that he remained in the Ile of *Cypres*, had no skill at all in the arte of Love, although it were more then

193

half proffered unto hym, was now become a scholler in Loves Schoole, and had alreadie learned his first lesson, that is, to speake pitifully, to looke ruthfully, to promise largely, to serve diligently, and to please carefully: Now he was learnyng his seconde lesson, that is to reward liberally, to give bountifully, to present willyngly, and to wryte lovyngly. Thus *Apolonius* was so busied in his newe studie, that I warrant you there was no man that could chalenge hym for plaiyng the truant, he followed his profession with so good a will: And who must bee the messenger to carrie the tokens and love letters, to the Ladie *Julina*, but *Silvio* his manne, in hym the Duke reposed his onely confidence, to goe betweene hym and his Ladie.

Now gentilwomen, doe you thinke there could have been a greater torment devised, wherewith to afflicte the harte of *Silla*, then her self to bee made the instrumente to woorke her owne mishapp, and to plaie the Attorney in a cause, that made so muche againste her self. But *Silla* altogether desirous to please her maister, cared nothyng at all to offende her self, [and] followed his businesse with so good a will, as if it had been in her owne preferment.

Julina now havyng many tymes, taken the gaze of this yong youth *Silvio*, perceivyng hym to bee of suche excellente perfecte grace, was so intangeled with the often sight of this sweete temptation, that she fell into as greate a likyng with the man, as the maister was with her self: And on a tyme *Silvio* beyng sent from his maister, with a message to the Ladie *Julina*, as he beganne very earnestly to solicet in his maisters behalfe, *Julina* interruptyng hym in his tale, saied: *Silvio* it is enough that you have saied for your maister, from henceforthe either speake for your self, or saie nothyng at all. *Silla* abashed to heare these wordes, began in her minde to accuse the blindnesse of Love, that *Julina* neglectyng the good will of so noble a Duke, would preferre her love unto suche a one, as Nature it self had denaied to recompence her likyng.

(1581 text; Lothian and Craik 1975: 164–6)

(C) *Twelfth Night* clearly uses the *Gl'Ingannati* plot, but the closely connecting web of texts deriving from the Italian play (for details see Bullough, ii, 270; Orr 1970: 42) makes its exact background hard to determine. Shakespeare used one or more of these texts, but perhaps not including *Gl'Ingannati* itself. Of the non-English narrative versions, those by Belleforest and Bandello are the most likely for him to have known, but whereas there is no categorical evidence for either of these, he certainly used Riche's version of 1581. The conclusive evidence consists of his repetition from *Apolonius and Silla* of four specialized words, 'coisterell', 'garragascoynes', 'pavion' and 'galliarde', which are found in *Twelfth Night* and nowhere else in Shakespeare. Verbal resemblances between *Gl'Ingannati* and *Twelfth Night*, though they include two references to the 'notte di beffana', one of the Italian names for the festival of Twelfth Night, are not decisive enough to show Shakespeare knew the Italian play (these resemblances are listed by Lothian and Craik 1966: xxxviii–xl).

Apart from the plot, nothing essential in *Twelfth Night* comes from *Gl'Ingannati* or, perhaps, from any of its imitations – though Bullough suggests Riche's *Apolonius and Silla* was 'the work which crystallized his ideas . . . [and] combined motifs already dear to him' from his previous plays (II, 277). *Gl'Ingannati* is earthy and bawdy whereas

> Riche's story has an overlay of elegance that reaches towards the sublime courtliness of Shakespeare's main plot. The tone of *The Deceived Ones* sounds more like that of the Sir Toby-Maria-Aguecheek subplot of *Twelfth Night*, and given that clue we can go on to find other relationships between *The Deceived Ones* and the *Twelfth Night* subplot as well.
> (Satin 1966: 315)

These are fairly loose and unimportant, but the apparently unusual tonal freedom of Shakespeare's handling of the subplot, for example with Malvolio, may be connected with the Italian play's unbuttoned quality. (The fifth story in *Riche his Farewell*, 'Two Brethren', is sometimes connected with the Malvolio plot too.) Where the main plot is concerned, the tonal propinquity between Riche's *Apollonius and Silla* and Shakespeare's play looks greater in comparison with the Italian source than it really is: Shakespeare changed the mood he found in Riche's story, especially in the parts involving the widow Julina, Olivia's original:

> Her hasty meeting, feasting, and bedding of Silvio is refined into Olivia's equally hasty but decorous marriage-ceremony, and in consequence there is no pregnancy, no desertion, and no imprisonment of the heroine; all that survives of this rather

sensational element of Riche's tale is Orsino's violent impulse, to slay
Olivia or to sacrifice Viola, in Shakespeare's last scene.

(Lothian and Craik 1975: xlvi)

The disguised Julia part of the plot of *The Two Gentlemen of Verona*
comes from *Gl'Ingannati* via **Montemayor**; some touches in *Othello* and
The Merry Wives of Windsor may derive from *Riche his Farewell* (Pruvost
1960 and Cranfill 1959: xlviii–lii present the respective cases).

(D)

Bullough, ii; Satin (1966).
Benson, Pamela Joseph, ed. (1996). *Italian Tales from the Age of Shakespeare*.
London.
Clubb, Louise George (1989). *Italian Drama in Shakespeare's Time*. New
Haven.
Cranfill, Thomas Mabry, ed. (1959). *Rich's Farewell to Military Profession,
1581*. Austin, TX.
Lothian, J. M., and T. W. Craik, eds (1975). *Twelfth Night* (Arden
Shakespeare). London.
Luce, M., ed. (1912). *Rich's 'Apolonius and Silla': An Original of Shakespeare's
'Twelfth Night'*. London.
Orr, David (1970). *Italian Renaissance Drama in England before 1625:
The Influence of 'Erudita' Tragedy, Comedy, and Pastoral on Elizabethan and
Jacobean Drama*. Chapel Hill.
Pruvost, René. (1960). '*The Two Gentlemen of Verona, Twelfth Night*, et
Gl'Ingannati.' Etudes Anglaises 13: 1–9.
Salingar, Leo (1974). *Shakespeare and the Traditions of Comedy*. Cambridge.
Scragg, Leah (1992). *Shakespeare's Mouldy Tales: Recurrent Plot Motifs in
Shakespearean Drama*. London.

Godfrey of Viterbo See **Gower, John**.

Golding, Arthur See **Ovid (Publius Ovidius Naso)**.

Googe, Barnaby See **Palingenius, Marcellus**.

Gower, John (*c.* 1330–1408), Poet

(A) Gower was a minor nobleman who came of a Kentish family and pursued a literary career in London. For his friend **Chaucer** he is 'moral Gower'. His major works are the *Speculum Meditantis* or *Mirour de l'Omme*, a 30,000-line allegory in French; the *Vox Clamantis*, a 10,000-line poem on the 1381 Peasants' Revolt in Latin elegiacs; and the *Confessio Amantis*, 33,000 lines of English octosyllabic couplets. This last, one of the great achievements of fourteenth-century poetry, is a collection of 141 tales with a framing narrative in which a lover, Amans/Gower, makes his confession to Genius, the priest of Venus. He is to be cured of his love-sickness by edifying stories (which turn out to be tales from classical and medieval sources) illustrating the Deadly Sins. One of these, occupying most of Book VIII (devoted to 'unlawful love', and concentrating on incest), is the story of 'Apollinus', i.e. Apollonius of Tyre, which Gower took mainly from Godfrey of Viterbo's twelfth-century version of this traditional tale (see Archibald 1991: 192).

(B) Gower's reputation was always linked to Chaucer's, not always as an inferior. For the sixteenth century he was with Chaucer the first founder of English poetry, and he is often spoken of as having 'refined' the language. **Sidney**'s *Apology for Poetry* calls the pair 'the first light-givers to ignorance'; Robert **Greene**'s *Visio* of 1592 makes Gower the speaker for morality in poetry, against Chaucer's recommendation of variety and invention. **Spenser** is thought to have used Gower, and **Jonson** cites him more often than any other writer in his English grammar – though in *Timber* he warns against too much exposure to his antique practices. This reservation becomes hostility in **Puttenham**'s attack on Gower in the *Arte of English Poesy* (1589): though he helped to establish English vernacular poetry, Gower's verse, says Puttenham, was 'homely and without good measure, his wordes strained much deale out of the French writers, his ryme wrested, and in his inventions [was] small subtillitie'. These remarks may show the beginnings of a general downgrading of the early English poets (so Pearsall 1983: 193), but more likely what is at issue is a contest between 'drab' puritan-associated poets such as Gower and Langland and on the other hand 'golden' writers such as (pre-eminently) Chaucer, who escaped the general wrack.

The *Confessio Amantis* was printed in 1483 (by **Caxton**), 1532 and 1554, but not within Shakespeare's lifetime. The 1532 text and its 1554 reprint was the one 'in which Gower was read, if he was read at all, until 1810' (Pearsall 1983: 190). In this passage from Book VIII, corresponding to the recognition scene in *Pericles* 5.1, Gower's Marina-figure encounters her father, awakening him from the death-like trance into which he has fallen:

With that he sobreth his corage,

¶Qualiter sicut deus destinavit patri filia
inventam recognovit.

¶And put away his hevie chere.
But of hem two a man mai lere,
What is to be so sibbe of bloode,
None wist of other howe it stoode,
And yet the father at laste
His herte upon this mayde caste,
That he hir loveth kyndely.
And yet he wist never why,
But all was knowe er that thei went.
For god wote her hole entent,
Her hertes both anone discloseth.
This kynge, unto this maide opposeth,
And asketh first, what is hir name,
And where she lerned all this game,
And of what kyn she was come.
And she that hath his wordes nome,
Answereth, and saith: my name is Thaise,
That was sometyme well at aise.
In Tharse I was forthdrawe and fedde,
There I lerned, till I was spedde
Of that I can: my father eke
I not where that I shulde hym seke,
He was a kynge men tolde me.
My moder dreint in the see.
Fro poynt to poynt all she hym tolde,
That she hath longe in herte holde,
And never durst make hir mone,
But onely to this lorde allone,

To whom hir herte can not hele,
Tourne it to wo, tourne it to wele,
Tourne it to good, tourne it to harme.
  And he tho toke hir in his arme,
But such a joye as he tho made,
Was never sene, thus ben thei glade,
That sory hadden be toforne,
For this daie fortune hath sworne
To set hym upwarde on the whele.
So goth the worlde, now wo, now wele.
        (1700–38; Gower 1554: sig. Hh3ᵛ)

(C) Muir (1977: 68) speculates that Shakespeare knew Gower's version of the Pyramus and Thisbe story (*Confessio Amantis* III, 1331–1494), and there is a similarity between part of Book v of the poem and the episode of the casket test in *The Merchant of Venice* (see Bullough, I, 459). *The Rape of Lucrece* may reflect details from Book VII, in which the Lucrece story is made an exemplum of lust: so Richard Hillman, who argues a wider significance for the affinities in the 'balance' with which the characters are treated, since the attention Gower gives to Tarquin's 'motivation and state of mind' is 'matched only by Shakespeare' (1990: 266). But Hillman finds no verbal echoes, and the overall reasoning, 'it must have been taken from Gower: there is no trace of the idea in the classical sources' (264), is faulty. Hillman's article on *Pericles* also assumes without clear support Shakespeare's wide knowledge of the *Confessio*, leading to his 'use of love themes as a means of exploring larger issues of human sexuality and self-realization' in the play (1985: 428).

The Apollonius story is the only part of the *Confessio Amantis* certainly known to Shakespeare. He probably knew Book VIII from an early point in his career, since one of its episodes, Apollinus' discovery of his wife in the temple at Ephesus, is probably used in the denouement of *The Comedy of Errors*. 'Like the Mother in Shakespeare she becomes "abbesse" of the Temple of Diana in Ephesus and is reunited to her husband and child after many years' (Bullough, I, 11). The debt in *Pericles* is acknowledged at the start, in a passage taken seriously by Archibald (1991: 100–1) as evidence about contemporary interpretation of the Apollonius story: Gower's prologue announces a tale that

> hath been sung at festivals,
> On ember-eves and holy-ales;
> And lords and ladies in their lives
> Have read it for restoratives.
>
> (1.1.5–8)

Pericles combines the main outline of Gower's plot with the version of the same story by Lawrence **Twine**, but there are notable new or much-expanded episodes including 1.2 (with Helicanus), 2.1 (the Fishermen's dialogue) and 4.3 (Dionyza and Cleon's argument). 'Generally speaking . . . it is some of the most striking episodes in the play that are least anticipated in Gower' (Hoeniger 1963: xv). There are also severe cuts of some of Gower's less promising material. Close verbal echoes are not frequent, even though quite a number of passages in Shakespeare are paraphrased from Gower (see Hoeniger 1963: xv).

The most striking difference between poem and play, however, may be the figure of Gower himself in the role of Chorus. DelVecchio and Hammond take this to be itself a product of the *Confessio*'s influence: 'like Genius in the *Confessio*, Gower is Shakespeare's ancient storyteller, shaping and giving life to the dramatic experience for the audience by engaging the help of their imagination' (1998: 5). But something like it was in any event dramatically required for condensing the long romance, 'a story to baffle dramaturgy', as Coghill calls it (1964: 33). Hence 'Gower, who had earlier told the same story, is introduced to fill in the background material, comment on the situation, and carry forward by recitation, often imitative of his own Medieval style, incidents of the plot which dramatic compression could omit' (Gesner 1970: 86–7). Finally, in the epilogue Gower comments on the poetic justice of the play; but this, 'however much it may recall Gower's manner, has little in common with Gower's ending' (Hoeniger 1963: xvi). Lynch (1998: 69) argues, in fact, that Shakespeare's presentation of Gower as a whole 'seems not only at odds with the play but at odds with . . . [Gower's] Confessor-narrator'.

It might be proposed that Gower's contribution to the distinctive quality of *Pericles* goes deeper. Comparison with the Chinese box structures of **Heliodorus** reflected in *Cymbeline* suggests that the limpidity of Gower's story and its affinities with the saint's life narrative may have had an effect. Less speculatively, it should be agreed that Shakespeare has by use of the archaic romance materials with their inevitable circular movement from prosperity and well-being through adversity to joy and prosperity again . . . infused the play with an air of oft-repeated ceremony and ritual, giving it the tone of old myth, the quality of pageant and spectacle re-enacting the predictable cycles of life.

(Gesner 1970: 88)

(D) Pearsall (1983) gives guidance on Gower's reputation up to the present. Archibald (1991) is comprehensive on the transmission of the Apollonius story. Bullough, VI, compares Gower, Twine and Shakespeare in some detail. Hoeniger's treatments (1963, 1982) of the Gower–Shakespeare relationship are standard; Hillman (1985) proposes major influence, especially thematic, on *Pericles*; Scragg's (1992) more recent account is more perfunctory.

Archibald, Elizabeth (1991). *Apollonius of Tyre: Medieval and Renaissance Themes and Variations*. Woodbridge.

Bullough, I, VI.

Coghill, Nevill (1964). *Shakespeare's Professional Skills*. Cambridge.

DelVecchio, Doreen, and Antony Hammond, eds (1998). *Pericles* (New Cambridge Shakespeare). Cambridge.

Garrett, R. M. (1912). 'Gower in *Pericles*.' *ShJ* 48: 13–20.

Gesner, Carol (1970). *Shakespeare and the Greek Romance: A Study of Origins*. Lexington, KY.

Goolden, Peter (1955). 'Antiochus' Riddle in Gower and Shakespeare.' *RES* 6: 245–51.

Gower, John (1554). *De Confessione Amantis*. London.

Hillman, Richard (1985). 'Shakespeare's Gower and Gower's Shakespeare: The Larger Debt of *Pericles*.' *ShQ* 36: 427–37.

—— (1990). 'Gower's Lucrece: A New Old Source for *The Rape of Lucrece*.' *Chaucer Review* 24: 263–70.

Hoeniger, F. David, ed. (1963). *Pericles* (Arden Shakespeare). London.

—— (1982). 'Gower and Shakespeare in *Pericles*.' *ShQ* 33: 461–79.

Lynch, Stephen J. (1998). *Shakespearean Intertextuality: Studies in Selected Sources and Plays*. Westport, CT.

Pearsall, Derek (1983). 'The Gower Tradition', pp. 179–97 in A. J. Minnis, ed., *Gower's 'Confessio Amantis': Responses and Reassessments*. Cambridge.

Scragg, Leah (1992). *Shakespeare's Mouldy Tales: Recurrent Plot Motifs in Shakespearean Drama*. London.

Grafton, Richard (*c*. 1512–1572), Chronicler

(A) Grafton, a native of Shrewsbury, is best known for his part in making the **Bible** available in English: he printed a version of the Great Bible in collaboration with Miles Coverdale and Edward Whitchurch in 1538–9. In 1543 he published John **Hardyng**'s Chronicle, the first of the sixteenth-century chronicles, incorporating Thomas **More**'s life of Richard III and his own prose continuation (covering the period from Edward IV). In 1548 he brought out the recently deceased Edward **Hall**'s Chronicle, *The Union of the Two Noble and Illustre Families*, again with his own continuation, for the years 1532–47. Hall's work was burnt for its uncompromising Protestantism under Mary, and Grafton suffered too. On the accession of Edward VI in 1547 he had been appointed Royal Printer, but on Edward's death in 1553 he printed the proclamation of Lady Jane Grey, signing himself 'the Queen's Printer', and as a result was for a time imprisoned by Mary.

He now turned to compiling his own full-scale chronicle. A preliminary *Abridgement of the Chronicles of England* was dedicated to Lord Robert Dudley in 1562, followed by *A Manuell of the Chronicles of England* in 1565, but the full-scale two-volume history itself appeared in 1568–9 and is titled *A Chronicle at Large and Meere History of the Affayres of England and Kinges of the Same, deduced from the Creation of the Worlde, unto the First Habitation of this Island: and so by Continuance unto the First Yere of the Reigne of our Most Deere and Sovereigne Lady Queene Elizabeth*. This follows More and Hall in its theatrical and analytical approach to historical writing, while as a post-Reformation work emphasizing more strongly history's demonstration of God's judgements.

(B) *A Chronicle at Large* was for much of its length so close a transcript of Hall that John **Stow** complained in his *Summary of Chronicles* that 'somebodye (without any ingenious and plaine Declaration thereof) hath published, but not without mangeling, maister Halles Booke for his owne', prompting Grafton to defend his 'allegement' (abridgement). He had, he justifiably claimed, left out Hall's rhetorical speeches and 'many obscure woordes' (Preface to *Abridgement of the Chronicles of England*, 1570); but Grafton made no significant contribution to the content itself in those large stretches of the *Chronicle* taken over from Hall. Nor were his continuations of any great account for other writers, since all the parts of English history that were widely taken up by the Elizabethans were covered by Hall. Grafton's main importance for historical knowledge in the latter part of the sixteenth century was to ensure that Hall's work, which had dated quickly in style, continued to be available.

(C) The large overlaps between Grafton's work and that of **Hall**, **Holinshed** and other chroniclers make it difficult to isolate Grafton's particular contribution to Shakespeare, and it may indeed be negligible. Though he has been canvassed as a source for, in particular, *Henry VI* (especially by Wilson 1952a–b), there is for the *Henry VI* plays almost 'nothing in Grafton that cannot be accounted for from Holinshed, Hall, and Fox' (Cairncross 1957: xl). For Shakespeare's historical works in general, 'Grafton's revision of Hall's text, except for an occasional passage, is not detectable in the plays; verbal comparisons indicate Hall as the usual source' (Zeeveld 1936: 319). It is true that the few small and otherwise insignificant verbal similarities Shakespeare shows with Grafton cannot be neatly accounted for except on the assumption that Shakespeare did consult the *Chronicle at Large* for at least *Henry VI*. In the end, however, this is a case in which modern tendencies to lay stress on individual authorship may be counter-productive. All the sources available to Shakespeare for the history of Richard III, for example, were in fact interlinked: More's *History* was incorporated into Grafton, while Hall had incorporated Polydore Vergil and was himself incorporated by Hardyng, Stow and Holinshed (see Churchill 1900: 208–11). 'Naturally, there are differences between these works, but the process of redaction would leave a dramatist in search of variety of information or of emphasis very little to go on' (Hammond 1981: 75).

(D)
Cairncross, Andrew S., ed. (1957). *The Second Part of King Henry VI* (Arden Shakespeare). London.
Campbell, Lily B. (1947). *Shakespeare's 'Histories': Mirrors of Elizabethan Policy*. San Marino, CA.
Churchill, George B. (1900). *Richard the Third up to Shakespeare*. Berlin.
Hammond, Antony, ed. (1981). *King Richard III* (Arden Shakespeare). London.

Wilson, John Dover, ed. (1952a). *Henry VI Part 1* (New Shakespeare). Cambridge.

—— ed. (1952b). *Henry VI Part 2* (New Shakespeare). Cambridge.

Zeeveld, W. Gordon (1936). 'The Influence of Hall on Shakespeare's English Historical Plays.' *ELH* 3: 317–53.

Grammaticus, Saxo See **Belleforest, François de**.

Greek Anthology See **Marianus Scholasticus**.

Greek Romance (Including Achilles Tatius, *Apollonius of Tyre*, Chariton, Heliodorus, Longus, Xenophon of Ephesus)

(A) 'Romance' is the modern name for a long story of love and adventure written in prose; the first extant examples are the Greek romances of the early Christian era (2nd to 3rd centuries AD). The best-known are the work of Chariton of Aphrodisia (*Chaereas and Callirhoe*), Xenophon of Ephesus (*Habrocomes and Anthia* or *Ephesiaca*), Heliodorus of Emesa (*Aethiopica*), Longus (*Daphnis and Chloe*) and an anonymous author (*Apollonius of Tyre*, a lost work only available through later retellings). The last three have proved the most popular. Additionally there is Achilles Tatius' *Clitophon and Leucippe*, a non-mainstream romance which in the past has been thought to be a parody of others. The stories were probably told for centuries before being written down, but these writers made them vehicles for a self-conscious display of elaborate rhetorical and stylistic effects. They have been looked upon as escapist writing for the naive, but also as expressions of the beliefs of mystery cults; each view seems to be suggested by the marvellously improbable action. The main common elements of the stories are the long separation of two lovers; their unflinching fidelity and chastity through temptation and trial; an extremely involved plot with many subplots; travel to distant lands; mistaken identity and disguise.

(B) The transmission of Greek romances to the Renaissance involves complex routes, and the complications are often relevant to an understanding of what sources writers of the period are using. For example, the story of Apollonius of Tyre probably derives from a Greek original of the third century AD, and was probably turned into Latin about the sixth century. It survived in Greek and Latin manuscripts through the Middle Ages, and was eventually incorporated into the **Gesta Romanorum**, perhaps in the fourteenth century. Thence it passed into the vernacular throughout Europe, though in England's case John **Gower**'s influential treatment in his *Confessio Amantis* (1393) derived mainly from the twelfth-century Latin *Pantheon* of Godfrey of Viterbo. (For the full history of the tale's transmission see Archibald 1991.)

The Greek romance was an important influence on Renaissance narrative and drama, in the work of major writers across Europe: such different figures as **Boccaccio** and **Cervantes** (from whom, in turn, later storytellers borrow) are examples. In Britain, 'Greek romance is a major fabric of Renaissance narrative and drama, and . . . many of the marvelous adventures and titillating plot motifs and patterns, especially those calculated to produce surprise and horror or to create a spectacular effect, derive from the novel of the Greek decadence' (Gesner 1970: viii). However, this derivation is usually indirect, even though English translations became available during Shakespeare's lifetime (having been preceded in most cases by Italian, French or Latin renderings). Thomas Underdowne's Heliodorus appeared in 1577 and was reissued five times by 1607, Angel Day's Longus in 1587, William Burton's Achilles Tatius in 1597.

One of the stories in Barnaby Riche's *Farewell to Militarie Profession* (1581) is probably the first Elizabethan work of fiction to show unambiguous and extended debts to the Hellenic romance, with apparent verbal echoes as well as plot material from Underdowne's Heliodorus. William Warner's story-collection *Albion's England* (1584) came under the same influence. Henceforward it is common for English stories to use some of the motifs or conventions of Greek romance, or to treat the material as a repertory of incident. The authors may or may not know any examples directly: for example, a number of **Greene**'s stories appropriate elements directly from Longus, Heliodorus and Achilles Tatius, while others are apparently based only on Boccaccio. On other occasions English writers take from the romance the suggestion of a heightened and elaborated 'long story' itself: **Sidney** used Heliodorus as a model of form in this way in the *Arcadia*.

A lost play called *Theagenes and Chariclea*, performed for Elizabeth I in 1572, perhaps from Heliodorus, may be the first dramatic example of a

Greek romance plot on the English stage. The affinity between Greek romances and drama was noted as long ago as Photius in the ninth century, who called them dramatic narratives. But again, when Greek romance material of whatever kind finds its way into Elizabethan drama, there is usually no sign of direct use of the Greek sources, in translation or otherwise.

(C) It is impossible to prove how much Shakespeare knew of Greek romances directly, in English translations or in other possible forms either English or European, and how much of his awareness of them came from the 'derived tradition'. However, the latter (involving such writers as Gower, Greene, Sidney and **Twine** (see (B)) accounts for most, perhaps all, of his knowledge, and this is treated in the appropriate entries elsewhere in this dictionary. The fact remains, however, that in one or two plays with recognized sources in the derived tradition, some details not anticipated in Shakespeare's accepted immediate sources are present in the romances themselves.

Leaving aside incidental and/or very probably indirect reflections elsewhere in Shakespeare's work, the Late Plays are the points at which the strongest connections can be found, the case for direct echoes being strongest with *Cymbeline* and *Pericles*. (Wolff 1912: 452–5 offers a now generally discounted suggestion about Day's *Daphnis and Chloe* as a source for *The Winter's Tale*.) *Cymbeline* shows links from the derived tradition to perhaps almost all the principal romances, but some analogues with Achilles Tatius are less easy to explain as arising indirectly. For example, in *Clitophon and Leucippe* the theme of mistaken death occurs several times, and at one point the lover, Clitophon, is deceived by a headless body dressed in Leucippe's clothing, the head having been cast into the sea (compare Guiderius on Cloten's head: 'I' ll throw't into the creek / Behind our rock, and let it to the sea', 4.2.152–3). (This can be paralleled from other possible sources; but see Gesner 1970: 95–8 for other affinities with Achilles Tatius.) *Pericles* is again a kind of composite of romance elements, with a few distinctive elements not in evidence in the derived tradition. In particular, because of coincidences with different known variants of the story of Apollonius, especially in characters' names, it is thought that Shakespeare must have known some lost folklore or other version of the tale as well as Gower's and Twine's (see Bullough, vi, 355).

As for the general 'romance properties' which many commentators have seen in some Shakespeare works (such as Adams 1967 on romantic love and the faithful heroine), these are invariably derivable from intermediate sources, though it is admittedly interesting to speculate about what Shakespeare might have felt was distinctive about the romances themselves. The nearest he comes to a discussion is in the *Pericles* prologue, since it does not refer only to the Gower version of the Apollonius story:

> To sing a song that old was sung,
> From ashes ancient Gower is come,
> Assuming man's infirmities,
> To glad your ear and please your eyes.
> It hath been sung at festivals,
> On ember-eves and holy-ales;
> And lords and ladies in their lives
> Have read it for restoratives.
> The purchase is to make men glorious;
> Et bonum quo antiquius, eo melius.
>
> (1–10)

'To make men glorious': did Shakespeare detect in the romances some resonance that has eluded later commentators? Terry Comito's answer is as follows:

For Shakespeare (or even for Fletcher) all their mazed complexity seems to have embodied an intuition about the rhythms of experience itself. The hard outlines of beginning, middle, and end begin to blur, as does the boundary between comedy and tragedy. No single episode will seem absolute when the world has become (as it has for Marina) a 'lasting storm, whirring' man from all fixity (*Pericles*, 4.1.198–20); or a labyrinth like the forest where Philaster loses his way in a 'mere confusion and so dead a chaos that love cannot distinguish' (*Philaster*, 3.2.138–40).

(Comito 1975: 60)

We may choose to believe that such was the overall impression Shakespeare acquired of Greek romance, whether or not his reading included any specimens at first hand.

207

(D)

Adams, Martha Latimer (1967). 'The Greek Romance and William Shakespeare.' *University of Mississippi Studies in English* 8: 43–52.

Archibald, Elizabeth (1991). *Apollonius of Tyre: Medieval and Renaissance Themes and Variations.* Woodbridge.

Comito, Terry (1975). 'Exile and Return in the Greek Romances.' *Arion* (2nd series) 2: 59–80.

Doody, Margaret Anne (1998). *The True Story of the Novel.* London (first published 1997).

Gesner, Carol (1970) *Shakespeare and the Greek Romance: A Study of Origins.* Lexington, KY.

Haight, Elizabeth Hazelton (1945). '*Apollonius of Tyre* and Shakespeare's *Pericles, Prince of Tyre*', pp. 142–89 in Haight, *More Essays on Greek Romances.* New York.

Wolff, Samuel Lee (1912). *The Greek Romances in Elizabethan Prose Fiction.* New York.

Greene, Robert (1560?–1592), Playwright, Novelist, Poet and Pamphleteer

(A) The son of a Norwich saddler, Greene attended St John's College and Clare Hall, Cambridge. From 1586 he quickly acquired a reputation as a playwright and reprobate, one of the University Wits. As a writer he had some real talents. He combined verse and prose in romances such as *Mamillia* (*c.* 1580) and the very popular *Pandosto* (1588). *Menaphon* (1589), including some attractive lyrics and carrying a prefatory epistle by **Nashe**, is a burlesque of the euphuistic romance. He may have collaborated with Shakespeare on *Henry VI* (and possibly elsewhere), and with **Lodge** on *A Looking Glasse for London and England.* His extant solo plays, mostly romantic comedies, probably all belong to his last years, beginning with *Alphonsus*, an absurd attempt to rival *Tamburlaine*; the others definitely ascribed to him are *Orlando Furioso, James IV* and *Friar Bacon and Friar Bungay*. It is a minority view that these constitute his best work; some of them were certainly popular. Though one of the best-known authors of the day, Greene did not become wealthy through his writing: over the years he approached sixteen different patrons for seventeen works. The more successful Shakespeare (the 'upstart crow') was famously disparaged in the 1592 tract *Greene's Groatsworth of Witte* (possibly by Henry Chettle). Ironically, he was called upon by Church authorities in the 1590s to defend the faith against the Puritan 'Martin Marprelate'. His end in squalid surroundings following 'a surfeit of pickle herring and Rennish wine' was described with relish by Gabriel **Harvey**, whose notorious quarrel with Nashe had been provoked by one of Greene's pamphlets.

(B) Greene's romance *Pandosto. The Triumph of Time*, the main source of *The Winter's Tale*, is an intricate and plausibly complicated story, drawing sometimes hackneyed material from a large number of previous narratives, especially of the Patient Grissel type (including, whether directly or indirectly, **Greek romances** and **Chaucer**'s *Clerk's Tale*: see Baldwin 1990). *Pandosto* reflected the tastes of the age, and its popularity led to more adaptations than one. In 1595 Francis **Sabie**, a Lichfield schoolmaster, turned it into two blank-verse narrative poems which Shakespeare also seems to have used. It is perhaps surprising Greene did not adapt it as a play himself – it is eventful and episodic. As it is, the tale is told with a speed and economy Greene's other work often lacks. *Pandosto*'s popularity outlasted that of almost all other Elizabethan fiction, despite mockery from some elite quarters: there were twenty-six editions by 1735, and it is alluded to later still in Richardson's *Clarissa* (for its later reputation see Newcomb 1997).

This sample shows several points of congruity with *The Winter's Tale*:

It happened not long after this, that there was a meeting of all the Farmers Daughters in Sycilia, whither Fawnia was also bidden as the mistres of the feast, who having attired her selfe in her best garments, went among the rest of her companions to the merry meeting: there spending the day in such homely pastimes as shephards use. As the evening grew on, and their sportes ceased, ech taking their leave at other, Fawnia desiring one of her companions to beare her companie, went home by the flocke, to see if they were well folded, and as they returned, it fortuned that Dorastus (who all that daye had bene hawking, and kilde store of game) incountred by the way these two mayds, and casting his eye sodenly on Fawnia, he was halfe afraid, fearing that with Acteon he had seene Diana: for hee thought such exquisite perfection could not be founde in any mortall creature. As thus he stood in a maze, one of his Pages told him, that the maide with the garland on her head was Fawnia the faire shepheard, whose beauty was so much talked of in the Court. Dorastus desirous to see if nature had adorned her minde with any inward qualities, as she had decked her body with outward shape, began to question with her whose daughter she was, of what age and how she had bin trained up, who answered him with such modest reverence and sharpnesse of witte, that Dorastus thought her outward beautie was but a counterfait to darken her inward qualities, wondring how so courtly behaviour could be found in so simple a cottage, and cursing fortune that had shadowed wit and beauty with such hard fortune. As thus he held her a long while with chat, Beauty seeing him at discovert, thought not to lose the vantage, but strooke him so deeply with an invenomed shafte, as he wholy lost his libertie, and became a slave to Love, which before contemned Love.

(Greene 1588: sigs D2^v–D3^r)

(C) It is supposed Shakespeare used one of the first three editions of *Pandosto* of 1588–95, rather than one of the later editions in which the Oracle is made to say 'The King shall die [not 'live'] without an heir.'

The *Pandosto* story falls into five phases. The first is a study of jealousy, as is underlined by Greene's opening paragraph on the 'infectious sore' this passion represents. Pandosto, King of Bohemia, resolves to have his old friend King Egistus of Sicily poisoned during a visit. His companion warns Egistus and assists his escape, but the innocent and pregnant Queen Bellaria is imprisoned and proclaimed an adulteress and traitor. The newborn daughter is cast adrift at sea. Bellaria is tried and condemned by Pandosto, but his nobles persuade him to consult the Oracle of Apollo, which declares Bellaria chaste, Egistus innocent, and Pandosto treacherous. Pandosto's remorse comes too late as his only son is reported dead and Bellaria herself collapses and dies; Pandosto erects a tomb for her. In the second phase, the infant daughter is picked up by Porrus, a poor shepherd with a shrewish wife, who brings up the girl, Fawnia, until she is sixteen. Third, Fawnia is wooed by Egistus' son Dorastus, against his father's will. At their second meeting she praises the simple country life, and, after a conflict between his love and his sense of rank, Dorastus dresses in shepherd's clothes to ask for Fawnia's hand. They decide to flee to Italy, but Porrus has meanwhile determined to inform the King how Fawnia was found. Instead he is lured onto the ship taking the lovers abroad by Dorastus' servant Capnio.

Egistus now falls ill with grief at the loss of his son, while the ship is driven onto the coast of Bohemia. Dorastus disguises himself, remembering the quarrel between his father and Pandosto, but Pandosto, hearing of Fawnia's beauty, has the couple brought before him. He conceives an 'unlawful lust' for the girl, and casts Dorastus into prison. In the fifth and last phase, Egistus sends ambassadors to request his son's freedom and Fawnia's execution. But Porrus finally tells the story of her finding, displaying the tokens by which Pandosto realizes she is his daughter. The youths' marriage is celebrated in Sicily, but Pandosto, struck anew with remorse at his incestuous impulse, commits suicide. His crown is assumed by Dorastus. Greene's moral, underlined in the Epistle Dedicatory and by his subtitle 'The Triumph of Time', is that 'time will tell'.

Shakespeare's play, then, reverses the locales: the King and Queen of Bohemia become monarchs of Sicily, while Greene's King of Sicily is made King of Bohemia. *The Winter's Tale* enriches *Pandosto* by adding fresh characters, most notably Paulina and Autolycus (the one character omitted is the shepherd Porrus' shrewish wife, slightly resembling Paulina; Autolycus is also slightly anticipated by Capnio, Dorastus' servant). And there are two crucial narrative departures. Greene's sombre resolution seems to most readers out of keeping with the rest of the story, and is described by Greene himself as a way 'to close up the Comedie with a Tragicall stratageme'. In Shakespeare the survival of the queen and the reconciliation of the family at the close are the most major changes to the plot. But the proximity of play to source is remarkable for Shakespeare, involving more verbal echoes than from any novel or romance he used on any other occasion. Pafford (1966: xxx–xxxi) lists strongly parallel passages: a comparison suggests that Shakespeare must not only have studied Greene's story first to work out his plot, but kept it by his side as he wrote. Since his use of it can only imply approbation of some kind, this seems to bring full circle his relation to his old collaborator (as it appears) and abuser. Even one of Shakespeare's character names, Mamillius, may have been taken from Greene's quite separate romance *Mamillia* (the rest are mostly from **Plutarch**).

On the other hand, there are also important ways in which *Pandosto* seems to have set Shakespeare's imagination to work without determining exactly what course it would take. Thus, for example,

when Bellaria asked that the Oracle might be consulted it was 'fearing more perpetual infamy than momentary death', and she fell down on her knees to make the request. Shakespeare develops the queen's attitude to infamy and death, but as for the act of kneeling, he gives this to the cowed courtiers pleading for the baby's life at II, iii, 152, where as the unanimous expression of horror and revulsion it is impressive. (Pyle 1969: 159–60)

Or the stimulus may operate in an opposite direction: Bellaria's tears in prison may have led to Hermione being 'not prone to weeping'.

Pandosto's lack of *The Winter's Tale*'s happiness and optimism is not a contrast in the plays' endings alone, since 'there is little in [Greene's] characters which shows the working of strength, loyalty, self-sacrifice, love, or other virtue' (Pafford 1966: xxxxiii). But as Bullough points out, the drastic change in *The Winter's Tale*'s denouement could be said to be dictated partly by the logic of Shakespeare's development, and partly too by the requirements of the dramatic presentation: if he was to repeat the reconciliatory type of ending he had already written in *Pericles* and *Cymbeline*, it would require a figure unlike the lustful and backsliding Pandosto, and 'to leave Leontes in penitential misery without any recompense would be both harsh and undramatic. A miracle was needed to make reconciliation and pardon possible' (Bullough, VIII, 132). A double denouement of the type found in *Pericles* is also made possible by the resuscitation of Hermione. Yet Shakespeare's innovative artistry should not be ignored through over-emphasis on the exigencies of plot, for reconciliation and unity are latent in much earlier scenes from Act 4: 'Shakespeare has taken the decisive step away from a merely dramatized narrative of love's young woes to the true art of the romance play, where the unity to be attained is focused in truths spoken unwittingly by youth and age alike' (Lawlor 1962: 99).

Further dimensions to the connection between the two works have been proposed. Lawlor stresses the reversal of the idea in *Pandosto*'s subtitle: Shakespeare shows 'not . . . the triumph of Time, but [of] the human wish to triumph over time' (1962: 105). Ewbank (1989) takes the point slightly further by suggesting that the triumph of patience (rather than time or fortune) means that *The Winter's Tale* harks back to pre-Greene versions of the story such as Chaucer's. Lynch (1998: 83–4) contends that Shakespeare 'writes against the linguistic assumptions' of *Pandosto* ('language as a fully reliable medium of representation').

A number of Greene's many other writings have been connected more locally with other Shakespeare plays. Autolycus' roguery may well draw details from Greene's popular series on the practices of contemporary thieves and other crooks, *The Art of Conny-Catching* (1591–2; excerpted by Bullough, VIII, 214–19). Greene's essay-collection *Euphues his Censure to Philautus* (1587) has long been considered a possible minor source for *Troilus and Cressida* (see Whitaker 1976; Palmer 1982); Greene presents four debates between Greeks and Trojans during a truce, with some verbal and topical similarities to various points in Shakespeare's play and as a whole conceivably forming a model for its otherwise unprecedented council scene.

It is easy to believe that Greene's plays must also have influenced Shakespeare in one way or another – though overly speculative suggestions such as Chandler (1995a–b) can be discounted. Greene's best efforts, *Friar Bacon* and *James IV*, came at a time when his younger contemporary would have been most receptive to innovative dramaturgical ideas. Greene's mixtures of tangled love story (with rural scenes), magic and fairy-lore, Plautine jokes, interlude devices, and reminiscences of the classics is not so far removed from the materials of Shakespeare's romantic comedies, in which he seems to have 'placed in juxtaposition similar temperaments, and created conflicts . . . characteristic of Greene's drama' (Tynan 1912: 258), including in particular his development of the triangular love-relationship out of the model first furnished on the stage by the two Greene plays just mentioned (see Dean 1982: 39–40). Some more specific similarities should also be noted. *James IV*'s structurally striking scene 1.1 may have been a model for the structure of *Julius Caesar* 1.2 (see Jones 1971: 22–3), and there are close parallels to the rhetorical arrangement of some of its heroine's speeches at one or two points in Helena's soliloquy at *All's Well* 3.2.102–16 (see Hunter 1987). Finally, if the two men did not, in fact, collaborate on *Henry VI*, Greene's influence may well lurk behind certain scenes in the trilogy none the less; one explanation of the 'upstart crow' attack is that he is accusing Shakespeare of plagiarizing his work in those plays.

(D) Cole (1973: 507–42) has a sharp reading of Greene's work as a whole. The text of *Pandosto* has been frequently reprinted, for example by Bullough, VIII, and Pafford (1966), who also provide two of the most extensive discussions of the romance's relation to *The Winter's Tale*. Lawlor's (1962) ambitious essay shows how Shakespeare's transformation of *Pandosto* can be a key to understanding the nature of his 'dogmatic romance' mode. A more diffuse but no less substantial treatment of the relationship goes on in the course of Pyle (1969).

Baldwin, Anna (1990). 'From the *Clerk's Tale* to *The Winter's Tale*', pp. 199–212 in Ruth Morse and Barry Windeatt, eds, *Chaucer Traditions: Studies in Honour of Derek Brewer*. Cambridge.

Bullough, VIII.

Carroll, D. Allen (1987). 'The Badger in *Greenes Groats-Worth of Witte* and in Shakespeare.' *SP* 84: 471–82.

Chandler, David (1995a). 'An Incident from Greene's *Alphonsus* in *As You Like It*.' *N&Q* 240: 317–19.

—— (1995b). 'The "Bed-Trick" in *Measure for Measure*: A Source Suggestion.' *N&Q* 240: 320–1.

Cole, Howard C. (1973). *A Quest of Inquirie: Some Contexts of Tudor Literature*. Indianapolis.

Dean, Paul (1982). 'Shakespeare's *Henry VI* Trilogy and Elizabethan "Romance" Histories: The Origins of a Genre.' *ShQ* 33: 34–48.

Ewbank, Inga-Stina (1989). 'From Narrative to Dramatic Language: *The Winter's Tale* and its Source', pp. 29–47 in Marvin Thompson *et al.*, eds, *Shakespeare and the Sense of Performance: Essays in the Tradition of Performance Criticism in Honor of Bernard Beckerman*. Newark, DE.

Greene, Robert (1588). *Pandosto. The Triumph of Time*. London.

Hunter, G. K. (1987). 'How Greene was my Shakespeare? K. M. Revisited', pp. 76–9 in *KM 80: A Birthday Album for Kenneth Muir*. Liverpool.

Jones, Emrys (1971). *Scenic Form in Shakespeare*. Oxford.

Lawlor, John (1962). '*Pandosto* and the Nature of Dramatic Romance.' *PQ* 41: 96–113.

Lynch, Stephen J. (1998). 'Language in *Pandosto* and *The Winter's Tale*', pp. 83–112 in Lynch, *Shakespearean Intertextuality: Studies in Selected Sources and Plays*. Westport, CT.

Mortenson, Peter, and Jo Ann Davis (1975). 'A Source for "Richard II", II.i.40–68.' *N&Q* 220: 167–8.

Newcomb, Lori Humphrey (1997). 'The Triumph of Time: The Fortunate Readers of Robert Greene's *Pandosto*', pp. 95–123 in Cedric C. Brown and Arthur F. Marotti, eds, *Texts and Cultural Change in Early Modern England*. Basingstoke.

Pafford, J. H. P., ed. (1966). *The Winter's Tale* (Arden Shakespeare). London.

Palmer, Kenneth, ed. (1982). *Troilus and Cressida* (Arden Shakespeare). London.

Pyle, Fitzroy (1969). *The Winter's Tale: A Commentary on the Structure.* London.

Tynan, Joseph L. (1912). 'The Influence of Greene on Shakespeare's Early Romance.' *PMLA* 27: 246–64.

Whitaker, Virgil K. (1976). 'Still Another Source for *Troilus and Cressida*', pp. 100–7 in Standish Henning *et al.*, eds, *English Renaissance Drama: Essays in Honor of Madeleine Doran and Mark Eccles.* Carbondale.

Grenewey, Richard See **Tacitus, Publius Cornelius or Gaius Cornelius.**

Grimald, Nicholas See **Cicero, Marcus Tullius;** *Tottel's Miscellany*.

Groto, Luigi (d. 1624), Italian Dramatist Groto's play *La Hadriana* (1578), drawn from a version of the Romeo and Juliet story, shows one or two small local similarities to Shakespeare's play, but it is unlikely Shakespeare would have known it.

Orr, David (1970). *Italian Renaissance Drama in England before 1625: The Influence of 'Erudita' Tragedy, Comedy, and Pastoral on Elizabethan and Jacobean Drama*, p. 127. Chapel Hill.

Guarini, Giovanni Battista (1538–1612), Italian Poet and Playwright

(A) A native Ferrarese, Guarini became a courtier and diplomat, adopted as court poet there when Tasso fell into disgrace. His famous pastoral play *Il pastor fido* ('The Faithful Shepherd'), based on Tasso's hugely successful drama *Aminta* (1573), was composed in the early 1580s, first published in 1589, and performed in 1595. With its associated critical writings, notably the *Compendio della poesia tragicomica* (issued with later editions), it is Guarini's only literary work to be remembered today, though he also wrote a collection of *Rime*, a comedy (*L'Idropica*), letters, and treatises on politics. This 'five-act academic, Sophoclean pastoral tragicomedy in verse prepared for a royal wedding', as Clubb (1989: 6) strenuously describes it, tells an elaborately plotted romantic story set in Arcadia of a couple supposed to marry to avert a plague sent by Diana. Both boy and girl love elsewhere, but after narrow escapes from compromising situations as well as capital punishment, and a discovery of hidden ancestry, the lovers' permutations are brought into harmony with their inclinations. The play, today accorded no more than historical importance, is characterized by wordy monologues, narrations, sententiae and other features in which its high style can be displayed.

(B) In Italy *Il pastor fido* was an immediate but controversial success, Guarini doing all he could to fan the controversy with defences of the tragicomic form he had pioneered, on the grounds of Aristotelian 'truth to life'. Within forty years there had been translations into German, Spanish, Dutch and Portuguese. It would be a large task to trace the aftermath of *Il pastor fido* over Europe: the play became the single most influential example of stage pastoral, and of the new Italian mixture of tragedy and comedy, so baptizing if not actually giving birth to Renaissance tragicomedy.

English printings of Guarini's play began as early as 1591, when an edition paid for by Giacopo Castelvetri, an Italian tutor to the aristocracy who was keen to convey fashionable masterpieces into his pupils' hands, was printed in London. An English translation of 1602 is ascribed to Sir John Dymock; Sir Richard Fanshawe produced another in 1647; and one ?W. Quarles translated the work into Latin for a Cambridge performance in about 1604. There are nine seventeenth-century editions of translations by five separate hands, whereas no other Italian play can show more than a single translation, and most were not Englished at all.

As early as 1605, **Jonson**, like some continental critics, attacks imitators of Guarini (in *Volpone* 3.4.86–92), who have already supposedly slackened the sinews of English poetry with their emulation of his smooth and 'feminine' style. Such properties come over only crudely in the 1602 English version:

> Cruell *Amarillis*, that with thy bitter name
> Most bitterly dost teach me to complaine

216

Whiter then whitest Lillies and more faire,
But deafer and more fierce than th'adder is.
Since with my words I do so much offend,
In silence will I die; but yet these plaines
These mountaines and these woods, shal cry for me,
Whom I so oft have learned to resound
That loved name. For me my plaints shall tell
The plaining fountains and the murm'ring windes:
Pittie and griefe shall speake out of my face,
And in the end though all things else prove dombe,
My verie death shal tell my martirdome.
(1.2.1–13; Guarini 1602: sig. B3ᵛ)

Guarini's mode was more refined than anything preceding it in English drama, at a distance from the tragedy of blood or the homely japes of earlier English (or Italian) stage comedy. But to a writer of Jonson's cast, its faults included a moral evasiveness and transgressions against the principles of decorum.

As theatre it proved not directly assimilable to the English tradition. The title of Fletcher's *The Faithful Shepherdess* (1608) alludes to Guarini, and this play attempted a similar sophistication, which, however, its disastrous reception showed its audience unprepared for: the public took tragicomedy to be **Sidney**'s 'mongrel' genre, mixing comedy and clowns with tragedy and kings. More oblique ways of capitalizing on Guarini's innovations had better success. Other English playwrights to immerse themselves in the theory and practice of the new genre, though not uncritically so, were John **Marston**, whose *The Malcontent* (?1603), entered as a 'tragicomoedia' in the Stationers' Register, incorporates many literal quotations from the 1602 English translation of *Il pastor fido*, and Samuel **Daniel**, who imitated Guarini's play in his 'pastoral tragicomedy' (as he termed it) *The Queene's Arcadia* (1605), and is sometimes assumed to be the main target of Jonson's irony in the *Volpone* passage. Guarini's impact may also have contributed importantly to a wider change in the Elizabethan public repertory in the early 1600s 'away from the grand confrontation that *Hamlet* had implied and toward the compromise by which justice and forgiveness could be embodied in the action' (Hunter 1973: 137).

(C) Guarini's effect on Shakespeare partly equates to that of the theatrical movement in which he was so influential, a movement which 'in Italy produced neat intrigue comedies in the early Cinquecento and later romantic comedy, and experiments with tragedy, as well as a pastoral drama that was cultivated with an intent to stage the kinds of visions at which Shakespeare eventually excelled' (Clubb 1989: 23). A general debt of this kind can be claimed at least for any of Shakespeare's 'problem comedies' and 'green world' plays. Henke, for example, accepts that *The Winter's Tale* 'exemplifies the "unwritten poetics" of [Guarini and others] . . . probably independently of direct influence' (1993: 214); there has, indeed, always been precious little documentary proof of direct borrowing or physical contact between Italian comedians and Elizabethan playwrights. Great caution is also needed in evaluating similarities because of the common raw materials found in Latin comedy and Italian *novelle*. But such indirect or 'generalized' influence may hold more significance than anything traditional source studies could establish. There is evidence that the genres, topoi and commonplaces of Cinquecento theatre were 'known or known of in England without reference to any particular playwright', evidence which is arguably 'especially important for doing justice to Shakespeare, whose work . . . demands recognition as avant-garde drama in which the latest theatrical fashions were appropriated in dazzlingly new combinations' (Clubb 1989: 157). In the early 1600s, no fashion was more prominent on the European stage than the new Italian tragicomedy of which *Il pastor fido* was paradigmatic. The point is taken further still by Doran (1954), who suggests that if there is a theoretical foundation for Shakespeare's work in general, it is to be found in Guarini's theory of mixed genres.

Guarini's direct influence on Shakespeare has been claimed too, on no less an authority than G. K. Hunter's. The approximate coincidence of the dates of the 1602 translation and (by some chronologies at least) the writing of the first play normally connected with *Il pastor fido, All's Well that Ends Well*, may suggest the English version was of more significance than Guarini's original Italian for Shakespeare. Perhaps the former helped him use the latter. Hunter's proposed verbal similarities (1973: 138–44) with the Italian in *All's Well*, especially the *anagnorisis* of 5.3.232–74, are not compelling (for one or two more see Whitfield 1976: 34). But the case for Guarini's part in this play may be bolstered by another factor: a tonal similarity in this scene – of 'tragic urgency' with 'cumbrous levity', in Hunter's terms – and correspondingly, at the level of the drama's structure as a whole, Shakespeare's presentation not merely of mixed joy and sorrow, but of an action which arrives at a comic resolution providentially, despite or even because of its tragic potential – as Guarini's theory dictated tragicomedies should. Kirsch glosses thus: 'it was Guarini's most significant discovery that the characteristic peripeteia of tragicomedy could be related to a substantial motif of human experience – namely the Christian apprehension of *felix culpa*, the achievement of joy not only through suffering but partly because of it' (1972: 10). The last lines of *All's Well* make direct reference to such a process:

> All yet seems well; and if it end so meet,
> The bitter past, more welcome is the sweet.
> (5.3.326–7)

These lines, as commentators seem to have neglected to mention, bear some resemblance to the close of *Il pastor fido*:

> Non è sana ogni gioia,
> né mal ciò che v'annoia.
> Quello è vero gioire,
> che nasce da virtù dopo il soffrire.
> (ed. Whitfield 1976: 410)

– translated by Fanshawe (more closely than Dymock had managed):

> All is not joy
> That tickles us: Nor is all that annoy
> That goes down bitter. 'True joy is a thing
> 'That springs from Vertue after suffering.
> (ed. Whitfield 1976: 411)

Intriguing as the possibility may be that the germ of the structures which the King's remark reflects in *All's Well* can be found in Guarini, however, the observation may of course be felt to rest rather on human experience at large.

Measure for Measure can be said to be Guarinian by virtue of its final denouement as well as its modality, and Lucio's 'prattle' in 5.1 can be explained as a bold imitation of the pointedly mixed emotion ('sdegno e riso') in Guarini's unknottings. If Guarini is a source, though, he is one which Shakespeare's play overgoes: 'the sharp contrasts, moral, tonal, structural, social, even ontological, in *Measure for Measure* distinguish it from Guarini's version of tragicomedy' (Clubb 1989: 85). In general, while the formal principle of Shakespearean tragicomedy (especially in *All's Well* and *Measure for Measure*) has often been descried in Guarini's widely influential theory and practice, there is no evidence that any Shakespeare play was specifically written to his formula. Nor, in considering the background of these English plays, should the history of previous Italian attempts to mingle tragedy and comedy, and to work out how best to represent such an idea as providence, be ignored.

In their generic self-consciousness and generic contamination, their related patterns of happiness destroyed then restored by virtue and nature with divine aid, and their pastoral ingredients, the Late Plays employ elements conspicuous in Cinquecento tragicomedy. Considerably more specific similarities can be noted also. *The Winter's Tale* employs several more commonplaces of the genre in the decisive third-act techniques for balancing tragedy and comedy: the story, the dream and the comic rustic. Some of the Shakespearean thematic material, such as the philosophical topic of Nature against Art, and narrative ingredients such as the symbolic temporary relocation of characters in the country, is conspicuous in Guarini too. All this proves regrettably little, but if it is not possible to contend that Guarini must be given priority over other possible Late Play sources, it is at least arguable that these works are the closest approximations to Guarini among the English tragicomedies, as for example with the ending of *Cymbeline*, which 'approximates the drawn-out final episode of testimonies, misinterpretations, and revelations that Guarini contrives' uniquely well (Turner 1983: 201).

One earlier Shakespeare play has been associated with Guarini. But Leslie (1996) does his largely unprecedented case for the Italian's direct influence on *A Midsummer Night's Dream* no service by listing indiscriminately all similarities, even the vaguest. Though it is not to be denied that the two works 'inhabit the same aesthetic world' (463), many of these 'shared elements' – such as 'implied danger' and 'comedy' – are manifestly of no account as evidence.

(D) Perella (1960) and Staton and Simeone (1964: ix–xvi) are among discussions of Guarini's reputation in the sixteenth and seventeenth centuries. Weinberg (1961) covers the theoretical debate to which *Il pastor fido* led in the 1590s; Kirkpatrick (1995) deals with Guarini's theoretical position and the Marston and Fletcher imitations too. Clubb (1989) compares Shakespearean and Cinquecento drama thoroughly, including Guarini, addressing issues of influence incidentally but illuminatingly. Hunter (1973) argues for the direct impact of *Il pastor fido* on *All's Well* and *Measure for Measure*, whereas Kirsch (1972) is more circumspect on *All's Well* only. For the Late Plays generally see Henke (1996, 1997); for *Cymbeline*, Turner (1983).

Clubb, Louise George (1989). *Italian Drama in Shakespeare's Time*. New Haven.

Doran, Madeleine (1954). *Endeavors of Art: A Study of Form in Elizabethan Drama*. Madison, WI.

Guarini, Giovanni Battista (1602). *Il Pastor Fido: or the Faithfull Shepheard. Translated out of Italian into English*. London.

Henke, Robert (1993). '*The Winter's Tale* and Guarinian Dramaturgy.' *CompD* 27: 197–217.

—— (1996). '"Gentleman-like Tears": Affective Response in Italian Tragicomedy and Shakespeare's Late Plays.' *Comparative Literature Studies* 33: 327–49.

—— (1997). *Pastoral Transformations: Italian Tragicomedy and Shakespeare's Late Plays*. Newark, DE.

Herrick, Marvin T. (1955). *Tragicomedy: Its Origins and Development in Italy, France, and England*. Urbana, IL.

Hunter, G. K. (1973). 'Italian Tragicomedy on the English Stage.' *RenD* 6: 123–48.

Kirkpatrick, Robin (1995). *English and Italian Literature from Dante to Shakespeare: A Study of Source, Analogue and Divergence*. London.

Kirsch, Arthur (1972). *Jacobean Dramatic Perspectives*. Charlottesville.

Leslie, Robert W. (1996). 'Shakespeare's Italian Dream: Cinquecento Sources for *A Midsummer Night's Dream*.' *CompD* 29: 454–65.

Lever, J. W., ed. (1965). *Measure for Measure* (Arden Shakespeare). London.

Mowat, Barbara A. (1987). 'Shakespearean Tragicomedy', pp. 80–96 in Nancy Klein Maguire, ed., *Renaissance Tragicomedy: Explorations in Genre and Politics*. New York.

Perella, Nicholas J. (1960). 'Amarilli's Dilemma: The *Pastor Fido* and Some English Authors.' *CompLit* 12: 348–59.

Staton, Walter F., and William E. Simeone, eds (1964). *A Critical Edition* of Sir Richard Fanshawe's 1647 Translation of Giovanni Battista Guarini's 'Il Pastor Fido'. Oxford.

Turner, Robert Y. (1983). 'Slander in *Cymbeline* and Other Jacobean Tragicomedies.' *ELR* 13: 182–202.

Weinberg, Bernard (1961). *A History of Literary Criticism in the Italian Renaissance*, 2 vols. Chicago.

Whitfield, J. H., ed. (1976). *Battista Guarini: Il Pastor Fido. The Faithful Shepherd, Translated (1647) by Richard Fanshawe*. Edinburgh.

Guazzo, Stefano (1530–1593), Italian Court Secretary and Author of *La Civile conversazione* Guazzo's popular courtesy book was translated by George Pettie and Bartholomew Yong in 1581–6; for its English readership see Sullivan (1925: I, xxxiv–xxxv). D'Alessandro contends for diffuse reflections of it in Shakespeare.

D'Alessandro, Ellis J. M. (1978). 'Guazzo and Shakespeare.' *Rivista di letterature moderne e comparate* 31: 85–108.

Sullivan, Sir Edward, ed. (1925). *The Civile Conversation of M. Steeven Guazzo*. London.

Guido delle Colonne See **Caxton, William**; **Lydgate, John**.

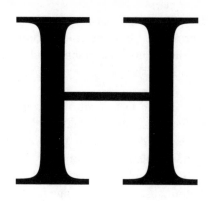

Hakluyt, Richard (*c.* 1552–1616), English Geographer A

well-known map of the world in projection which is associated with
Hakluyt's writings of 1599–1600 is a good candidate as Maria's 'new
map with the augmentation of the Indies' (*Twelfth Night* 3.2.74).

Hind, Arthur M. (1952–64). *Engraving in England in the Sixteenth and
    Seventeenth Centuries: A Descriptive Catalogue with Introductions*, 3 vols: I,
    178–81. Cambridge.

Hall (Halle), Edward (1498?–1547), Chronicler See also
More, Sir Thomas.

(A) Edward Hall, lawyer and historian, was educated at Eton, Cambridge and Gray's Inn, becoming a staunch supporter of Henry VIII
and the Tudor dynasty. His book *The Union of the Two Noble and Illustre
Families of Lancastre and Yorke* (posthumously published by Richard
Grafton in 1548), usually referred to as Hall's Chronicle, is a narrative
of fifteenth-century English history from Henry IV to Henry VIII
created by tracing the consequences of a single act, the usurpation of
Henry Bolingbroke. It is based on Polydore Vergil's *Historia Anglica*, the
first consecutive narrative account of fifteenth-century English history,
drawing also on other sources, but Hall is 'the first English chronicle-
writer to show in all its completeness that new moralizing of history
which came in with the waning of the Middle Ages' (Tillyard 1944: 42).

223

The *Union* was the most ideologically weighted of all the major sixteenth-century chronicles. It treats the period as a whole as an object lesson in the disastrous consequences of civil strife, finding a providential pattern in English history.

(B) Hall was fortunate not to live on into the reign of Mary, since his uncompromising Protestantism and unqualified support for Henry VIII would have meant his persecution. His Chronicle was burnt, but it seems in any case to have fallen quickly under a cloud as stylistically an example of 'indenture English', as Ascham called it, the language of legal deeds. Hall certainly uses such language freely, but there are more appealing ingredients (and more enthusiastic readers, such as the authors of **A Mirror for Magistrates**). An example of Hall's dramatic portrayal of events (discussed by Tillyard 1944: 48) is in his presentation of Buckingham's long speech to Bishop Morton on his claims to the title of heir to the House of Lancaster prior to the Battle of Bosworth:

> But whyther God so ordeyned, or by fortune it so chaunced, while I was in a mase, other to conclude sodaynlie on this title, and to sett it open a mongeste the common people, or to kepe it secrete a while, se the chaunce: as I rode betwene worceter and bridgenorthe, I encountered with the lady Margariete, countesse of Richemonde, nowe wyfe to the lorde Stanley, whiche is the very daughter and sole heyre, to lorde Jhon duke of Somersett my grandfathers elder brother. Whiche was as cleane out of my mynde as though I had never sene her, so that she and her sonne the Earle of Richemonde be bothe bulwarcke and portecolice betwene me, and the gate, to entre into the majestie royall and gettynge of the crowne. And when we had commoned a litle concernyng her sonne, as I shal showe you after, and were departed she to oure ladie of worceter, and I towarde Shrewsberie: I then newe chaunged and in maner amased, began to dispute with my selfe, litle considerynge that thus my earnest title was turned even to a tittyl not so good as, *est amen*.

> (ed. Ellis 1809: 388)

Hall's Chronicle was pillaged for material in the 1560s and 1570s by **Grafton** and **Holinshed**, who tempered the florid and often cloudy style as well as adding new material for later reigns. Where they did use

Hall they did no more than edit him, rather than producing their own accounts with his help, so that Hall's work was being read, in original or adapted form, throughout the second half of the sixteenth century. Hall survived in this way largely because of the continuing utility of his pro-Tudor presentation of history in a climate which remained uneasy. His importance as a source for later writers in all genres is firstly that he presented the period of English history most often dealt with in the literature of the sixteenth century (for example, **Daniel**'s *Civil Wars* and *A Mirror for Magistrates*), secondly that as well as narrating he described, analysed, explained, 'probed for the causes of events [and] emphasized the end of the action and the manner of a man's death as revealing the judgement finally imposed in a moral universe' (Campbell 1947: 70). 'Every Elizabethan writer who thought at all deeply on the subject owed something, and most of them a great deal, to the Hall–More–Vergil reconstruction of the events preceding the accession of the Tudors', and 'it was not only in Hall that it was lovingly elaborated into a series of moral judgements and delivered in a fine spirit of oracular conviction' (Reese 1961: 52).

(C) Shakespeare had access to Hall directly as well as through Grafton and Holinshed. Thus it is often impossible to tell which authority Shakespeare used; but it is certain that he did know and use all three, because he sometimes draws on material unique to each one. And as the basis of the later chronicles, Hall is often Shakespeare's ultimate if not immediate source, though careless collation has in the past some-times led to underestimation of his importance. Shakespeare 'shows intimate and easy familiarity with the whole chronicle. It was from Hall, more than from any other source, that he drew his interpretation of the Plantagenet dynasty, the chain of nemesis . . . and his conception of the leading characters' (Cairncross 1957: xli).

It is clear that many items of historical information and pieces of phraseology are taken by Shakespeare from Hall (sometimes via Grafton and Holinshed, sometimes not) in *1–3 Henry VI*, *1–2 Henry IV*, *Henry V*, *Richard II* and *Richard III*. Particularly telling as evidence of Shakespeare's long-term acquaintance with Hall is the fact that he often uses material Hall mentions in contexts other than the historical episode Shakespeare is dealing with (see Cairncross 1957: xli). There are also ways in which Shakespeare appears to give dramatic expression to some of the qualities of Hall's style: 'oration and rhetorical figure, liveliness of narrative detail, development of character and motive, and the domination of theme in the establishment of continuity in fifteenth-century history' (Zeeveld 1936: 325). This is especially significant in that Shakespeare's taste is for elements Hall's rewriters Grafton and Holinshed tend to ignore and omit. For example, Hall – but not Grafton or Holinshed – elaborately describes the lamentation in France after Agincourt:

> And yet the dolor was not onely his, for the ladies souned for the deathes of their husebandes, the Orphalines wept and rent their heares for the losse of their parentes, the faire damosells defied that day in the whiche they had lost their paramors, the servantes waxed mad for destruccion of their masters, and finally, every frend for his frend, every cosyn for his alye, every neighbor for his neighbor, was sorry, displeased and greved.
>
> (ed. Ellis 1809: 73)

Shakespeare makes Exeter threaten the French *before* the battle in similar terms:

> on your head
> Turning the widows' tears, the orphans' cries,
> The dead men's blood, the privy maidens' groans,
> For husbands, fathers, and betrothed lovers,
> That shall be swallowed in this controversy.
>
> (*Henry V*, 2.3.105–8)

Hall's influence on Shakespeare's treatment of character is more difficult to demonstrate, but the chronicler's positive portrayal of Margaret of Anjou has been seen behind Shakespeare's favourable presentation of her in *1 Henry VI*, and his negative ones of Edward, Talbot and Warwick as relevant to Shakespeare's in *2–3 Henry VI* (Zeeveld 1936: 337–41). Candido (1987) finds the sudden transformation of Richard III on assuming the throne to be owing to 'the strange literary alchemy' that joined **More**'s unfinished life of Richard to Hall's moralistic historical mode as sources for this play: the Chronicle incorporated a version of More's *History of Richard III*, concluding with the flight of Buckingham, and the narrative was continued by Hall himself. As for the effect of Hall's use of 'theme in the establishment of continuity in fifteenth-century history', it can be argued that 'to read continuously in the Chronicles is to discover that they exemplify less the grand historical design than the complexity, dispersal, randomness, even incomprehensibility of actual happenings' (Hunter 1990: 18). But no reader could miss in Hall the 'imperative lesson . . . of the destruction that follows rebellion and dissension in a realm' (Campbell 1947: 68), and evidence that Shakespeare found at least hints in Hall for a unified view of historical purpose and continuity in the histories may be found in his suggestions of a revenge motive in the actions of Margaret of Anjou and elsewhere.

Hall is the main source for *Sir Thomas More* (see Metz 1989: 174–82).

(D) For Hall's Chronicle and its context see Reese (1961). The modern groundwork on Shakespeare's use of Hall was done in the 1930s, by King (1934), Zeeveld (1936) and others. A curiosity, a copy of Hall annotated by an Elizabethan hand, is discussed by Keen (1954). The widest-ranging recent reassessments are Tomlinson (1984) and Hunter (1989), but they deal with Hall together with other chronicles.

Bullough; Muir (1977); Tillyard (1944).

Beer, Jurgen (1992). 'The Image of a King: Henry VIII in the Tudor Chronicles of Edward Hall and Raphael Holinshed', pp. 129–49 in Uwe Baumann, ed., *Henry VIII in History, Historiography and Literature*. Frankfurt.

Begg, Edleen (1935). 'Shakespeare's Debt to Hall and Holinshed in *Richard III.*' *SP* 32: 189–96.

Cairncross, Andrew S., ed. (1957). *The Second Part of King Henry the Sixth* (Arden Shakespeare). London.

Campbell, Lily B. (1947). *Shakespeare's "Histories": Mirrors of Elizabethan Policy*. San Marino, CA.

Candido, Joseph (1987). 'Thomas More, The Tudor Chronicles, and Shakespeare's Altered Richard.' *ES* 68: 137–41.

Ellis, Henry, ed. (1809). *Hall's Chronicle; Containing the History of England, during the Reign of Henry the Fourth, and the Succeeding Monarchs*. London.

Hardin, Richard F. (1989). 'Chronicles and Mythmaking in Shakespeare's Joan of Arc.' *ShSu* 42: 25–35.

Hunter, G. K. (1989). 'Truth and Art in History Plays.' *ShSu* 42: 15–24.

Keen, Alan (1954). *The Annotator: The Pursuit of an Elizabethan Reader of*

> *Halle's Chronicle, involving some surmises about the early life of William Shakespeare.* London.

King, Lucille (1934). 'The Use of Hall's Chronicles in the Folio and Quarto Texts of *Henry VI*.' *PQ* 13: 321–32.

Matheson, Lister M. (1995). 'English Chronicle Contexts for Shakespeare's Death of Richard II', pp. 195–219 in John A. Alford, ed., *From Page to Performance: Essays in Early English Drama*. East Lansing.

Metz, G. Harold, ed. (1989). *Sources of Four Plays Ascribed to Shakespeare*. Columbia, MI.

Patterson, Annabel (1994). *Reading Holinshed's 'Chronicles'*. Chicago.

Reese, M. M. (1961). *The Cease of Majesty: A Study of Shakespeare's History Plays*. London.

Tomlinson, Michael (1984). 'Shakespeare and the Chronicles Reassessed.' *Literature and History* 10: 46–58.

Zeeveld, W. Gordon (1936). 'The Influence of Hall on Shakespeare's English Historical Plays.' *ELH* 3: 317–53.

Hardyng, John (1378–1465?), Chronicler The chronicle written by this loyal retainer of Hotspur's, though it would have been available to Shakespeare only in manuscript, is closer to the action of *1 Henry IV* than other sources for aspects of the rebellion leading to the Battle of Shrewsbury.

West, Gilian (1990). 'Hardyng's Chronicle and Shakespeare's Hotspur.' *ShQ* 41: 348–51.

Harington, Sir John See **Ariosto, Ludovico.**

Harsnett, Samuel (1561–1631), Archbishop of York
(A) Harsnett (born Halsnoth) belonged to family of bakers in Colchester. He was educated at Cambridge, where he was considered an outstanding scholar, and had become a priest by 1586. After conflicts with the authorities over church practices, a spell as a schoolmaster followed, after which in 1588 he commenced an academic career at Cambridge. From 1597 he was given a series of increasingly important church appointments, culminating in 1602/3 in the archdeaconry of Essex,

through his friend Richard Bancroft, Bishop of London, to whom he became a chaplain in 1597. Now an obviously rising clerical politician, he went on to become Master of Pembroke Hall, Cambridge (1605), Bishop of Chichester (1609; in both these offices he was the successor to Launcelot Andrewes), Bishop of Norwich (1619), and eventually Archbishop of York (1629), the second-highest position in the Church of England, as well as, intermittently, Vice-Chancellor of Cambridge University. He sat in Parliament for twenty-one years, and for the last two years of his life was a privy counsellor. Though a learned, eloquent man of taste and imagination, his manner was forthright and he was no stranger to controversy; at one point in 1616, the Fellows of Pembroke petitioned to the king against their Master.

Harsnett was one of the most capable leaders of the generation which established the style and tone of the religion now known as Anglicanism. His book *A Declaration of Egregious Popish Impostures, to withdraw the Harts of her Majesties Subjects from their Allegeance, and from the Truth of Christian Religion professed in England* (London, 1603) is a long diatribe against a group of recusant Catholic priests who, in a series of incidents in 1585–6, had claimed to exorcise demons from seven individuals mostly in the town of Denham, Buckinghamshire, in the process drawing large audiences and making some converts. The book includes depositions, summaries of other books, and so on, which are extensively paraphrased and reproduced in Appendices.

(B) The *Declaration* plays on Protestant fears by linking Catholic tradition to superstition and paganism. It was a contribution to a contemporary crisis, and followed Harsnett's *Discovery of the Fraudulent Practises of One John Darrel*, 1599, on another convicted exorcist. Both are propagandistic works officially sponsored by the Anglican Church, in which Harsnett attempts 'to cap permanently the great rushing geysers of charisma released in rituals of exorcism' associated with Catholicism (Greenblatt 1985: 105; for the full context see Thomas 1997: 477–92). The *Declaration* was by no means an obscure book in its time, even though it was not necessarily widely read (there were reissues in 1604 and 1605). It was 'the climax to ... major political and religious campaigns waged by a powerful bishop; the power of the Court of High Commission, the voice of the Crown itself in ecclesiastical affairs, validated its findings' (Brownlow 1993: 118). Since its publication was an act of state, a dramatist making casual use of it may even have risked appearing impudent. Shakespeare's interest in Harsnett is not matched by contemporary playwrights; it may possibly result from family connections to one or more of the exorcists (see Brownlow 1993: 108–10).

This passage from Chapter 6 (on the priests' 'waies of catching and inveigling theyr disciples') illustrates Harsnett's normal tactics – the use of allegedly documentary detail, a hectoring tone and heavy sarcasm. The 'Master Maynie' referred to is Richard Mainy, younger son of a well-known Kentish family and the most inventive of the supposedly possessed individuals involved in the episode.

Our late popish Exorcists, have certaine new devised signes of their owne observation, more fitting the times, and effectuall for the gra-cing their gracelesse profession. Theyr Empericall signes be these. 1, If the partie affected, cannot for burning abide the presence of a Catholique priest. 2, If shee will hardly be brought to blesse herselfe with the signe of the Crosse. 3, If a casket of reliques beeing brought her, shee turne away her face, and cry that they stinke. 4, If S. *Johns* Gospel being put in a Casket, and applied unto her, she rubbe, or scratch any part of her body, and cry it burnes, it is an evident demonstration, that the enemie dooth lurke in that part. 5, If she can hardly be brought to pronounce these words, *Ave Maria, the mother of GOD*, and most hardly *the Catholique Church*. 6, If a Casket of reliques covered with red, doe seeme white unto her. 7, If shee tumble, and be vexed, when any goe to confession. 8, If shee have a shivering at Masse. 9, If shee fleere, and laugh in a mans face.

But our holy Tragaedians heere had hast of theyr sport, and there-fore they would not stay the trying of any such curious signes, but tooke a shorter cut. *Marwood, Westons* patient, beeing pinched with penurie, and hunger, did lie but a night, or two, abroad in the fieldes, and beeing a melancholicke person, was scared with lightning, and thunder, that happened in the night, and loe, an evident signe, that the man was possessed. The priests must meet about this pittifull creature. *Edmunds* must come, the *holie Chaire* must be fetcht out, the holy budget of sacred reliques must be opened, and all the enchaunting mysteries applied about the poore man.

Ma: *Maynie* had a spice of the *Hysterica passio*, as seems from his youth, hee himselfe termes it the Moother (as you may see in his confession) and saith, that hee was much troubled with it in Fraunce,

and that it was one of the causes that mooved him to leave his holy
order whereinto he was initiated, and to returne into England. For
this, and for leaving the order of *Bonhommes*, see here an evident
signe, that *Maynie* had a devil: whatsoever hee did or spake, the devil
did, and spake in him: the horse that he rid upon to *Denham*, was no
horse, but the devil: *Maynie* had the devils in livery-coates attending
upon him: and all this tragicall out-cry, for leaving his order, and a
poore passion of the Mother, which a thousand poore girles in
England had worse, then ever Ma: *Maynie* had.

(Harsnett 1603: 24–5)

In this passage should be noted in particular: the equivalence suggested,
as throughout the *Declaration*, between the exorcising priests and theatrical performers ('our holy Tragaedians'); the 'Moother' or *Hysterica passio*
for Lear's 'O, how this mother swells up toward my heart! / Hysterica
passio – down, thou climbing sorrow' (2.4.55–6, a unique use of the
Latin phrase in Shakespeare); and perhaps the priests' *'holie Chaire'*
(presented later in the book as a torture) for the chair in which
Gloucester's eyes are put out (3.7).

(C) Lewis Theobold in his eighteenth-century edition of Shakespeare
was the first to point out the anticipations of *King Lear* in the *Declaration
of Egregious Popish Impostures*, but the beginnings of modern interest
come with the comprehensive collection of verbal echoes by Muir 1951
(listed with cross-references to *Lear* in Muir 1972: 239–42). For some
time afterwards, commentators (Elton 1966; Milward 1973; Murphy
1984) tended to see mainly local or conventionally 'contextual' significance in them, but the nature of the relationship has been questioned
again in recent years by, in particular, Greenblatt (1985) and Brownlow
(1993). It seems clear that Shakespeare read the *Declaration* just before
writing *King Lear*. A minor echo in *Othello* is not found in the quarto and
so is probably a later interpolation (see Brownlow 1979; Brownlow
1993: 118).

As the passage in (B), above, suggests, some of the parallels identified
in *Lear* represent simply the adoption of a striking word or the use of
recondite terminology or information. The names of Edgar's familiar
spirits, for instance, are all derived from the devils who supposedly
possessed the Denham demoniacs, and Harsnett twice uses the
expression 'the prince of darknes' (Muir 1951: 15):

231

EDGAR   This is the foul fiend Flibbertigibbet; he begins at cur-
few, and walks till the first cock; he gives the web and the
pin, squences the eye, and makes the hare-lip; mildews
the white wheat, and hurts the poor creature of earth.

> Swithold footed thrice the 'old;
> He met the nightmare and her nine-fold;
> Bid her alight
> And her troth plight,
> And aroint thee, witch, aroint thee!

KENT   How fares your Grace?

LEAR   What's he?

KENT   Who's there? What is't you seek?

GLOUCESTER   What are you there? Your names?

EDGAR   Poor Tom; that eats the swimming frog, the toad, the
tadpole, the wall-newt, and the water; that in the fury
of his heart, when the foul fiend rages, eats cow-dung
for sallets, swallows the old rat and the ditch-dog,
drinks the green mantle of the standing pool; who is
whipp'd from tithing to tithing, and stock-punish'd,
and imprison'd; who hath had three suits to his back,
six shirts to his body –

> Horse to ride, and weapon to wear;
> But mice and rats, and such small deer,
> Have been Tom's food for seven long year.
> Beware my follower. Peace, Smulkin; peace, thou
> fiend!

GLOUCESTER   What, hath your Grace no better company?

EDGAR   The prince of darkness is a gentleman;
Modo he's call'd, and Mahu.

(3.4.113–40)

Sometimes Shakespeare seems to go further. Edgar's words at
4.1.59–64 are again an undoubted and explicit reference to Harsnett,
and to the historical actuality on which his *Declaration* is based: the supposedly possessed 'chambermaids and waiting-women', Sara Williams,
Friswood Williams and Anne Smith of Denham, the full records of
whose legal examinations are appended to Harsnett's book:

Five fiends have been in poor Tom at once: of lust, as Obidicut; Hobbididence, prince of dumbness; Mahu, of stealing; Modo, of murder; Flibertigibbet, of mopping and mowing, who since possesses chambermaids and waiting-women.

(4.1.58–63)

But the explicitness makes it possible to read this speech as a meta-theatrical moment which violates the historical setting 'in order to remind the audience of the play's conspicuous doubleness, its simul-taneous distance and contemporaneity' (Greenblatt 1985: 113). It may also be said to 'translat[e] the girls' possessions out of the metaphorical theater of Harsnett's diatribe into the real tragic theater, [and] restore to them the potentiality of generating significance, which Harsnett had tried to negate' (Brownlow 1993: 122).

'The undisputable borrowings from Harsnett are confined to Poor Tom's part in the storm scenes and some passages connected with it psychologically', especially episodes of sadism and moral perversion (Salingar 1983: 156). But it has recently been argued that Harsnett's book as a whole affected Shakespeare's imagination, perhaps suggest-ing even such major elements of *Lear* as the Fool and the storm, and affecting the play's very purpose. If so, the book 'is not in the ordinary sense a source at all. Rather the play is the result of an encounter with another text: a kind of dialogue has taken place' (Brownlow 1993: 118). For Greenblatt, adopting the traditional position that Shake-speare subordinated his art to the myths of the Tudor monarchy, what is central is the equivalence, posited by Harsnett and in some sense accepted by Shakespeare, between the imposture of possession and theatricality. *King Lear* offers 'a double corroboration of Harsnett's arguments': Edgar's possession is fictional, and 'the play itself is bounded by the institutional signs of fictionality' (the playhouse walls, etc.). So Shakespeare 'dutifully reiterates' Harsnett's position, though in the process the 'demonic principle' is inevitably 'reconstituted as theatre' (Greenblatt 1985: 115–16, 122). A more engaged Shake-speare is posited by Brownlow: far from dutiful acceptance of Harsnett's position, he found it disturbing in that 'it issues from, and gives expression to, an authoritarianism as offensive as anything that its author attacks in the name of skeptical enlightenment'. Harsnett 'gave Shakespeare a microcosm of the claim to authority and its results', but 'the insincerity and violence Harsnett attributes to [the demoniacs]

233

recoil upon himself and the state he serves', and Shakespeare responds by composing

> a romantic tragedy of outrageous indecorum, appropriating or engulfing Harsnett's own book, and situating its contents in a landscape of violence and alienation that, whether we read it as pre- or post-Christian, offers a devastating commentary on the spiritual condition of contemporary England.
>
> (1993: 127–8)

(D) Easily the most thorough treatment both of Harsnett and of his impact on *Lear* is Brownlow (1993), containing a complete text of the *Declaration* and taking full account of previous published work. A different tack is followed by Greenblatt (1985, developed from Greenblatt 1982; see above). The main novelty of the only post-Brownlow study, Wolf (1998), is the suggestion that Harsnett's lack of interest in the actual maladies of the 1585–6 exorcists' victims is deliberately 'undermined' by *Lear*'s 'world in which sympathy is the key to the understanding of suffering' (261). But this is largely anticipated by Bullough.

Brownlow, F. W. (1979). 'Samuel Harsnett and the Meaning of Othello's "Suffocating Streams".' *PQ* 58: 107–15.

—— (1993). *Shakespeare, Harsnett, and the Devils of Denham.* Newark, DE.

Bullough, VIII, 299–302.

Elton, William (1966). *King Lear and the Gods.* San Marino, CA.

Greenblatt, Stephen (1982). '*King Lear* and Harsnett's "Devil Fiction".' *Genre* 15: 239–42.

—— (1985). 'Shakespeare and the Exorcists', pp. 101–23 in Gregory S. Jay and David L. Miller, eds, *After Strange Texts: The Role of Theory in the Study of Literature.* New York.

Harsnett, Samuel (1603). *A Declaration of Egregious Popish Impostures.* London.

Milward, Peter (1973). *Shakespeare's Religious Background.* London.

Muir, Kenneth (1951). 'Samuel Harsnett and *King Lear*.' *RES* 2: 11–21.

—— ed. (1972). *King Lear* (Arden Shakespeare). London.

Murphy, John L. (1984). *Darkness and Devils: Exorcism and 'King Lear'.* Athens, OH.

Salingar, Leo (1983). '*King Lear*, Montaigne and Harsnett.' *The Aligarh*

Journal of English Studies 8.ii: 124–66 (also published in *Anglo-American Studies*, 3 (1983)).

Thomas, Keith (1997). *Religion and the Decline of Magic: Studies in Popular Beliefs in Sixteenth and Seventeenth Century England.* London (first published 1971).

Wolf, Amy (1998). 'Shakespeare and Harsnett: "Pregnant to Good Pity"?' *SEL* 38: 251–64.

Harvey, Gabriel (1550–1630), Academic and Poet Tobin's discoveries, not uniformly accepted, are all of small-scale similarities to works by Harvey in *Hamlet*.

Tobin, J. J. M. (1985). 'Gabriel Harvey: "Excellent Matter of Emulation".' *Hamlet Studies* 7: 94–100.

—— (1980). 'Harvey and Hamlet.' *ANQ* 18: 86–7.

Heliodorus, of Emesa See **Greek Romance**.

Henryson, Robert (*c.* 1425–*c.* 1505), Scottish Poet
(A) Very limited biographical information has come down to us about Henryson. Evidence suggests he was a schoolmaster in Dunfermline, and he was definitely a notary. His canon is also uncertain, but unambiguously ascribed to him are three extended works and twelve short ones. The subjects of the longer poems are all from antiquity: *The Morall Fabillis of Esope the Phrygian*, *Orpheus and Erudices* and *The Testament of Cresseid*. The last is a reminder of the now old-fashioned title for Henryson's school, the 'Scottish Chaucerians': Chaucerian features in his verse include the use of a poetic *persona* and a preference for Chaucerian stanza-forms over couplets.

(B) Shakespeare's contemporaries may have taken little interest in Henryson's work as a whole, but the pathos and stark beauty of *The Testament of Cresseid* (*c.* 1490), a sequel to **Chaucer**'s *Troilus and Criseyde*, appealed strongly to them. It is a 616-line poem narrating the punishment of Criseyde for her infidelity. Though Chaucer's poem was also extremely familiar in the sixteenth century, it is clear that, for example,

235

George Turberville's reference to his treacherous mistress as 'faire Cressid's heire' (1575), and George Whetstone's warning against the archetypal 'cunning' of Cressida in the preface to his own version of 'Cressid's Complaint' (1576), reflect Henryson's work rather than Chaucer's. On the other hand, Henryson's presentation of Criseyde is by no means the extreme negative depiction sometimes assumed in modern interpretation of it, which often 'over-emphasizes the sexual elements of Cresseid's fall, and under-emphasizes her lack of honour, her faithlessness in a moral and intellectual sense. It also misunderstands the nature and significance of Cresseid's suffering and death' (Smith 1982: 71).

The *Testament* was printed in Thynne's 1532 edition of Chaucer and in all subsequent editions of Chaucer until 1721, including that of Thomas Speght, whose 1598 *Workes of Chaucer* may have been the form in which Shakespeare read the poem. Hence readers of Chaucer tended to have read Henryson too. The following stanzas from near the close of the pathos-drenched 'Complaint of Cresseid' (given in Speght's rather corrupt text) bring the story down to her death. Cresseid speaks:

> Lovers beware, and take good hede about
> Whom that ye love, for whan ye suffer pain
> I let you wit there is right fewe throughout
> Whom ye may trust to have true love again
> Prove whan ye woll your labour is in vain
> Therefore I rede ye take them as ye finde
> For they are sad as Wedercocke in winde.

> Bicause I know the great unstablenesse
> Brittle as glasse, unto my selfe I saie
> Trusting in other as great brutelnesse
> As inconstant, and as untrue of faie
> Though some be true, I wot right few are they
> Who findeth truth, let him his lady ruse
> None but my selfe as now I woll accuse.

> Whan this was said, with paper she sat doun
> And in this maner made her testament
> Here I bequeth my corse and carioun
> With wormes and with Toodes to be rent

My cuppe, my clapper, and mine ornament
And all my gold, these lepre folke shal have
Whan I am dedde, to burie me in grave.

This roiall ring set with this Rubie redd
Which Troilus in dowrie to me sende
To him again I leave it whan I am dedde
To make my carefull death unto him kende
Thus I conclude shortly and make an ende
My spirit I leave to Diane where she dwels
To walke with her in wast wodes and welles.

O Diomede thou hast both broche and belte
Which Troilus gave me in tokening
Of his true love, and with that word she swelt
And sone a leaper man toke of the ring
Than buried her withouten tarying
To Troilus forthwith the ring he bare
And of Creseide the death he can declare.
(561–95; ed. Speght 1598: fo. 197ʳ)

(C) *The Testament of Cressid* is the sole Henryson work associated with Shakespeare, but though Shakespeare may well have read it, the nature of its impact on him (in *Troilus and Cressida*) is unclear. Bayley (1963) makes the most extensive claims; at the other extreme Bullough (v, 215–19) prints an excerpt only as an analogue, not a source. The old suggestion that the mere appearance of the *Testament* in a volume called *The Works of Chaucer* would have led Shakespeare to assume it was Chaucer's work, and hence to acquire a distorted notion of Chaucer's heroine, exercises Donaldson, in particular, who rightly observes that 'to suppose that Shakespeare thought Chaucer wrote *The Testament* is to attribute to him not only little Latin and less Greek, but minimal English and no sense' (Donaldson 1985: 76). Donaldson suggests Shakespeare did know Henryson's poem but had fairly full awareness of its status.

Exiguous parallels of phrasing mentioned by commentators and editors include Cressida's expression of grief at the prospect of being handed over to the Greeks at 4.2.104–5, 'Tear my bright hair, and . . . Crack my clear voice with sobs', possibly from Henryson's 'vois sa clear' and/or 'clear voice' (338, 435): if this were all the effect Henryson's poem had on Shakespeare's play the matter would be of small concern. But doubts remain that a more considerable debt may be owed. The static and declamatory quality of Henryson's tale, as against Chaucer's much more flowing narrative, does seem to present an affinity with the play. More tangibly, there is the point in Cressida's last scene at which she tells Diomed the token he is angling for belongs to one 'that lov'd me better than you will' (5.2.88). This apparent insight into the future, and hence the fatalistic frame of mind in which we leave Cressida, may arise from a memory of Henryson's apparent addition to the story, in which his Diomedes rejects Cresseid near the start of the *Testament*: 'When Diomeid had all his appetite, / And more, fulfilled of this faire ladie . . . [he] hir excluded fro his company' (71–5). Similarly, Chaucer's Troilus may be true in love, but 'nowhere does Chaucer convert him into a byword for truth . . . Henryson is the first considerable poet to celebrate Troilus' truth and to counterbalance it rhetorically with Cressida's falseness' (Donaldson 1985: 101). It may be to Henryson, then, that we should look for the origins of such a passage as this well-known exchange:

> True swains in love shall in the world to come
> Approve their truth by Troilus, when their rhymes,
> Full of protest, of oath, and big compare,
> Want similes, truth tir'd with iteration –
> As true as steel, as plantage to the moon,
> As sun to day, as turtle to her mate,
> As iron to adamant, as earth to th' centre –
> Yet, after all comparisons of truth,
> As truth's authentic author to be cited,
> 'As true as Troilus' shall crown up the verse
> And sanctify the numbers.

CRESSIDA   Prophet may you be!
> If I be false, or swerve a hair from truth,
> When time is old and hath forgot itself,
> When waterdrops have worn the stones of Troy,
> And blind oblivion swallow'd cities up,
> And mighty states characterless are grated
> To dusty nothing – yet let memory
> From false to false, among false maids in love,

Upbraid my falsehood when th' have said 'As false
As air, as water, wind, or sandy earth,
As fox to lamb, or wolf to heifer's calf,
Pard to the hind, or stepdame to her son' –
Yea, let them say, to stick the heart of falsehood,
'As false as Cressid'.

(3.2.169–92)

(D)

Bayley, John (1963). 'Shakespeare's Only Play', pp. 58–83 in Nevill Coghill and Berners A. W. Jackson, eds, *Stratford Papers on Shakespeare*. Toronto.

Bullough, VI.

Donaldson, E. Talbot (1979). 'Briseis, Briseida, Criseyde, Cresseid, Cressid: Progress of a Heroine', pp. 3–12 in Edward Vasta, Zacharias P. Thundy and Theodore M. Hesburgh, eds, *Chaucerian Problems and Perspectives: Essays Presented to Paul E. Beichner, C.S.C.* Notre Dame.

Donaldson, E. Talbot (1985). *The Swan at the Well: Shakespeare Reading Chaucer*. New Haven.

Smith, Valerie (1982). 'The History of Cressida', pp. 61–79 in J. A. Jowitt and R. K. S. Taylor, eds, *Self and Society in Shakespeare's 'Troilus and Cressida' and 'Measure for Measure'*. Bradford.

Speght, Thomas, ed. (1598). *The Workes of our Antient and Learned English Poet, Geffrey Chaucer*. London.

Thompson, Anne (1978). *Shakespeare's Chaucer: A Study in Literary Origins*. Liverpool.

Herbert, Mary Sidney See **Garnier, Robert**.

Herodian, of Syria (*fl. c.* AD 230), Historian of Rome
Herodian's *History*, translated by Nicholas Smyth about 1550, may hold some significance for *Titus Andronicus* as a 'picture of decadent imperial family disputes'.

Hunter, G. K. (1984). 'Sources and Meanings in *Titus Andronicus*', pp. 171–88 in J. C. Gray, ed., *Mirror up to Shakespeare: Essays in Honour of G. R. Hibbard*. Toronto.

Herodotus (*c.* 490–*c.* 425 BC), **Greek Historian** Dean's pamphlet suggests some material Shakespeare could have derived from Herodotus, but is unable to show the derivation is ever direct.

Dean, John (1977). *Shakespeare's Romances and Herodotus' Histories.* Salzburg.

Higgins, John See *Mirror for Magistrates*.

Hoby, Sir Thomas See **Castiglione, Baldassare.**

Holinshed, Raphael (*c.* 1528–*c.* 1580), **Chronicler** See also **Buchanan, George**; **Fabyan, Robert**; **Foxe, John**; **Grafton, Richard**; **Hall, Edward**; **Stow, John**.
(A) Holinshed was apparently from a Cheshire family, and perhaps educated at Cambridge. The *Chronicles of England, Scotland, and Ireland* which now go under his name started life as a projected universal history and cosmography organized by the printer Reginald Wolfe. Wolfe died in 1573, and Holinshed, his assistant or translator, became the editor or co-ordinator of the venture, now altered in scope to become a geographical description and history of England, Scotland and Ireland from their first inhabitation to the present. The first edition appeared in two volumes in 1577, and was presented as the work of a group, almost a committee, and beyond that group as the culmination of centuries of historical writing (the work begins with a two-page listing of sources). A second edition, expanded to three volumes though frequently bound in two, was published after Holinshed's death in 1587. This was subjected to government censorship for reasons not altogether clear (for a recent discussion see Patterson 1994: 234–63; Holinshed 1807–8 represents the uncensored 1587 edition).

The text runs to about 3,500,000 words, 'roughly equal to the total of the Authorized Version of the Bible, the complete dramatic works of Shakespeare, *Clarissa*, Boswell's *Life of Johnson*, and *War and Peace* combined' (Booth 1968: 1). Like other Tudor chronicles, it gives generous attention to a wide range of material including spectacles both civil (such as pageants) and natural (such as beached whales), notorious crimes, urban government and price fluctuations, as well as the fortunes of kings and dynasties. In the historical sections, Holinshed and his collaborators and successors draw constantly and explicitly for material, in some cases also methodology, on **Fabyan**, **Foxe**, **Grafton**, **Stow** and especially **Hall** (for England), as well as lesser sources and other sources for Scotland and Ireland (notably George **Buchanan** and Richard Stanyhurst; see respectively Mapstone 1998, Maley 1997), all slightly adapted and sometimes overlapped for deliberate contrast. Though Holinshed's own writing seldom wins plaudits, the volume's comprehensiveness and up-to-dateness ensured its utility and its wide influence – it is sufficiently clearly the greatest of the Elizabethan chronicles.

The first edition of the Chronicle was Holinshed's only published work. He subsequently became steward on the estate of Thomas Burdett of Bramcote, Warwickshire, dying there shortly after it was published. In this capacity he presided over the manor court at Packwood, so it is conceivable that Shakespeare met him before his death.

(B) The second edition of Holinshed of 1587 was a work of some complexity, bringing together a diverse mass of material built up in several layers. Already in 1577, 'what Holinshed wrote was, in his own phrase, a 'collection of histories'; the pluralism attached both to the variety of sources drawn on and to the collaborative effort that went into the production, and both these point away from explanatory clarity' (Hunter 1989: 18). In 1587 this 'collection' was augmented and annotated by Abraham Fleming, a Cambridge-trained antiquary, and others, who brought the narrative down to 1587 and whose apparatus added extensive indices, Latin tags and conspicuous morals in the margins for narratives and narrative episodes (such as, for example, 'The outward and inward troubles of tyrants by means of a grudging conscience').

The result is, and was in the sixteenth century, sometimes seen as incoherent; alternatively as reflecting a 'complex process of compilation, aggregation, and ideological negotiation' with the reader being asked to 'be his own historian [as] part of a coherent agenda: to educate Elizabethan citizens in political and legal reality' (Patterson 1996: 153–5). In either case the tendency would be for the material to raise questions in the reader's mind, in for instance the markedly

241

non-committal way in which the vicissitudes of the succession question in Henry VIII's reign are outlined, or in the tensions between the Protestant sources of the Scottish material on the reign of Mary Queen of Scots (**Boece**, Buchanan) and the editorial endeavour to please Elizabethan authorities by no means generally prepared to countenance the deposition of monarchs. For writers disposed to make use of it, the work constituted a huge storehouse of characters, lineages, dates, battles, discussions of motivation, Tudor political doctrine, and rhetoric. The importance of Holinshed (and other chronicles) as a source of material for Elizabethan playwrights must be seen generally as a result of the nationalistic spirit promoted by Elizabeth in the country at large, which was at its height following the defeat of the Armada in 1588. Dramatists, such as some of those responsible for **Chronicle History Plays**, focused strongly on the Hundred Years' War for the French succession, 1337–1453, when English armies repeatedly conquered large parts of France during the reigns of Edward III, Richard II, Henry IV, Henry V and Henry VI. Holinshed was also a suitable quarry for quite different kinds of drama, as in the anonymous play *Arden of Faversham* (1591), which draws on material he worried was 'impertinent' to his compilation, concerning a small-town murder case.

The following passage indicates exactly how far, in the episode of *Henry V* which has now become one of the more controversial parts of the Histories, Shakespeare is following Holinshed, who in his turn is following Hall (there is also a possibility that Shakespeare turned in this episode to an alternative source, Richard **Crompton**'s *Mansion of Magnanimitie*). The page containing the conclusion of this passage is shown in Fig. 7; the marginal headings ('A right wise and valiant challenge of the king', etc.) should be noted as part of Holinshed's text.

> In the meane season, while the battell thus continued, and that the Englishmen had taken a great number of prisoners, certeine Frenchmen on horssebacke, whereof were cepteins Robinet of Bornevill, Rifflart of Clamas, Isambert of Agincourt, and other men of armes, to the number of six hundred horssemen, which were the first that fled, hearing that the English tents and pavilions were a good waie distant from the armie, without anie sufficient gard to defend the same, either upon a covetous meaning to gaine by the spoile, or upon a desire to be revenged, entred upon the kings campe, and there spoiled the hails, robbed the tents, brake up chests, and

242

Englishmen disposed themselues in order of battell, readie to abide a new field, and also to inuade, and newlie set on their enimies, with great force they assailed the earles of Marle and Fauconbridge, and the lords of Louraie, and of Thine, with sir hundred men of armes, who had all that daie kept togither, but now slaine and beaten downe out of hand. ¶ Some write, that the king perceiuing his enimies in one part to assemble togither, as though they meant to giue a new battell for preseruation of the prisoners, sent to them an herald, commanding them either to depart out of his sight, or else to come forward at once, and giue battell: promising herewith, that if they did offer to fight againe, not onelie those prisoners which his people alreadie had taken; but also so manie of them as in this new conflict, which they thus attempted should fall into his hands, should die the death without redemption.

The Frenchmen fearing the sentence of so terrible a decree, without further delaie parted out of the field. And so about foure of the clocke in the after none, the king when he saw no apperance of enimies, caused the retreit to be blowen; and gathering his armie togither, gaue thanks to almightie God for so happie a victorie, causing his prelats and chapleins to sing this psalme: *In exitu Israel de Aegypto,* and commanded euerie man to kneele downe on the ground at this verse: *Non nobis Domine, non nobis, sed nomini tuo da gloriam.* Which doone, he caused *Te Deum,* with certeine anthems to be soong, giuing laud and praise to God, without boasting of his owne force or anie humane power. That night he and his people tooke rest, and refreshed themselues with such victuals as they found in the French campe, but lodged in the same village where he laie the night before.

In the morning, Montioie king at armes and foure other French heralds came to the K. to know the number of prisoners, and to desire buriall for the dead. Before he made them answer (to vnderstand what they would saie) he demanded of them whie they made to him that request, considering that he knew not whether the victorie was his or theirs? When Montioie by true and iust confession had cleered that doubt to the high praise of the king, he desired of Montioie to vnderstand the name of the castell nere adioining: when they had told him that it was called Agincourt, he said, Then shall this conflict be called the battell of Agincourt. He feasted the French officers of armes that daie, and granted them their request, which busilie sought through the field for such as were slaine. But the Englishmen suffered them not to go alone, for they searched with them, & found manie hurt, but not in ieopardie of their liues, whom they tooke prisoners, and brought them to their tents. When the king of England had well refreshed himselfe, and his souldiers, that had taken the spoile of such as were slaine, he with his prisoners in good order returned to his towne of Calis.

When tidings of this great victorie, was blowne into England, solemne processions and other praisings to almightie God with boune-fires and ioifull triumphes, were ordeined in euerie towne, citie, and burrow, and the maior & citizens of London went the morow after the daie of saint Simon and Iude from the church of saint Paule to the church of saint Peter at Westminster in deuout maner, rendring to God hartie thanks for such fortunate lucke sent to the king and his armie. The same sundaie that the king remoued from the campe at Agincourt towards Calis, diuerse Frenchmen came to the field to vew againe the dead bodies; and the pesants of the countrie spoiled the carcasses of all such apparell and other things as the Englishmen had left: who tooke nothing but gold and siluer, iewels, rich apparell

and costlie armour. But the plowmen and pezants left nothing behind, neither shirt nor clout: so that the bodies laie starke naked vntill wednesdaie. On the which daie diuerse of the noble men were conuaied into their countries, and the remnant were by Philip earle Charolois (sore lamenting the chance, and moued with pitie) at his costs & charges buried in a square plot of ground of fifteene hundred yards; in the which he caused to be made three pits, wherein were buried by account fiue thousand and eight hundred persons, beside them that were caried awaie by their freends and seruants, and others, which being wounded died in hospitals and other places.

After this their dolorous iournie & pitifull slaughter, diuerse clearks of Paris made manie a lamentable verse, complaining that the king reigned by will, and that councellors were partiall, affirming that the noble men fled against nature, and that the commons were destroied by their prodigalitie, declaring also that the cleargie were dumbe, and durst not saie the truth, and that the humble commons dulie obeied, & yet euer suffered punishment, for which cause by diuine persecution the lesse number vanquished the greater: wherefore they concluded, that all things went out of order, and yet it was there no man that studied to bring the vnrulie to frame. It was no maruell though this battell was lamentable to the French nation, for in it were taken and slaine the flower of all the nobilitie of France.

There were taken prisoners, Charles duke of Orleance nephue to the French king, Iohn duke of Burbon, the lord Bouciqualt one of the marshals of France (he after died in England) with a number of other lords, knights, and esquiers, at the least fifteene hundred, besides the common people. There were slaine in all of the French part to the number of ten thousand men, whereof were princes and noble men bearing baners one hundred twentie and six, to these, of knights, esquiers, and gentlemen, so manie as made vp the number of eight thousand and foure hundred (of the which fiue hundred were dubbed knights the night before the battell) so as of the meaner sort, not past sixteene hundred. Amongst those of the nobilitie that were slaine, these were the cheefest, Charles lord de la Breth high constable of France, Iaques of Chatilon lord of Dampier admerall of France, the lord Rambures master of the crossebowes, sir Guischard Dolphin great master of France, Iohn duke of Alanson, Anthonie duke of Brabant brother to the duke of Burgognie, Edward duke of Bar, the earle of Neuers an other brother to the duke of Burgognie, with the erles of Marle, Vaudemont, Beaumont, Grandprée, Roussie, Fauconberge, Fois and Lestrake, beside a great number of lords and barons of name.

Of Englishmen, there died at this battell, Edward duke Yorke, the earle of Suffolke, sir Richard Kikelie, and Dauie Gamme esquier, and of all other not aboue fiue and twentie persons, as some do report; but other writers of greater credit affirme, that there were slaine aboue fiue or six hundred persons. Titus Liuius saith, that there were slaine of Englishmen, beside the duke of Yorke, and the earle of Suffolke, an hundred persons at the first incounter. The duke of Glocester the kings brother was sore wounded about the hips, and borne downe to the ground, so that he fell backwards, with his feet towards his enimies, whom the king bestrid, and like a brother valiantlie rescued from his enimies, & so sauing his life, caused him to be conueied out of the fight, into a place of more safetie. ¶ The whole order of this conflict which cost manie a mans life, and procured great bloudshed before it was ended, is liuelie described in *Anglorum prælijs,* where also, besides the manner of disposing

Figure 7   Raphael Holinshed, *The Third Volume of Chronicles* (London, 1587), p. 555 (actual size 350 × 228 mm).

Margin notes:

A fresh onset.

A right wise and valiant challenge of the king.

Thanks giuen to God for the victorie.

A worthie example of a godlie prince.

Titus Liuius.

The battell of Agincourt.

The same day that the new maior went to Westminster to receiue his oth, the aduertisement of this noble victorie came to the citie in the morning betimes per men sent vp from their beds. Register of maiors.

Three graues that held fiue thousand and eight hundred couples.

Noble men prisoners.

The number slaine on the French part. Englishmen slaine.

Englishmen slaine.

Rich. Grafton, Titus Liuius.

Abr. Fl. out of Anglorum prælijs sub Hen. 5.

caried awaie caskets, and slue such servants as they found to make anie resistance. For which treason and haskardie in thus leaving their campe at the verie point of fight, for winning of spoil where none to defend it, verie manie were after committed to prison, and had lost their lives, if the Dolphin had longer lived.

But when the outcrie of the lackies and boies, which ran awaie for feare of the Frenchmen thus spoiling the campe, came to the kings eares, he doubting least his enimies should gather togither againe, and begin a new field; and mistrusting further that the prisoners would be an aid to his enimies, or the verie enimies to their takers in deed if they were suffered to live, contrarie to his accustomed gentlenes, commanded by sound of trumpet, that everie man (upon paine of death) should incontinentlie slaie his prisoner. When this dolorous decree, and pitifull proclamation was pronounced, pitie it was to see how some Frenchmen were suddenlie sticked with daggers, some were brained with pollaxes, some slaine with malls, other had their throats cut, and some their bellies panched, so that in effect, having respect to the great number, few prisoners were saved.

When this lamentable slaughter was ended, the Englishmen disposed themselves in order of battell, readie to abide a new field, and also to invade, and newlie set on their enimies, with great force they assailed the earles of Marle and Fauconbridge, and the lords of Lauraie, and of Thine, with six hundred men of armes, who had all that daie kept togither, but now slaine and beaten downe out of hand.

¶Some write, that the king perceiving his enimies in one part to assemble togither, as though they meant to give a new battell for preservation of the prisoners, sent to them an herald, commanding them either to depart out of his sight, or else to come forward at once, and give battell: promising herewith, that if they did offer to fight againe, not onelie those prisoners which his people alreadie had taken; but also so manie of them as in this new conflict, which they thus attempted should fall into his hands, should die the death without redemption.

The Frenchmen fearing the sentence of so terrible a decree, without further delaie parted out of the field. And so about foure of the clocke in the after noone, the king when he saw no apperance of enimies, caused the retreit to be blowen; and gathering his armie togither, gave thanks to almightie God for so happie a victorie, causing his prelats and chapleins to sing this psalme: *In esitu Israel de*

Aegypto, and commanded everie man to kneele downe on the ground at this verse: *Non nobis Domine, non nobis, sed nomini tuo da gloriam*. Which doone, he caused *Te Deum*, with certeine anthems to be soong, giving laud and praise to God, without boasting of his owne force or anie humane power.

(Holinshed 1587: III, 554)

(C) Shakespeare used the 1587 edition of Holinshed, and used it as a source for over a third of his plays: all ten earlier Histories, those later plays drawing on English historical material *King Lear*, *Macbeth* and *Cymbeline*, the likely collaborations *Edward III* and *Henry VIII* (but see **Stow**), perhaps also in revising *Sir Thomas More*. The sweep of the vast Chronicle can be exciting, and Shakespeare evidently took it up not only or even perhaps primarily as a reference tool, but for wide and enthusiastic browsing – at least after *Henry VI*, where the use of Holinshed is restricted. This reading might even, by linking the Wars of the Roses with the arrival of Elizabeth's age of 'concord' and 'unity', have 'given Shakespeare his cue for his civil war plays' (Jones 1977: 122). Once embarked on a play, and with other source-materials to hand, it may well be that Shakespeare dipped and skimmed in Holinshed, allowing himself to be guided by the marginal notes and by what happened to fall under his eye (Black 1948: 212–13 performs some calculations regarding such matters as how much time was required to read the sections involved). In any case, it is obvious that a playwright can only make successful use of it by rigorous exclusion. Richard II ascended the throne in the Chronicle in 1377, but Shakespeare's play begins in 1398, two years before the end of his reign. In *Henry IV*, Holinshed's account of events during Bolingbroke's kingship is virtually narrowed down to the rebellions, and three of these are telescoped into one. On other occasions Shakespeare's suppression of what Holinshed says has a more specific dramatic purpose. Where the Chronicle clearly identified the envy of the Percies and the King's fear of Mortimer's right to the throne as the reasons for the behaviour of these individuals, Shakespeare clouds these matters in the opening scenes of *1 Henry IV* so as to allow a fuller treatment of the ethics of rebellion and usurpation.

Corresponding to the omissions and contractions, there are of course many ideas in the Shakespeare plays not found in Holinshed. Shakespeare virtually invents the Bastard in *King John* (see Braunmuller 1988), and in *Richard II* John of Gaunt. In *Henry IV* Hal and Hotspur (owing,

245

it seems, to the influence of **Daniel**) become contemporaries and so parallel figures, whereas in the Chronicle Hotspur was a generation older. Such changes are important 'in tracing sources and analyzing dramatic technique'; but as Lily B. Campbell wrote (1947: 229),

> making Henry, the rebel, to be plagued by rebellion; showing Henry, the regicide, as hoping vainly to placate an avenging King of kings by a pilgrimage to the Holy Land; picturing Henry, the usurper, as sorrowing over his disobedient son and fearful that he may try to supplant him: these changes indicate the moral universe in which Shakespeare set his characters and give meaning to the plot.

This observation is a reminder that the meanings of Shakespeare's historical plots do not come primarily from his historical sources.

The relevant later Shakespeare plays use Holinshed in various ways. Law (1952) gives a tabulation of the Holinshed correspondences in *Macbeth* (though sometimes the source may well be one of the Chronicle's own sources, used directly; see **Buchanan**), as well as thirty-five incidents in the play which are not found in Holinshed. There are indeed many telling changes to the narrative: Muir (1990: xxxvii) even suggests that the Chronicle's marginalia, which 'read almost like a running commentary on the play', may have been more decisive for Shakespeare than the narrative itself. In Holinshed Duncan is younger and weaker, while Macbeth, though cruel, is assertive enough both to assist Duncan before his murder and to rule satisfactorily for ten years after it. Macbeth's possibly justifiable grievances against Duncan and his collusion with Banquo in the murder are, of course, omitted altogether, while Lady Macbeth's part is worked out from a single sentence to the effect that she 'lay sore upon him to attempt the thing, as she that was very ambitious'. A number of the play's incidents seem to derive from sections of the Chronicle unconnected with the Macbeth story.

In both *Lear* and *Cymbeline* Shakespeare works at a considerably greater distance from Holinshed. Perhaps he distinguished sharply between the Tudor and the much earlier material he found there, and did not feel obliged to treat the latter with the respect due to history as opposed to legend. He doubtless read Holinshed's account of Lear's reign, but its overall narrative outline overlaps with other accounts he is known to have used, and the details it lends to *Lear* are few – though some, such as Cordeilla's description of Lear as 'my naturall father' and the chronicler's of 'the unnaturalnesse which he found in his two daughters', seem important. Holinshed's narrative of Brute, grandson of Aeneas, which forms the opening section of his English history, contains all the historical or pseudo-historical matter that appears in *Cymbeline*, an 'account of a reign so uneventful that it had defeated the inventive powers of generations of quite imaginative chroniclers' (Nosworthy 1969: xviii). But again, apart from supplying the names of most of the characters (and incidentally of Iago in addition: Woodson 1978), there is little specific in this use of Holinshed. Much of 3.1, depicting the defiance of Caesar's ambassador by 'Kymbeline', and some of the report of the battle in 5.3, reflect the Chronicle text, though the latter scene is transposed by Shakespeare from a completely different part of Holinshed's book dealing with the Scottish defeat of the Danes in AD 976. (This, and the fact that the names borrowed for *Cymbeline* are widely distributed in the Chronicle, suggests the browsing habits of Shakespeare as a reader of Holinshed.) Less direct, but, if accepted, more important links are also suggested for *Cymbeline*: Shakespeare's story is 'not owed to, but consonant with the strange adventures of Brute' (Brockbank 1958: 43); he 'echoes' the attitudes towards Rome which he discovered in the Chronicle and may have 'found within his historical material the suggestions of a romance' (Rossi 1978: 111).

Henry VIII is often said to show a dependence unusual for Shakespeare on the actual words of the 1587 Chronicle, from appropriation of single expressions in marginal comments (such as the unusual word 'arrogancy' which is imported into a speech of Katherine's at 2.4.110) to close following of whole speeches. Anderson (1984: 131) argues this away, whereas for other commentators it gives rise to 'the frightening specter of creativity in abeyance', exorcised by 'claiming that the play condenses the disordered largesse of Holinshed into a tightly focussed and causally satisfying drama' (Patterson 1996: 148). But *Henry VIII* uses more procedures than one in refashioning the Holinshed material. For example, as well as following the absolute necessity of condensing and unifying, the play transposes incidents from one historical episode to another to suit the dramatist's purpose. Wolsey's downfall through mistakenly sending the king an inventory of his goods is in fact reported by Holinshed of Thomas Ruthall, Bishop of Durham, whose death Wolsey brought about. The play also combines Holinshed's material with the work of other historians (definitely Foxe, arguably Hall, **Speed**, and Stow). Even the speeches which are little more than versifications

247

of Holinshed 'show characteristic emphases or additions that make a dramatic point or give shape to the material' (Foakes 1968: xxxvii, with examples; Foakes' Appendix II contains all main Holinshed passages used for the play). And among other shifts of tone and interpretation, the sympathetic light in which Wolsey and Buckingham are presented in their falls seems to be entirely Shakespeare's own.

Many accounts of Shakespeare's use of Holinshed's Chronicle urge his overall 'freedom' or, alternatively, his 'indebtedness'. Both descriptions are correct in differing respects. Given the drastic selection of a small segment of Holinshed's narrative, Shakespeare often follows the sequence of events with great scrupulousness, but this is not remarkable – 'For the most part [in *Richard II*] he does what anyone attempting to dramatize historical narrative would be forced to do: he selects the scenes by means of which the story might be acted; in terms of the narrative itself, he both compresses and expands' (Trousdale 1982: 66). The literal use of Holinshed is not seldom responsible, in fact, for anomalies in the play texts, as Trousdale goes on to illustrate. As for offering new perspectives and interpretations (as opposed to new material), Shakespeare's 'varying' of his themes will normally lead to the discovery of new topics in the story, but this does not mean that the plays dramatize various views of history where the Chronicle offered only one, for the Chronicle was already multivocal – Holinshed's preface gave notice that he had 'chosen to shew the diversitie' of opinion among his predecessors (Holinshed 1587: III, sig. A3ᵛ), and his collaborators did likewise. Hence in using the 1587 volume 'what Shakespeare had before him as he wrote was a lively representation of how historians diverge on the issue of evaluation, and how strenuous is the pull of ideological bias' (Patterson 1996: 150). In this sense, some at least of the freedom of interpretation and emphasis found in Shakespeare's use of Holinshed was already exemplified there.

(D) Boswell-Stone (1907) and Nicoll (1927) arrange selections from Holinshed in the chronological order of Shakespeare's plays, making it easy to find a passage from the corresponding lines in a play, the former with running quotation from and commentary on the relevant Shake-speare history plays and an especially useful index to personages and events. Hosley (1968) uses Holinshed's chronological order instead, giving more of the sequence, flavour and format of Holinshed's own work. Booth (1968) and Patterson (1994) are very different full-length treatments of Holinshed's volume, seen in recent years as a more self-conscious and sophisticated work in its own right. Cole (1973: 36–55) asks simple but important questions about what type of insights the study of Holinshed can give rise to. For individual plays and groups of plays, see below.

Bullough; Jones (1977); Tillyard (1944).

Anderson, Judith H. (1984). *Biographical Truth: The Representation of Historical Persons in Tudor-Stuart Writing*. New Haven.

Beer, Jurgen (1992). 'The Image of a King: Henry VIII in the Tudor Chronicles of Edward Hall and Raphael Holinshed', pp. 129–49 in Uwe Baumann, ed., *Henry VIII in History, Historiography and Literature*. Frankfurt.

Black, Matthew W. (1948). 'The Sources of Shakespeare's *Richard II*', pp. 199–216 in James G. McManaway *et al.*, eds, *Joseph Quincy Adams Memorial Studies*. Washington.

Booth, Stephen (1968). *The Book Called Holinshed's Chronicles: An Account of its Inception, Purpose, &c.* San Francisco.

Boswell-Stone, W. G. (1907). *Shakespeare's Holinshed: The Chronicle and the Plays Compared*. London.

Boyd, Brian (1995). '*King John* and *The Troublesome Raigne*: Sources, Structure, Sequence.' *PQ* 74: 37–56.

Braunmuller, A. R. (1988). '*King John* and Historiography.' *ELH* 55: 309–32.

Brockbank, J. P. (1958). 'History and Histrionics in *Cymbeline*.' *ShSu* 11: 42–9.

Campbell, Lily B. (1947). *Shakespeare's "Histories": Mirrors of Elizabethan Policy*. San Marino, CA.

Champion, Larry S. (1990). '*The Noise of Threatening Drum*': *Dramatic Strategy and Political Ideology in Shakespeare and the English Chronicle Plays*. Newark, DE.

Cole, Howard C. (1973). *A Quest of Inquirie: Some Contexts of Tudor Literature*. Indianapolis.

Donno, Elizabeth Story (1987). 'Some Aspects of Shakespeare's Holinshed.' *HLQ* 50: 229–48.

Foakes, R. A., ed. (1968). *King Henry VIII* (Arden Shakespeare). London (first published 1957).

Goldberg, Jonathan (1987). 'Speculations: *Macbeth* and Source', pp. 38–58 in Christopher Norris and Richard Machin, eds, *Post-Structuralist*

Readings of English Poetry. Cambridge (also as pp. 242–64 in Jean E. Howard, ed., *Shakespeare Reproduced: The Text in History and Ideology*, New York, 1987).

Hardin, Richard F. (1989). 'Chronicles and Mythmaking in Shakespeare's Joan of Arc.' *ShSu* 42: 25–35.

Holinshed, Raphael (1587). *The First and Second Volumes of Chronicles . . . The Third Volume*, 3 vols. London.

—— (1807–8). *Chronicles of England, Scotland and Ireland*, 6 vols. London.

Hosley, Richard, ed. (1968). *Shakespeare's Holinshed: An Edition of Holinshed's Chronicles (1587), Source of Shakespeare's History Plays, King Lear, Cymbeline, and Macbeth*. New York.

Hunter, G. K. (1989). 'Truth and Art in History Plays.' *ShSu* 42: 15–24.

Kim, Yun-Cheol (1989). 'Shakespeare's Unhistorical Inventions and Deviations from Holinshed, and Their Dramatic Functions in *Richard II*.' *Journal of English Language and Literature* (Seoul), 35: 747–58.

Law, Robert A. (1934). 'Holinshed as a Source of *Henry V* and *King Lear*.' *University of Texas Bulletin* 14: 38–44.

—— (1950). 'Deviations from Holinshed in *Richard II*.' *University of Texas Studies in English* 29: 91–101.

—— (1952). 'The Composition of *Macbeth* with Reference to Holinshed.' *University of Texas Studies in English* 31: 35–41.

—— (1954). 'The Chronicles and the "Three Parts" of *Henry VI*.' *University of Texas Studies in English* 33: 13–32.

—— (1957). 'Holinshed and *Henry the Eighth*.' *University of Texas Studies in English* 36: 3–11.

Maley, Willy (1997). 'Shakespeare, Holinshed and Ireland: Resources and Con-Texts', pp. 27–46 in Mark Thornton Burnett and Ramona Wray, eds, *Shakespeare and Ireland: History, Politics, Culture*. Basingstoke.

Mapstone, Sally (1998). 'Shakespeare and Scottish Kingship: A Case History', pp. 158–89 in Sally Mapstone and Juliette Wood, eds, *The Rose and the Thistle: Essays on the Culture of Late Medieval and Renaissance Scotland*. East Linton.

Matheson, Lister M. (1995). 'English Chronicle Contexts for Shakespeare's Death of Richard II', pp. 195–219 in John A. Alford, ed., *From Page to Performance: Essays in Early English Drama*. East Lansing.

Muir, Kenneth, ed. (1990). *Macbeth* (Arden Shakespeare). Walton-on-Thames (first published 1951).

—— ed. (1972). *King Lear* (Arden Shakespeare). London.

Nicoll, Allardyce, and Josephine Nicoll, ed. (1927). *Holinshed's Chronicle as used in Shakespeare's Plays*. London.

Norbrook, David (1987). '*Macbeth* and the Politics of Historiography', pp. 78–116 in Kevin Sharpe and Steven N. Zwicker, eds, *Politics of Discourse: The Literature and History of Seventeenth-Century England*. Berkeley.

Nosworthy, J. M., ed. (1969). *Cymbeline* (Arden Shakespeare). London.

Patterson, Annabel (1994). *Reading Holinshed's 'Chronicles'*. Chicago.

—— (1996). '"All Is True": Negotiating the Past in *Henry VIII*', pp. 147–66 in R. B. Parker and S. P. Zitner, eds, *Elizabethan Theater: Essays in Honor of S. Schoenbaum*. Newark, DE.

Rackin, Phyllis (1990). *Stages of History: Shakespeare's English Chronicles*. London.

Rossi, Joan Warchol (1978). '*Cymbeline*'s Debt to Holinshed: The Richness of III.i', pp. 104–12 in Carol McGinnis Kay and Henry E. Jacobs, eds, *Shakespeare's Romances Reconsidered*. Lincoln, NE.

Tomlinson, Michael (1984). 'Shakespeare and the Chronicles Reassessed.' *Literature and History* 10: 46–58.

Trousdale, Marion (1982). *Shakespeare and the Rhetoricians*. London.

Woodson, William C. (1978). 'Iago's Name in Holinshed and the Lost English Source of *Othello*.' *N&Q* 223: 146–7.

Holland, Philemon See **Camden, William**; **Livy (Titus Livius)**; **Pliny (Gaius Plinius Secundus)**; **Plutarch**; **Suetonius (Gaius Suetonius Tranquillus)**.

Homer (probably 8th Century BC), Greek Epic Poet
(A) Homer is the shadowy figure traditionally regarded as the author of the *Iliad* and *Odyssey* and so the founder of Western epic. The *Iliad* deals with the story of the Siege of Troy (Ilium), and the disastrous consequences of the wrath of Achilles, champion of the besieging Greeks. The *Odyssey* (probably not known to Shakespeare in any form; see Baldwin 1944: II, 660) narrates Odysseus' journey home after the Trojan War. Aristotle's is the classic description of Homer's characteristics as a poet: he attributes to him distinction in all the arts of epic, namely high seriousness and nobility, unity of action combined with variety of incident, dramatic vividness and authorial self-effacement.

But the *Iliad* can also be described generically as 'heroic tragedy': 'the Homeric-Sophoclean image of the tragic hero [is] the concept ... usually implied when we speak of "tragedy" in western literature' (Brower 1971: 80).

(B) Homer is a relatively late acquisition for the English Renaissance. Though his importance was recognized in the Middle Ages, his work was known only at second hand through Latin imitations and summaries, for which there was still a demand well into the Renaissance. Some of these have their merits – Ezra Pound, for instance, used Andreas Divus' *Odyssey* (1538) as the basis for his *Canto I*. Praise of Homer from humanists such as **Erasmus** and Sir Thomas **Elyot** contributed to his establishment as a school text. It was usually the *Iliad* rather than the *Odyssey* that was read in Elizabethan grammar schools, often in Latin translation (Baldwin 1944: II, 653–4).

Homer's *Iliad* and *Odyssey* were first Englished during Shakespeare's lifetime. Various unpublished, small-scale, indirect or unsuccessful translations of the *Iliad* in the second half of the sixteenth century were all superseded by George **Chapman**'s version published 1598–1611; his *Odyssey* followed in 1614–15. The only part of Chapman's work which could be relevant for Shakespeare is the first section published, the *Seaven Bookes of The Iliades* (i.e. Books I–II and VII–XI) of 1598; the rest of the translation almost certainly appeared too late to have been a significant source, and is largely ignored in what follows below.

Chapman's metre is the fourteener, and his style is not an easy one. The idiosyncratic detail is apt to obscure syntactic connections and impede narrative flow. His fidelity to Homer has been much debated. Chapman's Homer possesses poetic energy in abundance, but though a distinctive writer Chapman is here a decidedly uneven one. There is also a clear moralizing impetus – his 1598 volume is dedicated 'To the most honoured now living instance of the Achillean virtues eternized by divine Homer, the Earl of Essex' – to turn Homer into a 'mirror for princes'. All these features can be seen in Achilles' final rebuke to Agamemnon in Book I:

> Thou mightst esteeme me base
> And cowardlie to let thee use thy will in my disgrace;
> To beare such burthens never were my strength and spirites combinde,
> But to reforme their insolence, and that thy soule should finde

Were it not hurt of common good more than mine owne delight.
But I, not soothing Nestor's sute, for right's sake reverence right,
Which thou dost servilely commend but violate it quite.
And this even in thy intrayles print – I'le not prophane my hand
With battell in my lust's defence: a gyrle cannot command
My honour and my force like thine, who yet commandes our hoast.
Slave live he to the world that lives slave to his lusts engrost.
But feed it, come, and take the dame; safe go thy violent feete,
But whatsoever else thou findst aborde my sable fleete
Dare not to touch without my leave, for feele my life mischance
If then thy blacke and lust-burnt bloud flow not upon my Lance.
    (1598 text, 302–16; ed. Nicoll 1957: i, 517–18; roman for italic)

(C) Despite commentators' assertions, Shakespeare's knowledge of Homer remains unproven. Though there are in the corpus, unsurprisingly, some references to Homeric episodes, none can be shown to depend on direct knowledge of Homer either in Greek or in translated form. To Brower, Chapman's Homer is significant not because Shakespeare read it but as a help 'in placing and defining certain attitudes and modes of expression in the major tragedies. If Chapman's reading of Homer is not Shakespeare's, it is a version by one of his contemporaries, and much nearer to his reading than any translation since the reign of James I' (1971: 78–9). What is meant here is such matters as the penchant for meditative analysis shared by Shakespeare's and Chapman's heroes – 'a Renaissance Achilles or Hector . . . would be, for example, the Antony of *Antony and Cleopatra*' (Brower 1971: 80–1). But such connections are tenuous in the extreme. Claimed verbal echoes of Chapman's *Seaven Bookes of the Iliades* are no more conclusive. Potentially the most extensively Homeric work of Shakespeare's is *Troilus and Cressida*: for a listing of possible echoes here see Palmer (1982: 33–7) and for a fuller treatment Presson (1953). Tantalizingly, it remains 'likely that Shakespeare knew more of Homer than he read, and possible that he read more than we know about' (Henderson 1935: 142).

(D) For the English Renaissance Homer, including Chapman, see especially Sowerby (1994).

Baldwin (1944).

Brower, R. A. (1971). *Hero and Saint: Shakespeare and the Graeco-Roman Heroic Tradition*. Oxford.

Henderson, W. B. Drayton (1935). 'Shakespeare's *Troilus and Cressida*: Yet Deeper in its Tradition', pp. 127–56 in Hardin Craig, ed., *Essays in Dramatic Literature: The Parrott Presentation Volume*. Princeton (reprinted New York, 1967).

Nicoll, Allardyce, ed. (1957). *Chapman's Homer*, 2 vols. London.

Palmer, Kenneth, ed. (1982). *Troilus and Cressida* (Arden Shakespeare). London.

Presson, Robert K. (1953). *Shakespeare's 'Troilus and Cressida' and the Legends of Troy*. Madison, WI.

Root, Robert K. (1903). *Classical Mythology in Shakespeare*. New York.

Smith, Valerie (1982). 'The History of Cressida', pp. 61–79 in J. A. Jowitt and R. K. S. Taylor, eds, *Self and Society in Shakespeare's 'Troilus and Cressida' and 'Measure for Measure'*. Bradford.

Sowerby, Robin (1994). *The Classical Legacy in Renaissance Poetry*. London.

Homilies

(A) A homily is anciently a simple dilation on a scriptural text; the items which formed the Tudor books called *Certain Sermons or Homilies* (1547) and *The Seconde Tome of Homilies* (1563) are instead expositions on topics deemed significant for churchgoers, which use Scripture along with other authorities and techniques to develop their themes. They were first introduced under Edward VI as part of a programme to enforce religious conformity. Thomas Cranmer edited the strongly Protestant first series, and wrote three of its twelve discourses (subdivided into thirty-one in later editions). The first three homilies were titled 'A Fruitefull Exhortacion to the Readyng of Holye Scripture', 'Of the Misery of All Mankynde' and 'Of the Salvacion of All Mankynde'. This book was suppressed under Mary, but reissued under Elizabeth, in whose reign any clerical resistance to its weekly reading was not tolerated. The second book of homilies of 1563, again strongly anti-Roman, contained twenty new discourses dealing with doctrinal and moral topics; and from 1571 a long and transparently propagandistic homily 'Against Disobedience and Wylfull Rebellion' was added to new editions of the second book (as well as being issued independently) in the wake of the Northern Rebellion, the Queen's excommunication and the various ensuing plots. Hence the homilies in use from 1571 amounted to thirty-three items, many of them subdivided into parts which constituted up to six separate readings. All were eventually collected into a single volume in 1623.

(B) From 1547, a homily, or a fixed part of one of the longer homilies, was delivered at all Sunday and holy day services in the majority of English churches instead of a sermon, following the order and rotation prescribed in the manual's Preface, meaning that on average an English adult would probably have heard each homily about once a year. Only licensed preachers (whose learning and loyalty to the established church were assured) were entitled to deliver sermons of their own composition, and few such clergymen were available, especially rurally (though the town of Stratford had one in Henry Heycroft from 1569 to 1584). The responsibility of reading a homily was binding upon unlicensed clergy. Liturgical function apart, 'the book of homilies came to be regarded as a benchmark of reformed belief in England' (Bond 1987: 5): the Forty-Two Articles of 1552 referred to and took for granted the authority of the homilies in doctrinal matters, and it was quickly realized that 'they could be used as a standard for measuring conformity and controlling maverick preachers of whatever persuasion' (Bond 1987: 5–6).

This was why Elizabeth, who 'regarded the enforced reading of the homilies as a crucial component of ecclesiastical polity' (Bond 1987: 11), and felt three or four licensed preachers enough for a county, was probably the most enthusiastic patron of the homilies of her time. But there was plenty of opposition. Richard **Hooker**, sometimes considered an apologist for the Elizabethan settlement, preferred the much more flexible sermon form, as encouraging 'aptnes to followe particular occasions presentlie growinge, to put life into wordes by countenance voice and gesture, to prevaile mightelie in the suddaine affections of men' (ed. Hill 1977: 100). Such views were common among sixteenth-century Puritans, whose increasingly loud complaint that the homilies were an impediment to the creation of a preaching ministry was acknowledged at the 1604 Hampton Court Conference – though the plan the King announced on this occasion to promote preaching instead was to be only half realized. However, over the seventeenth century, with better-educated parish clergy, and decreasing governmental interference in their work, the Church's dependence on the homilies dwindled, notwithstanding conservatives' attempts to revive and supplement them into the early eighteenth century.

The inclusion in the collection of the last homily, 'Against Disobedience and Wylfull Rebellion', made it clear that the Elizabethan government thought of homilies as political measures. It was divided into six parts, each followed by a prayer for Queen and country. The first of them engages with an issue explored in several of the Histories, the problem of the bad ruler:

> But what if the prince be undiscrete and evyll in deede, and it also evident to all mens eyes that he so is? I aske agayne, what if it be long of the wickednesse of the subjectes, that the prince is undiscrete or evyll? Shall the subjectes both by their wickednesse provoke God for their deserved punishment to geve them an undiscrete or evyll prince, and also rebell against hym, and withall against God, who for the punishment of their sinnes dyd geve them suche a prince? Wyll you heare the Scriptures concerning this point? God (say the Holy Scriptures) maketh a wicked man to raigne for the sinnes of the people. Agayne, God geveth a prince in his anger (meaning an evyll one) and taketh away a prince in his displeasure (meaning specially when he taketh away a good prince for the sinnes of the people): as in our memorie he toke away our good Josias, Kyng Edwarde, in his young and good yeres for our wickednesse . . . Wherefore let us turne from our sinnes unto the Lorde with all our heartes, and he wyll turne the heart of the prince unto our quiet and wealth: Els for subjectes to deserve through their sinnes to have an evyll prince, and then to rebell against hym, were double and treble evyll, by provoking God more to plague them.
>
> (1571 text, ed. Bond 1987: 214–15)

(C) Shakespeare's one reference to homilies in general, suggesting the common attitude to their reading in church, comes in Rosalind's response to Orlando's verses as declaimed by Celia:

> O most gentle pulpiter! What tedious homily of love have you wearied your parishioners withal, and never cried 'Have patience, good people'.
>
> (*As You Like It* 3.2.145–8)

256

Elsewhere, however, 'precisely because their language and ideas were so widely known as to be in the air of the time, it is hardly possible to prove a link between lines in the plays and similar homiletic passages' (Rosinger 1975: 299) – a difficulty too often ignored by commentators who take similarity for evidence of direct influence. A good example is the attempt made several times by different scholars to trace the notion of hierarchy from the homily 'Concernyng Good Ordre and Obedience to Rulers and Magistrates' to the words of such characters as Ulysses, Titania and Coriolanus. And Shaheen's (1999: 831–2) list of almost 200 Shakespeare 'parallels' to the homilies is too generous to give even a rough indication of the position, failing to distinguish between probably direct echoes and mere set phrases and terms popularized by the homilies (the overwhelming majority of his thirty-six references for the homily 'Against Swearyng and Perjurie', for instance, are simple cases of the use of two or three of the words 'swear', 'forswear', 'oath' and 'perjury'). Nevertheless, enough verbal and other signs of the homilies' effect on the plays exist to suggest that they leave some mark over the range of the Shakespeare canon.

As Hart (1934) pointed out, ideas, and to a lesser extent expressions, from the 1547 'Exhortacion concernyng Good Ordre and Obedience' and the long 1571 homily 'Against Disobedience and Wylfull Rebellion' have many parallels in the Histories, notably on the topics of passive obedience, the evils of rebellion, and the divine right of kings. Hart's belief that Shakespeare derived some of these concepts specifically from these homilies is unverifiable, even if their expression is sometimes similar. The real importance of these homily texts may lie rather in their status as knowledge common to all members of the playhouse audience, meaning that Shakespeare can evoke a deep penumbra of context and connotation extremely economically. Nor is the relevance of these homilies confined to the Histories. In 'Against Disobedience', the rebellious are worthy of a 'horrible and dreadful damnation' that 'no mortal man can express with words, nor conceive in mind'; Macduff's exclamation on finding his murdered king is 'O horror, horror, horror! Tongue nor heart / Cannot conceive nor give thee name' (*Macbeth* 2.3.61–2). Milward also suggests a looser echo of this homily in Camillo's resolution to do his king's bidding (*The Winter's Tale* 1.2.357–61; Milward 1973: 120–1).

The more disparate echoes of other homilies can only be exemplified,

257

not enumerated, here. Often these are of little further significance, but sometimes they suggest the direction the playwright's mind took, and sometimes they clarify his meaning. Phrasing from the 'Homelie of Whoredom and Unclennesse' (also known as 'Against Adultery') in *The Comedy of Errors* is echoed by, and helps explain, Adriana's own speeches on adultery (see Baldwin 1965: 169–71). The same homily contains a passage reasoning that 'If whoredom had not been syn, surely S. Jhon Baptist would never have rebuked King Herode for takyng his brothers wife' (Bond 1987: 176). Perhaps Hamlet in his remark to the Players, 'It out-herods Herod' (3.2.13), while referring principally to the Herod of the **Mystery Plays**, was at some level recalling this association (so Rosinger 1975). Finally, the Clown's complaint to the Countess in *All's Well* that 'service is no heritage' (1.3.23) is exactly paralleled verbally in the homily 'Against Idleness'.

(D) Bond (1987) supplies a thorough discussion of the general history and significance of the homilies, especially regarding their compilation and early use. Shaheen's (1999) listing of homily echoes, though recent, is flawed by its inclusion of much material with no necessary connection and the omission of some interesting parallels, such as Rosinger's (1975) and Baldwin's (1962, 1965).

Baldwin, T. W. (1962). 'Three Homilies in *The Comedy of Errors*', pp. 137–47 in Richard Hosley, ed., *Essays on Shakespeare and the Elizabethan Drama in Honor of Hardin Craig*. Columbia.

—— (1965). *On the Compositional Genetics of The Comedy of Errors*. Urbana, IL.

Bond, Ronald B., ed. (1987). *'Certain Sermons or Homilies' (1547) and 'A Homily against Disobedience and Wilful Rebellion': A Critical Edition*. Toronto.

Hart, Alfred (1934). *Shakespeare and the Homilies and Other Pieces of Research into the Elizabethan Drama*. Melbourne.

Hill, W. Speed, ed. (1977). *Of the Laws of Ecclesiastical Polity, Book V*. Cambridge.

Milward, Peter (1966). 'The Homiletic Tradition in Shakespeare's Plays with Special Reference to *Hamlet*.' *Shakespeare Studies* (Japan) 5: 72–87.

—— (1973). *Shakespeare's Religious Background*. London.

Rosinger, Lawrence (1975). 'Hamlet and the Homilies.' *ShQ* 26: 299–301.

Shaheen, Naseeb (1999). *Biblical References in Shakespeare's Plays*. Newark, DE.

Hooker, Richard (1553/4–1600), Theologian Hooker's thought on social hierarchy, in particular, has been regarded as underlying Shakespeare's, but direct use has not been clearly established. Hooker is one of many antecedents cited for Ulysses' 'Degree' speech in *Troilus and Cressida* (1.3).

Cohen, Eileen Z. (1970). 'The Visible Solemnity: Ceremony and Order in Shakespeare and Hooker.' *TSLL* 12: 181–95.

Milward, Peter (1973). *Shakespeare's Religious Background*, pp. 134–43. London.

Horace (Quintus Horatius Flaccus) (65 BC–8 BC), Roman Poet

(A) The son of a freedman from Apulia, Horace was educated at Rome and later Athens. In 44–42 BC he served in Brutus' army, and, he tells us, ran away at the battle of Philippi in 42. He obtained a pardon for his republican soldiering but was stripped of his family property, and then obliged to write in order to live. About 38 BC he was introduced to Maecenas, the great Roman patron, who took him under his protection and provided him with his famous Sabine villa. During the 30s Horace wrote his seventeen meditative, often ironic *Epodes*, miscellaneously on love, politics and his personal enemies, and his two Books of *Satires* or *Sermones*, traditionally seen as the urbane and mocking antithesis in satire to the scurrilous and personal invective of **Juvenal**. He then published the first three Books of his *Odes* or *Carmina* in 23. This varied collection contains moods varying from Stoic gravity to Epicurean gaiety in poems on public themes, *carpe diem* poems, celebrations of the country life, the joys of wine, and poetry itself, poems of moral reflection, of love, and of friendship. The first Book of his *Epistles*, hexameter poems ostensibly written to friends on the morals of everyday life, was next to appear; a further Book of *Epistles* and a fourth of *Odes* followed, and his *Ars Poetica* (*Art of Poetry*) is assigned to his last years. Though many qualities have been construed in his work, and different parts of that work prioritized, over the centuries, Horace's unfluctuating status since the Renaissance as one of the very greatest of Roman poets is broadly founded on what Quintilian describes as his quality of being 'plenus . . . iucunditatis et gratiae et variis figuris et verbis felicissime audax' ('full of delight and charm, with great variety of figures and bold but very apt use of words'), together with a supreme poetic craftsmanship manifesting itself especially in his use of metres, and an urbane wit which permits or constructs several angles at once from which to see the world.

(B) **Erasmus** included Horace among his list of authors suitable for school use in *De Ratione Studii*, and Baldwin (1944: II, 497) found that of more than two dozen pre-1600 English grammar school curricula he examined, only three failed to specify Horace in one form or another. In some schools the *Epistles* were used to assist in training with epistolary writing; others specified the *Satires* and *Odes*; there is evidence of the teaching of the *Ars Poetica*; and so on. While the *Odes* were evidently used as stylistic models in education, for their matter the 'instructive' *Satires* and *Epistles* were given preference; by the late sixteenth century Horace had for long been regarded as primarily a moralist. The use of the lyric poetry even as a metrical model was new in England – through the Middle Ages such a practice would have had little purpose, since Latin prosody was barely understood – and, because Horace's special poetic qualities had no great appeal to pre-Renaissance tastes, he was in general rated very far behind **Virgil**, and usually **Ovid**, as a Latin poet until the seventeenth century. Even in satire, **Juvenal** was frequently preferred as more direct and cutting.

A lost translation of the *Satires* by Lewis Evans in 1565 was the first substantial English rendering of Horace. Thomas Drant, Archdeacon of Lewes, translated the *Epistles*, *Satires* and *Ars Poetica* in cumbersome fourteeners in 1566–7, but did not venture into the *Odes* and *Epodes*. Drant's tastes squared with those of Lambinus, the editor of Horace whose text of 1561 became the most widely used one in the late sixteenth century, whom Drant quotes in his dedicatory epistle:

> If we wey both profytte and delectation Lambinus wrote truly, emongst latin poetes Horace hath not his felowe. This is he whome great Augustus writte shoulde be loked to as him selfe, whom Maecenas loved as himselfe, ripe, pythye, excellent for moral preceptes, full of pretye speaches, full of Judgement.
>
> (Drant 1567: sig. *3ᵛ; roman for italic)

In Renaissance Europe as a whole, the *Satires* and *Epistles* were translated entire three times as often as the *Odes* and *Epodes*. Drant's Horace was to be the last large-scale English translation for some seventy years, though less ambitious attempts in the interim included a partial version of the *Ars Poetica* by Queen Elizabeth herself.

Horace was an unavoidable presence in the education of the literate classes of the English Renaissance, but how far was this matched by his presence in the work of English writers? Before Shakespeare's time he had been in this respect too the poet of the *Satires* and *Epistles* for a few pioneers, notably Sir Thomas Wyatt, whose own epistolary satires, though not translations of Horace's, are inconceivable without them. **Sidney** is the first English poet to translate a Horatian Ode (ii.10, as 'You better sure shall live', late 1570s) in such a way as to create an independent English poem, but lesser talents were at a loss for the style and sophistication required. It was Ben **Jonson** who first, and influentially for later generations, made use of the full range of Horace's work. His creative imitations naturalized it in such poems as 'To Penshurst', 'To Sir Robert Wroth' and 'Inviting a Friend to Supper'. His translations too (several *Odes* and *Epodes*, *Satire* i.9, *Ars Poetica*), as well as his deliberate modelling of his poetic personality on Horace's, helped earn him the name of 'the English Horace'. It was in the early seventeenth century that Horace came to be felt as important a lyric poet as a satirist, indeed the 'prince of lyrics'; but Jonson's Horace also commanded respect as a moralist:

> Such was *Horace*, an Author of much Civilitie; and (if any one among the heathen can be) the best master, both of vertue, and wisdome; an excellent, and true judge upon cause, and reason; not because he thought so; but because he knew so, out of use and experience.
>
> (*Discoveries*; ed. Herford and Simpson 1925–51: viii, 642)

Jonson's work also indicates, finally, more of the reasons for Shakespeare's tendency to avoid the Horatian model: 'Jonson's study of Horace ... led him to favour concision, strength, and restraint over exuberant verbal embroidery – significantly he was in general not much interested in the works of Ovid – or elaborate metaphor of the Shakespearean type' (Martindale 1992: 201).

Drant's Horace is sometimes thought to have been known to Shakespeare (as by Turner 1957), but on no good evidence. Although some of

261

Horace (Quintus Horatius Flaccus)

Jonson's Horace translations were in existence during Shakespeare's lifetime, there are no signs he knew them either. But it is not unlikely he knew the Latin poem, *Ode* IV.1, which Jonson is translating here, even if its fame belongs more to later eras, and even if we choose not to credit claims of echoes from it in *Hamlet* (see C):

> *Venus*, againe thou mov'st a warre
> Long intermitted, pray thee, pray thee spare:
>   I am not such, as in the Reigne
> Of the good *Cynara* I was: Refraine,
>   Sower Mother of sweet Loves, forbeare
> To bend a man, now at his fiftieth yeare
>   Too stubborne for Commands so slack:
> Goe where Youths soft intreaties call thee back.
>   More timely hie thee to the house,
> With thy bright Swans, of *Paulus Maximus:*
>   There jest, and feast, make him thine host,
> If a fit livor thou dost seek to toast;
>   For he's both noble, lovely, young,
> And for the troubled Clyent fyl's his tongue,
>   Child of a hundred Arts, and farre
> Will he display the Ensignes of thy warre.
>   And when he smiling finds his Grace
> With thee 'bove all his Rivals gifts take place,
>   He'll thee a Marble Statue make
> Beneath a Sweet-wood Roofe, neere *Alba Lake:*
>   There shall thy dainty Nostrill take
> In many a Gumme, and for thy soft eares sake
>   Shall Verse be set to Harpe and Lute,
> And *Phrygian* Hau'boy, not without the Flute.
>   There twice a day in sacred Laies,
> The Youths and tender Maids shall sing thy praise:
>   And in the *Salian* manner meet
> Thrice 'bout thy Altar with their Ivory feet.
>   Me now, nor Wench, nor wanton Boy,
> Delights, nor credulous hope of mutuall Joy,
>   Nor care I now healths to propound;
> Or with fresh flowers to girt my temple round.
>   But why, oh why, my *Ligurine,*

Flow my thin teares, downe these pale cheeks of mine?
   Or why, my well-grac'd words among,
With an uncomely silence failes my tongue?
   Hard-hearted, I dreame every Night
I hold thee fast! but fled hence, with the Light,
   Whether in *Mars* his field thou bee,
Or *Tybers* winding streames, I follow thee.
                  (ed. Herford and Simpson 1925–51: VIII, 292–3)

(C) Horace has been one of the best-known of classical authors during the rise of modern literary scholarship, leading to more opportunities for discoveries of parallels in Shakespeare than with most other sources. Much ingenuity has been expended on showing what exactly Shakespeare knew and recalled of Horace, but many echoes or claimed echoes have little or no other significance. A fairly good knowledge of the text of Horace's *Odes*, with more mixed levels of awareness of his other works, is evident in Shakespeare, but he is, *tout court*, no Horatian writer. There are some cases, however, in which echoes of Horace can be said to offer additional understanding of or interpretative possibilities for a passage.

When Timon of Athens cites *Epistle* I.2 (at 1.2.28) he quotes an extremely familiar work which educated members of the audience are expected to recognize instantly, but its familiarity means the citation shows nothing about Shakespeare's direct knowledge of Horace. When Demetrius reads out the first two lines of *Ode* I.22 in *Titus Andronicus*, in a message from Titus, Chiron's ability to identify them displays only a rudimentary level of training, and the quotation again establishes nothing about Shakespeare's familiarity with Horace since these verses were indeed quoted, twice, in William Lily's Latin grammar, the *Brevissima Instituto*:

DEMETRIUS   What's here? A scroll, and written round about.
            Let's see:
            [*Reads*] 'Integer vitae, scelerisque purus,
            Non eget Mauri iaculis, nec arcu.'
CHIRON   O, 'tis a verse in Horace, I know it well;
            I read it in the grammar long ago.
                                          (4.2.18–23)

Even the non-explicit use of Horace's *Ode* III.30, 'Exegi monumentum',

263

at the start of Sonnet 55 ('Not marble, nor the gilded monuments / Of princes, shall outlive this powerful rhyme'), involves a passage so commonplace that it supplies no evidence Shakespeare knew the Latin, though it is *prima facie* likely he did (see also on this passage Baldwin 1950: 260–3). Shakespeare's most obviously Horatian lines are not the most revealing, nor, as a rule, those where knowledge of the source tells the reader anything new.

Discounting references to Horace likely to arise from intermediate sources or commonplaces, there are at least some passages in Shakespeare which seem to have been affected directly by the *Odes*. Perhaps the most famous comes in Henry IV's contrast between himself and his subjects, in which the following lines seem full of Horatian ideas creatively used:

> Why rather, sleep, liest thou in smoky cribs,
> Upon uneasy pallets stretching thee,
> And hush'd with buzzing night-flies to thy slumber,
> Than in the perfum'd chambers of the great,
> Under the canopies of costly state,
> And lull'd with sound of sweetest melody?
> O thou dull god, why liest thou with the vile
> In loathsome beds, and leav'st the kingly couch
> A watch-case or a common 'larum-bell?
>
> > (*2 Henry IV*, 3.1.9–17)

Horace's *Ode* III.1 famously deals with the theme that it is tranquillity of mind and not wealth that makes for happiness; the relevant lines (17–24) are quoted here in Sir Richard Fanshawe's seventeenth-century rendering:

> Over whose head hangs a drawn sword,
> Him cannot please a Royal feast:
> Nor melody of lute or bird,
> Give to his eyes their wonted rest.
> Sleep, gentle sleep, scorns not the poor
> Abiding of the Plough-man: loves
> By sides of Rivers shades obscure:
> And rockt with West-windes, Tempe Groves.
>
> > (ed. Carne-Ross 1996: 91)

Another apparently direct debt to the *Odes* involves the famous 'Pyrrha' poem (1.5) and Hastings' lament over his airy hopes in *Richard III* 3.4.98–103 (noted by Johnson: see Baldwin 1944: II, 500). But in this and most other examples, the echo of Horace seems not to make any perceptible creative or interpretative difference (Baldwin exaggerates in claiming the *Richard III* passage cannot be understood without Horace's; see also the over-generous collection of other examples in his full discussion, II, 497–525). In some instances the exact nature of Shakespeare's borrowing from the *Odes* appears to signal his use of the extensive glosses and commentary of Lambinus.

Among Horace's other works, echoes of the *Ars Poetica* – sometimes generically classed, and printed, with the *Odes* – are fairly frequent in Shakespeare, echoes of the *Epistles* (including the direct quotation in *Timon*, above) and *Satires* considerably less so. One obvious explanation is that Shakespeare's knowledge was picked up not from the air, which should have contained a more even distribution of material, but from a grammar school training which, as was normal, involved some Horace, but which happened to concentrate on the *Odes*. Inconclusive signs of Shakespeare's knowledge of the *Ars Poetica* are scattered widely, as in for example the commonplace about the mountain bringing forth a mouse at *Love's Labour's Lost* 5.2.518, but there is more tangible evidence (because of resemblances of detail) for his use of its famous passage on the ages of man (158–74). This lies in the background of more than one of Shakespeare's treatments of the theme: in *As You Like It* 2.7 it is echoed (through Lambinus) together with related passages from Ovid, **Palengenius** and others (see Baldwin 1944: I, 652–73), whereas in *Macbeth*, for Macbeth's *ennui* at 5.3.22–6, Shakespeare seems, reasonably enough, to expect some members of his audience to have a fairly close recollection of the Horatian passage alone (see Hammond 1989).

Perhaps significantly, Horatian echoes have been discerned in almost all the tragedies, though again the evidence usually falls short of adequate proof of a relationship. A set of small verbal echoes in *King Lear* 3.4 seems to show reminiscences in Lear's words to Edgar/Poor Tom of stray lines from two of the *Epistles* and one of the *Odes*, in one case via a quotation in Samuel **Harsnett**. Lear sees his position in particular through Horace's *Epistle* II.1, especially the lines (210–13) translated by Drant thus:

That poet on a stretched rope may walke and never fall,
That can stere up my passions, or quicke my sprytes at all.
Stere me, chere me, or with false feares of bugges fill up my brest,
At *Athens* now, and now at *Thebes*, by charminge make me rest.

(Drant 1567: sig. G7ʳ)

The collocation here of several apparently disparate ideas in the protagonist's words shows 'a unity between the scattered eccentricities of Lear' (Blunden 1934: 202). In *Hamlet* we may choose to see an echo of *Ode* iv.1's 'Me nec femina nec puer' ((C), above; so Mangold 1908), adding sarcastic point to one of Hamlet's remarks to Rosencrantz at 2.2.317–23; an allusion to Drant's version of *Satire* iii.3 (Turner 1957); and memories of Horace's character in Horatio (Kilpatrick 1982). It is, however, unclear why Shakespeare might have expected detailed knowledge of Drant from his audience, and little seems to be added to the play if the Horatio character is thought of as Horatian.

The possibility, more pleasant than plausible, that the bear in *The Winter's Tale* was suggested by the reference in *Epistle* ii.1 to the rabble at the theatre calling for bears or boxers instead of good drama has of course been canvassed (Randall 1985). The most intriguing remaining connections are with *Antony and Cleopatra*, though it seems unlikely they could be securely confirmed. Shakespeare might have arrived unassisted at his conception of the dying Cleopatra as a paradoxical Stoic, but it is not available in **Plutarch**, and he could easily have derived it from Horace's *Ode* i.37 (see Westbrook 1947; Martindale 1990: 186–9). A surmise of Emrys Jones' (1977: 43–6) would make Horace's *Odes* the underlying model for the play's style as a whole, 'with its firmly moulded phrasing, its small-scale figurative effects, and its sustained musicality', also perhaps connecting with some of the play's themes (empire, love and wine). Horace was a contemporary of Antony and Cleopatra's.

(D) Carne-Ross (1996) assembles Renaissance and later translations of Horace. Edden (1973) surveys attitudes to and English renderings of Horace down to 1666, and is supplemented by Jiriczek (1911) on Drant. The work of the Martindales (1990, 1992, 1993) covers Horace's influence on Jonson and his immediate successors in more detail. The only synoptic account of Shakespeare and Horace is Baldwin (1944), which also explores bibliographical contexts for Shakespeare's knowledge; other commentators all operate at the level of individual passages or plays, though in some cases more far-reaching effects on Shakespeare than Baldwin claims are proposed. The Horatian tradition as it affects the *Sonnets* – but only marginally Horace's direct influence on them – is extensively addressed in Leishman (1961).

Baldwin (1944), II, 497–525; Martindale (1990); Muir (1977).

Baldwin, T. W. (1950). *On the Literary Genetics of Shakspere's Poems and Sonnets*. Urbana, IL.

Blunden, Edmund (1934). 'Shakespeare's Significances', pp. 195–215 in *The Mind's Eye: Essays*. London.

Carne-Ross, D. S., and Kenneth Haynes, eds (1996). *Horace in English*. Harmondsworth.

Drant, Thomas (1567). *Horace his Arte of Poetrie, Pistles, and Satyrs Englished*. London.

Edden, Valerie (1973). '*The Best of Lyrick Poets*', pp. 135–60 in C. D. N. Costa, ed., *Horace*. London.

Hammond, Paul (1989). 'Macbeth and the Ages of Man.' *N&Q* 234: 332–3.

Herford, C. H., Percy and Evelyn Simpson, eds (1925–51). *Ben Jonson*, 8 vols. Oxford.

Jiriczek, O. L. (1911). 'Der Elisabethanische Horaz.' *ShJ* 47: 42–63.

Jones, Emrys, ed. (1977). *Antony and Cleopatra* (New Penguin Shakespeare). Harmondsworth.

Kilpatrick, Ross (1982). 'Hamlet the Scholar', pp. 247–61 in Pierre Brind' Amor and Pierre Senay, eds, *Mélanges offerts en hommage au Révérand père Etienne Gareau*. Ottawa.

Leishman, J. B. (1961). *Themes and Variations in Shakespeare's Sonnets*. London.

Mangold, W. (1908). 'Zu *Hamlet*, II, 2, 321.' *ShJ* 44: 146–7.

Martindale, Charles (1992). 'Ovid, Horace, and Others', pp. 177–213 in Richard Jenkyns, ed, *The Legacy of Rome: A New Appraisal*. Oxford.

Martindale, Joanna (1993). 'The Best Master of Virtue and Wisdom: The Horace of Ben Jonson and his Heirs', pp. 50–85 in Charles Martindale and David Hopkins, eds, *Horace Made New: Horatian Influences on British Writing from the Renaissance to the Twentieth Century*. Cambridge.

Randall, Dale B. J. (1985). ' "This is the Chase": Or, the Further Pursuit of Shakespeare's Bear.' *ShJ* 121: 89–95.

Turner, Paul (1957). 'True Madness (A Note on "Hamlet," II, ii, 92–5).' *N&Q* 202: 194–6.
Westbrook, Perry D. (1947). 'Horace's Influence on Shakespeare's *Antony and Cleopatra*.' *PMLA* 62: 392–8.

Huon of Burdeux (**Anon. French Romance**) The usual assumption that in *A Midsummer Night's Dream* the figure (and name) of Oberon is taken from this romance, translated by Lord Berners before 1533, is supported by a few further local affinities between the two works.

Brooks, Harold F., ed. (1979). *A Midsummer Night's Dream* (Arden Shakespeare), pp. lix, 145–6. London.
Bullough, I, 370–1.

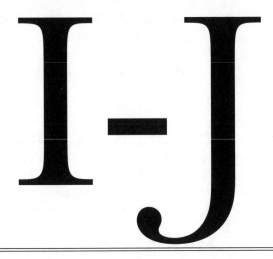

I-J

Impresa, Imprese See **Emblems**.

Interludes See **Morality Tradition**.

James I and VI (1566–1625), King of England, Scotland and Wales There are signs that three Shakespeare plays, *Macbeth*, *Othello* and *Measure for Measure*, are in different ways designed to pay compliments to James, and draw on his own published writings in order to do so.

Draper, J. W. (1938). '*Macbeth* as a Compliment to James I.' *Englische Studien* 72: 207–20.

Jones, Emrys (1968). ' "Othello", "Lepanto" and the Cyprus Wars.' *ShSu* 21: 47–52.

Stevenson, David Lloyd (1959). 'The Role of James I in Shakespeare's *Measure for Measure*.' *ELH* 26: 188–208.

Jodelle, Etienne (1532–1573), French Poet and Playwright There are a few points, especially in Act 3, at which *Antony and Cleopatra* looks closer in some details to Jodelle's play *Cléopâtre captive* (performed 1552–3, published 1574) than to its other sources. But these are much too slight to confirm an acquaintance.

Muir, Kenneth (1969). 'Elizabeth I, Jodelle, and Cleopatra.' *RenD* 2: 197–206.

Jonson, Ben (1573?–1637), Poet and Dramatist Jones (1971: 149–51) refers to the names Othello/Thorello and some other local similarities between passages in *Othello* and *Every Man in his Humour* (1601), and Taylor (1982) to miscellaneous similarities between *King Lear* and *Eastward Ho!* (1605), again perhaps merely coincidental.

Jones, Emrys (1971). *Scenic Form in Shakespeare.* Oxford.
Taylor, Gary (1982). 'A New Source and an Old Date for *King Lear.*' *RES* 33: 396–413.

Jourdain (Jourdan), Silvester (d. 1650) See **Bermuda Pamphlets**.

Juvenal (Decimus Junius Juvenalis) (*fl.* 2nd Century AD), Roman Satirist Kilpatrick's is the fullest recent treatment of the passing resemblances to Juvenalian lines in *Hamlet*, where most possible echoes of him have been found in Shakespeare; they are insufficient to establish direct acquaintance.

Kilpatrick, Ross (1982). 'Hamlet the Scholar', pp. 247–61 in Pierre Brind'Amor and Pierre Senay, eds, *Mélanges offerts en hommage au Révérand Père Etienne Gareau.* Ottawa.

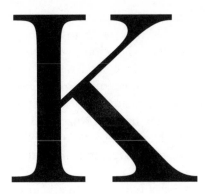

K

Krantz, Albert (Crantz; Albertius Kranzius) (d. 1517), German Theologian, Diplomat and Chronicler Krantz's 1548 Latin account of the Hamlet story might have been available to Shakespeare, but Olsson's case for the playwright's use of it is predicated on the assumption that he did not know enough French to read **Belleforest**'s.

Olsson, Yngve B. (1968). 'In Search of Yorick's Skull: Notes on the Background of Hamlet.' *ShSt* 4: 183–220.

Kyd, Thomas (1558–1594), Playwright
(A) The son of a successful scrivener (legal scribe), Kyd attended the recently founded Merchant Taylors' School, but is not known to have entered university. Most of his original work seems to have been done before 1588, perhaps including the lost play more or less tentatively assigned to him, the so-called Ur-*Hamlet*. As well as evidently lost plays there may well have been others never assigned to him at all after the sixteenth century. His brilliantly innovative *Spanish Tragedy*, first performed at some point between 1582 and 1592, was an influential adaptation of some of the ingredients of Senecan tragedy – such as ghosts and a revenge plot – to the English stage. Kyd later published translations of Italian and French plays; his closet tragedy *Cornelia* (probably written in 1593), from **Garnier**, was in keeping with current courtly fashion.

271

Other courtly closet dramas, including his blank verse *Pompey the Great*, do not survive. During 1587–8 he seems to have become a secretary to an unknown lord, and by 1590 to have joined the service of Essex as a secret agent. In 1593 the Privy Council had his lodgings searched in connection with charges of 'libels' apparently laid against his sometime roommate **Marlowe**, in which he was implicated. A heretical essay was found which Kyd, probably under torture, attributed to Marlowe. But Marlowe was exonerated, and Kyd, who was disowned even by his own family, died in disgrace and poverty little more than a year later.

(B) Early references suggest Kyd was seen as a dramatist of importance, lending support to the hypothesis that he was responsible for more plays than are known to later times. But *The Spanish Tragedy* alone achieved an unrivalled success on the Elizabethan and Jacobean stage (for the stage history see Freeman 1967: 120–31), and its popularity lasted until the 1630s, with ten separate editions being issued from 1592 to 1633. It was revised for a revival in 1602, acquiring 320 fresh lines by one of several candidates including **Jonson**, **Dekker**, Webster and (according to Stevenson 1968) Shakespeare. Its influence in a general sense can be traced or assumed in all later Elizabethan revenge tragedies, and allusions, echoes and parodies of it are ubiquitous on the stage for decades. In 1614 Jonson characterized an old-fashioned playwright as one who would swear that '*Jeronimo* [*The Spanish Tragedy*] and *Andronicus* were the best plays yet'.

The deeply motivated vigour of Hieronimo's dramatic idiom as he prepares his vengeance for his son Horatio's murder was of great significance for later writers (see (C)). It is illustrated in this soliloquy:

> See, see, oh see thy shame *Hieronimo*,
> See heere a loving Father to his sonne:
> Beholde the sorrowes and the sad laments,
> That he delivereth for his sonnes dicease.
> If loves effects so strives in lesser things,
> If love enforce such moodes in meaner wits,
> If love expresse such power in poore estates:
> *Hieronimo*, When as a raging Sea,
> Tost with the winde and tide ore turnest then
> The upper billowes course of waves to keep,
> Whilest lesser waters labour in the deepe.

Then shamest thou not *Hieronimo* to neglect,
The sweet revenge of thy *Horatio*.
Though on this earth justice will not be found:
Ile downe to hell and in this passion,
Knock at the dismall gates of *Plutos* Court,
Getting by force as once *Alcides* did,
A troupe of furies and tormenting hagges,
To torture *Don Lorenzo* and the rest.
Yet least the triple headed porter should,
Denye my passage to the slimy strond:
The *Thracian* Poet thou shalt counterfeite:
Come on olde Father be my *Orpheus*,
And if thou canst no notes upon the Harpe,
Then sound the burden of thy sore harts greefe,
Till we do gaine that *Proserpine* may graunt,
Revenge on them that murdred my Sonne,
Then will I rent and teare them thus and thus,
Shivering their limmes in peeces with my teeth.
        (3.13.95–123; Kyd 1592: sigs H2^v–H3^r)

(C) The hypothesis that Kyd's hand was at work in some Shakespeare plays, notably *Hamlet* and *Titus Andronicus*, was once found more credible than it now seems, and theories about the authorship of *Hamlet*'s predecessor-play have come and gone. It would now be unusual to hold that *The Taming of a Shrew* both predated Shakespeare's play and was written by Kyd. But doubts about such connections need not reduce Shakespeare's debt to Kyd to the mere *schema* of revenge tragedy: he is likely to have been impressed by his predecessor well beyond this level. The Ur-*Hamlet*, being only hypothetically reconstructable, cannot readily be analysed as source-material at all, and indications of the effects of other Kyd plays on Shakespeare are faint – most concretely, there is a reference to Basilico, one of the principal characters in the 1589 play often ascribed to Kyd, *Soliman and Perseda*, in *King John*, 1.1.244. But *The Spanish Tragedy* is in itself an influence of sufficient moment to give Kyd an important bearing on the shape of Shakespeare's work, in a mixture of direct and less direct ways. The many parallels in incident and situation between it and *Hamlet* (Bullough, VII, 16–17 lists twenty items) need not suggest conscious emulation: such resemblances can be accounted for as the combined result of a powerful impression from a

273

recent or not-so-recent performance, and the effect of *The Spanish Tragedy* on contemporary audience tastes and the norms of dramatic practice and convention. The first could explain, for example, the duplicated incident of an oath taken on the cross of a sword-hilt, and the second the appearance in both works of a vengeance-seeking ghost and an inset play (even though the last device had been used several times previously by Shakespeare). As evidence of Kyd's impact on *Hamlet*, these parallels are reinforced by a few verbal similarities mainly found in the Q1 text of Shakespeare's play.

Certain details in a number of Shakespeare plays can with some plausibility be attributed to memories of *The Spanish Tragedy*: for these, see as well as the commentators mentioned below Edwards (1959: xxvi–xxvii), Boas (1955: introduction), and Jacobs (1975). Some apparent echoes in *The Taming of the Shrew* have been taken as supporting a very early date for the Shakespeare play, but Thompson's (1984) strongest evidence, Christopher Sly's evidently unintentional allusions to the currently famous play in the Induction (especially his 'Go by, Saint Jeronimy', 7), is unpersuasive, since such echoes are common for many years in other playwrights' work (Freeman 1967: 134 lists six instances of 'go by' from 1602 to 1630). The relationships of Kyd's play to *Titus Andronicus*, recently analysed by Jonathan Bate, and *Richard III*, suggestively explored by Emrys Jones, are of greater interest. *Titus Andronicus* seems to involve not only an equivalent for Kyd's framing devices and a patterning of Titus' idiom on Hieronimo's (see below) but also many more local points of contact. There is found in both, to take a variety of examples, 'a fascination with speech and silence, with tongues removed and acts of inscription', emblematic props, and 'assumed madness and theatre' as the means the revenger takes of speaking and acting in public (Bate 1995: 86). As with *Hamlet*, these similarities very likely result from a combination of direct and indirect influence from Kyd, though the earlier date of *Titus* may affect the proportion of each by bringing the play nearer (perhaps very near) in time to the earlier phases of *The Spanish Tragedy*'s impact.

As well as sharing at a fairly superficial level 'a certain hard metallic eloquence, a liking for repetitive rhetorical schemes and patterns, [and] a high incidence of latinate formality', all of which Kyd had drawn from Seneca more fluently than any English dramatist before him, *The Spanish Tragedy* has in common with *Richard III* 'fundamentals of conception and structure' (Jones 1977: 200). In particular, the presentation of figures who act as embodiments of memory – Revenge, Andrea, Hieronimo himself – seems to be reflected in Shakespeare's Margaret (whose inclusion in the play's action is unhistorical), functioning to recall the past and call for judgement. Kyd's effect of a supernatural order supervening on the main action, achieved through the framing presence of Andrea's Ghost and Revenge, is on Jones' view a direct inspiration for the dream scenes in *Richard III*, with Clarence in 1.4 and Richard in 5.3.

More important still, it seems likely that *The Spanish Tragedy*, perhaps in conjunction with other Kyd plays now lost, would have acted also as a powerful influence on Shakespeare (as well as many other contemporary writers) in wider formal and stylistic ways. For example, it offered the first significant deployment on the English tragic stage of framing devices, in the choric figures and inset play. Such devices were useful as solving dramaturgical problems and extending possibilities: frames

> could elicit moral meanings from the welter of dramatic actions, they could point the tale, and they could even lead the audience to consider its own place in the *theatrum mundi*, as *Hamlet's* dumb show and inner play do . . . they offered exposition and causal explanations that the dramatist could not locate, or did not choose to locate, in the represented action.   (Braunmuller 1984: 108)

Shakespeare, though rarely employing formal choruses, prologues, epilogues or full frames, gains their advantages by converting the frame into an 'inner play'. Something of this has already been noted above with *Richard III*; in *Titus Andronicus*, Titus too is a play-maker, inviting his family to help him 'Plot some device of further misery' (3.1.134) and overtly directing other characters, especially in the masque-like show he creates in 5.2.

A example must also have been set by Kyd's development of the figurative language required for dramatic expression of the self. From Gavin **Douglas**' **Virgil** and from the ***Mirror for Magistrates***, Kyd fashioned the idiom of Hieronimo's suffering, a vehicle for expressing emotion through the 'imagery necessary for a metaphorical journey of the troubled spirit'. Kyd would thus seem to have laid the foundations for Shakespeare's figurative blank verse, in which the motions of the spirit express themselves often in passages of extended and mounting

275

intensity; the idiom of Hieronimo's agonies 'very soon became the language of the most intense parts of new and greater plays' (Baker 1967: 163–4). In technical terms, the lines given in (B) are hard to distinguish from similar lines of Shakespeare's.

(D) For Kyd's impact on Elizabethan dramatists other than Shakespeare, see Edwards (1966), and, more briefly and factually, Freeman (1967: 131–7).

Bullough, vii; Jones (1977).

Baker, Howard (1967). 'The Formation of the Heroic Medium', pp. 126–68 in Paul J. Alpers, ed., *Elizabethan Poetry: Modern Essays in Criticism*. Oxford (first published in Baker, *Induction to Tragedy*, 1939).

Bate, Jonathan, ed. (1995). *Titus Andronicus* (Arden Shakespeare). London.

Boas, F. S. (1955). *The Works of Thomas Kyd*, corrected edition. Oxford.

Braunmuller, A. R. (1984). 'Early Shakespearian Tragedy and Its Contemporary Context: Cause and Emotion in *Titus Andronicus, Richard III*, and *The Rape of Lucrece*', pp. 96–128 in Malcolm Bradbury and David Palmer, eds, *Shakespearian Tragedy* (Stratford-upon-Avon Studies, 20). New York.

Edwards, Philip, ed. (1959). *The Spanish Tragedy*. London.

—— (1966). *Thomas Kyd and Early Elizabethan Tragedy*. London.

Freeman, Arthur (1967). *Thomas Kyd. Facts and Problems*. Oxford.

Jacobs, Edward Craney (1975). 'An Unnoted Debt to Kyd in *King Lear*.' *ANQ* 14: 19.

Kyd, Thomas (1592). *The Spanish Tragedie, Containing the Lamentable End of Don Horatio, and Bel-Imperia: with the Pittiful Death of olde Hieronimo*, 2nd edn. London.

Law, Robert Adger (1948). 'Belleforest, Shakespeare, and Kyd', pp. 279–94 in James G. McManaway *et al.*, eds, *Joseph Quincy Adams Memorial Studies*. Washington.

Stevenson, Warren (1968). 'Shakespeare's Hand in *The Spanish Tragedy* 1602.' *SEL* 8: 307–21.

Thompson, Ann (1984). '*The Taming of the Shrew* and *The Spanish Tragedy*.' *N&Q* 229: 182–4.

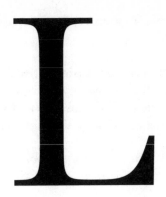

La Primaudaye, Pierre de (1546–1619), Author of
L'Académie françoise La Primaudaye's prose compendium of
scientific, moral and philosophical knowledge was translated into
English from 1586 and may have supplemented **Palingenius** as a
Shakespearean source in various plays.

Hankins, John Erskine (1953). *Shakespeare's Derived Imagery*. Lawrence,
KA.

**Lavater, Lewes (Ludwig) (1527–1586), German Theo-
logical Writer** Lavater's treatise on spirits, Englished in 1572, may
have suggested some details for the ghosts and ghostly imaginings in
Hamlet and *Macbeth*.

Maguin, Jean-Marie (1972). 'Of Ghosts and Spirits Walking by Night:
A Joint Examination of the Ghost Scenes in Robert Garnier's
Cornélie, Thomas Kyd's *Cornelia* and Shakespeare's *Hamlet* in the
Light of Reformation Thinking as Presented in Lavater's Book.'
CahiersE 1: 25–40.
Slater, Ann Pasternak (1978). 'Macbeth and the Terrors of the Night.'
EinC 28: 112–28.

Leigh, Nicholas See **Erasmus, Desiderius.**

Le Loyer, Pierre (Peter de Loier), Sieur de la Brosse (*fl.* 1586) Le Loyer's treatise *Discours et histoires de spectres*, translated into English in 1605, was a Catholic answer to **Lavater**; some distant echoes have been identified in *Macbeth*'s ghostly imaginings.

Paul, Henry N. (1950). *The Royal Play of Macbeth: When, Why, and How it was written by Shakespeare*, pp. 57–9. New York.

Leo, John (Joannes), *Africanus* See **Africanus, Leo**.

Leslie (Lesley), John (1527–1596), Bishop of Ross Leslie's *De Origine Scotorum* (1578), available to Shakespeare only in Latin, contains a genealogical tree of the royal Stuarts (reproduced by Bullough) which has been thought to have influenced the imagery of *Macbeth* 3.1, in which Banquo sees himself as 'the root and father of many kings'. The case is not compelling.

Bullough, VII, 441–3.
Paul, Henry N. (1950). *The Royal Play of Macbeth: When, Why, and How it was written by Shakespeare*. New York.

Lewkenor, Sir Lewis (*c.* 1556–1626), Diplomat and Translator Lewis' 1599 translation of Gasparo Contarini, *The Commonwealth and Government of Venice*, was used in *Othello* for information about Venice and for Othello's defence against the charge of witchcraft.

Drennan, William R. (1988). ' "Corrupt means to aspire": Contarini's *De Republica* and the Motives of Iago.' *N&Q* 233: 474–5.
Sipahigil, T. (1972). 'Lewkenor and "Othello": An Addendum.' *N&Q* 217: 127.
Whitfield, Christopher (1964). 'Sir Lewis Lewkenor and *The Merchant of Venice*: A Suggested Connexion.' *N&Q* 209: 123–33.

Livy (Titus Livius) (59 BC–AD 17), Roman Historian

(A) Livy was born in Padua, came to Rome as a young man, and by the age of thirty had commenced his 142-Book *Historiarum ab Urbe Condita* ('History of Rome from her Foundation'), the first adequate treatment of the subject, published in instalments to immediate acclaim. Livy seems not to have held public offices, but devoted himself to his writing as an orator or moralist, without personal experience of war or politics. He began and remained on good terms with Augustus, surviving him by three years. Livy's stated general purpose is a moral one: to narrate history from which lessons can be drawn. His highly expressive prose discloses reverence for the old Roman character, fervent championship of the republican state on which his work is the great repository of information, and a belief in the inherent nobility of humanity.

(B) Livy's *History* covered the period from the fabled arrival of Aeneas in Italy to the death of Drusus in 9 BC, but only a quarter of it (Books I–IX, XXI–XLV) has ever been extant in modern times. It was little mentioned in the Middle Ages, but enthusiastically taken up in the Renaissance following an *editio princeps* of 1469. There were London-printed editions from 1589. Ascham (*Schoolmaster*) and Hoole (*New Discovery*) promote Livy as a model for imitation; **Jonson** (*Timber*) urges 'the best authors to youth first, . . . the openest and clearest. As Livy before Sallust.' The interest is mainly in his eloquence, hence in the orations; that is, not in Livy as a historian but 'as moralizable matter for literary exercises' (Baldwin 1944: II, 568) – a standard Elizabethan attitude to historical writing in general, but especially pronounced here. He was also admired as a counsellor of policy: Sir Anthony Cope's version of the stories of Scipio and Hannibal (*The Historie of Two the Moste Noble Capitaines*, 1544), he told Henry VIII in his dedication, was intended to help men 'doe displeasure to theyr ennemies, and to avoyde the crafty and daungerous baites, which shall be layde for theim'.

The English were fortunate that the first complete translation was by Philemon Holland (1552–1637; for his life and work see Matthiesson 1930), an able Latinist with a good ear for his own language. His 1600 translation, *The Roman Historie*, has many admirable qualities, though they are not always those of Livy. The following excerpt (II, 32) displays Holland's characteristic phrase-making in his version of a famous part of the Coriolanus story.

Whilome (quoth he) when as in mans bodie, all the parts thereof agreed not, as now they do in one, but ech member had a several intent and meaning, yea and a speech by it selfe: so it befel, that all other parts besides the belly, thought much and repined that by their carefulnes, labor, and ministerie, all was gotten, and yet all little enough to serve it: and the bellie it selfe lying still in the mids of them, did nothing else but enjoy the delightsome pleasures brought unto her. Wherupon they mutined and conspired altogether in this wise, That neither the hands should reach and convey food into the mouth, not the mouth receive it as it came, ne yet the teeth grind and chew the same. In this mood and fit, whiles they were minded to famish the poore bellie, behold other lims, yea and the whole bodie besides, pined, wasted, and fel into an extreme consumption. Then it was well seen, that even the very belly also did no smal service, but fed the other parts, as it received food it selfe: seeing that by working and concocting the meal throughlie it digesteth and distributeth by the veins into all parts that fresh and perfect blood whereby we live, we like, and have our full strength.

A much smaller-scale translation from Livy is found in a book Shakespeare certainly knew, William **Painter**'s *Palace of Pleasure* (1566–75). This collection of stories contains a fairly close version of Livy's narrative in I, 57–60 of the *History*, the story of the rape of Lucrece, as Painter's second 'novel'. Part of the latter section is given here. As the concluding paragraphs suggest, the episode in Livy's interpretation is important for the transition from tyranny under the Tarquins to Roman republicanism. Lucrece 'receives nothing in the way of psychological depiction but assumes the person of a martyr to the cause; an almost equal emphasis is placed on Lucius Junius Brutus, who leads the successful revolt' (Roe 1992: 35).

Then every one of them gave her their faith, and comforted the pensive and languishing lady, imputing the offence to the authour and doer of the same, affirming that her bodye was polluted, and not her minde, and where consent was not, there the crime was absente. Whereunto she added. I praye you consider with your selves, what punishmente is due for the malefactour. As for my part, though I cleare my selfe of the offence, my body shall feele the punishment; for no unchast or ill woman, shall hereafter impute no dishonest act

280

to Lucrece. Then she drewe out a knife, which she had hidden secretely, under her kirtle, and stabbed her selfe to the harte. Which done, she fell downe grovelinge uppon her wound and died. Whereupon her father and husband made great lamentation, and as they were bewayling the death of Lucrece, Brutus plucked the knife oute of the wound, which gushed out with abundance of bloude, and holding it up said. I sweare by the chast bloud of this body here dead, and I take you the immortall Gods to witnes, that I will drive and extirpate oute of this Citie, both L. Tarquinius Superbus, and his wicked wife, with all the race of his children and progenie, so that none of them, ne yet any others shall raigne anye longer in Rome. Then hee delivered the knife to Collatinus, Lucretius, and Valerius who merveyled at the strangenesse of his words: and from whence he should conceive that determination. They all swore that othe, and followed Brutus as their Captaine, in his conceived purpose. The body of Lucrece was brought into the market place, where the people wondred at the vilenesse of that facte, every man complayning uppon the mischiefe of that facinorous rape, committed by Tarquinius. Whereupon Brutus perswaded the Romaynes, that they should cease from teares and other childishe lamentacions, and to take weapons in their handes, to shew themselves like men . . .

[At Rome] the people out of all places of the Citie, ranne into the market place. Where Brutus complained of the abhominable Rape of Lucrece, committed by Sextus Tarquinius. And thereunto he added the pride and insolent behaviour of the king, the miserie and drudgerie of the people, and howe they, which in time paste were victours and conquerours, were made of men of warre, Artificers and Labourers. He remembred also the infamous murder of Servius Tullius their late kinge. These and such like he called to the peoples remembraunce, whereby they abrogated and deposed Tarquinius, banishing him, his wife, and children . . .

When Tarquinius was come to Rome, the gates were shutte against him, and he himselfe commaunded to avoide into exile. The campe received Brutus with great joye and triumphe, for that he had delivered the citie of such a tyraunte. Then Tarquinius with his children fledde to Caere, a Citie of the Hetrurians. And as Sextus Tarquinius was going, he was slaine by those that premeditated revengemente, of olde murder and injuries by him done to their predecessours. This L. Tarquinius Superbus raigned xxv. yeares. The raigne of the kinges from the first foundation of the Citie continued CCxliiii. yeares. After which governmente two Consuls were appointed, for the order and administration of the Citie. And for that yeare L. Junius Brutus, and L. Tarquinius, Collatinus.

(Painter 1575: sigs 6^r–7^r)

(C) Shakespeare seems to have had some first-hand knowledge of Livy, certainly of the Lucrece story. This 'fairly certainly' dates from school training, according to Baldwin (1944: II, 573), who also carefully investigates the copious amount of Livy Shakespeare could have found in the extensive notes to Marsus' standard 1550 edition of **Ovid**'s *Fasti* (Baldwin 1950: 97–106). Although there have been attempts at political interpretation of the poem, and although the kind of mixed state Livy's republic represents was for various reasons attracting much attention in Jacobean England, in *Lucrece* the psychological drama is in obvious ways to the fore (in particular the part played by conscience). Overall, then, Livy's interests served Shakespeare's purposes less well than those of Ovid, whose *Fasti* was a more significant source for him. Livy's revolutionary climax 'is very subdued, as is the entire political dimension of the story', which is mentioned 'almost as a narrative afterthought' (Donaldson 1982: 43), or perhaps rather in a very conspicuously cursory fashion. One or two touches are owing to Livy nevertheless. (The 'Argument' to the poem, perhaps not by Shakespeare, contains phrasing from Painter's rendering: see Bush 1932: 150.) Livy contrasts the evil that has overtaken Lucrece's body with her inviolate mind, and she identifies her suicide as a defence of the good name of Roman women. This surfaces in Shakespeare as

'No, no,' quoth she 'no dame hereafter living
By my excuse shall claim excuse's giving.
(1714–15)

'Her resolve matches the tenor of public responsibility which Livy is eager to cultivate, and emphasises that personal conscience accords with devotion to the good of the *patria*' (Roe 1992: 36).

There have been suggestions that Livy's Lucrece narrative also contributes to the Brutus of *Julius Caesar* (Berman 1972), and that the severe virtue of the Andronici in *Titus Andronicus* owes something to Livy's early Books (Hunter 1984). The other Shakespeare work with a clear debt to Livy is *Coriolanus*. The main incidents of this play are taken from **Plutarch**'s *Life of Coriolanus*, but decisive resemblances to Livy are afforded by Shakespeare's version of the fable of the Body's Members as narrated by Menenius in 1.1. This probably draws on several sources: the story is told by Sir Philip **Sidney**, by **Erasmus**, by **Camden**, and others. Shakespeare knew Livy's version and possibly Holland's recently published translation in (B) (Muir 1953; Muir 1977: 238).

> With a kind of smile,
> Which ne'er came from the lungs, but even thus –
> For look you, I may make the belly smile
> As well as speak – it tauntingly replied
> To th' discontented members, the mutinous parts
> That envied his receipt; even so most fitly
> As you malign our senators for that
> They are not such as you . . .
> Your most grave belly was deliberate,
> Not rash like his accusers, and thus answered.
> 'True is it, my incorporate friends,' quoth he
> 'That I receive the general food at first
> Which you do live upon; and fit it is,
> Because I am the storehouse and the shop
> Of the whole body. But, if you remember,
> I send it through the rivers of your blood,
> Even to the court, the heart, to th' seat o' th' brain;
> And, through the cranks and offices of man,
> The strongest nerves and small inferior veins
> From me receive that natural competency
> Whereby they live. And though that all at once
> You, my good friends' – this says the belly; mark me.

I CITIZEN   Ay, sir; well, well.

MENENIUS   'Though all at once cannot
> See what I do deliver out to each,
> Yet I can make my audit up, that all
> From me do back receive the flour of all,
> And leave me but the bran.'

(1.1.105–12, 126–44)

Conformities here are useful in demonstrating Shakespeare's know-ledge of Livy in *Coriolanus*, but it has been forcefully argued that 'they matter far less than a series of overall attitudes, attitudes peculiar to this play, which ... Shakespeare owed not to any one, particular passage in Livy, but to his history as a whole' (Barton 1985: 116). The events in Livy's Book II narrative of the troubles afflicting Rome after the expulsion of the Tarquins are all reported by Plutarch, but the emphasis and context are very different. Livy's Book II is devoted to showing how *libertas* was achieved in Rome, at both institutional and individual level. Here Livy 'patiently teases out the intimate connec-tion, unfolding over a vast stretch of years, between Rome's need to cultivate the arts of peace as well as war, and the internal struggle between her patricians and plebeians' (Barton 1985: 120). *Coriolanus* may be seen as a play specifically about the *polis*, focusing on Rome herself at a moment of transition, with the protagonist exemplary only as a figure who finally learns what is outdated about his attitudes – none of which would have been suggested by Plutarch's quite different presentation of the story.

(D)

Baldwin (1944); Baldwin (1950); Bullough, v; Muir (1977).

Barton, Anne (1985). 'Livy, Machiavelli, and Shakespeare's "Coriola-nus".' *ShSu* 38: 115–29.

Berman, Ronald (1972). 'A Note on the Motives of Marcus Brutus.' *ShQ* 23: 197–200.

Brockbank, Philip, ed. (1976). *Coriolanus* (Arden Shakespeare). London.

Burke, Peter (1966). 'A Survey of the Popularity of Ancient Historians, 1450–1700.' *History and Theory* 5: 135–52.

Bush, Douglas (1932). *Mythology and the Renaissance Tradition in English Poetry*. London.

Donaldson, Ian (1982). *The Rapes of Lucretia: A Myth and its Transform-ations*. Oxford.

Holland, Philemon (1600). *The Roman Historie written by T. Livius*. London.

Hunter, G. K. (1984). 'Sources and Meanings in *Titus Andronicus*', pp. 171–88 in J. C. Gray, ed., *Mirror up to Shakespeare: Essays in Honour of G. R. Hibbard*. Toronto.

Matthiesson, F. O. (1931). *Translation: An Elizabethan Art*. Cambridge, MA.

Muir, Kenneth (1953). 'Menenius's Fable.' *N&Q* 198: 240–2.

Painter, William (1575). *The Palace of Pleasure Beautified, Adorned, and Well Furnished with Pleasaunt Histories and Excellent Novels.* London.

Roe, John, ed. (1992). *The Poems* (New Cambridge Shakespeare). Cambridge.

Lodge, Thomas (1558?–1625), Poet, Playwright and Romance Writer

(A) Lodge's father was a grocer, sometime Lord Mayor of London, then a bankrupt. The son attended Merchant Taylors' School and Trinity College, Oxford, followed by admission to Lincoln's Inn in 1578. He served in the navy, 1588–91, immediately before and after which period his only two extant plays were published, the second a collaboration with Robert **Greene**. His writing, the extent and diversity of which was partly a response to financial pressures, includes *Scillae's Metamorphosis* (1589), the first erotic epyllion in English verse; *Phillis* (1593), a sonnet cycle; and *Rosalynde* (1590), one of the most polished prose romances of its time (also including a succession of lyrics in mid-Elizabethan style), which used the name of **Lyly**'s hero to attract a similar readership, but otherwise had little to do with *Euphues*. Several other prose romances followed, including *Euphues Shadow* (1592) and *Margarite of America* (1596). Lodge also published satires in the Horatian manner, moral dialogues, and treatises and disquisitions on various, often topical, subjects. He became a Catholic convert and in 1596 wrote a devotional work on the Virgin Mary; in the same year he published a treatise on the Seven Deadly Sins. In 1597 he abandoned Grub Street to take further degrees in medicine at Avignon and Oxford. In his later years he spent periods abroad as a recusant, and practised medicine. During these phases he wrote *A Treatise of the Plague* (1603) and published several translations – of Josephus, the Jewish historian (1602), of **Seneca** (1614), and of the theological writer Simon Goulart.

(B) *Rosalynde* was popular enough to go through nine editions in the half-century after its 1590 publication. This sample passage recounts Rosader (Orlando)'s appearance at King Torismond (Duke Senior)'s feast on arrival in Arden with his old servant, Adam Spencer.

Whatsoever thou be that art maister of these lustie squiers, I salute

thee as graciously, as a man in extreame distresse may: knowe that I
and a fellow friend of mine, are here famished in the forrest for
want of foode: perish wee must unlesse relieved by thy favours.
Therefore if thou be a Gentleman, give meate to men, and to suche
as are everie way woorthie of life: let the proudest squire that sits at
thy table, rise and incounter with mee in anie honourable point of
activitie whatsoever, and if hee and thou proove me not a man,
send me away comfortlesse. If thou refuse this, as a niggard of thy
cates, I will have amongst you with my sword: for rather will I dye
valiantly, then perish with so cowardly an extreame. *Gerismond* looking him earnestly in the face, and séeing so proper a Gentleman in
so bitter a passion, was mooved with so great pitie, that rising from
the table, he tooke him by the hand and badde him welcome . . .
Well to be short, those hungry squires fell to their victuals, and
feasted themselves with good delicates, and great store of wine.
Assoone as they had taken their repast, *Gerismond* (desirous to heare
what hard fortune drave them into those bitter extreames)
requested *Rosader* to discourse, (as it wer not any way prejudicall
unto him) the cause of his travell. *Rosader* (desirous anie way to
satisfie the curtesie of his favourable host, (first beginning his
exordium with a volley of sighes, and a fewe luke warme teares)
prosecuted his discourse, and told him from point to point all his
fortunes, how hee was the yongest sonne of Sir *John* of *Bourdeaux*,
his name *Rosader*, how his brother sundry times had wronged him,
and lastly, how for beating the Sheriffe, and hurting his men, hee
fled: and this old man (quoth he) whom I so much love and honour,
is surnamed *Adam Spencer*, an old servant of my fathers, and one
(that for his love) never fayled me in all my misfortunes. When
Gerismond hearde this, hee fell on the necke of *Rosader*, and next
discoursing unto him, how he was *Gerismond* their lawfull King
exiled by *Torismond*, what familiaritie had ever been betwixt his
father sir *John* of *Bourdeaux* and him, how faithfull a subject hee
lived, and how honourably he died: promising (for his sake) to give
both him and his friend such curteous intertainment, as his present
estate could minister: and upon this made him one of his forresters.
Rosader seeing it was the King, cravde pardon for his boldnesse, in
that he did not doo him due reverence, and humbly gave him
thankes for his favourable curtesie.

(Lodge 1592: sigs G1ʳ–G2ʳ)

(C) *Rosalynde* begins with the tale of the three sons of Sir John of Bordeaux and their father's deathbed wishes; Saladyne, the eldest, seeks to retain all the land their father divided between them. He arranges for a wrestler to injure Rosader, the youngest son, in the sports arranged by the bad King Torismond, usurper of the good King Gerismond's throne. Rosader beats and kills the champion, watched by Alinda, Torismond's daughter, and Rosalynde, Gerismond's daughter. Rosader and Rosalynde fall in love; Rosader quarrels with Saladyne and is chained up as a lunatic, but defeats the local sheriff his brother calls in and escapes to Arden with the help of his aged servant Adam Spencer. Meanwhile Rosalynde is banished together with Alinda, who tries to defend her.

As this summary of only the first part of the action indicates, Shakespeare's debts in terms of plot are considerable. But it can also be seen that omissions are effected to make the play more manageable and more suited to the stage, such as the sheriff's men's defeat by Rosader – 'much that is violent and sensational, distanced by the artificiality of tone and style in Lodge, does not appear at all' (Latham 1975: xliv). Both major and minor adjustments in plot and emphasis occur throughout: a substantial example is that Alinda always takes the lead in Lodge's narrative, Rosalynde being a subordinate page whose courtship is treated more incidentally. A highly effective minor adjustment is to make Duke Senior a friend of the dead Sir Rowland, creating an immediate tie between Rosalind and Orlando which makes her falling in love a subtle modulation rather than a sudden unexplained passion, and complicates it with an element of melancholy.

In terms of everything other than plot, Lodge's relationship to Shakespeare is much more superficial: it is that of talent to genius. For one thing, Lodge's work never questions the conventions on which it is based, whereas in Shakespeare Rosalind's role is in one sense precisely this, to test Orlando's rhapsodizing or Phoebe's beauty against common sense. Her language explores the boundaries of its mode, whereas the pastoral-euphuistic patterning of Rosalynde's speech exists for its own sake (indeed, the speech habits of Lodge's characters are largely undifferentiated). It is often felt, in fact, that *As You Like It* amounts in part to a parodic treatment of Lodge's formal rhetorical mode, and, more than this, of the 'typical procedure (and unintended absurdity) of romance, where formal rhetoric is utterly dissynchronized from the situation, time and place of the narrative action' (Gibbons 1987: 66). For example,

Duke Senior's mock-solemn response to Orlando's intrusion on the courtly exiles in 2.7 looks like a reaction against the ethos of Lodge's version of the episode ((B), above). Jacques and Touchstone, two main foci of critical or sceptical attitudes in *As You Like It*, simply do not exist in *Rosalynde*; and in the development of Lodge's Coridon into Corin is created a vehicle 'to reinforce the play's underlying base of contemporary reference and social commentary which distinguishes Shakespeare's treatment of the story from Lodge's' (Daley 1990: 17). The elaborate steps by which Lodge's Alinda and Saladyne pair off, complete with sonnet-writing and lengthy confessions of mutual love, are dazzlingly compressed such that, as Rosalind later tells Orlando, Celia and Oliver 'no sooner met but they look'd; no sooner look'd but they lov'd' (4.2.31–3).

But *As You Like It* is not ultimately, or not dominantly, a 'satire' on Lodge, on romance, or on pastoralism. Tolerant laughter at the diversity of people is often felt to be of its essence. The real narrowness of Lodge's work in comparison to Shakespeare's is perhaps that Lodge's characters are diversely situated rather than fundamentally different, whereas in Shakespeare 'we see persons in relation, contrasted or paralleled not only situationally but in thought, feeling, mood, temperament, character and idiom. This constitutes the play's individuality' (Latham 1975: xlvi). It is inevitably harsh to Lodge's merits to place the two works in immediate juxtaposition, but to do so is to see that it is simply not the case, for example, that Shakespeare's Rosalind is 'less complex and less true to nature than Lodge's' (Mincoff 1966: 88) – which is not to say that Lodge's figure lacks life and motion.

Shakespeare must certainly have known at least one other of Lodge's works. *Scillae's Metamorphosis* forms part of the context of *Venus and Adonis* by virtue of being a pioneering, and in its time somewhat sensational, domestication of the Ovidian epyllion. *Venus and Adonis*' six-line stanza may well derive from it, and Lodge's poem also contains a passage on Venus and the death of Adonis which may have stirred Shakespeare's imagination, sounding 'so many of the keynotes of his own work – the colour contrasts of pallor and blood, the pathos of the delicate flower-like youth, the helpless grief of the bereaved goddess' (Clark 1994: xxxiii). The most important other relationship between the two writers involves *King Lear* and Lodge's 1591 prose romance *The Famous True and Historicall Life of Robert Second Duke of Normandy*. This is an example of one relative of the medieval 'Robert of Sicily' tale; another, which is also sometimes associated with *Lear*, is the 'Robert the Devil' story which became popular in the early sixteenth century. In outline the story is that a materialistic king has his place taken by an angel in his likeness. The real king asserts his identity but is denied entry to his palace, appointed court fool, and in other ways humiliated. Eventually he comprehends his situation and repents. Several emphases of Lodge's particularly elaborate version, notably the burden of redemption placed on children who have suffered from and inherited the sins of their fathers, seem – though it can be put no more strongly – to be reflected in Shakespeare's play: see Hamilton (1974).

(D) Comparison of *Rosalynde* and *As You Like It* lends itself to development in a number of directions. Mincoff (1966) concentrates on structure and plot. Two contrasting studies of the respective female leads are Berry (1980) and Lynch (1998); Daley (1990) focuses on the Corin figure to emphasize differences of modality. Whitworth (1977) points out that too many commentators read *Rosalynde* through spectacles created by *As You Like It*; Muir (1977), one of his targets, gives a blow-by-blow account of Shakespeare's changes, as does Whitworth (1997) in a more detailed and analytical fashion. Perhaps the best single account is Latham (1975).

Bullough, II; Muir (1977), 125–31.

Berry, Edward I. (1980). 'Rosalynde and Rosalind.' *ShQ* 31: 42–52.

Brissenden, Alan, ed. (1993). *As You Like It* (Oxford Shakespeare). Oxford.

Clark, Sandra, ed. (1994). *Amorous Rites: Elizabethan Erotic Narrative Verse*. London.

Cuvelier, Eliane (1975). 'Sur la metaphore du jardin dans *Richard II* et un poème de Thomas Lodge.' *CahiersE* 8: 76–8.

Daley, A. Stuart (1990). 'Shakespeare's Corin, Almsgiver and Faithful Feeder.' *ELN* 27: 4–17.

Gibbons, Brian (1987). 'Amorous Fictions and *As You Like It*', pp. 52–78 in John W. Mahon and Thomas A. Pendleton, eds, *"Fanned and Winnowed opinions": Shakespearean Essays Presented to Harold Jenkins*. London.

Hamilton, Donna B. (1974). 'Some Romance Sources for *King Lear*: Robert of Sicily and Robert the Devil.' *SP* 71: 173–91.

Latham, Agnes, ed. (1975). *As You Like It* (Arden Shakespeare). London.

L[odge], T[homas] (1592). *Rosalynde*. London (first published 1590).

Lynch, Stephen J. (1998). 'Representing Gender in *Rosalynde* and *As You Like It*', pp. 5–34 in Lynch, *Shakespearean Intertextuality: Studies in Selected Sources and Plays*. Westport, CT.

Mincoff, Marco (1966). 'What Shakespeare Did to *Rosalynde*.' *ShJ* 96: 78–89 (reprinted in Jay L. Halio, ed., *Twentieth-Century Interpretations of 'As You Like It'*, Englewood Cliffs, 1968).

Pierce, Robert B. (1971). 'The Moral Languages of *Rosalynde* and *As You Like It*.' *SP* 68: 167–76.

Whitworth, Charles, Jr (1977). '*Rosalynde*: As You Like It and as Lodge Wrote It.' *ES* 58: 114–17.

Whitworth, Charles (1997). 'Wooing and Wedding in Arden: *Rosalynde* and *As You Like It*.' *Etudes Anglaises* 50: 387–99.

Longus See **Greek Romance**.

Lope de Vega (Carpio), Felix (1562–1635), Spanish Dramatist McGrady quashes speculation about Lope's contribution to *Romeo and Juliet*.

McGrady, Donald (1969). 'Romeo and Juliet has no Spanish Source.' *ShSt* 5: 20–4.

Lucan (Marcus Annaeus Lucanus) (AD 39–65), Latin Epic Poet

(A) Lucan, nephew of **Seneca the Younger**, was born at Corduba in Spain, educated in Rome and Athens, and for a time greatly admired by Nero. A voluminous writer, his sole surviving work is the unfinished epic *Bellum Civile* or *De Bello Civili* (*The Civil War*, *c.* AD 62–5; in Shakespeare's time the poem was known as the *Pharsalia* after the name of the battle at its climax). It is an account of the period of civil war between Julius Caesar and Pompey the Great which historically precedes the action of Shakespeare's *Julius Caesar* – Pompey's defeat at the Battle of Pharsalius occurred in 48 BC, Caesar's assassination in 44. Formally the *Bellum Civile* is a historical poem, but it can also be described as political, an impassioned attack on the unchecked rule of the state by one individual. Perhaps because of its politics, or perhaps because Nero was jealous of his literary success, Lucan was forbidden to publish the work or write others. He joined Piso's conspiracy to overthrow Nero, and, like the younger Seneca, was forced to commit suicide, his poem incomplete, when the plot was discovered.

(B) The *Bellum Civile* is a grand and flawed poem, historically always seen as a foil to the *Aeneid*, and as the greatest Latin epic after **Virgil**'s. It includes passages of forceful declamatory eloquence – there are over a hundred speeches – and in the Renaissance Lucan was usually thought of more as a model for the orator than the poet. A conspicuous place is given to Lucan by Renaissance educators such as Sir Thomas **Elyot** (see Baldwin 1944: II, 550) and men of letters, and in the late sixteenth and early seventeenth centuries the poem was widely read and imitated. But Lucan has always had his critics. He spurns conventional poetic embellishment, preferring a self-conscious directness which has affronted many readers from antiquity onwards. His realism can be seen as degenerating into the grotesque, his pathos into sentimentality. There is no detached Virgilian understatement in Lucan – characteristic instead is prodigious rhetoric constantly bordering on hyperbole. To some (Harington, **Nashe**, **Sidney**) he was a historiographer and not a literary artist. **Jonson**'s judgement in his *Conversations* was that 'Lucan, taken in parts, was good divided, read altogether merited not the name of a poet'.

English versions begin with **Marlowe**'s *Lucans First Booke Translated Line for Line*, published 1600, and continue with a complete rendering by Sir Arthur Gorges, friend of Ralegh and **Spenser**, in 1614. Gorge's translation is too late to have been used by Shakespeare but its publication helps indicate Lucan's currency during his lifetime. This version is militant and republican in spirit, and any reading of Lucan was apt to be politically charged. At a rudimentary level the *Pharsalia*'s stress on the horrors of civil war must have seemed pertinent to those familiar with the copious Tudor propaganda on this subject. Moreover Lucan was an 'angry young man' whose religion was scepticism and who delighted in the esoteric and macabre; on all these counts his appeal to Elizabethan poets is obvious, and he is acknowledged to be one of the chief patrons of epical expression in the sixteenth century. The taste for English civil war poetry developed by **Daniel** (*Civil Wars*, 1595) and **Drayton** (*Baron's Wars*, 1603) owes much to Lucan: both these writers draw upon him freely. On the stage, the Caesar of the *Pharsalia* is evidently a prototype for the Elizabethan villain (see Blissett 1956); in Marlowe's *The Massacre at Paris*, on the French civil wars, he is the pattern for the Catholic leader Guise.

Jonson commended the 'admirable height' of Marlowe's version; Lucan's extravagance and hyperbole finds an echoing taste in this first English translator, whose choice of blank verse is historically significant and perhaps politically pointed (see Norbrook 1994):

> Now *Caesar* overpast the snowy *Alpes*,
> His mind was troubled, and he aim'd at war,
> And comming to the foord of *Rubicon*,
> At night in dreadful vision fearefull *Roome*,
> Mourning appear'd, whose hoary hayres were torne,
> And on her Turret-bearing head disperst,
> And armes all naked, who with broken sighes,
> And staring, thus bespoke: what mean'st thou *Caesar*?
> Whether goes my standarde? Romans if ye be,
> And beare true harts, stay heare: this spectacle
> Stroake *Caesars* hart with feare, his hayre stoode up,
> And faintnes numm'd his steps there on the brincke.
> He thus cride out: Thou thunderer that guardst
> *Roomes* mighty walles built on *Tarpeian* rocke,
> Ye gods of *Phrigia* and *Júlus* line,
> *Quirinus* rites and *Latian Jove* advanc'd
> On *Alba* hill, ô *Vestall* flames, ô *Roome*,
> My thoughts sole *goddes*, aid mine enterprise,
> I hate thee not, to thee my conquests stoope,
> *Caesar* is thine, so please it thee, thy soldier;
> He, he afflicts *Roome* that made me *Roomes* foe.
> This said, he laying aside all lets of war,
> Approcht the swelling streame with drum and ensigne,
> Like to a Lyon of scortcht desart *Affricke*,
> Who seeing hunters pauseth till fell wrath
> And kingly rage increase, then having whiskt
> His taile athwart his backe, and crest heav'd up,
> With jawes wide open ghastly roaring out;
> (Albeit the *Moores* light Javelin or his speare
> Sticks in his side) yet runs upon the hunter.
>
> (185–214; 1600 text, ed. Bowers 1973: 296–7)

(C) Shakespeare's works include one direct quotation from Lucan. A slightly inaccurate version of a line from the *Pharsalia* appears in *2 Henry VI* as Suffolk is being led to his execution:

WHITMORE   Come, Suffolk, I must waft thee to thy death.
SUFFOLK   Gelidus timor occupat artus: it is thee I fear.

(4.1.117)

Lucan's line (I, 246) reads 'gelidus pavor occupat artus'. To Dover Wilson (1952: l–liii) this allusion, like the rest of the display of classical learning in *2 Henry VI*, is evidence of another hand than Shakespeare's at work in the play; but other commentators have thought differently.

Baldwin cites a few more phrases (mainly in the Roman Plays) which seem to echo the *Pharsalia*, and takes the view that 'Shakespeare certainly knew something of Lucan'. But this knowledge, Baldwin surmises, is only at the level of tags; Shakespeare had no 'direct and detailed knowledge of Lucan's tumid embroidery [i.e. of his distinctive style], whether in the original or through other sources' (Baldwin 1944: II, 551). Similarities other than phraseological can perhaps be explained by Lucan's extensive influence over pre-Shakespearean drama, especially on the Elizabethan stage villain. Though Shakespeare's Caesar is less malicious than Lucan's, his Bolingbroke crosses a very Lucanian Rubicon, and his Richard III and Macbeth are in some sense part of this tradition (see Blissett 1956).

A different kind of case is outlined in Jones (1977: 273–7). Shakespeare's frequent concern with fame, Jones argues, can be connected with Lucan's constant references to the eyes of posterity watching his characters; this may have 'helped to shape the scene of Caesar's death, and probably of much in *Henry V* and *Antony and Cleopatra*, plays of famous victories and defeats'. Further, the strange and distinctive style of the speech on the fall of Troy recited by Hamlet and the Player (2.2.445–512), which has been variously accounted for, is seen by Jones as a deliberate imitation of Lucan's:

> The rugged Pyrrhus, he whose sable arms,
> Black as his purpose, did the night resemble
> When he lay couched in the ominous horse,
> Hath now this dread and black complexion smear'd
> With heraldry more dismal; head to foot

> Now is he total gules, horridly trick'd
> With blood of fathers, mothers, daughters, sons,
> Bak'd and impasted with the parching streets,
> That lend a tyrannous and damned light
> To their lord's murder.
>
> (445–55)

This, in Jones' view, 'is probably the best Elizabethan pastiche of Lucan, perhaps the best in English' (277).

(D)

Baldwin (1944); Jones (1977).

Blissett, William (1956). 'Lucan's Caesar and the Elizabethan Villain.' *SP* 53: 553–75.

Bowers, Fredson, ed. (1973). *The Complete Works of Christopher Marlowe*, 2 vols. Cambridge.

Gorges, Sir Arthur (1614). *Lucan's Pharsalia: Containing the Civil Warres betweene Caesar and Pompey*. London.

Logan, George M. (1976). 'Lucan – Daniel – Shakespeare: New Light on the Relation Between the *Civil Wars* and *Richard II*.' *ShSt* 9: 121–40.

Norbrook, David (1994). 'Lucan, Thomas May, and the Creation of a Republican Literary Culture', pp. 45–66 in Kevin Sharpe and Peter Lake, eds, *Culture and Politics in Early Stuart England*. Basingstoke. (A version appears also as Ch. 1 of Norbrook, *Writing the English Republic: Poetry, Rhetoric and Politics, 1627–1660*, Cambridge, 1999.)

Ronan, Clifford J. (1988). 'Lucan and the Self-Incised Voids of *Julius Caesar*.' *CompD* 22: 215–26.

Wilson, John Dover, ed. (1952). *Henry VI Part 2* (New Shakespeare). Cambridge.

Lucian (*c.* AD 117 – after 180), Greek Satirist

(A) He was born in Syria, educated in rhetoric, and travelled in Greece, Italy and southern Gaul before settling in Athens about 155. He was a professional rhetorician who ghosted speeches for use in court, and gave exhibitions of his skill publicly as he wandered these regions. He is known to have written some eighty works in lucid Attic prose, in diverse genres but usually satirically humorous: essays and letters, dialogues and speeches, stories resembling novellas. Lucian's two best-known works in later ages are the wry *Mortuorum Dialogi* (*Dialogues of the Dead*), imaginary dialogues between real-life figures (such as Alexander and Achilles) in the Underworld, and the *Vera Historia* (*True History*), a parody of travellers' tales including a journey to the Moon. **Rabelais** and Swift's *Gulliver's Travels* both stand in his long shadow.

(B) Lucian was lost sight of during antiquity, and with him the aesthetic purposes of the satirical dialogues for which he was rediscovered later. Hence

> neither the Byzantines nor the Renaissance Italians were equipped to see Lucian as other than a moralist who happened to write in a particularly entertaining way ... It was a Lucian filtered via such channels who was to reach the Europe of the Northern Renaissance. The bizarre effect of this is that we must turn our backs on the real Lucian, and substitute for him a series of shifting masks, whose common feature is the element of derision (however light) and of moral intent (however negative). (Robinson 1979: 65–6)

About 1504 an Aldine Lucian came into the hands of **Erasmus**, who, ably supported by his friend Sir Thomas **More**, became the greatest and most influential of all Renaissance Lucianists. For the spread of knowledge of Lucian, Erasmus' and More's translations of some of the Greek dialogues into Latin (first published in a joint volume in 1506) were second in importance only to the references to and imitations of Lucian in Erasmus' *Adagia,* in the dialogues of his *Colloquies* and in his *Encomium Moriae* (*Praise of Folly*). There were, of course, other translators and imitators in England and Europe, especially frequently of the *Vera Historia,* and Lucian figured plentifully in pedagogical vehicles including Tudor school curricula and the school edition owned by **Jonson**, *Luciani Samosatensi Dialogi Octo* (Paris, 1530). Though as this suggests he was a widely read author, he was popularly seen as an enemy of Christianity. He tended to be deployed in times of stress as a lever to upset hierarchies, as by Erasmus, who describes him as a defence against superstition and an exposer of hypocrisy – and whose work Luther disparaged as 'stinking of Lucian'. But Lucian's tones were sometimes found too mordant for the taste of quieter periods. He is not a frequent source for dramatists: Jonson's use of Lucianic material is uniquely extensive on the English stage (Robinson 1979: 104).

More's Latin translations of Lucian of 1505–6 were the first by an Englishman to be printed, and they were reprinted more often than any of More's other writings during his lifetime. But the first complete English translation came from Francis Hickes (1566–1631), post-humously published in 1634. Thus it was not available to Shakespeare; but the following excerpt from it reflects what he may have read or heard of in another version (see (C)):

Timon. Behold a third man, Demeas, the Rhetorician with a decree in his hand, who professeth himselfe to bee one of our kinred: I payed to the citie for this fellow, eleven talents in one day, which hee was fin'd in, and committed untill hee should make payment: and for pittie set him at libertie: yet the other day, when it was his lot to distribute dole money among the Erechthean tribe, and I came to him to crave my share, hee said he could not tell whether I were a cittizen.

Demeas. All haile, Timon, a bounteous benefactor towards your kindred, the bulwarke of Athens, and the ornament of Greece

. . .

Timon. I know not whether it will be your fortune ever to come to marriage, friend mine, if this blow with my Mattocke do but fall aright.

Demeas. Alas, alas: what meanest thou by this? dost thou tyrannize, Timon, and beate freemen, that art no true freeman, nor cittizen they selfe? but be sure of it, I will crie quittance with thee out of hand one way or other: especially for burning the castle.

Timon. No such matter: for that thou seest stands sunburnt, and therefore thou showest thy selfe a plaine sycophant.

Demeas. But thou art rich, and hast broken in thorow the backe doore.

Timon. Neither is that broken up: and therefore thou art idle every way.

Demeas. But broken up it will be: and thou hast already got into thy hands all the riches that were within it.

Timon. Take one more blow for that.

Demeas. O my backe: what shall I doe?

Timon. Dost thou crie? I have yet a third blow to bestow upon thee if thou tarry, it would be a shame for thee, that could cut in pieces two companies of the Lacedaemonians without armes and should not now be able to confound one withered fellow.

(Lucian 1634: 164–6)

(C) Leaving aside a refuted case for Lucian's part in two lines of *Cymbe-line* (Kott 1972; Haffenreffer 1976), the sole Shakespeare text behind which Lucian stands is *Timon of Athens*. But the nature of the relation-ship is not clear. Shakespeare's principal source for the story is in **Plutarch**. Lucian's dialogue *Timon, or the Misanthrope* had given rise to several other works, including **Boiardo**'s late fifteenth-century play *Timone* and an English academic play of uncertain date (versions of both are printed in Bullough, v). These are very unlikely to have been used by Shakespeare, but no pre-Shakespearean English translation of Lucian is known. 'We must assume, therefore, that Shakespeare read Lucian in French, Italian or Latin versions, or in the Greek original, or that Boiardo's by no means widely circulated play transmitted the rele-vant matter from the dialogue, or that Shakespeare could lay his hands on a lost English Lucian' (Honigmann 1961: 3). Deighton (1905: xxviii–xxx) lists verbal parallels with the Greek which prove unconvincing (for reasons summed up by Oliver 1959), and half-proposes that Apemantus is based on a character in another of Lucian's dialogues, Diogenes in *The Sale of Creeds*. Honigmann more constructively posits Shakespeare's use of Filbert Bretin's *Les Oeuvres de Lucian* (Paris, 1582/3) and lists parallels suggesting various kinds of detailed borrowing (for imagery, aspects of Timon's behaviour, etc.). Bullough (v, 239–40) summarizes elements for which it appears Lucian must be 'the final source', for example 'Shakespeare's Timon frees Ventidius from imprisonment for debt . . . as Lucian's Timon has helped Demeas' ((B), above). It might be added that Lucian's dialogues are closer to drama in form than Plutarch's *Lives* are. But Lucian's mixture of cynicism and joviality of tone is not Shakespeare's, and in the end it may be a fair assessment that *Timon* is 'Lucianic only in some second-hand and relatively insignificant way' (Robinson 1979: 104).

(D)
Bullough, vi.
Deighton, K. (1905). *Timon of Athens* (Arden Shakespeare). London.
Fritsche, F. (1870). *De Timone Luciani et Shakespearii*. Rostock.
Haffenreffer, Karl (1976). 'Jan Kott's "Lucian in *Cymbeline*".' *YES* 6: 38–40.
Honigmann, E. A. J. (1961). '*Timon of Athens*.' *ShQ* 12: 3–20.
Kott, Jan (1972). 'Lucian in *Cymbeline*.' *MLR* 67: 742–4.
Lucian, translated by Francis Hickes (1634). *Certain Select Dialogues of*

Lucian: Together with his True Historie, Translated from the Greek into English.
Oxford.
Oliver, H. J., ed. (1959). *Timon of Athens* (Arden Shakespeare). London.
Robinson, Christopher (1979). *Lucian and his Influence in Europe*. London.

Lupton, Thomas (*fl.* 1583), Miscellaneous Writer
Lupton's *Siquila. Too Good to be True* (1580–1) is a relatively detailed version of the *Measure for Measure* story which Shakespeare could have known.

Bawcutt, N. W., ed. (1991). *Measure for Measure* (Oxford Shakespeare), p. 21. Oxford.

Lydgate, John (*c.* 1370–1451), English Poet
(A) Born at Lydgate, near Newmarket, he may have attended the Universities of Oxford, Paris and Padua. In 1397 he took holy orders, and subsequently lived in the monastery at Bury St Edmunds, but this did not prevent his spending much of his time staging pageants for the London guilds. Lydgate was a friend and admirer of **Chaucer**. One of his patrons was Humphrey, Duke of Gloucester, who appears as a character in four Shakespeare plays, and through whose patronage he became for a time official poet of Henry VI's Court.

His total verse production of some 130,000 lines includes three longer works in particular. His *Troy Book* (printed 1513 and 1555 as *The Hystorye Sege and Dystruccyon of Troye*) of 1412–20, running to 26,626 lines, was, according to the Prologue, commissioned by Henry V. It is a free and colourful version of Guido delle Colonne's standard *Historia Troiana* which moralizes the subject, stressing the evils of war, the sway of Fortune, and the transience of human life. *The Story of Thebes* followed *c.* 1420. In 1431–8 Lydgate translated, again with much latitude, and from an intermediary French version, **Boccaccio**'s *De Casibus Virorum Illustrium* ('On the Fate of Illustrious Men'), printed 1494 as the *Fall of Princes*, turning the stories in the process into crudely didactic moral exempla.

(B) Lydgate's stature was at its peak in the late fifteenth and early sixteenth centuries, when he was probably as highly regarded as Chaucer. By the later sixteenth century he was established as one of the few early

English classics: Francis Meres writes of England's 'three ancient poets, Chaucer, Gower, and Lydgate', and the same trinity is invoked by **Nashe** as models which the English can oppose to the Italians'. The *Fall of Princes* remained popular into the earlier sixteenth century, and was republished in 1527, but the book was significantly taken up again about 1555, when a printer, John Wayland, conceived the idea of reissuing it with a continuation into British history of more recent times. After various mishaps this continuation became the enormously popular ***Mirror for Magistrates***, 1559 (for the initial publishing history see Campbell 1960: 5–10). Henceforward the *Mirror* eclipsed Lydgate's book, which was not reprinted again until the twentieth century, while owing to Lydgate's work its conception and form.

Lydgate's *Troy Book* was only one of many literary treatments of the Troy legend available in the Middle Ages and Renaissance. But it was one of only two popular English versions of Guido della Colonne's famous Latin prose treatment of 1287 (**Caxton**'s was the other popular rendering, at second hand from a French version). Lydgate's narrative is much longer than its model, and precedes and follows the Troy story with related ones. It fancifully elaborates and romanticizes the chivalric elements of the material: Hector kills twice ten thousand men single-handed in one battle, Troilus later performing similar feats. But Lydgate also moralizes at length, condemning the war as springing from a trivial cause, blaming Priam for embarking on it, and insisting on the sinfulness of Helen's abduction.

This passage presents Achilles' killing of Hector, for the barbarity of which Lydgate explicitly condemns him, elsewhere reproaching **Homer** for having made Achilles his hero. As in Shakespeare (5.8.1), Hector has just taken possession of the body and spoils of a Greek king he has defeated on the field, and he too is reprimanded for his greed. Shakespeare may have known the *Troy Book* in either the 1513 or 1555 edition; this text is from the 1513 printing.

> Lyke as ye may now of Ector rede
> That sodaynely was brought to his endynge
> Oonly for spoylynge of this ryche kynge.
> For of desyre to hym that he hadde
> On hors backe out whan he hym ladde
> Reklesly, the storye maketh mynde,
> He caste his shelde at his backe behynde

To welde hym selfe at more lyberte,
And for to have opportunyte,
To spoyle hym and for no wyght spare;
So that his breste disarmed was and bare.
Except his plates there was no diffence
Agayne the stroke to make resystence.
Alas, why was he tho so rekles,
This floure of knyghthode, of manhode pereles,
Whan that his foo all that ylke day
For hym alone in awayte so lay,
If in myschefe of hate and of envye
In the felde he myght hym ought espye.
This Achylles, cruell and venymous,
Of hertely hate moste melancolyous,
Whiche covertly hovynge hym besyde,
Whan that he sawe Ector disarmed ryde
He hente a spere sharpe grounde and kene,
And of Ire in his hatefull tene
All unwarely or Ector myght adverte,
Alas the whyle! he smote hym to the herte
Thorugh out the breste, that dede he fylle downe
Unto the erthe, this Troyan champyowne,
Thorugh neclygence oonly of his shelde.
(iii, 5370–99; ed. Bullough, vi, 178–9, punctuation
modernized)

(C) The identifiable effect of the *Fall of Princes* on Shakespeare is confined to its status as the model for *A Mirror for Magistrates*. The *Troy Book*,
on the other hand, would have offered character sketches for all the
principal figures in *Troilus and Cressida*, plenty of suggestions for
incidents, and 'speeches that are often on the edge of high drama'
(Henderson 1935: 128). It has been suggested Shakespeare read the
poem early: 'we shall never get *Troilus and Cressida* right unless we think
of a Shakespeare steeped as a youth in the antique and venerable and
quaint world of Lydgate's Troy' (Tillyard 1965: 45). But there is too
much overlap between Lydgate, Caxton and other possible sources
(notably Homer) of the Trojan War material for any certainty as to
what Shakespeare owes to each, and commentators disagree considerably. While Palmer (1982: 30) suggests Lydgate may have led to 'the

conflated and contradictory Shakespearean Ajax' and the ordering of the incident in which Hector's family dissuades him from fighting (5.3), Bullough (VI, 93) proposes him as a possible source for the account of Troilus' character at 4.5.95–102, the episode of Hector and the resplendent knight (5.6, 5.8), and Achilles' order to his Myrmidons (5.7). Sometimes it is suggested Shakespeare owes nothing to Lydgate at all (Stein 1930), sometimes on the contrary that Shakespeare went to Caxton for factual detail but 'found Lydgate much more useful in suggesting ideas and motivation' (Tillyard 1965: 43).

Since Caxton (indirectly) and Lydgate (directly) both draw from the same source, Guido's *Historia Troiana*, the narrative material of battles, truces, and so on is necessarily very similar. Hence, too, Shakespeare's manipulation of elements common to all sources is normally what matters in his use of them – he 'has given a different interpretation of both the epic and the erotic theme from those he found in his sources, while basing that interpretation on points of character and incident he found there' (Bullough, VI, 107). But while the material may be in common, the sources do differ in tone and emphasis, and Lydgate's sometimes critical attitude to the failings of the treacherous Greeks (especially Achilles), in particular, seems to anticipate Shakespeare's presentation. On the other hand, this criticism is fairly isolated, and cannot be used to support the position that the play is a thoroughgoing satire – 'the notion of wholesale belittling is [not] applicable to Lydgate's *Troy Book*' (Sacharoff 1970: 127). Henderson goes furthest in associating the two writers, arguing that the connections are in terms of their 'Philosophy of Values', the passions of love and war being 'treated so philosophically that they become parties to the greater war between Individualism and Society' (1935: 128). Tillyard, more concretely and more modestly, gives one example of how 'close study would reveal many ways in which Lydgate could explain difficulties of detail in *Troilus and Cressida*' (1965: 147), suggesting that Shakespeare's reference to a truce in the council scene of 1.3, incompatible with the battle in his previous scene, is owing to a recollection of Lydgate's specification that a similar Greek council takes place during a truce.

(D)
Bullough, VI.

Campbell, Lily B., ed. (1960). *The Mirror For Magistrates*. New York (edition first published 1938).

Farnham, Willard (1956). *The Medieval Heritage of Elizabethan Tragedy*. Oxford (first published 1936).

Henderson, W. B. Drayton (1935). 'Shakespeare's *Troilus and Cressida*: Yet Deeper in its Tradition', pp. 127–56 in Hardin Craig, ed., *Essays in Dramatic Literature: The Parrott Presentation Volume*. Princeton (reprinted New York, 1967).

Palmer, Kenneth, ed. (1982). *Troilus and Cressida* (Arden Shakespeare). London.

Presson, Robert K. (1953). *Shakespeare's 'Troilus and Cressida' and the Legends of Troy*. Madison, WI.

Sacharoff, Mark (1970). 'The Traditions of the Troy-Story Heroes and the Problem of Satire in Troilus and Cressida.' *ShSt* 6: 125–35.

Stein, Elizabeth (1930). 'Caxton's *Recuyell* and Shakespeare's *Troilus*.' *MLN* 45: 144–6.

Tillyard, E. M. W. (1965). *Shakespeare's Problem Plays*. Harmondsworth (first published 1950).

Lyly, John (*c.* 1554–1606), Novelist and Dramatist

(A) Lyly's grandfather and founder of the family's fortunes was William Lily, a noted scholar and teacher who became High Master of St Paul's School in London. John Lyly's father, Peter, was a minor ecclesiastical official in Canterbury; John may well have attended the Cathedral Grammar School there, overlapping if so with **Marlowe**. Afterwards he followed his grandfather to Magdalene College, Oxford, graduating in 1575. He settled in London, and in 1578–80 published the first two parts of his prose romance *Euphues*, a cautionary tale of a prodigal son (named from the Greek εὐφυής, 'well-endowed' or 'good-natured') which is made a vehicle for moral debate about wit and wisdom. Its extravagant new form of English, developed at this time by Lyly and several contemporaries, was studded with puns, high-flown rhetoric, alliteration, allusion and other stylistic features so ostentatiously collected together as to call for the invention of the term 'euphuism'; the mode acquired great fashionability for a few years.

In 1583 Lyly married an heiress and gained control of the new Blackfriars theatre as a kind of impresario. He now sought patronage from Lord Burghley, a family connection, and Edward de Vere, Earl of Oxford, whose 'servant' – perhaps secretary – he became, and who must have financed his debut in the theatre: he was paid in 1584 for performances at court by Oxford's boys' company. The company was playing the first of a sequence of courtly prose romances and pastorals which Lyly wrote for the boys' companies, including the oldest surviving examples of court plays, *Campaspe* and *Sapho and Phao*. By 1590 his dramatic oeuvre also included *Gallathea, Endimion, Midas, Mother Bombie* and *Love's Metamorphosis*. At this date he had no rival as a court dramatist, and his fame on the public stage was outshone only by Marlowe's. Lyly's innovations in drama included fuller attention to the architecture of a play, for example by delaying and building up climaxes, and the differentiation of characters by differentiation of their dialogue.

(B) The rise and fall of Lyly's reputation follows that of his *Euphues*; first printings of the plays in the 1590s probably reflect the romance's popularity. *Euphues* took by storm the court at which it was directed; its first editor of 1632 wrote that 'all our ladies were then his scholars, and that Beauty in court which could not then parley Euphuism was as little regarded as she which now there speaks no French' (quoted from Hunter 1962: 72). *Euphues, the Anatomy of Wit* was immediately imitated in Anthony **Munday**'s *Zelauto* and Austen Saker's *Narbonus*, both 1580. The first part of Robert **Greene**'s *Mamillia* probably belongs to the same year. By 1581 five editions of *Euphues, The Anatomy of Wit* had been published, together with four of its 1580 sequel, *Euphues and his England*. Further imitations followed: in 1581 Barnaby Riche's *Don Simonides*, in 1584 Brian Melbanke's *Philotimus*.

'Up to this point the fashion for love-stories moralized in the manner of Lyly would seem to be in full flood; thereafter, in the long series of Greene's romances we can see a recession from it' (Hunter 1962: 258). Detractors included **Sidney**, **Nashe**, **Jonson** and **Drayton**, whose 'Epistle to Henry Reynolds' shows how Lyly's wit came to be seen by the Jacobeans as mere courtly artificiality: it was Sidney, Drayton writes, who

> did first reduce
> Our tongue from *Lillies* writing then in use;
> Talking of Stones, Stars, Plants, of fishes, Flyes,
> Playing with words, and idle Similies . . .
> So imitating his ridiculous tricks,
> They spake and writ, all like meere lunatiques.
> (89–92, 95–6; ed. Hebel 1932: III, 228)

Though *Euphues* was being printed down to 1716, the later versions were modernized; and the plays, more closely linked to the court, did not enjoy even the limited bourgeois afterlife of the romance. Lyly's career as a court dramatist was over by 1590, and his last few years' work for the stage is evidently out of tune with the tastes of the late sixteenth century (Hunter 1962: 291–7 tellingly compares *Endimion* with *Cynthia's Revels*). In his heyday the court plays had attracted imitators too, however: Greene, for example, seized on the possibility of 'translating' *Campaspe* onto the popular stage in his *Friar Bacon and Friar Bungay* (*c.* 1589).

This sample from *Euphues, the Anatomy of Wit*, in which the hero woos Lucilla, illustrates how the euphuistic style combines a range of devices – stylistic effects such as antithesis, alliteration and *parison* (balance between grammatical parts of a sentence); rhetorical figures such as simile; and other flourishes such as references to classical history and mythology:

> It is your beautie (pardon my abrupte boldnesse) Ladye that hath taken every part of mee prisoner, and brought me to this deepe distresse, but seeinge women when one praiseth them for their desertes, deeme that hee flattereth them to obteine his desire, I am heere present to yelde my selfe to such tryall, as your courtesie in this behalfe shall require: Yet will you commonly object this to such as serve you and sterve to winne your good wil, that hot love is soone colde, that the Bavin though it bourne bright, is but a blaze, that scaldinge water if it stande a while tourneth almost to yse, that pepper though it be hot in the mouth is colde in the mawe, that the faith of men though it frye in their woordes, it freeseth in theire works: Which things (*Lucillia*) albeit they be sufficient to reprove the lightnesse of some one, yet can it not convince every one of lewdenes, neither ought the constancie of all, to be brought in question through the subtiltie of a fewe. For although the worme entereth almost into every woode, yet he eateth not the *Ceder* tree: Though the stone *Cylindrus* at every thunder clappe, rowle from the hill, yet the pure sleeke stone mounteth at the noyse, though the rust fret the hardest steele, yet doth it not eate into the Emeraulde, though *Polypus* chaunge his hew, yet the *Salamander* keepeth his coulour, though *Proteus* transforme himselfe into every shape, yet *Pygmalion* retaineth his olde forme, though *Aeneas* were to fickle to *Dido*, yet *Troylus* was to

faithfull to *Craessida*, thoughe others seeme counterfaite in their deedes, yet *Lucilla* perswade your selfe that *Euphues* will bee alwayes curraunt in his dealinges.

(1578 text, ed. Bond 1902: I, 218–19)

(C) A long-recognized morsel apparently from Lyly in Shakespeare is the lark at 'heaven's gate' in Sonnet 29:

> Like to the lark at break of day arising
> From sullen earth, sings hymns at heaven's gate

Campaspe contains (5.1) a song which includes the lines:

> Brave prick song! who is't now we heare?
> None but the Larke so shrill and cleare;
> How at heavens gats she claps her wings,
> The Morne not waking till shee sings.
>   (ed. Bond 1902: ii, 351)

But only one clear reference to Lyly occurs in Shakespeare's plays, and that, if anything, negative: Falstaff's justly famous parody of euphuism in *1 Henry IV*, 2.4 (first performed in 1597, by which time Lyly's mannerisms were becoming outdated). Lyly is probably not the sole target here, but he can be assumed to be a principal one among exemplars of the idiom of the time, and specific references seem to be intended to several passages in *Euphues*. First there is 'though the Camomill, the more it is trodden and pressed downe, the more it spreadeth, yet the violet the oftner it is handled and touched, the sooner it withereth and decayeth' (ed. Bond 1902: i, 196), second, another two passages (ed. Bond 1902: i, 250, 320) rhetorically employing the biblical saying about the defiling effects of pitch (see Humphreys 1974: 79). Falstaff's words are:

> Harry, I do not only marvel where thou spendest thy time, but also how thou art accompanied; for though the camomile, the more it is wasted the sooner it grows, yet youth, the more it is wasted the sooner it wears . . . Shall the blessed son of heaven prove a micher and eat blackberries? A question not to be ask'd. Shall the son of England prove a thief and take blackberries? A question to be ask'd. There is a

305

thing, Harry, which thou hast often heard of, and it is known to many in our land by the name of pitch. This pitch, as ancient writers do report, doth defile; so doth the company thou keepest; for, Harry, I do not speak to thee in drink, but in tears; not in pleasure, but in passion; not in words only, but in woes also.

(2.4.386–404)

There are, in fact, several Lylian ideas in the Histories. The comic euphuism and actual gift for pithy phrase of Lyly's foolish Sir Thopas in *Endimion*, who 'thinks himself the valiantest man in the world if he kill a woman', sometimes anticipate Falstaff, though at other times Thopas resembles Pistol more strongly. The Archbishop's discourse on the commonwealth of bees in *Henry V*, 1.2.187–204, can be related to sources in **Virgil** and **Elyot**, but, since Shakespeare knew the *Euphues*, its treatment of the subject (ed. Bond 1902: II, 44–6) is also pertinent.

But it is in the comedies that Lyly's influence is most readily detectable. 'What Shakespeare retains from Lyly', it can be argued, 'and develops to the utmost, though with a certain satirical twist at the end, is the comedy of courtship – the capers of the men as they strut and preen themselves, the coquetry of the girls, who pretend they will not when they would and plague their lovers' (Mincoff 1961: 19). Two factors complicate matters. Since no court plays previous to Lyly's are extant, it is possible that what appear to be Lylian elements in Shakespeare derive from other sources. Second, parallels of plot and language may be concrete but the borrowing they indicate is small-scale, whereas to identify more substantial debts entails comparison of evanescent features such as emphasis and tone. For example, it is hard to think of another English author who preceded Shakespeare in using 'the mere fact of being in love almost as a comic situation' (Mincoff 1961: 15), but equally hard to show that Lyly's work determined this central feature of Shakespearean comedy. This is also the reason why estimates of Lyly's impact on Shakespeare, both as a whole and in individual plays, vary so wildly, for example in respect of *Love's Labour's Lost* between the extremes of Mincoff's 'the very nucleus of the play . . . is taken from Lyly, as are the characters, and the contrapuntal structure, and the static scenes of wit' (1961: 19), and Richard David's view that since Lyly's dramas 'belong to an older and more courtly *genre* even than *Love's Labour's Lost*, Shakespeare's most courtly play', there is 'no real similarity' between *Love's Labour's Lost* and Lyly's work (1968: xxxi).

Given all this, it is as well to bear in mind that the importance of this subject does not lie in the number of parallels that can be assembled, but ultimately in the ways Shakespeare develops his model. *Euphues* is a different case from Lyly's plays in this regard: many local similarities of phrasing can be discovered in Shakespeare (parallel passages are given by Bond 1902: I, 163–75), almost all of which may or may not be merely coincidental, but there are few signs of the work's influence on him at any deeper level.

More detailed accounts of the pattern of Shakespeare's use of Lyly tend to suggest what may be a suspiciously neat bell curve in level of engagement over time. Early comedies such as *The Comedy of Errors* and *The Taming of the Shrew* are less strongly related to Lyly's plays, though in the latter Lucentio's lessons in the *Heroides* (3.1) appear to be modelled on scene 1.3 of Lyly's *Mother Bombie* (Velz 1973). But for *The Two Gentlemen of Verona*, according to Bullough, 'Lyly served Shakespeare as a master in the dramatic use of the courtly and amorous code' (I, 205); Shakespeare seems 'conscious of the glamour of *Euphues*' (Hunter 1962: 313), meaning that this is a play which rates elegance highly, but not that Shakespeare merely follows Lyly's leads in style or structure. Possible specific echoes include a scene in *Sapho to Phao* (2.4), in which Phao is counselled by Sibilla, for Valentine's naive advice to the Duke on winning a lady (3.1.89–105), and the love-versus-friendship clash in the plot of Lyly's *Endimion*. Some of the Shakespeare play's comic devices, such as the two comic servants (Launce and Speed), can also be paralleled from *Endimion*.

Such early comedies may show a gradual approach to Lyly's kind of love comedy, but it is not until *Love's Labour's Lost* that Shakespeare follows him closely in terms of detail (as well, perhaps, as in employing mock-euphuistic styles for the dialogue). Here, as is routinely pointed out, the figure and the history of Armado seem indebted to *Endimion*'s braggart soldier Sir Thopas (though a minority view is that the figures resemble one another because of a common origin). Shakespeare's treatment is more complex, however: 'the function of Armado is more difficult to see schematically than is that of Thopas . . . Shakespeare handles his multiple plots to suggest the variety of social experience at different levels' – 'the *different* responses which make up a unified though wide-ranging social scene' (Hunter 1962: 317). Structurally, too, *Love's Labour's Lost* seems close to Lyly's 'fugal method in which whole groups of characters had been developed in parallel lines' (Mincoff 1961: 22), perhaps especially the method of *Endimion* and *Gallathea* (Scragg 1982). *Love's Labour's Lost* is arguably the most fundamentally Lylian play in the Shakespeare canon, though once again representing a development, not a mere following, of his predecessor. '[Lyly's] characters merely voice current attitudes towards love, whereas Shakespeare's characters express these ideas as if they were their own' (Stevenson 1966: 172). And whereas Lyly's combats of wit are intellectual contests as ends in themselves, Shakespeare's are used to convey restraint in the face of emotion, and as points of self-realization.

For *A Midsummer Night's Dream*, Lyly's *Gallathea* (first performed 1588?), a play Shakespeare would have been familiar with early in his career, has been proposed as a principal source. The main evidence on one account is that the plays are tied together thematically by their 'vision of "translation"' (Scragg 1977: 128), but structural similarities between the *Dream* and Lyly's work in general may be stronger. The complex and episodic Shakespearean plot is constructed in the Lylian manner by balancing several self-contained groups against one another; for example, the Mechanicals are handled as Lyly handles his parodies of master by servant-figure, keeping them apart and distinct until the final Act. Or we may note a wealth of Lylian motifs in the theme of parental opposition, the debate subject of imagination versus reason, and so on – 'the very profusion of Lylian motifs in this play might seem to turn it into a cento, were it not that this profusion is itself unLylian' (Hunter 1962: 319). Other Lyly plays perhaps have some bearing on *Midsummer Night's Dream* too: *Sapho and Phao* for the epilogue, *Midas* for the ass's head.

On the reasonable assumption that Shakespeare's undoubted early knowledge of Lyly was 'internalized' and summoned up, often unconsciously, in later years, diminishing echoes may be found in *Twelfth Night* and *The Merry Wives of Windsor* – though it is hard to be sure one is hearing them. Viola's wooing of the Duke by innuendo involves verbal parallels with *Gallathea* 3.2 which Scragg (1982) uses as the basis for extensive claims of shared preoccupations in the two plays with role-playing and transmutation by time. The Falstaff of *Wives* is if anything even more Sir Thopas-like than his earlier incarnations (both are also punished by fairies). An assortment of possible Lylian touches has been traced in *As You Like It*, the most plausible of them associated with Rosalind from the 1593 or 1594 play *The Woman in the Moon* (see Latham 1975) and with the amatory situations from *Gallathea* again, perhaps reinforced and sometimes mediated by **Lodge**'s use of this play for his *Rosalynde* (so Scragg 1982: 85ff.). For suggestions on affinities with Lyly in the Late Plays, see Scragg (1982).

(D) Bond's 1902 edition of Lyly includes generous comment on matters such as his biography, bibliography and reputation, as well as an over-generalized account of his effect on Shakespeare. Mincoff (1961: 15) notes that early investigations of Lyly's relationship to Shakespeare 'tended to concentrate rather on concrete parallels than on funda-mental principles', but unintentionally reveals why this was so by con-structing too speculative a survey. Further 'concrete parallels', mostly very minor, are still being discovered (as by Andrews 1984). The final chapter of Hunter (1962), still the best book-length study of Lyly, is a full and forceful overview stressing differences between Lyly and Shake-speare in a more or less play-by-play treatment. Scragg (1982) is a most extensive treatment of the impact of the single play *Gallathea*, with an introduction reviewing twentieth-century work on Shakespeare–Lyly connections at large.

Andrews, Michael Cameron (1984). 'The Owl's "Merry Note".' *N&Q* 229: 187–8.

Bevington, David (1989). ' "Jack Hath Not Jill": Failed Courtship in Lyly and Shakespeare.' *ShSu* 42: 1–13.

Bond, R. Warwick, ed. (1902). *The Complete Works of John Lyly: Now for the First Time Collected and Edited from the Earliest Quartos*, 3 vols. Oxford.

Borinski, Ludwig (1958). 'The Origin of the Euphuistic Novel and its Significance for Shakespeare', pp. 38–52 in Don Cameron Allen, ed., *Studies in Honor of T. W. Baldwin*. Urbana, IL.

Bullough.

David, Richard, ed. (1968). *Love's Labour's Lost* (Arden Shakespeare). London (first published 1951).

Hebel, J. William, ed. (1932). *The Works of Michael Drayton*, 4 vols. London.

Humphreys, A. R., ed. (1974). *King Henry IV Part I* (Arden Shakespeare). London.

Hunter, G. K. (1962). *John Lyly: The Humanist as Courtier*. London.

Latham, Agnes, ed. (1975). *As You Like It* (Arden Shakespeare). London.

Mincoff, Marco (1961). 'Shakespeare and Lyly.' *ShSu* 14: 15–24.

Scragg, Leah (1977). 'Shakespeare, Lyly and Ovid: The Influence of *Gallathea* on *A Midsummer Night's Dream.*' *ShSu* 30: 125–34.

Scragg, Leah (1982). *The Metamorphoses of Gallathea: A Study in Creative Adaptation*. Washington, D.C.

Stevenson, David Lloyd (1966). *The Love-Game Comedy*. New York.

Velz, John W. (1973). 'Gascoigne, Lyly, and the Wooing of Bianca.' *N&Q* 218: 130–3.

M

Machiavelli, Niccolò (1469–1527), Italian Statesman and Political Philosopher

(A) Machiavelli was born in Florence, where he was among these who rose to power in the new republic established in 1498, becoming its second chancellor. He led important embassies to Louis XII of France, the Emperor Maximillian and Cesare Borgia. On the accession to power of the Medici in 1512 he was imprisoned on a charge of conspiracy against the new regime, and tortured. Though soon pardoned, he was obliged to withdraw from public life, and devoted himself to study. His major theoretical works were written in retirement and aimed in part at obtaining employment under the new regime, which was not forthcoming. The original and controversial *Il Principe* ('The Prince'), written 1513 and published 1532, was intended as a handbook for rulers (specifically the new rulers of Florence), and the *Discorsi sopra la prima deca di Tito Livio*, published 1531, is a large commentary on the first ten Books of **Livy** and hence on the principles of republican government. He also wrote a treatise on the art of war, a comic play, a history of Florence and several more minor literary and historical works.

(B) *Il Principe* was available in printed form from 1532. Though Machiavelli was not immediately perceived as an enemy of Christianity, the Jesuits' efforts led to his works being placed on the first Papal Index of 1559, preventing the open dissemination of them in Catholic countries. Pious Protestants such as Roger Ascham also took a dim view of

311

Machiavelli on account of his atheism, as well as for the different reason that he was associated with Italy. Ascham provides in his *Report and Discourse . . . of the Affairs and State of Germany* (*c.* 1570) an early example of a prevalent view, complaining of those who 'with consciences confirmed with *Machiavelles* doctrine . . . thincke say and do what soever may serve best for profit and pleasure'. And Innocent Gentillet's widely-known *Discours . . . Contre Machiavel* (written 1576; English translation 1602), a long-winded refutation ascribing to Machiavelli's influence not only the Massacre of St Bartholomew but the whole of French policy from Henry II to Charles IX, encouraged anti-Machiavellianism in England. Other readers, of course – famously, in the early phases of the English reception, Francis Bacon – were more accepting of Machiavelli's secular political world; Bacon argued that at least the knowledge of evil was useful. Few generalizations are worth hazarding as to English opinions: 'the ability of sixteenth-century writers to combine apparently irreconcilable attitudes' in this regard has been remarked (Bawcutt 1970: 12).

The English government did know its mind: it refused to licence the printing of *Il Principe* or the *Discorsi* until well into the seventeenth century. The public was supplied with Italian-language editions carrying false imprints by the London printer John Wolfe in the 1580s. These circulated widely, together with copies of pre-Index Latin and French editions, and manuscript English translations of both works from 1585 or a few years later, some of which still survive (see Craig 1944; Raab 1964: 52–3). This situation is partly a reflection of the idea, recorded in the Preface to Wolfe's illicit editions, that Machiavelli's works carried a hidden republican ideology (see Donaldson 1988: 86–110). The less controversial *Art of War* and *Florentine History* were printed in English translation in 1560–2 and 1595 respectively.

It was undoubtedly via the stage that his name was first heard by most Englishmen. But the Elizabethan stage Machiavel was not a wholly new figure: he was a blend of one of the more negative current interpretations of Machiavelli with the Vice, the humorous villain from the medieval **Morality Tradition** (and perhaps with Machiavellian elements in **Seneca** and **Cinthio**'s plays mixed in too: see D'Andrea 1980). This figure also diverged further and further from the content of Machiavelli's own writings over time. Much of the dramatists' work can be traced back to a surge of interest in Machiavelli around 1580 affecting Gabriel **Harvey**, Robert **Greene** (who both refer to him at this

312

time), and others including **Marlowe**, the first to bring a Machiavel figure onto the stage when the murderous Nick Machevill introduced *The Jew of Malta* (1588), and eventually the heaviest investor in them (Barabas, Tamburlaine, Faustus). **Jonson**, **Marston** and Webster are further playwrights readily associated with the phenomenon. Machiavelli's use as a stock stage villain does not indicate that the dramatists, or other English readers, were unfamiliar with what he had actually written: on the contrary, writers such as Jonson, **Kyd**, Marston, **Nashe**, Ralegh and **Sidney** clearly knew his work at first hand – which is not to say they approved of it. In some respects Machiavelli's prose is often inherently dramatic or theatrical, and he is by no means only an abstract or theoretical writer even in *Il Principe*, since he includes a wealth of historical stories and examples to enforce his points. Such features do much to account for his popularity, though it is not usually these which resurface in English writers' work.

(C) The traditional Machiavels of Shakespeare's plays have been widely written on, and they do not derive directly from Machiavelli. This discussion does not deal with Shakespeare's Iagos, Aarons and Edmunds (for which see rather Praz 1928).

On balance, 'it would be more surprising if it could be proved that Shakespeare had managed to avoid reading Machiavelli than if concrete evidence were to turn up that he had' (Barton 1985: 122). But his several passing uses of Machiavelli's name itself, for example in *1 Henry VI*, 5.4.74, as a synonym for 'cunning and ruthless', are unrevealing, and specific reference to Machiavelli's work is nowhere obvious in Shakespeare. One trouble with scholarship on the subject is that specific reference is also rare there, commentators usually comparing only generally 'Machiavellian' principles of character and action with the content of the plays. Where this is not the case, a converse problem besets investigation: since Machiavelli says so much about kings, governance, rebellion, and so on, not only in *Il Principe* but also in the *Discorsi* and the *Florentine Histories*, it is all too easy to isolate parallels in his writings for attributes and behaviour found at one point or another in the many Shakespeare plays which involve similar elements. In addition, apparent parallels very often turn out either to be already present in the historical sources, or to derive from the popular Machiavelli myth. All positions on the spectrum have been adopted over the years regarding the positiveness or otherwise of Shakespeare's response to the

Italian writer. It is possible he knew Gentillet's *Contre Machiavel*, which gives an idea (if a biased one) of Machiavelli's arguments, rather than *Il Principe* itself.

The range of plays in which Machiavellian elements have been discerned runs from early to fairly late works, beginning naturally enough with the Histories. Henry VI is sometimes seen as an illustration of Machiavelli's thesis in *Il Principe* about the enfeebling effects of Christianity on modern rulers, and his contention (*Discorsi* I.9) that only a single concentrated authority could reform a decaying political order. Perhaps the presentation of the French in *Part I* reflects a 'divided attitude toward the Machiavellian ethic they embrace' (Wineke 1983). Henry V, naturally enough, has been identified both as a Machiavellian figure (D'Amico 1986) and as an anti-Machiavellian one. A stronger, because more detailed, case can be made for the Bolingbroke of both *Richard II* and *Henry IV* (one is outlined by Ribner 1948), but there is no proof that the figure is directly inspired by Machiavelli. *Macbeth* shows at least three possible models of kingship (Duncan, Macbeth, Malcolm) and so lends itself to similar speculation (as by Riebling 1991). Malcolm's successful seizure of power seems more authentically Machiavellian in procedure than Macbeth's own manoeuvres (Sahel 1978). Machiavelli's view of Coriolanus in his *Discorsi*, which stands in an interesting relationship to Shakespeare's but can only tentatively be proposed as a shaping influence on it, is discussed by Barton (1985).

A different kind of link exists between the plot of *Measure for Measure* and the story recounted in Chapter 7 of *Il Principe*. Cesare Borgia, the ostensible hero of Machiavelli's book, brought order to the Romagna by placing in authority the Spaniard Remirro de Orco, renowned as a cruel governor, and giving him *carte blanche*. Remirro's harsh methods made the country peaceful and united, upon which Cesare reintroduced civil authority and, to win over the people, had Remirro executed. Even if this story's resemblance to that of Vincentio and Angelo 'cannot be coincidental' (Jaffa 1981: 189), there is a strong possibility it reached Shakespeare through intermediate sources (so Holland 1959; Hager 1990). Even so, Shakespeare may have assumed his audience's knowledge of it principally from Machiavelli.

One overall view is offered by Robert Ornstein, who sees Shakespeare as conscious of the challenge Machiavelli posed to traditional assumptions but resistant to his conclusions:

Addressing himself always to fact and historical example, Machiavelli thought there could be no appeal from the dictates of Necessity; Shakespeare realized, however, that Necessity is as the mind conceives and rationalizes it. Where Machiavelli insisted that seeing was believing, Shakespeare understood that in politics believing is often seeing . . . Whatever role the Prince may play – magus or scapegoat – the King's Body is the living presence of the nation and his royal We a communion of multitudes.

(Ornstein 1972: 30)

(D) Raab (1964) and more recently Donaldson (1988) deal with Machiavelli's reception among English political writers and polemicists of the sixteenth and seventeenth centuries; Bawcutt's survey (1970) is usefully more miscellaneous. On Shakespeare, the quantity of work is disproportionate to the security with which any direct use of Machiavelli can be demonstrated. Other treatments are found in the course of wider-ranging studies on Elizabethan and Jacobean drama not listed below.

Barton, Anne (1985). 'Livy, Machiavelli, and Shakespeare's "Coriolanus".' *ShSu* 38: 115–29.

Bawcutt, N. W. (1970). 'Machiavelli and Marlowe's *The Jew of Malta.*' *RenD* 3: 3–49.

Craig, Hardin, ed. (1944). *The Prince: An Elizabethan Translation.* Chapel Hill.

D'Amico, Jack (1986). 'Moral and Political Conscience: Machiavelli and Shakespeare's *Macbeth* and *Henry V.*' *Italian Quarterly* 27: 31–41.

D'Andrea, Antonio (1980). 'Giraldi Cinthio and the Birth of the Machiavellian Hero on the Elizabethan Stage', pp. 605–18 in Maristella de Panizza Lorch, ed., *Il Teatro Italiano del Rinascimento.* Milan.

Donaldson, Peter S. (1988). *Machiavelli and the Mystery of State.* Cambridge.

Hager, Alan (1990). 'Shakespeare's Disassembly and Reassembly of Montaigne's Utopia and Machiavelli's Anti-Utopia.' *Machiavelli Studies* 3: 79–93.

Holland, Norman N. (1959). '*Measure for Measure*: The Duke and the Prince.' *CompLit* 11: 16–20.

Jaffa, Harry V. (1981). 'Chastity as a Political Principle: An Interpretation of Shakespeare's *Measure for Measure*', pp. 181–213 in John Alvis and Thomas G. West, eds, *Shakespeare as a Political Thinker*. Durham, N.C.

Lupton, Julia (1987). 'Truant Dispositions: Hamlet and Machiavelli.' *JMRS* 17: 59–82.

Ornstein, Robert (1972). *A Kingdom for a Stage: The Achievement of Shakespeare's History Plays*. Cambridge, MA.

Praz, Mario (1928). *Machiavelli and the Elizabethans*. London (reprinted in Praz, *The Flaming Heart: Essays on Crashaw, Machiavelli, and other Studies in the Relations between Italian and English Literature from Chaucer to T. S. Eliot*, New York, 1958).

Raab, Felix (1964). *The English Face of Machiavelli: A Changing Interpretation 1500–1700*. London.

Ribner, Irving (1948). 'Bolingbroke, A True Machiavellian.' *MLQ* 9: 177–84.

Riebling, Barbara (1991). 'Virtue's Sacrifice: A Machiavellian Reading of *Macbeth*.' *SEL* 31: 273–86.

Sahel, Pierre (1978). 'Machiavelisme vulgaire et machiavelisme authentique dans *Macbeth*.' *CahiersE* 14: 9–22.

Wineke, Donald R. (1983). 'The Relevance of Machiavelli to Shakespeare: A Discussion of *1 Henry VI*.' *CLIO: A Journal of Literature, History, and the Philosophy of History* 13.i: 17–36.

Mantuan (Giovanni Baptista Spagnuoli) (1448–1516), Italian Neo-Latin Poet

(A) Of partly Spanish descent, he was born in Mantua, studied there and in Padua, then entered the Carmelite order, of which he became Vicar-General in 1483. As well as a prominent ecclesiastical administrator, he was a scholarly figure in the culture of the Italian Renaissance. Mantuan's prolific writings include *silvae* and many religious poems, but his fame has rested from the first on his *Bucolics* or *Eclogues*, printed in 1498. They are ten didactic poems making up a short book, with a range of themes and tones: against illicit love and the looseness of women, the neglect of poets, the evils of the city. Four deal directly with aspects of the religious life. All are aphoristic, verbally vivid, and moralistic or satirical. On their account Mantuan has sometimes been called 'the second **Virgil**': their classical quality was quickly acknowledged by wide acclaim, a learned commentary, and adoption for teaching. A modern edition, including English translation, is Piepho (1989).

(B) Mantuan's *Eclogues* had achieved great popularity and pre-eminence by the second half of the sixteenth century, owing in large part to their blend of classical form with edifying Christian content. They were often prescribed for use in English schools. In his poem 'To Henry Reynolds' **Drayton** recalls, or imagines, his instruction when at 'scarce ten yeares of age' he asked his 'deare master' to make him a poet:

> shortly he began,
> And first read to me honest *Mantuan*,
> Then *Virgils Eclogues*, being entred thus
> Me thought I straight had mounted *Pegasus*,
> And in his full Careere could make him stop,
> And bound upon *Parnassus* by-clift top.
> (35–40; ed. Hebel 1932: iii, 226–7)

The use of Mantuan for the teaching of elementary prosody is fully documented in Hoole's *New Discovery of the Old Art of Teaching School* (see Baldwin 1944: i, 646–8). William Webbe writes more formally in his discussion of the eclogue in his *Discourse of English Poetry* (1586):

> After *Virgyl* in like sort writ *Titus Calphurnius* and *Baptista Mantuan*, wyth many other both in Latine and other languages very learnedlye. Although the matter they take in hand seemeth commonlie in appearaunce rude and homely, as the usuall talke of simple clownes: yet doo they indeede utter in the same much pleasaunt and profitable delight. For under these personnes, as it were in a cloake of simplicitie, they would eyther sette foorth the prayses of theyr freendes, without the note of flattery, or enveigh grievously against abuses, without any token of bytternesse.
>
> (ed. Arber 1870: 52)

Mantuan had expanded the pastoral mode to a point at which it could be used as a vehicle for virtually any material, especially satirical. Many sixteenth-century English pastorals, such as Alexander Barclay's *Five Eclogues* (1513–14), Barnabe Googe's *Eglogs* (1563), Francis **Sabie**'s *Pan's Pipe* (1595), and most importantly parts of **Spenser**'s *Shepheardes Calendar* (1579), are modelled on Mantuan's.

There are six known English printings of Mantuan's *Eclogues* from 1569 to 1600, as well as two editions of the translation by George

Mantuan (Giovanni Baptista Spagnuoli)

Turberville first published in 1567. This is the start of Eclogue I, which turns out an uncharacteristically sunny poem on the consummation of honourable love, in Turberville's energetic Englishing:

The speakers names.

Fortunatus. Faustus.

Fortunat'   Frend Faustus, pray thee, since our flock
    in shade and pleasaunt vale
Doth chewe the cudde: of auncient love
    let us begin to tale.
Least if by hap unhappy sleepe
    our senses should begyle,
Some savage beast in sprouted corne
    our cattell catch the while:
For many such about the fields
    do lurking lye in wayte.
Wherfore to watch is better far
    than sleepe in my conceyte.

Faustus   This place, this self same shady bushe
    that shrowds us from the heate,
Knows how I haue been cloyd with cares
    and *Cupids* coales yfreat
These .iiii. yeares space, or .ii. at least
    if I remember well.
But synce we are at leasure both,
    and pleasaunt is to tell:
I will begin the whole discourse
    and shewe thee how it fell.
Here I, whilst in my tender youth
    of cattell should had care,
Would spread my garment on the soyle,
    and bolte upright would stare
Into the open Skyes alofte:
    with dolefull drops of bryne
And heavy playnt recounting of
    this curssed fate of myne.

(Mantuan 1567: sig. B1ʳ⁻ᵛ)

(C) Like every grammar school boy, Shakespeare would have been drilled in Mantuan's *Eclogues* in the Latin (there is no sign of his having known Turberville's rendering). Holofernes in *Love's Labour's Lost*, abstracted, as usual, in his discussion with Nathaniel, supplies the only certain allusion to Mantuan in Shakespeare's work:

> Fauste, precor gelida quando pecus omne sub umbra
> Ruminat –
> and so forth. Ah. good old Mantuan! I may speak of thee as the traveller doth of Venice:
> > Venetia, Venetia,
> > Chi non ti vide, non ti pretia.
> Old Mantuan, old Mantuan! Who understandeth thee not, loves thee not –
> > Ut, re, sol, la, mi, fa.
>
> > (4.2.89–95)

Holofernes' first quotation is the first line of the *Eclogues*, a line as familiar to Elizabethan schoolboys as Virgil's 'Tityre, tu patulae' (Eclogue I). It had recently been deployed in literary skirmishes between Gabriel **Harvey** and Thomas **Nashe**. In Harvey's *Foure Letters* (1592) he attacks Nashe, whose 'margine is as deeplie learned, as *Fauste precor gelida*', i.e. very superficially learned. Nashe replied in like vein, mentioning the line again. 'Here we have the words classified, by two of the chief writers before the public, as the one tag that even the worst of Grammar School dunces might be expected to remember' (David 1968: 81). Mantuan's line was evidently used to describe a beginner in poetry. Shakespeare's reference to Mantuan in *Love's Labour's Lost* seems at least half affectionate, but Baldwin sees the allusion as indicating on Shakespeare's part what would have been thought a reprehensibly frivolous attitude towards a writer of 'awesome dignity in school circles' (1944: I, 646); it would seem that 'Shakespeare did not share his pedantic schoolmaster's enthusiasm for this staple of the grammar-school curriculum' (Sowerby 1994: 216).

Baldwin (I, 649–52) suggests some remote small-scale Shakespearean parallels with Mantuan, or rather, for the most part, with materials brought together in the annotations of his editor Josse Bade (Badius, also Ascensius), who explains Mantuan's extensive classical allusions. On the whole, it is in any case clear that Shakespeare's pastoral world, usually an idyllic contrast to the court or city, is radically unlike Mantuan's, where suffering and danger are still present.

(D)

Arber, Edward, ed. (1870). *William Webbe, Graduate: A Discourse of English Poetrie, 1586.* London.

Baldwin (1944).

David, Richard, ed. (1968). *Love's Labour's Lost* (Arden Shakespeare). London (first published 1951).

Hebel, J. William, ed. (1931–41). *The Works of Michael Drayton*, 5 vols. Oxford.

Mantuan, translated by George Turberville (1567). *The Eglogs of the Poet B. Mantuan Carmelitan, Turned into English Verse.* London.

Piepho, Lee, ed. (1989). *Adulescentia: The Eclogues of Mantuan / Baptista (Spagnuoli) Mantuanus.* New York.

Sowerby, Robin (1994). *The Classical Legacy in Renaissance Poetry.* London.

Marguerite, de Navarre See **Painter, William**.

Marianus Scholasticus (5th Century AD?), Byzantine Poet

A six-line Greek Anthology epigram attributed to this poet may be rather more than an analogue for Sonnets 153 and 154; Shakespeare could have known it from a translation in one of several modern languages or in Latin.

Hutton, James (1941). 'Analogues of Shakespeare's Sonnets 153–4: Contributions to the History of a Theme.' *MP* 38: 385–403 (reprinted in Hutton, *Essays on Renaissance Poetry*, Ithaca, 1980).

Marlowe, Christopher (1564–1593), English Poet and Dramatist See also **Ovid (Publius Ovidius Naso)**.

(A) Marlowe was born the son of a Canterbury shoemaker, two months before Shakespeare. He attended the King's School, Canterbury, and from 1580 Bene't (now Corpus Christi) College, Cambridge, on a scholarship founded by Archbishop Parker primarily for those intending to take holy orders. He received his first degree in 1584, by which time he may have begun to work as a government spy. His play *Dido, Queen of Carthage* may have been composed as early as 1586, in collaboration with **Nashe**. Having held his scholarship for the maximum six years, Marlowe graduated MA after the intervention of the Privy Council on his behalf, and despite rumours that he had joined the Catholic seminary at Rheims; this may mean he had attempted to infiltrate the expatriate English Catholic community. In the summer of the same year, 1587, his *Tamburlaine* was produced to great acclaim. He was soon writing for the Admiral's Company, apparently becoming in some sense its 'answer' to Shakespeare. He soldiered in the Netherlands, whence he was deported for counterfeiting, and probably worked as a spy both at home and abroad for Elizabeth's government. He joined the group of freethinkers around Sir Walter Ralegh. When in 1593 some heretical papers were found in the possession of **Kyd**, with whom Marlowe shared lodgings, Kyd attributed them to Marlowe and he was summoned to appear before the Privy Council on a charge of heresy. But a few days later, while on bail, he was stabbed to death in a Deptford tavern, reportedly in a dispute over the bill but perhaps in connection with clandestine activities in government service.

His plays after *Tamburlaine* (with dates of composition rather than the usually somewhat later publication) are *Doctor Faustus*, 1588–9, *The Jew of Malta*, *c.* 1590, *Edward II*, 1592, and *The Massacre of Paris*, 1593 (the last jointly with Nashe). He was also responsible for translations from **Ovid**, a long but unfinished version of Musaeus' poem *Hero and Leander*, and some shorter poems.

(B) Marlowe's influence on contemporary drama in general was extensive. With Kyd, he virtually invented Elizabethan tragedy and secured the role of blank verse as the standard medium for the stage, leading English drama away once and for all from 'the jigling vaines of rhyming mother-wits', as the Prologue to *Tamburlaine* puts it. Marlowe's plays remained a powerful presence on the stage into the seventeenth century, and **Chapman**, in particular, carried forward the development of the aspiring heroic character for which his drama is renowned. Marlowe's contemporaries were unanimous: he was the Muses' darling, but his personal faults were clear – as the authors of *The Second Part of the Return from Parnassus* (1603) put it, 'Pity it is that wit so ill should dwell, / Wit lent from heaven, but vices sent from hell.' Today Marlowe's apparent sexual, political and religious nonconformities, and the supposed 'subversiveness' of his work, are made prominent in critical accounts, but the fact of his plays' publication in itself may suggest it is 'reasonable to consider him, even if somewhat unorthodox, as well within the spectrum of opinion that authority "allowed"' (Dutton 1993: 27).

Marlowe's distinctive style was perceived thus by Joseph Hall in his *Virgidemiarum* (1597):

One higher pitch'd doth set his soaring thought
On crowned kings that Fortune hath low brought:
Or some upreared, high-aspiring swaine
As it might be the Turkish *Tamberlaine.*
Then weeneth° he his base drink-drowned spright,°   *thinks; spirit*
Rapt to the threefold loft of heavens hight,
When he conceives upon his fained stage
The stalking steps of his great personage,
Graced with huf-cap° termes and thundring threats   *blustering*
That his poore hearers hayre quite upright sets. . . .
There if he can with termes Italianate,
Big-sounding sentences,° and words of state,   *aphorisms*
Faire patch me up his pure *Iambick* verse,
He ravishes the gazing Scaffolders°   *spectators in the gallery*
          (1598 text, I.3; ed. Davenport 1949: 14, glosses added)

Marlowe's 'mighty line', as **Jonson** called it in his sonnet to Shakespeare ('in its narrowest form a balanced line in which the first part plays against the last part either verbally or alliteratively and often in both ways', Baker 1967: 131), is the basis of Tamburlaine's famous lament over the dead Zenocrate. This may be directly echoed in Morocco's richly lyrical speeches in *The Merchant of Venice* (see (C), below).

          Blacke is the beauty of the brightest day,
          The golden balle of heavens eternal fire,
          That danc'd with glorie on the silver waves:
          Now wants the fewell that enflamde his beames
          And all with faintnesse and for foule disgrace,
          He bindes his temples with a frowning cloude,
          Ready to darken earth with endlesse night:
          Zenocrate that gave him light and life,
          Whose eies shot fire from their Ivory bowers,

And tempered every soule with lively heat,
Now by the malice of the angry Skies,
Whose jealousie admits no second Mate,
Drawes in the comfort of her latest breath
All dasled with the hellish mists of death.
Now walk the angels on the walles of heaven,
As Centinels to warne th' immortall soules,
To entertaine devine Zenocrate.
Apollo, Cynthia, and the ceaslesse lamps
That gently look'd upon this loathsome earth,
Shine downwards now no more, but deck the heavens
To entertaine divine Zenocrate.
The christall springs whose taste illuminates
Refined eies with an eternall sight,
Like tried silver runs through Paradice
To entertaine divine Zenocrate.
The Cherubins and holy Seraphins
That sing and play before the king of kings,
Use all their voices and their instruments
To entertaine divine Zenocrate.
And in this sweet and curious harmony,
The God that tunes this musicke to our soules:
Holds out his hand in highest majesty
To entertaine divine Zenocrate.
Then let some holy trance convay my thoughts,
Up to the pallace of th' imperiall heaven:
That this my life may be as short to me
As are the daies of sweet Zenocrate:
Phisitions, wil no phisicke do her good?
                    (1592 text; *2 Tamburlaine* 2.4.1–38)

(C) Marlowe's and Shakespeare's names are apparently linked as early as 1592, when their fellow playwright Robert **Greene** famously refers to Shakespeare as the 'upstart crow' in addressing the 'famous gracer of tragedians', presumed to be Marlowe. Their relationship has usually been seen in terms of a rivalry in the course of which they borrow from each other in turn. Henry VI's weakness is in contrast to Tamburlaine's will to power; *Edward II*, Marlowe's riposte to *Henry VI*, is indebted to *Richard III* (see Brooke 1961; Brooks 1968), but lacks the perspective of a whole nation's plight presented in Shakespeare's next play, *Richard II*. The plot of *Richard II*, in its turn, has many parallels with that of *Edward II*, but drastically reduces the homosexual elements. In a word, 'the two dramatists, contending with and reacting from each other, select their material to make contrasting effects' (Bradbrook 1980: 196). In this sense it can be agreed that in general Marlowe was 'hardly a source . . . rather a model' for Shakespeare (Charney 1997: 213).

But discussion of the relationship between Shakespeare and Marlowe has to contend with the special problem that Marlowe's own writing may actually be included within texts attributed to Shakespeare. The notion that they collaborated on *Henry VI*, in particular, is an old, though unproven one. The 'disintegrators' who believe Shakespeare was not the writer of the works assigned to him use either biographical clues or internal evidence on the characteristics of respective parts of the works themselves, and on both counts Marlowe has always been among the alternative authors proposed. The latest version of the latter kind of investigation is computational analysis, the more sophisticated examples of which (such as Merriam 1996) have hypothesized that many plays dated to the early years of Shakespeare's career, in particular *1–3 Henry VI*, *Titus Andronicus*, *Richard II* and *Richard III*, incorporate an unknown quantity of original writing by Marlowe – though there is no external evidence that the two playwrights ever collaborated. All this makes it extremely difficult to determine, for Shakespeare's plays up to 1593, whether similarities with Marlowe's work (generically or in terms of individual plays) represent normal echoes, parody, Marlowe's writing itself, Marlowe's writing revised by Shakespeare, or some combination.

Phoebe, in *As You Like It*, quotes Marlowe's *Hero and Leander* in apostrophizing the author of this pastoral poem as 'Dead shepherd', and in so doing makes Shakespeare's only definite reference to a contemporary poet (a less conclusive one occurs at 3.3.12):

> Dead shepherd, now find I thy saw of might:
> 'Who ever lov'd that lov'd not at first sight?'
> (3.5.80–1)

Hero and Leander is often assumed to have been a model for *Venus and Adonis* (for comparisons see Bradbrook 1980), but in fact there is no evidence to prove which was written first. There are, however, a number of certain quotations from Marlowe elsewhere in Shakespeare, for example *A Midsummer Night's Dream*, 1.1.170 (for a list of Marlowe echoes in this play see Brooks 1979: lxiv), and Pistol's parody of Tamburlaine's among other contemporary dramatic styles in *2 Henry IV* (compare *2 Tamburlaine* 4.3.1–2):

> Shall packhorses,
> And hollow pamper'd jades of Asia,
> Which cannot go but thirty mile a day,
> Compare with Caesars, and with Cannibals,
> And Troiant Greeks?
>
> (*2 Henry IV*, 2.4.154–8)

In the characters of Tamburlaine, the Guise (in *The Massacre at Paris*), and most famously Barabas (in *The Jew of Malta*), Marlowe established the theatrical Machiavel – 'ruthless and magnetic, self-delighting and self-destructive' (Ure 1971: 212). Such a figure is found, with whatever Marlovian colouring, in such Shakespearean creations as Richard III, Edmund and Iago, but perhaps the most Marlowesque example (if a distinction may be so made) is Aaron in *Titus Andronicus*. His opening soliloquy contains no specific echoes of Shakespeare's contemporary, but the manner is extremely close. To Brooke, it is 'impossible to hear this, and not think of Marlowe. Overall there is a sustained rhythmic splendour moving from hyperbole to hyperbole; but the relationship is patent also in every significant detail' (1961: 35):

> Now climbeth Tamora Olympus' top,
> Safe out of Fortune's shot, and sits aloft,
> Secure of thunder's crack or lightning flash,
> Advanc'd above pale envy's threat'ning reach . . .
> Then, Aaron, arm thy heart and fit thy thoughts
> To mount aloft with thy imperial mistress,
> And mount her pitch whom thou in triumph long
> Hast prisoner held, fett'red in amorous chains,
> And faster bound to Aaron's charming eyes
> Than is Prometheus tied to Caucasus.
> Away with slavish weeds and servile thoughts!
> I will be bright and shine in pearl and gold,
> To wait upon this new-made emperess.
>
> (2.1.1–4, 12–20)

Yet there are two apparently opposed ways of reading such similarities. We may see the superb assurance of these lines as showing that Marlowe 'pushed Shakespeare into a further degree of inventiveness' (Bradbrook 1980: 195), or we may read them as a kind of parody: 'Shakespeare is erupting in the Tamburlaine style as a form of parody. If Aaron begins in the style of Tamburlaine, it is only as a magnificent example of rhetorical display' (Charney 1997: 215). Perhaps these alternatives are only apparently in conflict. It may be that Shakespeare's recognition of the imaginative force of Marlowe's Machiavels goes with a moral rejection of them, leading to an equivocal presentation of their qualities in his own characters; this is what Brooke means by observing 'if this is to be called pastiche, it must be with the recognition that it is re-creation with original force' (1961: 36).

After Aaron, the closest character parallels are with Richard of Gloucester as developed in both *3 Henry VI* and *Richard III*. In fact, Margaret's ghost in the latter play describes him by echoing Barabas' 'We Jews can fawn like spaniels when we please, / And when we grin we bite' (*The Jew of Malta*, 2.3.20–1): 'O, Buckingham! take heed of yonder dog: / Look, when he fawns, he bites' (1.3.289–90). Richard's Marlovian vitality, unlike Aaron's, is 'always contained within the compass of his perversion', so that he 'never sets a healthy human instinct at odds with the moral scheme' and in the end the Marlowe-derived element is 'entirely new-created to Shakespeare's own purpose in a very different context'. In *Richard II*, similarly, the Marlovian mode of Mowbray and Bolingbroke's headstrong speeches in the first scene is not invoked 'in such a way as to disturb us: for the rhetoric is so decisively placed as blood-ruled . . . that it is felt almost as a parody (not comic of course) rather than echo' (Brooke 1961: 37–9). The play as a whole responds to *Edward II* in a manner that reveals 'dynamic tensions' between the two writers (Skura 1997: 41). Some such conclusion about Shakespeare's use of Marlowe in general is, in fact, widely felt though variously expressed: put at its simplest, 'what Shakespeare learned from Marlowe . . . was shown . . . in reaction' (Bradbrook 1980: 203). *Henry V*, a few years apart from the earlier histories, seems to show Shakespeare happy to write within rather than against the Marlovian historical mode (perhaps specifically within the framework of the 'Conqueror play' of which *Tamburlaine* was the leading examplar): common ingredients include the chorus and the episodes of unexpected cruelty.

Outside the Histories, Marlovian elements have been detected more occasionally. The largest-scale case is *The Merchant of Venice*. Shakespeare and Marlowe were the only two dramatists of their time to make a Jew the central figure of a play; their characters are by no means similar, but Shylock's language, and the use made of him to criticize Christian hypocrisy, is reminiscent of Barabas. *The Jew of Malta* is the source also for the atmosphere, though not the plot itself, of Jessica's rebellious relationship with Shylock, and an apparently deliberate invocation of Marlowe is involved in the surprisingly poetic qualities of the relatively minor characters Morocco and Arragon (Brooke 1961; see also Bradbrook 1980). The *Merchant* is perhaps Shakespeare's 'most Marlovian play', by virtue not of assimilation but of 'a subversion that works in both directions' (Shapiro 1998: 269).

Elsewhere in the Shakespeare corpus, the horse-stealing episode in *The Merry Wives of Windsor* has for long been associated with *Doctor Faustus* (see Smith 1992), and other snatches of Marlowe here include a quotation from his poem *The Passionate Shepherd* (see Shapiro 1991: 112–15). *Romeo and Juliet* is said to show the after-effects of *Hero and Leander* in a general way – in the elevation and assurance of Juliet's 'Gallop apace, you fiery-footed steeds' (3.2.1ff.), in Mercutio's bawdy wit, or, more modishly, in its distinctive way of converting 'Marlovian homosexuality into phallocentric male friendship charged with erotic overtones' in Mercutio's relationship with Romeo (Porter 1989: 138). Marlovian rhetoric seems to be given a negative function in *Julius Caesar*: it is used according to Brooke (1961: 42–3) 'to discriminate between the valid greatness assumed to be [Caesar's], and the vulgar egotism superficially indistinguishable from it', with 'the placing of Caesar's crazy ambition in the ascent of a Marlovian rhetorical mountain'. But by the time of *As You Like It*, at the latest, Marlowe's presence is so spectral that it is not clear whether Shakespeare's audience is meant to register it.

These scattered indications of Marlowe's continuing presence are often thought to be exhausted by the later phases of Shakespeare's career, though one exception is the reminiscences of *Dido, Queen of Carthage* in the tale of Troy as retold in *Hamlet* (2.2.440–2; see Black 1994, Shapiro 1991: 126–32). Brooke is categorical is stating that Shakespeare's 'later plays never . . . show any direct dependence' (1961: 44), and Shapiro sees no reason to demur, observing that his 'engagement with Marlowe appears to come to an end . . . around the turn of the century' (1991: 89). Naturally this has not prevented others from making their cases on later plays, though as yet these have tended not to allow for various kinds of coincidence. *Tamburlaine* has been offered as a shadow behind *Lear*, both in points of detail and in structural patterns, with the effect, among other things, of contributing to 'debate about the existence of God and of divine providence' and 'an anatomization of . . . desire' (Hopkins 1996: 113, 119). No less predictably, there have also been attempts to find *Faustus* in *Macbeth* (such as Nosworthy 1984).

(D) The literature on Marlowe–Shakespeare connections is large. Ure (1971) and at greater length Bradbrook (1980) provide brief overviews; Brooks (1968) gives a more substantial treatment of Marlowe in the early Shakespeare with special reference to traditional dramatic features and 'multiple influence' in conjunction with others. Much modern commentary is indebted to Brooke (1961). Shapiro's respected full-scale 1991 study deals with Shakespeare's impact on Marlowe as well as vice versa, and develops a unified argument about the development of Shakespeare's response over time. Cartelli (1991) is especially alert to matters of staging and stage history. Otherwise, much useful article-sized material has been published: titles below will identify work on each Shakespeare, or Marlowe, text.

Baker, Howard (1967). 'The Formation of the Heroic Medium', pp. 126–68 in Paul J. Alpers, ed., *Elizabethan Poetry: Modern Essays in Criticism*. Oxford (first published in Baker, *Induction to Tragedy*, 1939).

Battenhouse, Roy (1974). 'The Relation of Henry V to Tamburlaine.' *ShSu* 27: 71–80.

Black, James (1994). 'Hamlet Hears Marlowe, Shakespeare Reads Virgil.' *Renaissance and Reformation* 18.iv: 17–28.

Bradbrook, M. C. (1980). 'Shakespeare's Recollections of Marlowe', pp. 191–204 in Philip Edwards, Inga-Stina Ewbank and G. K. Hunter, eds, *Shakespeare's Styles: Essays in Honour of Kenneth Muir*. Cambridge.

Brooke, Nicholas (1961). 'Marlowe as Provocative Agent in Shakespeare's Early Plays.' *ShSu* 14: 34–44.

Brooks, Harold F., (1968). 'Marlowe and the Early Shakespeare', pp. 67–94 in Brian Morris, ed., *Christopher Marlowe*. London.

—— ed. (1979). *A Midsummer Night's Dream* (Arden Shakespeare). London.

Bullough, I, 454–7.

Cartelli, Thomas (1991). *Marlowe, Shakespeare and the Economy of Theatrical Experience*. Philadelphia, PA.

Charney, Maurice (1979). 'Jessica's Turquoise Ring and Abigail's Poisoned Porridge: Shakespeare and Marlowe as Rivals and Imitators.' *RenD* 10: 33–44.

—— (1994). 'Marlowe's *Edward II* as Model for Shakespeare's *Richard II*.' *Research Opportunities in Renaissance Drama* 33: 31–41.

—— (1997). 'The Voice of Marlowe's Tamburlaine in Early Shakespeare.' *CompD* 31: 213–23.

Clemen, Wolfgang (1972). 'Shakespeare and Marlowe', pp. 123–32 in Clifford Leech and J. M. R. Margeson, eds, *Shakespeare 1971*. Toronto.

Davenport, A., ed. (1949). *The Collected Poems of Joseph Hall, Bishop of Exeter and Norwich*. Liverpool.

Dutton, Richard (1993). 'Shakespeare and Marlowe: Censorship and Construction.' *YES* 23: 1–29.

Egan, Robert (1968). 'A Muse of Fire: *Henry V* in the Light of *Tamburlaine*.' *MLQ* 29: 15–28.

Fleissner, Robert F. (1990). 'Dr. Faustus as a Source for Hamlet.' *Literatur in Wissenschaft und Unterricht* 23: 68–71.

Garber, Marjorie (1979). 'Marlovian Vision / Shakespearean Revision.' *Research Opportunities in Renaissance Drama* 22: 3–7.

Hopkins, Lisa (1996). ' "Lear, Lear, Lear!" Marlowe, Shakespeare, and the Third.' *Upstart Crow* 16: 108–23.

MacIntyre, Jean (1986). '*Doctor Faustus* and the Later Shakespeare.' *CahiersE* 29: 27–37.

Marlowe, Christopher (1592). *Tamburlaine the Great*. London.

Merriam, T. V. N. (1993). 'Marlowe's Hand in *Edward III*.' *Literary and Linguistic Computing* 8: 59–72.

Merriam, Thomas (1996). 'Tamburlaine Stalks in *Henry VI*.' *Computers and the Humanities* 30: 267–80.

Nosworthy, James M. (1984). '*Macbeth, Doctor Faustus*, and the Juggling Fiends', pp. 208–22 in J. C. Gray, ed., *Mirror up to Shakespeare: Essays in Honour of G. R. Hibbard*. Toronto.

Porter, Joseph (1989). 'Marlowe, Shakespeare, and the Canonization of Heterodoxy.' *South Atlantic Quarterly* 88: 128–40.

Porter, Joseph (1989). *Shakespeare's Mercutio*. Chapel Hill.

Ross, A. Elizabeth (1996). 'Hand-Me-Down-Heroics: Shakespeare's Retrospective of Popular Elizabethan Heroical Drama in *Henry V*', pp. 171–203 in John W. Velz, ed., *Shakespeare's English Histories: A Quest for Form and Genre*. Binghamton.

Shapiro, James (1991). *Rival Playwrights: Marlowe, Jonson, Shakespeare*. New York.

—— (1998). '"Which is *The Merchant* here, and which *The Jew?*": Shakespeare and the Economics of Influence.' *ShSt* 20: 269–77.

Skura, Meredith (1997). 'Marlowe's *Edward II*: Penetrating Language in Shakespeare's *Richard II*.' *ShSu* 50: 41–55.

Smith, Robert A. H. (1992). '*Doctor Faustus* and *The Merry Wives of Windsor*.' *RES* 43: 395–7.

—— (1997). '*Julius Caesar* and *The Massacre at Paris*.' *N&Q* 242: 496–7.

Ure, Peter (1971). 'Shakespeare and the Drama of his Time', pp. 211–21 in Kenneth Muir and S. Schoenbaum, eds, *A New Companion to Shakespeare Studies*. Cambridge.

Marston, John (1576–1634), Poet and Playwright

(A) Marston's father was a prosperous lawyer, his mother the daughter of an Italian doctor. After Brasenose College, Oxford, Marston proceeded to the Middle Temple, but quickly discovered a preference for writing over the law. He cultivated a satirical bent in his first published works in 1599, *The Metamorphosis of Pigmalion's Image* and *The Scourge of Villainy*. These figured later that year on a list of thirteen satirical publications condemned as an affront to public decency and burned in the yard of the Stationers' Hall by the common hangman. Marston's career in the playhouse included spells as a writer for the Admiral's Men, the Boys of St Paul's and the Queen's Revels, in which company he owned a share. The core of his theatrical work is the sequence of plays *Antonio and Mellida* (1599 or 1600), *Antonio's Revenge* (1600 or 1601), *Jack Drum's Entertainment* (1600), *The Malcontent* (?1603) and *Sophonisba* (1606). He involved himself in a long-running battle with **Jonson**, which is referred to in his *Histriomastix* (1599), but during a later truce collaborated with **Jonson** and **Chapman** on *Eastward Ho!* (1605). In 1608 he was jailed on an unknown charge, and subsequently abandoned poetry and drama for the Church, taking orders in 1609.

(B) Marston was well known to contemporaries both as a playwright and a satirist. He is reckoned among 'the best for satire' (Francis Meres in *Palladis Tamia*, 1598), an English **Horace** (John Weever in *Epigrams*,

1599). His enemies also had their say: Crispinus vomiting words from *Histriomastix* in Jonson's *Poetaster* identifies his stylistic vice as linguistic dissipation. But he was clearly seen as a leading literary figure at the turn of the century, and beyond – **Camden**, in 1605, classes him with another dozen well-chosen names as the 'most pregnant wits of these our times, whom succeeding ages may justly admire' (*Remains Concerning Britain*). In a more extended description in the second part of the *Return from Parnassus* (first performed 1603), if the satirical overlay is subtracted, Marston's writing is characterized in terms of its directness and audacity:

> Tut what cares he for modest close couch termes,
> Cleanly to gird our looser libertines.
> Give him plaine naked words strippt from their shirts
> That might beseeme plaine dealing *Aretine*:
> I there is one that backes a paper steed
> And manageth a penknife gallantly.
> Strikes his poinado at a buttons breadth,
> Brings the great battering ram of tearmes to townes
> And at first volly of his Caunon shot,
> Batters the walles of the old fusty world.
>
> (Anon. 1606: sig. B2ᵛ)

(C) All the cases of Marston's possible influence on Shakespeare involve cross-fertilization between plays first staged very close to each other in time, and the respective arguments for such influence usually rely on contestable assumptions about their dates and order of appearance. However, the chronological proximity of the plays can also work to support hypotheses on influence in other ways. The bearing of Marston's *Antonio and Mellida* and its sequel, *Antonio's Revenge*, upon *Hamlet* is particularly problematic in such respects: the reconciliation of external and internal details (including textual cruxes, issues of revision and the possible use of common sources) which is required to establish even the possibility of Marston's influence on Shakespeare here takes considerable effort. Indeed, Felix Pryor (1992) treats the subject almost as detective work, while Harold Jenkins (1982: 7–13) attempts to demonstrate that *Hamlet* influenced *Antonio's Revenge* and not vice versa. Pryor, starting from the idea that Marston's writing for the Boys of St Paul's (and not Jonson's for the Boys of the Chapel Royal, as is usually assumed) was the object of Hamlet's remarks to the Players on the 'little eyases' (2.2.334), constructs a more ingenious than convincing case for the extensive impact of Marston on Shakespeare's play. This includes the claims, for example, that the Player's speech on Troy is a parody of Marston's manner, and that the famous crux about knowing 'a hawk from a handsaw' (2.2.175) is an allusion to the Marston family crest. Marston's strained and laboured follow-up, *Antonio's Revenge*, seems to draw among many other sources on the Ur-*Hamlet*, the lost pre-Shakespearean play sometimes attributed to **Kyd**, and this would explain most if not all of the apparent echoes in or of Shakespeare's *Hamlet*. But, depending on what view is adopted of the dating of each work, it may still be argued that Shakespeare was 'reacting strongly against the facile attitudes towards revenge found in Marston's play'; in particular, 'Antonio's idea of an avenger's obligation to evince extreme emotion could well be the source of such an obligation in the "rogue and peasant slave" soliloquy at the end of Act 2' (Edwards 1985: 7). The suggestion (as by Taylor 1986) that *The Malcontent* was also an influence on *Hamlet*, for the antic disposition, imagery and other features, is based on evidence which on current consensus datings of the two plays would normally be taken to suggest influence in the opposite direction.

Other than the complicated case of *Hamlet*, Marston has been proposed as one of Shakespeare's models in three other plays. In some cases, there is little more to be said than that resemblances exist, since there is insufficient data to draw further inferences. *Cymbeline* contains, unusually, a spoken rather than a sung dirge; so too do *The Spanish Tragedy* and *Antonio's Revenge* (see Hunter 1964). The Marston–Chapman–Jonson collaboration *Eastward Ho!* has some structural parallels with *King Lear* (Taylor 1982); a similarity has also been noted between an episode in *The Malcontent* and Gloucester's suicide attempt. And *The Malcontent* may have furnished a different kind of model for *Measure for Measure*. Together with **Middleton**'s *The Phoenix*, it is one of as few as two previous plays employing the 'disguised monarch' figure which enjoyed some popularity in a range of dramas produced from 1603–4 onwards. Marston's disguised Malevole, like Shakespeare's Duke, foils the intended villainies and preserves the intended victims. Pendleton (1987) assembles some other likenesses between the plays in 'small matters of language, theme, and situation', together with theatrical links between Shakespeare and Marston's play via the King's Men, but these are not enough to clinch the matter. The main similarity is itself of unclear significance: for one thing, Shakespeare had already used a disguised monarch himself – albeit in a different way – in *Henry V*.

Finally, persistent suggestions of a link between Marston and Jacques have been made over the years (summed up by Latham 1975: xlviii–li, with references to which Fink 1935 should be added). The claim that Malevole is the prototype of Shakespeare's figure has to contend with the difficulty that both the plays and the characters are in most ways completely different. The idea that Jacques is in part a version of Marston himself can be made to seem somewhat more plausible through various kinds of links to Marston's work and reputation.

(D)

Anon. (1606). *The Returne from Pernassus: or the Scourge of Simony* [Part 2]. London.

Edwards, Philip, ed. (1985). *Hamlet, Prince of Denmark* (New Cambridge Shakespeare). Cambridge.

Fink, Z. S. (1935). 'Jacques and the Malcontent Traveller.' *PQ* 14: 237–52.

Hunter, G. K. (1964). 'The Spoken Dirge in Kyd, Marston and Shakespeare: A Background to "Cymbeline".' *N&Q* 209: 146–7.

Jenkins, Harold, ed. (1982). *Hamlet* (Arden Shakespeare). London.

Latham, Agnes, ed. (1975). *As You Like It* (Arden Shakespeare). London.

Pendleton, Thomas A. (1987). 'Shakespeare's Disguised Duke Play: Middleton, Marston, and the Sources of *Measure for Measure*', pp. 79–98 in John W. Mahon and Thomas A. Pendleton, eds, *'Fanned and Winnowed Opinions': Shakespearean Essays Presented to Harold Jenkins*. London.

Pryor, Felix (1992). *The Mirror and the Globe: William Shakespeare, John Marston and the Writing of 'Hamlet'*. London.

Taylor, Gary (1982). 'A New Source and an Old Date for *King Lear*.' *RES* 33: 396–413.

Taylor, James (1986). '*Hamlet*'s Debt to Sixteenth-Century Satire.' *Forum for Modern Language Studies* 22: 374–84.

Masuccio, of Salerno (*c.* 1415–*c.* 1477), Italian Novelist

(A) Masuccio belonged to the noble Guardati family of Salerno, and became the earliest of the southern Italian *novellieri*. He was at some point secretary to Roberto di Sanseverino, and many of his stories were dedicated to prominent Neapolitans, so it is assumed he spent his life mainly in or near Naples. His *Novellino* or *Cinquante Novelle* (1476) is a skilfully written collection of a hundred stories, each separate and followed by the writer's comments. Many of the stories can be found in other forms in the work of earlier writers or in folklore. Luigi Pulci, the contemporary Italian epic poet, speaks of Masuccio as an imitator of **Boccaccio**. One of his principal themes, the vices of the clergy, is announced in the prologue, where he proclaims himself, more emphatically and more earnestly than his models or successors in the novella tradition, a *censor morum*. His often blunt realism is compounded by frequent references to actual persons, setting his work apart from the pure fiction of Boccaccio or **Fiorentino**.

(B) Masuccio's name was well known to Shakespeare's contemporaries. Some ten Italian editions had appeared by the end of the sixteenth century, and readers had largely to be content with these: *Il Novellino* was not, as far as can be established, available in English in Shakespeare's time. The first Elizabethan English rendering is a prose one of Novel 41, *c.* 1565 (Scott 1916: 113). One or two other individual tales were translated or adapted in the following years, such as the seventeenth novel, given (perhaps via a French version) both as 'The Doctor of Laws' in William **Painter**'s *Palace of Pleasure* (1566), and as 'The Dutch Courtesan' by John **Marston** (1604). But Masuccio's work is very little associated with the Elizabethan or Jacobean stage, and the first complete English translation belongs to the late nineteenth century.

(C) *Romeo and Juliet* and *The Merchant of Venice* are the Shakespeare texts which may have a connection with Masuccio, but in both cases it is tenuous, and has been made to seem more so by the traditional, though weakening, belief that Shakespeare could read no Italian (see here **Fiorentino** (Giovanni) and Shaheen 1994). The *Romeo and Juliet* story derives from folklore and romance material which was developed by a series of European writers of *novelle* in the fifteenth and sixteenth centuries, of which Masuccio seems to have been the first. His tale (Novel 29) of the clandestine romance and marriage of Mariotto Mignarelli and Giannozza Saraceni of Siena, with a bribed friar assisting at the nuptials, is substantially the story of *Romeo and Juliet*, but it ends with

Giannozza dying of grief in a convent after the beheading of her exiled husband, who has been apprehended while trying to open her tomb. The several other treatments of the story available to Shakespeare (see **Brooke**) leave no unique links between his work and Masuccio's. There is a discussion and bibliography of the relationship between the two texts in Jonas (1917).

Masuccio's Novel 14 concerns a youth from Messina who falls in love with the daughter of a miser from whom he borrows money. He robs the miser and elopes with the daughter. Comparison with *The Merchant of Venice* gives in the Italian tale: a young girl closely guarded by her father, a miser (but not a Jew); a young man who uses his female servant to persuade the girl to elope with him; her theft of her father's jewels and cash; their welcome by the lord of the country they elope to, who is a friend of the young man's. 'The character of the miser and his outcries at the loss of his money, jewels, and daughter also serve to bind this source to the main plot' (Satin 1966: 118). An English translation of this story is given in Satin (1966) and Bullough, I, 497–505, who holds that the elopement of Jessica 'came directly or indirectly' from Masuccio.

(D)

Bullough, I; Satin (1966).

Jonas, Maurice, ed. (1917). *The Thirty-Third Novel of Il Novellino . . . From Which is Probably Derived the Story of Romeo and Juliet*. London.

Scott, Mary Augusta (1916). *Elizabethan Translations from the Italian*. Boston, MA.

Shaheen, Naseeb (1994). 'Shakespeare's Knowledge of Italian.' *ShSu* 47: 161–9.

Middleton, Thomas (*c*. 1570–1627), Dramatist Middleton was responsible for one of the very few plays employing the 'disguised monarch' figure to predate *Measure for Measure*, his *The Phoenix* (1604).

Pendleton, Thomas A. (1987). 'Shakespeare's Disguised Duke Play: Middleton, Marston, and the Sources of *Measure for Measure*', pp. 79–98 in John W. Mahon and Thomas A. Pendleton, eds, *"Fanned and Winnowed Opinions": Shakespearean Essays Presented to Harold Jenkins*. London.

Miracle Plays See **Mystery Plays**.

Mirror for Magistrates, A

(A) As published in 1559, having been printed but suppressed for four years under the Marian regime, *A Mirror for Magistrates* was an anthology of nineteen first-person verse narratives called 'tragedies' or 'complaints'. In them the ghosts of certain eminent statesmen mainly belonging to the period of English history from Richard II onwards were imagined as describing the manner of their downfall to a group of listeners, the actual authors of the stories. The original contributors were William Baldwin (the editor, known as a philosopher, poet, printer and playwright), George Ferrers, Thomas Phaer, John Skelton and others (some unidentified). Almost all were of good birth, had positions at court, and were political moderates. It was hoped at this date that the series would be augmented, so as 'to searche and dyscourse oure whole storye [history] from the fyrst beginning of the inhabitynge of the yle' (ed. Campbell 1960: 70). The second edition of 1563 included seven more narratives and Thomas Sackville's famous *Induction* to his own contribution, the *Complaint of Buckingham*. There were seven editions by 1587, several edited by John Higgins, an antiquarian and classical scholar. Higgins added to the original collection in 1574 his *Firste Parte*, made up of a proem and sixteen long verse fables on the 'infortunate Princes' and heroes of early Britain, 'from the comming of Brute to the incarnation of our saviour', including the story of 'Leire' and 'Cordila' (ed. Campbell 1946: 30). For later editions he provided a further twenty-four fables, almost all on classical figures including Julius Caesar. Other writers, including Thomas Blenerhasset and Thomas Churchyard, added still more; about half the writers overall can be identified.

The *Mirror* was intended, and presented, as a sequel to **Lydgate**'s popular *Falls of Princes*, and for their materials the contributors drew principally on **Hall**'s Chronicle. The stories are for the most part ponderously didactic, aiming to demonstrate the mutability of the world and show magistrates and others in authority who may be possessed of any vice, 'as in a loking glas . . . howe the like hath bene punished in other heretofore' (ed. Campbell 1960: 65). Seventeenth-century editions up to the final one of 1610 added stories of virtue rewarded to the old ones of wickedness punished. The *Mirror* was also dedicated to the use of history 'to teach the political lessons which its authors reckoned most pertinent to the understanding of political events in their own day' (Campbell 1947: 109), and hence events which might be used to exemplify contemporary affairs were sometimes given prominence, and others omitted. Twentieth-century tastes have usually been antipathetic to the work's literary qualities, but more positive estimates are possible; Sackville's *Induction* is regularly singled out, and Tillyard (1944 and 1959) notes the aesthetic appeal of the stories' metrical variety.

(B) The popularity of the *Mirror* was long-lived as well as great, as witnessed by the number of editions and by Sir Philip **Sidney**'s inclusion of it in his most select list of English poems in the *Apology for Poetry*. It was imitated almost from the start, in the 1570s, in the form both of collections of historical 'tragic' narratives and poems written as single complaints. Both traditions were developed further in later decades, the former by such writers as Samuel **Daniel**, William Warner and Michael **Drayton**, the latter notably by Daniel in his *Complaint of Rosamond*, and subsequent followers (see Farnham 1956: 304–39). The *Mirror*'s procedure of drawing historical lessons for the present was first applied to dramatic work by one of its contributors, Sackville, whose *Gorboduc* (1565) expounds the danger to a kingdom when the succession is not clear. More than thirty historical plays of Shakespeare's time are on subjects covered in the *Mirror*, and 'certainly many of them were affected by [its] purposes and methods', including its principal novelty for work of its kind, first-person monologue (Campbell 1947: 111). But the dramatists' debt to the book is wider than this. It made an 'inspired discovery . . . that British history and legend were an almost inexhaustible well of tragical matter, waiting to be drawn upon'; and, together with its imitations, it 'taught the Elizabethan public that tragical moralizing had newly moving appeal when brought close home' in narratives of personal misfortune (Farnham 1956: 271). It also laid very strong emphasis on a central conception in tragedy, the clash between human designs and non-human agency (see Tillyard 1944: 76–9).

The story of *Cordila*, not definitely used by Shakespeare, belongs to Higgins' 1574 additions. It runs to 371 lines in which she is persuaded, in prison, to take her own life by a 'gryzely ghost' called Despair. Before these melodramatic events she calls to mind the past:

But while that I these joyes enjoyd, at home in *Fraunce*
My father *Leire* in *Britayne* waxed aged olde,
My sisters yet them selves the more aloft t'advaunce,
Thought well they might, be by his leave, or sans so bolde:
To take the realme and rule it as they wold.
They rose as rebels voyde of reason quite,
And they deprivde him of his crowne and right.

Then they agreed, it should be into partes equall
Devided: and my father threscore knightes and squires
Should alwayes have, attending on him still at cal.
But in six monthes so much encreasid hateful Ires,
That *Gonerell* denyde all his desires,
So halfe his garde she and her husband refte:
And scarce alowde the other halfe they lefte.

Eke as in *Scotlande* thus he lay lamenting fates,
When as his daughter so, sought all his utter spoyle:
The meaner upstarte gentiles, thought themselves his mates
And betters eke, see here an aged prince his foyle.
Then was he faine for succoure his, to toyle.
With all his knightes, to *Cornewall* there to lye:
In greatest nede, his *Raganes* love to trye.

And when he came to *Cornwall*, *Ragan* then with ioye,
Received him and eke her husbande did the lyke:
There he abode a yeare and livde without a noy,
But then they tooke, all his retinue from him quite
Save only ten, and shewde him dayly spite,
Which he bewailde complayning durst not strive,
Though in disdayne they laste alowde but five.

On this he deemde him, selfe was far that tyme unwyse,
When from his doughter *Gonerell* to *Ragan* hee:
Departed erste yet eache did him poore king despise,
Wherfore to *Scotlande* once againe with hir to bee
And bide he went: but beastly cruell shee,
Bereavde him of his servauntes all save one,
Bad him content him self with that or none.

Eke at what time he askte of eache to have his garde,
To garde his grace where so he walkte or wente:
They calde him doting foole and all his hestes debarde,
Demaunded if with life he could not be contente.
Then he to late his rigour did repente,
Gainst me and sayde, *Cordila* now adieu:
I finde the wordes thou toldste mee to to true.
        (1574 text, 120–60; ed. Campbell 1946: 150–2)

(C) Shakespeare is generally assumed to have known the *Mirror* well, and from an early date, partly *prima facie* on the grounds of its evidently wide and enthusiastic readership. He would have been 'just of an age to be subject to the popularity of the enlarged issues of the Mirror in 1574 and 1587' (Tillyard 1959: 13). Most tangibly, it is a source for plot and character details in his plays on British history, including *King Lear* and *Cymbeline*, with very occasional and minor echoes elsewhere (as in *Julius Caesar*: see Muir 1977: 121–2). It is often used in conjunction with **Holinshed** and other chroniclers, creating difficulties in determining which of several overlapping sources was primary. It has been observed that Shakespeare's combination in many of the Histories of the documentary sweep which distinguishes them from the Tragedies with an unusually compelling characterization of a principal figure corresponds to 'the broad viewpoint of the chronicles, on the one hand, and the individual focus of the *Mirror*, on the other' (Crane 1985: 298). On another level, the *Mirror*'s tendency to overlay its Christian homiletics with Virgilian and Senecan tropes, as in Sackville's *Induction*, may be important for Shakespeare's rapprochement between chronicle history and something resembling a classical tragic tenor in the Histories.

King John is sometimes thought of as an anthology of falls, like the *Mirror*, but no specific echoes are evident. In the Second Tetralogy, *1 Henry IV* may well show the influence of Thomas Phaer's 'tragedy' of Owen Glendower, for the figures of Glendower and Hotspur (Bullough, IV, 164–5), and the traitors' conspiracy in *Henry V* owes something to the story of Richard, Earl of Cambridge, in the *Mirror* (Bullough, IV, 357–8). More extensive material was available in the *Mirror* for *Richard II* and *Richard III*; many figures belonging to the period of both plays appear in the early editions, though not the first edition. For *Richard III* there are the complaints of Henry IV; George, Duke of Clarence; Edward IV; Sir Anthony Woodvile; Lord Rivers; Lord Hastings;

Henrie, Duke of Buckingham; Richard Plantagenet, Duke of Gloucester; and Shore's Wife. From these narratives Shakespeare did not take over the *Mirror*'s laboured moralizing but 'accepted the general contemporary notions of kingship which it embodies' and adopted its 'sense of moral retribution', this perhaps reinforcing his impressions from Hall (Bullough, III, 229–33). To these historically relevant sections may be added the *Induction* as a likely influence on Clarence's dream, and the complaint of *Claudius Tiberius Drusus* as a source in Richard's first accounts of his deformity (so Jones 1977: 217). For *Richard II* the relevant complaints were those of Thomas of Gloucester; Thomas Mowbray, the Earl of Norfolk; the Earl of Northumberland; and Richard himself. But here, despite a few possible verbal echoes, there is 'not enough to prove any reliance on the *Mirror*', which 'is more significant as showing that Shakespeare departed from a well-known view of Richard when he set over the King's follies a sympathetic analysis of his agony in defeat' (Bullough, III, 7).

The complicated transmission of the *Lear* story in many versions all deriving from **Geoffrey of Monmouth** includes several tellings known or perhaps known to Shakespeare, among them those of Geoffrey himself, **Camden**, **Spenser**, Holinshed, *Albion's England*, and, in the *Mirror*, the tragedy of Cordila in the 1574 and 1587 editions (see Perrett 1904, summarized in Muir 1972: xxxi–xxxiv, who also discusses the two editions). Among the distinctive features in Higgins' narrative used by Shakespeare are the progressive reduction in the number of Lear's knights (see (B)), references to the King of France and to Cordila's dowry, and the identities of Gonerell and Ragan's husbands. Other important elements such as the love-test are also found in the *Mirror* version, but not uniquely.

The *Mirror* had two versions of the Cymbeline story, given as the 'tragedies' of Guiderius, respectively by Thomas Blenerhasset and John Higgins, the latter following Geoffrey of Monmouth. The speeches in the council scene of *Cymbeline* 3.1 have been thought to recall ideas and scraps of phrasing from both writers; other possible echoes of these and related *Mirror* tragedies are found elsewhere in the play. All of these were expounded by Harold F. Brooks in Nosworthy (1976: 205–9), and are summarized in Bullough (VIII, 9) and Muir (1977: 261–2), but the verbal parallels, at least, are less striking than is generally admitted. The words 'did extort', 'tribute' and 'free' in 3.1.46–7, for example, seem to represent not so much Brooks' 'unmistakabl[e] echoes' as four words

340

not unlikely to occur together in any literary character's reference to the payment of a tribute.

(D) Campbell's 1946 and 1960 editions of the *Mirror* supply full textual history. Farnham (1956) and Tillyard (1944 and 1959) both provide analysis of the *Mirror*'s reputation and qualities. Bullough gives the fullest account of its impact on the Histories, with further consideration of *Richard II* by Hamilton (1983). Perrett (1904) is still useful, indeed exhaustive, on the many historical sources of *King Lear*, and Nosworthy's (1976) appendix on *Cymbeline*. Dubrow (1986) deals with Shakespeare's modifications to the 'complaint' genre as derived from the *Mirror* in *The Rape of Lucrece*.

Bullough, iii, iv, vii, viii; Jones (1977); Muir (1977); Tillyard (1944).

Campbell, Lily B., ed. (1946). *Parts Added to The Mirror for Magistrates by John Higgins and Thomas Blenerhasset*. Cambridge.

—— (1947). *Shakespeare's "Histories": Mirrors of Elizabethan Policy*. San Marino, CA.

—— ed. (1960). *The Mirror For Magistrates*. New York (first published 1938).

Crane, Mary Thomas (1985). 'The Shakespearean Tetralogy.' *ShQ* 36: 282–99.

Dubrow, Heather (1986). '"A Mirror for Complaints": Shakespeare's Lucrece and Generic Tradition', pp. 399–417 in Barbara Kiefer Lewalski, ed., *Renaissance Genres: Essays on Theory, History, and Interpretation*. Cambridge, MA.

Farnham, Willard (1956). *The Medieval Heritage of Elizabethan Tragedy*. Oxford.

Hamilton, Donna B. (1983). 'The State of Law in *Richard II*.' *ShQ* 34: 5–17.

Muir, Kenneth, ed. (1972). *King Lear* (Arden Shakespeare). London (first published 1952).

Nosworthy, J. M., ed. (1976). *Cymbeline* (Arden Shakespeare). London (first published 1955).

Perrett, Wilfrid (1904). *The Story of King Lear from Geoffrey of Monmouth to Shakespeare*. Berlin.

Tillyard, E. M. W. (1959). '*A Mirror for Magistrates* Revisited', pp. 1–16 in [Herbert Davis and Helen Gardner, eds,] *Elizabethan and Jacobean Studies Presented to Frank Percy Wilson*. Oxford.

Moffett (Moufet, Muffet), Thomas (1553–1604), Physician and Occasional Writer

Duncan-Jones disposes of the hypothesis that Moffett's poem *Of the Silkworms* (published 1599) might be a source for *A Midsummer Night's Dream*.

Duncan-Jones, Katherine (1981). 'Pyramus and Thisbe: Shakespeare's Debt to Moffett Cancelled.' *RES* 32: 296–301.

Monmouth, Geoffrey of See **Geoffrey of Monmouth**.

Montaigne, Michel Eyquem de (1533–1592), French Essayist

(A) Montaigne was born the third son of the Seigneur de Montaigne at the family château near Bordeaux. He was educated privately and at the Collège de Guyenne, noted for its early training of other distinguished figures, and where George **Buchanan**'s time as a tutor overlapped with his. He entered the magistrature by becoming a member of the Board of Excise, and in 1557 became a city counsellor in Bordeaux. In 1559–60 he spent some time at the court of Francis II. He married in 1565, and in 1568 succeeded to the family estates as the eldest surviving son, taking up residence at Château Montaigne as a country gentleman. He sold his seat in the Bordeaux Parliament, giving himself over to his study. Montaigne now began the *Essais* which created his reputation and which defined the term 'essay' by creating the form. But their form is less remarkable than their character, in which candid self-analysis and independent philosophical thought are married to an attentive interest in men and morals and in literature. He first exhibited his sceptical philosophical outlook in his *Apology for Raimond Sebond*, separately published in 1576 but eventually forming the longest of the *Essais*. The first two volumes of the collection were published in 1580, a third added in 1588, and the work eventually totalled 107 pieces of varying length. He toured Italy, Germany and Switzerland in 1580–1, returning to France on his unanimous election (against his wishes) as Mayor of Bordeaux, an office his father had held before him and which he occupied until 1585.

(B) The *Essais* were immediately popular in France, though not all readers showed the enthusiasm of Marie de Gournay, who fainted from excitement on first perusing them and became Montaigne's advocate and editor. In her 1595 edition (which included Montaigne's last revisions) she presented them as blows against the 'blind tyranny of custom', but most of her contemporaries preferred to see in them a familiar type of stoicism rather than a highly individual philosophical outlook. Hence the *Essais* were most usually regarded as a repository of orthodox wisdom, though religious writers such as Blaise Pascal began to attack their scepticism as anti-Christian in the seventeenth century.

In England, 'every phase of his broad philosophy struck some responsive note . . . The sane penetration of his scepticism was what her thinkers wanted' (Matthiesson 1931: 105). He was fortunate to have as his translator John **Florio** (*c.* 1553–1625), a lexicographer and translator now chiefly remembered for his version of the *Essais* of 1603 (revised 1613). Florio's rich Elizabethan English achieves good equivalence with Montaigne's liveliness of wit and metaphor. His work, introduced by a poem of Samuel **Daniel**'s praising Montaigne as one who 'Hath more adventur'd of his owne estate / Then ever man did of himselfe before', and (following Marie de Gournay) who attacked '*Custome*, the mightie tyrant of the earth' (Montaigne 1603: sig. ¶1ʳ), was widely read by English writers, including **Jonson**, **Marston** and Webster among the dramatists (see Villey 1917), and was reprinted up to 1632. But 1603 probably does not represent the earliest date at which Montaigne was available in English. Florio's translation was entered in the Stationers' Register in 1600, and may have been in progress from as early as 1598. Some other non-extant English translations may be referred to in a Stationers' Register entry of 1595 and in the essayist Sir William Cornwallis' reference to reading an English version in 1600.

A controversial signature, possibly Shakespeare's, is found in a British Library copy of Florio's volume (see Thompson 1917). The translation is illustrated here by the one passage certainly used by Shakespeare, from essay I.30, 'Of the Caniballes':

Al our endevours or wit, cannot so much as reach to represent the neast of the least birdlet, it's contexture, beautie, profit and use, no nor the webbe of a seelie spider. *All things* (saith *Plato*) *are produced, either by nature, by fortune, or by arte. The greatest and fairest by one or the other of the two first, the least and imperfect by the last.* Those nations seeme therefore so barbarous unto mee, because they have received very-little fashion from humane wit, and are yet neere their originall naturalitie. The lawes of nature do yet commaund them, which are but little bastard-ized by ours. And that with such puritie, as I am sometimes grieved the knowlege of it came no sooner to light, at what time ther were men, that better than we could have judged of-it. I am sorrie, *Lycurgus* and *Plato* had it not: for me seemeth that what in those nations wee see by experience, doth not onelie exceede all the pictures wherewith licentious Poesie hath prowdly imbellished the golden age, and al hir quaint inventions to faine a happy condition of man, but also the conception and desire of Philosophie. They could not imagine a genuitie so pure and simple, as we see it by experience; nor ever beleeve our societie might be maintained with so little arte and humane combination. It is a nation, would I answere *Plato*, that hath no kinde of traffike, no knowledge of Letters, no intelligence of numbers, no name of magistrate, nor of politicke superioritie; no use of service, of riches, or of poverty; no contracts, no successions, no dividences, no occupation but idle; no respect of kinred, but common, no apparrell but naturall, no manuring of lands, no use of wine, corne, or mettle. The very words that import lying, falshood, treason, dissimulation, covetousnes, envie, detraction, and pardon, were never heard-of amongst-them. How dissonant would hee finde his imaginary common-wealth from this perfection?

(Montaigne 1603: 102)

(C) Shakespeare and Montaigne very obviously share important inter-ests if not a complete cast of mind, and so their expressing the same sentiments is not evidence of a direct relationship. Shakespeare did not need to read Montaigne before he could write that 'there is nothing either good or bad but thinking makes it so' (*Hamlet* 2.2.29–30). Many claimed verbal echoes can be seen to be equally spurious given the possibilities of coincidence between two large *oeuvres* involving (in Florio's version) exactly contemporary English. For example, Taylor (1925: 17) adduces an observation in an otherwise unrelated context in Florio, 'it is the mindes priviledge to renew and recover it selfe on olde age', as a source for Troilus' imagining of a woman who will 'keep her constancy in plight and youth, / Outliving beauty's outward, with a mind / That doth renew swifter than blood decays!' (*Troilus and Cressida* 3.3.157–9). But the two shared words 'mind' and 'renew' are common ones, and the subject in each passage quite different. This is a mild example of the extravagances of certain commentators of the late

344

nineteenth and earlier twentieth century, who tended to discover Montaigne everywhere in Shakespeare.

A further danger in assessing Montaigne's importance for Shakespeare is that of ignoring the many collections of usually classical sayings (precepts, aphorisms, etc.) which both writers certainly used, and which would have allowed them to arrive independently at a large number of the correspondences noted between their work. One example of many given on this point by Harmon (1942) is the Duke's speech on death in *Measure for Measure*, often thought indebted to Montaigne, but in which the similarities are at least as likely to result from shared knowledge of classical aphorisms current as *loci communes*. Harmon's work requires some qualification: Shakespeare's acquaintance with classical writers quoted by Montaigne (and translated by Florio) may sometimes be a result specifically of the essayist's use of them, so that certain parallels between, for example, Shakespeare and **Seneca** or Lucretius may after all be an aspect of Montaigne's influence on the playwright. Further qualifications are suggested by Ellrodt (1975: 39–40).

The one certainty to emerge from many years of discussion of this subject has been that Florio's Montaigne is echoed in *The Tempest*. Gonzalo's description of his imaginary commonwealth shows a debt to the essay 'Of the Cannibals' ((B), above) which is accepted by even sceptical commentators:

> I' th' commonwealth I would by contraries
> Execute all things; for no kind of traffic
> Would I admit; no name of magistrate;
> Letters should not be known; riches, poverty,
> And use of service, none; contract, succession,
> Bourn, bound of land, tilth, vineyard, none;
> No use of metal, corn, or wine, or oil;
> No occupation; all men idle, all;
> And women too, but innocent and pure;
> No sovereignty –

SEBASTIAN   Yet he would be king on't.

ANTONIO   The latter end of his commonwealth forgets the
           beginning.

GONZALO   All things in common nature should produce
           Without sweat or endeavour. Treason, felony,

345

> Sword, pike, knife, gun, or need of any engine,
> Would I not have; but nature should bring forth,
> Of its own kind, all foison, all abundance,
> To feed my innocent people.
> SEBASTIAN No marrying 'mong his subjects?
> ANTONIO None, man; all idle; whores and knaves.
> GONZALO I would with such perfection govern, sir,
> T' excel the golden age.
>
> (2.1.141–62)

A further clear echo from Montaigne in Prospero's lines on 'the rarer action' (5.1.27), this time from essay II.11, 'Of Crueltie', has been identified more recently (Prosser 1965); other possible echoes in *The Tempest*, from essay III.5, 'Of Diverting and Diversions', are canvassed by Paster (1984).

Gonzalo's exposition on the commonwealth, taken together with the unimaginative but in the end not unintelligent scepticism of Antonio and Sebastian, involves a combination of engagement with and recoil from Montaigne which can be seen as indicative of a Shakespearean attitude, though it is also in part a reflection of drama's characteristic multivocality. G. F. Parker notes the slight dilution of Montaigne's radicalism in Gonzalo – the nakedness ('no apparell but naturall') has become 'innocence', and overall 'Montaigne's affirmation of a radical naturalness, of the sovereignty of our "puissant mother nature", cannot be so vigorously affirmed in Shakespeare; it has to be hedged a little by Gonzalo, and provokes in reaction a destructive, cynical voice altogether foreign to Montaigne.' He goes on to generalize with further examples from *Othello*, *Measure for Measure* and *Lear*: 'the Montaignean vision of radical naturalness, of unaccommodated man, both fascinates certain of Shakespeare's characters, and generates a kind of recoil' (Parker 1999: 3–5).

Outside *The Tempest*, Shakespeare's use of Montaigne as a direct source is a matter of speculation only. But the speculation has tended to concentrate on a small number of plays, especially in recent years. The Problem Plays (including *Hamlet*) have usually seemed most in keeping with the spirit of the *Essais*, as in Barbara Everett's characterization of *All's Well* (1970: 9): 'If France in this play is sometimes reminiscent of a feudal Waste Land, its *genius loci* (so to speak) is the great creator of an intensely modern sceptical self-consciousness, Shakespeare's contemporary Montaigne'. One explanation is that following the stimulus of Florio (perhaps somewhat before 1603 if the use of a manuscript text is posited), a sceptical exploration of the nature of the self reaches a peak; later, 'Shakespeare the tragedian had to part company with Montaigne', since 'the full tragic response calls for a heightened consciousness of identity – evident in Lear, Othello, or Macbeth – not for the kind of self-consciousness that may dissolve identity' (Ellrodt 1975: 49). Exploration of Montaigne's impact on the Problem Plays has taken the form of analysis of the confluence of Montaigne's and Shakespeare's thought (Deutschbein 1944–5; Reyher 1947; Ellrodt 1975; Knowles 1999), but also of formal and stylistic matters such as methods of characterization (Fricker 1951; Schmid 1945–6).

A large number of verbal echoes have also been claimed in one later play, *King Lear*, but many are of doubtful validity and significance. Salingar (1983, following especially Henderson 1939–40) finds echoes from essay II.8, 'Of the affection of fathers to their children', II.12, the 'Apologie of *Raymond Sebond*', and others, but downplays the likelihood that two writers discussing similar matters (for example, the procedures by which one can give one's goods away to one's children) will arrive at some of the same points, and use some of the same words, independently. Other claims for verbal echoes in this discussion are baseless – it is not likely Edgar's description to Gloucester of his forged letter as Edgar's 'essay or taste of my virtue' (1.1.44) carries Montaigne's meaning for 'essay' when both Folio and Quarto texts actually read 'assay' – though Salingar's suggestions as to similarity of thought do not stand or fall by this evidence. Muir's account (1972: 235–9) is more cautious on verbal similarities, despite which it concludes that Montaigne had 'a substantial influence on the thought of *King Lear*' (239) whereas Salingar suggests the borrowings 'are felt as marginal commentaries rather than essential to the action' (154). There is scope for further investigation.

(D) Taylor's (1925) notes and Tannenbaum's (1942: 37–46) bibliography list many earlier studies of the subject, most of them seriously outdated; for the period 1940–75 see Ellrodt's (1975) notes. Flygare's (1983) notably idiosyncratic volume offers a large table of the verbal parallels thitherto discovered between Montaigne and Shakespeare, keyed to an annotated bibliography of the discovers' work, as well as 'a Shaksperean Montaigne' and 'A Montaignean Shakspere', i.e. comprehensive sequences of excerpts from each writer accompanied by marginal references to the other. Taylor (1925) additionally offers appendices of words and phrases found in Florio/Montaigne and used by Shakespeare only after 1602, but these rely on sometimes antiquated assumptions about the chronology of the plays. One of the most widely ranging recent contributions, dealing with Montaigne less as a direct source than comparatively, is Parker (1999); like Salingar's single-play discussion (1983), this stresses the importance but also the ultimately limited nature of the affinities between the thought of the two writers. For a short account of Florio and his work as a translator see Matthiesson (1931).

Deutschbein, M. (1944–5). 'Shakespeares Hamlet und Montaigne.' *ShJ* 80–1: 70–107.

Ellrodt, Robert (1975). 'Self-Consciousness in Montaigne and Shakespeare.' *ShSu* 28: 37–50.

Everett, Barbara, ed. (1970). *All's Well that Ends Well* (New Penguin Shakespeare). Harmondsworth.

Flygare, William (1983). *Montaigne–Shakspere–Studies*. Kyoto.

Fricker, R. (1951). *Kontrast und Polarität in der Characterbildern Shakespeares*. Bern.

Harmon, Alice (1942). 'How Great was Shakespeare's Debt to Montaigne?' *PMLA* 57: 988–1008.

Henderson, W. B. Drayton (1939–40). 'Montaigne's *Apology of Raymond Sebond*, and *King Lear*.' *Shakespeare Association Bulletin* 14: 209–25 and 15: 40–54.

Hodgen, Margaret T. (1952). 'Montaigne and Shakespeare Again.' *HLQ* 16: 23–42.

Knowles, Ronald (1999). '*Hamlet* and Counter-Humanism.' *RenQ* 52: 1046–69.

Levin, Harry (1959). *The Question of Hamlet*. New York.

Matthiesson, F. O. (1931). *Translation: An Elizabethan Art*. Cambridge, MA.

Montaigne, Michel de (1603). *The Essayes or Morall, Politike and Millitarie Discourses . . . done into English by . . . John Florio*. London.

Muir, Kenneth, ed. (1972). *King Lear* (Arden Shakespeare). London.

Parker, G. F. (1999). 'Shakespeare's Argument with Montaigne.' *Cambridge Quarterly* 28: 1–18.

Paster, Gail Kern (1984). 'Montaigne, Dido, and *The Tempest*: "How Came That Widow In?"' *ShQ* 35: 91–4.

Prosser, Eleanor (1965). 'Shakespeare, Montaigne, and "the rarer action".' *ShSt* 1: 261–4.

Reyher, Paul (1947). *Essai sur les idées dans l'oeuvre de Shakespeare.* Paris.

Salinger, Leo (1983). '*King Lear*, Montaigne and Harsnett.' *Aligarh Journal of English Studies* 8.ii: 124–66.

Schmid, Eduard Eugen (1945–6). 'Shakespeare, Montaigne und die schauspielerische Formel.' *ShJ* 82–3: 103–35.

Tannenbaum, S. A. (1942). *Michel Eyquem de Montaigne: A Concise Bibliography.* New York.

Taylor, George Coffin (1925). *Shakspeare's Debt to Montaigne.* Oxford.

Thompson, E. Maunde (1917). 'Two Pretended Autographs of Shakespeare.' *The Library*, July: 193–217.

Villey, Pierre (1917). 'Montaigne et les poètes dramatiques anglais du temps de Shakespeare.' *Revue d'histoire littéraire de la France* 24: 357–93.

Montemayor, Jorge de (*c.* 1521–1561), Hispanic Novelist

(A) Born in Portugal, Montemayor settled in Spain after visiting Italy. Also a poet, singer and composer of music, he became famous throughout Europe for his romance *Diana Enamorada*, first published about 1559. In Italy he had witnessed the popularity of Sannazaro's *Arcadia*, and took from it his pastoral setting, numerous incidents and an overall emphasis on love. The chief innovation of Montemayor's seven-book work – written in Castilian – is structural: it is a continuous story with main plot and subplots, making up a much more intricate fabric than earlier romances tended to achieve. The principal narrative concerns Diana and Syrenus, a couple who part when Syrenus has to leave the kingdom; Diana marries another. The secondary narrative (occupying Book II with a continuation in Book VII) is the story of Felismena and Felix. The former disguises herself as a boy, becomes her lover's page and is employed by him to woo Celia. Celia falls in love with the disguised Felismena, but dies of chagrin on finding her feelings unreciprocated. Felix disappears but is later rescued from several knights by Felismena disguised as a shepherdess, and they are united. Several loose ends were left in the plot following Montemayor's premature death in 1561.

(B) The *Diana* became famous throughout western Europe: demand for its characters' elegant rusticity, complicated intrigues and amorous sensibility outstripped supply, and a highly successful continuation by Gaspard Gil Popo which tied up some of the incomplete strands was published in 1574. Calderon was an admirer of Montemayor's work, using some of the *Diana*'s interspersed poems and verse passages in his plays. **Cervantes** tried to emulate it in his novel *La Galatea* (1585), and it turns up in *Don Quixote* (1605–15), where, after its rescue (as the best exemplar of its genre) from the burning of the books, it is the inspiration for Quixote to turn from knight to shepherd (ii.67). Translations were widely attempted: into Latin; into French (by Nicholas Colin, 1578); and into English – English-speaking readers included **Sidney**, Drummond of Hawthornden, perhaps **Spenser** – by more than one writer. Barnaby Googe put a small portion into eclogue form in 1563, and an early sample of a translation by one Edward Paston (not eventually completed) is commended by Bartholomew Yong in the preface to his complete rendering, finished in 1583 and printed in 1598. Thomas Wilson had meanwhile produced a version of Book i, dedicating his work to the Earl of Southampton, but it was never printed or concluded. The most important source of the novel's fame and influence in sixteenth-century England was perhaps Sidney's then widely recognized use of it as a model in the *Arcadia*. Milton cited the two books together in describing village ballads as 'the Countrymans *Arcadia's* and his *Monte Mayors*' (*Areopagitica*). But although a new abridgement appeared as late as 1737, the *Diana*'s fame slowly declined along with the pastoral tradition in which it stands, and Yong's translation, which remained the sole complete English one, was never reprinted until the late twentieth century.

Yong (1560–1606), a London grocer's son and occasional poet, produced an expansive rendering, sometimes awkward but by no means pedestrian, before reaching the age of twenty-three. In this passage, Celia recounts the letter episode, corresponding to 1.2 of *The Two Gentlemen of Verona*:

> love (me thought) did put a certaine desire into my minde to see the letter, though modestie and shame forbad me to aske it of my maide, especially for the wordes, that had passed betweene us, as you have heard. And so I continued all that day untill night, in varietie of many thoughts. But when *Rosina* came to helpe me to bedde, God knowes how desirous I was to have her entreat me againe to take the letter, but she woulde never speake unto me about it, nor (as it

seemed) did so much as once thinke thereof . . . that (me thought) was the longest and most painfull night, that ever I passed. But when with a slower pace (then I desired) the wished day was come, the discreet and subtle *Rosina* came into my chamber to helpe me to make me readie, in dooing whereof, of purpose, she let the letter closely fall, which when I perceived, what is that that fell downe (said I,) let me see it. It is nothing, Mistresse, saide she. Come, come, let me see it (saide I) what, moove me not, or else tell me what it is. Good lord Mistresse (saide she) why will you see it: it is the letter I would have given you yesterday. Nay that it is not (saide I) wherefore shew it me, that I may see if you lie or no. I had no sooner said so, but she put it into my handes, saying: God never give me good, if it be anie other thing; and although I knewe it well indeede, yet I saide, what, this is not the same, for I know that well enough, but it is one of thy lovers letters, I will read it, to see in what neede he standeth of thy favour.

(1598 text; ed. Kennedy 1968: 84–5)

(C) In one form or another, Book ii of the *Diana* is an acknowledged source for *The Two Gentlemen of Verona*, but the range of possible forms is wide. Shakespeare may have known about the Court production of a lost play evidently based on Montemayor's Book ii which is mentioned in the Revels Accounts for 1585, *The Historie of Felix and Philomena*; but although this may have suggested to him the dramatic possibilities of the tale, it is for various reasons unlikely he drew on this particular version. The outline of the well-known narrative Montemayor was handling also underlies **Bandello**'s novel ii.36 and the play *Gl'Ingannati* (and its derivatives). Shakespeare does show awareness of some of these other versions, but it would seem that 'he depended most of all upon the prose story of Montemayor, probably because of the dramatic advance of the Spaniard over his predecessors and followers in handling a well-known story' (Harrison 1926: 252). For this, Shakespeare may have had access to a manuscript version of Yong's translation, to one of the other English renderings, or even to the original Spanish text. But Leech (1969) is 'almost certain' he knew Yong, and the evidence in Perry (1989) that he also used the Spanish is meagre.

For *The Two Gentlemen of Verona* Montemayor's tale suggested the Julia–Silvia–Proteus triangle, not only in outline but several of the incidents. Both writers include, for example, the episode in which the enamoured maid, urged by an innkeeper to listen to some brave music, hears her lover serenading her unknown rival, and before that Shakespeare's Julia plays a variant of Montemayor's scene (in (B)) over the letter. Perhaps the character of Lucetta 'borrows Rosina's lively repartee, her pert familiarity, and her knowledge of psychology' (Kennedy 1968: xliv). However, the *Diana* provides no Valentine figure and hence none of the conflict between love and friendship that Shakespeare shows; Felix is only a lustful and faithless aristocrat, Felismena by no means the tenderly pathetic figure Julia is; and the fact that Shakespeare's lady fails to fall in love with the page is the more surprising since she had done so in the Spanish tale.

Given that Shakespeare knew the Montemayor story as early as *The Two Gentlemen of Verona*, it is easy to believe that he recalled it in a fairly general way in some later plays, though the difficulty of proof makes somewhat tendentious Bullough's remark that for a time 'Montemayor's *Diana* became his text-book of amorous entanglements and sentiment' (I, 211). *As You Like It* and *Twelfth Night* seem plausible cases in point since they involve comparable structures of sexual relationships and boy/girl disguise. In fact, the effect of the *Diana* on **Lodge**'s *Rosalynde* is more pertinent to the former than the suggestions of direct influence that have been advanced now and again, but the latter actually reverts to the Montemayor plot element of having the lady fall for the page which had been suppressed in *The Two Gentlemen* – almost as though Shakespeare had deliberately saved it for a later occasion. A case is also mounted for Montemayor's Book I as the source for the main plot of *A Midsummer Night's Dream* by Kennedy (1968: xlvii), but the structural similarities are generic rather than precise. Many more modest types of parallel (listed by Brooks 1979: lxiv, n. 1) do suggest, however, that features of the *Diana* such as its emphasis on love, its mention of magical agency, and the presentation of an Amazon, though individually found in many other possible sources, may well be relevant to the play.

(D) The fullest treatment of Montemayor's reputation and influence in England is in the introduction to Kennedy (1968).

Bullough, I.

Brooks, Harold F., ed. (1979). *A Midsummer Night's Dream* (Arden Shakespeare). London.

Harrison, T. P., Jr (1926). 'Concerning *Two Gentlemen of Verona* and Montemayor's *Diana*.' *MLN* 41: 251–2.

Kennedy, Judith M., ed. (1968). *A Critical Edition of Yong's Translation of George of Montemayor's 'Diana' and Gil Polo's 'Enamoured Diana'*. Oxford.

Leech, Clifford, ed. (1969). *The Two Gentlemen of Verona* (Arden Shakespeare). London.

Perry, Thomas Amherst (1989). '*The Two Gentlemen of Verona* and the Spanish *Diana*.' *MP* 87: 73–6.

Shin, Woong-jae (1989). '*Two Gentlemen of Verona* and *Diana enamorada*: Shakespeare's Class-Oriented Modifications of His Sources.' *Journal of English Language and Literature* (Seoul) 35: 717–33.

Morality Tradition (including Interludes) See also **Chronicle History Plays**; **Mystery Plays**.

(A) Under this heading are included morality plays strictly speaking, and plays in the morality tradition down to the rise of the regular Elizabethan theatre. Definitions, and nomenclature, have always been problematic in this area; for convenience and completeness of reference a number of separable categories are here taken together:

1   Morality plays as such were in some ways a development of the Miracle or **Mystery Plays**, now no longer based on biblical stories but with characters representing abstract concepts (Chastity, Good Deeds, Everyman, etc.) in a vaguely contemporary setting. In one way or another the plot aimed at moral edification through allegory, usually involving a contest for the soul of a 'mankind' figure. The earliest extant example is *The Castle of Perseverance* of *c.* 1405, the best-known *Everyman* of *c.* 1500; but these plays were being written down to the 1520s and printed down to 1557.

2   By some accounts, the rise of the 'interlude', a short secular play exemplified by John Heywood's *Four PP*, occurs towards the end of the fifteenth century, and interludes continue to be written until the Elizabethan drama itself begins. 'Interludes' are lively and realistic farces which have freed themselves from allegorical abstraction. However, in so far as the term is used in the sixteenth century it refers to the most orthodox of moralities too; it is, in fact, applied indiscriminately to 'any kind of dramatic performance whatever' (Chambers 1903: ii, 183). In any case, the interludes 'owe a great

deal to the morality play in moral purpose, and in the characterization which depended upon this', and 'the moral doctrines of the Old Church and the New are the main subject matter of the interludes' (Happé 1972: 12–13). The term is now sometimes avoided as patronizing.

3   The didactic purpose of calling a sinner to repentance evolves into socio-political purposes via transitional works of the mid-sixteenth century by such writers as John Skelton, Henry Medwall, Sir David Lindsay, John Bale and Nicholas Udall (sometimes called 'political morality plays'). The central 'Humanum Genus' or 'Mankind' figure becomes an emblematic ruler and the ancillary characters take their places in a courtly setting. But the characters presented are still universalized figures, not historical or real ones – King Correction, Verity, Sedition.

4   The so-called 'historical moralities' or 'hybrid' plays (i.e. containing both classical and popular elements) of the 1560s deal with historical or legendary material. Among several other works of these years, 'it is in three "classical plays" of the 1560's that the morality stands closest to those popular tragedies which are immediately pre-Shakespearean' (Farnham 1956: 251): *Apius and Virginia*, by 'R.B.', *Horestes*, by John Pickering, and *Cambyses*, by Thomas Preston. Preston's characters in the most sophisticated of these works stand halfway between morality figures and historical actualities: Cambises was supposedly a historical king of Persia, but the stage figure inherits the representative function of the Mankind character. The play also offers a Vice figure (Ambidexter, who 'plays with both hands', doing both good and evil though always intending mischief). *Cambyses* is both a moral play and a tragedy of sorts, concluding with the rewards of sin for the protagonist.

Various kinds of lists and other details of these plays are given by Southern (1973) and Bevington (1962: 66–7, 265–78). The circumstances of their performance vary from public squares to schools, colleges, banqueting halls and court, but all were performed by itinerant players – 'minstrels' or later 'interluders'.

(B) Morality plays proper (type 1 in the above list) were still being performed in the late sixteenth century, but their popularity was rapidly fading. Many of their successors in the tradition, on the other hand, were still recent works: there are perhaps twenty-eight extant texts of plays in types 2–4 written in the period 1558–86, and a large number of others can be assumed to be lost (Potter 1975: 105–6).

The few recorded comments on these largely home-grown works, from such figures as **Puttenham**, **Sidney** and Whetstone, tend to be dismissive, but this is to be expected from writers concerned to promote the literature of classical antiquity. Practising dramatists were aware of, and did not disdain to use, the morality tradition. Internal evidence from plays contemporary with Shakespeare shows they could rely on their audience's familiarity with standard elements in the old-fashioned moralities of type 1, while older members of the late sixteenth-century audience, at least, would almost inevitably have had some experience of later types. Some of Shakespeare's contemporaries drew heavily on the moralities for their own dramatic idiom; **Marlowe**'s *Faustus* is the Elizabethan work most similar to a morality play proper.

As with English drama as a whole until the seventeenth century, plays in the morality tradition were not generally known through printed editions but performances. They tended to be printed either not at all (some remained in manuscript until twentieth-century printings) or only many years after they began to be staged. While there is every likelihood that Shakespeare witnessed performances of these plays by itinerant players in his youth, perhaps in the town of Coventry, near Stratford, he would have been very unusual for his time if he read them as well. This account of a performance given in the 1560s or 1570s, recorded by an exact contemporary of Shakespeare's, one R. Willis, in his old age in the 1630s, is thus perhaps more useful than a section of a play-text as an indication of how these works were experienced by most of their audience and by Shakespeare (the play Willis saw, *The Cradle of Security*, is now lost).

> In the city of *Gloucester* the manner is (as I think it is in other like corporations) that when Players of Enterludes come to towne, they first attend the Mayor to enforme him what noble-mans servants they are, and so to get licence for their publike playing; and if the Mayor like the Actors, or would shew respect to their Lord and Master, he appoints them to play their first play before himselfe and the Aldermen and Common Counsell of the city; and that is called the Mayors play, where every one that will comes in without money, the Mayor

giving the players a reward as hee thinks fit to shew respect unto them. At such a play, my father tooke me with him and made mee stand betweene his leggs, as he sate upon one of the benches where wee saw and heard very well. The play was called 'the Cradle of security,' wherin was personated a King or some great Prince with his Courtiers of severall kinds, amongst which three Ladies were in speciall grace with him; and they keeping him in delights and pleasures, drew him from his graver Counsellors, hearing of Sermons, and listning to good counsell, and admonitions, that in the end they got him to lye downe in a cradle upon the stage, where these three Ladies joyning in a sweet song rocked him asleepe, that he snorted againe, and in the meane time closely conveyed under the cloaths where withall he was covered, a vizard like a swines snout upon his face, with three wire chaines fastned thereunto, the other end whereof being holden severally by those three Ladies, who fell to singing againe, and then discovered his face, that the spectators might see how they had transformed him, going on with their singing, whilst all this was acting, there came forth of another doore at the farthest end of the stage, two old men, the one in blew with a Serjeant at Armes; his mace on his shoulder, the other in red with a drawn sword in his hand, and leaning with the other hand upon the others shoulder, and so they two went along in a soft pace round about by the skirt of the Stage, till at last they came to the Cradle, when all the court was in greatest jollity, and then the foremost old man with his Mace stroke a fearfull blow upon the Cradle; whereat all the Courtiers with the three Ladies and the vizard all vanished; and the desolate Prince starting up bare faced, and finding himselfe thus sent for to judgement, made a lamentable complaint of his miserable case, and so was carried away by wicked spirits. This Prince did personate in the morall, the wicked of the world; the three Ladies, Pride, Covetousnesse, and Luxury, the two old men, the end of the world, and the last judgement. This sight tooke such impression in me, that when I came towards mans estate, it was as fresh in my memory, as if I had seen it newly acted.

(Willis 1639: 110–14)

As a sample of such a play's content, an excerpt is given here from an early example, *Mankind*. In this episode the invisible Titivillus (a devil, 'the Fend of helle') prevents Mankind from carrying out his due labour and interrupts his devotions (Mankind's saying his prayers outside a church is a sign of yielding to temptation).

[*Exeunt all but* TITIVILLUS]

To speak with Mankind I will tarry here this tide,°	*time*
And assay his good purpose for to set aside.	
The good man Mercy shall no longer be his guide.	
I shall make him to dance another trace!°	*dance*
Ever I go invisible – it is my jet° –	*fashion*
And before his eye thus I will hang my net,	
To blench° his sight. I hope to have his	*deceive*
foot-met.°	*measure*
To irk him of his labour I shall make a frame:°	*device*
This board shall be hid under the earth, privily.°	*secretly*

[*Places a board in the earth*]

His spade shall enter, I hope, unreadily!°	*with difficulty*
By then° he hath assayed, he shall be very	*by the time that*
angry,	
And lose his patience, pain of shame.°	*for fear of shame*
I shall meng° his corn with drawk° and with	*mix; weed*
darnel;	
It shall not be like° to sow nor to sell.	*suitable*
Yonder he cometh! I pray of counsel.°	*please keep it secret*
He shall ween grace were wane.°	*think grace absent*

[*Enter* MANKIND *with a bag of grain.* TITIVILLUS *is invisible to him*]

MANKIND	Now, God, of his mercy, send us of his sand!°	*bounty*
	I have brought seed here to sow with my land.	
	While I over-delve° it, here it shall stand.	*dig over*

[*Puts the bag down and prepares to* dig. TITIVILLUS *steals it*]

In nomine Patris, et Filii, et Spiritus Sancti, now I will begin.

357

[The spade strikes against the board]

This land is so hard it maketh me unlusty and
      irk! °   *dull and sore*
I shall sow my corn at a venture, and let God work.

[Looks for the bag]

Alas, my corn is lost! Here is a foul work!
I see well, by tilling little shall I win.
Here I give up my spade for now and for ever!
Here TITIVILLUS *goeth out with the spade [which* MANKIND
    has thrown down]
To occupy my body I will not put me in dever;° *endeavour*
I will hear my evensong here, ere I dissever.°   *depart*
This place I assign as for my kirk.°   *church*

[Kneels and takes up his rosary]

Here, in my kirk, I kneel on my knees.
Pater noster, qui es in caelis . . .

[Enter TITIVILLUS]

TITIVULLUS   I promise you, I have no lead on my heels!   *[To audience]*
                 I am here again to make this fellow irk.
                       (525–56; ed. Lester 1981: 33–4, glosses added)

(C) Most of the relationships between Shakespeare's works and plays
in the morality tradition are of a general kind. For example, Othello is
often said to resemble the Humanum Genus figure in the moralities at
large, and the Vice figure is discerned in such characters as Aaron,
Falstaff, Richard III, Parolles and Iago (see Righter 1962; Spivack 1958;
Dessen 1986). There are also a number of more or less explicit allusions
to the morality tradition. Hal describes Falstaff as 'that reverend vice,
that grey iniquity, that father ruffian, that vanity in years' (*1 Henry IV*,
2.4.438–9), and earlier in the same scene Falstaff offers to speak 'in
King Cambyses' vein' (2.4.376) in reference to Thomas Preston's *Cam-*
byses – though in this case what Shakespeare parodies is more fustian
blank verse than Preston's style (see Craig 1966: 53). Many explicit

references in Shakespeare are assembled by Gatch, who sees them as specifically 'allusions to dramatic practice', 'intended to call up visual memories of the stage business of . . . moralities' that Shakespeare's older contemporaries could have seen (1928: 27).

The moralities, but no single morality play, seem in fact to lie somewhere behind many recurrent elements in Shakespearean drama, some major and some minor. The following non-exhaustive list is supplied by Potter (1975: 124; for additions see Dessen 1986: 134–60).

1   The moral prologue which outlines the whole of the play's action in advance (e.g. the prologues to *Romeo and Juliet* and *Pericles*).
2   The instruction of the hero by good counsel (e.g. Gaunt to Richard II, Polonius to Laertes).
3   The conspiracy of vice, disguising itself as virtue (e.g. Richard III and Buckingham, the Witches in *Macbeth*.
4   The initiation of the naive hero into experience (e.g. Brutus in *Julius Caesar*, Troilus in *Troilus and Cressida*).
5   Virtue unjustly cast out (e.g. Adam in *As You Like It*, the Soothsayer in *Julius Caesar*).
6   The delinquent hero's recognition of his state of sin (e.g. Antony in Egypt, Clarence's dream in *Richard III*).
7   The providential intervention of God's mercy (e.g. the rebirth of Hermione in *The Winter's Tale*, Portia in *The Merchant of Venice*).
8   The formal confession and repentance of the hero (e.g. Kate's recantation in *The Taming of the Shrew*, Richard II in the tower).
9   The unmasking and punishment of disguised vice (e.g. Malvolio in *Twelfth Night*, Iago's unmasking by Emilia).
10 The moralizing epilogue, implicating the audience (e.g. Feste in *Twelfth Night*, Prospero in *The Tempest*).

Potter suggests the difficulty of making firm connections by adding that these items are examples of 'otherwise inexplicable bits and pieces' of the Shakespeare plays, which some plainly are not. The fundamental difficulty in analysing such 'general' use of the morality tradition in Shakespeare is that postulations about it are based not on evidence but on our perception of comparable figures or patterns, which may very well not be the same as Shakespeare or his audience's perceptions.

Shakespeare's Histories are particularly rich in morality tradition elements. For *Richard III* Hammond lists Richard's Vice-like attributes at length: 'strange appearance, use of asides, discussion of plans with the audience, disguise, long avoidance, but ultimate suffering of punishment', and others (1981: 101). Spivack's discussion is the best-known; it concludes: 'for as long as the archaic role grips [Richard] he is compelled by its homiletic principle to display himself as the type of villainy' (1958: 403–4). This seems to say that for some (presumably the first half) of the play, Richard *is* a Vice; and few would accept this when put so reductively. Nevertheless, the interpretative possibilities of the association are many and various. Dessen, for example, shows how the 'two phased structure' of the play, with Richard's success collapsing after a peak in Act 3, can be seen as a traditional pattern that includes the arrest and punishment of the Vice (1986: 49ff.).

Henry IV (especially Part 1) offers probably the best-known and most contested example of a claimed morality framework which seems to affect interpretation radically. Just as Falstaff can be seen as a Vice figure (depending on how seriously we take apparent cues like Hal's description, above), Hal is said to be 'Every Prince', or in Dover Wilson's terms *Henry IV* has its archetype in the Prodigal Son play (like *Youth*, *c.* 1520) involving 'the tempter, the younker ['young gentleman'], and the father with property to bequeath and counsel to give' (Wilson 1943: 22). This approach has found favour, but its limitations, and its tendency to simplify the play, have been firmly pointed out by, for example, Somerset (1977) and Powell (1980: 61–2). Potter suggests that 'the tradition out of which *Henry IV, Part One* emerges seems not so much that of "youth" plays as of the political morality' (1975: 133–4). Dessen stresses other 'morality' patterns, such as the conflicts set in motion between the 'dual protagonists' Hal and Hotspur (1986: 66–90). It seems clear that both the likeness and unlikeness of *Henry IV* to a morality ought to be recognized, morality elements helping to make the play what it is but in the process being transcended; certainly all modern commentators are concerned to avoid 'yet another reductive treatment of Shakespeare's rich characters and images, a scholarly melt-down to some irreducible allegorical core' (Dessen 1986: 2).

Middle-period Shakespeare provides further cases of morality-influenced plays. The basic similarities of *Measure for Measure* and *Timon of Athens* to moralities in terms of framework and, to some degree, character types, are fairly self-evident. It has been argued that *Timon* specifically draws on *Magnyfycence* (Levitsky 1978). *All's Well that Ends Well* provides a more often discussed and perhaps more interesting example. This is largely because identifying Parolles (at some level) with the public Vice, and Bertram (at some level) as a Humanum Genus figure undergoing his development towards virtue, seems to solve the problems – for a psychologically realistic reading – of the hero's unlikeability and of his rapid conversion. Readings on these lines, such as Dessen's (1986), are not accepted by all, but many commentators agree that the morality pattern operates as background or 'blueprint' in *All's Well* (for example Tillyard 1965: 108–9). *Troilus and Cressida* as a whole is sometimes considered partly akin to the morality; according to Tillyard (1965: 52), one scene in particular, 3.2, sees Pandarus, Troilus and Cressida 'emerge from their own distinctive and dramatic characters to become types: Pandarus as the Bawd, Troilus as Fidelity in Love, Cressida as Falsehood in Love'.

Almost all Shakespeare's tragedies can be said to contain morality elements, but to what extent and effect is variously estimated, and connections are hard to demonstrate. For example, *Macbeth* has been seen as 'a morality play written in terms of Jacobean tragedy' (Farnham 1950: 79), but its protagonist's self-awareness is not matched in typical moralities, though Creeth (1976) finds it paralleled in *The Castle of Perseverance*. This and further correspondences, too loose or inconclusive to count as specific echoes but including for example Lear's humbling before the approach of death (see Jones 1971: 157–8), do help to stress the proximity of *Macbeth* and *Lear* – *Othello* is less convincing – to moralities more generally. Shakespeare's tragedies – unlike other Tudor plays, with exceptions such as *Doctor Faustus* – seem to recall these 'prototypes' in their 'universality of scope and . . . religious meaning', sharing their 'grandeur and moral seriousness' (Creeth 1976: 40). In such a play as *Lear* there are, of course, many stubbornly realistic and literal features which are irreducible to what is traditionally thought of as morality play modality: 'the bare outlines of the dramatic type have been overlaid and often obscured by the fullness of the plot and the intricacies of the relationship between the characters. The personifications of the medieaval play have grown into human beings as complicated and unpredictable as men and women usually are' (Campbell 1948: 108). On the other hand, morality play modality is not necessarily simple and uniform, since moralities themselves sometimes mix 'imitative forms and functions . . . with transmuted ritual' (Weimann 1978: 69), and there are a number of indubitable 'personifications', and other non-representational elements, in *Lear*. The best-recognized is the 'Pity in

361

the Stocks' emblem with Kent in 2.2 (see Riebanz 1974, and for other morality details Muir 1972: xxv–xxix). Herein lies a challenging area for criticism, in the region between the clearly non-morality overall effect and the morality elements and devices incorporated at a more local level. *Lear*'s presentation of questions about identity, about evil and retribution, penance and despair, all invite the question not of how far we should read the text as a morality play, but of 'how a morality play has been transformed into *King Lear*' (Potter 1975: 152; whose discussion goes on to offer one of the most convincing answers to the question to date).

Finally, in relation to Shakespeare's drama as a whole, there is a possibility of major structural influences from the morality tradition. Baldwin (1947) attends to the rise of the five-act structure in these dramatic predecessors of Shakespeare's. Weimann (1978) considers the dramaturgy of space (*platea* and *locus*). More specifically, basic morality structures may be discerned below a number of Shakespeare plays and parts of plays. Dessen (1986) on *Richard II* is noted above; for a different kind of example, the morality play dramatizes alternatives between virtue and vice by presenting 'alternating scenes of seriousness and riot that give dramatic point to a series of analogies or correspondences between radically opposed alternatives', and hence 'perhaps *1 Henry IV*'s greatest debt to the morality is to be found in its alternations between the serious plot of Henry IV and Hotspur . . . and the comic plot of Hal and Falstaff' (Bevington 1987: 26).

(D) On the earlier drama itself, Southern (1973) is the most comprehensive factual guide. The widest general study of the influence of the morality tradition is Potter (1975), but this also includes excellent treatment of *Henry IV* and *Lear* (with an excursion on the play within the play of *Hamlet*). Spivack (1958) and Schell (1983) both concentrate on the tradition more than on Shakespeare, Spivack on the Vice, Schell confining his Shakespearean analysis to *Richard II* and *Lear*. Bevington (1962) deals authoritatively with the tradition and with Shakespeare's contemporaries but only incidentally with Shakespeare himself. Dessen's (1986) subtle study is especially concerned with the Histories and *All's Well*, and with the more oblique ways in which the morality tradition bears on Shakespeare's work.

Among accounts of individual plays, a main point of departure for modern work on *Richard II* here is Rossiter (1961), just as most studies of *Henry IV* and the morality start from Dover Wilson (1943). Later material on the latter play by Boughner (1954), Spivack (1957) and Levin (1977) is notable. For *All's Well*, standard are Tillyard (1965), Bradbrook (1950), G. K. Hunter (1959) and R. G. Hunter (1965), with Godshalk (1974) offering a contrary reading; for *Timon*, see Walker (1979) and Levitsky (1978). Scragg (1968) deals with Iago, the most-canvassed morality element in *Othello*. Campbell's (1948) well-known article on *Lear* treats the play as 'a morality . . . upon which has been grafted a view of the unwise man of stoic morality', and Schell (1983) argues for substantial influence on the play from the moralities.

Bullough; Muir (1977).

Baldwin, T. W. (1947). *Shakspere's Five-Act Structure: Shakspere's Early Plays on the Background of Renaissance Theories of Five-Act Structure from 1470.* Urbana, IL.

Bass, Eben (1963). 'Falstaff and the Succession.' *College English* 24: 502–6.

Bergeron, David (1967). '"Timon of Athens" and Morality Drama.' *College Language Association Journal* 10: 181–8.

Bevington, David M. (1962). *From 'Mankind' to Marlowe: Growth of Structure in the Popular Drama of Tudor England.* Cambridge, MA.

—— ed. (1987). *Henry IV, Part I* (Oxford Shakespeare). Oxford.

Boughner, Daniel C. (1954). 'Vice, Braggart, and Falstaff.' *Anglia* 72: 35–61.

Bradbrook, M. C. (1950). 'Virtue is the True Nobility: A Study of the Structure of *All's Well That Ends Well.*' *RES* 1: 289–301.

Campbell, Oscar James (1948). 'The Salvation of Lear.' *ELH* 15: 93–109.

Chambers, E. K. (1903). *The Medieval Stage*, 2 vols. Oxford.

Craig, T. W. (1966). 'The Tudor Interlude and Later Elizabethan Drama', pp. 37–57 in John Russell Brown and Bernard Harris, eds., *Elizabethan Theatre* (Stratford-upon-Avon Studies, 9). London.

Creeth, Edmund (1976). *Mankynde in Shakespeare.* Athens, GA.

Dessen, Alan C. (1978). 'Homilies and Anomalies: The Legacy of the Morality Play to the Age of Shakespeare.' *ShSt* 11: 243–58.

—— (1986). *Shakespeare and the Late Moral Plays.* Lincoln, NE.

Eccles, Mark, ed. (1969). *The Macro Plays: The Castle of Perseverance, Wisdom, Mankind.* Oxford.

Farnham, Willard (1950). *Shakespeare's Tragic Frontier.* Berkeley.

—— (1956). *The Medieval Heritage of Elizabethan Tragedy.* Oxford.

Farnham, Willard (1971). *The Shakespearean Grotesque: Its Genesis and Transformations*. Oxford.

Gatch, Katherine Haynes (1928). 'Shakespeare's Allusions to the Older Drama.' *PQ* 7: 27–44.

Godshalk, W. L. (1974). '*All's Well That Ends Well* and the Morality Play.' *ShQ* 25: 61–70.

Grantley, Darryll (1986). '*The Winter's Tale* and Early Religious Drama.' *CompD* 20: 17–37.

Hammond, Antony, ed. (1981). *Richard III* (Arden Shakespeare). London.

Happé, Peter, ed. (1972). *Tudor Interludes*. Harmondsworth.

Hunter, G. K., ed. (1959). *All's Well That Ends Well* (Arden Shakespeare). London (first published 1959).

Hunter, Robert Grams (1965). *Shakespeare and the Comedy of Forgiveness*. London.

Jones, Emrys (1971). *Scenic Form in Shakespeare*. Oxford.

Lancashire, Anne (1970). '*Timon of Athens*: Shakespeare's *Dr. Faustus*.' *ShQ* 21: 35–44.

Lester, G. A., ed. (1981). *Three Late Medieval Morality Plays: Mankind, Everyman, Mundus et Infans*. London.

Levin, Lawrence L. (1977). 'Hotspur, Falstaff, and the Emblems of Wrath in *1 Henry IV*.' *ShSt* 10: 43–65.

Levitsky, Ruth (1978). '*Timon*: Shakespeare's *Magnyfycence* and an Embryonic *Lear*.' *ShSt* 11: 107–22.

Mack, Maynard (1965). *King Lear in Our Time*. Berkeley.

Muir, Kenneth, ed. (1972). *King Lear* (Arden Shakespeare). London.

Potter, Robert (1975). *The English Morality Play: Origins, History and Influence of a Dramatic Tradition*. London.

Powell, Raymond (1980). *Shakespeare and the Critics' Debate: A Guide for Students*. London.

Ribner, Irving (1960). *Patterns in Shakespearean Tragedy*. London.

Riebanz, John (1974). 'Theatrical Emblems in *King Lear*', pp. 39–51 in Rosalie Colie and F. T. Flahiff, eds, '*Some Facets of King Lear*': *Essays in Prismatic Criticism*. Toronto.

Righter, Anne (1962). *Shakespeare and the Idea of the Play*. Cambridge.

Rossiter, A. P. (1961). *Angel with Horns: Fifteen Lectures on Shakespeare*. London.

Schell, Edgar (1983). *Strangers and Pilgrims: From 'The Castle of Perseverance' to 'King Lear'*. Chicago.

Scragg, Leah (1968). 'Iago – Vice or Devil?' *ShSu* 21: 53–65.

Shirley, John W. (1938). 'Falstaff, an Elizabethan Glutton.' *PQ* 17: 271–87.

Somerset, J. A. B. (1977). 'Falstaff, the Prince, and the Pattern of "2 Henry IV".' *ShSu* 30: 35–45.

Southern, Richard (1973). *The Staging of Plays before Shakespeare*. London.

Spivack, Bernard (1957). 'Falstaff and the Psychomachia.' *ShQ* 8: 449–59.

—— (1958). *Shakespeare and the Allegory of Evil: A History of a Metaphor in Relation to his Major Villains*. New York.

Tillyard, E. M. W. (1965). *Shakespeare's Problem Plays*. Harmondsworth (first published 1950).

Velz, John W. (1981–2). 'From Jerusalem to Damascus: Biblical Dramaturgy in Medieval and Shakespearean Conversion Plays.' *CompD* 15: 311–26.

Walker, Lewis (1979). '*Timon of Athens* and the Morality Tradition.' *ShSt* 12: 159–78.

Weimann, Robert, ed. Robert Schwartz (1978). *Shakespeare and the Popular Tradition in the Theater: Studies in the Social Dimension of Dramatic Form and Function*. Baltimore.

Whitaker, Virgil (1965). *The Mirror up to Nature*. San Marino, CA.

Wickham, Glynne (1959). *Early English Stages, 1300 to 1660*, 3 vols: Vol. 1. London.

W[illis], R. (1639). *Mount Tabor. Or Private Exercises of a Penitent Sinner*. London.

Wilson, J. Dover (1943). *The Fortunes of Falstaff*. Cambridge.

More, Sir Thomas (1478–1535), Writer and Statesman

(A) Born the son of a Justice of the King's Bench in London, the young More was sent to live as a page in the Lambeth household of Archbishop John Morton, who discerned his talents and advised his starting at Oxford at the age of sixteen. In his twenties More coupled with a successful career in the law friendships with such leading lights of humanism as **Erasmus** (his senior by seventeen years), John Colet and William Lily. He became a Member of Parliament at the age of twenty-four, then Undersheriff of London, and in 1518 Privy Councillor to Henry VIII. From this point he rose quickly at Court, ultimately following Wolsey as Lord Chancellor in 1529. After conflicts over the King's legitimacy as sole head of the Church he resigned this office in

1532 and retired, subsequently engaging in disputes over the emerging doctrines of Protestantism. Refusing to impugn the pope's authority in religious matters or to support Henry's divorce from Katherine of Aragon, he was indicted for treason and executed in 1535.

More was an internationally renowned scholar and a prolific writer. His *Utopia* (1516) is only his best-known work, part of a generically diverse range of writings mainly in Latin, amounting so far to fifteen volumes in the ongoing modern edition, including biography, tracts, treatises, apologiae, a large collection of letters and another of epigrams, poems in Latin and English, and his *Dialogue of Comfort against Tribulation*, composed during his imprisonment in the last fourteen months of his life. He was canonized in 1935.

(B) More's posthumous position in the cultural life of the later sixteenth century was unique. His problematic status as a Catholic martyr in Protestant Tudor England was one complicating factor. His life story was suppressed in the histories of **Hall** and **Foxe**, and a planned biography by William Rastell was aborted with the early death of Mary I, but, outside the authorized media, tales of his wit and wisdom flourished. As well as the interest attaching to his life – also the subject of the play *Sir Thomas More* (which Shakespeare is believed to have been partly responsible for revising in the Jacobean period) – much fascination and influence was exercised by his writings. The 1551 English translation of the *Utopia* was often reprinted, the *Dialogue of Comfort* was issued for the first time in 1553, and More's complete English works were first collected in 1557. The unfinished *History of King Richard III* (1514–18; the title is not More's), written in slightly differing English and Latin forms, the only work of More's used as a source by Shakespeare, was first published, garbled and corrupted, in its English variant by **Grafton** as part of his addition to **Hardyng**'s Chronicle in 1543. It was then incorporated, still with certain inaccuracies, in Hall's Chronicle of 1548. A superior text of the English version was published by William Rastell, More's nephew, in his 1557 *Works* of More; and the Latin version was printed in a later (1565) edition of More's works (a full textual history is given in Sylvester 1963: xvii–lix). In later decades More's *History* was incorporated into the chronicles of **Holinshed** (who modified Hall's text by reference to Rastell's edition) and **Stow**.

The *History of King Richard III* was clearly well known and highly regarded within a short time after its first publication (for uses of it as an example in rhetorical works see Donno 1982: 442–3). In the sense that it sealed the reputation of its protagonist – it is a work of propaganda, not an impartial study – it was one of the most influential books of its era. The eventual effect of More's innovative approach to historical writing in this relatively short narrative would also be difficult to over-state, though its precocity made it slow to be assimilated: 'Homely, aphoristic, jocular, alive with delicate and moving strokes of character, this was a remarkable book by a remarkable man, and in an aesthetic sense it was too special to have any immediate effect on the writing of history' (Reese 1961: 46). But Roger Ascham clearly saw More's importance, writing in 1553:

> Syr *Thomas More* in that pamphlet of *Richard* the thyrd, doth in most part I beleve of all these pointes so content all men, as if the rest of our story of England were so done, we might well compare with *France*, *Italy*, or *Germany* in that behalfe.
>
> (ed. Wright 1904: 126)

Ascham explains the reasons why an approach like More's is so effect-ive: it records not only deeds but the causes they result from; it provides 'for every issue' a 'generall lesson of wisedome and warines, for lyke matters in time to come'; it gives 'lively' description not only of the protagonists' physical appearance 'but also ... the inward disposition of the mynde' (ed. Wright 1904: 126). More's *History* was also an incitement to more than one playwright to compose 'dramatically rather than anecdotally ... to get close to [More]'s matter and to treat it primarily as human happenings and only secondarily as a repertory of morals or a mere series of events' (Tillyard 1944: 40). Nevertheless, the style blends classical formality with the informal realism – Hunter (1989) and Jones (1977) note influences from **Tacitus** and **Suetonius**, and Donno (1982) would have it a formal *vituperatio*.

The episode of the stage-managed request to Richard to assume the throne, corresponding to Shakespeare's 3.7, is given here in the Hall version of More's text. The passage is part of the most compelling section of More's *History*, covering Richard's acquisition of the crown, and it illustrates especially clearly how 'the magnificent tension of More's prose in the *History* arises from ... dramatized conflicts between public show and private perception. Irony is everywhere and our sense of danger is only heightened by our growing awareness that we ought to

367

be able to laugh at Richard even as we shudder at his calculated crimes'
(Sylvester 1976: xviii).

> the protectoure made greate difficulte to come doune to theim,
> excepte he knewe some parte of their errande, as thoughe he
> doubted and partely mistrusted the commynge of suche a numbre to
> hym so sodainely, without any warnyng or knowlege, whether they
> came for good or harme. Then when the duke had shewed this too
> the Mayre and other, that thei mighte there by se how litle the protec-
> tour loked for this matter, they sente again by the messenger such
> lovynge message, and there with so humbly besoughte hym to vouch-
> safe that thei mighte resorte to his presence to purpose their entent of
> wich thei woulde to none other persone any parte disclose. At the last
> he came out of his chambre, and yet not doune to theim, but in a
> galary over theim with a bishop on every hande of hym, where thei
> beneth might se hym and speke to hym, as thoughe he woulde not yet
> come nere them til he wist what they meante. And there upon, the
> duke of Buckyngham firste made humble peticion to hym on the
> behalfe of theim all, that his grace woulde pardon theim and licence
> them to purpose unto his grace the entent of their commyng without
> his displeasure, without whiche pardon obteined, they durst not bee
> so bold to move hym of that matter. In whiche, albeit they meante as
> muche honoure to his grace as wealth to all the realme beside, yet
> were thei not sure how his grace would take it, whom they would in
> no wise offende. Then the protectour, as he was verie gentle of hym
> selfe and also longed sore apparantly to know what they meante, gave
> hym leave to purpose what hym liked, verely trustynge for the good
> minde that he bare them all, none of theim any thyng woulde
> entende to hym warde, wherewith he thought to bee greved. When
> the duke had this leave and pardon to speake, then wexed he bolde to
> shewe hym their entente and purpose, with all the causes movyng
> theim thereto, as ye before have harde. And finally, to beseche his
> grace that it would like hym of his accustomed goodnesse and zeale
> unto the realme now with his yie of pitie to beholde the long con-
> tinued distresse and decaie of the same, and to set his gracious hande
> to the redresse and amendemente therof by takynge upon hym the
> croune and governaunce of the realme accordyng to his right and
> title laufully discended unto hym . . .
> When the protector had harde the proposicion, he loked very

strangely therat and made answere, that albeit he knewe partely the thynges by theim alleged to bee true, yet suche entiere love he bare to kynge Edward and his children, and so muche more regarded his honour in other realmes aboute, then the croun of any one, of whiche he was never desyrous, so that he could not finde in his harte in this poinct to incline to their desire, for in al other nacions where the truth were not wel knowen, it shoulde paraventure bee thoughte that it were his awne ambicious mynde and devise to depose the prince and to take hym selfe the croune, with which infamy he would in no wise have his honour steined for any croune, in which he had ever perchaunce perceyved muche more labour and pein, then pleasure to hym that so would use it as he that would not and were not worthy to have it. Notwithstandyng, he not onely pardoned them of the mocion that they made hym, but also thanked them for the love and harty favoure they bare hym . . .

Upon this answer geven, the duke of Buckyngham . . . shewed aloude unto the protectour, for a finall conclusion that the realme was apointed that kynge Edwarde his line should no longer reigne upon them

(Hall 1548: 'The pitifull life of kyng Edward the .v.', fos 23ʳ–24ʳ)

(C) Shakespeare is known to have read Hall, whose text is also the source of More's material for later chroniclers such as Holinshed. Shakespeare used both Hall and Holinshed for *Richard III* (see Begg 1935). There is no evidence that he knew the markedly different version of More's narrative in the 1557 *Works*. More is acknowledged in the margin of the 1548 Hall volume as responsible for the Life of Edward V and 'some parte of kinge Richard the .iii.' (it is in fact the greater part).

Shakespeare's extensive use of More's accounts of both Edward V's and Richard III's reigns for narrative ingredients is only the most basic, and not necessarily the most faithful way in which Shakespeare follows More. Nor is it consistent: though Act 3 is close to the *History*, Act 1 is largely fictional, Act 2 allows only a subordinate role for Richard, and Act 4 veers away from the chronicles in giving the female characters more prominence. And the final three scenes of the play derive from Hall exclusively, since More's narrative ends with Buckingham's flight; this can be seen as decisive for Richard's presentation in that the vibrant figure More delineates is replaced after this point by 'the shadow of Hall's heavy didacticism, with the once hasty and reckless king paralyzed by depression' (Candido 1987: 141). Equally, Shakespeare omits material More had included.

Nevertheless, until Act 5 Shakespeare is in important respects 'true to the tone of the book: his emphases are More's, though they are modified by the technique of dramatization' (Hammond 1981: 74). Centrally, Shakespeare presents a witty villain in ironic terms, as More had been the first within the tradition of historical writing on this figure to do. (Shakespeare's exaggeration of some of these emphases, by adding further and greater villainies, for example, is consistent with a conception of history as general truth rather than individual fact, though the play shows some awareness that individual facts matter.) Jones suggests Shakespeare's presentation of a histrionic, role-playing Richard may even have derived quite specifically from the episode of the staged usurpation given in (B), above, meaning that the sequence of scenes culminating in 3.7, 'so like a play within a play in that its chief speakers perform before a stage audience, was the original nucleus of *Richard III*' (1977: 215). On this point a short passage from 3.7 may be sufficient for comparison with the More/Hall version in (B):

> *Enter* GLOUCESTER *aloft, between two Bishops.*
> CATESBY *returns.*

MAYOR	See where his Grace stands 'tween two clergymen!
BUCKINGHAM	Two props of virtue for a Christian prince,
	To stay him from the fall of vanity;
	And, see, a book of prayer in his hand,
	True ornaments to know a holy man.
	Famous Plantagenet, most gracious Prince,
	Lend favourable ear to our requests,
	And pardon us the interruption
	Of thy devotion and right Christian zeal.
GLOUCESTER	My lord, there needs no such apology:
	I do beseech your Grace to pardon me,
	Who, earnest in the service of my God,
	Deferr'd the visitation of my friends.
	But, leaving this, what is your Grace's pleasure?
BUCKINGHAM	Even that, I hope, which pleaseth God above,
	And all good men of this ungovern'd isle.
GLOUCESTER	I do suspect I have done some offence

> That seems disgracious in the city's eye,
> And that you come to reprehend my ignorance.
> BUCKINGHAM   You have, my lord. Would it might please your Grace,
> On our entreaties, to amend your fault!
> GLOUCESTER   Else wherefore breathe I in a Christian land?
> BUCKINGHAM   Know then, it is your fault that you resign
> The supreme seat, the throne majestical,
> The scept'red office of your ancestors,
> Your state of fortune and your due of birth,
> The lineal glory of your royal house,
> To the corruption of a blemish'd stock;
>
> (3.7.95–122)

At all events, the quasi-Senecan scenario of manipulative villain surrounded by victims is already in place for More's reader, who

> could find that everything in Richard's reign happened as it did because of the kind of person Richard was. His will, or rather his obsession, his manipulative drive, undiverted by social loyalties to brother, mother, wife, benefactor, comrade-in-arms, can be shown directing the passive world around him to the ends he alone foresees. All the others . . . are cajoled, bribed, terrified, deceived, magnetized into compliance.
>
> (Hunter 1989: 21)

Shakespeare probably draws from More the strong sense of how it feels to be Richard's victim in his treatment of Hastings (perhaps the germ of the ideas elaborated in 1.2 and 1.4). And many of Richard's remarks and asides seem to embody in 'internalized' form the irony and sarcasm of More's comments. Concomitantly, Shakespeare seems to respond to 'the artful, sometimes devious, manipulation of language for it[s] affective value'; 'to Richard's reliance on verbal skills to achieve his ends, Shakespeare adds echo, recapitulation, and prophecy, thus intensifying the concern with language that runs throughout the play' (Donno 1982: 43–4).

(D) Begg (1935) lists definite uses of Hall/More in *Richard III*. Donno (1982) and Anderson (1984) outline modern views on the nature and circumstances of More's *History*. Hammond (1981) has a full review of the facts of its relationship with Shakespeare's play, but the text of the Hall version given in his appendix is error-prone.

Jones (1977), 211–18; Tillyard (1944).

Anderson, Judith H. (1984). *Biographical Truth: The Representation of Historical Persons in Tudor–Stuart Writing*. New Haven (Chs 6–7 on More and Shakespeare's *Richard III*).

Begg, Edleen (1935). 'Shakespeare's Debt to Hall and Holinshed in *Richard III.' SP* 32: 189–96.

Berkowitz, Steven (1986). '"Men Were Deceivers Ever" (*Much Ado* 2.3.63): Buchanan's Baptistes, Shakespeare's Richard III and the Uses of Deception from More to Shakespeare', pp. 39–53 in *A Collection of Papers Presented in the First National Conference of English and American Literature*. Taichung, Taiwan.

Campbell, Lily B. (1947). *Shakespeare's 'Histories': Mirrors of Elizabethan Policy*. San Marino, CA.

Candido, Joseph (1987). 'Thomas More, The Tudor Chronicles, and Shakespeare's Altered Richard.' *ES* 68: 137–41.

Donno, Elizabeth Story (1982). 'Thomas More and *Richard III*.' *RenQ* 35: 401–47.

Hall, Edward (1548). *The Union of the Two Noble and Illustre Famelies of Lancastre and Yorke*. London.

Hammond, Antony, ed. (1981). *King Richard III* (Arden Shakespeare). London.

Hanham, Alison (1975). *Richard III and his Early Historians*. Oxford.

Hunter, G. K. (1989). 'Truth and Art in History Plays.' *ShSu* 42: 15–24.

More, Sir Thomas (1557). *The Works of Sir Thomas More Knyght . . . Wrytten by him in the Englysh Tongue*. London.

Reese, M. M. (1961). *The Cease of Majesty: A Study of Shakespeare's History Plays*. London.

Sylvester, Richard S., ed. (1963). *The Yale Edition of the Complete Works of St. Thomas More*, Vol. 2: *The History of King Richard III*. New Haven.

—— ed. (1976). *St. Thomas More: The History of King Richard III and Selections from the English and Latin Poems*. New Haven (version of previous item 'for the general reader').

Wright, William Aldis, ed. (1904). *The English Works of Roger Ascham: Toxophilus, Report of the Affaires and State of Germany, The Scholemaster*. Cambridge.

Mosse, Miles (*fl.* 1580–1614), Divine Mosse's treatise *The Arraignment and Conviction of Usurie* (1595) offers two references to the biblical episode debated by Antonio and Shylock, one of them in its preface.

Holmer, Joan Ozark (1985). ' "When Jacob Graz'd His Uncle Laban's Sheep": A New Source for *The Merchant of Venice.' ShQ* 36: 64–5.

Munday (Mundy), Anthony (*c.* 1560–1633), Poet and Playwright
(A) Munday was the son of a London stationer, a published poet at the age of seventeen, and elsewhere in his earlier years an apprentice printer, apparently a child actor, and a spy. In the early 1580s he was employed in government service in the detection and prosecution of recusants, infiltrating the English college at Rome, and taking a prominent part in the capture and trials of the Jesuits who followed the Catholic martyr Edmund Campion to England. As a reward for these services, it is supposed, he was given a Court office as 'messenger of the Queen's Chamber' in 1584. His career as a dramatist began in the mid-1580s, and from 1594 to 1602 he wrote for Henslowe and the Admiral's Company. Late in the 1590s he seems to have been touring with Pembroke's Men. During the latter part of his life he is said to have become a tradesman, but he was still writing pageants for the Lord Mayor at least as late as 1623.

Munday tried his hand at every popular literary genre. He was responsible for some eighteen plays, many now lost. Several were very successful, including the part-authored *Sir Thomas More* and a two-part play on John Oldcastle which was published in 1600 with Shakespeare's name on the title page (but which is now assigned to Munday and three others). He also wrote numerous ballads and songs, an imitation of *A Mirror for Magistrates*, and translations of romances, and was responsible for re-editing his friend **Stow**'s *Survey of London*. His work is today considered to fall short of distinction, much of it considerably so. His play *John a Kent and John a Cumber* is one of very few manuscript plays of the period which survive in the hand of their author.

(B) Few individuals contributed more to popular entertainment in his time, and Munday was an extremely well-known figure among his

373

contemporaries. Francis Meres described him in 1598 as one of 'the best for comedy' and 'our best plotter' (probably meaning 'provider of scenarios for development'). Webbe's *Discourse of English Poetry* (1586) praises his lyrics as in an 'exquisite vaine', and **Marston**'s comedy *Histriomastix* (1599) introduces him as 'great in plotting new plays that are old ones, and uses no luxury or blandishment, but plenty of old England's mother-words'. In Marston's play Munday is given employment by the strolling players in preference to **Jonson**: the two were rivals, and Jonson ridiculed Munday for dullness and lack of originality from the time of his earliest dramatic work, *The Case is Altered* (1599).

(C) There are probably coincidental affinities with works by Munday in *Much Ado about Nothing*, *As You Like It*, *The Winter's Tale*, *The Tempest* and elsewhere. In the first case, *Fedele and Fortunio* (1585), a play adapting Luigi Pasqualigo's *Il Fedele* (1579) which is tentatively attributed to Munday, is 'just possibl[y]' the source of the comical arrests by Dogberry and Verges in Act 5, but 'the parallel is very distant' (Bullough, II, 70) and often discounted altogether (as by Prouty 1950). Munday and Chettle's two-part play on Robin Hood of 1598, *The Downfall and the Death of Robert, Earl of Huntington, Otherwise called Robin Hoode of Merrie Sherwodde*, has possible echoes in the pastoral element of *As You Like It*. The faint connections (especially in suggestions of a theme of resurrection) between *The Winter's Tale* and some of Munday's civic pageants of the early seventeenth century are, as Bergeron (1973, 1978) himself largely concedes while drawing attention to them, at least as likely to indicate Shakespeare's influence on Munday as the converse. Munday's play *John a Kent and John a Cumber* is given as an analogue to *The Tempest* (for Ariel) by Bullough (VIII, 259), but *The Tempest* has also been connected with Munday's translation of an anonymous Spanish romance, *Primaleon, Prince of Greece*, as *Primaleon*, published 1595–1619. Schmidgall (1986) offers seventeen parallels, but most flow naturally enough from the shared premise of people shipwrecked on an island ruled by a benevolent magician, and the date of publication (1619) of the parts supposed to have affected Shakespeare's play means, as Schmidgall concedes, that Shakespeare would need to have read Munday's translation before it was printed.

Further miscellaneous points of contact with Shakespeare are easily hypothesized: Shapiro (1961) even discusses what Shakespeare might have learned from now lost history plays which Munday may have written in the 1580s and 1590s. But Munday is rather more securely linked with two further Shakespeare works. *The Merchant of Venice* offers close local parallels with Munday's story of a (non-Jewish) money-lender, *Zelauto, or The Fountaine of Fame* (1580), notably in Shakespeare's courtroom scene (see Bullough, I, 452–3; epitome of text in Brown 1961: 156–68) and perhaps for the Jessica-Lorenzo plot. Much the most extensive Munday material in Shakespeare, however, is (probably) to be found in *A Midsummer Night's Dream*, which has large 'situational' over-laps with Munday's *John a Kent and John a Cumber*. This, one of Munday's better dramatic efforts, is a comedy about a forced double wedding involving two nobles (and their respective partners), who engage the services of the folk-magician John a Kent, while their parents pit another magician, John a Cumber, against him. The dating of the text is crucial to the Shakespearean connection: though taken in the past to belong to the mid-1590s, the play is now with some reservations thought to date from 1589–90, in which case the direction of influence must run from Munday to the *Dream* (for the dating see Brooks 1979: lxvi). Shakespeare may either have seen a performance or read a manu-script. Munday's play supplied the following elements (listing adapted from the extensive discussion in Coghill 1964: 52):

1   Lovers in flight from parental opposition to their love.
2   Moonlit woods through which they flee to join their lovers.
3   A mischievous fairy imp, in service to a magician.
4   Clowns who organize buffoonish entertainment in honour of their territorial overlord on the occasion of a double wedding; contention for the leading part; malapropisms.
5   Young men led by an invisible voice until they fall exhausted.
6   A 'happy ending' with lovers correctly paired and wedded.

These elements 'make up a dramatic vehicle, a *schema*' (Coghill 1964: 52), on current showing 'the nearest thing, in fact, to the comprehensive source which beyond this the *Dream* does not have' (Brooks 1979: lxv). Further evidence of the connection lies in three verbal echoes identified by Brooks (1979: lxv–lxvi); Shapiro (1961: 28–9) speculates about more general similarities.

(D)
Bergeron, David M. (1973). 'Shakespeare and Munday Again.' *ANQ* 12: 28–32.

Bergeron, David M. (1978). 'The Restoration of Hermione in *The Winter's Tale*', pp. 125–33 in Carol McGinnis Kay and Henry E. Jacobs, eds, *Shakespeare's Romances Reconsidered*. Lincoln, NE.

Brooks, Harold F., ed. (1979). *A Midsummer Night's Dream* (Arden Shakespeare). London.

Brown, John Russell, ed. (1961). *The Merchant of Venice* (Arden Shakespeare). London (first published 1955).

Bullough, VIII.

Coghill, Nevill (1964). *Shakespeare's Professional Skills*. Cambridge.

Collier, J. Payne, ed. (1851). *John a Kent and John a Cumber; A Comedy, by Anthony Munday . . . With Other Tracts by the Same Author*. London.

Prouty, Charles Tyler (1950). *The Sources of Much Ado About Nothing: A Critical Study, Together with the Text of Peter Beverley's Ariodanto and Ieneura*. New Haven.

Schmidgall, Gary (1986). '*The Tempest* and *Primaleon*: A New Source.' *ShQ* 37: 423–39.

Shapiro, I. A. (1961). 'Shakespeare and Mundy.' *ShSu* 14: 25–33.

Mush, John (*fl.* 1601), Catholic Controversialist A 1601/2 pamphlet by Mush which formed part of the Archpriest Controversy shows some anticipations of *Measure for Measure* in discussions of ethics, doctrine and attitudes to priests.

Kaula, David (1970). 'Measure for Measure and John Mush's Dialogue.' *ShSt* 6: 185–95.

Mystery Plays See also **Morality Tradition**.

(A) The mystery plays (or, often synonymously for English authorities, 'miracle plays'), the principal form of drama in medieval Europe, had their origins in the ceremonies and festivals of the Church, but from the thirteenth century they began to be disjoined from the liturgy and to pass out of ecclesiastical control. In their golden age from the mid-fourteenth century to the early sixteenth, performances were mounted in England by the craft guilds, and in continental Europe by fraternities of laymen. There are four surviving English cycles: the Chester, York, Coventry, and Towneley or Wakefield cycles. These are linked series of plays each traditionally performed as a group in a particular town or its locality, in the open air, often over several days, on the occasion of a festival such as Corpus Christi or Whitsun. Each traces the history of the world according to the Scriptures from the Creation to the Last Judgement, including some obligatory and some optional episodes but in all cases with a full narrative of the life of Christ, and particular elaboration of the Passion sequence. Mystery plays are always anonymous, and with some exceptions show few signs of individual authorship: their cross-influences and borrowings reflect an international tradition.

(B) The mystery tradition was moribund in the second half of the sixteenth century, and no new plays were written. But there are well-attested performances of the old ones throughout the period. For example, parts of the Coventry cycle were performed at Kenilworth, near Stratford, in 1575, and in Coventry itself still later; others were given at York at least as late as 1579, Newcastle 1589, and Chester 1600. But the Reformation frowned on the mystery plays, and they faded away during the rise of the regular English theatre (talk of 'suppression' may exaggerate the matter, but see Ingram 1982 and Gardiner 1967). Suspicions of popish tendencies in the texts are attested by the preparation of notes, still extant, on aspects of the York cycle touching on doctrinal matters by Archbishop Grindal for Elizabeth I.

One of the traditional elements in the Passion section of the cycles was the tormenting of Christ by his accusers. The play *Coliphizacio* ('The Buffeting [of Christ]') in the Wakefield group is wholly given over to this subject. The following excerpt, in which the writer's sophistication is indicated by the metrical virtuosity alone, consists of the longest speech in it, made by Caiphas to Jesus.

Hear'st thou, harlot, of all?° Of care may thou sing!   *Do you hear every-*
                                                          thing, rascal?
How durst thou thee call either emperor or king?
I do fie° the!   *say fie to*
What the devil dost thou here?
Thy deeds will do° thee dear.   *cost*
Come near and roun° in mine ear,   *whisper*
Or I shall ascry° the.   *denounce*

Illa-hail was thou° born! Hark, says he ought again? *it's bad luck you were*
Thou shall once ere° to-morn to speak be full fain.   *sometime before*
This is a great scorn and a false train;°   *trick*

Now wolf's-head and outhorn on thee be ta'en,°   *may you be hunted like*
                                                                        an outlaw
Vile faitour!°   *impostor*
One word might thou speak ethe,°   *easily*
Yet might it do thee some leath;°   *ease*
Et omnis qui tacet
Hic consentire videtur.°   *And all those who remain silent consent to this*

Speak on one word, right in the devil's name!
Where was thy sire at board° when he met with thy dame?   *living*
What, neither booted nor spurred, and a lord of name?
Speak on in a turd, the devil give thee shame,
Sir Sybré!°   [*mocking the obscurity of Christ's birth(?)*]
Perdé, if thou were a king,
Yet might thou be riding.
Fie on thee, foundling!°   *bastard*
Thou lives but by brib'ry.°   *you live only by theft*

Lad, I am a prelate, a lord in degree:
Sits in mine estate, as thou may see,
Knights on me to wait in diverse degree.
I might thole thee abate,° and kneel on thy knee   *allow you to humble*
                                                                           yourself
In my presence.
As ever sing I mass,
Whoso keeps the law, I guess,
He gets more by purchase
Than by his free rent.

The devil give thee shame that ever I knew thee!
Neither blind nor lame will none pursue° thee.   *persecute*
Therefore I shall thee name – that ever shall rue thee –
King Coppin° in our game; thus shall I endue° thee   *Coxcomb(?); invest*
For a fatour.°   *impostor*
Say, dare thou not speak for fear?
I shrew him thee lered!°   *I curse him that taught you*
Weme!° the devil's dirt in thy beard,   [*expression of impatience*]
Vile false traitor!
                (128–71; modernized from Cawley 1958: 81–2, glosses added)

(C) Much of what he knew of the mystery plays must have come down to Shakespeare through the **Morality Tradition**, but there are some signs of a more direct awareness of them, most conspicuously in the form of allusions to mystery play material. Henry V's threats to the citizens of Harfleur, for example, are likely to be more strongly related to the old plays than the **Bible** itself, because Herod and the Massacre of the Innocents were so strikingly portrayed in them (there are mystery plays specifically on this theme):

> Your naked infants spitted upon pikes,
> Whiles the mad mothers with their howls confus'd
> Do break the clouds, as did the wives of Jewry
> At Herod's bloody-hunting slaughtermen.
>
> (3.3.38–41)

'What we should envisage', contends Emrys Jones (1977: 51), 'is Shakespeare's possibly knowing a number of these cycles, and, having seen one or more of them several times, reaching the kind of unthinking effortless familiarity with them that anyone in the historical period may arrive at with works of popular entertainment – especially when they have been experienced uncritically early in life.'

Jones emphasizes throughout his discussion Shakespeare's use, as he sees it, of the mysteries' 'scenic form' or configuration of events (and not the events which they depict as such), first in two cases in the Histories which can be related to the Passion plays in the mystery cycles. The tragedy of Humphrey, Duke of Gloucester in *2 Henry VI* is, he suggests, affected in conception and structure by the traditional dramatization of Christ's victimization in Jerusalem, in 'the stress on the enemies of the victim-protagonist, and on their virulent malice; the conspiratorial method of their undertaking against him[;] the legalistic procedure they find it expedient to adopt, with a consequential wide range of speech-tones; and the progressive isolation of the hero' (Jones 1977: 52). In *3 Henry VI*, probably the most striking episode is Margaret's taunting speech to York, placed on the molehill, during which she sets a paper crown on his head. Jones argues that this 'recalls more than one of the violent torture scenes in the mysteries', and at times comes particularly close to the tone and substance of Caiaphas' diatribe against Christ in *Coliphizacio* ((B), above), comparing especially

the jeering to the effect 'How dare you call yourself a king'. 'In view
of the prominence given in the mysteries to the malice of Christ's
accusers . . . it seems likely that something of this ritual of torment was
carried over into Margaret's role in this scene' (Jones 1977: 54–6):

> What, was it you that would be England's king?
> Was't you that revell'd in our parliament
> And made a preachment of your high descent?
> Where are your mess of sons to back you now?
> The wanton Edward and the lusty George?
> And where's that valiant crook-back prodigy,
> Dicky your boy, that with his grumbling voice
> Was wont to cheer his dad in mutinies?
> Or, with the rest, where is your darling Rutland?
> Look, York: I stain'd this napkin with the blood
> That valiant Clifford with his rapier's point
> Made issue from the bosom of the boy;
> And if thine eyes can water for his death,
> I give thee this to dry thy cheeks withal.
> Alas, poor York! but that I hate thee deadly,
> I should lament thy miserable state.
> I prithee grieve to make me merry, York.
> What, hath thy fiery heart so parch'd thine entrails
> That not a tear can fall for Rutland's death?
> Why art thou patient, man? Thou should'st be mad;
> And I to make thee mad do mock thee thus.
> Stamp, rave, and fret, that I may sing and dance.
> Thou would'st be fee'd, I see, to make me sport;
> York cannot speak unlesse he wear a crown.
> A crown for York! – and, lords, bow low to him.
> Hold you his hands whilst I do set it on.

> [*Putting a paper crown on his head.*

> Ay, marry, sir, now looks he like a king!
> Ay, this is he that took King Henry's chair,
> And this is he was his adopted heir.
> But how is it that great Plantagenet
> Is crown'd so soon and broke his solemn oath?

As I bethink me, you should not be King
Till our King Henry had shook hands with death.
And will you pale your head in Henry's glory,
And rob his temples of the diadem,
Now in his life, against your holy oath?
O, 'tis a fault too too unpardonable!
Off with the crown and with the crown his head;
And, whilst we breathe, take time to do him dead.
(1.4.70–108)

Jones finds further mystery play elements in the Tragedies. In *King Lear* the baiting of the king by his daughters again corresponds to the tormenting of Jesus, and the ensuing scenes on the heath, imbued with a cataclysmic effect comparable to the treatment of Christ's sufferings, correspond to the Crucifixion play that enacted them. Coriolanus' exile, Timon's passion and Caesar's betrayal echo, fairly incidentally, other parts of the Gospel story, but there is no very strong connection with the dramatic treatment of these narratives in the mysteries. There are somewhat better grounds for connecting Macbeth with the Herod figure, perhaps especially in the slaughter of the innocent Duncan, leading to what could be regarded as re-dramatizations of the Last Supper, the Harrowing of Hell, and the Last Judgement (see Ide 1975).

Elsewhere in the Shakespeare corpus, traces of the miracle plays have been discerned in such unlikely places as *The Comedy of Errors* (Kinney 1988), and more predictably in *Measure for Measure*. The mystery play subjects of the Woman Taken in Adultery (versions of which survive in three of the extant cycles) and the Repentance of Mary Magdalene (in two cycles), with their oppositions of old and new law and their 'convergence of the sublime and the humble' (Cox 1983: 13), are in some sense part of *Measure for Measure*'s background, and the play may also be said to be 'fully eschatological as a mystery cycle is eschatological – foreshadowing Judgment long before it occurs and exploiting the attendant ironies as cycles do' (Velz 1992: 316). But it is not possible to conclude that Shakespeare had mystery plays directly in mind in writing it: 'we are dealing with a dramatic tradition as a source in the broadest sense . . . none of these plays is a source or analogue in the strict sense of those terms' (Cox 1983: 2).

(D) Relatively little work has appeared on this topic. Matthews (1962)

381

was pioneering, but limited by a tendency to make all actions in a play symbolic or allegorical, to think in terms of moral theology and not dramaturgy. The suggestive investigations of Jones (1977) have encouraged a few others, but to date the only other substantial publications specifically in this area are those of Cox (1983), Guilfoyle (1990), and somewhat tangentially Kinney (1988) and Velz (1992); and some of these treat only a single Shakespeare text. Hence the unpublished dissertations of Morrison (1978) and Stone (1973) are useful.

Cawley, A. C., ed. (1958). *The Wakefield Pageants in the Towneley Cycle.* Manchester.

Cox, John D. (1983). 'The Medieval Background of *Measure for Measure.*' *MP* 81: 1–13.

Gardiner, Harold C. (1967). *Mysteries' End: An Investigation of the Last Days of the Medieval Religious Stage.* Hamden, CT (first published 1946).

Guilfoyle, Cherrell (1990). *Shakespeare's Play within Play: Medieval Imagery and Scenic Form in 'Hamlet', 'Othello', and 'King Lear'.* Kalamazoo.

Ide, Richard S. (1975). 'The Theatre of the Mind: An Essay on *Macbeth.*' *ELH* 43: 338–61.

Ingram, R. W. (1982). 'Fifteen-seventy-nine and the Decline of Civic Religious Drama in Coventry', pp. 114–28 in G. R. Hibbard, ed., *The Elizabethan Theatre VIII.* Port Credit.

Jones (1977).

Kinney, Arthur F. (1988). 'Shakespeare's *Comedy of Errors* and the Nature of Kinds.' *SP* 85: 29–52.

Matthews, Honor (1962). *Character and Symbol in Shakespeare's Plays: A Study of Certain Christian and Pre-Christian Elements in their Structure and Imagery.* Cambridge.

Matus, Irvin Leigh (1989). 'An Early Reference to the Coventry Mystery Plays in Shakespeare?' *ShQ* 40: 196–7.

Morrison, George Peter (1978). 'Shakespeare's Lancastrian Tetralogy in the Light of the Medieval Mystery Cycles: A Theory for Unity.' PhD diss. State University of New York.

Sierz, Krystyna (1984). 'Some Medieval Concepts in Shakespeare's Plays.' *Studia Anglica Posnaniensia: An International Review of English Studies* 17: 233–49.

Stone, Charles R. (1973). 'Dramas of Christian Time: Temporal Assumptions and Dramatic Form in the Medieval Mystery Cycle, the

Morality Play, and Shakespeare's Second Tetralogy.' PhD diss. University of Minnesota.

Velz, John W. (1992). '"Some shall be pardon'd, and some punished": Medieval Dramatic Eschatology in Shakespeare.' *CompD* 26: 312–29.

Weimann, Robert, revised and translated by Robert Schwartz (1978). *Shakespeare and the Popular Tradition in the Theater: Studies in the Social Dimension of Dramatic Form and Function*. Baltimore.

N

Nannini (or Fiorentino), Remigio (1521–1581), Italian Historical Writer Nannini's 1563 work translated into English in 1601 as *Civil Considerations upon Many and Sundrie Histories*, a compendium of advice to princes and military commanders, has been insecurely linked to *Hamlet* and *The Tempest*.

Ormsby-Lennon, Theresa Suriano (1977). ' "Piccolo, ma con gran vaghezza": A New Source for *Hamlet?' Library Chronicle* (Philadelphia) 41: 119–48.

Slights, William W. E. (1985). 'A Source for *The Tempest* and The Context of The *Discorsi.' ShQ* 36: 68–70.

Nashe, Thomas (1567–*c*.1601), Playwright and Satirist
(A) Nashe was born into a clerical family in Lowestoft and educated at St John's College, Cambridge. At Cambridge he met Robert **Greene**, to whose prose romance *Menaphon*, 1589, Nashe contributed a preface in which he claimed membership of the circle of University Wits and attacked the players. He became notorious as a reckless and biting pamphleteer, employed by Archbishop Whitgift against 'Martin Marprelate', then on his own account against Richard and **Gabriel Harvey** and the Puritans. His *Have with You to Saffron-Walden* was the culmination of this later pamphlet war in 1599.

His first really successful publication was *Pierce Penilesse his Supplication to the Divil* (1592), a virtuoso piece of no particular genre in which the author-persona Pierce requests a loan from the Devil and composes a satirical commentary on society. *The Unfortunate Traveller*, a picaresque forerunner of the modern adventure novel, appeared in 1594 but enjoyed little success in its own day. The same applies to Nashe's treatise on apparitions of the same year, *The Terrors of the Night*. As a dramatist he wrote only one piece indubitably all his own, the satirical masque *Summer's Last Will and Testament* (1592), but he collaborated with **Greene**, and on another occasion with **Marlowe** on *Dido, Queen of Carthage* (1594). *The Isle of Dogs* (1597), a work begun by Nashe and completed by other hands, was the most scandalous of Elizabethan plays, seen by the Privy Council's informer as 'lewd', 'seditious' and 'sclanderous', and rigorously suppressed. Unlike three of the actors, Nashe escaped gaol by fleeing London, but when he returned in 1599 he faced a wholesale government condemnation of his writings. His last work, published presumably before the official prohibition came into effect, was *Lenten Stuffe* (1599), a burlesque panegyric on Yarmouth and its red herrings. His eclectic writings are hard to characterize, tending to be *sui generis* or at least to fall outside the mainstream of work in their genres, but his untrammelled, exuberant, digressive style has immediate appeal: 'impromptu and searching, Nashe's prose often seems, not a *first* anything, but a last high achievement of the impromptu and searching vigor exemplified in Tyndale's Bible' (Berryman 1967: 12).

(B) The epitaph which occurs as part of the review of various writers' reputations in *The Second Part of the Return from Parnassus* (first performed 1603) is for its time not untypically favourable on Nashe as a satirist:

INGE[NIOSO]. *Thomas Nash.*
        I, here is a fellow *Judicio* that carried the deadly stocke
        in his pen, whose muse was armed with a gag tooth,
        and his pen possest with *Hercules* furyes.
JUDICIO.   Let all his faults sleepe with his mournfull chest,
        And then for ever with his ashes rest,
        His stile was witty, though he had some gall,
        Something he might have mended, so may all.
        Yet this I say, that for a mother wit,
        Few men have ever seene the like of it.
                    (1606 text; Anon. 1606: sig. B3ʳ)

385

Nashe himself realized that *Pierce Penilesse*, published when he was twenty-five years old, was his most popular work. In *Have with You to Saffron-Walden* he accused Gabriel Harvey of using the name of Pierce to increase the sales of his *Pierce's Supererogation*. By this time, in 1599, there had been five editions of Nashe's pamphlet, three of them in 1592 alone; as late as 1606 there appeared an anonymous 'continuation' of it. Nashe's identification with it lasted until the end of his life and 'to maintain and exploit the personality of Pierce became increasingly his main endeavour' (Hibbard 1962: 84). *Pierce* was enjoyed for what the continuation calls 'variation of humours', as a brilliant display of wit on a wide variety of topics. One of Pierce's seven 'complaints' against his times gives a fair sample of the energetic hotchpotch that is Nashe's prose. The last section here has been considered a source for Hamlet's comments on the 'dram of eale' (1.4.23–38; see Davenport 1953; Evans 1953):

> From Gluttony in meates, let me descend to superfluitie in drinke: a sinne, that ever since we have mixt our selves with the Low-countries, is counted honourable: but before we knew their lingring warres, was held in that highest degree of hatred that might be. Then if we had seene a man goe wallowing in the streetes, or lie sleeping under the boord, we would have spet at him as a toade, and cald him foule drunken swine, and warnd al our friends out of his company: now he is no body that cannot drinke *super nagulum*, carouse the Hunters hoop, quaffe *upsey-freze crosse*, with healthes, gloves, mumpes, frolickes, and a thousand such dominiering inventions. He is reputed a pesaunt and a boore that wil not take his licour profoundly. And you shall heare a Cavalier of the first feather, a princockes that was but a Page the other day in the Court, and now is all to be frenchified in his Souldiers sute, stand uppon termes with Gods wounds you dishonour me sir, you do me the disgrace if you do not pledge me as much as I drunke to you: and in the midst of his cups stand vaunting his manhood: beginning everie sentence, with when I first bore Armes, when he never bare any thing but his lords rapier after him in his life. If he have beene over and visited a towne of Garrison as a travailer or passenger, he hath as great experience as the greatest Commander and chiefe Leader in *England*. A mightie deformer of mens manners and features, is this unnecessary vice of all other. Let him bee indued with never so many vertues, and have as much goodly proportion and

favour as nature can bestow uppon a man: yet if hee be thirstie after his owne destruction, and hath no joy nor comfort, but when he is drowning his soule in a gallon pot, that one beastly imperfection, will utterlie obscure all that is commendable in him: and all his good qualities sinke like lead down to the bottome of his carrowsing cups, where they will lie like lees and dregges, dead and unregarded of any man.

(Nashe 1592: sigs E3^v–E4^r)

(C) It has sometimes been thought that personal relations between Nashe and Shakespeare were such as to have resulted in Nashe's collaboration in several Shakespeare plays (see e.g. Wilson 1952a: xxi–xxxi; Wilson 1952b: xxxvii–xliii), and even Nashe's representation as a character, Moth, in another (see Yates 1936: 4–5). But there are other possible explanations for the links which are certainly present between Nashe and Shakespeare in the early plays in question, *Henry VI* and *Love's Labour's Lost*, and recent scholarship has often either discounted these suggestions or regarded them as not proven (see e.g. Cairncross 1962: xxx–xxxv; Harlow 1965; Hattaway 1990: 41–3).

Dozens of very small-scale and scattered verbal echoes of Nashe have been proposed by scholars mainly of recent years. But commentators have insufficiently heeded the caveats of Davenport (1953: 374): 'Parallels such as [these] are tricky things. It is very easy to miss seeing them, and it is equally easy to fancy a causal connection where none exists.' Davenport's parallels between *Pierce Penilesse* and *Hamlet/Macbeth* invoke context as well as verbal resemblances, but are still as likely as not to be fortuitous, though the *Hamlet* ones are accepted by Jenkins (1982: 104–6). *Pierce Penilesse* and *Have with You to Saffron-Walden* have, however, accumulated more supposed Shakespearean echoes than any of Nashe's other works, and these pamphlets are indeed likely to have passed through Shakespeare's hands. The former has long been connected with *Love's Labour's Lost*, and the latter, one of the most notorious books of its decade, refers to leading actors by name and contains a spirited defence of the stage. Shakespeare's plays around the time of *Twelfth Night* show particular affinities with these two Nashe works. Some of these amount to little more than bare indications of Shakespeare's acquaintance with Nashe in echoes of rare or otherwise distinctive words and phrases. Others suggest Shakespeare's use of him for substantive material, including according to Holmer (1995a, 1995b) the figure of Mercutio, conceivably a Nashe type, but most convincingly for Malvolio's humiliations. Shakespeare, it has been argued, 'found in the figure of Harvey as gull, with his characteristics of egocentricity, puritanism, and social presumption a workable model for the creation of Malvolio' (Tobin 1980, who also demonstrates verbal parallels and contends for further echoes of *Lenten Stuff* and other Nashe works in *Twelfth Night*). But even Tobin, a long-term proponent of Nashe's influence on Shakespeare, finds it necessary to qualify the word 'model'; even here we are dealing at most only with hints and small-scale suggestions, recalled at a distance of several years.

(D) The apparently large literature resolves itself into a small number of full-length articles and many recordings of tiny echoes (or apparent echoes), most of them the latter by the indefatigable John Tobin (his larger collection of echoes in *Dream, Merchant, Henry V, Julius Caesar* and *Macbeth* is in Tobin 1992).

Anon. (1606). *The Returne from Pernassus: or the Scourge of Simony* [Part 2]. London.

Berryman, John, ed. (1967). *The Unfortunate Traveller*. New York.

Cairncross, Andrew S., ed. (1962). *The First Part of King Henry VI* (Arden Shakespeare). London.

Davenport, A. (1953). 'Shakespeare and Nashe's "Pierce Penilesse".' *N&Q* 198: 371–4.

Ebbs, E. C. (1951). 'A Note on Nashe and Shakespeare.' *MLN* 66: 480–1.

Evans, G. Blakemore (1953). 'Thomas Nashe and the "Dram of Eale".' *N&Q* 198: 377–8.

Harlow, C. G. (1965). 'The Source for Nashe's *Terrors of the Night*, and the Authorship of *1 Henry VI*.' *SEL* 5: 31–47 and 269–81.

Hattaway, Michael, ed. (1990). *The First Part of King Henry VI* (New Cambridge Shakespeare). Cambridge.

Hibbard, G. R. (1962). *Thomas Nashe: A Critical Introduction*. London.

Holmer, Joan Ozark (1995a). 'Nashe as "Monarch of Witt" and Shakespeare's *Romeo and Juliet*.' *TSLL* 37: 314–43

—— (1995b). 'No "Vain Fantasy": Shakespeare's Refashioning of Nashe for Dreams and Queen Mab', pp. 49–82 in Jay L. Halio, ed., *Shakespeare's 'Romeo and Juliet': Texts, Contexts, and Interpretation*. Newark, DE.

Jenkins, Harold, ed. (1982). *Hamlet* (Arden Shakespeare). London.

Nashe, Thomas (1592). *Pierce Penilesse his Supplication to the Divell*, 3rd edn. London.

Schrickx, W. (1969). '*Titus Andronicus* and Thomas Nashe.' *ES* 50: 82–4.

Slater, Ann Pasternak (1978). 'Macbeth and the Terrors of the Night.' *EinC* 28: 112–28.

Tobin, J. J. M. (1978). 'Nashe and *As You Like It*.' *N&Q* 223: 138–9 (Tobin has been responsible for some fifteen other notes of this kind published in this journal and others since 1978).

—— (1980). 'Gabriel Harvey in Illyria.' *ES* 61: 318–28.

—— (1992). 'Nashe and Shakespeare: Some Further Borrowings.' *N&Q* 237: 309–20.

Wilson, John Dover, ed. (1952a). *Henry VI Part 1* (New Shakespeare). Cambridge.

—— ed. (1952b). *Henry VI Part 2* (New Shakespeare). Cambridge.

Yates, Frances (1936). *A Study of 'Love's Labours Lost'*. Cambridge.

York, E. C. (1953). 'Shakespeare and Nashe.' *N&Q* 198: 370–1.

Newton, Thomas See **Cicero**, **Marcus Tullius**; **Seneca, Lucius Annaeus**.

North, Sir Thomas See **Plutarch**.

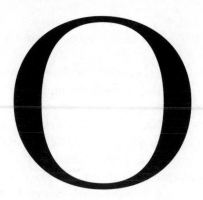

Ovid (Publius Ovidius Naso) (43 BC–AD 18), Roman Poet
(A) Ovid was a leading figure in the literary and social life of Rome
when in AD 8 Augustus suddenly banished him to Tomis, a remote
outpost on the Black Sea. His extant work consists of: a collection of
love elegies, the *Amores*; two mock-didactic poems for lovers, the *Ars
Amatoria* and *Remedia Amoris*; a collection of the fictional correspondence
of mythological heroines, the *Heroides*; a poem on Roman festivals, the
Fasti; two collections of personal poems written during the poet's exile
near the Black Sea, *Tristia* and *Ex Ponto*; a short personal invective, *Ibis*;
and a mythological poem in fifteen Books on transformation and
change, the *Metamorphoses*. Of these, much the most important for
Shakespeare and his time is the last.

Although of epic dimensions and written in the hexameters expected
for epic, the *Metamorphoses* is quite unlike the epics of **Homer** and
Virgil. It does not involve a unified action and theme, but consists of a
series of self-contained narratives cleverly woven together and included
within a rough chronological sequence which extends from the Creation to the poet's own day. The *Metamorphoses* is one of the world's
great source-books, a poetic handbook of mythological stories. But
there were other compilations of mythological stories available to the
Renaissance; Ovid's poetic character is the real reason for his centrality
to the period and to Shakespeare's work. Different aspects of this character present themselves to Shakespeare and his contemporaries at different times, but there is wide agreement that a kind of playful

390

exuberance – called by Quintilian (X.1.88) *lascivia* – is a central Ovidian quality.

(B) Ovid was a major literary figure in England throughout the Middle Ages: the troubadours, clerics, historians and moralists of the period all attest the appeal of the schoolmaster of the art of love, the narrative poet, the mythologist and the painter of female nature. **Chaucer** was notably attracted to Ovid's brand of playful wit, so that Ovid's influence on Shakespeare may sometimes be mediated through him, for example via *Troilus and Criseyde* in *Troilus and Cressida*. This is also the case with **Gower** (*Confessio Amantis*, 1386–93) and with **Lyly**, the stylistic prodigality of whose *Euphues* (1578) is in a tradition deriving from Ovid's *Heroides*. Ovid's assured place in the literary canon meant that he was heavily represented in school textbooks, so much so that it may even be imagined that 'Shakespeare's first lessons in poetry were lessons in the imitation of Ovid' (Bate 1993: 22). Shakespeare's contemporaries described Ovid's poetry in such terms as 'conceited', 'silver-tong'd', and, in versification, 'prompt'. His abundant influence on writers of the period can be readily documented for all his major works. He had a powerful effect on **Spenser**: the *Metamorphoses* for mythological, allegorical and other elements in *The Faerie Queene*, and perhaps the *Fasti* for *The Shepheardes Calendar*. **Drayton**'s collection *England's Heroical Epistles* (1597) is modelled on the *Heroides*, an important book also for the fiction of such writers as **Greene** and Pettie; **Jonson** and his followers come under the Ovidian spell in various ways; **Marlowe**'s *Ovid's Elegies* is part of a substantial fashion in love elegy.

Historically the dominant tradition in reading Ovid had been an allegorical one, in which moral and even Christian meanings were everywhere discovered. This way of reading the *Metamorphoses*, in particular, was in decline in Shakespeare's day but had not disappeared: the preface to Golding's translation of 1567 offers specifically Christian interpretations of the stories. This tradition is important for Shakespeare because it creates meanings for mythological allusions which are available to sophisticated Renaissance audiences, and more widely important as a distraction from the customary censure of Ovid for his licentiousness. A related tradition is iconographic; Fig. 8 shows one example of a conventional way of representing the transformation of Actaeon (*Metamorphoses* V), with stag's head, human body and hunter's

Figure 8 La Metamorphose d'Ovide figurée (Lyons, 1557), sig. C5ᵛ.

clothes, which has been thought to underlie Shakespeare's presentation of Falstaff in his burlesque of the Actaeon myth in the last Act of *The Merry Wives of Windsor* (see Steadman 1963). However, there is a demonstrable shift in the focus of reading in Ovid over the sixteenth century onto his poetic, especially rhetorical, qualities, and away from allegory. This is reflected in Holofernes' heavily humorous pedagogic comment

392

(punning on Ovid's cognomen 'Naso', connected with the Latin for 'nose'):

> for the elegancy, facility, and golden cadence of poetry . . . Ovidius Naso was the man. And why, indeed, 'Naso' but for smelling out the odoriferous flowers of fancy, the jerks of invention?
>
> *(Love's Labour's Lost*, 4.2.116–19)

As well as the rise of the 'rhetorical' as against the 'moral' or allegorical Ovid, there is particular interest in Shakespeare's time in what might be called the 'amoral' Ovid. In 1582 the Privy Council prescribed patriotic literature for grammar schools in place of 'Ovid de arte amandi, de tristibus or such lyke'. But this was to little avail in view of the tide of Ovidian verse in the following two decades. Not the least significant part of this was the 1590s series of Ovidian 'epyllia', short narrative poems, usually of a strongly erotic cast, reflecting Ovid's grotesqueness, brittle pathos, lyricism and elegance – Marlowe's *Hero and Leander* is the best-known example apart from *Venus and Adonis* (Keach 1977 is standard on both the Ovidian and English contexts of Shakespeare's poem). To some of the sterner Elizabethan literary sensibilities, Ovid was for such reasons a less important figure than those Augustan poets whose work is in more elevated styles and genres. Jonson's *Poetaster*, for instance, presents Ovid as a character banished by Augustus for daring to imitate the gods in a masquerade – and there is little complaint about Ovid's punishment.

English versions of Ovid's tales had begun with Chaucer and Gower in the fourteenth century, but direct translations of the Latin did not arrive until the sixteenth. Important translations for Shakespeare and his contemporaries are Arthur Golding's *Metamorphoses* (1565–7) and Marlowe's *Amores* (*c.* 1595). Golding's, once labelled by Ezra Pound 'the most beautiful book in the language', was a major and enduring Elizabethan achievement (for early responses see Taylor 1989: 55). Golding's closing 'epistle' describes his translation as intended to direct 'every man['s] . . . mynd by reason in way of vertue', and provides exemplary readings of many of the tales, sometimes involving Christian allegory, but Golding's translation itself is substantially free of moralistic intrusion. It follows the Latin closely except for the incorporation of explanatory glosses within the text and some wordy local padding. Golding naturalizes Ovid, giving English equivalents for some mythological names (e.g. 'Penthey' for 'Penthius') and incorporating homely English diction and folklore. Golding's fourteener couplet has inbuilt disadvantages, and the translation can seem quaint; but there is a vigorous narrative drive. Sixteenth-century readers would have responded more warmly than is now common to the 'gusto', 'racy speech' and 'energetic doggerel' that J. F. Nims (1965: xxxi) finds in the translation (specimens in (C)).

Marlowe's version of Ovid's *Amores*, titled *Ovid's Elegies*, was apparently the catalyst that led to the burst of enthusiasm for licentious Ovidian poems mentioned above which forms part of the context for *Venus and Adonis*. Marlowe's translations, which probably circulated in manuscript after being composed in the 1580s, are extremely spirited, energetic, and plausible recreations of Ovid's sophisticated style in verse of great dexterity. The young Shakespeare used a couplet from Ovid's *Amores* (I.xv.35–6) as the epigraph to *Venus and Adonis*; it is easy to imagine him responding to Marlowe's version of the passage in which it occurs, though there are many more attractive still in Marlowe's translation:

> Therefore when flint and yron weare away,
> Verse is immortall, and shall nere decay.
> Let kings give place to verse, and kingly showes,
> And banks ore which gold bearing *Tagus* flowes.
> Let base conceited wits admire vilde things,
> Fair *Phoebus* leade me to the Muses springs.
> About my head be quivering Mirtle wound,
> And in sad lovers heads let me be found.
> The living, not the dead can envie bite,
> For after death all men receive their right:
> Then though death rackes my bones in funerall fier,
> Ile live, and as he puls me downe, mount higher.
>   (31–42; ed. Bowers 1973: II, 339)

(C) Shakespeare's knowledge of Ovid is not out of step with his contemporaries'. He knew the *Metamorphoses* and the *Heroides*, the *Fasti*, and at least parts of the *Amores*, *Ars Amatoria* and *Tristia*. All of these were available to him in English translation except the *Fasti*, untranslated until 1640. But the effect Ovid had on Shakespeare has always been recognized as more extensive and more important than for comparable writers. In his survey of contemporary literature published in 1598, *Palladis Tamia*, Francis Meres writes of Shakespeare as a reincarnation of Ovid:

> As the soule of Euphorbus was thought to live in Pythagoras: so the sweete wittie soul of Ovid lives in mellifluous and hony-tongued Shakespeare, witness his *Venus and Adonis*, his *Lucrece*, his sugred *Sonnets* among his private friends, etc.
>
> (ed. Smith 1904: II, 317–18)

The immediate references are to:

1 *The Rape of Lucrece*, based partly on Ovid's *Fasti*, II, 721–852 (and apparently partly on **Livy**, I, 57–9).
2 Shakespeare's *Sonnets*, which make use of the *Metamorphoses*, especially the philosophical speech of Pythagoras in Book XV.
3 *Venus and Adonis*, which blends several Greek myths found in the *Metamorphoses*. The tale of Venus and Adonis (*Met.* X, 519–59, 705–39) is the main source, but in Ovid Adonis is not the cold figure Shakespeare makes him. His resistance to love is taken from Ovid's tale of Hermaphroditus and Salmacis in *Met.* IV, 285–388. Shakespeare's description of the raging boar derives from another passage in the *Metamorphoses*, VIII, 284–6, probably in Golding's version (Root 1903: 31–3). Other Ovidian contexts also surround the text (see Bate 1993: 48–65). Overall, the result of Shakespeare's huge expansion of the Adonis story (less than a hundred lines to more than a thousand) is that Ovid's text becomes a framework for a display of Shakespeare's own rhetorical skills.

But Meres' comments do not mean that Ovid's influence on Shakespeare was restricted to his non-dramatic works, or to matters of style and subject. Meres takes metempsychosis, the notion of the transmigration of souls expounded by Ovid himself in *Metamorphoses* XV, as a figure for the translation of one poet into another. Deep affinities are indeed implied by the range of similarities between Shakespeare and Ovid suggested by Bate (1993: 3):

> a method of composition which involves shaping inherited stories in such a way that they are wrought completely anew; a refusal to

submit to the decorums of genre, a delight in the juxtaposition of contrasting tones . . .; an interest above all else in human psychology, particularly the psychology of desire in its many varieties; an exploration of the transformations wrought by extremes of emotion; a delight in rhetorical ingenuity, verbal fertility, linguistic play; variety and flexibility as fundamental habits and mind and forms of expression.

Moving to particulars, there are several direct quotations from Ovid in the plays: in *The Taming of the Shrew*, for example, Lucretio's pose as a Latin tutor leads to his quoting *Heroides*, 1.33–4 at 3.1.26–7 (for other direct quotations see Highet 1957: 204). Ovid is also the only classical author named by Shakespeare, in *Love's Labour's Lost* (see (B)). Shakespeare's characters do not read many books; of the few examples, two read the same passage of the *Metamorphoses*, the story of Tereus, Procne and Philomela from Book VI (*Titus Andronicus* 4.1, *Cymbeline* 2.2). Barkan suggests that because this story is not one of the Renaissance Ovidian cliches (like those of, say, Narcissus, or Phaethon) we should infer 'that Shakespeare knew his Ovid at first hand and that he read the *Metamorphoses* with a deliberate and original purpose' (Barkan 1986: 243). But Ovid may have been mediated through other writers: the versions of this story by Chaucer and Gower were well known.

Three plays are singled out in what follows to indicate something of the range of uses to which the English poet puts the Roman one. The use of the *Metamorphoses* as an on-stage prop in *Titus Andronicus* 4.1, the quintessentially self-conscious literary moment in which Lavinia reveals the perpetrators of her outrage (as just mentioned), is only the most obvious element of Ovidian allusion in this play, allusion which is strongly focused on the Philomel tale (*Metamorphoses* VI) as pattern and precedent, but not confined to it (it notably involves also the legend of the world's four ages and Io's method of revealing her rapist). '*Titus* is to Ovid's Philomel story what *Venus and Adonis* is to Ovid's Venus and Adonis, what *Lucrece* is to Ovid's *Fasti*', and Lavinia's reading of Ovid 'signals that the play is itself . . . a revisionary reading of the Ovidian text' (Bate 1993: 104). Revision involves variation: for one thing, competition with the Ovidian model results in exaggeration of it. Demetrius and Chiron correspond to Tereus, Lavinia to Philomel, Titus to Pandion and then Procne. But as Titus says to Demetrius and Chiron, 'Far worse than Philomel you us'd my daughter, / And worse than Progne I will be reveng'd' (5.2.195–6). He is as good as his word, butchering two corpses to Procne's one. Clearly, too, where the Ovidian tale had released Philomel's tragic potentiality into Orphic song with her metamorphosis into the nightingale, Shakespeare's reworking concentrates on the tragedy (for further discussion of *Titus*' variations on Ovid see Bate 1993: 103–17).

The *Metamorphoses* is also 'primary' for the very different world of *A Midsummer Night's Dream*, arguably 'Shakespeare's fullest attempt to respond to the inspirations afforded by Ovidian materials and to translate them into his own mythic language' (Barkan 1986: 252). The play is full of explicitly named mythical figures, and its action is both explicitly and implicitly based on Ovidian metamorphosis. Characteristically of Shakespeare's use of Ovid, the exercise of imitation once again involves the dynamic of competition and transformation, so that the mythical figures are not simply assimilated but 'translated' by Shakespeare from the Ovidian materials. With Theseus and Hippolyta, for example, Shakespeare avoids the considerable body of negative associations surrounding the figures, or else presents the characters as having been educated out of such attitudes towards love. For this purpose, Chaucer and perhaps **Plutarch** join with Ovid in the background to the play. Similarly with Shakespeare's use of metamorphic events. Bottom's transformation comically revises the tale of Diana and Actaeon while probably borrowing also from **Apuleius**, and for the business of the love-juice Shakespeare creates a myth that corresponds to no particular Ovidian example but produces rather 'an original etiology in Ovidian mode' (Barkan 1986: 257) in Oberon's tale of love-in-idleness (2.1.148–72).

Ovid is so much in vogue at Theseus' palace that for the Duke's wedding-night entertainment he can reject the subjects of the battle of the Centaurs and Lapinths and the dismemberment of Orpheus to hear instead the 'antic' re-enactment of the famous episode of Pyramus and Thisbe (from *Metamorphoses* IV, 55–166). This parody version may in some sense be aimed at Golding's *Metamorphoses* (see Muir 1977: 68–77 for a full discussion), the opening of whose Pyramus and Thisbe story is given here:

> Within the towne (of whose huge walles so monstrous high and
> thicke
> The fame is given Semyramis for making them of bricke)

Dwelt hard together two yong folke in houses joynde so nere
That under all one roofe well nie both twaine conveyed were.
The name of him was Pyramus, and Thisbe calde was she.
So faire a man in all the East was none alive as he,
Nor nere a woman maide nor wife in beautie like to hir.
This neighbrod bred acquaintance first, this neyghbrod first did
    stirre
The secret sparkes, this neighbrod first an entrance in did showe,
For love to come to that to which it afterward did growe.
And if that right had taken place they had bene man and wife,
But still their Parents went about to let which (for their life)
They could not let. For both their heartes with equall flame did
    burne.
No man was privie to their thoughts. And for to serve their turne
In steade of talke they used signes. The closlier they supprest
The fire of love, the fiercer still it raged in their brest.
The wall that parted house from house had riven therein a crany
Which shronke at making of the wall.
                                 (IV, 67–84; Golding 1567: fo. 43ᵛ)

In Shakespeare, Wall picks up the word 'crany', used only by Golding among the possible sources, though admittedly a standard translation for the word *rima* used in Ovid's text:

> In this same interlude it doth befall
> That I, one Snout by name, present a wall;
> And such a wall as I would have you think
> That had in it a crannied hole or chink,
> Through which the lovers, Pyramus and Thisby,
> Did whisper often very secretly.
> This loam, this rough-cast, and this stone, doth show
> That I am that same wall; the truth is so;
> And this the cranny is, right and sinister,
> Through which the fearful lovers are to whisper.
>   (5.1.154–63; roman for italic)

Golding's characteristic overuse of the auxiliary 'did' shown in his lines 74–6 here also seems to be reflected in Quince's prologue:

> This grisly beast, which Lion hight by name,
> The trusty Thisby, coming first by night,
> Did scare away, or rather did affright;
> And as she fled, her mantle she did fall;
> Which Lion vile with bloody mouth did stain.
> (5.1.138–42; roman for italic)

However far this burlesque is directed towards Golding (other less well-known English versions of the story are certainly involved), 'Shakespeare can scarcely have despised Golding's translation of the *Metamorphoses*; nor is its telling of the Pyramus story by any means despicable' (Brooks 1979: lxxxvi–lxxxvii). In any case, Golding's translation has a considerable role in the wider Ovidianism of the *Dream* (see especially Forey 1998).

Prospero's speech 'Ye elves of hills' is probably the most familiar and most powerful Ovidian imitation in Shakespeare's plays. It also shows how Shakespeare uses both Latin and English texts for his purposes. Though much of his vocabulary is borrowed from Golding, Shakespeare apparently goes to the Latin for other details such as the type of tree ('Jove's stout oak'):

Ye Ayres and windes: ye Elves of Hilles, of Brookes, of Woods alone,
Of standing Lakes, and of the Night approche ye everychone.
Through helpe of whom (the crooked bankes much wondring at the
    thing)
I have compelled streames to run cleane backward to their spring.
By charmes I make the calme Seas rough, and make the rough Seas
    plaine,
And cover all the Skie with Cloudes and chase them thence againe.
By charmes I raise and lay the windes, and burst the Vipers jaw.
And from the bowels of the Earth both stones and trees doe draw.
Whole woods and Forestes I remove: I make the Mountaines shake,
And even the Earth it selfe to grone and fearfully to quake.
I call up dead men from their graves: and thee O lightsome Moone
I darken oft, though beaten brasse abate thy perill soone.
Our Sorcerie dimmes the Morning faire, and darkes the Sun at
    Noone.
(VII, 265–77; Golding 1567: fo. 83ᵛ)

> Ye elves of hills, brooks, standing lakes, and groves;
> And ye that on the sands with printless foot
> Do chase the ebbing Neptune, and do fly him
> When he comes back; you demi-puppets that
> By moonshine do the green sour ringlets make,
> Whereof the ewe not bites; and you whose pastime
> Is to make midnight mushrooms, that rejoice
> To hear the solemn curfew; by whose aid –
> Weak masters though ye be – I have be-dimm'd
> The noontide sun, call'd forth the mutinous winds,
> And 'twixt the green sea and the azur'd vault
> Set roaring war. To the dread rattling thunder
> Have I given fire, and rifted Jove's stout oak
> With his own bolt; the strong-bas'd promontory
> Have I made shake, and by the spurs pluck'd up
> The pine and cedar. Graves at my command
> Have wak'd their sleepers, op'd, and let 'em forth,
> By my so potent art.
>
> (5.1.33–50)

Once again, Shakespeare's adumbration of Ovid/Golding, adding in for example the native fairy lore, is apparent. The grandeur, sonority and striking imagery of Prospero's speech seem to recall Ovid's verse rather than Golding's fourteeners. But it is less easy to be sure how much Shakespeare's audience was supposed to discern in such an imitation. All commentators believe that 'educated members of the audience would recognize the presence of Ovid'; the question is whether there is as much 'complex interplay between the divergent meanings of the two texts as our more ingenious critics suppose' (Martindale 1990: 23). To some, precisely such 'complex interplay' is Shakespeare's principal interest (e.g. Bate 1993: 9–11, 251–5; Brown 1994: 9–19). It is also debatable how much of the Ovidian context is pertinent. This may be crucial here in determining how layered the allusion is: 'if in *The Tempest* Shakespeare is calling up the whole context of Medea's speech, and not its imagery of witchcraft alone, then he is associating Prospero's magic with the power to go back to one's youth, the power to be rejuvenated by a daughter-figure' (Parker 1995: 131).

(D) Brewer (1933–57) addresses the European Ovidian context. For the

400

impact of Golding's translation on Shakespeare see especially Brown (1994) and Forey (1998). On Shakespeare's Ovidianism generally, Bate's (1993) admirable book-length work is comprehensive, and carries a full bibliography which supplements the present one, but his study by no means supersedes all previous material. Among the most suggestive general accounts are Barkan (1986), Velz (1986) and Parker (1995). Selected work on individual plays and poems also appears below.

Barkan, Leonard (1980). 'Diana and Actaeon: The Myth as Synthesis.' *ELR* 10: 317–59.

—— (1981). '"Living Sculptures": Ovid, Michaelangelo and *The Winter's Tale.*' *ELH* 48: 639–67.

—— (1986) *The Gods Made Flesh: Metamorphosis and the Pursuit of Paganism.* New Haven.

Barnett, Louise. (1979). 'Ovid and *The Taming of the Shrew.*' *Ball State University Forum* 20.iii: 16–22.

Barroll, J. L. (1967). 'Shakespeare's Other Ovid: A Reproduction of the Commentary on Metamorphoses I–IV.' *ShSt* 3: 173–256.

Bate, Jonathan (1989). 'Ovid and the Sonnets; or, Did Shakespeare Feel the Anxiety of Influence?' *ShSu* 42: 65–76.

—— (1993). *Shakespeare and Ovid.* Oxford.

Boas, F. S. (1947). *Ovid and the Elizabethans.* London.

Bowers, Fredson, ed. (1973). *The Complete Works of Christopher Marlowe*, 2 vols. Cambridge.

Braden, Gordon (1973). *The Classics and English Renaissance Poetry: Three Case Studies.* New Haven.

Brewer, Wilmon (1933–57). *Ovid's Metamorphoses in European Culture*, 3 vols. Francistown, N.H.

Brooks, Harold F., ed. (1979). *A Midsummer Night's Dream.* London.

Brown, Sarah (1994). 'Ovid, Golding, and *The Tempest.*' *Translation and Literature* 3: 3–29.

Cantelupe, Eugene B. (1963). 'An Iconographical Interpretation of *Venus and Adonis*, Shakespeare's Ovidian Comedy.' *ShQ* 14: 141–51.

Dean, Paul (1991). '*Antony and Cleopatra*: An Ovidian Tragedy?' *CahiersE* 40: 73–7.

Donaldson, Ian (1982). *The Rapes of Lucretia: A Myth and its Transformations.* Oxford.

Findlay, L. M. (1978). 'Enriching Echoes: *Hamlet* and Orpheus.' *MLN* 93: 982–9.

Forey, Madelaine (1998). ' "Bless Thee, Bottom, Bless Thee! Thou art Translated!": Ovid, Golding, and *A Midsummer Night's Dream*.' *MLR* 93: 321–9.

Fripp, E. I. (1930). 'Shakespeare's Use of Ovid's *Metamorphoses*', pp. 98–128 in Fripp, *Shakespeare Studies, Biographical and Literary*. London.

Golding, Arthur (1567). *The XV. Bookes, Entituled Metemorphosis, translated oute of Latin*. London.

Hamilton, Donna B. (1973). '*Antony and Cleopatra* and the Tradition of Noble Lovers.' *ShQ* 24: 245–51.

Highet, Gilbert (1957). *The Classical Tradition: Greek and Roman Influences on Western Literature*. New York.

James, Heather (1997). *Shakespeare's Troy: Drama, Politics and the Translation of Empire*. Cambridge.

Keach, William (1977). *Elizabethan Erotic Narratives: Irony and Pathos in the Ovidian Poetry of Shakespeare, Marlowe, and their Contemporaries*. London.

Lamb, M. E. (1980). 'Ovid's *Metamorphoses* and Shakespeare's *Twelfth Night*', pp. 63–77 in Maurice Charney, ed., *Shakespearean Comedy*. New York.

——— (1989). 'Ovid and *The Winter's Tale*: Conflicting Views Toward Art', pp. 69–87 in W. R. Elton and W. B. Long, eds, *Shakespeare and the Dramatic Tradition: Essays in Honor of S. F. Johnson*. Newark, DE.

Martindale (1990).

Mueller, Martin (1971). 'Hermione's Wrinkles, or, Ovid Transformed: An Essay on *The Winter's Tale*.' *CompD* 5: 226–39.

Nims, John Frederick, ed. (1965). *Ovid's Metamorphoses: The Arthur Golding Translation*. New York.

Nosworthy, J. M. (1982). 'Shakespeare's Pastoral *Metamorphoses*', pp. 90–113 in G. R. Hibbard, ed., *The Elizabethan Theatre, VIII*. Port Credit.

Parker, Fred (1995). 'Regression and Romance in Shakespeare's Late Plays.' *Cambridge Quarterly* 24: 112–32.

Root, R. K. (1903). *Classical Mythology in Shakespeare*. London.

Smith, G. Gregory, ed. (1904). *Elizabethan Critical Essays*, 2 vols. Oxford.

Staton, W. F., Jr (1962–3). 'Ovidian Elements in *A Midsummer Night's Dream*.' *HLQ* 26: 165–78.

Steadman, John M. (1963). 'Falstaff as Actaeon: A Dramatic Emblem.' *ShQ* 14: 231–44.

Tarantino, Elisabetta (1997). 'Morpheus, Leander, and Ariel.' *RES* 48: 489–98.

Taylor, A. B. (1989). 'Golding, Ovid, Shakespeare's "Small Latin", and the Real Object of Mockery in "Pyramus and Thisbe".' *ShSu* 42: 53–64.

—— (1991). 'Shakespeare and Golding.' *N&Q* 236: 492–9 (Taylor has been responsible for some fifteen other notes and articles on this topic since 1977).

Thomson, Ann (1978). 'Philomel in *Titus Andronicus* and *Cymbeline*.' *ShSu* 31: 23–32.

Velz, John W. (1986). 'The Ovidian Soliloquy in Shakespeare.' *ShSt* 18: 1–24.

Willson, Robert F. (1969). 'Golding's *Metamorphoses* and Shakespeare's Burlesque Method in *A Midsummer Night's Dream*.' *ELN* 7: 18–25.

P-Q

Painter (Paynter), William (1540?–1594), English Translator See also **Boccaccio, Giovanni**; **Cinthio, Giovanni Baptista Giraldi**; **Livy (Titus Livius)**.

(A) Painter came from Kent and was educated at St John's College, Cambridge. He became headmaster of a school and later Clerk of the Ordnance at the Tower of London, a position he retained until his death despite charges of corruption. Among a number of translations, literary and otherwise, easily his most popular, and today his only remembered work, was the *Palace of Pleasure* (1566–7, then finally expanded 1575). This was an anthology of generally faithful and accurate versions of, eventually, 101 'pleasant histories and excellent novels' by Roman, Greek, English, Italian and French writers including **Livy**, **Plutarch**, **Cinthio**, **Fabyan**, **Xenophon**, **Apuleius**, **Froissart**, **Belleforest**, **Fiorentino**, **Masuccio** and **Boccaccio**. It gave readers the first large-scale collection in English of the novella literature which had been circulating in other languages since the time of **Chaucer**.

(B) The publication record of Painter's *Palace* suggests its popularity: his first volume was reprinted, a second added, then the whole reissued in less than a decade. A similar impression is given by the condemnations of the work's immorality by Ascham in *The Schoolmaster* and by Stephen Gosson in his *Theatre Plays Confuted*, 1582, calling it one of the books 'ransacked to furnish the Play houses in London'. It is confirmed by the quick appearance of other story collections which followed Painter's lead and included translations from the Italian: the anonymous *Sackful of Newes* (1573) and *The Forest of Fancy* (1579), Barnabe Riche's *Farewell to Militarie Profession* (1581), George Whetstone's *Heptameron of Civill Discourses* (1582) and *Tarlton's News out of Purgatorie* (anon., 1590).

As Gosson said, many Elizabethan and Jacobean playwrights (such as Webster, Massinger and **Marston**) drew plots from Painter; Scott (1916: 12) lists forty-three Elizabethan plays of this kind. Painter may also be held largely responsible for the extreme frequency of Italian settings on the Elizabethan stage. Lewis (1954: 309) sees this as the main function of the novella in England – 'to serve as dung or compost for the popular drama'. The *Palace* also had a major influence on story-writers, and shaped the English conception of the novella. Because of Painter's use of French intermediaries, this meant, in particular, that 'the Italian "novel" made its appearance in England already split in the French fashion' (Rodax 1968: 99), between the cynicism and licentiousness of the original tales and the moralism and 'refinement' which the French versions tended to superimpose.

An excerpt from the *Palace* is given under **Boccaccio**.

(C) Shakespeare very likely used the *Palace of Pleasure* version of Boccaccio's tale of Giletta de Nerbone for *All's Well*: for this – easily Shakespeare's most extensive use of Painter, if his source was indeed the English rather than the Italian and/or French which Painter himself worked from – see **Boccaccio**. Here may be noted Price's (1978) perhaps improbable suggestion that it is specifically Painter, in the form of his version of the story of Ermino Grimaldi (*Palace* I, 31; *Decameron* I, 8), that is drawn upon briefly in the King's speech to Bertram at 1.2.31–48.

There are also some signs of Shakespeare's awareness of Painter in the background of *The Rape of Lucrece* (see **Livy**), *Romeo and Juliet*, *The Merry Wives of Windsor*, *Much Ado about Nothing* and *Timon of Athens*. They are very small and in unimportant areas, and would hardly have been held to suggest an acquaintance with the *Palace* were it not for the near-certainty that Shakespeare knew other parts of the book. Painter's version of the Romeo and Juliet story (the twenty-fifth novel in his collection) was translated from **Belleforest**'s handling, as was Shakespeare's principal source in this play, Arthur **Brooke**'s verse tale *The Tragicall Historye*. The one apparent echo of it in Shakespeare is the resemblance between Painter's '40 hours at the least' and Shakespeare's 'two and forty hours' anticipated for Juliet's drugs to wear off, a detail not given in Brooke or the other available versions. *The Merry Wives of Windsor* may reflect knowledge of Giovan **Straparola**'s tale of Filenio Sisterno, which forms Painter's I, 49 (printed in Bullough), though stories of the 'duped lover' type were available in some abundance. Beatrice and Benedick's relationship in *Much Ado* shows some similarity with that between the two lovers in Painter's I, 61, from Marguerite of Navarre's *Heptameron* (the female one sometimes identified with Marguerite herself); see Richmond 1991: 193–4.

Finally, Painter's twenty-eighth story 'Of the straunge and beastlie nature of Timon of Athens, enemie to mankinde, with his death, burial, and epitaph' (printed in Bullough) was drawn from **Plutarch** and others. As with *Romeo and Juliet*, the case for Shakespeare's acquaintance with it consists of the circumstantial evidence of his having used other parts of the *Palace of Pleasure* together with a duplicated detail or piece of phrasing. Timon's epitaphs in Shakespeare are taken verbatim from North's Plutarch except for one alteration, the use of the expression 'wicked caitiffs' in place of North's 'wicked wretches' at 5.4.71, which matches Painter's phrasing ('wretched catife') at this point. But it would seem that for *Timon of Athens* 'Painter had nothing of importance to offer that was not in Plutarch' (Bullough, VI, 239).

(D) For Painter's technique as a translator see especially Rodax (1968: 96–100).

Benson, Pamela, ed. (1996). *Italian Tales from the Age of Shakespeare*. London.

Bullough, II, VI.

Kirkpatrick, Robin (1995). *English and Italian Literature from Dante to Shakespeare: A Study of Source, Analogue and Divergence*. London.

Lewis, C. S. (1954). *English Literature in the Sixteenth Century including Drama*. Oxford.

Price, John Edward (1978). 'Painter's "Ermino Grimaldi" and Shakespeare's "All's Well that Ends Well".' *N&Q* 223: 141–3.

Richmond, Hugh M. (1991). 'Shakespeare's *Verismo* and the Italian Popular Tradition', pp. 179–203 in J. R. Mulryne and Margaret Shewring, eds, *Theatre of the English and Italian Renaissance*. Basingstoke.

Rodax, Yvonne (1968). *The Real and the Ideal in the Novella of Italy, France and England*. Chapel Hill.

Scott, Mary Augusta (1916). *Elizabethan Translations from the Italian.* Boston, MA.

Palingenius, Marcellus (*fl.* 1531), Author of *Zodiacus Vitae*

(A) 'Palingenius' is usually taken to be the pseudonym of Pietro Angelo Manzoli of Stellata, near Ferrara, the only certain historical fact about whom is that his bones were exhumed and burnt, and his book the *Zodiacus Vitae* ('The Zodiac of Life') placed upon the Papal Index as heretical, in 1558. Beyond this, his identity, his supposed profession of medicine, and even the date of his sole book's appearance (1531 or 1535) are all in doubt. The *Zodiacus Vitae* is a verse compendium of astronomical, moral and philosophical thought couched in the form of a dialogue and in a 'vision' framework, generically within the medieval tradition of philosophical poetry. Palingenius' more minor offences against the Church would have included his open discussions of sensitive areas (such as the eternity of the world, the creation *ex nihilo* and its necessity), often under the guidance of his 'divine Plato'; but it is uncertain what more specific outrages he was supposed to have committed – they may lie in his 'relationships to 15th and 16th century Averroistic thought . . . even perhaps in his relationship to the quarrels between Averroists of various stripes' (Tuve 1947: xxiii).

(B) Palingenius' book was reprinted in its Latin form at least thirty times before the sixteenth century was out, some ten of the Latin editions being issued in England, with her 'affection for heretics, if only they might be Roman heretics' (Tuve 1947: xxiv). It was also widely taught in the early years of English grammar school, using both Latin editions (such as the Basle 1574 one, addressed to the *moderatores* of Christian youth) and English translations. Gabriel **Harvey** saw it as a 'most learned' and 'pregnant introduction into Astronomie, and both philosophies'. Barnaby Googe, a strongly Protestant admirer of the work, translated it into English in 1560–5, commencing his task at the age of nineteen. Both original and translation were praised by such as Francis Meres, while Thomas Digges, the eminent English scientist whose son Leonard was acquainted with Shakespeare, learned the eleventh chapter of the Latin by heart. The Elizabethans 'ranked Palingenius high among the minor Latin poets and considered Googe's translation of

him to be good if not great verse' (Hankins 1953: 14); the poem 'did not
. . . form men's styles, but it helped to shape the thinking of very many
English writers and readers' (Tuve 1947: v).

Googe's unrhymed verse translation appeared incomplete in 1560
and 1561, with the full text published in 1565, 1576 and 1588. The
passage given below is closely followed by Palingenius' description of
man's life as a series of five ages each with its specific evils (Palingenius
1576: 100–1):

> Wherfore if thou dost well discerne, thou shalt behold and see
> This mortall lyfe that here you leade, a Pageant for to bee.
> The divers partes therein declarde, the chaunging world doth showe,
> The maskers are eche one of them with lively breath that blowe.
> For almost every man now is disguised from his kinde,
> And underneth a false pretence they sely soules do blinde.
> So move they Goddes above to laugh wyth toyes and trifles vayne,
> Which here in Pageants fond they passe while they doe life retayne.
>
> (Palingenius 1576: 99)

(C) Shakespeare would probably have read either the 1576 edition of
Googe or the very similar 1588 reprint. These were the first to include
the marginal notes which offer parallels for several points in the plays.
The 1576 edition appeared when Shakespeare was ten or eleven years
old, and this would have been what he used if, as is likely, he
encountered Googe during a study of the Latin *Zodiacus* at school
(as commonly in the third form). Several of the verbal parallels are
reminiscent of Googe rather than the Latin.

'Many of the images and ideas of the *Zodiake* are acknowledged
commonplaces, though they may have seemed less commonplace to
Shakespeare than they do to us, since his own use of them has served to
popularize them' (Hankins 1953: 15). Minor and unconnected parallels
(such as in the suggestion by Camden 1957 that Albany's proverb 'Filths
savour but themselves', *Lear* 4.2.38, derives from Googe) may be overlooked, then. But Palingenius' description of the world as a stage, and
Googe's accompanying marginal annotation, 'The world a stage play'
(appearing beside the first two lines in the passage in (B), above), have
attracted the attention of Shakespeare scholars on several occasions
from at least the mid-nineteenth century, principally but not exclusively
in connection with Jacques in *As You Like It*. Though on the face of it

these are also common enough ideas, there are very few pre-Shakespearean loci in which the world-stage and the ages of man ideas appear together, and none of them are so likely to have been known to him as Palingenius. For Jacques' speech, one of Palingenius' own models, **Ovid**'s comparison of life with the four seasons (used by Shakespeare on several previous occasions), is mixed with the *Zodiacus*, and Shakespeare's seven (as opposed to five) ages seem to have come from Proclus (see Baldwin 1944: I, 666–7).

Shakespeare compares life to a play and/or the world to a stage in a number of other places, of which two are particularly likely examples of direct borrowing because they incorporate both these ingredients and their contexts involve additional elements from the passage in Palingenius. Near the start of *The Merchant of Venice*, in Antonio's 'I hold the world but as the world . . . / A stage, where every man must play a part' (1.1.77–8), the assignation of specific parts to individuals can be paralleled from the *Zodiacus*. Lear's stage reference in 'When we are born, we cry that we are come / To this great stage of fools' (4.6.183–4) is preceded by the same image as precedes in Palingenius, of the babe who cries at birth for fear of the world's evils – a popular idea, but nowhere else associated with that of the world-stage. Several dozen further parallels or apparent parallels examined by Hankins (1953) are often likely to be mere coincidences, as for example when Hamlet's 'sea of troubles' is associated with Palingenius on the 'troublous seas' of man's 'present life' in a context contemplating escape through death (but not suicide).

(D) For Palingenius' continental reputation and influence see Borgiani (1912); for Googe and his translation, Tuve (1947: vii–xv). Burrow (1986) does not mention Palingenius, but offers a wealth of other material Shakespeare's ages of man may draw on.

Baldwin (1944).

Borgiani, G. (1912). *Marcello Palingenio Stellato e il suo poema lo 'Zodiacus Vitae'*. Città di Castello.

Burrow, J. A. (1986). *The Ages of Man: A Study in Medieval Writing and Thought*. Oxford.

Camden, Carroll (1957). 'Three Notes on Shakespeare.' *MLN* 72: 251–3.

Hankins, John Erskine (1953). *Shakespeare's Derived Imagery*. Lawrence, KA.

Palingenius, Marcellus (1576). *The Firste Syxe Bokes of Marcellus Palingenius, Called the Zodiake of Life. Newly translated out of Latine into Englishe by Barnabe Googe.* London.

Tuve, Rosemond, ed. (1947). *The Zodiake of Life, by Marcellus Palingenius; Translated by Barnabe Googe* (facsimile of 1576 edn.). Delmar, N.Y.

Watson, Foster (1908). *The 'Zodiacus Vitae' of Marcellus Palengenius Stellatus: An Old School-Book.* London.

Paradin, Claude See **Emblems**.

Paris, Matthew (d. 1259), Chronicler Several details of incident and perhaps of phrasing in *King John* parallel Paris' Latin *Historia Major* (1571) sufficiently closely to make it seem almost certain Shakespeare knew it. **Holinshed** did too, but his reworking omits points common to Paris and Shakespeare.

Honigmann, E. A. J., ed. (1954). *King John* (Arden Shakespeare), xv–xvii. London.

Persius Flaccus, Aulus (AD 34–62), Roman Satirist A few phrases and figures, in later Shakespeare especially, may have a provenance in Persius.

Baldwin (1944), ii, 542–7.

Pescetti, Orlando (1556–1624), Italian Dramatist Pescetti's *Il Cesare* (printed 1594) offers parallels to *Julius Caesar*, but almost all can be explained by common sources such as **Plutarch** and **Appian**. His *La regia pastorella* (1589) has more recently been speculatively linked to *The Winter's Tale* by Clubb (1989: 161–71).

Clubb, Louise George (1989). *Italian Drama in Shakespeare's Time.* New Haven.

Herrick, Marvin T. (1965). *Italian Tragedy in the Renaissance*, pp. 156–7. Urbana, IL.

410

Orr, David (1970). *Italian Renaissance Drama in England before 1625: The Influence of 'Erudita' Tragedy, Comedy, and Pastoral on Elizabethan and Jacobean Drama*, pp. 128–9. Chapel Hill.

Petrarch (Petrarca), Francesco (1304–1374), Italian Poet and Scholar

Petrarch's poetry would have been known to Shakespeare in some form, and may have had some direct effect on the *Sonnets*, but influence is hard to demonstrate: Kennedy (1989) mounts the fullest study.

Kennedy, William J. (1989). ' "Sweet Theefe": Shakespeare Reading Petrarch.' *Annals of Scholarship: An International Quarterly* 6: 75–91.
Leishman, J. B. (1961). *Themes and Variations in Shakespeare's Sonnets.* London.
Roche, Thomas P., Jr (1981). 'How Petrarchan is Shakespeare?', pp. 147–64 in Wendell M. Aycock, ed., *Shakespeare's Art from a Comparative Perspective.* Lubbock, TX.

Pettie, George See **Guazzo, Stefano.**

Phaer, Thomas See *Mirror for Magistrates*; Virgil (Publius Vergilius Maro).

Philostratos, of Lemnos (b. *c.* AD 191), Author of *Eikones*

Philostratos, who could by 1578 be read in French as well as in Latin and Greek, has a brief *ekphrasis* on a painting of the siege of Thebes which shows some similarities to the Troy passage in lines 1366–1428 of *The Rape of Lucrece*.

Hulse, S. Clark (1978). ' "A Piece of Skilful Painting" in Shakespeare's "Lucrece".' *ShSu* 31: 13–22.

Plato (*c.* 428–*c.* 348 BC), Greek Philosopher

The main subject of Shorey's survey is Renaissance Platonism rather than Plato's works directly; for Shakespeare see pp. 175–236. Jones (1977: 20–1) notes a curious parallel between Falstaff's death and Socrates' in the *Phaedo*. Some links between Shakespeare and Plato probably come about through **Erasmus**.

Jones (1977).
Shorey, Paul (1938). *Platonism and English Literature*. Berkeley.

Plautus, Titus Maccius (*c.* 254–184 BC), Roman Playwright

(A) Plautus was born in Umbria, travelled to Rome when young, and found some kind of work in connection with the stage. He was later reduced to grinding corn for a baker, in which circumstances in *c.* 224 BC he wrote three plays. These he sold to the managers of the public games for enough money to enable him to leave the mill, and he continued to write comedies for the rest of his life. Twenty-one plays were identified as his genuine work by Varro, and these seem to be the ones which survived into modern times from a larger total once attributed to him. They are all adaptations of Greek works from the New Attic Comedy, in particular ones by Menander, and are characterized by a cynical tone, complex plots and stock characters. Some are farcical, others are on social or sentimental themes; among the best-known today are the *Menaechmi*, which exploits the possibilities of confusion between two identical twins; the *Amphitryon*, a burlesque of the legend of Alcmena's seduction by Jupiter, assuming the form of her husband; and the *Miles Gloriosus* ('Boastful Soldier'), based on the familiar stock figure. Plautus' work was very popular in republican Rome, but considered unpolished by the age of Augustus.

(B) Plautus' disinterment in the Renaissance – he was known only by repute before twelve texts were recovered in 1429 – was a strong stimulus to modern literature throughout Europe, especially on account of his realism. Thus his sixteenth-century editor Camerarius was able, in the essay 'De Carminibus Comicis', to define a comedy as 'a complete poem intricate in action or knit together by its characters, concerning a fictitious plot, about things, incidents and affairs taken from common life and resembling everyday occurrences' (translated Bullough, I, 5). On the stage Italy led the way, with the production of Plautus'

Menaechmi in Italian at the ducal court of Ferrara in 1486, and in the early sixteenth century the Italian public could enjoy numerous examples of a new form of drama, the *commedia erudita* ('learned comedy'), imitating Plautus and **Terence** (see **Ariosto**). Moralists complained, predictably, about Plautus' frivolity; Martin Luther, however, whose Plautus was one of only two books he owned on entering the monastery at Erfurt, stressed the playwright's pedagogical uses as a mirror of morality.

In Britain, Plautus' plays were staged or publicly recited in Latin from as early as the 1520s, continuing well into the Elizabethan era with seventeen recorded performances in Oxford and twenty in Cambridge from 1549 to 1583 (Boas 1914: 386–9). The *Menaechmi* was 'probably the best-known of all classical plays in the sixteenth century, by way of stage revivals and imitations' (Salingar 1974: 88). In sixteenth-century schools, too, the *Menaechmi* was almost universally prescribed and translated, with *Amphitryon* and other Plautine plays very likely to be read too. Plautus was evidently very familiar to Shakespeare's audience, otherwise Polonius could not make his observations on the versatility of the Players: 'Seneca cannot be too heavy nor Plautus too light' (2.2.396).

Francis Meres' well-known praise of Shakespeare begins 'As Plautus and Seneca are accounted the best for Comedy and Tragedy among the Latines: so Shakespeare among the English is the most excellent in both kinds for the stage.' The first English dramatic comedy, Nicholas Udall's *Ralph Roister Doister* (1537), is based on Plautus' *Miles Gloriosus*, and Plautus became the model *par excellence* for stage comedy in Elizabethan England. There is an apparent paradox here, for the ever-present cash nexus and heartless atmosphere of the New Comedy contrast strongly with the generally expansive sentiment of the Elizabethans. But Doran (1954: 174–81) has demonstrated that Plautus' and Terence's drama was perceived as essentially romantic, as containing love stories leading to marriage; and the links between Roman and Elizabethan comedy are tangible enough if considered in terms of structure rather than atmosphere (the Jacobean city comedy of **Jonson** and others is another matter). At least thirteen Elizabethan plays take either a general situation or a specific scene from Plautus, and several more (other than Shakespeare's) adopt a plot wholesale (Hosley 1966: 132). Beyond this, the use of stock figures by English playwrights often implies a Plautine background. And play-writing in the Plautine

413

mould must be seen as a European phenomenon: the descendants of *Mostellaria*, for instance, include, as well as Jonson's *Alchemist* and Shakespeare's *Taming of the Shrew*, Bentivolgio's *I Fantasmi*, Jefferay's *The Bugbears*, Heywood's *The English Traveller* and Larivey's *Les Esprits*, while there are half a dozen versions of the *Menaechmi* in Italian and Spanish alone.

Sixteenth-century English translations (or close and complete adaptations) of Plautus were, however, few. The anonymous *Jack Juggler* of 1555 and Edward Courtney's *Amphitryon* of 1562–3 are both from the same play, the former using part only. The more sophisticated William Warner's *Menaechmi* was registered 10 June 1594, six months before the first performance of *The Comedy of Errors*. It is a good example of Tudor translation, highly theatrical, and sometimes thought even livelier than its original. This scene, the opening of Act 2, in which the second Menechmus (the Antipholus figure) arrives from abroad, displays Plautus' realistic mode and Warner's vigorously colloquial style:

ACT TWO
Scene i Enter Menechmus, Socicles. Messenio his servant, and some Saylers

MEN.   Surely *Messenio*, I thinke Sea-fairers never take so comfort-
          able a joy in any thing, as when they have bene long tost
          and turmoyld in the wide seas, they hap at last to ken land.

MESS.   Ile be sworn, I shuld not be gladder to see a whole Country
          of mine owne, then I have bene at such a sight. But I pray,
          wherfore are we now come to *Epidamnum*? must we needs go
          to see everie Towne that we heare off?

MENECH.   Till I finde my brother, all Townes are alike to me: I must
          trie in all places.

MESS.   Why then let's even as long as wee live seeke your brother:
          six yeares now wee have roamde about thus, *Istria, Hispania,
          Massylia, Ilyria*, all the upper sea, all high *Greece*, all Haven
          Towns in *Italy*, I think if we had sought a needle all this
          time, we must needs have found it, had it bene above
          ground. It cannot be that he is alive; and to seek a dead
          man thus among the living, what folly is it?

MEN.   Yea, could I but once find any man that could certainly
          enforme me of his death, I were satisfied; otherwise I can
          never desist seeking: Litle knowest thou *Messenio* how neare
          my heart it goes.

414

MESS. This is washing of a Blackamore. Faith let's goe home, unlesse ye meane we should write a storie of our travaile.

MEN. Sirra, no more of these sawcie speeches, I perceive I must teach ye how to serve me, not to rule me.

MESS. I, so, now it appears what it is to be a servant. Wel yet I must speake my conscience. Do you heare sir? Faith I must tell ye one thing, when I looke into the leane estate of your purse, and consider advisedly of your decaying stocke, I hold it verie needful to be drawing homeward, lest in looking for your brother, we quite lose ourselves. For this assure your selfe, this Towne *Epidamnum*, is a place of outragious expences, exceeding in all ryot and lasciviousnesse: and (I heare) as full of Ribaulds, Parasites, Drunkards, Catchpoles, Cony-catchers, and Sycophants, as it can hold: then for Curtizans, why here's the currantest stamp of them in the world. Ye must not thinke here to scape with as light cost as in other places. The verie name shews the nature, no man comes hither *sine damno*.

MEN. Yee say very well indeed: give mee my purse into mine owne keeping, because I will so be the safer, *sine damno*.

MESS. Why Sir?

MEN. Because I feare you wil be busie among the Curtizans, and so be cosened of it: then should I take great paines in belabouring your shoulders, so to avoid both these harms, Ile keep it my selfe.

(1595 text; ed. Bullough, I, 17–18)

(C) Shakespeare is often thought to have read Plautus in the Latin. Baldwin (1947: 667–8) discusses available editions, proposing Lambinus, one of the title-pages from whose Lugduni Batavorum 1577 edition is shown in Fig. 9, as Shakespeare's; see also Foakes (1968: xxviii). The main Plautine plays associated with him are the *Menaechmi, Amphitryon, Mostellaria, Captivi, Miles Gloriosus, Casina* and *Rudens*. The many Renaissance adaptations of Plautus mean that elements from these plays also reached Shakespeare indirectly via the German and Dutch humanists' Latin drama, or, more importantly, Italian comedies. For example, one of the main sources for *The Taming of the Shrew*, Ariosto's *I Suppositi*, was based on Plautus' *Captivi*. Other debts are vaguer: one may argue for example that Shakespeare's braggart soldier figures (such as Don Armardo, Parolles, Bardolph, Pistol and Falstaff) have their

A & refidet in ara?fed videtur legendum.*Hem fe viden vt iaſlat furcifer?* Tv QVIESCE HANC REM MODO, &c. } tu
modò Callidamate,inquit Theuropides,fac finem iftius rei petendæ.hoc eſt,define pro Tranione deprecari.NE QVIC-
QVAM NEVIS.}fruſtra non vis *neuis*,fecunda perſona verbi *nolo*.HANC MODO VNAM NOXIAM: VNAM QVAE-
so}ſubintellige ignoſce,aut coudona Tranioni,ſi vnquam poſthàc tale aliquid peccarit,occidito.ſic ſuprà.FAC CAV-
SA MEA.}fac quod abs te peto,cauſa mea.QVID GRAVARIS? QVASI NON CRAS,&c.}quid grauaris hanc culpám
mihi remittere,ſeu condonare?profectò grauari non debes.nam ſi idcirco mihi ignoſcere non vis,quod hoc pacto,tibi
de me pœnas ſumere integrum non erit.exiſtimare debes,me cras aliám noxiam commeriturum,ita tibi & hoc pecca-
tum vetus,& illud recens animaduertere,atque vlciſci licebit.

B

M E N AE C H M I.

DRAMATIS PERSONAE.

C

PENICVLVS	paraſitus.
MENAECHMVS	ſurreptus.
EROTIVM	meretrix.
CYLINDRVS	coquus.
MENAECHMVS	ſoſicles.
MESSENIO	ſeruos.
MVLIER	vxor.
ALIVS SERVOS.	
ANCILLA	SENEX.
MEDICVS	LORARII.

ARGVMENTVM.

D

ERCATOR Siculus,cui erant gemini filij,
Ex illis ſurrepto altero mortem oppetit,
Nomen ſurreptitij indit illi qui domi eſt,
Auos paternus,facit Menæchmum Soſiclem.
Et is germanum,poſtquam adoleuit,quæritat
Circum omneis oras.pòſt Epidamnum deuenit:
Hîc fuerat auctus ille ſurreptitius.
Menæchmum ciuem credunt omnes aduenam.
Eúmque appellant,meretrix,vxor & ſocer,
Ij ſe cognoſcunt fratres poſtremò inuicem.

E

ERCATOR SICVLVS,}Moſchus nomine. GEMINI FILII}Soſicles,& Menæchmus.Ex ILLIS
SVRREPTO ALTERO.} altero ex illis geminnis ei ſurrepto,vididelicet Menæchmo.NOMEN SVR-
REPTITII INDIT ILLI QVI DOMI EST AVOS PATERNVS.} auus paternus mortuo filio ſuo.
geminorum patre,imponit nomen Menæchmi,qui ſurreptus erat,illi,qui domi eſt,videlicet Soſicli: &
ita Soſiclem,Menæchmum ..... & ipſe Menæchmus eodem nomine vocabatur. FACIT ME-
NAECHMVM SOSICLEM.}Soſiclem facit Menæchmum.ET IS GERMANVM POSTQVAM ADO-
LEVIT QVAERITAT.}& is Soſicles, nomine mutato , Menæchmus factus , germanum , hoc eſt, fratrem ex vtraque
parente diligenter quærit circum regiones omneis orbis terrarum.EPIDAMNVM DEVENIT}Dyrrachium venit.Sed
Steph.de vrbibus docet duas Epidamnos eſſe,vnam in Illyrico, alteram in ſinu Ionio.Sic ille , Ἐπίδαμνος, πόλις ἰλλυρίδος
uera,ſeu creuerat ſurreptitius ille Menæchmus,atque adeò ciuitate donatus erat. MENAECHMVM CIVEM CRE-
DVNT OMNEIS ADVENAM}omnes credunt Menæchmum aduenam.qui fratrem circum omneis terras quæritabat,
eſſe ciuem Menæchmum. EVMQVE APPELLANT MERETRIX ET VROR.}eúmque,qui erat aduena,pro Me-
næchmo ciue alloquuntur & accipiunt.meretrix, vxor,& ſocer Menæchmi ciuis. II SE COGNOSCVNT FRATRES
POSTREMO INVICEM}poſtremò ij Menæchmi cognoſcunt inter ſe,fratres ſe eſſe.

Mm iiij

Figure 9 M. Accius Plautus ... Dionys. Lambinii Monstroliensis emendatus: ab eodemque commentariis explicatus (Leyden, 1577), p. 415 (printed area actual size 270 × 150mm).

ancestry in Plautus' *miles gloriosus* and 'parasite' figures via the Italians; that 'the English clown [is] developed in part from the resourceful servant of Italian comedy who in turn is derived from the *serenus* of Roman comedy'; and even that 'romantic love and romantic adventure came into English comedy from the Italian plays which were modeled upon classical comedy' (Duckworth 1952: 411). It is such general resemblances that connect Plautus with Shakespeare comedies like *The Two Gentlemen of Verona* and *Much Ado about Nothing*, in which 'the influence of New Comedy . . . does not derive from a single discrete text . . . with a recoverable itinerary [but] provides structures and principles by which Shakespeare organizes his novella material' (Miola 1994: 80).

Other plays do have strong specific connections. The *Taming of the Shrew* can be seen as a sophisticated combination of New Comedy with native tradition. As well as showing signs of indirect use of Plautus, numerous details may be directly adapted from the *Mostellaria*, including the names of the characters Tranio and Grumio. But Shakespeare's use of Plautus seems to go beyond details, to the recovery of the Plautine Tranio beyond Ariosto's Dulipo, for example – both Tranios, but not Dulipo, have an able defender (Lucentio/Callidamates) and emerge scot-free and impenitent. Shakespeare might, it is suggested, have deduced such original features from Ariosto without necessarily reading Plautus' play. Such intuitive recovery of an earlier dramatic context behind a later work is also at issue in suggestions, highly speculative but intriguing, that Plautus opened a window for Shakespeare onto Menander and the rest of the world of Greek New Comedy, only fragments of which have come down to modern times, with possible effects on a range of his plays (see Nuttall 1989: 6–10).

Shakespeare's most obviously Plautine work is *The Comedy of Errors*, for which *Menaechmi* was the principal source (for a summary of correspondences see Foakes 1968: 109–12). *Menaechmi* supplies the main plot of the long-separated twins mistaken for each other; Shakespeare multiplies the confusions and adds the pathetic notes on the separation and the father in 1.1. Sometimes Shakespeare takes his extra materials from other sources, but he borrows the central enlargement from Plautus himself, by going to *Amphitryon* for the second set of twins who become the servants (Dromios). *Errors* is thus a *contaminatio*, a recombination of separate works, and Shakespeare does not merely appropriate discrete elements from the two plays but blends them together more organically. *Menaechmi* is a play which 'in dramatic terms does not

417

pretend to be anything more than a heartless romp performed by two-dimensional comic types' (Rudd 1994: 57), and its appeal lies mainly in its verbal wit. Shakespeare did not take this over, though he mastered Plautus' plot and surpassed him in characterization, for instance in transforming the flat Plautine Medicus into the figure of Pinch. Overall, 'Shakespeare modified the Plautine attitude to life, and here his divergence from the academic dramas which often sought to recreate the Roman scene in scholarly fashion, is noteworthy. He tells his Ephesian tale in terms of the modern *novella*' (Bullough, I, 8). There are signs that Shakespeare used a Latin text of Plautus' play, but this does not preclude his having seen Warner's too (Bullough, I, 3–4). Verbal parallels between *Errors* and Warner's *Menaechmi* are sometimes seen as evidence that Shakespeare used Warner (so Riehle 1990: 279–83), sometimes that Warner used Shakespeare (so Baldwin 1928).

Recent commentators have attempted to overturn or at least qualify an older assumption that Plautus' influence on Shakespeare is largely confined to the earlier plays. Even the tragedies have sometimes become hunting-grounds for Plautine elements: Polonius as *senex*, Laertes as comic *adulescens*, Edgar's feigned madness foreshadowed by Menaechmus'. But even if felt plausible, these links may tell us little. A different and clearer kind of Plautine debt can be argued for *The Merry Wives of Windsor*: 'if [Shakespeare] was indeed faced with a commission to write a court play at short notice about the fat knight in love, the most promising model to consider would have been Plautus's *Braggart Soldier*' (Salingar 1974: 231–2). This character type was familiar enough in England for use of it not necessarily to imply recourse to Plautus himself, but the *miles gloriosus*, Salingar continues, 'could have furnished . . . also the character of the Host', and anticipates the main lines of Shakespeare's play in general structure – 'there is a static opening scene showing off the role of Pyrgopolynices, then comes the first of the two intrigues against him, the intrigue involving the invention of a double identity for the heroine . . . whom he will agree in the course of the second intrigue to release'. It is possible that *Wives* draws also on Plautus' *Casina*, in which a husband and wife argue over a girl's marriage, like Anne's parents, and in which Shakespeare could have found suggestions for Falstaff's drubbing in the clothes of 'the fat woman of Brainford' (Bullough, II, 9; for detailed comparisons see also Forsythe 1921).

Finally, there is a basis for seeing Plautus as at least an overall model in the Romances. In a general way, the *Amphitryon* prologue would have interested Shakespeare for its comments on tragicomedy. *The Tempest* has been associated particularly with *Rudens* (see especially Svendsen 1983), a play highly esteemed by the humanists, involving an exiled father and his daughter. With the exception of one or two close verbal similarities, however, the supposed parallels (of 'tone' or 'theatricality') are vague, or easily explained as fortuitous. More substance attaches to claims of New Comedic structural influence on the Romances, notably in the configuration of *senex, virgo* and *adulescens* in both *The Tempest* and *Pericles*. The relevance of such basic elements in Plautus to Shakespeare's Romances is suggested, as Miola (1994) shows, by Scaliger's description of New Comedic plot:

> In New Comedy then, marriages and love affairs are the chief subjects. There are many jealous rivalries. Virgins are brought from bawds so that they may be free; some may be discovered to be free by a ring, by rattles or amulets, by nurses, recognized by a father, mother, lover, or brother, always to the great discomfort of the bawds.
>
> (translated Miola 1994: 140)

(D) Some older studies, such as Gill's (1925, 1930), are still useful. Riehle (1990) is comprehensive but often too ready to identify material in Shakespeare as Plautine. Miola's (1994) is a subtler treatment using a broad conception of literary influence; there is perhaps again some tendency to over-enthusiasm. Other helpful general accounts of Shakespeare's use of Plautus are Salingar (1974) for elements such as disguise, tricksters and fortune (as well as general context), and Brooks (1961) for plot. Baldwin (1965) has the fullest account of the sources of *The Comedy of Errors*, Riehle some more recent suggestions including the notion that Plautus is partially responsible for Shakespeare's 'scenic dramaturgy' – use of locale and space on stage – in this work (Riehle 1990: 77ff.).

Arthos, John (1967). 'Shakespeare's Transformation of Plautus.' *CompD* 1: 239–53.

Barber, Lester E. (1970). '*The Tempest* and New Comedy.' *ShQ* 21: 207–11.

Baldwin, T. W., ed. (1928). *The Comedy of Errors* (Heath's American Arden Shakespeare). Boston.

——(1965) *On the Compositional Genetics of 'The Comedy of Errors'.* Urbana, IL.

Boas, F. S. (1914). *University Drama in the Tudor Age.* Oxford.

419

Braunmuller, A. R. (1987). 'Plautus, Abraham Fleming, and *King John*', pp. 18–19 in *KM 80: A Birthday Album for Kenneth Muir*. Liverpool.

Brooks, Harold F. (1961). 'Themes and Structures in *The Comedy of Errors*', pp. 54–71 in John Russell Brown and Bernard Harris, eds, *Early Shakespeare* (Stratford-upon-Avon Studies, 3). London.

Bruster, Douglas (1990). 'Comedy and Control: Shakespeare and the Plautine Poeta.' *CompD* 24: 217–31.

—— (1991). ' "Nor Plautus Too Light": *Hamlet* 1.2.184–5 and Plautus's *Pseudolus*.' *ANQ* 4.iii:118–19.

Bullough.

Coulter, Cornelia C. (1920). 'The Plautine Tradition in Shakespeare.' *JEGP* 19: 66–83.

Doran, Madeleine (1954). *Endeavors of Art: A Study of Form in Elizabethan Drama*. Madison, WI.

Duckworth, George Eckel (1952). *The Nature of Roman Comedy: A Study in Popular Entertainment*. Princeton.

Foakes, R. A., ed. (1968). *The Comedy of Errors* (Arden Shakespeare). London (first published 1962).

Forsythe, R. S. (1921). 'A Plautine Source of *The Merry Wives of Windsor*.' *MP* 18: 401–22.

Gill, E. M. (1925). 'A Comparison of the Characters in *The Comedy of Errors* with those in the *Menaechmi*.' *University of Texas Studies in English* 5: 79–95.

—— (1930). 'The Plot-Structure of *The Comedy of Errors* in Relation to its Sources.' *University of Texas Studies in English* 10: 13–65.

Harrold, William E. (1970). 'Shakespeare's Use of *Mostellaria* in *The Taming of the Shrew*.' *ShJ* 106: 188–94.

Heilman, Robert B. (1979). 'Farce Transformed: Plautus, Shakespeare, and Unamuno.' *Comp. Lit* 31: 113–23.

Hosley, Richard (1966). 'The Formal Influence of Plautus and Terence', pp. 131–46 in John Russell Brown and Bernard Harris, eds, *Elizabethan Theatre* (Stratford-upon-Avon Studies, 9). London.

Knox, Bernard (1955). ' "The Tempest" and the Ancient Comic Tradition', pp. 52–73 in W. K. Wimsatt, ed., *English Stage Comedy* (English Institute Essays, 1954). New York.

Miola, Robert S. (1994). *Shakespeare and Classical Comedy: The Influence of Plautus and Terence*. Oxford.

Nevo, Ruth (1980). 'Shakespeare's Comic Remedies.' *New York Literary Forum* 5–6: 3–15.

Nuttall, A. D. (1989). *The Stoic in Love: Selected Essays on Literature and Ideas.* London.

Riehle, Wolfgang (1990). *Shakespeare, Plautus and the Humanist Tradition.* Woodbridge.

Rudd, Niall (1994). *The Classical Tradition in Operation: Chaucer/Virgil; Shakespeare/Plautus; Pope/Horace; Tennyson/Lucretius; Pound/Propertius.* Toronto.

Salingar, Leo (1974). *Shakespeare and the Traditions of Comedy.* Cambridge.

Shaw, Catherine M. (1980). 'The Conscious Art of *The Comedy of Errors.*' *New York Literary Forum* 5–6: 17–28.

Svendsen, James T. (1983). 'The Fusion of Comedy and Romance: Plautus' *Rudens* and Shakespeare's *The Tempest*', pp. 121–34 in Karelisa V. Hartigan, ed., *From Pen to Performance: Drama as Conceived and Performed.* Lanham, MD.

Plessis-Mornay, Philippe du, Sieur de Marlay (1549–1623), Huguenot Theologian

His short treatise translated by Mary Sidney as *A Discourse of Life and Death* in the same volume as her *Antonius* (1592 edition; see **Garnier**) can be linked to the Duke's 'Be absolute for death' in *Measure for Measure* (3.1.5–41).

Duncan-Jones, Katherine (1977). 'Stoicism in *Measure for Measure*: A New Source.' *RES* 28: 441–6.

Pliny (Gaius Plinius Secundus) ('The Elder') (AD 23–79), Roman Writer on Natural History

(A) Pliny came of a wealthy north Italian family with estates at Como, where he was born. He was educated in Rome, saw active service in the army, and became the commander of a cavalry regiment and a comrade of the future Emperor Titus. He made scientific tours to German parts; he died during a relief mission after an investigation of an eruption of Vesuvius. His writings included a history of the Germanic wars, works on oratory and grammar, and a continuation of a history of Rome. But his principal and only surviving work is the monumental *Naturalis Historia*, completed AD 77. This took a lifetime's effort and extended to thirty-seven volumes. It is an encyclopedic compilation of information on all things of natural or non-artificial origin, with digressions on human inventions and institutions. It is by no means the impersonal kind of production later 'encyclopedias' became: on the contrary, it is extremely idiosyncratic and riddled with Pliny's prejudices. In some ways it transcends its function as a collection of data and second-hand report through what have been called its 'poetical-philosophical' qualities.

(B) The frequently unique (if spectacularly unreliable) information found in the *Historia* was enough to render it useful, often fascinating, to early modern readers in spite of its sometimes tedious manner. Pliny's tracks can be traced in a great many later compendia and other works on diverse subjects, and in innumerable local images and ideas in literature. Sixteenth-century editions are abundant and indices were available, including one by Delacampius which has been associated with Shakespeare (Baldwin 1935).

The first English version, by 'I.A.' (John Alday?), of 1565, was reprinted twice in Shakespeare's lifetime, but is merely a sampler from an earlier and fuller French rendering. It is the 1601 rendering by Philemon Holland (1552–1637), the 'translator-general of his age', that familiarized Pliny to English-speaking readers. This is a characteristic Renaissance product, its crowded pages recording Holland's struggles to gloss and correct the hotchpotch of information in his interpolations and marginal notes.

This passage from VII, 2 is an example of Holland's Pliny at its most fantastical.

¶ *Of the Scythians, and the diversitie of other nations.*

That there bee Scythians, yea, and many kinds of them that feed ordinarily of mans flesh, wee have shewed alreadie in our former discourses. A report haply that would be thought incredible, if we did not consider and thinke withall, how in the very middle and heart of the world, even in Sicily and Italy, here hard by, there have beene such monsters of men, namely, the Cyclopes and Lystrigones: nay, if we were not credibly informed, that even of late daies, and go no farther than to the other side of the Alpes, there be those that kill men for sacrifice after the manner of those Scythian people; and that wants not much of chewing and eating their flesh. Moreover, neere unto those Scythians that inhabit toward the pole Articke, and not far from that climate which is under the very rising of the North-east wind, and about that famous cave or whole out of which that wind is said to issue, which place they call Gesclithron, [*i.* the cloister or key of the earth] the Arimaspians by report do dwell, who as we have said before, are known by this marke, for having one eie only in the mids of their forehead: and these maintain war ordinarily about the mettall mines of gold, especially with griffons, a kind of wilde beasts that flie, and use to fetch gold out of the veines of those mines (as commonly it is received:) which savage beasts (as many authors have recorded, and namely, *Herodotus* and *Aristeas* the Proconnesian, two writers of greatest name) strive as eagerly to keepe and hold those golden mines, as the Arimaspians to disseize them therof, and to get away the gold from them. Above those, are other Scythians called Anthropophagi, where is a countrie named Abarimon, within a certain vaile of the mountain Imaus, wherin are found savage and wild men, living and conversing usually among the bruit beasts, who have their feet growing backward, and turned behind the calves of their legs, howbeit they run most swiftly. These kind of men can endure to live in no other aire nor in any clime else than their own, which is the reason that they cannot be drawne to come unto other kings that border upon them, nor could be brought unto *Alexander* the great: as *Beton* hath reported, the marshall of that princes campe, and who also put down his gests and journies in writing. The former Anthropophagi or eaters of mans flesh, whom we have placed about the North-pole, ten daies journie by land above the river Borysthenes, use to drink out of the skuls of mens heads, and to weare the scalpes haire and al, in stead of mandellions or stomachers before their breasts, according as *Isogonus* the Nicean witnesses.

(Pliny 1635: 153–4)

(C) There has been disagreement over how Shakespeare read Pliny – in Latin (Baldwin 1935), in Holland (Thomson 1952: 127, but specifically rebutted by Baldwin), or in the earlier French version (Muir 1957: 128)? Perhaps he did not read him at all: almost anything one looks for can, it seems, be found somewhere in Pliny's book, and equally, much of Pliny's material is recycled by later writers (see Stroup 1938). If Shakespeare perused the *Naturalis Historia* at all, this probably happened before or during the composition of *Othello*, since (*pace* Simmons 1976 and Schanzer 1956, mentioning tenuous links elsewhere) Shakespeare's apparent echoes of Pliny are largely confined to this play. It may be significant that *Othello* is dated to immediately after the first appearance of Holland's translation. The apparent echoes, some seeming to reflect Holland's phrasing, are all in matters of detail. Indications of Pliny's presence behind Othello's defence of his conduct to Brabantio in 1.3 include, according to Meyerstein (1942), his denial of magical practices; more famously and more probably, the marvels Othello encountered in his travels, with the famous 'Anthropophagi' (1.3.144), resemble elements in Holland's VII, 2 (above) and other passages. The other well-known borrowing, or apparent borrowing, is from II, 919, translated by Holland 'And the sea Pontus evermore floweth and runneth out into Propontis, but the sea never retireth backe againe within Pontus':

> Like to the Pontic sea,
> Whose icy current and compulsive course
> Ne'er feels retiring ebb, but keeps due on
> To the Propontic and the Hellespont;
> Even so my bloody thoughts, with violent pace,
> Shall ne'er look back, ne'er ebb to humble love,
> Till that a capable and wide revenge
> Swallow them up.
>
> (3.3.57–64)

(D) The basic claims for Pliny's presence in Shakespeare, largely summed up in Muir (1957), are now old; they have begun to be reduced (Boose 1981; Stroup 1938) or, on occasion, speculatively extended (Simmons 1976).

Baldwin, T. W. (1935). 'A Note upon William Shakspere's Use of Pliny', pp. 157–82 in Hardin Craig, ed., *Essays in Dramatic Literature: The Parrott Presentation Volume*. Princeton (reprinted New York, 1967).

Boose, Lynda E. (1981). 'Othello's "Chrysolite" and the Song of Songs Tradition.' *PQ* 60: 427–37.

Bullough, VII.

Meyerstein, E. H. W. (1942). 'Othello and C. Furius Cresinus.' *TLS* 7 Feb: 72.

Muir, Kenneth (1953). 'Holland's Pliny and "Othello".' *N&Q* 198: 513.

—— (1957). *Shakespeare's Sources, I: Comedies and Tragedies*. London.

Pliny, translated by I. A. (1565). *A Summarie of the Antiquities and Wonders of the World, Abstracted out of the Sixteene First Bookes of Plinie, translated oute of French*. London.

Pliny, translated by Philemon Holland (1635). *The Historie of the World: Commonly called, the Naturall Historie of C. Plinius Secundus*, 2 vols. London (first published in one volume, 1601).

Schanzer, Ernest (1956). '"Anthony and Cleopatra" and the Countess of Pembroke's "Antonius".' *N&Q* 201: 152–4.

Simmons, J. L. (1976). 'Holland's Pliny and *Troilus and Cressida*.' *ShQ* 27: 329–32.

Stroup, Thomas B. (1938). 'Shakespeare's Use of a Travel-Book Commonplace.' *PQ* 17: 351–8.

Thomson, J. A. K. (1952). *Shakespeare and the Classics*. London.

Plutarch (*c.* AD 46–*c.* 120), Greek Biographer, Historian and Moral Philosopher

(A) Born in provincial Boeotia, Plutarch studied philosophy at Athens, visited Egypt and Italy, and taught at Rome, but his was eventually, and largely, a life of quiet cultivation in Boeotia under the *Pax Romana*. Here he wrote his diverse collection of *Moralia* ('Moral Essays'), mostly treatises on philosophical and rhetorical subjects, displaying a great breadth of interest in and curiosity about the world, and his *Parallel Lives of the Ancient Greeks and Romans*, twenty-three paired biographies of notable figures of antiquity, nineteen of them with attached comparisons assessing the virtues and vices of each subject against its Greek/Roman counterpart (there are also a few single lives). Together these two works transmitted to Europe more knowledge of the moral and historical aspects of classical antiquity, and probably more stimulus to imaginative treatment of antiquity in works of art, than any other authority, largely because Plutarch is one of the most charming and readable of classical writers. He takes history to be the biographies of great men, but his declared object in each Life is to bring out the moral character in question, for educational purposes (he tells us in the *Life of Pericles*), rather than to provide a history of events of the figure's times. Plutarch is, however, no simple didactic moralist. He shows himself much interested in men's habits and way of living, and aware of the complex and paradoxical nature of the human beings he writes of, making him at times suspend or disarm his moral judgement, and making his characterizations seem in some respects often surprisingly modern.

(B) It was for his moral emphasis and his wise sayings that Plutarch was in general valued throughout the Renaissance, so that the *Moralia* were on the whole better-known than the *Lives*. But the *Lives* were increasingly used educationally. Not prescribed in **Elyot'**s *Governour* (1531), nor in Ascham's *Schoolmaster* (1570), their fortunes were evidently changing in later decades, with **Montaigne**'s praise of them in his essay 'On the Education of Children', Sir Francis Walsingham's recommendation of them to his nephew, and **Jonson**'s reference in *The Devil is an Ass*, where a character has named his child 'Plutarchus':

> That yeere Sir,
> That I begot him, I bought *Plutarch's* lives,
> And fell s' in love with the booke, as I call'd my sonne
> By 'his name: In hope he should be like him:
> And write the lives of our great men!
> (3.2.21–5; ed. Herford and Simpson 1925–51: vi, 212)

Indeed, 'the popularity of Plutarch [appears] related to his educational importance' – 'himself a teacher, Plutarch was especially appreciated by other teachers' (Burke 1966: 143), an obvious example being his French translator Jacques Amyot of Melun, professor at Bourges. As an interpreter rather than a mere reporter of events (like the chroniclers), he also qualified as a good historian, but here, it has been felt, he ranked behind **Suetonius** and **Tacitus**: 'it was the busts of the Twelve Caesars that decorated almost every palace in Europe ... and it required a considerable intellectual feat to substitute the Plutarchan vision of Rome (mostly republican) for the customary line of the Imperial Caesars' (Spencer 1957: 31). In contrast to the *Moralia*, no handy selections from Plutarch's *Lives* were available; the cumbrous continental folio editions of the sixteenth century betokened a book not in demand from the ordinary cultivated reader.

The record of early English translations shows a similar concentration on the *Moralia*. Wyatt's *Quiet of Minde*, 1528, from *De Tranquillitate Animi*, stands at the head of what becomes a fairly extensive tradition of single-text translations in the sixteenth century, extending to one example by Queen Elizabeth herself, though it did not produce a complete version. As for the *Lives*, they had early been turned from Greek into Latin, but it was at the point when a full range of Roman historians in complete translations was about to be opened up to English readers in their own tongue (Tacitus in 1591 and 1598; **Livy** in 1600) that the famous rendering of Sir Thomas North (*c.* 1535–*c.* 1601) appeared, in

1579. To judge by the European bibliographical record, Plutarch's popularity in vernaculars was far greater than in the original, even more exaggeratedly so compared to most other Greek historians (see Burke 1966: 138–9). Even so, and notwithstanding that figures treated in the *Lives* acquired some popularity as subjects for writers (as in the Roman plays composed in emulation of **Garnier**), neither North nor Plutarch became by any means household names in Shakespeare's time. This, of course, makes it very unlikely that any of the cases of close verbal following of the text of the *Lives* in Shakespeare constitute imitations which the audience is meant to recognize as such.

North's translation was taken almost exclusively from Amyot's French version of 1559, commonly regarded as one of the all-time master-pieces of French prose. North himself, who translated a number of other major works from the Spanish and Italian as well as the French, was in France in the entourage of his elder brother, Roger Lord North, on an embassy to the French court in 1574, when Amyot's book would have been fresh in Paris. He subsequently prospered and was eventually knighted by Queen Elizabeth, to whom he dedicated the third edition of his *Lives* in 1603. North was by no means a scholar of Amyot's class, but since Amyot had already supplied the scholarship (including many original emendations and interpretations), he could concentrate on turning Plutarch into a contemporary, deploying a rich Elizabethan idiom and modern tone. Amyot had already tended to expand and explain Plutarch, whom he observed to write 'doctement et gravement' rather than 'doucement et facilement'. North's forceful and picturesque language sometimes replaces less colourful expression in the French, though its clarity is not always unimpeachable (Russell 1973: 150–8 carries out a stylistic comparison of the two translations via a case study of Chapter 29 of the *Life of Antonius*, concluding in both cases that their 'differences from the real Plutarch may well be reckoned pure gain').

The appeal of Plutarch's *Parallel Lives* cannot be illustrated by a single passage, for their attractions are too various, including the 'little homely citations of mere gossip, the accounts of venturesome exploits stirring to the reader's imagination, the frequent parentheses, the constant bias towards ethical judgements', all of which features 'have their own integrity as parts of a method of portraiture which has delighted students of human motives, reasonings, and deeds' (Shackford 1929: 9). North's translation is illustrated here instead, by one or two of the pages which underlie what may be, in all the playwright's work, 'the longest continuous passage in which Shakespeare relies closely on a particular source' (Heuer 1957: 52), in *Coriolanus* 5.3. It is a case in which North proffers an emphasis which Amyot had not, and one taken up by Shakespeare. The adverb applied by Volumnia to Coriolanus in her complaint that he 'unnaturally sheweth all ingratitude' substitutes for the French 'asprement' (corresponding to the Greek πικρῶς), with the consequence that 'the conflict, conceived psychologically or rather logically in the French version as one between "rigeur" and "raison", is now being transferred to a different plane . . . The disruption of the natural bonds and of the naturally inherent order of human existence has become the decisive issue' (Heuer 1957: 52).

'My sonne, why doest thou not aunswer me? doest thou thinke it good altogether to geve place unto thy choller and desire of revenge, and thinkest thou it not honestie for thee to graunt thy mothers request, in so weighty a cause? doest thou take it honorable for a noble man, to remember the wronges and injuries done him: and doest not in like case thinke it an honest noble mans parte, to be thankefull for the goodnes that parents doe shewe to their children, acknowledging the duety and reverence they ought to beare unto them? No man living is more bounde to shewe him self thankefull in all partes and respects, then thy selfe: who so unnaturally sheweth all ingratitude. Moreover (my sonne) thou hast sorely taken of thy countrie, exacting grievous payments apon them, in revenge of the injuries offered thee: besides, thou hast not hitherto shewed thy poore mother any curtesie. And therefore, it is not only honest, but due unto me, that without compulsion I should obtaine my so just and reasonable request of thee. But since by reason I cannot persuade thee to it, to what purpose do I deferre my last hope?' And with these wordes, her selfe, his wife and children, fell downe upon their knees before him. Martius seeing that, could refraine no lenger, but went straight and lifte her up, crying out: Oh mother, what have you done to me? And holding her hard by the right hande, oh mother, sayed he, you have wonne a happy victorie for your countrie, but mortall and unhappy for your sonne: for I see my self vanquished by you alone.

(1579 text; Plutarch 1895–6: ii, 185–6)

(C) Shakespeare would have read parts of several of the classical historians in Latin at school, but comparison between his early, non-Plutarchan, attempt at a Roman setting in *Titus Andronicus*, and the later ones from *Julius Caesar* onwards, suggests North induced a fresh interest in the matter of Rome. The playwright may have worked from any or indeed all of the first three editions of 1579, 1595 and 1603 at one time or another (see MacCallum 1967: 152), though his use of the second alone, possible on current chronologies for the relevant plays, is sometimes proposed. There are no clear signs of his independent knowledge of any French, Latin or Greek Plutarch texts. His reading possibly led first to the use of the *Life of Theseus* for the figure of Theseus, some character names, and other details in *A Midsummer Night's Dream* (see Nosworthy 1982: 104–5), though other explanations for these correspondences can be found. Three subsequent plays were constructed very squarely on Plutarch: *Julius Caesar*, *Antony and Cleopatra* and *Coriolanus*; *Timon of Athens* draws on two brief segments of the *Lives*. Shakespeare worked from several Lives eclectically where relevant material was found in more than one: *Julius Caesar*, for instance, involves events appearing in the narratives of Brutus, Antony and Caesar himself. The care with which he approached North's volume, rearranging and combining what he found in different Lives with other sources (such as **Appian**), is apparent.

Several reasons can be advanced to account for Shakespeare's initial attraction, and regular recurrence, to the *Lives*. The qualities of North's prose made the English Plutarch often highly adaptable for theatrical use – at the extreme, Shakespeare needs only to versify the sentences he finds, and by keeping close to North achieves some fine local effects. Second, Plutarch's history is focused on individual lives, and hence tends to offer a dramatic, indeed tragic, shape, where a chronicle, say, does not. G. K. Hunter takes this point further in observing that Plutarch offers 'a concentration on the inexplicable individuality of personal lives, seen together with the tortuousness of the process by which subjective traits become objective and politically significant facts' (Hunter 1977: 20). And Plutarch concerns himself with issues that interested the Renaissance and which seem to have interested Shakespeare: the nature of heroism in an unheroic world, the limitations of Stoic doctrine, the individual's relation to the state. Such interests associate Plutarch strongly with other writers on Shakespeare's shelf, for example Montaigne, another notable admirer of Plutarch.

There has been much discussion of what material, other than the obvious, Shakespeare might have known in the *Lives*. Honigmann (1959) is rightly insistent that his use of the comparisons at the end of each pair of lives can be crucial (Plutarch's comparisons were, however, unavailable in a few cases, including that of Alexander and Caesar, because they had been lost in ancient times; Renaissance editors often inserted their own speculative reconstructions, but North did not include these). The Greek half of each of the principal pairs of Lives Shakespeare read may sometimes have supplied supplementary or contrastive detail, so that he may draw some negative characteristics of Brutus, for example, from Plutarch's parallel description of Dion (so Homan 1975, but contradicted by Humphreys 1984: 23). At one time or another it has been suggested that Shakespeare also knew many more of the *Lives* – of Cicero, Pompey, Cato the Younger, Cato the Elder, etc.; this is obviously always possible, but the evidence advanced (e.g. in Hanna 1994 on *The Life of Timoleon*) sometimes falls short of what is required. In other words, the knowledge that the playwright read some of the *Lives* cannot in itself imply he read all of them, so the strongest cases for influence are built upon lives he is known to have studied or those strongly associated with them – their paired counterparts or others which he might easily have been led on to.

It is often supposed that Shakespeare first read Plutarch about the time of composing *Julius Caesar* and *Henry V* (see below for the latter), *c.* 1599. Though almost all significant narrative material in *Julius Caesar* derives from Plutarch, Shakespeare was to follow his source more closely in later dealings with him. From the first three-quarters of Caesar's long *Life* he took only a few details, drawing for the most part only on the last quarter, and combining it almost seamlessly with episodes from *Brutus* and *Antonius* (Maguin 1973: 34–49 and Humphreys 1984: 10–23 provide scene-by-scene comparative analysis). Sometimes Shakespeare flatly contradicts Plutarch: Plutarch's Caesar suspects only Cassius where the play's Caesar suspects both Brutus and Cassius, and the play's dispute between Octavius and Antony about leading the right wing of the army takes place between Brutus and Cassius in the Greek text. Ultimately, Shakespeare's creative originality leads to a work less with different emphases than a different orientation:

> Plutarch furnished the play's grand strategy and many of its infillings – the main character evaluations, the sense of shaping destiny, and a lucidity of style which suited – even perhaps prompted – the play's

'classical' distinction. But . . . Shakespeare leaves out many particulars, to create a plot comprising the conspiracy's rise and fall, and Caesar's bodily defeat and spiritual triumph. As a dramatist must, he sees history as relationships, not only as aims and strategies. Far more than in Plutarch do we sense what the conspirators meant to each other, and to Caesar, and he to them and to Antony, and Brutus to Portia.

(Humphreys 1984: 23–4)

The second and longer phase of Shakespeare's work with the *Lives* comes in the group of plays assigned to the years 1606–7, *Antony and Cleopatra, Coriolanus* and *Timon of Athens*. (There is, as the dates imply there may be, some cross-pollination in Shakespeare's use of the Lives which form these plays' respective principal sources. For purely decorative reasons, it seems, the parts in *Timon* involve six proper names from the *Life of Marcus Antonius*.) In *Antony and Cleopatra* he submits himself to history rather than imposing his own patterns, particularly so in Act 5, and this offers an explanation for the play's hard-to-follow scenic structure and its unemphatic quality: the Antonius narrative, though 'full of compelling circumstantial detail', is 'lacking in a clearly visualizable shape', tending to follow 'the wavering course of Antony himself' (Jones 1971: 225). Even where Shakespeare's invention is called upon, Plutarch often provides its starting-points. The first Act, though largely Shakespeare's own material, evokes the lovers' way of life, 'which', says North, 'they called Amimetobion (as much to say, no life comparable and matcheable with it)' (Plutarch 1895–6: VI, 27). Enobarbus, though developed from only two sentences in the Life, is as a choric figure in some ways an equivalent for the authorial voice of Plutarch (as for Shakespeare himself), and in his ambivalence towards the lovers he merely exaggerates tendencies already present in the narrative (and in the accompanying comparison between Antony and Demetrius). While Plutarch generally, and on some views uncharacteristically, adopts distinctly 'Roman' attitudes towards them and their 'childish sports', it is part of his charm that he presents some episodes – their practical jokes, for example – in much more genial tones. In *Antony and Cleopatra* the verbal echoes of North are, however, more restricted than in the other Plutarchan plays; in spite of the famously close borrowings from the passage on Cleopatra at Cydnus, the play 'adheres most closely to the narrative of the biographer, which is altered mainly by the omission of details unsuitable for the purposes of the dramatist; but the words, phrases, constructions, are for the most part conspicuously Shakespeare's own' (MacCallum 1967: 166).

Other non-narrative elements shared with Plutarch here are the Rome–Alexandria axis – though Shakespeare develops and complicates the contrast, and Plutarch's development of a distinctive atmosphere for Greece is ignored – and an interest in Antony's mental struggle, introduced very early in the play ('These strong Egyptian fetters I must break', 1.2.113) but not followed through very fully by Shakespeare. The strains of Antony's marriage are inspired by Plutarch's juxtapositions of Octavia and Cleopatra, this subject also being dealt with more insistently in the play than the Life. Still, there is in Shakespeare's treatment of Antony 'the same expansiveness, nobility, generosity, and largeness of spirit – though not quite the simplicity which is important in Plutarch', a simplicity which is precisely what renders him vulnerable to Cleopatra's wiles. As for Cleopatra, 'Plutarch's figure is sometimes enigmatic . . . but far less so than Shakespeare's: in a quite different way from Plutarch's figure, one can understand why she captivated a hero of Antony's stature' (Pelling 1988: 42, 44).

Coriolanus was a much more obscure narrative for Shakespeare to choose, much further from the beaten track than his previous selections, even if the story of Rome's ingratitude and Coriolanus' revenge had been told by Livy and in **Painter**'s *Palace of Pleasure*. 'Dozens of poetasters could write plays on Julius Caesar or on Cleopatra. Dozens did. But to write *Coriolanus* was one of the great feats of the historical imagination in Renaissance Europe' (Spencer 1957: 35). Plutarch couples Coriolanus in his *Life* with Alcibiades as two different types brought into conflict with their own countrymen, the one successful and the other unsuccessful at retaining popular favour (he implies that Coriolanus' errors result from the early loss of his father, though his generous and noble nature was never wholly suppressed), and Shakespeare also draws on Plutarch's comparison between them – for verbal and other echoes of it see Honigmann 1959.

In Plutarch's *Coriolanus*, as was not the case with the *Life of Antonius*, 'the tormented genius of the young aristocrat is beautifully presented, and the material is set out in such a way that it was easy for later dramatists to organize it into tragedy for the stage' (Bullough, v, 473). At a superficial level Shakespeare treats his source carefully, for example in preserving Roman manners and allusions; but on other levels new perspectives are opened up. The introduction of the concept of mercy, too little of which Coriolanus is said to have shown towards the people, and to which Volumnia appeals, is a divagation from Plutarch and North as 'implying an extension of mercy beyond the narrow scope of class bias' (Heuer 1957: 57). Correspondingly, Aufidius is brought in much earlier than in Plutarch to establish what North terms the 'marvellous private hate' between them. And, though the debt to North/ Plutarch (shown in (B)) in the set-piece interview with Volumnia is evident, the emphases are different: 'Shakespeare entirely excises the religious aura surrounding this appeal, the vision which moves Valeria to suggest the women's deputation to Martius, and the subsequently pious thanksgiving . . . Shakespeare makes the characters in his play frequently appeal to the gods, but he is more interested in the awe that they feel towards and inspire in each other' (Poole 1988: 12).

The story of Timon of Athens occurs as a digression in the *Life of Marcus Antonius*, recounting how after the battle of Actium Antony lived in 'his solitary house he had built by the sea, which he called Timoneon' and followed Timon's example. Plutarch's description of Timon, less than 500 words in North, gave the basic data – Alcibiades and Apemantus as the only people Timon tolerated, his invitation to the Athenians to hang themselves on his fig tree, and two epitaphs, both of which, confusingly, Shakespeare uses in the final scene of the play. Since Plutarch's *Life of Alcibiades* formed the counterpart of his *Coriolanus* it is natural to assume Shakespeare read it. This cannot be categorically proved, but the rather formless *Alcibiades* does provide all the facts in Shakespeare's portrait of the character, together with the ambivalence towards him which Aristophanes must have felt when in the *Frogs* he proposed him as a suitable subject for two contrasting dramatic interpretations, comic and tragic respectively. A third and last possible Plutarchan locus among the sources is the 'Comparison of Alcibiades with Martius Coriolanus', drawn on for *Coriolanus*, which may be verbally echoed once in the play (Honigmann 1959: 29). 'If, however, North's *Plutarch* gave Shakespeare what may be called his premises' for *Timon*, 'it did not give him a plot of anything like the completeness of the plots he normally followed' (Oliver 1959: xxxv).

Shakespeare's use of Plutarch goes well beyond these four plays. Plutarch's presence in Shakespearean drama on English history is partly an aspect of the sixteenth-century European habit of seeing ancient history as the grammar for its vernacular descendents.

433

Mossman (supplemented by Tiffany 1999) shows in detail how Plutarch may be a model for style and structure as well as narrative content in *Henry V*, which she contends 'has the structure of a classic Plutarch life' and draws on Plutarch's *Life of Alexander* 'not only for filling out the subtle texture of the Alexander comparisons but also for suggesting ways in which a portrait of a national hero could be made more memorable, more moving, more universal' (1994: 73). More lightheartedly, Fluellen's famous comparison between Henry and Alexander is often taken to be a kind of parody of the Plutarchan 'comparisons'. Elsewhere, Shakespeare returns again and again to the *Life of Brutus* over a ten-year period, especially the pages dealing with Brutus and Portia's relationship. These seem to leave their mark on Lady Percy in *Henry IV* and Portia in *The Merchant of Venice*, while Hamlet and Macbeth can be seen as developments of a Shakespearean concern with interiority that begins with the Brutus of *Julius Caesar* (see Mueller 1991).

It has proved tempting to look for Plutarchan ingredients in altogether remoter parts of the Shakespeare canon. This game is sometimes not worth the candle – though J. M. Nosworthy (1982: 102–10), for example, rightly points out that the use of six names from Plutarch in *The Winter's Tale* may imply other as yet undiscovered debts. In some cases standing rather as testaments to the ingenuity of scholars than major aids in the interpretation of Shakespeare are studies of Plutarch and *Hamlet* (Freeman 1974), Plutarch and *Othello* (Graves 1973), Plutarch and *Cymbeline* (Lees 1976), and so forth.

(D) For Plutarch's place among historians in the Renaissance see Shackford (1929), Burke (1966) and Hunter (1977); for North's life and work see Matthiesson (1931). Spencer (1964) is the standard modern edition of selections showing the Shakespearean material in Plutarch (in a modernized 1579 text), with the linguistically or narratively closest parallel passages from the plays quoted at the foot of many pages. The range of ways in which Shakespeare uses Plutarch – as source, background, subtext – is explored by Miola (1987). Though most studies concentrate on a single Shakespeare play or occasionally a single Plutarch life, investigation can also be carried out thematically: Dillon (1979), for example, discusses 'solitariness' as a theme Shakespeare developed from Plutarch. Other modern editions of the four principal Plutarchan plays as well as those listed have useful discussions of the relationships for these individual works. Green (1979) is a recent attempt to deal at the length of a short monograph with the Roman plays collectively as Plutarch-based works.

Bullough, v.

Burke, Peter (1966). 'A Survey of the Popularity of Ancient Historians, 1450–1700.' *History and Theory* 5: 135–52.

Dillon, Janette (1979). ' "Solitariness": Shakespeare and Plutarch.' *JEGP* 78: 325–44.

Freeman, James A. (1974). 'Hamlet, Hecuba, and Plutarch.' *ShSt* 7: 197–202.

Graves, Wallace (1973). 'Plutarch's *Life of Cato Utican* as a Major Source for *Othello*.' *ShQ* 24: 181–7.

Green, David C. (1979). *Plutarch Revisited: A Study of Shakespeare's Last Roman Tragedies and their Source*. Salzburg.

Hanna, Sara (1994). 'Voices against Tyranny: Greek Sources of *The Winter's Tale*.' *Classical and Modern Literature* 14: 335–44.

Herford, C. H., Percy and Evelyn Simpson, eds (1925–51). *Ben Jonson*, 8 vols. Oxford.

Heuer, Hermann (1957). 'From Plutarch to Shakespeare: A Study of Coriolanus.' *ShSu* 10: 50–9.

Homan, Sidney (1975). 'Dion, Alexander, and Demetrius – Plutarch's Forgotten *Parallel Lives* – as Mirrors for Shakespeare's *Julius Caesar*.' *ShSt* 8: 195–210.

Honigmann, E. A. J. (1959). 'Shakespeare's Plutarch.' *ShQ* 10: 25–33.

—— (1961). '*Timon of Athens*.' *ShQ* 12: 3–20.

Humphreys, Arthur, ed. (1984). *Julius Caesar* (Oxford Shakespeare). Oxford.

Hunter, G. K. (1977). 'A Roman Thought: Renaissance Attitudes to History exemplified in Shakespeare and Jonson', pp. 93–118 in Brian S. Lee, ed., *An English Miscellany: Presented to W. S. Mackie*. Cape Town.

Jones, Emrys (1971). *Scenic Form in Shakespeare*. Oxford.

Lees, Francis Noel (1976). 'Plutarch and *The Winter's Tale*.' *N&Q* 221: 161–2.

MacCallum, M. W. (1967). *Shakespeare's Roman Plays and their Background*. London (first published 1910).

Maguin, Jean-Marie (1973). 'Preface to a Critical Approach to *Julius Caesar*, with a Chronological Catalogue of Shakespeare's Borrowing from North's Plutarch.' *CahiersE* 4: 15–49.

Matthiesson, F. O. (1931). *Translation: An Elizabethan Art*. Cambridge, MA.

Miola, Robert S. (1987). 'Shakespeare and his Sources: Observations on the Critical History of "Julius Caesar".' *ShSu* 40: 69–76.

Mossman, Judith (1994). '*Henry V* and Plutarch's Alexander.' *ShQ* 45: 57–73.

Mueller, Martin (1991). 'Plutarch's "Life of Brutus" and the Play of Its Repetitions in Shakespearean Drama.' *RenD* 22: 47–93.

Neill, Michael, ed. (1994). *Antony and Cleopatra* (Oxford Shakespeare). Oxford.

Nosworthy, J. M. (1982). 'Shakespeare's Pastoral Metamorphoses', pp. 90–113 in George R. Hibbard, ed., *The Elizabethan Theatre VIII*. Port Credit.

Oliver, H. J., ed. (1959). *Timon of Athens* (Arden Shakespeare). London.

Pelling, C. B. R., ed. (1988). *Plutarch: Life of Antony*. Cambridge.

Plutarch (1895–6). *Lives of the Noble Grecians and Romans Englished by Sir Thomas North anno 1579* (The Tudor Translations, VIII), 6 vols. London.

Poole, Adrian (1988). *Coriolanus* (Harvester New Critical Introductions to Shakespeare). London.

Rothschild, Herbert B., Jr (1976). 'The Oblique Encounter: Shakespeare's Confrontation of Plutarch with Special Reference to *Antony and Cleopatra*.' *ELR* 6: 404–29.

Russell, D. A. (1973). *Plutarch*. London.

Shackford, Martha Hale (1929). *Plutarch in Renaissance England, with Special Reference to Shakespeare*. Wellesley, MA.

Spencer, T. J. B. (1954). 'The Vile Name of Demetrius.' *MLR* 49: 46–8.

—— (1957). 'Shakespeare and the Elizabethan Romans.' *ShSu* 10: 27–38.

—— ed. (1964). *Shakespeare's Plutarch: The Lives of Julius Caesar, Brutus, Marcus Antonius, and Coriolanus in the translation of Sir Thomas North*. Harmondsworth.

Stirling, Brents (1964). 'Cleopatra's Scene with Seleucus: Plutarch, Daniel, and Shakespeare.' *ShQ* 15.i: 299–311.

Tiffany, Grace (1999). 'Shakespeare's Dionysian Prince: Drama, Politics, and the "Athenian" History Play.' *RenQ* 52: 366–83.

Porter, Henry (*fl.* 1589), Playwright Porter's *The Two Angry Women of Abingdon* (played by 1590?) has a range of perhaps entirely coincidental similarities with *Romeo and Juliet*, while its sequel, a lost work, is hypothetically connected with *The Merry Wives of Windsor* by Nosworthy (1965). Reservations in the latter case are noted by Oliver (1971: lx–lxi).

Nosworthy, J. M. (1952). 'The Two Angry Families of Verona.' *ShQ* 3: 219–26.

—— (1965). *Shakespeare's Occasional Plays: Their Origin and Transmission*, pp. 93–114. London.

Oliver, H. J., ed. (1971). *The Merry Wives of Windsor* (Arden Shakespeare). London.

Pory, John See **Africanus, Leo**.

Preston, Thomas See **Morality Tradition**.

Primaudaye, Pierre de la See **La Primaudaye, Pierre de**.

Proverbs See also **Culmann, Leonhard**; **Erasmus, Desiderius**; **Publilius Syrus**.

Dent, R. W. (1981). *Shakespeare's Proverbial Language*. Berkeley.

Tilley, M. P. (1950). *A Dictionary of the Proverbs in England in the Sixteenth and Seventeenth Centuries*. Ann Arbor.

Wilson, F. P. (1969). 'The Proverbial Wisdom of Shakespeare', pp. 143–75 in Helen Gardner, ed., *Shakespearian and Other Studies by F. P. Wilson*. Oxford.

Ptolemaeus, Claudius (Ptolemy) (*fl.* AD 139–161), Roman Astronomer and Geographer Maps printed in the many Renaissance editions of Ptolemy's *Geography* often include one or two features, such as 'anthropophagi', which appear in Othello's account of his travels.

French, J. Milton (1934). 'Othello among the Anthropophagi.' *PMLA* 49: 807–9.

Publilius Syrus (1st Century BC), Writer of Latin Mimes

At least a part of Publilius Syrus' collection of proverbs, including many *sententiae* from other writers, was almost universally studied by Renaissance schoolboys in some form.

Smith, Charles George (1963). *Shakespeare's Proverb Lore: His Use of the Sententiae of Leonard Culman and Publilius Syrus.* Cambridge, MA.

Puttenham, George (or Richard) (*c.* 1530–1590), Author of *The Arte of English Poesie*

(A) Either of two brothers, George and Richard Puttenham, may have been the author of the originally anonymous *Arte of English Poesie*, published in 1589 (but attributed at some points in the past to other authors altogether: see Willcock and Walker 1936: ixff.). Both were nephews of Sir Thomas **Elyot**, who dedicated to their mother, his sister, his *Education for the Bringing up of Children*. George, now considered the stronger candidate, was trained at Cambridge and the Middle Temple. He was also responsible for an (unprinted) 'Apologie' for Queen Elizabeth's treatment of Mary Queen of Scots.

The *Arte* particularizes fine distinctions of critical terminology. Book I is on the nature of poetry, its dignity, antiquity, educative power, and so on, dealing also with generic classes of it. Book II is on metre, anagrams, pattern-poetry, and other devices; Book III moves on to figures of speech and rhetoric, presenting English equivalents for the Greek terms – not the least valuable of the treatise's features.

(B) The *Arte*'s reputation, particularly in fashionable literary circles, was high during Shakespeare's later years and beyond; it is still a 'book that goes about' in **Jonson**'s 1619 conversations with Drummond. Jonson's copy, quoted here, is in the British Library. The final chapter (III. 25) is titled: '*That the good Poet or maker ought to dissemble his arte, and in what cases the artificiall is more commended then the naturall, and contrariwise*'. Puttenham is aiming here to distinguish the bases for a description of the poet's art.

In some cases we say arte is an ayde and coadjutor to nature, and a furtherer of her actions to good effect, or peradventure a meane to supply her wants, by renforcing the causes wherein shee is impotent and defective . . .

In another respect arte is not only an aide and coadjutor to nature in all her actions, but an alterer of them, and in some sort a surmounter of her skill, so as by meanes of it her owne effects shall appeare more beautifull or straunge and miraculous . . . And the Gardiner by his arte will not onely make an herbe, or flowr, or fruite, come forth in his season without impediment, but also will embellish the same in vertue, shape, odour and taste, that nature of her selfe woulde never have done: as to make the single gillifloure, or marigold, or daisie, double: and the white rose, redde, yellow, or carnation, a bitter melon sweete; a sweete apple, soure; a plumme or cherrie without a stone; a peare without core or kernell, a goord or coucumber like to a horne, or any other figure he will: any of which things nature could not doe without mans help and arte. These actions also are most singular, when they be most artificiall.

(Puttenham 1589: 253–4)

(C) Richard Field, the original printer of the *Arte* in 1589, was also responsible for printing Shakespeare's first published work, *Venus and Adonis*, four years later. It is often supposed Shakespeare and Field were friends rather than mere business associates (there are other family connections). This may be how Shakespeare encountered the *Arte*, though no good textual evidence is available for his knowledge of it until *King Lear*, over fifteen years later. At 3.2.79–95 of this play is found a speech given to the Fool which is usually taken to be a parody of some lines of verse given illustratively in the *Arte* and attributed there to **Chaucer** (see Muir 1977: 104).

Other than this, Puttenham's possible effects on Shakespeare are divisible into two kinds: echoes of Puttenham's thought or phraseology as such, and the use of figures and other devices explained or recommended by him (for example, the 'climbing' figure in which each term is a 'ladder' to the next, as in Rosalind's 'no sooner met but they look'd; no sooner look'd but they lov'd; no sooner lov'd but they sigh'd', *As You Like It* 5.2.31). Cases of the second kind, however plausible they may seem at times, are incapable of verification because Puttenham invents no new figures: Shakespeare could have found an explanation, and in probably every instance examples, of any given figure in another authority and/or in several literary works (in English or otherwise).

For the other type of debt, only one instance is widely considered both plausible and significant today: Puttenham's discourse on art and nature ((B), above) forms one of the several likely sources of the discussion between Perdita and Polixenes in *The Winter's Tale*, 4.4. In the chapter as a whole Puttenham distinguishes six different relationships between nature and art (art as 'aide and coadjutor', and so on). The commonplace nature of the thinking – the horticultural applications are scarcely unusual either – makes it difficult to say how much influence the passage has had on the dialogue, but Puttenham's perhaps somewhat solemn and didactic tone is the kind of thing the dramatist can be imagined as responding to with detached amusement. 'It would be in keeping with the quality of Shakespeare's wit to play lightly upon Puttenham's theme and provide a summary comment upon it, delivered with the grave urbanity of a Polixenes' (Wilson 1943: 118).

(D) The only lengthy account of Puttenham's effect on Shakespeare is Rushton (1909), and the length results from Rushton's far greater willingness to see the *Arte* behind Shakespearean phraseology, especially of rhetorical kinds, than is found in any more recent authority. His long essay consists almost entirely of juxtaposed passages linked by a few words of comment; some of the many parallels might bear re-examination today, but for the most part his procedure is fatally flawed by a failure to consider alternative explanations.

[Puttenham, George?] (1589). *The Arte of English Poesie*. London.

Rushton, William Lowes (1909). *Shakespeare and 'The Arte of English Poesie'*. Liverpool.

Willcock, Gladys Doidge, and Alice Walker, eds (1936). *The Arte of English Poesie by George Puttenham*. Cambridge.

Wilson, Harold S. (1943). '"Nature and Art" in *Winter's Tale* IV, iv, 86ff.' *Shakespeare Association Bulletin* 18: 114–19.

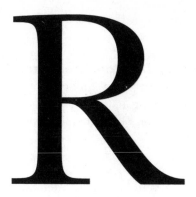

R

Rabelais, François (?1494–?1553), French Satirist A few possible allusions to and echoes of Rabelais in Shakespeare have never been felt to be of much consequence, and do not necessarily indicate direct knowledge. Some direct contact with Rabelais' words was, however, offered by quotations in the French language manuals of John **Eliot** (Thomas 1971).

Brown, Huntingdon (1933). *Rabelais in English Literature*, Appendix A. Cambridge, MA.

Prescott, Anne Lake (1998). *Imagining Rabelais in Renaissance England*. New Haven.

Thomas, David H. (1971). 'Rabelais in England: John Eliot's *Ortho-Epia Gallica.*' *Etudes Rabelaisiennes* 9: 97–118.

Rainolde, Richard (d. 1606), English Clergyman and Rhetorician Rainolde is one of the many possible sources for the 'degree' speech in *Troilus and Cressida* 1.3. His quite separate importance as a representative of a tradition in rhetoric that certainly affected Shakespeare is explained by Trousdale (1982).

Ronan, Clifford J. (1985). 'Daniel, Rainolde, Demosthenes, and the Degree Speech of Shakespeare's Ulysses.' *Renaissance and Reformation* 9: 111–18.

Trousdale, Marion (1982). *Shakespeare and the Rhetoricians*. Chapel Hill.

Rare Triumphes of Love and Fortune, The (Anon. Play, 1589) This play has 'so many minor points of resemblance to *Cymbeline* that it is tempting to regard it as an influence on Shakespeare, by contra-suggestion rather than by direct imitation' (Bullough, VIII: 21).

Bullough, VIII.
Nosworthy, J. M., ed. (1969). *Cymbeline* (Arden Shakespeare), xxv–xxviii. London.

Riche, Barnaby See *Gl'Ingannati*.

Robinson, Richard See *Gesta Romanorum*.

Ronsard, Pierre de (1524–1585), French Poet Leishman suggests that Ronsard influenced Shakespeare's *Sonnets* in somewhat more specific ways than merely by constituting part of the sonnet tradition.

Leishman, J. B. (1961). *Themes and Variations in Shakespeare's Sonnets*. London.

Roper, William (1496–1578), Biographer of Sir Thomas More Roper's manuscript biography of *c.* 1556–7 is one of five Lives of **More** which are considered possible sources for *Sir Thomas More*.

Metz, G. Harold, ed. (1989). *Sources of Four Plays Ascribed to Shakespeare*. Columbia, MI.

Rowley, Samuel (d. *c.* 1630), Playwright Rowley's *When You See Me You Know Me* (1605), a 'chronicle history' of Henry VIII, is an acknowledged source for the Shakespeare play, though very many points of similarity were inevitable in two works on the same subject.

Bullough, IV: 441–2.

Rowley, William See **Chronicle History Plays**.

Sabie, Francis (*fl.* 1595), Author of *The Fisher-Man's Tale* Sabie's two blank verse narrative poems *The Fisher-Man's Tale* and its sequel *Flora's Fortune* (both 1595) offer moderate similarities to *The Winter's Tale*, but the picture is clouded by Sabie's following of **Greene**'s *Pandosto* for incident and often for phraseology.

Bullough, VIII.
Honigmann, E. A. J. (1955). 'Secondary Sources of *The Winter's Tale.*' *PQ* 34: 27–38.
Stanford, Anne (1964). 'Shakespeare and Francis Sabie.' *ShQ* 15.i: 454–5.

Saint's Play, Medieval Emrys Jones suggests that the Saint's Play (or Passion Play) was paradigmatic for Shakespearean tragedy in 'the native late-medieval conception of the God-man hero' (1977: 84).

Jones (1977).

Savile, Henry See **Tacitus**, **Publius Cornelius (or Gaius Cornelius)**.

Saviolo, Vincentio (*fl.* 1595), Italian Fencing Master

Some specialist knowledge of fencing techniques, terminology and etiquette in *Romeo and Juliet* could be drawn from the English translation of Saviolo's fencing manual, *V. Saviolo his Practise*, 1594–5.

Holmer, Joan Ozark (1994). ' "Draw, if you be men": Saviolo's Significance for *Romeo and Juliet*.' *ShQ* 45: 163–89.

Saxo, *called* Grammaticus See Belleforest, François de.

Scève, Maurice (1510–1564), French Poet Jacques' image of the suffering lover in *As You Like It* 2.7.147–9 has been traced to one of Scève's poems.

Kastan, David Scott, and Nancy J. Vickers (1980). 'Shakespeare, Scève, and "A woeful ballad".' *N&Q* 225: 165–6.

Scot (Scott), Reginald (1538?–1599), Author of *The Discovery of Witchcraft*

(A) Scot's Kentish origins and his pursuits as a country gentleman are reflected in his first book, *The Perfect Platform of a Hoppe-Garden*, a treatise on hop-growing published in 1574. He attended Hart Hall, Oxford, appears to have been a lawyer and Justice of the Peace, and became Member of Parliament for New Romney, 1588–9. His large and learned book *The Discoverie of Witchcraft, wherein the Lewde dealing of Witches and Witchmongers is notablie detected . . . [with] a Treatise upon the Nature and Substance of Spirits and Divels* was published in 1584.

(B) *The Discoverie of Witchcraft* is 'important as a thorough-going demonstration of the marginal elements in medieval Catholicism and their affiliation with other contemporary kinds of magical activity' (Thomas 1997: 54). But it is chiefly remembered as an enlightened attack on the superstition that condemned 'witches' – often the poor or mentally unfit – to severe punishments. Scot argued that once we grant witches have no real power to do harm, we must also reject the usual secondary reason for witch trials, that the accused hoped or intended to cause harm – for 'to will a thing unpossible, is a signe of a mad man, or of a foole, upon whom no sentence or judgement taketh hold' (ed. Nicholson 1973: 11). Scot's work, however, 'upheld and defended a heresy, the existence and diabolical powers and practices of witches being believed in and guarded against, by the Queen, the bishops, and the people' (Nicholson 1973: xxxvii), and hence it was attacked by 'authorities' on witchcraft, including **James VI** of Scotland, who in 1597 published his less progressive *Daemonologie* and, on his accession to the throne of England in 1603, ordered Scot's book to be burned.

The reputation of Scot's work was for a time considerable – we are told by near-contemporaries it made 'great impressions on the Magistracy and Clergy' (Nicholson 1973: xxxvii), and Scot's admirers included Samuel **Harsnett**, later Archbishop of York. It was reprinted into the seventeenth century and it provided material for **Middleton**'s play *The Witch* (c. 1626).

This passage is one of three in which reference is made to 'Robin good-fellow'. As well as giving a remarkable catalogue of sixteenth-century 'bugs', it clearly illustrates the sceptical tenor of Scot's work:

Of vaine apparitions, how people have beene brought to feare bugges, which is partlie reformed by preaching of the gospell, the true effect of Christes miracles.

But certeinlie, some one knave in a white sheete hath cousened and abused manie thousands that waie; speciallie when Robin good-fellow kept such a coile in the countrie. But you shall understand, that these bugs speciallie are spied and feared of sicke folke, children, women, and cowards, which through weaknesse of minde and bodie, are shaken with vaine dreames and continuall feare. The *Scythians*, being a stout and a warlike nation (as divers writers report) never see anie vaine sights or spirits. It is a common saieng; A lion feareth no bugs. But in our childhood our mothers maids have so terrified us with an ouglie divell having hornes on his head, fier in his mouth, and a taile in his breech, eies like a bason, fanges like a dog, clawes like a beare, a skin like a Niger, and a voice roring like a lion, whereby we start and are afraid when we heare one crie Bough: and they have so fraied us with bull beggers, spirits, witches, urchens, elves, hags, fairies, satyrs, pans, faunes, sylens, kit with the cansticke, tritons, centaurs, dwarfes, giants, imps, calcars, conjurors, nymphes, changlings, *Incubus*, Robin good-fellowe, the spoorne, the mare, the man in the oke, the hell waine, the fierdrake, the puckle, Tom thombe, hob gobblin, Tom tumbler, boneles, and such other bugs, that we are

446

afraid of our own shadowes: in so much as some never feare the divell, but in a darke night; and then a polled sheepe is a perillous beast, and manie times is taken for our fathers soule, speciallie in a churchyard, where a right hardie man heretofore scant durst passe by night, but his haire would stand upright. For right grave writers report, that spirits most often and speciallie take the shape of women appearing to monks, &c: and of beasts, dogs, swine, horsses, gotes, cats, haires; of fowles, as crowes, night owles, and shreeke owles; but they delight most in the likenes of snakes and dragons.

(VII.15; 1584 text, ed. Nicholson 1973: 122–3)

(C) Shakespeare is widely assumed to have known the *Discoverie of Witch-craft*. Muir (1977: 216) observes vaguely that he 'probably derived some of his information' on witches in *Macbeth* from Scot, and Gulstad (1994) argues that the treatise was in Shakespeare's mind as a source of details for Lear's mock trial of his daughters (3.6). But it has a stronger and longer-established connection to *A Midsummer Night's Dream*, with two main aspects: Scot's discussion of beliefs about the 'hob gobblin' Robin Goodfellow (IV.10, VII.2, and VII.15, above), and his references to asinine transformations (v.3, XIII.19). Neither is quite conclusive as a Shakespeare source. Muir accepts a debt to Scot for Puck but finds it 'likely that Shakespeare's character is derived from folk-lore rather than books, and that Robin is fused with the puckle' (a kind of hobgoblin mentioned in the Scot passage quoted in (B)). Brooks, however, finds further close connections, including a mention of ventriloquism in Scot's discussions. Similar kinds of conclusion emerge from these two commentators on Scot's ass transformations, with Muir rightly observing that Shakespeare is likelier to have used **Apuleius**, but Brooks finding tiny correspondences perhaps sufficient to reopen the question (Muir 1977: 68; Brooks 1979: lx–lxi). Bullough's view is that the super-stitious nonsense Scot presents on asinine metamorphoses 'must have amused the poet, who laughingly answers Scot by showing transform-ations happening'; and where Puck is concerned, 'as Scot declares . . . Robin Goodfellow was no longer as terrible and credible as he used to be', Shakespeare 'presents a somewhat obsolescent bugbear and shows him as more genial than tradition made him' (I, 373).

(D)
Bullough, I; Muir (1977).

Brooks, Harold F., ed. (1979). *A Midsummer Night's Dream* (Arden Shakespeare). London.

Gulstad, William (1994). 'Mock-Trial or Witch-Trial in *King Lear*?' *N&Q* 239: 494–7.

Nicholson, Brinsley, ed. (1973). *The Discoverie of Witchcraft, by Reginald Scot, Esquire, Being a Reprint of the First Edition Published in 1584*. Wakefield (edition first published 1886).

Thomas, Keith (1997). *Religion and the Decline of Magic: Studies in Popular Beliefs in Sixteenth and Seventeenth Century England*. London (first published 1971).

Secchi, Nicolò (1500–1560), Italian Playwright Two of Secchi's plays, *Gl'Inganni* and *L'Interesse*, show some points of contact with *Twelfth Night*, especially in the treatment of women and romantic love.

Kaufman, Helen Andrews (1954). 'Nicolò Secchi as a Source of *Twelfth Night*.' *ShQ* 5: 271–80.

Melzi, Robert C. (1966). 'From Lelia to Viola.' *RenD* 9: 67–81.

Seneca, Lucius Annaeus, the Elder (*c*. 55 BC–*c*. AD 39), Roman Rhetorician The court scene in *The Merchant of Venice* follows some of the legal protocols expounded by the Elder Seneca; his *Controversia* is also a source of **Silvayn**'s *Orator*, and Waith (1951) suspects the apparent debt to Silvayn in *Pericles* is in fact an illusion created by the common origins.

Schlauch, Margaret (1960). 'Roman "Controversiae" and the Court Scene in Shakespeare's "Merchant of Venice".' *Kwartalnik Neoofilologiczny* 7: 45–56.

Waith, Eugene M. (1951). '*Pericles* and Seneca the Elder.' *JEGP* 50: 180–2.

Seneca, Lucius Annaeus, the Younger (*c*. 4 BC–AD 65), Roman Philosopher and Playwright
(A) The aristocratic son of the famous rhetorician whose name he

shared, the Younger Seneca also acquired fame in this field. Born in Spain, he was taken to Rome as a child. His success in oratory aroused Caligula's jealousy, and on the accession of Claudius in 41 BC the Empress Messalina had him exiled to Corsica. In 49 he was recalled to became tutor to Nero, the future emperor, under whom he was later to serve as a minister. He was caught up in some of Nero's crimes, for example in writing a defence of Nero's murder of his own mother. Forced to commit suicide after being implicated in a conspiracy against his master, Seneca did so with a composure that became legendary.

Seneca's writings consist of prose works (notably 124 letters and a series of treatises on ethical subjects) and eight extant tragedies in verse: *Hercules Furens, Troades, Medea, Phaedra* (= *Hippolytus*), *Oedipus, Agamemnon, Thebais* (= *Phoenissae*) and *Thyestes*. Two other plays were ascribed to him in the Renaissance: *Hercules Oetaeus* and *Octavia*. The plays follow Greek tragedy in subject matter and in some formal features. They deploy choruses and stichomythia; they are tightly structured in five Acts, and observe the 'classical' unities of time, place and action. Supernatural agency consists of ghosts and magic, the plots often arising from ghosts demanding vengeance. They are probably closet dramas – though this was not understood in the Renaissance – and abound in narrative and moralizing speeches a little like operatic arias, at the expense of stage action. Their tone evokes 'the overwhelming threatening presence of evil, the fearful insecurity of the powerful and the powerless, and the impotence of the good who can only maintain their integrity and self-respect by dying well' (Sowerby 1994: 87).

(B) Seneca's prose works held considerable appeal in the Renaissance and were widely translated (first in fairly complete form by Thomas **Lodge** in 1614). But their significance for Renaissance dramatists was in interaction with his plays, which exerted extensive influence partly because they were the only widely known examples of classical tragedy. Among classical dramatists, 'whatever criterion we use – date of the *editio princeps*, number of translations, number of vernacular imitations, success in production – Seneca's preeminence in the Renaissance is beyond dispute' (Smith 1988: 203).

Since as long ago as Dryden, criticism has viewed Seneca as an inferior dramatist – artificial, strained, derivative. This has made it hard to see why early modern writers might have been interested in him. One reason is simply that they delighted in the soaring excesses of the rhetoric which now seems merely overblown. Another is that his philo-sophical works expound a Stoicism assimilable in some respects to Christian doctrine – of all the philosophical schools, Jerome says in his commentary on Isaiah (4: 11), the Stoics have most in common with us. This does not mean there are not serious conflicts between the classical revenge action of Seneca's plays and conventional Christian morality – conflicts out of which the energies of Shakespeare's tragedies are sometimes said to issue.

Senecan plays were being staged in Latin at Oxford and Cambridge by the 1550s. The first English imitations were by the early dramatists of the Inns of Court such as Thomas Sackville and Thomas Norton, whose joint work *Gorboduc* (1562) is often called the first English tragedy (see Baker 1939). Like the later closet dramatists of the Mary Sidney circle (Samuel **Daniel**, Thomas **Kyd**, Abraham Fraunce), such play-wrights attempted close Senecan imitation. But 'after the opening of the public theatres in 1576, the dramaturgical response, although extensive, was more indirect, complex, and creative' (Boyle 1997: 143), partly because by this time Senecan materials had become mixed and mingled with other elements. This is true even of the standard English version of Seneca's plays, *Seneca: His Tenne Tragedies*, containing work in what has been called 'a rhetorical mode which would seem to be dir-ectly opposite to Seneca's' (Hunter 1974: 187). This is an exaggeration, but the taut structures of the Latin are sometimes hard to discern beneath the overlay of a homelier idiom. The *Tenne Tragedies* was a collection of English versions by Jasper Heywood, Alexander Nevile, Thomas Nuce and John Studley, and previously published from *c.* 1560 onwards, assembled by Thomas Newton in 1581, who added his own *Thebais*. Newton's gathering contains the only printed translations available to the Elizabethans, though there were other manuscript renderings of Seneca including a fragment from *Hercules Oetaeus* by Queen Elizabeth herself.

Around 1590 there is explicit redeployment of phrases and motifs from Senecan tragedy in important plays such as Kyd's *Spanish Tragedy* and **Marlowe**'s *Edward II*. Works by **Chapman**, Fulke Greville, **Jonson**, **Marston** and Webster also involve Senecan ideas or other borrowings; among the best-known are the use of pithy Senecan phrases by Webster's Duchess of Malfi – 'I am Duchess of Malfi still' (4.2.142; 'Medea superest', *Medea*, 166) – and Tamburlaine (*2 Tamburlaine* 4.1.116–20; compare *Hercules Furens* 958–61). Kyd, in particular, is responsible for popularizing the revenge motif and its sanguinary consequences in *The Spanish Tragedy*. Thomas **Nashe**, in the preface to **Greene**'s *Menaphon* (1589), makes a famous attack on the habit of borrowing from Seneca in a playwright (perhaps Kyd), or possibly in contemporary playwrights generally:

English *Seneca* read by candle light yeeldes manie good sentences, as *Bloud is a begger*, and so foorth; and, if you intreate him faire in a frostie morning, he will affoord you whole *Hamlets*, I should say hand-fulls of tragicall speeches.

As the date of Nashe's remarks and of other responses to Seneca mentioned above suggest, much of Shakespeare's work appears after the first flow of Senecan influence on English drama.

The following sample from *Seneca: His Tenne Tragedies* is taken from John Studley's version of *Hercules Oetaeus*. This passage, in which the Nurse advises Deianira to use magic to punish Hercules for his infatuation with Iole, contains little-noticed echoes of Prospero's speech 'Ye elves of hills' (*Tempest* 5.1.33–50) not present in its main source, Golding's *Metamorphoses* – 'Arte', 'roring', 'oape', 'noontyde'. Bottom's undertaking to speak in 'Ercles vain' (*A Midsummer Night's Dream* 1.2.34) is sometimes interpreted as a reference to Studley's translation.

NU[TRIX].   It is almost a common guise, that wedded wyves doe
        haunte,
        Theyr husbands hearts by magicke Arte, and witchcraft to
        enchaunte.
        In winter coulde I charmed have the woods, to make
        them sprout,
        And forst the thunder dint recoyle, that hath bin boulting
        out.
        With waltring surges I have shooke the seas amid the
        calme,
        I smoothed have the wrastling waves, and layde downe
        every walme.
        The dry ground gaped hath like gulphs, and out new
        springs have gusht,
        The roring rocks have quaking sturd, and none thereat
        hath pusht.

451

> Hell gloummy gates I have brast oape, where grisly ghosts all husht
>
> Have stood and aunswering at my charme the goblins grim have scoulde.
>
> The threefolde headded hounde of hell with barking throates hath houlde.
>
> Thus both the seas, the lande, the heavens, and hell bowe at my becke.
>
> Noone day to midnight, to and froe turnes at my charming checke.
>
> At my enchauntment every thing declynes from natures lawe.
>
> Our charme shall make his stomacke stoupe, and bring him more in awe.

DE[IANIRA]. What hearbes doe grow in Pontus sea? Or els on Pindus hill?

> To trownce this machelesse champion, where shall I finde the ill?
>
> The magicke vearse enchaunts the Moone from Starry skies to ground,
>
> And fruictfull harvest is thereby in barren winter found.
>
> The whisking flames of lightning leames oft sorcery doth stay,
>
> And noonetyde topsy turvy tost doth dim the dusky day.
>
> And leave the welkin to the starres, and yet not cause him stoupe.

NU[TRIX]. The Gods them selves by charme of love have forced bin to droupe.

DE[IANIRA]. Perhap hee shall be woon my one, and yeelde to her the spoyle.

> So love shall be to Hercules the last and latest toyle.

> > (1581 text; ed. Eliot 1927: II, 210–11)

(C) There has been much discussion of Shakespeare's relation to Seneca over the past century; there is still debate over how extensive and how direct the relation is, but the majority view now suggests more rather than less so. Earlier arguments for strong Senecan influence tended to be based on situational, character, and especially verbal similarities, which turned out often to be otherwise explicable; more spacious perspectives are now adopted, so that Senecanism may be discerned more diffusely. Also, where once it was often held that passages verbally echoing Seneca in Shakespeare were the result of reading only in indirect sources such as anthologies, it is now widely accepted that Shakespeare 'would have had a knowledge not merely of phrases from anthologies or of discrete passages but at least some entire plays' (Jones 1977: 268). One more development has been the realization that it may be a mistake to expect a similar kind of influence to be operative throughout Shakespeare's career. Seneca was being seen and used differently as time passed, with the early phase of interest followed by a later peak around 1600. 'This would suggest that one's critical suspicion that Seneca's influence on *Titus Andronicus* is superficial but that on *Macbeth* profound is in tune with history' (Daalder 1982: xxvi–xxvii).

It may be helpful to think in terms of two principal ways in which Seneca is found in Shakespeare: first in the use of Senecan dramatic modes, formal features, and specific elements from individual plays (words, characters, situations); second, and less demonstrably, in what T. S. Eliot called 'Senecan sensibility', deriving mainly from Seneca's prose works. Eliot describes Seneca's Stoicism, 'completely absorbed and transmogrified, because . . . already . . . diffused throughout Shakespeare's world', as 'an influence towards a kind of self-consciousness that is new; the self-consciousness and self-dramatization of the Shakespearean hero' (Eliot 1951: 139–40). Braden (1985: 69) follows this lead in observing that 'the sense of self implicit in the various morphologies of Senecan dramatic rhetoric is not unrelated to that evident in the various morphologies of Renaissance Stoicism'. This 'Senecan sensibility' is so widely reflected in the dramatic idiom of Shakespeare's time that almost any passage in which a suffering self speaks to the gods with rhetorical power and direct self-reference (as for instance Lear in Act 2) may reasonably, if not particularly usefully, be described as Senecan.

Where more local Senecan materials are concerned, it is possible, as Emrys Jones in particular has shown, to find 'glancingly rapid effects' (Jones 1977: 272) built on Seneca in unexpected places in Shakespeare, including comedies. The process of discovery is still continuing. Brooks (1979a: lxii–lxiii, 139–45) identifies fresh and suggestive parallels, some more than local, between *A Midsummer Night's Dream* and Seneca's *Hippolytus*, *Medea* and *Oedipus*, including for example the resemblance to Phaedra's of Helena's behaviour in love. Sheen (1992) argues strongly for a politically charged Senecan element in *Cymbeline*. But claims for Seneca's presence in the late tragedies are less unexpected. Boyle (1997: 147) notes *Hamlet* (*Thyestes, Agamemnon, Hercules Furens*) and *Lear* (*Thyestes, Agamemnon, Troades, Hercules Furens*), while Daalder finds in *Lear* the fundamental 'Senecan idea that good is . . . capable of enduring and protecting itself' (1982: xxxi). Ornstein (1958) and Wallace (1986) unusually suggest a specific Shakespearean source in perhaps Seneca's best-known prose work, *De Beneficiis*, for Brutus in *Julius Caesar* and for Timon in *Timon of Athens*, respectively. But three of Shakespeare's works seem to draw more heavily on Seneca than any others: *Titus Andronicus, Macbeth* and *Richard III*.

Titus Andronicus, sometimes considered the most Senecan of all Shakespeare plays – in spite of concerted attempts (notably Baker 1939) to sever the connection – quotes or misquotes *Phaedra* at 2.1.135 and 4.1.81–2, perhaps not to much effect. But more significant relationships are discernible. For Miola, *Troades* 'informs the symbolic design . . . as well as its dramatic configuration', in particular in its use of the tomb as 'a locus where the past, present, and future intersect, a symbol that mocks human struggle and achievement', while *Thyestes* is 'directly or indirectly . . . a deep source of its energy and its aesthetic of violence' (1992: 20–3). Arguably, the accommodation of the action to a Senecan pattern has an important overall impact in itself: 'such patterns . . . produce a curiously flattening effect: . . . they deprive the characters of their individuality and fix them as heroic types' (Smith 1988: 241).

Lady Macbeth's speech at 1.5.37–51 is perhaps the most familiar Senecan moment of the play:

> Come, you spirits
> That tend on mortal thoughts, unsex me here;
> And fill me, from the crown to the toe, top-full
> Of direst cruelty. Make thick my blood,
> Stop up th' access and passage to remorse,
> That no compunctious visitings of nature
> Shake my fell purpose nor keep place between
> Th' effect and it. Come to my woman's breasts,
> And take my milk for gall, you murd'ring ministers,
> Wherever in your sightless substances
> You wait on nature's mischief. Come, thick night,
> And pall thee in the dunnest smoke of hell,

That my keen knife see not the wound it makes,
Nor heaven peep through the blanket of the dark
To cry, 'Hold, hold'.

Ewbank (among others) compares these lines to Medea's very long Act 4 invocation to Hecate as translated by Studley, connecting the two speeches not by verbal echoes but by concatenation and configuration, closely linked images and ideas creating a 'train of associations' (Ewbank 1966: 85). Lady Macbeth may be meant expressly to recall Seneca's Medea, for example as found in the following excerpt from the invocation in Studley's translation:

Breath on these venoms Hecate, with deadly myght inspyre,
Preserve the touching poulder of my secret covert fyre,
O graunt that these my cloked craftes so may bewitch theyr Eyes,
That lykelyhoode of treason none they may heerein surmyse:
So worke that they in handling it may feele no kynde of heate:
Her stewing breast, her seathing vaynes, let fervent fyer freate
And force her rosted pyning lymmes to drop and melt away
                              (1581 text, ed. Eliot 1927: II, 91)

Further comparisons with *Medea* are made by Miola (1992: 106–7), who goes on to suggest parallels in imagery between *Macbeth* and other Senecan plays. He is joined by commentators such as Muir (1959: 112, 154), identifying specific echoes of Studley's *Agamemnon* in *Macbeth*. Others again relate Seneca's interest in the subjectivity of consciousness to the brooding self-awareness of Macbeth himself.

Finally, *Richard III* is distantly related to Seneca through its source *The True Tragedy of Richard III* (anonymous, 1594: see under **Chronicle History Plays**) which drew on *Richard Tertius* (1580), an academic Senecan tragedy in Latin on the same subject by Thomas Legge. Independently of this, *Richard III* is 'formally perhaps the most Senecanesque of Shakespeare's plays in its single action (there is no sub-plot), style and tone' (Boyle 1997: 148). Brooks (1979b, 1980) has added a number of meticulously traced local connections between tropes and ideas. With these points may be associated the inclusion of prologue, messenger, ghost, chorus and stichomythia, none of these links in itself conclusive but the precise form they take often suggesting a Senecan conjunction. An example may be helpful. The presence of stichomythia

455

does not in itself establish a Senecan background to a passage. But specific features in the following one from *Richard III* do seem to derive from Senecan technique, such as the pointed antithesis and the pivoting of each response on the wording of the proposition ('everlastingly . . . "ever" last', 'Harp not on that string . . . heartstrings'), turning the human conflict into elaborate verbal fencing:

KING RICHARD   Say she shall be a high and mighty queen.

QUEEN ELIZABETH   To wail the title, as her mother doth.

KING RICHARD   Say I will love her everlastingly.

QUEEN ELIZABETH   But how long shall that title 'ever' last?

KING RICHARD   Sweetly in force until her fair life's end.

QUEEN ELIZABETH   But how long fairly shall her sweet life last?

KING RICHARD   As long as heaven and nature lengthens it.

QUEEN ELIZABETH   As long as hell and Richard likes of it.

KING RICHARD   Say I, her sovereign, am her subject low.

QUEEN ELIZABETH   But she, your subject, loathes such sovereignty.

KING RICHARD   Be eloquent in my behalf to her.

QUEEN ELIZABETH   An honest tale speeds best being plainly told.

KING RICHARD   Then plainly to tell her tell my loving tale.

QUEEN ELIZABETH   Plain and not honest is too harsh a style.

KING RICHARD   Your reasons are too shallow and too quick.

QUEEN ELIZABETH   O, no, my reasons are too deep and dead –
Too deep and dead, poor infants, in their graves.

KING RICHARD   Harp not on that string, madam; that is past.

QUEEN ELIZABETH   Harp on it still shall I till heartstrings break.

KING RICHARD   Now, by my George, my garter, and my crown –

QUEEN ELIZABETH   Prophan'd, dishonour'd, and the third usurp'd.

KING RICHARD   I swear –

QUEEN ELIZABETH   By nothing; for this is no oath:
Thy George, profan'd, hath lost his lordly honour;
Thy garter, blemish'd, pawn'd his knightly virtue;
Thy crown, usurp'd, disgrac'd his kingly glory.
If something thou wouldst swear to be believ'd,
Swear then by something that thou hast not wrong'd.

(4.4.347–73)

(D) For a presentable modern equivalent of the verbal texture of

Senecan tragedy, there is Ted Hughes' translation of *Oedipus* (1969). Senecan influence on English Renaissance drama has been the subject of a separate bibliography: Kiefer (1978), supplemented in Kiefer (1985). This extends to some 115 entries (since 1900) and is excellently annotated. Hence only the most important items up to 1985, and a few overlooked by Kiefer, are listed below, and these notes are confined to major subsequent work. Martindale (1990: 29–41) reviews the literature at some length in reflecting on the nature of influence. Miola (1992) also summarizes the twentieth-century critical debate, then makes his own important contribution, an attempt 'to trace Seneca's influence on Shakespeare both in stylistic minutiae and in oblique, audacious effects' in an integrated account of Shakespeare's tragedies and tragicomedies. Helms (1997) has a more unorthodox treatment of specifically drama-turgical matters, only loosely centred on 'Senecan' effects, styles, char-acters, and so on, in Shakespeare and his contemporaries. The final sections of Boyle (1997) deal expertly with the Senecan tradition in European drama at large, with intermittent reference to Shakespeare.

Jones (1977); Martindale (1990).

Baker, Howard (1939). *Induction to Tragedy: A Study in a Development of Form in Gorboduc, The Spanish Tragedy and Titus Andronicus*. Baton Rouge.

Boyle, A. J. (1997). *Tragic Seneca: An Essay in the Theatrical Tradition*. London.

Braden, Gordon (1985). *Renaissance Tragedy and the Senecan Tradition: Anger's Privilege*. New Haven.

Brooks, Harold F., ed. (1979a). *A Midsummer Night's Dream* (Arden Shake-speare). London.

—— (1979b). '*Richard III*: Antecedents of Clarence's Dream.' *ShSu* 32: 145–50.

—— (1980). '*Richard III*, Unhistorical Amplifications: The Women's Scenes and Seneca.' *MLR* 75: 721–37.

Cohon, Bertram Jerome (1960). 'Seneca's Tragedies in *Florilegia* and Elizabethan Drama.' PhD diss. Columbia University.

Cunliffe, John W. (1893). *The Influence of Seneca on Elizabethan Tragedy*. London.

Daalder, Joost, ed. (1982). *Lucius Annaeus Seneca: Thyestes, translated by Jasper Heywood*. London.

Eliot, T. S., ed. (1927). *Seneca His Tenne Tragedies, edited by Thomas Newton anno 1581*, 2 vols. London.

457

Eliot, T. S. (1951). 'Shakespeare and the Stoicism of Seneca', pp. 126–40 in Eliot, *Selected Essays*. London (first published 1927).

Ewbank, Inga-Stina (1966). 'The Fiend-like Queen: A Note on *Macbeth* and Seneca's *Medea*.' *ShSu* 19: 82–94.

Helms, Lorraine (1997). *Seneca by Candlelight and Other Stories of Renaissance Drama*. Philadelphia, PA.

Hunter, G. K. (1967). 'Seneca and the Elizabethans: A Case-Study in "Influence".' *ShSu* 20: 17–26.

—— (1974). 'Seneca and English Tragedy', pp. 166–204 in C. D. N. Costa, ed., *Seneca*. London.

Kaufman, R. J. (1967). 'The Senecan Perspective and the Shakespearean Poetic.' *CompD* 1: 182–98.

Kiefer, Frederick (1978). 'Seneca's Influence on Elizabethan Tragedy: An Annotated Bibliography.' *Research Opportunities in Renaissance Drama* 21: 17–34.

—— (1985). 'Senecan Influence: A Bibliographical Supplement.' *Research Opportunities in Renaissance Drama* 28: 129–42.

Miola, Robert S. (1990). 'Othello Furens.' *ShQ* 41: 49–64.

—— (1992). *Shakespeare and Classical Tragedy: The Influence of Seneca*. Oxford.

Muir, Kenneth, ed. (1959). *Macbeth* (Arden Shakespeare). London (first published 1951).

Ornstein, Robert (1958). 'Seneca and the Political Drama of *Julius Caesar*.' *JEGP* 57: 51–6.

Sheen, Erica (1992). '"The Agent for his Master": Political Service and Professional Liberty in *Cymbeline*', pp. 55–76 in Gordon McMullan and Jonathan Hope, eds, *The Politics of Tragicomedy*. London.

Smith, Bruce R. (1988). *Ancient Scripts and Modern Experience on the English Stage 1500–1700*. Princeton.

Sowerby, Robin (1994). *The Classical Legacy in Renaissance Poetry*. London.

Wallace, John M. (1986). '*Timon of Athens* and the Three Graces: Shakespeare's Senecan Study.' *MP* 83: 349–63.

Sidney, Mary See **Garnier, Robert**; **Plessis-Mornay, Philippe du**.

Sidney, Sir Philip (1554–1586), Poet, Novelist and Critic

(A) The son of Sir Henry Sidney and Mary Dudley (sister to the Earl of Leicester), godson of Philip II of Spain, Sidney was educated at Shrewsbury School and Christ Church, Oxford. He travelled widely in Europe in 1572–5, impressing all he met. He was in Paris during the St Bartholomew's Day Massacre; he became a stout Protestant champion, promoting resistance to France and Spain. A political career did not develop, and his relations with the Queen were at times strained. Lacking employment, he sought secretly to join Drake's expedition to the Spanish coast in 1585, but instead was summoned to court and given a minor appointment in the Low Countries as Governor of Flushing, leaving England in 1585. He died of an infection from a wound received during an unimportant engagement with a Spanish supply convoy at Zutphen.

Sidney's works, none of which were printed in his lifetime, include the sonnet sequence *Astrophil and Stella* (printed 1591) and, with his sister Mary Sidney Pembroke, versions of the Psalms (not printed until the nineteenth century). The *Defence of Poesie*, or, in a slightly different version, *Apology for Poetry* (printed 1595), is effectively an epitome of Renaissance literary criticism, a defence of letters cast in the form of a classical oration, and drawing on authorities ancient and modern. The *Arcadia*, which introduced the Italian romance form to England but also entertains epic ambitions, exists in three different versions. As originally written for Mary Sidney in 1580–1 it is referred to as the *Old Arcadia*. This circulated in manuscript but was never printed in the sixteenth century. The second version, the *New Arcadia*, published posthumously in 1590, is Sidney's incomplete revision introducing new narratives and other major changes. Finally, in 1593 was published *The Countesse of Pembrokes Arcadia*, joining revised segment and unrevised remainder to make up a hybrid text, itself revised in the following decade.

(B) A mythologizing tendency helped determine the conduct of Sidney's life; it took over after his death, when he became a symbol of an idealized Elizabethan era – his poetry, wrote Samuel **Daniel**, showed 'what great Eliza's reign hath bred'. Lyric poets over the fifty years 1580 to 1630 regularly reflect the influence of *Astrophil and Stella* and often imitate it. The *Arcadia*, influential even before it was first printed, became enormously popular in late Elizabethan England and even more so in Caroline England, appealing to the taste for pastoral but also read as a courtesy book, a moral treatise, a discourse on love and philosophy, even as a rhetorical handbook. With the publication of the 1593 version, Sidney 'was being marketed . . . as the creator of a massive and complex work embracing both the heroic and romance traditions'. The publication of the folio edition of Sidney's major writings meant that 'these efforts to promote Sidney's image culminated in 1598 with the first literary collection in English to rival that of . . . Chaucer' (Stretkowicz 1986: 122).

This sample of the 1590 *Arcadia* is part of a dialogue interlude in *terza rima* about the rights and wrongs of suicide and the justice of the gods. The passage, from a segment of the narrative which for separate reasons it appears Shakespeare attended to, shows some verbal resemblances to parts of *King Lear* (see (C), below):

> What needed so high spirits such mansions blind?
>   Or wrapt in flesh what do they here obtaine,
>   But glorious name of wretched humaine-kind?
> Balles to the starres, and thralles to Fortunes raigne;
>   Turnd from themselves, infected with their cage,
>   Where death is feard, and life is held with paine.
> Like players pla'st to fill a filthy stage,
>   Where chaunge of thoughts one foole to other shewes,
>   And all but jests, save onely sorrowes rage.
> The child feeles that; the man that feeling knowes,
>   With cries first borne, the presage of his life,
>   Where wit but serves, to have true tast of woes.
> A Shop of shame, a Booke where blots be rife
>   This bodie is: this bodie so composed,
>   As in it selfe to nourish mortall strife.
> So divers be the Elements disposed
>   In this weake worke, that it can never be
>   Made uniforme to any state reposed.
> Griefe onely makes his wretched state to see
>   (Even like a toppe which nought but whipping moves)
>   This man, this talking beast, this walking tree.
> Griefe is the stone which finest judgement proves:
>   For who grieves not hath but a blockish braine,
>   Since cause of griefe no cause from life removes.
>   (ii.12; 1590 text, ed. Feuillerat 1939: i, 227, roman for italic)

(C) It is readily imaginable that Sidney's *Arcadia*, simply by virtue of its own remarkable artistic qualities, 'must have influenced Shakespeare at levels deeper than most of the materials from which he took his plots'. In the romantic comedies, in particular, it may have 'set an example in depicting processes of change, of growth, and capacity for love'; like Shakespeare, Sidney includes 'painful as well as ridiculous revelations about [the characters'] personal inadequacy, and the mingled yarn from which experience is made' and 'continuously alters the degree of sympathy with which the narrative engages the reader, and the angle of vision' (Gibbons 1987: 57–8). Nor is a creative response to Sidney's work necessarily likely to take shape in a prose mode, for another of the *Arcadia*'s qualities is that it is grounded in scenic form, and the five Books of the 1593 version are ordered according to Terentian five-act structure (with protasis, epitasis, catastrophe and Terentian double plot). Discussion of Sidney's possible impact on Shakespeare at this subterranean level has been undertaken by Brian Gibbons, whose observations are directed to *As You Like It* but could be applied elsewhere.

In the more orthodox sense, easily the most obvious of Shakespeare's borrowings from Sidney are in *King Lear*. Here he used, first, the tale of the blind Paphlagonian king and his family which made up the longest of the narratives freshly introduced into the *New Arcadia* of 1590. This story is told in instalments, beginning in II.10, to the heroes of Sidney's romance, after they meet the king being led by his good son Leonatus, who has refused to convey him to a high rock suitable for suicide. The Paphlagonian king has been deceived, blinded, and cast out by his bastard (and as Sidney calls him 'unnaturall') son Plexirtus, but Leonatus returns from exile and with foreign help thwarts the bastard, fighting him in person according to the rules of chivalry. The King of Paphlagonia dies, with strong verbal echoes of *Lear* 5.3.196–9, 'his hart broken with unkindnes and affliction, stretched so farre beyond his limits with this excess of comfort, as it was able no longer to keep safe his roial spirits' (ed. Feuillerat 1939: I, 212).

Shakespeare develops this narrative considerably. Edmund is derived from the non-speaking 'part' of Plexirtus, and Edgar from a character who sinks only to private soldiering, not to assumed madness and beggardom. *Lear*'s parallelism between the royal house and the house of Gloucester makes it obvious why Shakespeare introduced this story into the narrative of Lear and his daughters; it is also the case that

461

Shakespeare's deployment of a subplot paralleling his main plot resembles Sidney's technique, with the Paphlagonian story repeating the lessons on the resignation of power in the *Arcadia*'s main plot (see Ribner 1952). And the Paphlagonian king's misfortunes also seep into the Lear plot itself. Lear as well as Gloucester is turned out to wander by his enemies, and the 'extreame and foule' storm from which Sidney's 'poorely arayed' father and son shelter may have suggested Shakespeare's (there is also one in the *True Chronicle History of King Leir*). But as Sidney says, this matter is 'in it self lamentable, lamentably expressed', so it may be that 'sources of inspiration more potent than any detail were the theme itself and the moving quality of its narration' (Pyle 1948: 453). The epic sweep of Sidney's romance as a whole might also have helped Shakespeare to move away from the constricted world of the *Leir* chronicle history play and its analogues.

Further *Lear* material which may derive from the *Arcadia* supplements this. Like Gloucester, the King of Iberia in *Arcadia* II.15 is duped into believing that a murder plot has been hatched against him by his son Plangus, a detail absent from the Paphlagonian king story; like Cordelia, Plangus escapes overseas and seeks reconciliation (see McKeithan 1934). Some of Plangus' despairing reflections at an earlier stage, in II.12 of the *Arcadia* (given in (B), above), evoke the gods' malignity (for parallel passages in *Lear* see Muir 1972: xxxvii–xxxviii). And a famous dialogue in Sidney's III.10 is a demonstration of the dependence of nature on a benevolent order of things.

Other Shakespeare–Sidney connections are further to seek, and in the main less convincing when found (see Pyle 1948; Andrews 1972; Rees 1983; White 1986), but some firmer links to the *Arcadia* and *Astrophil and Stella* in Shakespeare's *Sonnets* bear closer inspection. Baldwin (1950: 194ff.) urges the influence of the *Arcadia* on the first group of *Sonnets* (specifically 3, 5–6, 8–9, and 13) as certain, citing a passage in *Arcadia* III.5 in which Cecropia urges her niece to marry. An excerpt most readily conveys the nature of the supposed debt:

> But my hart is already set (and staying a while on that word, she brought foorth afterwards) to lead a virgins life to my death: for such a vow I have in my selfe devoutly made. The heavens prevent such a mischiefe (said *Cecropia*.) A vowe, quoth you? no, no, my deere neece, Nature, when you were first borne, vowed you a woman, and as she made you the child of a mother, so to do your best to be mother of a

child: she gave you beautie to move love; she gave you wit to know love; she gave you an excellent body to reward love: which kind of liberall rewarding is crowned with unspeakable felicitie. For this, as it bindeth the receiver, so it makes happy the bestower: this doth not impoverish, but enrich the giver. O the sweet name of a mother: O the comfort of comforts, to see your children grow up, in whom you are (as it were) eternized: if you could conceive what a hart-tickling joy it is to see your own litle ones, with awfull love come running to your lap, and like litle models of your selfe, still cary you about them, you would thinke unkindnes in your own thoughts, that ever they did rebell against the mean unto it.

(1590 text, ed. Feuillerat 1939: i, 379)

There are close resemblances to Shakespeare in idea, and in image – Cecropia goes on to compare unmarried women to 'a pure Rosewater kept in a christal glas', like Shakespeare's rose in Sonnet 5, 'summer's distillation left, / A liquid prisoner pent in walls of glass'. Yet here, though the figures are the same, the applications, as Baldwin concedes, are different, and his overall assessment of the relationship as one of certain indebtedness is incautious. Quitslund's (1984: 115–19) proposal that Sonnets 84 and 85 wittily borrow their strategy from *Astophil and Stella* 3 and 35, which consider the same problem of how to praise a unique subject effectively, looks more secure.

(D) Texts of most of the parts of the *Arcadia* pertinent to *Lear* are given in Bullough, vii; of the Paphlagonian king story alone, in Satin (1966) and Muir (1972). Straightforward accounts of the *Lear–Arcadia* relationship are provided by Pyle (1948) and McKeithan (1934), while more recent treatments stressing particular aspects are Bono (1992) and Weiner (1991). For the *Arcadia* and other plays, see below. Any influence Sidney's other works had on Shakespeare seems to have been very limited, in spite of claims made by commentators such as Thaler (1947), for the *Apology for Poetry*.

Bullough; Muir (1977); Satin (1966).

Andrews, Michael C. (1972). 'Sidney's *Arcadia* and *The Winter's Tale.*' *ShQ* 23: 200–2.

Baldwin, T. W. (1950). *On the Literary Genetics of Shakspere's Poems and Sonnets*. Urbana, IL.

Bono, Barbara J. (1992). ' "The Chief Knot of All the Discourse": The Maternal Subtext Tying Sidney's *Arcadia* to Shakespeare's *King Lear*', pp. 105–27 in S. P. Ceserano and Marion Wynne-Davies, eds, *Gloriana's Face: Women, Public and Private, in the English Renaissance*. Detroit.

Buxton, John (1986). 'Shakespeare's *Venus and Adonis* and Sidney', pp. 104–10 in Jan van Dorsten *et al.*, eds, *Sir Philip Sidney: 1586 and the Creation of a Legend*. Leiden.

Feuillerat, Albert, eds. (1939). *The Complete Works of Sir Philip Sidney*, 4 vols. Cambridge.

Gibbons, Brian (1987). 'Amorous Fictions and *As You Like It*', pp. 52–78 in John W. Mahon and Thomas A. Pendleton, eds, *"Fanned and Winnowed Opinions": Shakespearean Essays Presented to Harold Jenkins*. London.

McKeithan, D. M. (1934). '*King Lear* and Sidney's *Arcadia*.' *University of Texas Studies in English* 14: 45–9.

Muir, Kenneth, ed. (1972). *King Lear* (Arden Shakespeare). London.

Parker, Barbara L. (1989). '*Troilus and Cressida*: A Further Source for Hector's Challenge (1.3.263–82).' *ANQ* 2.iv: 126–9.

Pyle, Fitzroy (1948). ' "Twelfth Night", "King Lear", and "Arcadia".' *MLR* 43: 449–55.

Quitslund, Jon A. (1984). 'Sidney's Presence in Lyric Verse of the Later English Renaissance', pp. 110–23 in Gary F. Waller and Michael D. Moore, eds, *Sir Philip Sidney and the Interpretation of Renaissance Culture: The Poet in His Time and in Ours. A Collection of Critical and Scholarly Essays*. London.

Rees, Joan (1983). 'Juliet's Nurse: Some Branches of a Family Tree.' *RES* 34: 43–7.

Ribner, Irving (1952). 'Sidney's *Arcadia* and the Structure of *King Lear*.' *Studia Neophilologica* 24: 63–8.

Stretkowicz, Victor (1986). 'Building Sidney's Reputation: Texts and Editors of the *Arcadia*', pp. 111–24 in Jan van Dorsten *et al.*, eds, *Sir Philip Sidney: 1586 and the Creation of a Legend*. Leiden.

Thaler, Alwin (1947). *Shakespeare and Sir Philip Sidney: The Influence of 'The Defence of Poesy'*. Cambridge, MA.

Vere, Charles (1994). 'Sir Philip Sidney Satirized in *Merry Wives of Windsor*.' *Elizabethan Review* 2.ii: 3–10.

Weiner, Andrew D. (1991). 'Sidney/Spenser/Shakespeare: Influence/Intertextuality/Intention', pp. 245–70 in Jay Clayton and Eric Rothstein, eds, *Influence and Intertextuality in Literary History*. Madison, WI.

White, R. S. (1986). 'Muscovites in *Love's Labour's Lost*.' *N&Q* 231: 350.

Woudhuysen, H. R., ed. (1998). *Love's Labour's Lost* (Arden Shakespeare). Walton-on-Thames.

Silva, Feliciano de See **Amadis de Gaule**.

Silvayn, Alexander (Alexandre Sylvain) (*c.* 1535– *c.* 1585), Flemish Moralist and Poet

(A) Alexandre Sylvain (anglicized as 'Silvayn') was the Latinized name of Alexandre van den Busche, the author of several works on polite conduct, poems, and other writings. He published in 1581 his *Epitomes de Cent Histoires, partie extraictes des Actes des Romains et autres, de l'invention de l'Autheur, avecq' les demandes, accusations, et deffences sur la matiere d'icelles.* This is a series of debates on moral issues which takes its cues from fictional stories and its form, ultimately at least, from **Seneca the Elder**'s controversiae. Each 'histoire' begins with a few lines of a summary narrative setting out the situation, then proceeds to a speech and a reply on the points of ethics and/or law which the situation raises.

(B) The *Cent Histoires* volume was translated into English in 1596 as *The Orator*. The translator is given as 'L.P.' and the dedicatory epistle is signed by 'Lazarus Piot' (a traditional identification of this figure with Anthony **Munday** was rejected by Thomas 1920: 310–15). The book seems not to have been reprinted.

The Orator contains as its ninety-fifth debate the details, as the heading puts it, 'Of a Jew, who would for his debt have a pound of the flesh of a Christian'. The narrative section sets out the flesh-bond arrangement and the judgement of a court in favour of the Christian. The Jew's appeal against the judgement and the Christian's speech in response are then given. This passage from the beginning of the debate includes about half of the Jew's speech.

> Impossible is it to breake the credite of trafficke amongst men without great detriment unto the Commonwealth: wherfore no man ought to bind himselfe unto such covenants which hee cannot or wil not accomplish, for by that means should no man feare to be deceaved, and credit being maintained, every man might be assured of his owne; but since deceit hath taken place, never wonder if

465

obligations are made more rigorous and strict then they were wont, seeing that although the bonds are made never so strong, yet can no man be very certaine that he shal not be a loser. It seemeth at the first sight, that it is a thing no lesse strange then cruel, to bind a man to pay a pound of the flesh of his bodie, for want of money: Surely, in that it is a thing not usuall, it appeareth to be somewhat the more admirable, but there are divers others that are more cruell, which because they are in use seeme nothing terrible at all: as to bind al the bodie unto a most lothsome prison, or unto an intollerable slaverie, where not only the whole bodie but also al the sences and spirits are tormented, the which is commonly practised, not only betwixt those which are either in sect or Nation contrary, but also even amongst those that are all of one sect and nation, yea amongst neighbours and kindred, and even amongst Christians it hath ben seene, that the son hath imprisoned the father for monie. Likewise, in the Roman Commonwealth, so famous for laws and armes, it was lawfull for debt, to imprison, beat, and afflict with torments the free Citizens: How manie of them (do you thinke) would have thought themselves happie, if for a small debt they might have ben excused with the paiment of a pound of their flesh? Who ought then to marvile if a Jew requireth so small a thing of a Christian, to discharge him of a good round summe? A man may aske why I would not rather take silver of this man, then his flesh: I might alleage many reasons, for I might say that none but my selfe can tell what the breach of his promise hath cost me, and what I have thereby paied for want of money unto my creditors, of that which I have lost in my credit: for the miserie of those men which esteeme their reputation, is so great, that oftentimes they had rather indure any thing secretlie then to have their discredit blazed abroad, because they would not be both shamed and harmed. Neverthelesse, I doe freely confesse, that I had rather lose a pound of my flesh, then my credit should be in any sort cracked: I might also say that I have need of this flesh to cure a friend of mine of a certaine maladie, which is otherwise incurable, or that I would have it to terrifie thereby the Christians for ever abusing the Jewes anie more hereafter: but I will onelie say, that by his obligation he oweth it me.

(Silvain 1596: 401–2)

(C) Silvayn's *Orator* has been most often associated with three Shakespeare plays: *Measure for Measure*, *The Merchant of Venice* and *Pericles*. For some more fragile links with *Othello* and *Coriolanus*, and between Silvayn's poems and *The Tempest*, see Nowottny (1965). It is unclear whether Shakespeare, if he did know Silvayn's work, would have used L.P.'s English or the original French version.

Measure for Measure offers parallels to no less than three of Silvayn's debates. These are debates on precisely the type of situations traditionally made up by moralists in order to illuminate ethical issues, so that the resemblances are in conformity with the view of the play as itself a type of ethical debate. But they are not close enough to indicate any debt. Declamation 54 concerns a man who persuaded his sister to bring about her ravisher's death; no. 61 is about two ravished maids, one of whom wants to marry the man responsible; and no. 68 presents a ravished maid who 'did first require her ravisher for her husband'.

Almost all the relevant parts of Declamation 95, the putative source for *The Merchant of Venice*, are included in the excerpt in (B), above. Possibly Shakespeare noticed the phraseology of the Jew's argument that there are worse punishments than taking a pound of flesh, such as keeping one's victim 'in intollerable slaverie', and used it for Shylock's speech at 4.1.90–5:

> You have among you many a purchas'd slave,
> Which, like your asses and your dogs and mules,
> You use in abject and in slavish parts,
> Because you bought them; shall I say to you
> 'Let them be free, marry them to your heirs –
> Why sweat they under burdens?'

Other than this, and the no more compelling point that 'the tone of Shylock's retorts at the trial is sometimes very close to that of Silvayn's Jew' (Mahood 1987: 6), there are some similarities in the arguments used on behalf of both Jews in the trial scene: about the 'credite' of the state and the point that he is not obliged to explain 'why I would not rather take silver . . . than his flesh' (compare 4.1.40–2). But there are significant divergences too: in Silvayn 'the Jew asserts that the debtor's duty is "to *give* me a pound of flesh" – the creditor need not cut it off' (Bullough, I, 452).

Finally, Silvayn's Declamation 53 is taken directly from the *Controversiae* of Seneca the Elder, and deals with a nun who was captured by pirates and sold to a brothel, where she killed a man about to violate her; the debate is on whether such a woman could properly become an abbess. This is clearly analogous to Mariana's history in *Pericles* (the similarities are enumerated by Elton 1949), but other sources, notably Lawrence **Twine**'s *Patterne of Painefull Adventures*, are closer to the details of Shakespeare's brothel episodes. The similarity with Silvayn's work can be explained by a common ancestry in **Greek romance** (so Waith 1951).

(D)

Bullough, I.

Elton, William (1949). '*Pericles*: A New Source or Analogue.' *JEGP* 48: 138–9.

Mahood, M. M., ed. (1987). *The Merchant of Venice* (New Cambridge Shakespeare). Cambridge.

Nowottny, Winifred (1965). 'Shakespeare and *The Orator*.' *Bulletin de la Faculté des Lettres de Strasbourg* 43.viii: 813–33.

Silvain, Alexandre, translated by L.P. (1596). *The Orator: Handling a Hundred Severall Discourses, in Forme of Declamations*. London.

Thomas, Henry (1920). *Spanish and Portugese Romances of Chivalry*. Cambridge.

Waith, E. M. (1951). '*Pericles* and Seneca the Elder.' *JEGP* 50: 180–2.

Skelton, John See ***Mirror for Magistrates, A***; **Morality Tradition**.

Skene, Sir John (1543?–1617), Scottish Legal Writer
Skene's Scots Acts (1597), as it was commonly known, was an official epitome or 'table' of the reigns of the kings of Scotland, containing some descriptive material on Macbeth and Duncan matching Shakespeare's narrative, in particular the 'traiterous' murder and the fact that Macbeth 'degenerates'.

Paul, Henry N. (1950). *The Royal Play of Macbeth: When, Why, and How it was written by Shakespeare*, pp. 220–2. New York.

Sophocles (*c.* 496–406/5 BC), Greek Tragedian Harvey's instances of possible Sophoclean influence on several Shakespearean tragedies form an engrossing but, as he acknowledges, ultimately inconclusive case.

Harvey, John (1977). 'A Note on Shakespeare and Sophocles.' *EinC* 27: 259–70.

Southwell, Robert (1561?–1595), Poet Fleeting echoes of Southwell seem to occur in *The Rape of Lucrece* and *King Lear*.

Brownlow, Frank (1987). 'Southwell and Shakespeare', p. 26 in *KM 80: A Birthday Album for Kenneth Muir*. Liverpool.

Speed, John (1552?–1629), Historian and Cartographer *Henry VIII* contains some verbal resemblances to passages in Speed's 1611 *History of Great Britaine*, but they are by no means conclusive as evidence of a relationship.

Foakes, R. A., ed. (1968). *Henry VIII* (Arden Shakespeare), pp. 112, 120. London (first published 1957).
Wiley, Paul L. (1946). 'Renaissance Exploitation of Cavendish's *Life of Wolsey*.' *SP* 43: 121–46.

Spenser, Edmund (*c.* 1552–1599), Poet Though Shakespeare may be assumed to have been conversant with *The Faerie Queene* (1590–6), its effect on him in any given work is hard to demonstrate. Watkins (1950) and Potts (1958) broadly see analogies in the comedies from *Much Ado* onwards and the Late Plays, primarily in 'the narrative or dramatic devices and procedures shared by Spenser and Shakespeare as poets of ethical action' (Potts 1958: 12). Previous studies are listed in Potts 1958: 7–8n. Shakespeare's debts are not confined to *The Faerie Queene*: Brooks (1979: lxi–lxii) explains some links between the *Shepheardes Calendar* (1579) and *A Midsummer Night's Dream*; Kerrigan (1999: 390–2) has a brief recent treatment of *The Ruins of Time* (1591) as a model for *A Lover's Complaint*.

Brooks, Harold F., ed. (1979). *A Midsummer Night's Dream* (Arden Shakespeare). London.
Kerrigan, John, ed. (1999). *The Sonnets and A Lover's Complaint.* Harmondsworth (first published 1986).
Potts, Abbie Findlay (1958). *Shakespeare and 'The Faerie Queene'.* Ithaca.
Watkins, W. B. C. (1950). *Shakespeare and Spenser.* Princeton.

Stapleton, Thomas (1535–1598), Catholic Controversialist If Stapleton's *Vita et Illustre Martyrium Thomae Mori* (1588) was used by the authors of *Sir Thomas More*, only the Latin text would have been available.

Metz, G. Harold, ed. (1989). *Sources of Four Plays Ascribed to Shakespeare.* Columbia, MI.

Stewart, William (1481?–1550?), Scottish Chronicler and Poet Stewart's *Buik of the Chronicles of Scotland*, not printed until the nineteenth century, contains some details conforming with *Macbeth*, but which also appear in one or more other sources.

Bullough, VII, 438.
Muir, Kenneth, ed. (1951). *Macbeth* (Arden Shakespeare), xxxix–xl. London.

Stow, John (*c.* 1525–1605), Historian See also **Elyot, Sir Thomas**.
(A) Stow, a Londoner by birth, was brought up to the trade of tailor, but turned antiquary in later life. In 1561 he published an edition of **Chaucer**, and in 1565 his *Summarie of Englyshe Chronicles* (in the process becoming a rival to Richard **Grafton** and starting an acrimonious exchange with him). The *Summarie* was expanded in 1580 into Stow's *Chronicles of England*, recast again in 1592 to become *The Annales or a Generale Chronicle of England from Brute until the Present Yeare of Christ.* Reissued in 1601 and 1605, and updated in 1615 and 1631, this was a connected narrative in the humanistic historical tradition, recording 'wise handling of weightie affaires, diligently to be marked and aptly to

be applied'. Stow also published a popular and historically still useful *Survey of London* in 1598.

Stow worked in the traditional chronicler's fashion, by judiciously culling from earlier chronicles and histories and reassembling the segments in a suitable order. He appropriated, for example, **More**'s *History of Richard III* almost wholesale, and became the first to introduce George Cavendish's *Life of Wolsey* (completed 1557) to print. He also assisted other contemporary historians personally, for example by purchasing part of John Leland's papers after the printer Reginald Wolfe's death, so being able to lend materials to the 1587 revisers of **Holinshed**'s Chronicle.

(B) Stow's work was being read almost from its first publication through other chroniclers' appropriations of it as well as in its original form. Its original form is represented here, by the opening of the extensive account of Thomas Wolsey and his rise and fall at the court of Henry VIII.

And here I think good to set down for example to posteritie, som part of the proceedings of this so oft named Thomas Wolsey archbishop, his ascending unto honorious estate, and sodeine falling againe from the same, as I have bin enformed by persons of good credite. Truth it is, this cardinall Wolsey was an honest poore mans son of Ipswich, in the county of Suffolk, and there born, and being but a childe, very apt to be learned, wherfore by the means of his parents, or of his good friends and masters, hee was conveyed to the Universitie of Oxford, where he shortly prospered so in learning, as himselfe reported, as he was made Bachelor of Art, when he passed not 15. yeeres of age, and was called most commonly through the University the boy Bacheler. Thus prospering in learning, he was made fellow of Maudelin colledge, and afterward appointed to be schoolmaster of Maudelin Schoole, at whiche time, the L. Marques Dorset had 3. of his sons there at schoole, committing unto him as well their education, as their instruction. It pleased the said L. Marques against a Christmas season to send aswel for the schoolmaster, as for his children home to his house for their recreation, in that pleasant and honorable feast. Then being there, the L. their father perceiving them to be right well employed in learning for their time, he having a Benefice in his gift being at that time void, gave the same to the schoolmaster in reward of his diligence, at his departure after Christmas to the Universitie, and having the presentation therof repaired to the Ordinary for his institution or induction, and being furnished of all his ordinary instruments, made speed to the benefice to take therof possession, and being there for that intent, one Sir Amias Poulet knight dwelling therabout, tooke an occasion of displeasure against him, upon what grounde I knowe not, but sir by your leave he was so bold to set the schoolmaster by the feete, during his pleasure, which after was neither forgotten not forgiven: for when the schoolmaster mounted the dignity to be Chancelor of England, he was not oblivious of his olde displeasure cruelly ministred unto him by M. Poulet: but sent for him, and after many sharpe words, enjoined him to attend until he were dismissed, and not to depart out of London without licence obtained, so that he continued there within the middle temple the space of 5. or 6. yeeres, who lay then in the gate-house next the streete, which he reedified very sumptuously, garnishing the same al over the outside with the cardinals armes, with his hat, cognisances, and other devises in so glorious a sort, that he thought therby to have appeased his old displeasure. Now may this be a good example, and president, to men in authoritie (which will sometime worke their will without wit) to remember in their authoritie, how authoritie may decaie: and whom they do punish of will, more then of justice, may after be advaunced to high honor and dignities in the common weales, and they based as low: who will then seeke the meanes to be revenged of such wrongs, which they suffered before.

(Stow 1592: 831–2)

(C) Owing to the extensive recycling of chronicle material from one writer to another in the sixteenth century, it cannot be demonstrated that Shakespeare ever read Stow's work. He may have used it for *Richard III*, though if he did it was for matter which derived directly from authorities Stow himself had used, in particular from More (see Churchill 1900: 223–7). There is some evidence that Stow's 1592 *Annales* were used for *Henry VIII*, in addition to the version of Stow's material given in Holinshed. (Stow's material here itself derives, like all other chronicles of the reign, from Cavendish's *Life of Wolsey*, but this dangerous work was available in its original form only in manuscript until the mid-seventeenth century, and the authors of *Henry VIII* are not thought to have known it directly; see Wiley 1946.)

This case is set out by Anderson (1984: 137):

In the absence of a Tudor printing of Cavendish's *Wolsey*, the undoubted influence of this work on *Henry VIII* would ordinarily suggest Shakespeare's knowledge of Stow, whose 1592 version of the *Wolsey* was the fullest in print available to Shakespeare; but many of Shakespeare's borrowings – the more striking ones often among them – occur in both editions of Stow and are copied from Stow's earlier edition by Holinshed 1587. Since there is no question of Shakespeare's familiarity with Holinshed's second edition, these borrowings are therefore usually taken to show another instance of it. The logic of this conclusion is more economical than necessary, but even allowing it, we find strong indications in Shakespeare's treatment of Cromwell's interview with Wolsey after the latter's fall that Shakespeare knew Stow's edition of 1592.

Even Stow's briefer narrative in his 1580 edition creates 'a wide place for the insertion of what amounted to a separate biographical sketch of the cardinal', making Wolsey 'the most prominent figure in the period of Henry VIII' and contributing to history a new 'character' (Wiley 1946: 129). In 1592 Stow makes much of 'the ambiguity of Wolsey's awareness that we find in Cavendish' (Anderson 1984: 136), which is only hinted at in Holinshed, and which implies the more ambivalent portrayal of Henry VIII also found in Stow. More specific material identified by Anderson as deriving from Stow in *Henry VIII* comes in the character of Cromwell: in 'the singular importance of Cromwell to Wolsey, the close nature of their relationship, and the rather tearful circumstances of their farewell' (Anderson 1984: 142). These resemblances are nevertheless inconclusive: the promotion of Cromwell's character has clear dramatic advantages for the playwright, and the other elements would follow naturally.

(D)
Anderson, Judith H. (1984). *Biographical Truth: The Representation of Historical Persons in Tudor-Stuart Writing*. New Haven.
Campbell, Lily B. (1947). *Shakespeare's "Histories": Mirrors of Elizabethan Policy*. San Marino, CA.
Churchill, George B. (1900). *Richard the Third up to Shakespeare*. Berlin.
Stow, John (1592). *The Annales of England, Faithfully Collected out of the*

most *autenticall Authors, Records, and Other Monuments of Antiquitie.*
London.

Wiley, Paul L. (1946). 'Renaissance Exploitation of Cavendish's *Life of Wolsey.*' *SP* 43: 121–46.

Strachey, William See **Bermuda Pamphlets**.

Straparola, Giovan Francesco (d. *c.* 1559), Italian Novelist See also **Painter, William**. Straparola's *Le piacevoli notti* (1550–3; French translation 1560–3) contains, ii.2, a 'duped lover' story which Shakespeare might have known in one form or another by the time he imagined Falstaff's discomfiture at the hands of the Merry Wives.

Bullough, ii.

Studley, John See **Seneca, Lucius Annaeus, the Younger**.

Suetonius (Gaius Suetonius Tranquillus) (*c.* AD 69– *c.* 140), Roman Historian

(A) Born, probably in Algeria, into an equestrian family, Suetonius studied law in Rome, a typical preparation for a political career. He became a friend of the Younger Pliny, who offered him a military post. Instead, in about 113 he became a secretary at the imperial palace, but in 121 or 122 he was dismissed by Hadrian for an alleged indiscretion with the Emperor's wife. His diverse writings included reference compilations and antiquarian works on ancient Greek and Roman customs and festivals, but to post-Byzantine history he is the greatest of the Roman biographers. His surviving works consist of parts of his *De Viris Illustribus* and the *De Vita Caesarum*. The former includes lives of **Horace**, **Lucan**, **Terence** and **Virgil**, which have been transmitted with the works of those authors, but Suetonius' reputation rests on the accounts he gives of Julius Caesar and the eleven succeeding Roman emperors. These contain lively description and often salacious or scandalous anecdote, and because they are not complete narrative histories, assuming rather the reader's prior knowledge of other sources, the *Lives of the Caesars* have been felt too preoccupied with trivia. Their unadorned style, with direct citations from documents and of Greek terms, has also seemed unattractive. But Suetonius' work is often best understood as a marshalling of material to make a case, regularly using standard rhetorical formats. His wit can be subtle.

(B) The *Lives of the Twelve Caesars* became a model for biographical narrative in the Middle Ages, and by the mid-sixteenth century in England it had become a usual part of the education of princes, as well as the less exalted pupils of the English grammar school. Copies of some of the 155 European editions from 1450 to 1700 (Burke 1966: 138) were owned by Edward VI; by **James VI** of Scotland, whose annual reading-list for 1580 included a *Commentaria in Suetonium* (Baldwin 1944: I, 552); and by Juan Luis Vives, who was involved in the education of the Princess Mary, and mentions him as a historian. Gabriel **Harvey** reckons Suetonius one of the best exemplars of Latin prose. The first English translation of Suetonius, Philemon Holland's 1606 *Historie of Twelve Caesars, Emperors of Rome*, comes considerably later than renderings into the other major European vernaculars.

(C) The possibility of echoes from Suetonius in Shakespeare has regularly been canvassed, with the Life of Claudius almost always proposed as Shakespeare's source. The exception is Julius Caesar's 'Et tu, Brute' (3.1.77), which parallels the Greek words Suetonius' Caesar speaks at this point, 'καὶ σύ, τέκνον', in the Life of Julius, 82. But versions of Caesar's dying words would of course have been known outside the Suetonian context. A few apparent echoes in *Richard III* may be coincidence or may be owing to an intermediate work such as the **Mirror for Magistrates** (Jones 1977: 217), as may Macbeth's resemblance to Claudius when both forgetfully expect men they have had killed to appear at entertainments (Jones 1977: 27).

The strongest case for Suetonius' direct contact with Shakespeare rests on *Hamlet*, though nothing conclusive can be established. No previous version of the story employing the name 'Claudius' being known (he is 'Feng' or 'Fengon' in Saxo Grammaticus and **Belleforest**), a connection with Suetonius has been hypothesized and worked out in terms of similarities of character traits, not however between the two Claudiuses, but between Suetonius' Claudius and Hamlet. The most prominent of these is the feigned madness. But neither this nor any of the other sixteen resemblances noted by Berry (1947) would strongly imply a connection, if taken individually; and Shakespeare's familiarity with the Emperor Claudius' name could be explained by his knowledge of **Plutarch** or **Seneca**. It is, rather, the collective case these similarities constitute that makes them seem more than coincidence. Even proponents of this theory concede, though, that without first-hand knowledge of the text of the Ur-*Hamlet* (see **Belleforest**) it cannot be determined whether these signs of a relationship derive from Shakespeare or his predecessor. At its strongest the argument is that 'besides Saxo and Belleforest we must also consider Suetonius' *Claudius* as a probable source and since the parallel elements in *Hamlet* and Suetonius do not appear in Saxo or Belleforest they must have been drawn from Suetonius by Thomas Kyd or by William Shakespeare himself' (Berry 1947: 81). Further parallels between Hamlet and Nero, such as that both wrote dramatic verse and acted (Montgomerie 1960: 70), are unconvincing.

(D)

Baldwin (1944); Jones (1977).

Berry, E. G. (1947–8). 'Shakespeare and Suetonius.' *The Phoenix* 2: 73–81.

Burke, Peter (1966). 'A Survey of the Popularity of Ancient Historians, 1450–1700.' *History and Theory* 5: 135–52.

Montgomerie, William (1960–1). 'More an Antique Roman than a Dane.' *Hibbert Journal* 59: 67–77.

Surrey, Henry Howard, Earl of See *Tottel's Miscellany*.

Sylvius, Aeneas (Enea Silvio Piccolomini) (1405–1464), Pope Pius II Guinn counts Sylvius as one of several influences on Shakespeare's handling of the letter device in Act 1 of *The Two Gentlemen of Verona*.

Guinn, John A. (1940). *The Letter Device in the First Act of the Two Gentlemen of Verona*. Austin, TX.

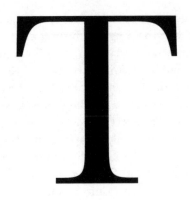

Tacitus, Publius Cornelius or Gaius Cornelius (*c.* AD 56– after 117), Roman Historian

(A) Surprisingly little is known about the life of Tacitus: even his full name is uncertain. He studied rhetoric at Rome, and pursued the normal career of a Roman aristocrat, holding office as quaestor, praestor, consul and provincial governor. He married the daughter of Julius Agricola, later Governor of Britain. His *Agricola*, a biography of his father-in-law, and *Germania*, on the ethnography of Germany, where Tacitus had travelled, were both published in the first century. But his most important writings are the later *Histories* and *Annals*, together covering the history of the Roman empire of the years 14–96. About a third of the former and a little more than half of the latter survive. Tacitus is usually thought of as the greatest of Latin historians, with a style at once complex, subtle and witty.

(B) 'Tacitus', the anonymous preface to Henry Savile's 1591 translation of the *Agricola* tells the reader, 'hath written the most matter with the best conceite in fewest words of any Historiographer ancient or modern. But he is hard. *Difficilia quae pulchra*.' Tacitus' difficulty prevented his becoming a standard teaching text in sixteenth-century schools, though excerpts were in use (see Baldwin 1956: II, 566). He was admired for his content as well as his style. His stature as a moralist was stressed by Bacon, who praised especially the 'characters' of Tiberius, Claudius and Nero. He was also appreciated as a political writer, both in a general sense, as attending to secret motives and hidden causes, and for a specific ideology. For the English avant-garde, 'Tacitus offered an acerb and disenchanted observation of the gradual strangulation, under the Empire, of all [the] ethical wonders of Republican Rome'. In comparison with the republican and radical Tacitus, 'Jonson and others clearly thought of Shakespeare and Plutarch as slow-witted provincials who hadn't caught up' (Hunter 1977: 104).

Savile's useful but aesthetically disappointing rendering of the *Agricola* and *Historiae* was reissued with Richard Grenewey's also unremarkable English translation of the *Germania* and *Annals* (significantly dedicated to Essex) in 1598, and the joint edition was standard through the seventeenth century. French, German and Italian translations were also available to the late sixteenth-century reader. **Jonson**'s high praise of Tacitus as the writer of the 'best Latin' he knows (*Conversations*) is matched by his extensive use of the *Annals*, including close translation, in his play *Sejanus* (1603); Jonson's dark and secretive atmospheres make him perhaps the most Tacitean of English writers of the age.

In this section of Grenewey's *Germania*, Germanicus ('Caesar') anticipates Shakespeare's Henry V in listening incognito to the remarks of his soldiers before battle:

When *Caesar* had passed the river Visurgis, he understoode by a fugitive from the enemie campe, what place *Arminius* had chosen to give battell: and that other nations were assembled in a wood consecrated to *Hercules*, with intention to assaile the camp by night. The runnagate was beleeved: lights were seene: and the espiales getting neerer, reported they heard a great confuse noise of men and horses. Being therefore at a jumpe to hazard all, thinking it convenient to sounde the soldiers minde, he bethought himselfe what was the fittest expedient to trie the truth. The Tribunes and Centurions brought him oftener pleasing then true newes: the freed men were of a servile disposition: in friends there was flatterie: if he should call an assembly, that which a few should begin, the rest would applaud. That their minds would be best knowen, when they were by themselves; not overlooked: in eating and drinking they would utter their fear or hope. As soone as it was night, going out at the Augural gate, accompanied with one alone, in secret and unknowen places to the watch: casting a savage beasts skin on his backe, he went from one place to another: stoode listning at the tents: and joyeth in the praise of himselfe: some extolling the nobilitie of their Captaine: others his comely personage: many his patience, and courtesie: that in sports and serious matters, he was still one man: confessing therefore that they thought it their parts, to make him some requitall in this battell, and sacrifice the traitors and peace-breakers to revenge and glory.

(Tacitus 1598: ii.3)

(C) Shakespeare may have used Tacitus' *Germania* for *Henry V* – or may not. There are parallels in the narratives of the Romans' warfare in Books i and ii for Henry's encouragement of his soldiers, his nocturnal walk around the camp, his meditation and his prayer (texts given in Bullough, iv, 408–11). Perhaps Shakespeare was struck 'not only by the device of the general's visiting his men in disguise, but also by likeness of character between Tacitus' hero and Harry the warrior-king' (Price 1961: 59). But 'all these elements . . . Shakespeare could have created for himself, given the King's circumstances and character', while King Henry's incognito meetings with the soldiers which seem to echo the passage in (B) may arise from a dramatic tradition 'in which a ruler in disguise mingles with his subjects' (Craik 1995: 10). Against the suggestion of influence can be cited the relative obscurity of these sections of Tacitus. Even if it is accepted, Shakespeare's deviations are significant; what Henry overhears from his troops is not conventional praise as in Tacitus, showing 'that Henry is not just an epic hero but also a modern ruler of a stiff-necked and highly critical nation' (Bullough, iv, 363).

A likely source in Tacitus has been proposed for one further episode in Shakespeare, that of the 'son that hath kill'd his father' in *3 Henry VI*, 2.5. It is suggested this was the result of his having read Savile's translation of the *Historiae* on its first appearance, and having found it germane to his subject 'because of its apposite theme of the calamities that overtake a state which mismanages its succession' (Womersley 1985: 471).

(D)
Baldwin (1956); Bullough, iv, 361–3.

Burke, Peter (1966). 'A Survey of the Popularity of Ancient Historians, 1450–1700.' *History and Theory* 5: 135–52.

Craik, T. W., ed. (1995). *Henry V* (Arden Shakespeare). London.

Hunter, G. K. (1977). 'A Roman Thought: Renaissance Attitudes to History Exemplified in Shakespeare and Jonson', pp. 93–118 in

Brian S. Lee, ed., *An English Miscellany: Papers Presented to W. S. Mackie*. Cape Town.

Price, George R. (1961). 'Henry V and Germanicus.' *ShQ* 12: 57–60.

Tacitus, translated by Richard Grenewey (1598). *The Annals of Cornelius Tacitus. The Description of Germanie*. London.

Womersley, D. J. (1985). '*3 Henry VI*: Shakespeare, Tacitus, and Parricide.' *N&Q* 230: 468–73.

Taming of a Shrew, The **(Anon. Play, 1594)** The vexed question of the relation between this play and Shakespeare's is handled authoritatively by Morris (1981).

Honigmann, E. A. J. (1954). 'Shakespeare's "Lost Source-Plays".' *MLR* 49: 293–307.

Morris, Brian, ed. (1981). *The Taming of the Shrew* (Arden Shakespeare). London.

Taverner, Richard See **Erasmus, Desiderius**.

Terence (Publius Terentius Afer) (*c*. 195–159 BC), Roman Playwright

(A) Born in Carthage, he became the slave of a Roman senator who brought him to Rome, educated him, and freed him. He began his career as a playwright with his *Andria* ('The Girl from Andros', 166 BC), an immediate success which gave him entrée into Roman high society. His five other extant comedies are *Eunuchus, Heauton Timoroumenos, Phormio, Hecyra* and *Adelphi*. Terence's plays seek to emulate the Greek New Comedy (only fragments of which are extant in post-classical times), especially that of Menander, whose work four of his plays adapt, preserving the Greek setting and overall ethos.

(B) Terence was thought of as an easy and essential author in the sixteenth century, and was often the first Latin writer to be tackled at grammar school, though his verse was frequently misinterpreted as prose. 'I learn'd *Terence*, i' the third forme at *Westminster*', says the boy in the induction to **Jonson**'s *The Magnetic Lady*. Ordinarily the schoolboy encountered him in the shape of Nicholas Udall's *Floures for Latine Spekinge Selected and Gathered oute of Terence*, 1533, which gave a Latin text and painstaking phrase-by-phrase English translations of excerpts from the *Andria*, *Eunuchus* and *Heauton Timoroumenos*, while ensuring by its format that the plays could not be enjoyed as drama. However, Terence, like **Plautus**, was comparatively often acted at schools and universities in sixteenth-century England, as well as at court.

This popularity was not only on account of his comic excellence and the suitability for deployment (or disguise) as moral instruction reflected in Udall's collection of *sententiae* and in **Sidney**'s references to him in his well-known defence of comedy in *The Defence of Poesy*. The purity and unique informality of his language, often associated with the refined colloquialism preferred by the great and good, was perhaps even more important a factor, and the principal reason why he was sometimes preferred to Plautus. He was thought by his mid-sixteenth-century editor Wagnerus 'profitable for the polishing of language, for the unlearning of rudeness, for the wealth and abundance of words and sentiments, for the invention of arguments for every kind of cause, for providing the knack of both speaking and writing' (translated Herrick 1950: 215). **Erasmus**, who knew all of Terence by heart, ranked him (in *De Ratione Studii*) first for the learning of Latin style; he was a model for writers in general, and comic dramatists in particular. Udall himself drew upon Terence's characters in his own play *Ralph Roister Doister* (1537); **Chapman**'s *All Fools* (1599) adapts his *Heauton* and *Adelphi*; and Jonson's comedy at large has Terentian features, though in his case as in many others Terence was of less importance than Plautus, usually thought the livelier comedian. It was prestigious to be compared to Terence: John Davies calls Shakespeare 'our English Terence', and the epistle before the 1609 quarto of *Troilus and Cressida* equates the play with the '*best Commedy in* Terence *or* Plautus'.

Terence monopolizes discussion of comic theory in the period. The extensive tradition of Renaissance commentary on his plays is documented by Baldwin (1947) and Herrick (1950). Especially significant, if only as indicating the widely held classical ideal in comic plays, are the brief essays on the history of classical drama *De Fabula*, by Evanthius, and *De Tragoedia et Comoedia*, attributed to Aelius Donatus. Often reprinted in editions of Terence (usually conflated as a single essay under the second title, and the name of Donatus), and used throughout the seventeenth as well as sixteenth century, they give between them a history and definition of stage comedy and a summary of the structure of a classical drama that proved influential for Renaissance practice (for modern translations see Hardison 1974: 39–49; for a summary of their content see Doran 1954: 106–8, and for suggestions as to their effect on Shakespeare, Snyder 1979: 40–2). Fig. 10 shows an image of a Roman theatre which was used to illustrate these essays in more than one early edition.

The extensive excerpts and collections of Terentian 'flowers' were not matched by full-scale translation in English. Thomas **More**'s friend, the lawyer John Rastell, produced an *Andria* in 1520, but no further published renderings are recorded until Maurice Kyffin's *Andria*, for school use, of 1588. The rest followed in 1598 with Richard Bernard's complete comedies. Bernard's preface describes Terence as being 'as ethical as Plato', and an entire sub-genre, 'Christian Terence', was developed by German and Dutch humanists to produce plays for the edification of youth. Early English imitators of Terence were also interested in using his protasis–epitasis–catastrophe structure to deliver moral lessons. The following self-justification by the character Parmeno in *Eunuchus* (who has mistakenly delivered his young charge to a loose woman) was very often cited in the Renaissance in defence of the pedagogical use of Terence's zestful depictions of lust, avarice and duplicity, on the principle that an acquaintance with wickedness is a prerequisite for shunning it:

> I have devised a way how a young man may know the naturall disposition and manner of queanes; to the intent that after he knowes them, he may for ever hate them as long as hee liveth. Who being abroad out of their owne houses, nothing in the world seemes to bee more cleane than they be, nor any thing more demure, nor more proper; who, when they sup with their lover, feed very nicely and daintily, and not but of the best: but to see them how uncleanly they bee, the ravening and manching, the sluttishnesse, penury, and what greedie gripes they are all alone at home; how they will slabber and sosse up browne bread in pottage, such as was left the day before; to know these things, are a singular profit to young men.
>
> (Terence 1614: 160)

(C) Shakespeare must have encountered Terence at school, and certainly derives material from him. But there is little good evidence of

482

Figure 10 Terence, *Comodiae VI. cum commentariis Aelii Donati, Guidonis Juvenalis, et Badii Ascensii* (Venice, 1499), fo. v^v (actual size 238 × 155mm).

first-hand borrowing, partly because knowledge of Terence was so widely diffused and so variously employed by other writers that Terentian linguistic, stylistic, character or narrative material need hardly ever come directly from the Terentian texts themselves, in Latin or in English:

> New Comedy influenced Propertius, Ovid, and Lucian, whose dialogues in turn supply character and situation to Erasmus and others. Boccaccio copied all of Terence by hand, remembering him significantly in the *Decameron*; Sidney's *Arcadia* (old version) orders its action according to the 'renaissance Terentian five-act structure,' with *protasis*, *epitasis*, and *catastrophe*, and features a Terentian double plot. Plautus and Terence shape tales in Bandello . . . The formative presence of New Comedy in these writers, so important to Shakespeare, argues for wider investigation.
>
> (Miola 1994: 14)

This is to say nothing of the lexicon of specifically dramatic possibility that Terence, with Plautus, created, and which was mediated to Shakespeare in part through the Italian theatre of the Cinquecento (see **Ariosto**). The often indistinguishable parts played by Terence and Plautus in Shakespeare's dramatic background also render it often impossible to isolate definitively Terentian features. With the four principal New Comedy elements discussed by Miola (1994), namely errors, intrigue, the *alazon* ('boaster') and romance, Terence's influence is probably inextricable from Plautus' in at least the second and third, while Plautus is much more clearly the originator of Shakespearean material in the first and last.

Thus, even though Shakespearean comedy as a whole has been called the 'function of . . . the Terentian formula for comic plots . . . and the battle of the sexes' (Nevo 1980: 3), the certainty that Shakespeare draws on Terence only means he is the ultimate source, as part of the comedic gene-pool, of some traditional or at least frequently recycled literary ingredients such as stock characters (e.g. the Prodigal Son figure: see Beck 1973) and expressions. For example, the above passage (B) on the necessity of learning from immodest sources was as long ago as the eighteenth century seen to lie behind Warwick's defence of Prince Hal to King Henry:

The Prince but studies his companions
Like a strange tongue, wherein, to gain the language,
'Tis needful that the most immodest word
Be look'd upon and learnt; which once attain'd,
Your Highness knows, comes to no further use
But to be known and hated.

(*2 Henry IV*, 4.4.68–73)

Such a connection is not capable of actual proof. But a more far-reaching, if altogether less tangible, effect of Terence's example on Shakespeare may have been in the overall structure of his plays. From his schooldays, it has been supposed, the sixteenth-century European dramatist felt the desire 'to imitate Terence, not merely in separate sections, but even in the writing of a whole play. When he thought of writing a play, he naturally thought of the one and only correct method, that which the teachers and commentators said was the way of Terence' (Baldwin 1947: 673), namely the 'five-act formula' into which the ancient grammarians had divided Terence's plays, and which is set out in the Renaissance by Landino and explained by Willich in his 1550 commentary on *Andria* (Act 3 has the 'sequence of perturbations', Act 4 exhibits the 'desperate state of the matter', and so on).

Baldwin shows that Terentian commentaries probably inspired Elizabethan five-act structure, but, since Shakespeare was not the first dramatist to write five-act plays, the hypothesis about Terence's effects on his dramatic structures has more substance when there are additional factors. Baldwin finds this to be the case in *Love's Labour's Lost*, which is 'not merely constructed principally from two plays of Plautus' but 'also analyses and reconstructs those plays into the *Andria* formula of Terentian structure' (Baldwin 1947: 666), i.e. the *duplex argumentum*, two closely related plots operating in tandem (see Levin 1971). This observation is a reminder that plot may in fact be the area in which Terence's effect on Shakespeare is at its strongest, both in the sense of overall scheme (benign doublings and redoublings, involutions and intrigues developing in certain ways at certain intervals) and individual ingredients (such as errors and lock-outs, twins and quasi-twins). This effect may not be confined to Shakespeare's comedies: as Miola notes apropos of the Late Plays, 'New Comedic romance generally features a pure female figure variously assaulted, journeys over sea and long time, reunions of parents and children' (Miola 1994: 195).

Two more conceivably important but, again, ultimately unprovable possibilities should be mentioned. It can be argued that the 'plot of the psyche' which emerges in Shakespeare's tragedies and Late Plays, which depends on the enormously important Renaissance rediscovery of the Aristotelian poetics of recognition, and of which the paradigm is the plot of mistaken identity, derives 'specifically from Terentian comedy as adapted for the education of Renaissance schoolboys using the *scholia* of Donatus' (Hutson 1994: 166). Finally, some of Terence's plays contain prologues discussing the nature of their adaptation of earlier plays which might be expected to have interested a dramatist like Shakespeare (is it theft, the *Adelphi* prologue asks, or an honour to the original?) – to what effect we can only speculate.

(D) Baldwin (1947) settled many major points concerning Terence's availability and importance to Shakespeare and his contemporaries. Miola (1994) is his most important and imaginative successor, expanding from the limited and often unconvincing lists of verbal echoes in such as Tschernjajew (1931) into an altogether wider conception of literary influence. Herrick (1950), Hosley (1966), Sowerby (1994) and Miola himself are useful on Terence's standing in the Renaissance generally.

Baldwin, T. W. (1947). *Shakspere's Five-Act Structure: Shakspere's Early Plays on the Background of Renaissance Theories of Five-Act Structure from 1470.* Urbana, IL.

Beck, Ervin (1973). 'Terence Improved: The Paradigm of the Prodigal Son in English Renaissance Comedy.' *RenD* 6: 107–22.

Doran, Madeleine (1954). *Endeavors of Art: A Study of Form in Elizabethan Drama.* Madison, WI.

Hardison, O. B., Jr (1974). *Medieval Literary Criticism: Translations and Interpretations.* New York.

Herrick, Marvin T. (1950). *Comic Theory in the Sixteenth Century.* Urbana, IL.

Hosley, Richard (1966). 'The Formal Influence of Plautus and Terence', pp. 131–46 in John Russell Brown and Bernard Harris, eds, *Elizabethan Theatre* (Stratford-upon-Avon Studies, 9). London.

Hutson, Lorna (1994). *The Usurer's Daughter: Male Friendship and Fictions of Women in Sixteenth-Century England.* London.

Levin, Richard (1971). *The Multiple Plot in English Renaissance Drama.* Chicago.

Miola, Robert S. (1994). *Shakespeare and Classical Comedy: The Influence of Plautus and Terence*. Oxford.

Nevo, Ruth (1980). 'Shakespeare's Comic Remedies.' *New York Literary Forum* 5–6: 3–15.

Shaw, Catherine M. (1980). 'The Conscious Art of *The Comedy of Errors*.' *New York Literary Forum* 5–6: 17–28.

Snyder, Susan (1979). *The Comic Matrix of Shakespeare's Tragedies: 'Romeo and Juliet', 'Hamlet', 'Othello', and 'King Lear'*. Princeton.

Sowerby, Robin (1994). *The Classical Legacy in Renaissance Poetry*. London.

Terence, translated by R[ichard] B[ernard] (1614). *Terence in English. Fabulae Comici Facetissimi et Elegantissimi Poetae Terentii Omnes Anglicae Factae*. London (first published 1598).

Tschernjajew, P. (1931). 'Shakespeare und Terenz.' *Anglia* 55: 282–95.

Thomas of Woodstock See under **Chronicle History Plays**.

Tottel's Miscellany

(A) Much of the mid-sixteenth century poetry of Henry Howard, Earl of Surrey (1517?–1547), Sir Thomas Wyatt (1503?–1542), and many anonymous contemporaries was published in 1557 by Richard Tottel (d. 1594), a mainly legal printer who also issued Surrey's *Aeneid* and Arthur **Brooke**'s *Romeus and Juliet*. Tottel's *Songes and Sonnettes, written by the Ryght Honorable Lorde Henry Haward late Earle of Surrey, and Other*, or *Tottel's Miscellany*, as it came to be known after a reprint of 1870, became the most famous and successful of the Elizabethan poetry miscellanies. The 271 pieces included in the first edition were ascribed as follows: 40 to Surrey, 97 to Wyatt, 40 to Nicholas Grimald (an associate of Tottel's in this venture, perhaps as editor), and the rest to 'uncertain authors'. These last include **Chaucer**; John Heywood; Thomas, Lord Vaux; Thomas Churchyard; and Sir John Cheke. Most seem to have been writers of C. S. Lewis' Drab Age, from towards the end of Henry VIII's reign onwards. The anthology occasioned the first appearance in print of Surrey's and Wyatt's poems, as well as being the first printed book to contain English sonnets.

Overall, most pieces are love lyrics, but satires, elegies and pastorals also figure in some quantity. Metrical experimentation is particularly frequent among its poets, especially Wyatt. There was no intention to create a collection of all the best verse of the era – for one thing, Tottel was concerned about possible censorship – and the selection mixes the more durable work of Wyatt and Surrey with some very dull material (it has been called 'the grave of Early Tudor poetry' – Mason 1959: 253). Moreover, although Wyatt and Surrey's work was brought to a new audience, Tottel's setting for it subtly altered its form and significance. Tottel's tastes, which depart from previous norms but were evidently shared by his readers, led him to rearrange many lines in Wyatt to increase their metrical smoothness and regularity; and to most of the poems in the collection he added titles which created a context of conventional courtly devotion (as in 'The lover sendeth sighes to mone his sute'), removing any hint of a political dimension. The best poetry in the volume thus became a glamorous and decorous illustration and model of supposedly actual courtly practice. The singling out of Surrey for mention on the title page is usually explained as owing to his aristocratic rank, but his execution had made him presentable as a Catholic hero under Mary in 1557, whereas Wyatt, whose son had been executed for treason in 1554, was presumably *non gratis* and so not mentioned on the title page despite his larger contribution.

(B) Tottel's volume was twice reprinted in 1557, and went through at least nine further editions before 1587, when the last sixteenth-century edition was issued. By this date, after additions and deletions of material, it took in a total of 310 poems. It helped create a vogue for anthologies generally over the succeeding decades, and several later collections follow its lead in specific ways. George **Gascoigne**'s *A Hundreth Sundrie Flowers* (1573) is an example: this also mimics aspects of a manuscript collection and adds titles which invite interpretation of the texts as responses to courtly situations, real or novelistic.

Tottel's first-generation followers, earlier Elizabethan poets such as Barnaby Googe, Thomas Sackville and George Turberville, had insufficient talents to reach their model's highest level; they confined themselves to the simpler metres, like poulter's measure, and developed their craft distinctly slowly. The book can, in fact, be held responsible for the vast stretches of monotonous long-lined verse of the era. Yet Tottel had also made available the work of Surrey and Wyatt and so enhanced their reputations, even if it appeared in an inauthentic form. Wyatt was known to the public at large almost solely through the miscellany – **Puttenham**'s comments on Wyatt, Surrey and Tottel in his *Arte of*

English Poesie (1589) show its effects here. The appearance of new editions until 1587, 'when the magnificent outburst of Elizabethan lyricism had begun', kept Tottel's influence 'constant and potent', and the *Miscellany* can be considered so 'largely responsible for this great outburst' that 'adequately to discuss its influence would be almost to write a history of the first three decades of Elizabethan poetry' (Rollins 1965: ii, 107–8).

Wyatt's and Surrey's work is widely available in modern printings. This sample of one of the two poems included by Thomas, Lord Vaux (no. 212 in Rollins 1965; originally printed anonymously) is quoted here from one of the 1557 editions.

> *The aged lover rounounceth love*
>
> I lothe that I did love,
> In youth that I thought swete:
> As time requires for my behove
> Me thinkes they are not mete,
>   My lustes they do me leave,
> My fancies all be flede:
> And tract of time begins to weave
> Gray heares upon my hedde.
>   For age with stelyng steppes,
> Hath clawed me with his cowche:
> And lusty life away she leapes,
> As there had bene none such.
>   My muse dothe not delight
> Me as she did before:
> My hand and pen are not in plight,
> As they have bene of yore.
>   For reason me denies,
> This youthly idle rime:
> And day by day to me she cryes,
> Leave of these toyes in time.
>   The wrincles in my brow,
> The furrowes in my face:
> Say limpyng age will hedge him now,
> Where youth must geve him place.
>   The harbinger of death,

> To me I see him ride:
> The cough, the colde, the gaspyng breath,
> Dothe bid me to provide.
>   A pikeax and a spade,
> And eke a shrowdyng shete,
> A house of claye for to be made,
> For such a gest most mete.
>
> (Tottel 1557: sig. X3^{r–v})

(C) Many books in modern libraries have Shakespeare's signature forged by a later hand. A copy of a 1557 Tottel now in an American collection, given according to a family tradition by Shakespeare to an ancestor of the poet Alexander Brome, has a more satisfactory provenance than most (see Fleming 1964). Perhaps, however, what needs explanation is why the volume was given away – that Shakespeare once possessed a copy of Tottel might almost have been assumed *a priori*.

There are two explicit allusions to the volume and its contents in Shakespeare's plays. Slender, left on his own during the first scene of *The Merry Wives of Windsor*, wishes for his copy of Tottel (under its then standard title) to entertain himself – 'I had rather than forty shillings I had my Book of Songs and Sonnets here' (1.1.179–80). One of the Gravediggers in *Hamlet* sings versions of the first, third and eighth stanzas from Vaux's poem in (B), above (5.1.61ff.); his version is distant enough to show that the playwright was working from memory, or at least did not take the words directly from the *Miscellany*. There are also snatches of phraseology from Tottel items that crop up from time to time in the poems and plays. Some very out-of-the-way material is involved here, such as phrasing from Grimald's translation of Gautier de Châtillon's Latin in *Macbeth* 1.2 (see Mason 1959: 253). Moore's (1998) speculations about two of Hamlet's speeches and two works of Surrey's, one of them in Tottel, are, however, far-fetched.

But neither Shakespeare's explicit references to Tottel's collection nor his distant echoes of some of its words really hint at what it seems safe to say must have been, however indirectly, the principal effect of the book on him as on others: an expansion, for all Tottel's straitjacketing of the work he printed, of the perceived possibilities of English verse. Shakespeare, not alone among his contemporaries, saw further possibilities in the directions Tottel's best poets had taken. Even if Tottel did not make the sonnet an immediately popular form (for a while the term meant only 'lyric'), the final sixteenth-century editions came at a time when the rage for sonnet sequences was beginning. More specifically, a number of Surrey's Tottel sonnets use the English sonnet form eventually adopted by Shakespeare; Surrey, and the miscellany's influence, can be said to have established this form's availability in the English tradition. Again, the two set pieces Tottel included from Nicholas Grimald, *The Death of Zoroas* and *Cicero's Death*, can together with Surrey's *Aeneid* be considered the earliest English examples of blank verse; new ground had again been broken, even though it is unlikely these works played much part in the eventual popularization of the form.

Although these and other innovations do not give the anthology much direct importance for Shakespeare, then, it is on a wide view by no means the least significant of his books. Its significance is largely summed up by **Jonson**'s comments on the poetry of Wyatt and Surrey: 'for their times admirable: and the more, because they began Eloquence with us' (*Conversations*).

(D) Rollins (1965) supplies in his second volume a full account of Tottel's volume, its contributors, and its history.

Fleming, John F. (1964). 'A Book from Shakespeare's Library Discovered by William Van Lennep.' *ShQ* 15.ii: 25–7.
Mason, H. A. (1959). *Humanism and Poetry in the Early Tudor Period: An Essay*. London.
Moore, Peter R. (1998). '*Hamlet* and Surrey's Psalm 8.' *Neophilologus* 82: 487–98.
Rollins, Hyder Edward, ed. (1965) *Tottel's Miscellany (1557–1587)*, revised edn, 2 vols. Cambridge, MA (first published 1928–9).
Tottel, Richard, ed. (1557). *Songes and Sonnettes, written by the Ryght Honorable Lorde Henry Haward late Earle of Surrey, and Other*. London (first 1557 edn; Rollins 1557A).

Troublesome Reigne of King John, The See **Chronicle History Plays**.

True Chronicle History of King Leir, The See **Chronicle History Plays**.

True Tragedie of Richard III, The See **Chronicle History Plays**.

Turberville, George See **Mantuan (Giovanni Baptista Spagnuoli)**.

Twine, Lawrence (fl. 1564–76), Translator

(A) The elder brother of Thomas Twine (see **Virgil**), he attended the Canterbury Grammar School, of which his father was headmaster, before admission to All Souls, Oxford, where he graduated and became a fellow in 1564. He registered for publication in 1576 *The Patterne of Painefull Adventures . . . that befell unto Prince Apollonius*, his prose translation – not the first into English – of the 153rd tale in the **Gesta Romanorum** of Apollonius of Tyre, done via a French version. If it was published at this date, no copy has survived: the first known edition dates from *c*. 1594. This book is Twine's only claim to literary notice. He is said to have become a rector in Sussex in 1578.

(B) A reprint of 1607 seems to have sparked interest in *The Patterne of Painefull Adventures*, but because *Pericles* cannot be certainly dated more precisely than 1606–8 it is not possible to determine whether the reprint was inspired partly by the appearance of the play, or whether the play followed the new edition. The minor dramatist George **Wilkins** appropriated many passages of Twine's story for his verse play *The Painfull Adventures of Pericles Prince of Tyre*, published 1608, drawing at the same time either on *Pericles* itself or an earlier, now lost play on the same theme.

A full text of Twine's story (in the edition of *c*. 1594) is given in Bullough (VI), and excerpts of the passages relevant to Shakespeare in Hoeniger (1963). Most of Chapter 14 is printed here:

> *How Tharsia withstoode a second assault of her virginitie, and by what meanes she was preserved.*

When night was come, the master bawd used always to receive the money, which his women had gotten by the use of their bodies the day before. And when it was demaunded of Tharsia, she brought him the mony, as the price and hire of her virginitie. Then said the bawd unto hir: It is wel doone Tharsia, use diligence hencefoorth, and see that you bring mee thus much mony every day. When the next day was past also, and the bawd understoode that she remained a virgin stil, he was offended, and called unto him the villaine that had charge over the maides, and said unto him: Sirra, how chanceth it that Tharsia remaineth a virgin still? Take her unto thee, and spoile her of her maidenhead, or be sure thou shalt be whipped. Then said the villaine unto Tharsia, tel me, art thou yet a virgin? She answered, I am, and shalbe as long as God will suffer me. How then, said he, hast thou gotten all this mony? She answered, with teares falling downe upon her knees, I have declared mine estate, humbly requesting all men to take compassion on my virginitie. And nowe likewise, falling then downe at his feete also, take pitty on me, good friend, which am a poor captive, and the daughter of a king, and doe not defile me. The villaine answered: Our master the bawd is very covetous and greedie of money, and therefore I see no meanes for thee to continue a virgin. Whereunto Tharsia replied: I am skilful in the liberal sciences, and well exercised in all studies, and no man singeth or playeth on instruments better than I, wherefore bring mee into the market place of the citie, that men may heare my cunning. Or let the people propound any maner of questions, and I will resolve them: and I doubt not but by this practise I shall get store of money daily. When the villaine heard this devise, and bewailed the maidens mishappe, he willingly gave consent thereto, and brake with the bawd his master touching that matter, who hearing of her skill, and hoping for the gaine, was easily perswaded.

(1607 text; ed. Hoeniger 1963: 170)

(C) *Pericles* owes much more to **Gower**'s than Twine's version of the Apollonius story, but there are a number of episodes in which the influence of *The Patterne of Painefull Adventures* seems palpable, especially in Act 4 and especially involving Lysimachus (the Governor of Mytilene, Twine's Athanagoras). The brothel scenes in Twine's version of the story are more conspicuous than Gower's, forming a lively and at times oddly humorous part of the narrative, and Shakespeare appears to have followed his lead.

One further suggestion about Twine's part in *Pericles* is made by DelVecchio and Hammond (1998: 8):

Rather than seeing Gower's and Twine's works as sprawling narratives incompatible with the stage and the requirements of drama, it is preferable to credit Shakespeare with a new insight into the handling of his sources for dramatic purposes. Although of course he took from Gower and Twine the elements of the story, perhaps their most instrumental influence on him was the potential he found there for presenting narrative as a dramatic form . . . What Shakespeare dramatises in *Pericles* is *the storytelling process itself.*

(D)

Bullough, vi.

DelVecchio, Doreen, and Antony Hammond, eds (1998). *Pericles* (New Cambridge Shakespeare). Cambridge.

Hoeniger, F. D., ed. (1963). *Pericles* (Arden Shakespeare). London.

Twyne, Thomas See **Virgil (Publius Vergilius Maro)**.

Tyndale, William See **Bible**.

U-V

Udall, Nicholas See **Erasmus, Desiderius**.

Ur-*Hamlet* See **Belleforest, François de.**

Virgil (Publius Vergilius Maro) (70–19 BC), Roman Poet
(A) Born near Mantua, Virgil was educated in Cremona and Mediola-
num (Milan) and later studied philosophy and rhetoric at Rome, where
he became one of the poets patronized by the statesman Maecenas. He
published to great acclaim in 37 BC his ten *Eclogues* or pastorals (or
'bucolics'). Soon afterwards, thanks to Maecenas' sponsorship, he left
Rome for Campania. The four Books of *Georgics*, on the art of hus-
bandry, followed in 30 BC, confirming him as the foremost poet of his
time. The last eleven years of his life were devoted, by the command of
Augustus, to the composition of a national epic based on the story of
Aeneas, the mythical founder of the Roman nation and of the Julian
family. This was said not to have been finished to Virgil's satisfaction at
his death. The *Aeneid* tells in twelve Books Aeneas' story from the fall of
Troy to his arrival in Italy, his wars and alliances with the native tribes,
and his final establishment of the new Italian kingdom.

(B) The enormous prestige of Virgil in the Middle Ages and Renaissance is well known. He had not only the name of a 'surpassing poet',

but also 'the fame of an odd [rare] orator, and the admiration of a profound philosopher' (as Richard Stanyhurst, his translator, put it in 1582), as well as a unique reputation among pagan writers as an honorary Christian – *anima naturaliter Christiana*, 'an instinctively Christian soul', in Tertullian's words. For poets he was the chief authority in epic (for **Ariosto**, Camoens, **Dante**, **Spenser**, Tasso) and pastoral (in Neo-Latin and in vernaculars). He was also the courtly classical poet *par excellence*, the uncrowned laureate of Rome, Minister of Arts to Augustus, strongly identified with ruling powers; and he was the refiner of the Latin language, giving him a special status in the humanist poetics of the Renaissance (see Sowerby 1994: 37–44). Playwrights of 'a preponderantly rhetorical drama like the early English tragedy' will inevitably make 'extensive use of epic fragments and epic technique' (Baker 1967: 141). More popularly, Virgil was still, if decreasingly, thought of, as sometimes in the Middle Ages, as a mage or sorcerer, magically helpful to readers through the *Sortes Virgilianae*, 'when by suddaine opening *Virgils* booke, they lighted upon some verse of his' for guidance (as **Sidney** dismissively describes the procedure in the *Apology for Poetry*). But, because 'many of the basic mythic and imaginative patterns underlying his poems proved especially amenable to the continuing Christian intellectual synthesis', the poems were 'allegorized and otherwise continually modernized so that they bore directly on the present concerns of his many interpreters in their times' (Low 1985: 3). In slightly different terms, because he was the central canonical figure for the Renaissance, to rework Virgil signalled 'the appropriation of a usable past in relation to some common pursuit of social purpose in the present' (Weimann 1988: 73). For the Elizabethans, this phenomenon embraced *inter alia* the association of the virgin Astraea, goddess of Justice (in Eclogue IV), with the Queen; Elizabeth's ties to another female who could be seen as founder of an empire, Dido (also known as Elissa); and the Troy legend, with the notion of the *translatio imperii* ('translation of empire'), 'a transnational, transhistorical model onto which poets . . . might graft indigenous myths of origin' for their own rulers or patrons (James 1997: 15). **James I** could and did identify himself both with Aeneas and Augustus (also, jokingly, with Latinus). The Troy legend was used more sceptically too, as for example by John Heywood to oppose Stuart absolutism (see James 1997: 21).

As a school author in the Renaissance, Virgil vied for prominence with **Ovid**, his perceived moral weight set against Ovid's charm and versatility. Pedagogically and otherwise he was encountered in many forms: in anthologies of *sententiae* and *florilegia*, in manuals of rhetoric, in paintings, woodcuts, and other illustrations, in classical dictionaries, and of course in editions and translations of his poems. Very few of the editions were English, and even those all drew on continental European commentaries, so that in many ways English readers necessarily received their Virgil from the European tradition (see especially Tudeau-Clayton 1998 and Baldwin 1944). Several very different English translations of Virgil had appeared by the later Tudor period. **Caxton**'s prose *Aeneid* of 1490 was not a translation from Virgil but had an itinerant ancestry, and few good qualities. Gavin **Douglas**' 1512 Scots version, in iambic pentameter couplets, was poetically far more successful; it was first printed in London in 1553, and included the supplementary Book XIII by Maphaeus Vegius. Henry Howard, Earl of Surrey's English rendering of Books II and IV of the 1540s, influenced by Douglas, is a crucial stage in the development of English blank verse (see Baker 1967; Jones 1964: xiiff.). Much more popular in its day, however, was the first complete English version of the *Aeneid* to be translated direct from the Latin, by Thomas Phaer, a Welsh polymath, and Thomas Twyne, a classical scholar who completed the work in 1584 by revising Phaer's Books I–IX of 1558–62 and adding his own translation of the rest, including Book XIII (for the complex textual history see Lally 1987: xxix–lxxi). This was the only complete English version of the *Aeneid* printed until the 1630s, and it was reissued four times up to 1620. Thomas **Nashe**'s copy of Phaer's first edition, 1558, is in the British Library. One or two pieces of Shakespeare's phrasing may just possibly reflect the use of Phaer (Baldwin 1944: 484; Taylor 1987). English versions of the *Eclogues* were not wanting: George Turberville (1567) and Abraham Fleming (1575) are the main Elizabethan translators, the latter extending his efforts ('in so plaine and familiar a sort, as a learner may be taught thereby to his profit', he writes) to the *Georgics* in 1589.

One of the best-known passages in the *Georgics* is IV, 153–68, the Commonwealth of the Bees. This anthology-piece is used by Shakespeare – perhaps via one or more intermediate versions – for Canterbury's speech in *Henry V*, 1.2.187–204. Fleming's version may not have been known to Shakespeare, but the Virgilian passage was (Baldwin 1944: 472–9):

The bees alone have their yoong ones bred common of them all,
The houses of their cities they as partners have and hold,
And often lead their lives under great lawes and government;
They only know their countrie and their certaine dwelling houses,
And being mindfull of the win-ter coming they take up paines
And fall to worke in sommer time; and they lay up in store
Their gettings for the common use and profit of them all.
For some do watch and toile for living, and are occupide
In feelds upon a bargaine or a league betweene them made:
Some other lay within the bounds or fenses of their houses
The juice of Narcisse, and the clam-mie gum from barke of tree,
The first foundation of their ho-niecombs; and afterwards
They hang or fasten thereupon wax sticking hard thereto.
Some other bring abrode the yoong ones now at perfect growth,
The hope of all the flocke (or swarmes:) others do thicken the
Finest and purest honie, and stretch out the little holes
Of their sweet honicombs with ho-ny liquid passing cleere.
Others there be unto whose lot warding at gates befals,
And they by turns do watch the raine and tempests of the wether;
Or else they take the burthens of the bees then comming home,
Or else with armie redie made, they drive away from hives
The drones, a lazie beast

(Virgil 1589: sig. Ii^{r-v})

One can do no better for a sample of the Phaer-Twyne *Aeneid* than
what Hamlet requests of the Player, 'Aeneas' tale to Dido, and there-
about of it especially where he speaks of Priam's slaughter' (2.2.440–2).
The Player's version, with a basis in **Lucan** and **Marlowe**'s *Dido, Queen
of Carthage* as well as Virgil, appears a few lines later in *Hamlet* (for the
relationships see Black 1994):

The fatall end of *Priam* now perhaps you will requier.
Whan hee the city taken saw and houses tops on fier,
And buildings broke, and round about so thicke his foes to rage,
His harneis on his shoulders (long on worn till than) for age
All quaking, on (good man) hee puts, to purpose small, and than
His sword him gyrt, and into death and enmies thicke he ran.
Amids the court right underneth the naked skies in sight,
An altar huge of sise there stoode, and by the same upright

An auncient Laurell tree did grow, that wide abroad was shed,
And it, and all the carvyd gods with broade shade overspred.
There *Hecuba* and her doughters all (poore soules) at the altars side
In heapes together affrayd them drew, like doves whan doth betide
Some storme them headlong drive, and clipping fast their gods did
    hold.
But whan shee *Priam* thus beclad in armes of youth so bold
Espied: what minde alas (quoth she) O wofull husband you
In harneis dight: and whither away with wepons run ye now?
Not men nor wepons us can save: this time doth axe to beare.
No such defence, no not if *Hector* mine now present were.
Stand here by mee, this altar vs from slaughters all shal shelde,
Or die together at ones we shall. So said she, and gan to welde
Him aged man, and in the sacred seat him set, and helde.

    Behold where skaping from the stroke of *Pirrhus* fers in fight
Polites, one of *Priams* sonnes, through foes and wepons pight,
Through galeries along doth run, and wide about him spies
Sore wounded than, but *Pirrhus* after him sues with burning eyes
In chase, and now welnere in hand him caught and held with spere,
Till right before his parents sight he came, than feld him there
To death, and with his gushing blood his life outright he shed.
There *Priamus*, though now for wo that time he halfe was dead,
Him selfe could not refraine, nor yet his voice nor anger holde.
But, vnto thee (O wretch) he cried, for this despite so bolde,
The gods (if any justice dwels in heaven or right regard)
Do yeeld thee worthy thankes, and thee do pay thy due reward,
That here within my sight my son hast slaine with slaughter vyle,
And not ashamd with lothsome death his fathers face to fyle.
Not so did hee (whom falsly thou beliest to be thy sier)
Achilles with his enmie *Priam* deale, but my desier
Whan *Hectors* corps to tombe he gave for golde, did entertaine
With truth and right, and to my realme restorde me safe againe.
So spake, and therwithall his dart with feeble force hee threw,
Which sounding on his brasen harneis hoarce, it backward flew,
And on his targat side it hit, where dintlesse downe it hing.
Than *Pirrhus* said, thou shalt go now therfore and tidinges bring
Unto my father *Achilles* soule, my dolefull deedes to tell.
Neptolemus his bastard is, not I, say this in hell.
Now die, and (as he spake that word) from the altar selfe he drew

Him trembling there, and deepe him through his sons blood did
   embrue.
And with his left hand wrapt his lockes, with right hand through his side
His glistring sworde outdrawen, he did hard to the hiltes to glide.
This ende had *Priams* destnies all, this chaunce him fortune sent,
Whan he the fier in *Troy* had seene, his walles and castels rent,
That somtime over peoples proud, and lands had reingd with fame ⎫
Of *Asia* emprour great, now short on shore he lieth with shame, ⎬
His head besides his shoulders laid, his corps no more of name. ⎭

               (1584 text, ɪɪ, 510–63; ed. Lally 1987: 42–3; italic for bold)

(C) There is reasonably good evidence that Shakespeare knew at least
some of Virgil – the *Aeneid* – at first hand in the Latin, as indeed any of
his contemporaries with a grammar-school education must have. A
quotation of four words in Latin in *2 Henry VI*, 2.1.24, and an apparent
linguistic echo ('fatal engine' / 'fatalis machina', *Aeneid* ɪɪ, 237) in *Titus
Andronicus*, 5.3.86, prove nothing in themselves, but Baldwin suggests
that the phrasing in Shakespeare's closely Virgilian passages sometimes
reflects the gloss for the Virgilian usage of a word in a Latin edition, or
in Thomas **Cooper**'s English–Latin *Thesaurus Linguae* (Baldwin 1944:
ɪɪ, 479–82, also 456–96 for detailed discussion of the use of excerpts,
annotations and editions in Shakespeare; for qualifications see Nuttall
1984: 71–2).

What parts of Virgil did Shakespeare know, and where did he use
Virgil in his poems and plays? He must have read at least the earlier
Books of the *Aeneid*. Books ɪ, ɪɪ, ɪv and vɪ were especially common study
texts, and Shakespeare's use of the poem tends to dry up after Book vɪ.
He has the Dido and Aeneas story (ɪv–vɪ) especially frequently in mind,
often in a romanticized form, in at least half a dozen plays including
Titus Andronicus, Hamlet, 2 Henry VI and 'a pre-Dido and a post-Dido in
Troilus and Cressida and *Antony and Cleopatra*'. Indeed, Dido 'appears allu-
sively in comedy, tragedy, history and romance – all the traditional
Shakespearean genres – and at all stages in the playwright's career'
(Savage 1998: 14, 18). The two other Virgilian episodes most frequently
referred to in direct Shakespearean allusions are the Sack of Troy and
Aeneas' visit to the Underworld, as for example in *1 Henry IV*, 1.1.70–4.

Shakespeare is very likely to have known much of Virgil's work other
than *Aeneid* ɪ–vɪ because of its general diffusion, but this very diffusion
makes it uncertain exactly which parts. For example, the steed of

Adonis in *Venus and Adonis* 289–300 may well owe something to Virgil's horse in *Georgics* III, 75–94; but Virgil's description was in the late sixteenth century the model 'commonplace' for a horse, cited as an example in all kinds of manuals of style, quoted in any number of commentaries on quite other texts, excerpted in *florilegia*, and so on. Hence Baldwin concludes of this passage that Shakespeare 'is here ultimately reflecting [the *Georgics*], . . . probably proximately, from grammar school, though there is no conclusive evidence in this passage that Shakspere modeled directly on the *Georgics* with the book before him, or that he was even conscious of any influence from that work' (Baldwin 1950: 25). Apart from the *Aeneid*, Shakespeare's knowledge of Virgil often reflects the type of excerpts presented in secondary compilations. But this is not incompatible with Shakespeare's having had direct knowledge of the original in the context of an edition of Virgil. This may well be the case with the Commonwealth of the Bees from *Georgics* IV ((B), above) used in *Henry V*, 1.2 (for the *Georgics* and *Eclogues* see Baldwin 1944: II, 464–79).

Shakespeare, despite his occasional (and highly tendentious) identification as the Virgil of **Jonson**'s *Poetaster*, is in his work as a whole clearly not a Virgilian poet. Though there are dozens of more or less plausible Virgilian moments in Shakespeare (tables are drawn up by Root 1903), the four most extensive and specific Virgilian loci can very quickly be listed, as follows:

1 *The Rape of Lucrece*, 1366–1526, for the story of the sack of Troy (in combination with Ovid, *Metamorphoses* XIII; see Allen 1962 and Baldwin 1950: 143–6).
2 The account of Aegeon's travels in *The Comedy of Errors*, 1.1.31–140, from Aeneas' narrative in *Aeneid* II, 13–267 (see Baldwin 1944: II, 485–7).
3 The Player's speech on Troy in *Hamlet*, 2.2 (see Black 1994).
4 *The Tempest*, in general (see below).

The collective significance of the specific Virgilian allusions in Shakespeare is not great because they are not usually 'integral to the fabric' of Shakespeare's work: 'These passages . . . are of their time: mannered, ornamental, clever – manifestly poetry of the English Renaissance. Shakespeare is seldom less Virgilian than when he is citing him' (Nuttall 1984: 73). On the other hand, these passages sometimes appear to be only the most conspicuous indication in the work of a more general permeation by Virgilian mood or matter. For example, the Virgilian presence in *The Tempest* is often of a 'spectral' kind, 'a half-seen image of death, or damnation, or despair at the back of an episode, a line, or even a single word' (Pitcher 1984: 197). To summarize Pitcher's example, there is reason to believe that in Prospero's boast of having 'to the dread rattling thunder / . . . given fire, and rifted Jove's stout oak / With his own bolt' (*Tempest* 5.1.44–6) is recalled the Sibyl's description of Salmoneus in Tartarus, 'in cruel wreake of turmentes just. / For he the flames of god, and thondring soundes would counterfeit' (Phaer-Twyne, VI, 620–1, translating *Aeneid* VI, 585–6; ed. Lally 1987: 137). So although Prospero, 'who also fakes tempests and who usurps the lightning of the gods, is at the summit of his authority in Act V . . . the fate of the overreaching Salmoneus, damnation for an impostor, hovers spectrally behind him' (Pitcher 1984: 197).

It may well be, then, that the more oblique and diffused kinds of Virgilianism count for more in Shakespeare than the direct and specific. Nor are these kinds always so attenuated, so 'spectral'. There are fairly few explicit Virgilian allusions in *Antony and Cleopatra*, but the Dido story has been felt as a deepening and enriching presence behind many episodes in the play, from Antony's first leave-taking of Cleopatra onwards; Brower goes so far as to call the play an 'imaginative sequel' to the *Aeneid* (1971: 351). But to recur to Nuttall's point, Shakespeare's use of Virgil here is for very un-Virgilian ends – namely, for the glamorization of Antony and Cleopatra, as in the reversal of *Aeneid* VI in Antony's 'Dido and her Æneas shall want troops, / And all the haunt be ours' (4.14.53–4).

For some other plays, there is little agreement on the purposes of Shakespeare's Virgilianism. *Titus Andronicus* is for Miola a 'comparatively clumsy and juvenile' attempt to 'invoke Vergil to help shape character and theme'; allusions to Aeneas and Lavinia are 'crudely and baldly inappropriate rather than ironic' (1986: 243). But for James, referring to the 'mutilation' and 'warping' of Virgil, the gaps between the world of *Titus* and the world of the *Aeneid* are highly meaningful: 'the play is set just before the fall of the Roman empire, and it is fitting that Vergilian values should survive only in empty forms', for example in that 'Vergilian *pietas* has ossified over the centuries'; 'the Vergilian virtues . . . emerge as bankrupt' (1997: 41, 52–3). Recent interest in Virgilian aspects of *Cymbeline* is at its strongest in James, who proposes that 'the play trains a relentless eye on the greatest fissure in the *Aeneid*'s commemoration of imperial Rome – Aeneas' abandonment of Dido – and uses it to propose a radical critique of Roman values' (1997: 167; for *Cymbeline* see also Miola 1983: 214ff.).

The role of Virgil in *The Tempest* has been much analysed, but the results are not always illuminating, and sometimes far-fetched. Is it limited to the first two scenes (Nosworthy 1948), or is the Dido and Aeneas story the shaping influence until Act 4 (Kott 1978), or does the whole play rely obliquely on the *Aeneid* (Still 1921, claiming that what Alonso's party experiences is comparable to Aeneas' journey to the Underworld)? Once again, the list of tangible, concrete borrowings is 'far shorter than we might reasonably expect: the storm itself, Alonso's journey, Ferdinand's first words to Miranda, the Harpy spectacle, bits of the wedding masque, the coastline of the island, the preservation of the mariners, and . . . widow Dido in Act II' (Pitcher 1984: 199). But once again, such a list arguably omits some of the broader Virgilian elements in the play, to which such direct allusions might be called 'points of entry' (Hamilton 1990: 21). For instance, it is claimed that the presence of the Dido story (beyond the old critical chestnut of the courtiers' baffling jokes at 2.1.70ff.) is 'unmistakably felt in *The Tempest* and . . . this example is meant to be rejected rather than be allowed to taint the union of Ferdinand and Miranda with its unsavoury associations' (Tarantino 1997: 495; see also Pitcher 1984). For Hamilton (1990) it is rather the Underworld of *Aeneid* VI that tends to provide the groundwork for the play, while for Miola what makes it Virgilian is ultimately that Shakespeare 'ponders an essentially Vergilian concern – the cost of civilization in human terms' (1986: 255). But none of these readings is irresistible. It could be argued instead that the *Aeneid*'s recycling of the wanderings of Odysseus in Book III is the most important Virgilian basis for *The Tempest*, in each work's decisive sense of revisiting and re-encountering the past; or indeed that the play may have deeper affinities with the *Aeneid*'s Odyssean sources than with the *Aeneid* itself (so Nuttall 1989: 9–10). *The Tempest* may 'represent . . . the culmination and conclusion of Shakespeare's relationship with Vergil' (Miola 1986: 255), perhaps even a self-conscious way of 'asserting himself over the poet whom he had confronted and rewritten . . . over his career' (Hamilton 1990: 134), but it is possible to over-emphasize Virgil's presence in it, as well as to underestimate the 'contamination' of the play's Virgil by Renaissance refashionings and representations of the *Aeneid*.

(D) The Virgil translations gathered in Gransden (1996) include snippets of the pre-Shakespearean ones. Baldwin (1944) and Tudeau-Clayton (1998) are especially useful on the contexts, pedagogical and bibliographical, in which Shakespeare is likely to have encountered Virgil. A general modern study of Virgil's impact on Shakespeare is lacking: most are thematic, or cover either a specified play or group of plays. Nuttall (1984) ought by his title to be an exception, but this is an account of 'resemblance, not influence'. The overview by Miola (1986) assumes an undemonstrated progression from Shakespeare's first steps to 'complex and controlled' Virgilian allusions later. A very different account of the earlier work is in James (1997), who continues on from *Titus Andronicus* to *Troilus, Antony and Cleopatra, Cymbeline* and *The Tempest* in her study of Shakespeare's use of Virgil to present the 'translation of empire'. Hamilton (1990) and Tudeau-Clayton (1998) both offer in their different, often opposing ways important revisionist studies of Virgil's relation to *The Tempest*. More conventional but still useful studies on the Virgilian strands in the play are Nosworthy (1948), Wiltenburg (1986) and Pitcher (1984).

For Virgilian texts other than the *Aeneid*, Baldwin (1944) covers echoes from the *Eclogues* and *Georgics*, and Bates (1967) sees Virgil's Eclogue II behind the 'plot' of Shakespeare's *Sonnets*.

Baldwin (1944); Baldwin (1950).

Allen, Don Cameron (1962). 'Some Observations on *The Rape of Lucrece.*' *ShSu* 15: 89–98.

Baker, Howard (1967). 'The Formation of the Heroic Medium', pp. 126–68 in Paul J. Alpers, ed., *Elizabethan Poetry: Modern Essays in Criticism*. Oxford (first published in Baker, *Induction to Tragedy*, 1939).

Bates, Paul A. (1967). 'Shakespeare's Sonnets and Pastoral Poetry.' *ShJ* 103: 81–96.

Betts, John H. (1968). 'Classical Allusions in Shakespeare's *Henry V* with Special Reference to Virgil.' *Greece & Rome* 15: 147–63.

Black, James (1994). 'Hamlet Hears Marlowe, Shakespeare Reads Virgil.' *Renaissance and Reformation* 18.iv: 17–28.

Bono, Barbara J. (1984). *Literary Transvaluation: From Vergilian Epic to Shakespearean Tragicomedy*. Berkeley.

Brower, Reuben A. (1971). *Hero and Saint: Shakespeare and the Graeco-Roman Heroic Tradition*. Oxford.

Gransden, K. W., ed. (1996). *Virgil in English*. Harmondsworth.

Hamilton, Donna B. (1990). *Virgil and 'The Tempest': The Politics of Imitation*. Columbus, OH.

Hulse, S. Clark (1978). ' "A Piece of Skilful Painting" in Shakespeare's "Lucrece".' *ShSu* 31: 13–22.

James, Heather (1997). *Shakespeare's Troy: Drama, Politics, and the Translation of Empire*. Cambridge.

Jones, Emrys, ed. (1964). *Henry Howard, Earl of Surrey: Poems*. Oxford.

Kott, Jan (1978). 'The *Aeneid* and *The Tempest*.' *Arion* 3: 425–51.

Lally, Steven, ed. (1987). *The 'Aeneid' of Thomas Phaer and Thomas Twyne: A Critical Edition Introducing Renaissance Metrical Typography*. New York.

Low, Anthony (1985). *The Georgic Revolution*. Princeton.

Miola, Robert S. (1983). *Shakespeare's Rome*. Cambridge.

—— (1986). 'Vergil in Shakespeare: From Allusion to Imitation', pp. 241–59 in John D. Bernard, ed., *Vergil at 2000: Commemorative Essays on the Poet and his Influence*. New York.

Nosworthy, J. M. (1948). 'The Narrative Sources of *The Tempest*.' *RES* 24: 281–94.

Nuttall, A. D. (1984). 'Virgil and Shakespeare', pp. 71–93 in Charles Martindale, ed., *Virgil and his Influence: Bimillennial Studies*. Bristol.

—— (1989). *The Stoic in Love: Selected Essays on Literature and Ideas*. London.

Pitcher, John (1984). ' "A Theatre of the Future": The *Aeneid* and *The Tempest*.' *EinC* 34: 193–215.

Root, R. K. (1903). *Classical Mythology in Shakespeare*. London.

Savage, Roger (1998). 'Dido Dies Again', pp. 3–38 in Michael Burden, ed., *A Woman Scorn'd: Responses to the Dido Myth*. London.

Sowerby, Robin (1994). *The Classical Legacy in Renaissance Poetry*. London.

Still, Colin (1921). *Shakespeare's Mystery Play: A Study of 'The Tempest'*. London (later revised as *The Timeless Theme*, London, 1936).

Tarantino, Elisabetta (1997). 'Morpheus, Leander, and Ariel.' *RES* 48: 489–98.

Taylor, Anthony Brian (1987). 'Thomas Phaer and Nick Bottom's "Hopping" Heart.' *N&Q* 232: 207–8.

Tudeau-Clayton, Margaret (1998). *Jonson, Shakespeare and Early Modern Virgil*. Cambridge.

Virgil, translated by Abraham Fleming (1589). *The Bucoliks . . . Together with Georgiks or Ruralls*. London.

Weimann, Robert (1988). 'Shakespeare (De)Canonized: Conflicting Uses of "Authority" and "Representation".' *New Literary History* 20: 65–81.

Wiltenburg, Robert (1986). 'The *Aeneid* in *The Tempest*.' *ShSu* 39: 159–68.

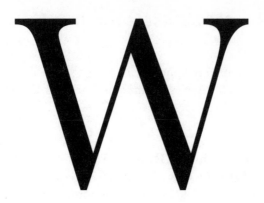

W

Wakefield Chronicle (16th Century Latin MS) This Latin manuscript chronicle contains a dating detail Shakespeare mentions for the death of Queen Eleanor which cannot be found in any other source known to have been available to him.

Honigmann, E. A. J., ed. (1954). *King John* (Arden Shakespeare), xvii–xviii. London.

Warning for Fair Women, A See **Bandello**, **Matteo**.

Whetstone, George See **Cinthio**, **Giovanni Baptista Giraldi**.

Whitney, Geoffrey See **Emblems**.

Wilkins, George (fl. 1603–8), Novelist and Dramatist Other than the vexed question of his part in the writing of *Pericles* and his adaptation of **Twine**'s *Pericles* source in his prose romance *The Painful Adventures of Pericles, Prince of Tyre* (1608; see Bullough), Wilkins is connected to Shakespeare as the author of *The Miseries of Inforst Marige* (written 1605/6, performed 1607), a play in which some passing resemblances to *King Lear* have recently been discerned by Taylor 1982.

Bullough, VI, 356–9 and Appendix I.
Taylor, Gary (1982). 'A New Source and an Old Date for *King Lear*.' *RES* 33: 396–413.

Willobie (Willoughby), Henry (1574?–1596?), Presumed Author of *Willobie His Avisa* There is a much-discussed relationship between Canto 47 of the 1594 complaint poem *Willobie His Avisa* and Poem 18 of *The Passionate Pilgrim*. Willobie's work may also be a minor source for *A Lover's Complaint* on the basis of devices such as the use of written verse in wooing.

Roe, John (1993). '*Willobie His Avisa* and *The Passionate Pilgrim*: Precedence, Parody, and Development.' *YES* 23: 111–25.

Woodstock See **Chronicle History Plays**.

Worde, Wynkyn de See *Gesta Romanorum*.

Wotton, Henry (*fl.* 1578), Translator The plot of the fifth story in Wotton's *A Courtlie Controversie of Cupids Cautels* (1578), a translation of Jacques d'Yver's *Le Printems d'Yver* (1572), may be a source, or merely an analogue, of *The Two Gentlemen of Verona*.

Atkinson, Dorothy F. (1944). 'The Source of *The Two Gentlemen of Verona*.' *SP* 41: 223–34.
Pogue, Jim C. (1962). '*The Two Gentlemen of Verona* and Henry Wotton's *A Courtlie Controversie of Cupid's Cautels*.' *Emporia State Research Studies* 10.iv: 17–21.

Wyatt, Sir Thomas See *Tottel's Miscellany*.

X-Y

Xenophon, of Ephesus See **Greek Romance**.

Xenophon (*c*. 428–*c*. 354 BC), Greek Historian and Miscellaneous Writer Renault suggests that Fluellen is airing a knowledge of Xenophon's *Anabasis* in his reference to the river in Macedon. She also mentions the more interesting prospect that Henry's incognito tour of his camp is connected with Xenophon's relation of how he roused his fellow-soldiers, the Ten Thousand; but for this episode **Tacitus** was nearer to hand.

Renault, Mary (1974). 'Shakespeare and Xenophon.' *TLS*, 12 July: 749.

Yong, Bartholomew See **Guazzo, Stefano**; **Montemayor, Jorge de**.

General Bibliography

This free-standing bibliography is provided for browsing, and for those wishing to assemble their own more selective bibliography under some heading other than that of a single source-author or source-text. The main 'Studies' section is largely composed of publications appearing within the preceding A–Z which make substantial reference to two or more sources as used by Shakespeare, though they are by no means all studies of Shakespeare's source-materials exclusively, or even of Shakespeare exclusively. Accounts of individual plays are listed here only if they fulfil the criterion of reference to two or more sources. Editions of plays (which routinely discuss a range of sources), and in Section II collections of source-texts for individual plays, are not included. Readers in search of information by play are referred particularly to the standard modern editions, especially Arden II and the Oxford Shakespeare, and to the compilations arranged on this principle, especially Bullough.

I. Bibliographies

Birmingham Public Libraries [and Waveney R. N. Fredrick, ed.] (1971). *A Shakespeare Bibliography: The Catalogue of the Birmingham Shakespeare Library*, 7 vols. London (includes sections on 'Sources of Shakespeare' in general, 'Sources and Background' for individual plays, etc.).

Carlsen, Hanne (1985). *A Bibliography to the Classical Tradition in English Literature*. Copenhagen (pp. 49–59 on Shakespeare).

Guttmann, Selma (1947). *The Foreign Sources of Shakespeare's Works: An Annotated Bibliography of the Commentary Written on the Subject between 1904 and 1940, together with Lists of Certain Translations available to Shakespeare*. New York.

Kallendorf, Craig (1982). *Latin Influences on English Literature from the Middle Ages to the Eighteenth Century: An Annotated Bibliography of Scholarship, 1945–1979*. New York (pp. 86–98 on Shakespeare are designed to supplement Velz 1968 by covering the years 1961–79).

McManaway, James G., and Jeanne Addison Roberts (1975). *A Selective Bibliography of Shakespeare: Editions, Textual Studies, Commentary*. Washington (pp. 239–41 on sources).

McRoberts, J. Paul (1985). *Shakespeare and the Medieval Tradition: An Annotated Bibliography*. New York.

Smith, Gordon Ross (1963). *A Classified Shakespeare Bibliography, 1936–1958*. University Park, PA (pp. 151–217 on Shakespeare's 'Sources, Literary Influences, and Cultural Relations').

Velz, John W. (1968). *Shakespeare and the Classical Tradition: A Critical Guide to Commentary, 1660–1960*. Minneapolis.

Watson, George, ed. (1974). *The New Cambridge Bibliography of English Literature*, Vol. 1: *600–1660*. Cambridge (columns 1575–80 on Shakespeare 'Sources and Influences').

II. Anthologies and Collections of Source-Texts

Benson, Pamela, ed. (1996). *Italian Tales from the Age of Shakespeare*. London.

Bullough, Geoffrey (1957–75). *Narrative and Dramatic Sources of Shakespeare*, 8 vols. London.

Chwalewik, Witold, ed. (1968). *Anglo-Polish Renaissance Texts for the Use of Shakespeare Students*. Warsaw (selections in facsimile from Belleforest, Munday, etc).

Collier, J. Payne, ed. (1850). *Shakespeare's Library: A Collection of the Ancient Novels, Romances, Legends, Poems and Histories used by Shakespeare*, 2 vols. London (revised by W. C. Hazlitt in 6 vols to include the plays, 1875).

Gollancz, Sir Israel, gen. ed. (1907–26). *The Shakespeare Classics*. 12 vols. London.

Griffin, Alice, ed. (1966). *The Sources of Ten Shakespeare Plays*. New York.

Lennox, Charlotte, ed. (1753–5). *Shakespeare Illustrated; or, the Novels and Histories on which the Plays . . . are Founded*, 3 vols. London.

Lockyer, Roger, and Gerald M. Pinciss, eds. (1990). *Shakespeare's World: Background Readings in the English Renaissance*. New York.

Metz, G. Harold, ed. (1989). *Sources of Four Plays Ascribed to Shakespeare: 'The Reign of King Edward III', 'Sir Thomas More', 'The History of Cardenio', 'The Two Noble Kinsmen'*. Columbia, MI (a supplement to Bullough).

N[ichols], J[ohn], ed. (1779). *Six Old Plays on which Shakespeare founded his Measure for Measure, Comedy of Errors, Taming the Shrew, King John, K. Henry IV and K. Henry V, King Lear*. London.

Satin, Joseph, ed. (1966). *Shakespeare and his Sources*. Boston.

Spenser, T. J. B., ed. (1968). *Elizabethan Love Stories*. Harmondsworth.

III. Studies

Allen, Percy (1928). *Shakespeare, Jonson, and Wilkins as Borrowers: A Study in Elizabethan Dramatic Origins and Imitations*. London.

Anderson, Judith H. (1984). *Biographical Truth: The Representation of Historical Persons in Tudor-Stuart Writing*. New Haven.

511

Armstrong, W. A. (1948). 'The Influence of Seneca and Machiavelli on the Elizabethan Tyrant.' *RES* 24: 19–35.

Baldwin, T. W. (1944). *William Shakspere's Small Latine and Lesse Greeke*, 2 vols. Urbana, IL.

Baldwin, T. W. (1947). *Shakspere's Five-Act Structure: Shakspere's Early Plays on the Background of Renaissance Theories of Five-Act Structure from 1470*. Urbana, IL.

Baldwin, T. W. (1950). *On the Literary Genetics of Shakspere's Poems and Sonnets*. Urbana, IL.

Baldwin, T. W. (1965). *On the Compositional Genetics of The Comedy of Errors*. Urbana, IL.

Beer, Jurgen (1992). 'The Image of a King: Henry VIII in the Tudor Chronicles of Edward Hall and Raphael Holinshed', pp. 129–49 in Uwe Baumann, ed., *Henry VIII in History, Historiography and Literature*. Frankfurt.

Begg, Edleen (1935). 'Shakespeare's Debt to Hall and Holinshed in *Richard III*.' *SP* 32: 189–96.

Bevington, David M. (1962). *From 'Mankind' to Marlowe: Growth of Structure in the Popular Drama of Tudor England*. Cambridge, MA.

Black, Matthew W. (1948). 'The Sources of Shakespeare's *Richard II*', pp. 199–216 in James G. McManaway *et al.*, eds., *Joseph Quincy Adams Memorial Studies*. Washington.

Boyce, Benjamin (1949). 'The Stoic *Consolatio* and Shakespeare.' *PMLA* 64: 771–80.

Bradbrook, M. C. (1951). *Shakespeare and Elizabethan Poetry: A Study of his Earlier Work in Relation to the Poetry of the Time*. London.

Brockbank, Philip (1953). *Shakespeare's Historical Myth: A Study of Shakespeare's Adaptations of his Sources in Making the Plays of 'Henry VI' and 'Richard III'*. Cambridge.

Brower, R. A. (1971). *Hero and Saint: Shakespeare and the Graeco-Roman Heroic Tradition*. Oxford.

Bush, Douglas (1927). 'Notes on Shakespeare's Classical Mythology.' *PQ* 6: 295–302.

Bush, Douglas (1932). *Mythology and the Renaissance Tradition in English Poetry*. London.

Campbell, Lily B. (1947). *Shakespeare's 'Histories': Mirrors of Elizabethan Policy*. San Marino, CA.

Churchill, George B. (1900). *Richard the Third up to Shakespeare*. Berlin.

Clubb, Louise George (1980). 'Shakespeare's Comedy and Late Cinquecento Mixed Genres.' *New York Literary Forum* 5/6: 129–39.

Clubb, Louise George (1989). *Italian Drama in Shakespeare's Time*. New Haven.

Cole, Howard C. (1973). *A Quest of Inquirie: Some Contexts of Tudor Literature.* Indianapolis.

Cole, Howard C. (1981). *The 'All's Well' Story from Boccaccio to Shakespeare.* Urbana, IL.

Cole, Howard C. (1983). 'Shakespeare's Comedies and their Sources: Some Biographical and Artistic Inferences.' *ShQ* 34: 405–19.

Craig, Hardin (1951). 'Motivation in Shakespeare's Choice of Materials.' *ShSu* 4: 26–34.

Crane, Mary (1985). 'The Shakespearean Tetralogy.' *ShQ* 36: 282–99.

Dean, Paul (1982). 'Shakespeare's *Henry VI* Trilogy and Elizabethan "Romance" Histories: The Origins of a Genre.' *ShQ* 33: 34–48.

Donaldson, E. Talbot (1979). 'Briseis, Briseida, Criseyde, Cresseid, Cressid: Progress of a Heroine', pp. 3–12 in Edward Vasta *et al.*, eds, *Chaucerian Problems and Perspectives: Essays Presented to Paul E. Beichner, C.S.C.* Notre Dame.

Doran, Madeleine (1954). *Endeavors of Art: A Study of Form in Elizabethan Drama.* Madison, WI (on Shakespeare's 'frame of artistic reference' as a whole).

Erskine-Hill, Howard (1983). *The Augustan Idea in English Literature.* London (sources of the Roman Plays).

Erskine-Hill, Howard (1996). *Poetry and the Realm of Politics: Shakespeare to Dryden.* Oxford (sources of the Histories).

Ettin, Andrew V. (1970). 'Shakespeare's First Roman Tragedy.' *ELH* 37: 325–41.

Ewbank, Inga-Stina (1989). 'From Narrative to Dramatic Language: *The Winter's Tale* and its Source', pp. 29–47 in Marvin Thompson *et al.*, eds, *Shakespeare and the Sense of Performance: Essays in the Tradition of Performance Criticism in Honor of Bernard Beckerman.* Newark, DE.

Farnham, Willard (1956). *The Medieval Heritage of Elizabethan Tragedy.* Oxford (first published 1936).

Gesner, Carol (1970). *Shakespeare and the Greek Romance: A Study of Origins.* Lexington, KY.

Gill, E. M. (1930). 'The Plot-Structure of *The Comedy of Errors* in Relation to its Sources.' *University of Texas Studies in English* 10: 13–65.

Hankins, John Erskine (1978). *Backgrounds of Shakespeare's Thought.* Hamden, CT.

Henderson, W. B. Drayton (1935). 'Shakespeare's *Troilus and Cressida*: Yet Deeper in its Tradition', pp. 127–56 in Hardin Craig, ed., *Essays in Dramatic*

Literature: The Parrott Presentation Volume. Princeton (reprinted New York, 1967).

Henke, Robert (1996). ' "Gentleman-like Tears": Affective Response in Italian Tragicomedy and Shakespeare's Late Plays.' *Comparative Literature Studies* 33: 327–49.

Highet, Gilbert (1957). *The Classical Tradition: Greek and Roman Influences on Western Literature*. New York (Ch. 11 on 'Shakespeare's Classics').

Hobsbaum, Philip (1978). *Tradition and Experiment in English Poetry*. London (Ch. 4 on Shakespeare's use of sources).

Hofele, Andreas (1997). 'Twentieth-Century Intertextuality and the Reading of Shakespeare's Sources.' *Poetica* 48: 211–27.

Honigmann, E. A. J. (1954). 'Shakespeare's "Lost Source-Plays".' *MLR* 49: 293–307.

Honigmann, E. A. J. (1955). 'Secondary Sources of *The Winter's Tale*.' *PQ* 34: 27–38.

Honigmann, E. A. J. (1961). '*Timon of Athens*.' *ShQ* 12: 3–20.

Hosley, Richard (1963–4). 'Sources and Analogues of *The Taming of the Shrew*.' *HLQ* 27: 289–308.

Hosley, Richard (1966). 'The Formal Influence of Plautus and Terence', pp. 131–46 in John Russell Brown and Bernard Harris, eds, *Elizabethan Theatre* (Stratford-upon-Avon Studies, 9). London.

Hunter, G. K. (1954). '*Henry IV* and the Elizabethan Two-Part Play.' *RES* 5: 236–48.

Hunter, G. K. (1971). 'Shakespeare's Reading', pp. 55–66 in Kenneth Muir and S. Schoenbaum, eds, *A New Companion to Shakespeare Studies*. Cambridge.

Hunter, G. K. (1977). 'A Roman Thought: Renaissance Attitudes to History exemplified in Shakespeare and Jonson', pp. 93–118 in Brian S. Lee, ed., *An English Miscellany: Presented to W. S. Mackie*. Cape Town.

Hunter, G. K. (1983). 'The Sources of *Titus Andronicus* – Once Again.' *N&Q* 228: 114–16.

Hunter, G. K. (1984). 'Sources and Meanings in *Titus Andronicus*', pp. 171–88 in J. C. Gray, ed., *Mirror up to Shakespeare: Essays in Honour of G. R. Hibbard*. Toronto.

Hunter, G. K. (1989). 'Truth and Art in History Plays.' *ShSu* 42: 15–24.

Jones, Emrys (1971). *Scenic Form in Shakespeare*. Oxford.
Jones, Emrys (1977). *The Origins of Shakespeare*. Oxford.
Jorgensen, Paul A. (1950). 'The Courtship Scene in *Henry V*.' *MLQ* 11: 180–8.

Kirkpatrick, Robin (1995). *English and Italian Literature from Dante to Shakespeare: A Study of Source, Analogue and Divergence*. London.

Langenfelt, Gösta (1955). 'The "Noble Savage" until Shakespeare.' *ES* 36: 222–7.

Law, Robert Adger (1943). 'The "Pre-Conceived Pattern" of *A Midsummer Night's Dream.*' *University of Texas Studies in English* 22: 5–14.

Leishman, J. B. (1961). *Themes and Variations in Shakespeare's Sonnets*. London.

Leon, Harry J. (1950). 'Classical Sources for the Garden Scene in *Richard II.*' *PQ* 29: 65–70.

Levenson, Jill L. (1984). 'Romeo and Juliet before Shakespeare.' *SP* 81: 325–47.

Lynch, Stephen J. (1998). *Shakespearean Intertextuality: Studies in Selected Sources and Plays*. Westport, CT.

McCabe, Richard A. (1993). *Incest, Drama and Nature's Law 1550–1700*. Cambridge.

MacCallum, M. W. (1967). *Shakespeare's Roman Plays and their Background*. London (first published 1910).

Marrapodi, Michele, *et al.*, eds (1993). *Shakespeare's Italy: Functions of Italian Locations in Renaissance Drama*. Manchester.

Martindale, Charles and Michelle (1990). *Shakespeare and the Uses of Antiquity: An Introductory Essay*. London.

Matthews, Honor (1962). *Character and Symbol in Shakespeare's Plays: A Study of Certain Christian and Pre-Christian Elements in their Structure and Imagery*. Cambridge.

Milward, Peter (1973). *Shakespeare's Religious Background*. London.

Miola, Robert S. (1983). *Shakespeare's Rome*. Cambridge.

Miola, Robert S. (1987). 'Shakespeare and his Sources: Observations on the Critical History of "Julius Caesar".' *ShSu* 40: 69–76.

Miola, Robert S. (1994). *Shakespeare and Classical Comedy: The Influence of Plautus and Terence*. Oxford.

Moore, Olin H. (1950). *The Legend of Romeo and Juliet*. Columbus, OH.

Mueller, Martin (1994). 'Shakespeare's Sleeping Beauties: The Sources of *Much Ado about Nothing* and the Play of their Repetitions.' *MP* 91: 288–311.

Muir, Kenneth (1957). *Shakespeare's Sources, I: Comedies and Tragedies*. London.

Muir, Kenneth (1960). 'Source Problems in the Histories.' *ShJ* 96: 47–63.

Muir, Kenneth (1974). 'Shakespeare's Roman World.' *Literary Half-Yearly* 15: 45–63.

Muir, Kenneth (1977). *The Sources of Shakespeare's Plays*. London (revision and expansion of Muir 1957).

Muir, Kenneth (1982). 'Shakespeare and the Tale of Troy.' *Aligarh Critical Miscellany* 5.ii: 113–31.

Mulryne, J. R., and Margaret Shewring, eds (1991). *Theatre of the English and Italian Renaissance*. Basingstoke.

Noble, Richmond (1935). *Shakespeare's Biblical Knowledge and Use of the Book of Common Prayer as Exemplified in the Plays of the First Folio.* London.

Nosworthy, J. M. (1948). 'The Narrative Sources of *The Tempest.*' *RES* 24: 281–94.

Nosworthy, J. M. (1982). 'Shakespeare's Pastoral Metamorphoses', pp. 90–113 in George R. Hibbard, ed., *The Elizabethan Theatre VIII.* Port Credit (on Ovid, Apuleius and Plutarch).

Orgel, Stephen, and Sean Keilen, ed. (1999). *Shakespeare and the Literary Tradition: The Scholarly Literature.* New York (collection of previously-published essays).

Ornstein, Robert (1986). *Shakespeare's Comedies: From Roman Farce to Romantic Mystery.* Newark, DE.

Orr, David (1970). *Italian Renaissance Drama in England before 1625: The Influence of 'Erudita' Tragedy, Comedy, and Pastoral on Elizabethan and Jacobean Drama.* Chapel Hill.

Osborne, Laurie E. (1990). 'Dramatic Play in *Much Ado about Nothing*: Wedding the Italian *Novella* and English Comedy.' *PQ* 69: 167–88.

Paul, Henry N. (1950). *The Royal Play of Macbeth: When, Why, and How it was written by Shakespeare.* New York.

Pearson, d'Orsay W. (1974). '"Unkind" Theseus: A Study in Renaissance Mythography.' *ELR* 4: 276–98.

Pendleton, Thomas A. (1987). 'Shakespeare's Disguised Duke Play: Middleton, Marston, and the Sources of *Measure for Measure*', pp. 79–98 in John W. Mahon and Thomas A. Pendleton, eds, *"Fanned and Winnowed Opinions": Shakespearean Essays Presented to Harold Jenkins.* London.

Perrello, Tony (1997). 'Anglo-Saxon Elements of the Gloucester Sub-Plot in *King Lear.*' *ELN* 35: 10–16.

Perrett, Wilfred (1904). *The Story of King Lear from Geoffrey of Monmouth to Shakespeare.* Berlin.

Potter, Robert (1975). *The English Morality Play: Origins, History and Influence of a Dramatic Tradition.* London.

Praz, Mario (1954). 'Shakespeare's Italy.' *ShSu* 7: 95–106 (reprinted in Praz, *The Flaming Heart: Essays on Crashaw, Machiavelli, and other studies in the Relations between Italian and English Literature from Chaucer to T. S. Eliot*, New York, 1958).

Presson, Robert K. (1953). *Shakespeare's 'Troilus and Cressida' and the Legends of Troy.* Madison, WI.

Prouty, Charles Tyler (1950). *The Sources of Much Ado about Nothing: A Critical Study, together with the text of Peter Beverley's Ariodanto and Ieneura.* New Haven.

Prouty, Charles Tyler (1960). 'Some Observations on Shakespeare's Sources.' *ShJ* 96: 64–77.

Rees, Joan (1983). 'Juliet's Nurse: Some Branches of a Family Tree.' *RES* 34: 43–7.

Reese, M. M. (1961). *The Cease of Majesty: A Study of Shakespeare's History Plays.* London.

Root, Robert K. (1903). *Classical Mythology in Shakespeare.* New York.

Sacharoff, Mark (1970). 'The Traditions of the Troy-Story Heroes and the Problem of Satire in *Troilus and Cressida.*' *ShSt* 6: 125–35.

Salingar, Leo (1974). *Shakespeare and the Traditions of Comedy.* Cambridge.

Salingar, Leo (1983). '*King Lear,* Montaigne and Harsnett.' *The Aligarh Journal of English Studies* 8.ii: 124–66 (also published in *Anglo-American Studies,* 3 (1983)).

Schanzer, Ernest (1963). *The Problem Plays of Shakespeare: A Study of Julius Caesar, Measure for Measure and Antony and Cleopatra.* London.

Schleiner, Louise (1990). 'Latinized Greek Drama in Shakespeare's Writing of *Hamlet.*' *ShQ* 41: 29–48.

Scragg, Leah (1992). *Shakespeare's Mouldy Tales: Recurrent Plot Motifs in Shakespearean Drama.* London.

Scragg, Leah (1996). *Shakespeare's Alternative Tales.* London.

Shaheen, Naseeb (1994). 'Shakespeare's Knowledge of Italian.' *ShSu* 47: 161–9.

Shapiro, Michael (1982). 'Boying Her Greatness: Shakespeare's Use of Coterie Drama in "Antony and Cleopatra".' *MLR* 77: 1–15.

Sierz, Krystyna (1984). 'Some Medieval Concepts in Shakespeare's Plays.' *Studia Anglica Posnaniensia* 17: 233–49.

Sledd, James (1951). 'A Note on the Use of Renaissance Dictionaries.' *MP* 49: 10–15.

Smith, Bruce R. (1988). *Ancient Scripts and Modern Experience on the English Stage 1500–1700.* Princeton.

Smith, Charles George (1963). *Shakespeare's Proverb Lore: His Use of the Sententiae of Leonard Culman and Publilius Syrus.* Cambridge, MA.

Smith, Valerie (1982). 'The History of Cressida', pp. 61–79 in J. A. Jowitt and R. K. S. Taylor, eds, *Self and Society in Shakespeare's 'Troilus and Cressida' and 'Measure for Measure'.* Bradford.

Sowerby, Robin (1994). *The Classical Legacy in Renaissance Poetry.* London.

Spenser, T. J. B. (1964). 'The Great Rival: Shakespeare and the Classical Dramatists', pp. 177–93 in Edward A. Bloom, ed., *Shakespeare 1564–1964: A Collection of Modern Essays by Various Hands.* Providence, R.I.

Spivack, Bernard (1958). *Shakespeare and the Allegory of Evil: A History of A Metaphor in Relation to his Major Villains.* New York.

Starnes, DeWitt T., and Ernest W. Talbert (1956). *Classical Myth and Legend in Renaissance Dictionaries: A Study of Renaissance Dictionaries in their Relation to the Classical Learning of Contemporary English Writers.* Chapel Hill.

Steppat, Michael (1987). 'Shakespeare's Response to Dramatic Tradition in *Anthony and Cleopatra*', pp. 254–79 in Bernhard Fabian and Kurt Tetzeli von Rosador, eds, *Shakespeare: Text, Language, Criticism: Essays in Honour of Marvin Spevack*. Hildesheim.

Stirling, Brents (1964). 'Cleopatra's Scene with Seleucus: Plutarch, Daniel, and Shakespeare.' *ShQ* 15: 299–311.

Stump, Donald V. (1983). 'Greek and Shakespearean Tragedy: Four Indirect Routes from Athens to London', pp. 211–46 in Stump *et al.*, eds, *Hamartia: The Concept of Error in the Western Tradition: Essays in Honor of John M. Crossett*. New York.

Thomson, J. A. K. (1952). *Shakespeare and the Classics*. London.

Tiffany, Grace (1999). 'Shakespeare's Dionysian Prince: Drama, Politics, and the "Athenian" History Play.' *RenQ* 52: 366–83.

Tillyard, E. M. W. (1944). *Shakespeare's History Plays*. London.

Tillyard, E. M. W. (1965). *Shakespeare's Problem Plays*. Harmondsworth (first published 1950).

Tomlinson, Michael (1984). 'Shakespeare and the Chronicles Reassessed.' *Literature and History* 10: 46–58.

Traugott, John (1982). 'Creating a Rational Rinaldo: A Study in the Mixture of the Genres of Comedy and Romance in *Much Ado about Nothing*.' *Genre* 15: 157–81.

Trousdale, Marion (1982). *Shakespeare and the Rhetoricians*. London.

Ure, Peter (1953). 'Shakespeare's Play and the French Sources of Holinshed's and Stow's Account of *Richard II*.' *N&Q* 198: 426–9.

Ure, Peter (1971). 'Shakespeare and the Drama of his Time', pp. 211–21 in Kenneth Muir and S. Schoenbaum, eds, *A New Companion to Shakespeare Studies*. Cambridge.

Velz, John W. (1992). '"Some shall be pardon'd, and some punished": Medieval Dramatic Eschatology in Shakespeare.' *CompD* 26: 312–29.

Weimann, Robert, revised and translated by Robert Schwartz (1978). *Shakespeare and the Popular Tradition in the Theater: Studies in the Social Dimension of Dramatic Form and Function*. Baltimore.

Weiner, Andrew D. (1991). 'Sidney/Spenser/Shakespeare: Influence/ Intertextuality/Intention', pp. 245–70 in Jay Clayton and Eric Rothstein, eds, *Influence and Intertextuality in Literary History*. Madison, WI.

Whitaker, Virgil K. (1953). *Shakespeare's Use of Learning: An Inquiry into the Growth of his Mind and Art*. San Marino, CA.

White, Howard B. (1970). '*Copp' d Hills towards Heaven*': *Shakespeare and the Classical Polity*. The Hague.

Wilson, Frank P. (1950). 'Shakespeare's Reading.' *ShSu* 10: 14–21.

Wilson, J. Dover (1957). 'Shakespeare's "Small Latin" – How Much?' *ShSu* 10: 12–26.

Yates, Frances A. (1942). 'Shakespeare and the Platonic Tradition.' *University of Edinburgh Journal* 12: 2–12.

Young, Alan R. (1975). 'The Written and Oral Sources of *King Lear* and the Problem of Justice in the Play.' *SEL* 15: 309–19.

Index

This is an index nominorum supplementing the A–Z entries. It includes references made to writers and works which have their own A–Z entries where they are mentioned in some connection other than as direct influences on Shakespeare; page numbers of their main entry are indicated by an asterisk. It also extends to figures associated with Shakespeare's books in such capacities as early commentators and editors, identified readers, translators and printers. Finally, it covers references to writers not known to be Shakespeare sources, whether predecessors or contemporaries, as well as later writers (such as, respectively, Aristotle, Webster and Milton). As in the A–Z, names are usually given in their most familiar form and under the most obvious initial letter, with alternatives supplied where it seems useful but without regard to consistency in adopting Latinized/vernacular forms, etc.